Regions, Resources, and Economic Growth

Regions, Resources, and Economic Growth

BY / *Harvey S. Perloff*

Edgar S. Dunn, Jr.

Eric E. Lampard

Richard F. Muth

PUBLISHED FOR *Resources for the Future, Inc.*

BY *The Johns Hopkins Press,* BALTIMORE

RESOURCES FOR THE FUTURE, INC., *Washington, D. C.*

Resources for the Future is a nonprofit corporation for research and education in the development, conservation, and use of natural resources. It was established in 1952 with the co-operation of The Ford Foundation and its activities since then have been financed by grants from that Foundation. Part of the work of Resources for the Future is carried out by its resident staff, part supported by grants to universities and other nonprofit organizations. Unless otherwise stated, interpretations and conclusions in RFF publications are those of the authors; the organization takes responsibility for the selection of significant subjects for study, the competence of the researchers and their freedom of inquiry.

This book is one of RFF's regional studies, which are directed by Harvey S. Perloff. The manuscript was edited by Martha Gibbon.

Staff Editors, Henry Jarrett and Vera W. Dodds

Preface

Economic growth in the United States has varied widely among the different geographic sections. Some regions have expanded rapidly, drawing in persons, materials, and capital in great quantities and enjoying high levels of living, at the same time that others are in various stages of relative decline.

The move of the Braves baseball team from Boston to Milwaukee and of the Dodgers and Giants across the continent to the West Coast might be said to symbolize two of the significant economic shifts of recent decades—the particularly rapid industrial growth of the western end of the Manufacturing Belt and the virtual flood of movement to the Far West, and especially California, from almost every other part of the country. The regional changes are not always so dramatic, but they are continuous and they play a large role in where and how our families live and in how they prosper.

This differential growth strongly influences the development and use of natural resources which, in turn, have an important effect on regional growth patterns. To understand the complicated interrelationships involved, it is necessary to see the natural resource activities—the farming, forestry, fishing, and mining, and the processing of their products—within the broad framework of over-all national and differential regional economic growth. The study presented here attempts to do this.

It was designed with two objectives in view:

One was to furnish information and insights that might be of value to the public and private groups concerned with various aspects of economic growth and decline as well as with natural resources. This is a field in which action programs seem to have grown at a much faster rate than the underlying knowledge essential to their effectiveness. Over 10,000 public and private agencies in the United States are concerned in one way or another with "area development." It has become increasingly evident—particularly to thoughtful persons with "area development" responsibilities—that efforts in the various sections of the country to attract industry and to raise levels of living can hope to be successful only if such policies are based firmly on a knowledge of industry requirements and impacts. It was our hope that the study could contribute to the knowledge needed for a sound policy approach to regional economic and resources planning and development.

The second objective was to provide a conceptual and methodological framework as a guide for our own future research in resources and regions and for possible use by scholars working in regional and developmental economics, business economics, geography, planning, and related fields, both in the United States and in other countries. While the study is concerned exclusively with developments in the U.S. economy, the conceptual and methodological problems involved in understanding the underlying forces at work have general relevance. In evolving our research approach, we have borrowed heavily from the work of scholars of many countries and we would hope that this study in turn can contribute something of value to those concerned with problems of subnational economic growth overseas.

Both objectives dictated a broad view of the subject, with a focus on economic growth as it takes place both over time and in space. Several assumptions growing out of our own previous research and that of others underlie our over-all approach:

(1) That regional economic growth in the *volume* of economic activities is subject to a different constellation of socio-economic forces than are the *welfare* aspects of growth. Both of these aspects received detailed attention in the study; all of Part V is devoted to welfare considerations, while Parts III and IV are chiefly concerned with a description and analysis of regional changes in the volume of economic activities. (2) That economic growth is an evolutionary process, with current development and future possibilities greatly influenced by the decisions and developments of the past—such as the existing size of markets as they have evolved in different regions of the country, the location of input sources, the economics of capital depreciation, and related considerations. Thus, in our research we sought an understanding of the regional settlement and growth patterns of the past as a necessary foundation for an understanding of present differential levels of living and rates of economic expansion.

(3) That the critical elements in the changing patterns of regional economic development are the locational and production decisions of business firms flowing from the input and market requirements of the major industries. This called for an overview of the key requirements of *each* of the major industry groups—a large task but, in our view, an essential one.

As the research unfolded, we found in certain of the initial findings a gold mine of knowledge and insight. This was true, for example, of our discovery, based on the application of a useful statistical tool, that the regions were growing in two distinctive ways: that certain regions were growing largely as a result of "within-industry" changes (of the type symbolized by the shift of cotton cultivation from the Southeast to the Southwest), while others were gaining from their particular industrial composition, that is, because they had an unusually high proportion of "rapid-growth" industries. So instructive was this distinction that it could be used as a generalized descriptive and analytical framework.

The book is divided into five parts. Part I presents the highlights in the story of regional economic growth in the United States since 1870, as well as a more detailed account of growth during the recent period 1939-54, as background for the analysis of the factors behind differential regional growth presented in later sections of the book. Part II discusses theories of growth and the conceptual and methodological framework employed in the study. Part III discusses the evolution of the subnational economy from the early part of the 19th Century, with a more detailed treatment of changes in the spatial distribution of population, income, natural resource activities, and other economic activities from 1870 to 1950. Part IV analyzes the forces behind the recent locational shifts in American industry and the impact of these shifts on differential regional economic growth. Part V is devoted to an analysis of the major causes of regional differentials in the level of per capita income and in the rates of growth in per capita income.

Summary statements are provided at several points. There is a summary of the key facts in regional economic development since 1870 in the last section of chapter 3. The emphasis here is on the growth indexes. A roundup of the main facts in the development of productive activities in the multistate regions of the country, and particularly the natural resources activities, is provided in chapter 18 at the end of Part III. A summary of the recent industrial shifts, of changes in the regional distribution of economic activities, and of the resulting regional patterns of growth is provided in chapters 19 and 26, the opening and closing chapters of Part IV. The central features of the regional variations in levels of living and of growth of per capita income are summarized at the end of each of the chapters in Part V and in more general terms in chapter 8 of Part II and chapter 34 of Part V.

The summary for the entire volume is provided in chapter 9, at the end of the conceptual discussion and preceding the detailed description and analysis of regional economic growth which are set out in Parts III, IV and V.

While each of the authors collaborating in this study has had major responsibility for certain sections of it, each has contributed ideas and materials to other parts of the book as well. Thus, the over-all design of the study and its direction were my main responsibility, as was the presentation of the introductory and conceptual material in Parts I and II, but each of the members of the group made important contributions to both of these tasks.

Eric E. Lampard brought together the historical data for the period 1870-1950, which involved the preparation of a number of new or improved historical series, and prepared Part III, weaving together many of the strands in the rich fabric of regional economic development in the United States.

Edgar S. Dunn, Jr., prepared Part IV, which analyzes the changes in the locational structure of American economic activity in the crucial years during and since World War II. This analysis is based on the remarkable feat of examining the key locational factors in each of the major industrial groups in the U. S. economy.

Richard F. Muth prepared most of Part V, in which the major causes of regional differentials in the level of per capita income and in the rates of growth in per capita income are analyzed, and provided valuable assistance to me in the preparation of chapter 29 of Part V, "Income and the Industrial Structure," chapter 33, "Migration and Income," and chapter 34, "Regions and Income: a summary."

Dunn and Lampard each took a year's leave from the University of Florida and Smith College respectively to work on the study full time at Resources for the Future; and both spent a further year completing their phases of the work after returning to their own institutions. During this period Muth was associated full-time with the Program of Regional Studies at Resources for the Future.

Throughout the book we have made use of materials focusing on the State Economic Areas (groups of counties with more or less common economic and social characteristics, as defined by the Bureau of the Census). These materials —relating to structure of economic activities, natural and human resources, migration, and levels of living—were prepared by Otis Dudley Duncan, who directed the work, Ray P. Cuzzort, and Beverly Duncan, under a grant to the Population Research and Training Center at the University of Chicago.

This volume is one of a series of Resources for the Future studies aimed at deepening our understanding of the role of natural resources in economic growth. These have been undertaken to help provide a foundation for policies and practices on the development, use, and conservation of natural resources which will contribute most to the general welfare.

A companion study, under Otis Dudley Duncan's direction, has just been published under the title, *Metropolis and Region*. This study deals specifically with the economic structure and functions of metropolitan communities and their relation to larger regions and to the nation. The two studies represent a loose division of labor between our own concentration on the state and the multistate region as a way of examining the subnational economy and the focus on the substate areas of the two efforts under Duncan's direction. As a result each group could study the subnational economy with fairly consistent types of data and thus hope to highlight somewhat different facets of the complex problems of regional economic structure and growth.

Attention in this book and in *Metropolis and Region* is directed to the continental United States. A separate study of economic development and resource problems in Alaska is being carried out by George W. Rogers under a grant from Resources for the Future to the Arctic Institute of North America.

Our study was undertaken during a period in which there has been a flowering of regional studies. This has provided a stimulus to our own research; it also made it unnecessary for us to cover all the major aspects of the subject in comparable detail. Those who can make the best use of material on regional economic growth are likely to examine at least the major studies as they become available.

Thus, we were fortunate in having at hand a prepublication copy of the University of Pennsylvania study (Kuznets, Thomas, Lee, Miller, Brainerd, Easterlin), *Population Redistribution and Economic Growth, United States, 1870-1950*, as well as a typescript copy of Frank A. Hanna's book, *State Income Differentials, 1919-1954*. We made extensive use of these materials in our research. At the same time, knowing that these volumes would be available before our own, we could touch lightly on the topics covered by these valuable studies without any sense of neglect.

The same was true of a number of other subjects important in the examination of regional economic growth. For example, during the period of our research we were in close touch with the group, under the direction of Raymond Vernon, carrying out the New York Metropolitan Region Study. Because we were aware of the very comprehensive treatment being given to problems of transportation and to the tertiary (service) activities in this study, which will be available at about the same time as our own, we felt that we could devote major attention to other aspects of greater direct importance to our central theme.

We gained greatly also from a number of preliminary unpublished studies, as well as published materials which were generously provided to us by Walter Isard and his associates at the University of Pennsylvania, William Nicholls and his associates at Vanderbilt University, and the regional-economics research group at Brown University.

We are very much in debt to the following persons who reviewed the entire manuscript and made many valuable suggestion: George Borts, O. Dudley Duncan, Richard A. Easterlin, Jerome L. Stein, Richard S. Thoman, Werner Z. Hirsch, and colleagues at Resources for the Future, Marion Clawson, Joseph Fisher, Henry Jarrett, and T. Lowdon Wingo, Jr. Wingo enriched his comments with new materials which we could use to great advantage in the book. Thoman also prepared a number of the charts used in the volume and provided materials drawn from the field of economic geography.

We are also indebted to the following scholars who reviewed one or several chapters in the field in which they have special competence or interest: Kenneth L. Bachman, Ronald L. Mighell, and R. Burnell Held on the agricultural sections; Charles H. Stoddard on forestry; Orris C. Herfindahl, Joseph Lerner, and Bruce C. Netschert on energy and mineral resources; Douglass C. North and William N. Parker on the historical materials of Part III; Harold J. Barnett, Paul H. Cootner, W. Lee Hansen, Douglass C. North, and Charles M. Tiebout on Parts I, II, and V. These reviews have contributed a great deal to improving the book.

Extremely able statistical assistance was provided by Mrs. Erna J. Peters, while the tremendous task of typing the many drafts of the book was done by, and under the supervision of, Mrs. Nadja Schocken. Miss Martha Gibbon did a thorough job of editing the volume. We were fortunate in having such competent assistance.

Harvey S. Perloff

Contents

*Part IV. The Regional Distribution of Economic Activities
in the United States, 1939–1954*

*Part V. Variations in Levels and Rates of Growth
of Per Capita Income*

TABLES

*Part V. Variations in Levels and Rates of Growth
of Per Capita Income*

STATISTICAL APPENDIX

FIGURES

Part I. An Historical Review of Regional Economic Growth

Part II. A Framework for Analysis

Part III. Regional Economic Development, 1870–1950

*Part IV. The Regional Distribution of Economic Activities
in the United States, 1939–1954*

Part V. Variations in Levels and Rates of Growth of Per Capita Income

Part

I / *Historical Review of*

Regional Economic Growth

1 / Introduction: a note on regions, time, and growth measures

National forces clearly dominate economic developments throughout the whole of the United States. Yet average levels of living vary significantly from one part of the country to another, and the various states and regions differ from one another widely in the size and in the rate of growth of their populations and in the scope of their economic activities. The main purpose of our study is to arrive at a better understanding of this phenomenon.

Here in Part I we shall bring together the key facts relevant to our inquiry, telling in broad outline the story of regional growth within the context of national economic growth in the United States since 1870. But first we shall briefly define the growth measures adopted, the regional groupings followed, and the time element employed throughout the study in our examination and presentation of the data that reflect the phenomenon with which we are concerned.

Measures of "Economic Growth"

Economic growth can be—and is—conceived of in many ways. Inherent in the very use of the term is some sense of significant changes in the way in which a people produce and consume, work and live and play. To record and measure a vast mosaic of change in the nation as a whole and in its various parts is no simple undertaking, and it is the better part of wisdom to appreciate that, even with our most advanced conceptual and statistical tools, we can grasp only the crudest notion of the nature and direction of these changes.

A useful starting point is to make a distinction between the changes that would seem to be associated with individual and family welfare and those associated with the *volume* of economic activities. The most commonly employed measures—really, crude indicators—of economic welfare, of improvement or decline in the average economic status of families and individuals, are the relative levels of per capita income and the changes in these levels. Different measures are needed in evaluating growth or decline in the volume of economic activities—the "more and bigger" aspect of economic growth as against the "better" aspect. Regional growth in volume might appropriately be measured by increases in population (i.e., number of persons, viewed as consumers and labor force), increases in total employment, and/or increases in total income produced or received within a given area. This distinction between the "welfare" measures and the "volume" measures of growth is important because it is possible for an area to have an increase in one without a corresponding increase in the other. In other words, an area may have an increase in population without an increase in average real per capita income; or an area may have a decrease in the volume of economic activities and population and yet enjoy an increase in average levels of living. This question is discussed in some detail at various points in this book.

Even when attention is focused on volume alone, the different measures of regional growth that might be used provide rather different results. Thus, somewhat different patterns may emerge if growth is measured by *absolute* increases in population and employment or by *relative* increases in population and employment, by *absolute* increases in total income or by *relative* increases in total income. To obtain anything resembling a rounded picture of regional economic growth, it is necessary to observe all of these various facets of expansion.[1] Also, somewhat different growth patterns may emerge when only the one or two most recent decades are considered and when a longer historical period is examined. For that reason, we shall examine both.

Concept of the Region

The term "region" is generally used to describe a group of geographically contiguous areas which have certain common or complementary characteristics or which are tied by extensive interareal activity or flows.[2] In economic analysis the investigator's choice of component areas (the "building blocks") depends both upon the extent to which such areas can be combined in terms of specified physical, socio-economic, or other criteria and on the form in which statistical data are available or can be made available for the purpose involved. This latter element imposes some serious constraints on choice.

For most of the subjects that are central to the problem to which we have

[1]The measurement of economic growth is discussed in some detail in Harvey S. Perloff, "Problems of Assessing Regional Economic Progress," *Regional Income*, National Bureau of Economic Research, *Studies in Income and Wealth*, Vol. 21 (Princeton: Princeton University Press, 1957), pp. 35-62. See also in the same volume discussions of various aspects of the measurement problem by Werner Hochwald, "Conceptual Issues of Regional Income Estimation," by Frank Hanna, "Analysis of Interstate Income Differentials: Theory and Practice," and by Abner Hurwitz and Carlyle P. Stallings, "Interregional Differentials in Per Capita Real Income Change."

[2]For a discussion of the various types of regions employed in economic analysis, see Joseph L. Fisher, "Concepts in Regional Economic Development," *Papers and Proceedings of the Regional Science Association*, Vol. 1 (1955), pp. W2-W20. Problems of spatial aggregation as related to analysis of trade patterns are discussed by Leon Moses, "The Stability of Interregional Trading Patterns and Input-Output Analysis," *American Economic Review*. Vol. 45 (December 1955), pp. 803-32.

addressed ourselves—such as income, natural resource activities, and industrial structure—data, and particularly historical series, are available only for the states. In several phases of our study—for example, in the discussion of industrial location—the subnational picture is drawn mainly in terms of the state units. At other points, we have focused on a "regional" grouping of states, as useful for both descriptive and analytical purposes. Thus, for example, in the historical section, Part III, we have adopted a consistent grouping of states as the only practical basis for statistical comparison over long periods of time and wide ranges of territory. The grouping is the one followed by the U.S. Department of Commerce in presenting its state personal income estimates. This was found to be appropriate for our purposes because of its rationale with regard to relative levels of living as among the various parts of the country and with regard to similarity of cultural-historical backgrounds. That is, this grouping follows the main tendencies of historical geographical development without doing grave injustice to either local sentiments or chronology of settlement.

A regional grouping of states was also found to be useful in the discussion in Part V of per capita income (actually the same grouping as in the historical section with one exception). In presenting data which describe the inter-state differences in income and its components, averages of income measures for regions or groups of states permit an economy in presentation and an easier comprehension of inter-state differences. In analyzing these inter-state differences, the use of regions provides a check on the completeness of the analysis. If the variables which account for the variation of the regional means about the national average fail to account for the variation of income measures within regions, we have omitted some significant variables from the analysis.

Figure 1. Regional Grouping of States.

Regional Grouping of States Employed[3]

The regional grouping of states that we have adopted for study and presentation purposes is as follows:

NEW ENGLAND: Maine, New Hampshire, Vermont, Massachusetts, Rhode Island, Connecticut

MIDDLE ATLANTIC: New York, New Jersey, Pennsylvania, Delaware, Maryland, District of Columbia

GREAT LAKES: Ohio, Indiana, Illinois, Michigan, Wisconsin

SOUTHEAST: Virginia, West Virginia, Kentucky, Tennessee, North Carolina, South Carolina, Georgia, Florida, Alabama, Mississippi, Arkansas, Louisiana[4]

PLAINS: Minnesota, Iowa, Missouri, North Dakota, South Dakota, Nebraska, Kansas

SOUTHWEST: Oklahoma, Texas, Arizona, New Mexico

MOUNTAIN: Montana, Idaho, Wyoming, Utah, Colorado

FAR WEST: Washington, Oregon, California, Nevada

For purposes of certain broad comparisons, we have grouped these eight regions into three "great regions," divided roughly along the courses of the Mississippi and Ohio rivers as follows:

THE NORTHEAST: embracing the New England, Middle Atlantic, and Great Lakes regions, and roughly comparable to the Manufacturing Belt.

THE SOUTHEAST: embracing the same area as the Southeast region above.

THE WEST: embracing the Plains, Mountain, Southwest, and Far West regions.

Thus the two great regions, the Northeast and the Southeast, may be conveniently termed the "eastern half" of the nation and the West the "western

[3]This grouping is one that was evolved by a committee composed of representatives of three Department of Commerce agencies, convened to consider the feasibility of standardizing the regional presentation of statistical data within the Department. The committee proposed a nine-region classification of geographically contiguous states after studying a large number of statistical series reflecting economic factors, particularly income and industrial employment, as well as selected noneconomic factors. We have departed from the proposed nine-region grouping by combining the committee's Upper and Lower South into one region, giving us eight instead of nine.

For a report on the Commerce committee's work, see Morris B. Ullman and Robert C. Klove, "The Geographic Area in Regional Economic Research," in *Regional Income*, National Bureau of Economic Research, *Studies in Income and Wealth*, Vol. 21 (Princeton: Princeton University Press, 1957), pp. 87-109. For the historical use of the terms "section," "division," "region," etc., see articles by F. Mood and V. Carstensen in M. Jensen, ed., *Regionalism in America* (Madison: University of Wisconsin Press, 1952), pp. 5-118. See also the revealing treatment of the subject in Otis Dudley Duncan, Ray P. Cuzzort and Beverly Duncan, *Statistical Geography: Problems in Analyzing Areal Data* (Glencoe, Ill.: Free Press, in press).

[4]For reasons noted later in the text, Louisiana will sometimes be classified with the Southwest rather than the Southeast.

half." Fortunately there have been few changes in state or territorial boundaries since 1870, with the exception of the division of the Dakota Territory and the Indian Territory (mostly Oklahoma); hence there has been little necessity for the retabulation of census data to accord with our chosen regional designation.[5]

For us, regional groupings are a device for study and presentation. Unlike the statistical agencies, which are necessarily concerned with general-purpose groupings that can be employed consistently for long periods of time, we are as much concerned with the intra-regional differences as with the similarities, with changes in areal patterning over time as with non-changing areal arrangements. Thus, to take an example, we are as much concerned with the aspects in which Florida departs significantly from other states in the Southeast, e.g., in income and migration, as with the aspects that distinguish the Southeast as a whole from the rest of the country. As a matter of fact, we employ the grouping described above merely as a point of departure and feel free to change the designation wherever this seems appropriate. Thus, in discussing certain subjects, we shall refer to the western end of the Manufacturing Belt, or upper New England, or the Atlantic coast states when it is useful to do so.

In the case of Louisiana, we found in studying economic development in the most recent period—over the past two or three decades—that this state had more characteristics in common with the Southwest than with the Southeast (particularly in the growth of the petroleum and oil-using industries). For this reason, we have included it with the Southwest in discussions of recent developments in Parts IV and V. Also this served as a useful self-discipline, as well as a way of alerting readers not to read more into a given regional grouping than the actual facts justify. The danger of coming to use a given grouping as more or less a final designation, rather than an initial point of reference, is so great that the introduction of this type of "change in mid-stream" seems not only justified but essential to focus attention on an important matter.

For certain subjects covered by our study, variations within the states as well as among states are analytically significant. We have attempted to get at such variations, where particularly significant, by focusing attention on State Economic Areas, which are groups of counties and are made up of metropolitan and non-metropolitan areas. (The metropolitan SEA is essentially the same as the Standard Metropolitan Area.)

Thus, we have attempted to develop an understanding of the subnational economy by focusing attention on various types of regional groupings, in each case seeking to employ the designation which is most revealing and most meaningful for the subject at hand. The groupings include the following:

1. The great regions: the Northeast, the Southeast, and the West.
2. Eight multi-state regions (particularly for the historical section).

[5]For a discussion of these and other problems of spatial and temporal units, see E. S. Lee, A. R. Miller, C. P. Brainerd and R. A. Easterlin, *Population Redistribution and Economic Growth, United States, 1870-1950* (Philadelphia: American Philosophical Society, 1957), pp. 10-14. Other historical data considerations are discussed in the statistical appendix to this study.

3. Modifications on the multi-state regions: as in reference to Upper New England or the North Plains or the Gulf Coast area.
4. The individual states.
5. State Economic Areas, made up of metropolitan and non-metropolitan SEA's.

Time Segments

Like a too rigid treatment of regions, a too rigid treatment of the time element can be misleading in economic description and analysis. There are important problems involved in the selection of the base year and in measuring values at two points in time. The length of the period of analysis is also significant in this regard. We might note as an example of this the significant difference that a single year can make with regard to the income picture. Between 1949 and 1950, state income increases ranged from a rise of 4% in Oklahoma to an increase of 23% in Montana. Thus, if Montana's income growth is assessed by comparing 1949 with, say 1940, an increase of 145% in total income payments will be recorded, but if 1950 is used, the increase over 1940 will be shown as 199%—a difference of 54 percentage points.

Since the problems referred to above are discussed in detail in the economic and statistical literature, we need not go into them here. However, we want to indicate that awareness of their importance has induced us to design our study so that subnational economic growth can be seen over various time segments, and with changes in base years and end points wherever appropriate for purposes of description and analysis. There are, of course, practical limits to the number of time variations that can usefully be employed in analysis, and—as in the case of regional designations—we have tried to strike a sensible balance. Thus, there are essentially two periods to which we have given our principal attention: the 80-year period between 1870 and 1950, which is the concern of Part III of the book, and the more recent period, 1939-54, which is employed for the analysis of locational shifts in Part IV. But we have also made use of other periods, either for purposes of testing or where the analysis could be enriched by doing so.

We hope that we have at least avoided some of the more damaging intellectual traps inherent in the subject which is the focus of our study.

2 / Economic growth since 1870[1]

(with a focus on the multi-state region)

At the end of the Civil War the United States was still a partially developed nation on the fringe of the European-dominated world economy. By 1957, it had become a major force in international economics, holding a first-rank position among the nations of the world in the production both of raw materials and of manufactured goods. Meanwhile, in spite of recurrent war and recession, its greatly enlarged population had come to enjoy the highest average level of living of any people in all history.

However, growth did not occur uniformly throughout the country. From the beginning, the extension of population and economic activities into "newer" areas, as well as the relative transformation of "older" and more developed regions, proceeded at markedly divergent rates. Some of this differentiation was doubtless due to the local effect of business fluctuations or to the incidence of such factors as war and politics, but most of it stemmed from the spread of a highly productive population and of capital into areas of relatively undeveloped natural resources in response to differential opportunities in various parts of the country. This territorial division of labor was undoubtedly one of the mainsprings of national economic growth.

We want first to examine the migration of people and shifts in economic activities within the United States during the period from 1870 to 1957 and to trace concomitant changes in the regional structure of the national economy. Our purpose here is to provide a picture of how the American economy evolved into its present geographic pattern. The broad outline of this evolution may be represented by several historical series reflecting population and income changes among the regions over these years. These permit the tracing of the physical occupation and settlement of the continental territory, the relative growth in economic activities, and the relative changes in levels of living over these years. The analysis of the changes observed is reserved for later chapters.

[1]Because of the lack of certain current data (i.e., post-1950 census), and for other reasons, the historical treatment of regional economic growth in Part III of this book covers the period 1870-1950. In this introductory section, however, certain of the more recent figures (for 1957) are included so that an up-to-date picture can be presented.

Growth and Shift of Population, 1870-1957

The movement of population and of economic activities in the United States since 1870 has been, in important part, a "spreading out" and "filling in," almost like the movement of flood waters over a rugged terrain. But it has not been simply a movement West, for there has been great and intensive development in the older settled sections of the East as well during these years. Thus, what we have is a nation still growing in all its parts.

Tables 1 and 2 and Figures 2 and 3 show the absolute numbers and relative rates of growth in population, by regions, between 1870 and 1957. The absolute increases were heaviest in the Southeast, Great Lakes, and Middle Atlantic regions throughout the period. The rates of increase, however, were highest in the Mountain, Southwest, and Far West regions. The regions east of the Mississippi surpassed the national *percentage* increases in only a few decades, and then only at slightly above average rates.

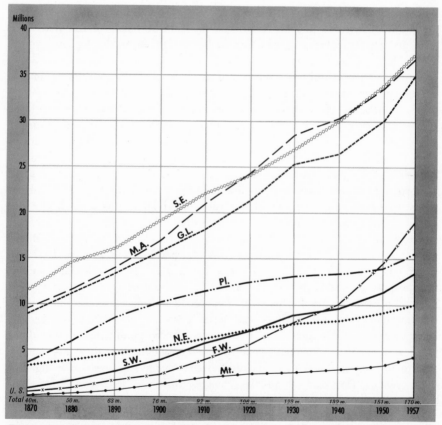

Figure 2. Population at Census Dates, by Region, 1870-1950 (and 1957).

Source: Table 1, note. Unless otherwise stated, sources for all charts are to be found in nearby tables.

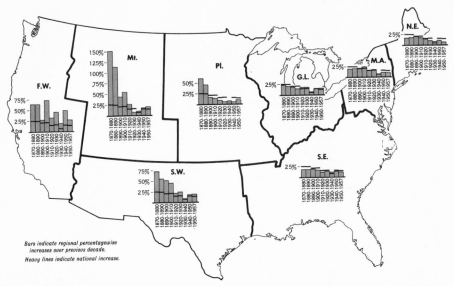

Figure 3. Decennial Rates of Population Increase, 1870-1950 (and 1950-57).

Before 1890 the Plains region also had a higher rate of population increase than the nation as a whole, but after 1890 it fell below the national average. In-migrants were fewer than out-migrants in Iowa and Missouri by the early twentieth century and in Minnesota, Nebraska, and Kansas by 1920. Since 1910 the proportion of the national population residing in the Plains states has declined by 4 percentage points. In recent decades the "westward" movement of population has been mostly towards the Far West, Southwest, and southern Mountain states.

Areas which consistently experienced the most rapid relative growth during these years were, on the whole, the least densely populated parts of the country. This is suggested by a comparison of the data in Table 2 with those in Table 3, which contrasts regional densities per square mile at various dates with the average density for the nation as a whole. As already noted, however, in *absolute* terms, the population increases were persistently heaviest in the Middle Atlantic, Great Lakes, and Southeast regions. In other words, the great bulk of the population continued to cluster in areas east of the Mississippi River. This can be seen in Figure 4, showing the regional distribution of the national population at various years since 1870, and in Figures 5 and 6[2], showing the patterns of settlement in 1900 and 1950.

The eastern part of the country—the New England, Middle Atlantic, Great Lakes, and Southeast regions—contained 85.5% of the nation's population in 1870, 74% in 1910, 71% in 1950, and 70% in 1957. In other words, the peopling of the West since 1870 has cost these four regions some 16 percentage

[2]Figures 5 and 6, prepared by the Bureau of the Census on the basis of data for minor civil divisions, highlight among other things the importance of water supplies in the settlement of the arid West.

Table 1. Regional distribution of U. S. population, 1870-1957, and population of regions, 1870 and 1957

Region	1870 (in thousands)	1870	1880	1890	1900	1910	1920	1930	1940	1950	1957	1957 (in thousands)
United States	39,818	100.0%	100.0%	100.0%	100.0%	100.0%	100.0%	100.0%	100.0%	100.0%	100.0%	170,337
New England	3,488	8.8	8.0	7.5	7.4	7.1	7.0	6.7	6.4	6.2	5.8	9,871
Middle Atlantic	9,848	24.7	23.4	22.5	22.5	23.0	23.1	23.3	23.0	22.3	21.5	36,722
Great Lakes	9,124	22.9	22.3	21.4	21.0	19.8	20.3	20.6	20.2	20.2	20.6	35,035
Southeast	11,600	29.1	27.3	25.5	25.1	23.9	23.0	22.2	22.9	22.4	21.8	37,193
Plains	3,857	9.7	12.3	14.2	13.6	12.7	11.9	10.8	10.3	9.3	9.0	15,309
Southwest	1,012	2.6	3.5	4.4	5.5	6.6	7.0	7.4	7.4	7.6	7.9	13,381
Mountain	171	0.4	0.9	1.4	1.7	2.2	2.4	2.2	2.3	2.3	2.4	4,146
Far West	718	1.8	2.3	3.1	3.2	4.7	5.3	6.8	7.5	9.7	11.0	18,680

SOURCE: Adapted from 17th U.S. Census of Population, 1950, Vol. II, Part 1, Table 6. Figures used are from the original census source, except for 1870. For that year, adjustments were made for underenumeration of 1,260,078 (mostly rural Negroes) in 13 Southern states. See U.S. Bureau of the Census, *Historical Statistics of the United States, 1789-1945* (Washington, GPO, 1949), Series B2, Note 11. This addition to national population has been distributed among the 12 states of our Southeast region and Texas in the Southwest region according to each state's share of enumerated Southeastern-plus-Texas population. This is, admittedly, a crude method of allocation, but data were not available for a more precise allocation. Figures for 1957 are from U.S. Department of Commerce, *Survey of Current Business*, August 1958, Table 3, p. 13.

Table 2. Percentage increases in population by census decades, by region, 1870-1950 (and 1950-57)

Region	1870-80	1880-90	1890-1900	1900-10	1910-20	1920-30	1930-40	1940-50	(1950-57)
United States	26.0	25.5	20.7	21.0	14.9	16.1	7.2	14.5	(13.0)
New England	15.0	17.2	19.0	17.2	12.9	10.3	3.3	10.4	(6.0)
Middle Atlantic	19.4	20.3	20.9	23.6	15.3	17.4	5.8	11.0	(9.2)
Great Lakes	22.8	20.3	18.6	14.2	17.7	17.8	5.3	14.2	(15.2)
Southeast	17.8	17.8	18.3	15.6	10.5	12.2	*10.6*	12.0	(10.1)
Plains	*59.7*	*45.1*	15.8	12.5	7.8	6.0	1.7	4.0	(8.9)
Southwest	*73.1*	*56.6*	*51.6*	*46.4*	*21.4*	*22.9*	7.7	16.3	(17.6)
Mountain	*151.4*	*113.1*	*43.1*	*53.7*	*26.9*	7.3	*9.3*	15.8	(19.0)
Far West	*64.0*	*64.5*	*27.0*	*73.8*	*32.1*	*46.8*	*18.8*	*48.8*	(*27.5*)

Figures in italics are above the national average.

SOURCE: See Table 1, note.

Table 3. Density of population, by region, 1870-1957

(Population per square mile of land area)

Region	Area*	1870	1890	1910	1930	1950	1957
United States	2,974,726 sq. mi.	13.4	21.2	30.9	41.3	50.7	57.3
New England	(2.12)	*55.2*	*74.4*	*103.7*	*129.3*	*147.5*	*156.3*
Middle Atlantic	(3.78)	*87.6*	*125.8*	*188.1*	*254.5*	*299.1*	*326.6*
Great Lakes	(8.23)	*37.3*	*55.0*	*74.5*	*103.3*	*124.1*	*143.1*
Southeast	(17.95)	21.7	*30.1*	*41.2*	*51.1*	*63.3*	*69.7*
Plains	(17.17)	7.6	17.5	22.8	26.0	27.5	30.0
Southwest	(19.08)	1.8	4.8	10.7	16.0	20.0	23.6
Mountain	(17.23)	0.3	1.8	3.9	5.4	6.8	8.1
Far West	(14.44)	1.7	4.5	9.9	19.3	34.1	43.5

*Figures in parentheses show proportion of total U. S. land area 1950. Figure in italics are above the national average.

Source: *Statistical Abstract of the United States, 1954,* Table 4, p. 10; also see Table 1, note.

points of their share of the nation's total population, and since 1910—it is particularly worth noting—only about 4 percentage points. The Great Lakes region, in fact, has a larger proportion of the nation's population at the present time than it had in 1910.

The region which secured the greatest share of the relative population losses of the East and the Plains region was the Far West. Its share of the national population increased from 4.7% to some 11% of the total between 1910 and 1957.

If regional growth is measured in terms of employed labor force rather than in terms of population, almost exactly the same pattern emerges—not unexpectedly. That is, between 1870 and 1957, the greatest relative expansion took place in the Far West, Southwest, and Mountain regions: the least, in the Southeast and New England.

The shares of the national labor force compare quite closely with the population shares for all regions (the greatest deviation being in the Southeast, where the influence of high birth rates emerges as significant). This can be seen by comparing the population and labor force shares of the Middle Atlantic, Far West, and Southeast regions for 1870 and 1950:

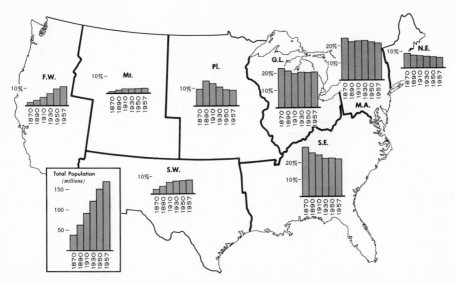

Figure 4. Regional Distribution of Total Population, 1870-1950 (and 1957).
Source: Table 1, note.

Share of U. S. Total	1870	1950
Middle Atlantic:		
Population	24.7%	22.3%
Labor force	25.2	23.5
Southeast:		
Population	29.1	22.4
Labor force	28.0	20.7
Far West:		
Population	1.8	9.7
Labor force	2.5	10.1

Urban Growth

Throughout the period under review there has been a continuous decline in the proportion of total population living in rural areas and a marked increase in urban population. The rate of urban increase has been positive in every region at every census since 1870. Urbanization in all parts of the country has been a central facet of recent American history. This significant change has accompanied the industrialization of the nation.

The decline in the share of the labor force engaged in resource activities (agriculture, forestry, mining, fishing) is traced in later chapters, as are the great increases in manufacturing and service employment. At this point we shall note only the profound effect that the changing structure of economic activities has had on the urban-rural pattern of population and in turn on the regional pattern of settlement. These are recorded here because of their significance for the analysis of regional economic growth which follows.

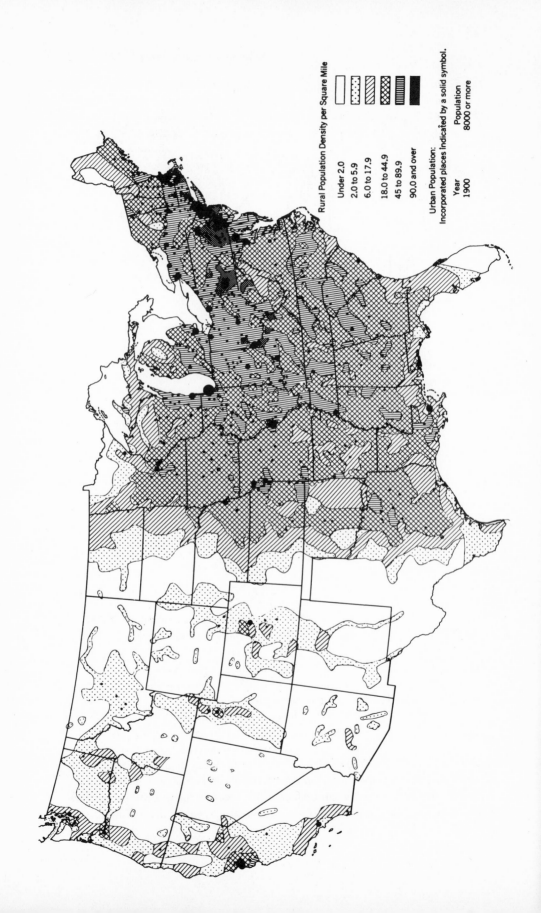

Rural Population Density per Square Mile

Under 2.0

2.0 to 5.9

6.0 to 17.9

18.0 to 44.9

45 to 89.9

90.0 and over

Urban Population:
Incorporated places indicated by a solid symbol.

Year
1900

Population
8000 or more

The increase in urban population within the various regions between 1870 and 1950 is summarized in Tables 4, 5, and 6.[3] The relative size of each region's urban population at various dates is shown in Table 4. By 1950, it can be seen, six of the eight regions had a larger urban than rural population. The decennial increases by regions are shown in Table 5. The rates of urbanization were higher in the "newer" and less developed regions, for the most part, than in the older and more developed areas of the country, though we tend to think of newly settled territory as largely rural.[4] Table 6 permits a comparison between the rates of urbanization and the proportion of urban residents in the total population of each of the regions. In spite of the very rapid increase in urban population in the West, the great bulk of the urban population resides in the East, and particularly in the Middle Atlantic and Great Lakes regions.

Viewed from the standpoint of city size (Table 7), the general process of urbanization has assumed different patterns in different regions. In 1870 only the Middle Atlantic and New England regions had the clearly defined beginnings of an "urban hierarchy"—that is, a broad base of many smaller-size urban centers underlying a smaller number of larger cities ranging up to a dominant regional metropolis. An emergent hierarchy was also evident in the Great Lakes region, but, in view of the much greater land area involved, these four or five midwestern centers with a population of over 50,000 could better be regarded as sub-regional centers in their own right with no one of them yet dominant over the others, though Chicago was already moving into that position. The same was broadly true of the urban scene in the South. Elsewhere in the country, the number of cities with more than 50,000 inhabitants could be counted on the fingers of one hand. In 1870, the Southwest and Mountain regions still had no center above 15,000 and the Plains had only three—St. Louis, St. Paul and Kansas City. In the Far West, San Francisco stood alone, rather like one of the great eastern coastal cities of colonial days.

By 1910 the force of urbanization was being felt throughout the entire country. The New England, Middle Atlantic, and Great Lakes regions had developed well-established urban hierarchies. The rest of the regions, with agriculture, forestry, and mining much more dominant than in the northeastern

---

[3] By 1950, the older census classification for presenting data on urban communities tended to understate the size of urban population, and a new classification in terms of "standard metropolitan areas" was introduced. In the present study, however, we have adhered to the older designation since it facilitated comparisons over time. For historical data based on the new designation, see Amos H. Hawley, *The Changing Shape of Metropolitan America: Deconcentration Since 1920* (Glencoe, Ill.: The Free Press, 1956).

[4] It is interesting to note that urbanization has proceeded in spurts, and has been cyclically oriented. Outstanding are the great spurts of the Mountain states during 1870-90, the Far West in 1870-90 and 1900-10, the Plains in 1880-90, and the Southwest over the four decades from 1870 to 1910.

Figure 5—opposite. Distribution of the Population, 1900.

Source: U. S. Bureau of the Census, *1900 Census of Population, Statistical Atlas*, plate 13.

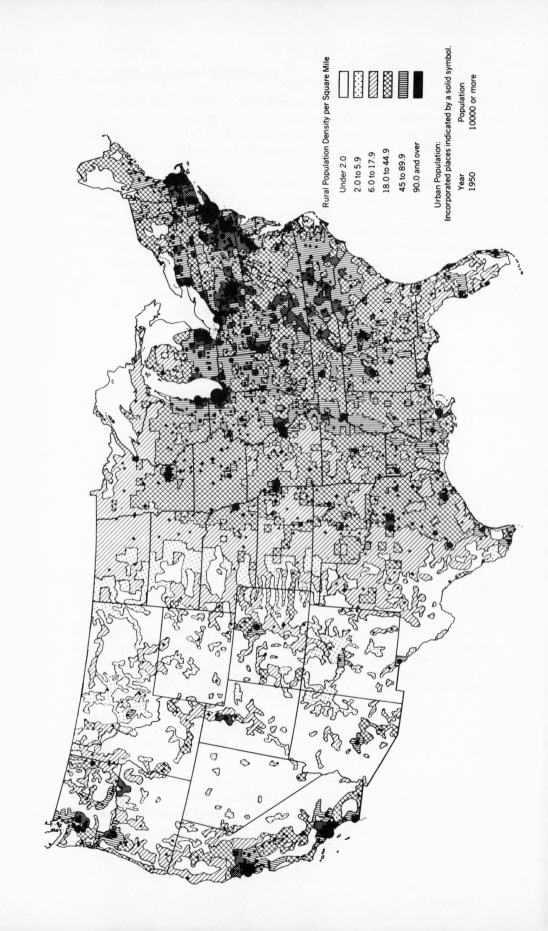

Rural Population Density per Square Mile

Under 2.0

2.0 to 5.9

6.0 to 17.9

18.0 to 44.9

45 to 89.9

90.0 and over

Urban Population:
Incorporated places indicated by a solid symbol.

Year   Population
1950   10000 or more

Table 4 Urban population as percentage of total population, by regions, 1870, 1910, and 1950

Region	1870 %	1910 %	1950 %
United States	25.2	45.7	59.0
New England	*44.4*	*73.3*	*74.3*
Middle Atlantic	*44.1*	*70.2*	*74.0*
Great Lakes	21.6	*52.7*	*65.7*
Southeast	9.5	19.4	42.5
Plains	18.9	33.2	49.9
Southwest	6.9	22.5	55.5
Mountain	13.9	40.7	51.8
Far West	*31.2*	*56.0*	62.7

Figures in italics are above the national average.

SOURCE: Adapted from 17th U. S. Census of Population, 1950, Vol. II, Pt. 1, Table 15. The additions to total population for the Southeastern states and Texas (see note to Table 1) for 1870 have been allocated as urban or rural according to the weight of the urban population shown in the original census report. This tends to exaggerate the absolute size of the urban population in some Southeastern states and in Texas but preserves the relative proportion in each case. The urban proportion in 1950 follows the standard census definition of "urban" (comparable with 1940) rather than the new definition adopted in the 17th U. S. Census, 1950. See also Tables P-4B and P-4C of E. S. Lee, A. R. Miller, C. P. Brainerd, and R. A. Easterlin, *Population Redistribution and Economic Growth, United States, 1870-1950* (Philadelphia: American Philosophical Society, 1957).

part of the nation and with huge land areas involved, were developing a different pattern of urban centers. There were several rapidly growing centers in each of these regions, but they were far smaller than the metropolitan communities of the Northeast and were not part of a clear-cut urban hierarchy. In the Southeast, for example, only New Orleans had a population of over 250,000 by 1910.

Figure 6—opposite. Distribution of the Population, 1950.

Source: Conrad and Irene Taeuber, *The Changing Population of the United States* (New York: John Wiley and Sons, 1958), Figure 3c.

Table 5. Decennial rates of increase of urban population, by region, 1870-1950

Region	1870-80	1880-90	1890-1900	1900-10	1910-20	1920-30	1930-40	1940-50
United States	41.0	56.5	36.4	39.3	29.0	27.3	7.9	19.5
New England	35.7	13.8	32.5	25.3	17.0	12.3	1.7	7.8
Middle Atlantic	34.7	39.6	35.0	34.6	22.7	20.7	4.8	8.0
Great Lakes	56.2	66.0	41.2	33.2	35.7	28.7	3.9	14.5
Southeast	16.2	63.8	37.1	48.3	36.0	39.3	18.6	33.5
Plains	53.1	106.2	27.7	31.3	22.2	17.6	7.9	17.1
Southwest	133.5	135.2	165.9	118.3	63.6	55.0	19.4	52.3
Mountain	351.5	197.9	51.6	68.6	23.8	14.7	18.1	31.0
Far West	89.1	94.1	37.4	112.1	45.1	60.3	14.9	43.6

Figures in italics are above the national average.

Source: See Table 4, note.

Table 6. Rank order of regions by rate of increase in urban population and regional proportions of U. S. urban population, 1870-1950

	1870-80 % Rate	1870 Proportion	1900-10 % Rate	1910 Proportion	1940-50 % Rate	1950 Proportion
(1)	Mt. 351.5	M.A. 43.4	S.W. 118.3	MA. 35.3	S.W. 52.3	M.A. 28.0
(2)	S.W. 133.5	G.L. 19.7	F.W. 112.1	G.L. 22.9	F.W. 43.6	G.L. 22.5
(3)	F.W. 89.1	N.E. 15.5	Mt. 68.6	N.E. 11.4	S.E. 33.5	S.E. 14.4
(4)	G.L. 56.2	S.E. 11.0	S.E. 48.3	S.E. 10.2	Mt. 31.0	F.W. 10.3
(5)	Pl. 53.1	Pl. 7.3	M.A. 34.6	Pl. 9.2	Pl. 17.1	Pl. 7.9
(6)	N.E. 35.7	F.W. 2.2	G.L. 33.2	F.W. 5.7	G.L. 14.5	N.E. 7.8
(7)	M.A. 34.7	S.W. 0.7	Pl. 31.3	S.W. 3.3	M.A. 8.0	S.W. 7.1
(8)	S.E. 16.2	Mt. 0.2	N.E. 25.3	Mt. 2.0	N.E. 7.8	Mt. 2.0
		100%		100%		100%

SOURCE: See Table 4, note.

Table 7. City size, 1870, 1910, and 1950

(Number of cities of certain size)

	1870					1910					1950				
	50,000–100,000	100,000–250,000	250,000–500,000	500,000–1,000,000	1,000,000+	50,000–100,000	100,000–250,000	250,000–500,000	500,000–1,000,000	1,000,000+	50,000–100,000	100,000–250,000	250,000–500,000	500,000–1,000,000	1,000,000+
New England	2	0	0	0	0	12	7	0	1	0	17	11	0	1	0
Middle Atlantic	3	4	1	1	1	18	5	4	2	2	23	13	3	4	2
Great Lakes	3	1	1	0	0	11	5	3	1	1	31	10	4	3	2
Southeast	1	2	0	0	0	6	6	1	0	0	23	15	4	1	0
Plains	0	0	1	0	0	5	3	1	1	0	9	4	3	2	0
Southwest	0	0	0	0	0	5	0	0	0	0	10	6	3	1	0
Mountain	0	0	0	0	0	1	1	0	0	0	2	1	1	0	0
Far West	0	1	0	0	0	1	4	2	0	0	11	5	5	1	1

SOURCE: 1870: *Statistical Abstract of the United States, 1921*, Table 35, pp. 58-60. 1910 and 1950: *Statistical Abstract of the United States, 1955*, Table 14, pp. 20-23.

By 1950 manufacturing activities had become significant in the Far West (particularly the Coast area) and in parts of the Southeast, and both of these regions had begun to develop more sharply defined urban "systems." In the rest of the country, except for eastern Texas, the larger cities tended to be more isolated regional centers (in some cases resembling "oasis cities"), with hardly a discernible hierarchy of smaller communities. Thus the population map of 1950 (see Figure 6) reveals three great urban masses highlighting the three great manufacturing zones of the nation—the major Manufacturing Belt of the Northeast and the lesser manufacturing zones of the Pacific Coast and the Southeast.

Changes in Total Income, 1880-1957[5]

One of the most comprehensive and suggestive measures of regional economic growth is provided by total personal income.[6] Table 8 presents data on changes in the regional distribution of the nation's total personal income between 1880 and 1957. In some important respects these data show an over-all pattern of differential regional growth similar to that shown by the data on population in Table 1. Like the changes in population, the changes in income reflect the impressive growth in volume of economic activities in the Far West and Southwest regions, the gradual decline in the volume shares of the New England and Middle Atlantic regions, and the stability of the Great Lakes region over the period as a whole.

A closer look at the data reveals, however, that the distribution of total income among the various regions does not correspond fully with the population distribution. This is particularly true for the Southeast. In 1880 this region had 27% of the nation's population but less than 14% of the total national income; and in 1957, while it had almost 22% of the total population, it had only some 15% of the total income. The differing pattern of regional shares reflects the sizeable differences in income-earning capacity of the activities dominant in the various regions. This was particularly important in the earlier part of the period.[7]

[5]Unfortunately, for the earlier part of the period under examination, the years for which income data are available do not coincide with the years for the population series discussed in the preceding sections. The best figures on state income available, those devised by Richard Easterlin of the University of Pennsylvania, begin with 1880 and proceed by two-decade intervals to 1920. Thereafter, income figures are available by decades in the Commerce series and after 1929, in fact, on an annual basis.

[6]Ideally, to measure growth in the volume of regional economic activities, we would want annual data on production—on net value produced—within each of the regions. But we do not have data on gross or net product for any subnational units. However, the Department of Commerce series on state personal income does provide a fairly close approximation to the desired measure.

[7]Cyclical movements, especially in agricultural prices, have also played a significant role in the levels of total income within the various regions.

Table 8. Regional distribution of total personal income, 1880-1957

(U. S. income in millions)

Region	1880*	1900*	1920*†	1930	1940	1950	1957
United States	$8,743 (100%)	$15,391 (100%)	$69,276 (100%)	$76,780 (100%)	$78,522 (100%)	$225,473 (100%)	$345,272 (100%)
New England	11.3	9.9	8.8	8.6	8.2	6.7	6.6
Middle Atlantic	32.6	30.8	30.2	33.3	30.5	26.4	25.5
Great Lakes	22.8	22.4	22.2	22.6	22.7	22.5	22.5
Southeast	13.7	12.0	13.0	11.2	13.2	15.2	15.4
Plains	11.1	13.3	10.3	8.9	8.3	8.8	8.1
Southwest	2.1	3.8	5.7	4.8	5.2	6.5	6.8
Mountain	1.4	2.5	2.5	1.9	2.0	2.2	2.2
Far West	5.0	5.3	7.4	8.8	9.9	11.7	13.0

*District of Columbia excluded.

† 1919-21 average.

SOURCE: Lee, Miller, Brainerd and Easterlin, (see note for Table 4), Table Y-1, p. 753; C. F. Schwartz and R. E. Graham, Jr., *Personal Income by States since 1929*, Office of Business Economics, U. S. Department of Commerce (Washington: Government Printing Office, 1956), Table 1; *Survey of Current Business* (August 1958), Table 1, p. 13.

Changes in Per Capita Income

The interplay between population growth and growth in total income within the various regions is reflected in the per capita income levels and rates of increase. Table 9 shows estimates of real income per capita (1929 dollars) over the 1880-1957 period in each of the regions. There has been a striking trend toward equalization among the regions. In 1880, regional averages ranged from 211% of the national average to 50%. In 1957 the highest regional income was only 119% of the national average and the lowest 70%.

Since 1920 the regions in which manufacturing and service activities are predominant have had considerably higher incomes than the less industrialized Mountain, Plains, Southwest, and Southeast regions. Before 1920 the advantage of the more urban-industrialized regions was by no means so consistent in this respect. In the last two decades of the nineteenth century the Far West and Mountain regions had the highest per capita real incomes in the country; it was only after 1900 that the industrial areas markedly improved their relative position. First the Middle Atlantic and New England regions, followed after World War I by the Great Lakes region, closed the gap between their income levels and those of the Far West. Between 1920 and 1940, the Middle Atlantic region was actually the pacemaker for the nation.

More recently, the states and regions appear to be grouping themselves into three categories with regard to per capita income levels (Figure 7). These groupings are: (1) the urban-industrialized-service regions of the Manufacturing Belt and the Far West, with per capita incomes above the national average, and mostly well above the average; (2) the Mountain, Plains, and Southwest

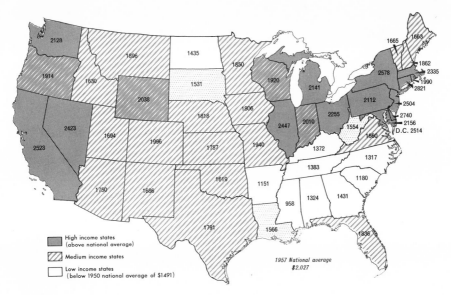

Figure 7. Per Capita Personal Income, 1957.

regions, northern New England and the peripheral Southeastern states of Florida and Virginia, with incomes somewhat below the national average; and (3) the greatest part of the Southeast, standing alone (except for the Dakotas) in terms of extremely low per capita income levels.[8]

The groupings are fairly well defined. Within the high-income areas, only three states in the Northeast (Indiana, Wisconsin, and Rhode Island) and only one state in the Far West (Oregon) were below the national average in 1957. In all the other states of the Northeast and the Far West, per capita income ranged from $2,112 to $2,821. The range in the low-income states of the Southeast was from under $1,000 (Mississippi) to slightly over $1,400 (Georgia); the average for this region in 1957 was below the *national* average of seven years before ($1,451). The middle-range group covered the relatively narrow range between $1,531 (South Dakota) and $1,996 (Colorado) in 1957.[9]

The depressing effect of population growth keeping close pace with the growth in total income is evident in the Southeast where, despite steadily increasing economic activity and increasing wage levels, per capita income continues to be far below the national average. In contrast, the slackening of population growth in the Plains states has helped to keep the level of real income per capita from falling sharply in relation to the national average in spite of a relatively slow growth in the volume of economic activities and total income.

[8]A few of the states are at the periphery of these major classes; these are shown on Figure 7 by dots in the case of the lowest income class and a break in the solid gray in the case of the states slightly under the level set for the highest income class (i.e., the national average per capita income in 1957).

[9]State per capita income figures for any one year inevitably reflect special circumstances, so that some variations are to be found from year to year. This is particularly true because of the wide cyclical swings in farm prices and farm incomes. For this reason, the states that are on the borderline between broad income categories are specially marked in Figure 7. For example, Wyoming, which was above the national average in 1957, was below the average in 1955 and 1956, and therefore is marked as borderline. This is true also of Indiana and Rhode Island which were just below the national average in 1957, but above the average in every other year between 1950 and 1956. Oregon was above the national average during the period 1950-53; just short of the average during 1954-57. The states of North Dakota, South Dakota, Louisiana, and West Virginia are borderline between the lowest and middle income categories if the standard of catching up with the national average of some years back is employed. Of these states, all but North Dakota were just above the 1950 national-average level (of $1,491) in 1957, but below this figure in 1955 and 1956. Of the Southeastern states, only Virginia and Florida can be said to fall clearly into the middle-income category.

Table 9. Regional income per capita, 1880-1957, and as percentage of national average

(Weighted average of state incomes per capita, 1929 dollars)

Region	1880		1900		1920		1930		1940		1950		1957	
		%		%		%		%		%		%		%
United States	$302.1		$414.0		$578.0		$640.0		$727.4		$1,062.7		$1,236.0	
New England	425.0	(140.7)	551.7	(133.3)	719.3	(124.4)	826.7	(129.2)	925.4	(127.2)	1,160.4	(109.2)	1,401.2	(113.4)
Middle Atlantic	422.8	(140.0)	570.2	(137.7)	772.5	(133.2)	912.9	(142.6)	965.8	(132.8)	1,255.2	(118.1)	1,459.7	(118.1)
Great Lakes	307.4	(101.8)	439.6	(106.2)	623.5	(107.9)	701.6	(109.6)	815.4	(112.1)	1,183.9	(111.4)	1,350.0	(109.2)
Southeast	150.6	(49.9)	197.7	(47.8)	326.2	(56.4)	321.0	(50.2)	419.3	(57.6)	719.2	(67.7)	870.1	(70.4)
Plains	271.2	(89.8)	401.5	(97.0)	501.0	(86.7)	523.1	(81.7)	590.5	(81.2)	1,003.6	(94.4)	1,111.6	(89.9)
Southwest	182.7	(60.5)	283.2	(68.4)	466.2	(80.7)	411.3	(64.3)	511.0	(70.2)	916.6	(86.3)	1,068.3	(86.4)
Mountain	501.5	(166.0)	601.0	(145.2)	590.7	(102.2)	551.8	(86.2)	649.2	(89.2)	1,017.8	(95.8)	1,137.2	(92.0)
Far West	638.2	(211.3)	674.6	(162.9)	780.6	(135.1)	837.0	(130.8)	959.7	(131.9)	1,279.4	(120.4)	1,467.7	(118.7)

Figures in italics are above the national average.

Deflators (1929 = 100):

1880– 57.3	1920–121.2	1940– 81.8	1957–164.0
1900– 48.9	1930– 97.5	1950–140.3	

1880–1920 are GNP deflators used by Easterlin.

1930–1957 are based on BLS Consumers Price Index, *Statistical Abstract of the United States 1958*, Table 419.

SOURCE: Unpublished data supplied by Richard Easterlin; *Personal Income by States since 1929* (see note for Table 8); *Survey of Current Business*, August 1958, Table 2.

3 / Economic growth, 1939-1954

(with a focus on the states)

Much of our analysis of the factors behind regional economic growth will concentrate on a recent period of relatively short duration—the 15-year period 1939-1954.[1] For this period we have examined in some detail the major elements suggesting changes in volume of economic activities within the states— population and total personal income—and changes in living levels as represented by per capita income. State data have been used in this examination to give a more detailed and particularized view than the regional data alone provide.

Measurement of Relative Change

A whole series of data on relative (percentage-wise) changes in population, total income, and per capita income are brought together in Figure 8 for the states and in Figure 9 for the multi-state regions in order to show the interplay of the key elements in regional growth. This technique of presentation, based on the "relative growth" chart developed by Edgar M. Hoover and Joseph L. Fisher,[2] has the important advantage of highlighting the wide variety of growth

---

[1]This period seemed to be appropriate for several reasons: (1) it coincides with two census dates for which considerable data are available of the type needed for the detailed analysis involved. (2) The years 1939 and 1954 have fairly comparable business-cycle (particularly unemployment) characteristics—a critical element in measurement and analysis of economic growth, although comparability of this type at best is highly tenuous. (3) Both the early part and the latter part of the period were influenced by war; first, World War II, and then the Korean War. Actually, of course, no years during the 20th century can be chosen (for growth comparisons) which can be considered to be really removed from the "unusual" factors associated with war and depression.

[2]Edgar M. Hoover, Jr., and Joseph L. Fisher, "Research in Regional Economic Growth," *Problems in the Study of Economic Growth,* Universities-National Bureau Committee on Economic Research (New York: The National Bureau of Economic Research, 1949), pp. 195-203.

In the two charts that we present here the solid horizontal axis measures 1954 population as a percentage of 1939 population and the solid vertical axis measures 1954 total personal

patterns within the national economy. The various combinations of increases or decreases relative to the national average are seen to be as follows:

I. *Above-average increases in population, total income, and per capita income:* The Southwestern states fall mainly into this category, with Arizona leading in both relative population increase and relative increase in total income. Florida follows closely on both these scores. In terms of relative increases in per capita income, however, the only states in this group that rank very high are New Mexico (seventh highest in the nation) and Texas (eleventh in rank).

II. *Above-average increases in total and per capita income; below-average increases in population:* Most of the Southeastern states fall into this group, and the Plains states are also strongly represented (Kansas, Nebraska, South Dakota). In two states—Mississippi and Oklahoma—population actually declined between 1939 and 1954, while total income and per capita income increased more rapidly than for the nation as a whole. Oklahoma had the third highest percentage increase in per capita income in the country and Mississippi the fifth highest.

III. *Above-average increases in per capita income; below-average increases in population and total income:* With the exception of Wisconsin, all of the states in this category are west of the Mississippi. The Plains states and the Mountain states (except Wyoming) that are not in either of the first two categories are in this one. When an average for the multi-state regions is struck, the Plains region is shown to be well below average in population growth, almost exactly average in growth of total income, and above average in per capita income increase, while the Mountain region had slightly above-average increases in all three over the 15-year period.

income in current prices as a percentage of 1939 total income. The data are plotted on a double logarithmic scale. The origin of the diagram (A) is at 100 for population, which represents population unchanged between the two dates, and at 207 for total personal income at current prices. Since prices increased 107% between the two dates, as measured by the Gross National Product deflator, an increase in total money income of 107% between 1939 and 1954 is the same as an unchanged total *real* income.

Each state (or region) is represented by a point on the graph with coordinates determined by its percentage changes in population and in total personal income between the two dates. Any point to the right of the solid vertical axis represents an increase in population and any point above the solid horizontal axis an increase in real total personal income.

The solid diagonal line drawn through the origin is the locus of all points on the chart for which per capita income in current dollars increased 107%, or for which per capita real income remained unchanged between 1939 and 1954. Any point above this line represents an increase in per capita real income.

In addition to the solid coordinate axes, dashed axes are shown. The origin of these (B) is the U.S. average increase—23% for population, 291% for total personal income in current prices, and 217% for per capita income in current prices. (In "real" terms, the national average increases were about 89% for total personal income and 53% for per capita income.) Any point to the right of the dashed vertical axis represents a population increase greater than the national average, and any point above the dashed diagonal axis a per capita income increase greater than the national average.

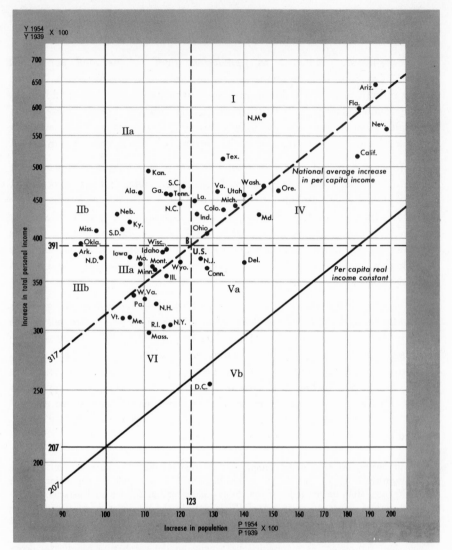

$\frac{Y\ 1954}{Y\ 1939}$ X 100

700
650
600
550
500
450
391
350
317
300
250
207
200
207

I
IIa
IIb
IIIa
IIIb
IV
Va
Vb
VI
B
U.S.

Ariz.
Fla.
Nev.
Calif.
N.M.
Tex.
National average increase in per capita income
Kan.
S.C.
Ga. Tenn.
Ala.
Va. Utah Wash.
La.
Mich. Ore.
Neb.
N.C.
Colo.
Ind.
Md.
Miss.
Ky.
Ohio
S.D.
Okla.
Wisc.
Ark.
Idaho
Iowa
N.D.
Mo. Mont.
Minn. Wyo.
Ill.
Conn.
N.J.
Del.
Per capita real income constant
W.Va.
Pa.
N.H.
Vt. Me.
R.I. N.Y.
Mass.
D.C.

123

90 100 110 120 130 140 150 160 170 180 190 200

Increase in population $\frac{P\ 1954}{P\ 1939}$ X 100

Increase in total personal income

Figure 8. Relative State Economic Growth, 1939-54.

Source: U. S. Bureau of the Census, *Personal Income by States since 1929*, Tables 1, 2, and 3.

The groups of states comprising the first three categories have the common feature of an above-average increase in per capita income. In the three remaining categories, per capita income increased less rapidly than for the nation as a whole.

IV. *Above-average increases in population and total income; below-average increases in per capita income:* The Far West falls into this category. Wash-

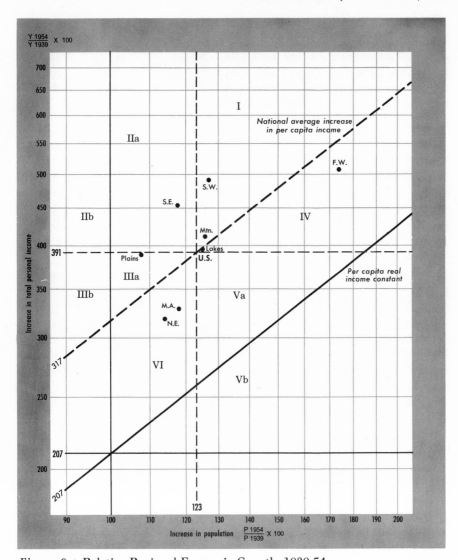

Figure 9. Relative Regional Economic Growth, 1939-54.

Source: U. S. Bureau of the Census, *Personal Income by States since 1929*, Tables 1, 2, and 3.

ington was the only state in the region with a per capita income increase equal to the national average.

V. *Above-average population increases; below-average increases in total and per capita income:* This category includes three small, largely urbanized states—New Jersey, Connecticut, and Delaware—and the District of Columbia. The District shows an actual drop in per capita income, evidently due to sub-urbanization and a change in the population structure of the city.

VI. *Below-average increases on all three counts:* All the New England states fall into this category except Connecticut (which reflects the special situation of the suburbanization of New York City). So also do the highly industrialized states, New York, Pennsylvania, and Illinois. On the basis of regional averages, the Middle Atlantic region is in this category; Maryland was the only state here that had an above-average increase in total income, a reflection in part at least of the suburbanization of Washington, D. C.

Percentage-wise increases in per capita income, it can be seen, have not been at all closely correlated with growth in population. Thus, of the twenty-nine states in which per capita income increased more rapidly than the national average, nineteen had a below-average increase in population. Of the six states with the highest relative increase in per capita income—Kansas, Alabama, Oklahoma, Nebraska, Mississippi, and Arkansas, in that order—all but two showed an actual decline in population; and in these two—Kansas and Alabama—the population increase was below the national average.[3]

The discussion to this point has emphasized *relative* state and regional growth. However, *absolute* numbers must also be considered to obtain a rounded picture of regional population and economic growth. The "size" of the state or region is, of course, significant in this regard. Thus, for example, the states with the highest percentage increases in population between 1939 and 1954, Nevada and Arizona, had total population gains of 105,000 and 446,000, respectively, while Pennsylvania, which ranked 36th among the states in percentage increase, had a population gain of 955,000. New York State, which was below the national average in percentage of population increase (117% against a national average of 123%), had the second largest absolute gain in the nation, a gain of 2,305,000. On the basis of absolute increments to population alone, the heavily populated states of Illinois, Massachusetts, New York, and Pennsylvania might be included among the "growth" states, even though each had a below-average percentage increase in population. A number of the more heavily populated states experienced sizeable population increases in both absolute and relative terms, particularly California, Florida, Texas, and Michigan. California's population gain was 5,723,000 out of a national total increase of 30,311,000—almost one-fifth of the total. The increase for

[3]The relationship between population numbers and income is, of course, highly complex—and will be discussed in some detail in Part V of this book. At this point, however, it is appropriate to note at least one aspect of this relationship. Parts of the West, including California, Nevada, and Oregon, show a tendency for population increases to run stronger than increases in total income earned, so that increments in per capita income fail to keep pace with the national average. This does not necessarily mean a poor balance between population and income growth, however. As long as employment opportunities are at least at the national average, and wages remain at above-average levels for comparable work, it may be that the loss in relative per capita income standing of these states is due to the in-migration of lower-income earning families at the same time that the older residents—those that were there before 1939—enjoy a rise in income at least comparable to the national average. However, the danger of imbalance does exist, and one would want to focus attention on changes in levels of real wages and similar indices to determine whether such imbalance has come into being.

Florida was 1,553,000; for Texas, 2,102,000; and for Michigan, 1,920,000.

These two significant dimensions of population growth can be combined by employing the "shift" method of presenting data.[4] Because this method of measurement is used throughout the study, we shall explain it here at this point, where it is first employed.

Population Shifts Among the States (Including a Note on Methodology)

The *net shifts* by which we measure state and regional growth or decline are the relative gains and losses among the states with regard to a given variable (such as population growth, as here) in comparison to the national figures. These relative changes are determined in the following way. In measuring the population changes between 1939 and 1954, for example, the percentage increase in national population for these years is applied to each state's population to give what might be called the *expected change* by 1954 if population had increased *uniformly* throughout the states. This *expected* population change for each state is then compared with the *actual* population change in each state as estimated by the United States Census Bureau for 1954. The fact that population did not increase uniformly throughout the states means that some states achieved more and others less than the *expected increase;* i.e., some states increased their numbers proportionally more than the ratio over the 15-year period; others increased their number proportionally less than the ratio. For example, California's *actual* increase over the period 1939-1954 was 4,152,000 more than it would have been if population had increased in the same proportion as the ratio (its *expected* change), whereas New York's increase in

Population	*United States*	*California*	*New York*
1939	130,880,000	6,785,000	13,523,000
1954	161,191,000	12,508,000	15,828,000
Actual Change:	+30,311,000	+5,723,000	+2,305,000
Expected Change: the percentage increase in national population applied to the states		+1,571,000	+3,132,000
Net Shift Among States, Upward and Downward	±9,458,000	+4,152,000	—827,000
State's % of Total Upward or Downward Shift		43.90%	—8.74%

[4]Earlier studies which have employed the "shift" technique of organizing substantial data include Daniel Creamer in National Resources Planning Board, *Industrial Location and Natural Resources* (Washington: U.S. Government Printing Office, December 1943), Chapter 4; Wilbur Zelinsky, "A Method For Measuring Change in The Distribution of Manufacturing Activity: The United States, 1939-47," *Economic Geography,* Vol. 34 (April 1958), pp. 95-126; Victor R. Fuchs, "Changes in the Location of U. S. Manufacturing Since 1929," *Journal of Regional Science,* Vol. 1 (Spring 1959), pp. 1-17.

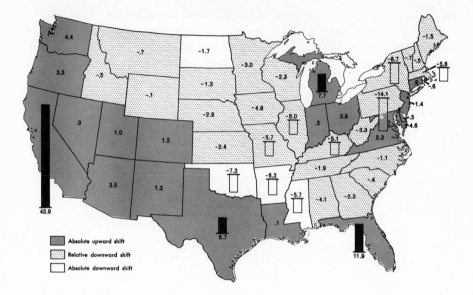

Figure 10. Net Shift in Total Population, 1939-54.

State figures represent % of total net shift. Total net shift as % of incremental change: 31.2. Total net shift as % of 1939 population: 7.2.

Source: Appendix Table H.

population was 827,000 less than it should have been to conform with the national increase. Thus, it can be said that California had a "net upward shift" of 4,152,000 people and New York a "net downward shift" of 827,000 over this period. California's *share* of the *total* net upward shift (that is, the sum of all state upward shifts) over the period was 43.9%, while New York sustained 8.74% of the *total* net downward shift (Figure 10).[5]

Figure 10 shows the net shift in population, by states, between 1939 and 1954. The states shown in dark color are those which had net upward shifts; the others all had net downward shifts. The percentage figure shown for each state is the proportion which its actual number is of the total net upward or downward shifts.

All states in the Far West and all except Oklahoma in the Southwest show relative population gains over these years. So also do the eastern Great Lakes

[5] Both the downward and upward shifts can further be classified as absolute or relative. An *absolute* downward shift is one in which all or some part of the downward shift was contributed by an actual decline in population. A *relative* downward shift is one in which there has been an increase in population, but one insufficient relative to the total increase to maintain that state's share of the total. An absolute upward shift is one in which all or some part of the shift was contributed by an actual increase in population. A relative upward shift is one in which there has been an actual decrease in the population but one that has been insufficient relative to the total decline to reduce that state's share of the total.

states and the Middle Atlantic seaboard states—Connecticut, New Jersey, Delaware, and Maryland; the gains in these Middle Atlantic states, as in Virginia in the Southeast, reflect the suburbanization effect noted earlier. Four states stand out: California, with 44% of the total net upward shift, Florida with 12%, Michigan with some 8%, and Texas with about 7%.

The group of states along the Appalachians—Kentucky, West Virginia, Pennsylvania, New York, and Massachusetts—together account for 37% of the net downward shift; Illinois, Iowa, and Missouri for 16%; and a tier of four states extending from Alabama through Oklahoma for another 23%. Together, these three groups make up three-quarters of the net downward shift.

In Table 10 the principal net population shifts among the states are examined for a somewhat longer time period—1910-1957—as a check on the findings for the shorter 1939-1954 period. The pattern of net upward shifts is generally similar for the two periods. The same four states—California, Florida, Michigan, and Texas—had the largest net upward population shifts between

Table 10. Principal population shifts among the states, 1910-1957

	Percentage net upward shift		Percentage net downward shift
California	43.11	Pennsylvania	14.28
Florida	12.24	Missouri	8.35
Michigan	11.77	Massachusetts	6.20
Texas	8.70	Iowa	5.98
New Jersey	4.20	Kentucky	5.44
Arizona	3.43	Arkansas	5.20
Washington	2.75	Mississippi	5.18
Oregon	2.37	Georgia	4.77
Maryland–District		Kansas	4.51
of Columbia	2.25	New York	4.49
North Carolina	1.87		

SOURCE: See Table 1, note.

1910-1957 as between 1939-1954. These states are clearly the outstanding population-growth states of the twentieth century.

With only slight modifications, also, the same groups of states had the greatest downward shifts in relative population standing in both periods.[6]

[6]This play-back over time, while complicating the presentation, is important as a continuing check on the growth patterns described, so that generalities with regard to growth experiences may be drawn with confidence. This is particularly important in the case of some series because, as mentioned at several points, beginning and/or terminal dates of an historical series can readily reflect the special circumstances of a single year or a very short period.

Relative Total Income Gains and Losses

When shift analysis is applied to the changes in relative standing among the states with regard to total personal income over the 1939-1954 period, California, Texas, Florida, and Michigan are found to have had the greatest net upward shifts. These are clearly the states that have made the greatest gains in volume of economic activities in recent years. On the other end of the scale, the four highly industrialized states of Illinois, Pennsylvania, New York and Massachusetts accounted for 80% of the net downward shift in total income. It should be emphasized again, however, that these were losses in relative standing only. All four of these states were in the top quarter of the states ranked according to absolute increments in total personal income. Moreover, at the end of the 1939-1954 period, each of them had a larger proportion of the nation's total income than of its total population.

The main divergences between changes in relative population standing and relative total income standing occurred in the Middle Atlantic seaboard states and in the Southeast (with the exception here of Florida and Virginia). Connecticut, New Jersey, and Delaware all show a net upward shift in population but some loss of standing in total income. (As explained later, however, this arises from special circumstances surrounding the period itself and is not representative of the growth patterns of the area generally.) The Southeastern states improved their relative standing on total income between 1939 and 1954 but had downward shifts in population. There was some divergence between population and total income changes in the Plains states also; all of these states had net downward shifts in population, but a number of them (particularly Kansas and Nebraska) improved their income standing somewhat during this period. World War II had a profound effect on the agriculture of the South and the West and also on the industry and services of these areas to the extent that interior locations for war-connected activities were favored over seaboard locations. An examination of the net shifts in total personal income for the postwar period alone shows that the main gains of these regions were made during the war and that the postwar pattern of income growth coincides fairly closely with the 1939-1954 pattern of population shift. For the postwar years, the Plains states show no gain in relative standing on total income; and this is true also for the states in the Deep South except Georgia and South Carolina. Furthermore, for the postwar years considered alone, the Middle Atlantic seaboard states show a gain in income standing and in fact claim some 15% of the nation's net upward shift in total income.

Table 11 shows the net upward and downward shifts in total income over a somewhat longer time period—the years from 1920 to 1957. Here the Middle Atlantic seaboard states—Connecticut, New Jersey, Maryland (and Virginia in the Southeast), together with the outstanding "growth states" of the shorter period examined—California, Florida, Michigan, and Texas—show up as having made the greatest improvements in relative position. Also, for this longer period, New York, Pennsylvania, Massachusetts, and Illinois show relative losses as in the shorter period. These four states, together with four Plains states, had the greatest net downward shifts between 1920 and 1957.

In general, then, it is clear that the World War II period has to be considered as special. The postwar period, however, exhibits the same pattern of differential gains among the states as does the longer-run period of 1920-1957.

Table 11. Principal shifts in total personal income among the states, 1920-1957

	Percentage net upward shift		Percentage net downward shift
California	40.72	New York	26.51
Florida	12.15	Pennsylvania	19.76
Texas	8.77	Massachusetts	13.32
Michigan	8.16	Illinois	6.85
Virginia	3.35	Iowa	3.72
North Carolina	3.20	Missouri	3.55
New Jersey	3.11	Oklahoma	3.09
Maryland–District		Kansas	2.99
of Columbia	2.30	Nebraska	2.10
Louisiana	2.25	Rhode Island	1.85
Connecticut	2.13		

SOURCE: See Table 8, note.

Per Capita Income

The evolving balance between population numbers and total income received is highly suggestive of the type of economic adjustment being made within a given state or region. Comparative percentage gains among the states in per capita income have already been presented. Figure 11 provides a useful additional view of the changing income picture. It shows the absolute increments to real per capita income from 1939 to 1954. This additional view is needed in order to avoid overstating the welfare advances of the areas starting with relatively low per capita incomes and understating the real advances of the "richer" and particularly the middle-income states.

Thus, the Southeast as a whole has had percentage increases in per capita income greater than the national average for every decade except one since 1900; yet, during the same period, there has been only one decade in which *absolute* increments in per capita income have exceeded the national average in any Southeastern state except Florida. This important feature of economic growth can be highlighted through an example, taking the richest of the Southeastern states. Between 1880 and 1950, the percentage increase in real per capita income for Florida was well above the national average; for every decade but one, the percentage increase for New York has been less than the national average. Yet in 1950 the absolute amount by which New York's per capita income exceeded that of Florida was $100 *greater* than it was in 1880. Of course, low income regions that realize a percentage rate of growth in real per capita income in excess of the national average over a sufficiently long period of time may ultimately liquidate the discrepancy in income. The starting point and rate of gain must, however, be considered to appreciate the length of time which might be involved in such equalization.

The regional pattern shown in Figure 11 differs from the one that emerges

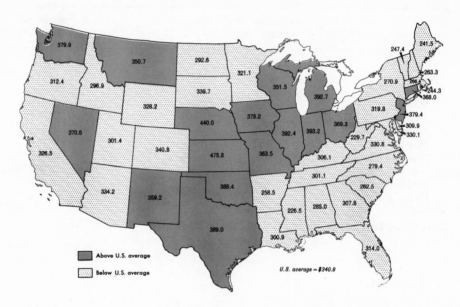

Figure 11. Absolute Increments to Real Per Capita Income, 1939-54.

Source: U. S. Bureau of the Census, *Personal Income by States since 1929,* Table 2.

when either *levels* of per capita income or *percentage rates of increase* in per capita income are recorded. And it is significantly different in certain respects from the pattern which emerges when growth in population and total income are set down. Possibly the most interesting feature of this particular measure of improvement in material welfare among the states, however, is the fact that, in absolute terms, the gains over the period 1939-1954 have been within a relatively narrow range. In only five states were the absolute gains in real income as much as 25% below the national average; and there were only two states with gains as much as 25% above the national average. *This suggests a remarkably uniform forward movement in absolute per capita income gains across the entire country during this 15-year period.* (The meaning of this forward movement is discussed in some detail in Part V of this book.)

Growth Profile Combining Multiple "Dimensions," 1939-1954

In presenting measures of regional growth, we have touched upon six "dimensions"—*absolute* increases in population, in total real personal income, and in per capita real income; *relative* increases in population, in total real personal income, and in per capita real income. None of these measures alone is adequate to describe even the crude outlines of economic growth. Each is subject to certain limitations and biases. Absolute measures tend to overstate the growth of big states such as Pennsylvania and understate the growth of little states such as Delaware. Relative measures tend to overstate the growth of areas with a low population or small income base and understate the growth of areas with a high population or large income base. Total income and population increments cannot indicate changes in individual and family welfare; and per capita income increments frequently do not correlate with other dimensions of growth.

In a situation such as this, one is tempted to try to combine the different variables into a combined index of growth. There is no possibility, however, of ever knowing the proper weights for combining these elements or the proper way to bring about an offsetting of bias. On the other hand, there does seem to be some advantage in bringing these measures together state by state into a kind of profile that will allow a comparison of the similarities and diversities that exist.

To this end, Figure 12 has been prepared. In it, we resort to the use of symbolic classification. Each state is assigned a plus or a minus for each of the six measures according to whether it ranks above or below the national average

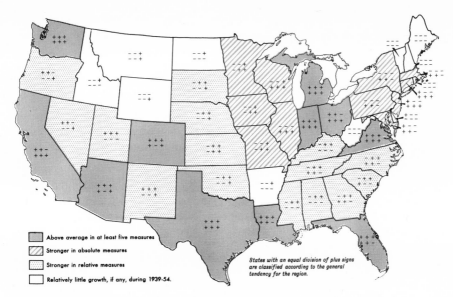

Figure 12. Profile of Growth Dimensions, by State, 1939-54.

or median for that measure. The symbols on the map read from left to right for (1) population, (2) total income, and (3) per capita income. The top row represents the relative measures; the bottom row, the absolute measures.[7]

Even as represented by these limited and relatively crude indicators, the states exhibit a wide variety of growth patterns. At one extreme are Texas, Michigan, Indiana, and Washington, that are above the average for every dimension; at the other extreme are Maine, New Hampshire, Vermont, Rhode Island, and West Virginia, that are below the average for every dimension. The mature industrial states of the Middle Atlantic region and the western Great Lakes states tend to be strong in absolute dimensions and weak in relative dimensions. In contrast, the agrarian states in the Southeast and Plains regions and the agrarian-mining states in the Southwest and the southern Mountain region tend to be strong in relative dimensions and somewhat weaker in absolute dimensions. The northern tier states in the New England, Plains, and Mountain regions tend to be weak in both.

A Sub-State View

Our investigation in this study is based mainly on state and regional data. However, at a number of points, we have examined data on sub-state areas, particularly the metropolitan communities and agricultural groups of counties. We have done so, first, as a check on whether the intra-state variations are too large to permit a meaningful description and analysis of the development of the sub-national economy and, second, as a way of enriching the information available, particularly in discussing economic activities that tend to be highly localized.

The smaller area figures that we have used are Bureau of Census data on the so-called State Economic Areas. These areas are groups of counties—either metropolitan or non-metropolitan—with similar economic and social characteristics.[8]

The extent to which these data can be used in checking the state view of income levels and economic growth is limited by the fact that they differ from the data available for the states both as to the measures employed (and the nature of the basic data) and as to the years covered. However, some meaningful comparisons are possible. Because of our concern with income levels, it is particularly important to compare the state and sub-state income figures to see whether the state and regional view of this critical variable is actually

[7]The method used has the obvious weakness of disregarding how much a state is above or below the average or median, but it did not seem advisable to elaborate the method. The only purpose is to present a simple impressionistic generalized picture of relative growth.

[8]These data have been brought together by Otis Dudley Duncan and his associates. The SEA system for which data are given here is based on *State Economic Areas* by Donald J. Bogue (Washington, D. C.: U. S. Government Printing Office, 1951). While some of these data are presented in the present volume, most of the sub-state material is presented and discussed in the volume *Metropolis and Region* (Baltimore: The Johns Hopkins Press, 1960), which is under the authorship of Duncan and his associates.

too gross for purposes of analysis. Such a comparison can be made for one year, 1949, when census data on median family incomes are available for State Economic Areas.[9] The data for that year are presented in Figure 13. This chart effectively serves the two purposes referred to above. First, it suggests that the state and regional figures on income levels—as shown in Figure 7, for example—do as a matter of fact provide a good general description of income levels in the sub-national economy. There is clearly a strong tendency for levels of living to be similar over wide stretches of territory. The Southeast, in this view as in the state view, is clearly in the lowest income category. The Manufacturing Belt and the Far West are seen to fall in the highest income classes, while the other three western regions generally fall into a middle income category.[10] In other words, it becomes evident that the state figures do describe the over-all income situation quite well.[11]

The sub-state data are particularly valuable from the standpoint of permitting a separate view of the urban and agricultural areas within the various states. How do levels of living and growth patterns differ as between these two major types of areas? The data in Figure 13 are revealing on this score. We can see that, in the richer parts of the nation—particularly in the Manufacturing Belt and the Far West—the differences in income levels as between city and countryside are not nearly so great as are the differences among the multi-state regions. In these richer sections, both non-metropolitan and metropolitan State Economic Areas fall within the highest income category.[12] In the middle-income regions, the urban areas tend to fall into the highest income category (highest, that is, when all the SEA's are classified in quintiles), while the rural zones tend to fall into somewhat lower categories. In the lowest income region, the Southeast, the urban areas tend to enjoy higher levels of living than the farming areas,

[9]Data were obtained from an unpublished series of data for State Economic Areas prepared by Donald J. Bogue and Calvin L. Beale and made available for the present study. Median family income for the SEA's has been determined on the basis of income distributions for the SEA as a whole. It has *not* been estimated by averaging median family incomes of the counties making up each SEA. In those cases where there were differences between the composition of SEA's used by Bogue and those used by the present authors, adjustments were made by recomputing median family income using the 1950 U. S. Census of Population.

[10]The high incomes shown for the Mountain SEA's for 1949 are not representative of income levels for this part of the nation generally. They reflect the unusually high farm prices and incomes which characterized the immediate postwar years. In a longer run view, the Mountain areas clearly fall into the middle income category.

[11]At the same time, the sub-state data provide useful additional information which is suggestive for a fuller view of sub-national economic growth. Thus, it can be seen from Figure 13 that Northern New England, the Northern Lakes area, and the Appalachian area of Pennsylvania and New York tend to have lower income levels than does the remainder of the Northeast. On the other hand, the *lower* Appalachian area, in the Southeast—which, as will be shown later, contains the greatest concentration of manufacturing activity in the Southeast—has a higher income level than the remainder of that region. The relatively wide range of income levels among the SEA's of Florida, Louisiana and Texas is suggestive of the significant economic transition that these "in-between" states are experiencing. Once brought to the forefront, sub-state materials of this kind can readily be taken account of in analyzing the differential growth of the various parts of the nation.

[12]Excepting only the cities in the "depressed" areas.

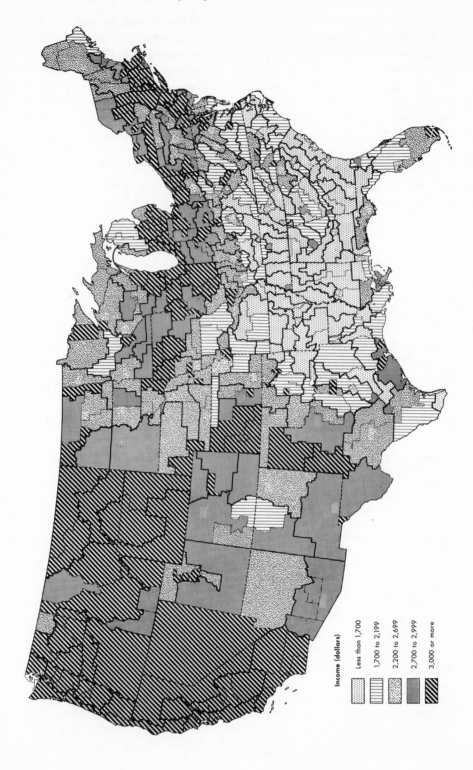

Income (dollars)

Less than 1,700

1,700 to 2,199

2,200 to 2,699

2,700 to 2,999

3,000 or more

but average income levels of the Southern cities are, on the whole, below those of cities in other parts of the country.

The sub-state data indicate that the growth of urban population, as well as average levels of living, has followed discernible regional patterns (but always with significant within-region variations). Figure 14 brings together data on the percentage increases in population for the larger metropolitan communities (actually Standard Metropolitan Areas, which are essentially the same as the metropolitan State Economic Areas) for the decade 1940-1950 and the 1949 data on median family income within metropolitan communities. When the data for these two variables are plotted on the same chart, there is a definite clustering which permits the drawing of boundary lines representing the "greater regions"—that is, the Northeast, Southeast, and West.

While the patterns are not entirely neat (the SMA's of the Plains region in particular tend to be scattered), the picture that emerges is quite similar to the one presented by the state data. The metropolitan communities of the Northeast have had far less population growth than those in the West and the Southeast. Within the Northeast, as marked off in the chart, the cities that have had an above-average growth are almost entirely within the Great Lakes region. For the Northeast, the range of percentage increases in population for the decade 1940-1950 has been relatively narrow, while income levels extend over a rather wide range. By contrast, the Western metropolitan communities fall within a narrow income range, while their population growth rates extend from a little above the median for the nation to truly phenomenal rates of growth (the population of Albuquerque, New Mexico, more than doubled within the decade). Income in the Southeast metropolitan communities is below the median for the nation with only one exception (Richmond, Virginia). While some southeastern cities have had a sizable growth in population, the greatest number outside of Florida experienced a rate of growth of modest dimensions, though largely above the average for the nation.

For the farming sections, sub-state data on levels of living are available over a fairly long period of time. A Farm-Operator Family Level-of-Living (FOLL) Index covering the State Economic Areas is available for 1930, 1940, 1950 and 1954.[13] Farm levels of living at the two ends of this period as shown by this index are set down in Figure 15 (for 1930) and Figure 16 (for 1954) for the

[13]This index, developed by Margaret Jarman Hagood, is a composite of several differently weighted variables related to levels of living: (1) percentage of farms with electricity; (2) percentage of farms with telephones; (3) percentage of farms with automobiles; and (4) average value of products sold or traded in the year preceding the census (adjusted for changes in purchasing power of the farmer's dollar). See Margaret Jarman Hagood, *Farm-Operator Family Level-of-Living Indexes for Counties of the United States, 1930, 1940, 1945, and 1950* (Washington: Department of Agriculture, Bureau of Agricultural Economics, 1952).

Figure 13—opposite.   Median Family Income, by State Economic Areas, 1949.

Source: An unpublished series of data for state economic areas prepared by Donald J. Bogue and Calvin L. Beale.

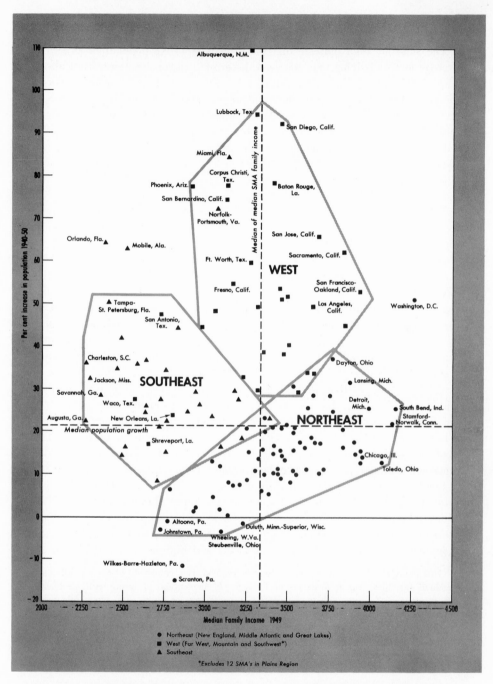

Figure 14. Regional Patterns of Family Income (1949) and Population Growth (1940-50) for SMA's of 100,000 or More Population.

Source: U. S. Bureau of the Census, *1950 Census of Population*, Vol. 11, Pt. 1, Tables 86 and 92.

non-metropolitan SEA's. During this period, the levels of living of farm operators had undergone a significant increase in every part of the country. And
yet, as is clear from these charts, the *relative* position of areas with respect to
levels of living of farm populations has remained much the same for nearly a
quarter of a century, if not longer. Regional differentials in 1930 and 1954
are strikingly similar. What has happened over the period is spelled out in
Table 12, which shows the means and standard deviations of the FOLL indexes
for the non-metropolitan SEA's.

Table 12. Means and standard deviations of farm-operator family level-of-
living indexes for 348 non-metropolitan state economic areas, 1930, 1940, 1945,
1950, and 1954

Year	Mean	Standard deviation
1930	76	36
1940	81	38
1945	102	44
1950	123	40
1954	142	36

SOURCE: M. J. Hagood, *Farm-Operator Family Level-of-Living Indexes for Counties of the
United States, 1930, 1940, 1945, and 1950* (Washington: Department of Agriculture,
Bureau of Agricultural Economics, 1952) ; and M. J. Hagood, G. K. Bowles, and R. R.
Mount, *Farm-Operator Family Level-of-Living Indexes for Counties of the United
States, 1945, 1950 and 1954* (Washington: Department of Agriculture, Agricultural
Marketing Service, 1957).

The dispersion of FOLL values around the mean, as measured by the standard
deviation, has remained remarkably constant over the interval. The equalization in levels of living among regions that has taken place has clearly come
about because of an over-all increase in levels of living *throughout the nation*
and not because of much more rapid increases specifically taking place in the
poorer areas. Greater increases in levels of living in the poorer areas would
have brought about an increase in the mean FOLL index, but the standard
deviation would have been reduced. This has not been the case. *Relative* positions of the various rural sections of the country have remained essentially
the same.

In spite of some significant intra-state variations, the picture that emerges
is quite similar to the one that was highlighted by the state and regional statistics. This brief excursion into the sub-state view, while it provides some enriching information, strongly suggests that sub-national economic growth can
be described (and analyzed) meaningfully by focusing mainly on state and
regional data. In the course of our study, our examination of the sub-state data
which was much more extensive and detailed than the data presented here
would reveal, gave us the assurance that it was sensible to center attention
mainly on developments as revealed by the state data.

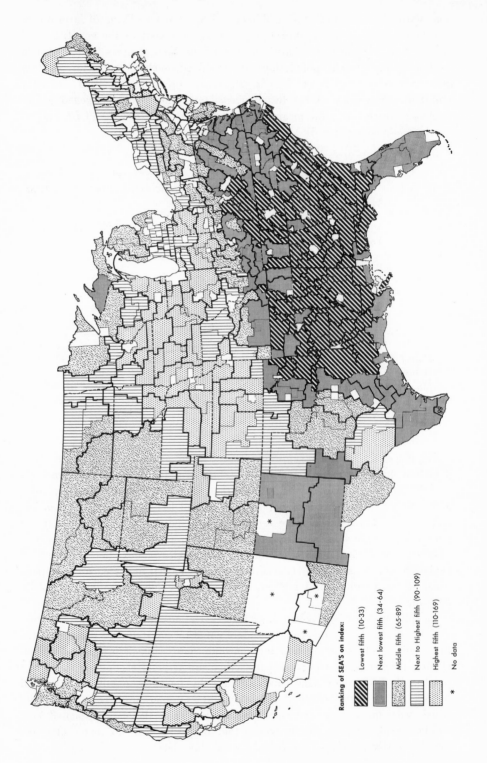

Ranking of SEA'S on index:

Lowest fifth (10-33)

Next lowest fifth (34-64)

Middle fifth (65-89)

Next to Highest fifth (90-109)

Highest fifth (110-169)

No data

*

Summary of Regional Economic Development, 1870-1957

The examination of growth indexes covering multi-state regions, states, and sub-state units for almost a century, as well as for short recent periods, provides a highly suggestive overview of economic growth in the United States. This overview can be summarized as follows:

Regional economic growth over the past century can be viewed appropriately only against the background of the phenomenal growth of the national economy. The population of the nation grew from 40 millions in 1870 to 170 millions in 1957. Total income of the nation increased in current dollars from less than $9 billion in 1880 to some $345 billion in 1957; even if account is taken of price increases, the growth in income has been truly remarkable. The gain in material welfare which has taken place because of the far more rapid growth in income than in population is suggested by the increase in real income per capita (in 1929 dollars) from $302 in 1880 to $1,236 in 1957. Even though at best this is a very rough estimate, particularly in consideration of the great changes in the "basket of goods" and of services consumed, the general order of magnitude is not likely to be too far off the mark.

Since 1870, the population of the United States has spread westward across the continent to occupy the remaining agricultural land and to tap other opportunities of the West. After 1910, however, the westward movement slackened until after World War II, when it was again revised mainly by the striking growth of California. In the period between 1870 and 1910, the proportion of the nation's population in the four Western regions increased from some 14% to 26% of the total; by 1957, it had gone up to 30%—that is, only 4 percentage points above the figure for 1910.

In absolute numbers, the steady growth of population *east* of the Mississippi has been unbroken in spite of a continuing exodus from northern New England and some parts of the South. After 1920, in fact, the greatest relative and absolute losses in population were recorded in the Mountain and Plains regions as people moved westward into California and some parts of the Southwest or eastward into the industrial areas of the Great Lakes and Middle Atlantic regions. In recent decades, a movement of population into Florida has become marked.

Since 1910 almost all interstate and intrastate migration has been into urban areas. Urbanization has continued, although at a declining rate, and the 1950 census reported that 64% of the entire national population resides in cities.[14] Only less significant than urbanization itself has been the growth of large and medium-sized cities which have come to dominate the pattern of settlement and

[14]Some 60% according to the older definition of urban.

Figure 15—opposite. Farm-Operator Family Level-of-Living Indexes for Nonmetropolitan Areas, 1930.

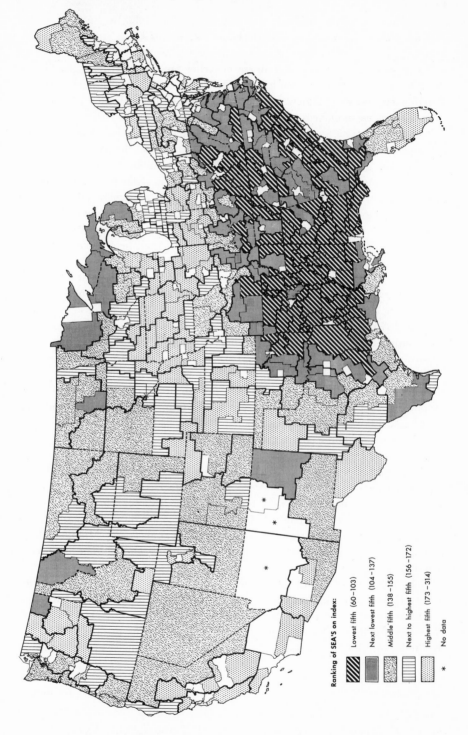

Ranking of **SEA'S** on index:

Lowest fifth (60-103)

Next lowest fifth (104-137)

Middle fifth (138-155)

Next to highest fifth (156-172)

Highest fifth (173-314)

No data   *

activities in their respective regions. Only 18 states in 1950 had more than half their population still living in rural areas; of these one was in New England, three were in the Mountain region, four in the Plains, and ten in the Southeast.

The growth in total personal income—a key measure of the expansion in volume of economic activities—has followed a pattern essentially similar to that of population growth as far as the East-West division is concerned. As recently as 1880, more than 80% of the total national income was received by the four Eastern regions (which contained at that time 81% of the total population). By 1920, the proportion had fallen to a little over 74%, most of the change taking place before the turn of the century. By 1957, some 70% of total personal income was still received by the Eastern regions; this was almost exactly the same proportion of the national total as in the case of population.

The record of relative regional growth lends itself to a choice of emphasis— either upon the West's remarkable growth or upon the East's equally remarkable

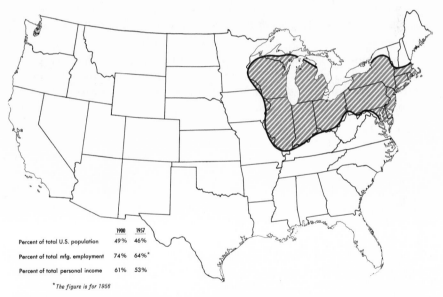

	1900	1957
Percent of total U.S. population	49%	46%
Percent of total mfg. employment	74%	64%*
Percent of total personal income	61%	53%

The figure is for 1956

Figure 17.   The Manufacturing Belt, 1900 and 1957.

maintenance of national dominance, especially that of the Manufacturing Belt. As Figure 17 shows, after more than a half-century of "filling in" and probing of new wealth and new opportunities across the vast continent, the Manufacturing Belt (covering roughly the three Northeastern regions *excluding* northern New England) in 1957 contained 46% of the total population of the nation,

Figure 16.   Farm-Operator Family Level-of-Living Indexes for Non-metropolitan Areas, 1954.

53% of the total income, and 64% of the total manufacturing employment.[15] Something over a half century ago, in 1900, the figures for the Manufacturing Belt were 49% of the nation's total population, 61% of the total income, and 74% of the manufacturing employment. In one sense, then, it can be said that there has been a remarkably small loss in relative standing over a half century of great national growth, and clearly *this area is still the very heart of the national economy and the very center of the national market for goods and services.*

On the other side, the gains of the remainder of the country, particularly of the Far West and the Southwest, are also strikingly demonstrated by these figures, and one can understand why the growth of the West should be made the central feature of many of the accounts of relative regional growth.

It seems sensible, we believe, to give full attention to both of these views of the same phenomenon and to weigh them properly in the larger context of over-all national economic growth.

When the focus is narrowed down from this very broad view to one encompassing the individual states (and groupings of states), and particularly when attention is devoted to the more recent decades, the data reveal several types of situations with regard to *growth in volume.* These can be briefly characterized as follows:

I. Four regions and one state can be identified as having had the greatest relative over-all expansion in population and economic activities generally in recent years. These are: the Far West, the Southwest, the eastern Lakes states, the Atlantic Seaboard states, and Florida.

II. The picture for regions of greatest relative decline—or least differential growth—is less clear-cut. There appear to be five groups of states in this category, some of which must be defined in special regional terms:

(1) New England (other than Connecticut);

(2) New York, Pennsylvania, West Virginia, and to a lesser extent Kentucky, which, together with Massachusetts, make up a band of states along the Appalachians which have declined in relative economic standing in the nation;

(3) The "Deep South" states of Mississippi and Arkansas, which, together with Oklahoma, had *absolute* losses in population over the period 1939-1954 and only slight gains in volume of economic activities relative to the rest of the nation;

(4) The northern Mountain states; and

(5) The Plains states.

These groups do not show decline on all scores by any means. The older and economically more advanced areas, in particular, rank high in absolute increases in population and total income. Excluding those states that show greatest absolute growth, four New England states, four northern tier states in the Mountain-Plains section of the country, the "Deep South" states, and West Virginia are the areas that show the least economic growth over the recent past. (Refer back to Figure 12.)

---

[15]The figure for manufacturing employment is for 1956, the latest available at the time of writing.

On the side of material welfare, as measured by per capita income levels and rates of growth, several features stand out from the preceding review:

1. All parts of the country have gained from the great increases in income that have accompanied the economic development of the United States; but in spite of some equalization, the three regions that were below the national average in per capita income in 1880 (the Southeast, Southwest, and Plains) were still below the national average in 1957—the poorest region, the Southeast, by 30%.

2. There has been a clear trend toward income equalization throughout the entire period. The most striking feature of this trend, however, has been a strong "pulling down" towards the national average of the highest income levels (mainly by a great inflow of population). The "upward push" of the low income regions has been much less strong. Thus, while real per capita income of the Far West was 211% of the national average in 1880, it was 135% of the average in 1920 and only 119% in 1957—even though it was still the highest per capita income of any region in the country. In the Mountain region, per capita income was 166% of the national average in 1880 (the second highest in the nation), 102% in 1920 (slightly above the national average) but only 92% in 1957 (below the average). On the other side, per capita income in the Plains was in the same relationship to the national average in 1957 (90%) as in 1880; the Southwest improved its relative position from 61% of the national average in 1880 to 86% in 1957 and the Southeast moved up from 50% in 1880 to 70% in 1957.

3. Relative levels of per capita income—again, in spite of the tendency toward equalization—have become strongly associated with the level of urbanization-industrialization, much more so than in the past. The highly industrialized and urbanized Middle Atlantic and New England regions have been well above the national average level of per capita income throughout the period since 1880, and the Great Lakes region joined their ranks as its industrialization gathered momentum. However, in the 1880-1900 decades, the two regions with the *highest* per capita incomes—the Far West and Mountain regions—were not industrialized. In the 20th century, the development of these two regions diverged.

After 1900 the Far West grew more in accordance with the pattern of the older urban-industrial regions of the East. The Mountain region, in contrast, declined steadily in relative levels of living, falling below the national average after 1920 and closely paralleling the agricultural regions. At some point between 1900 and the outbreak of World War I, the Far West appears to have crossed the threshold of urban-industrial society. In recent decades there has been a consistent division between the highly industrialized and the less industrialized regions with regard to relative levels of living.

4. The data, particularly those for the recent years, highlight the fact that there have been a variety of paths to increases in levels of per capita income. Some states and regions have experienced above-average increases in income either in relative or absolute terms, or both, while they have grown in population and economic activities. This has been the case with most of the Far West and

the Southwest, Florida and Virginia, and the eastern Great Lakes states. On the other side, some of the states have had gains in material welfare in the face of out-migration and relatively little over-all increases in population and economic activities, as is true of the Plains region generally and some of the Southeastern states. In a few instances—particularly Oklahoma, Arkansas, and Mississippi—there has been a substantial relative gain in per capita income levels accompanying an actual decline in population. Clearly, "sound economic adjustment" has a different meaning under different circumstances.

Part

II / *A Framework for Analysis*

4 / *Theories of regional economic growth*

The growth of economic activity and of per capita income, we have seen, has differed widely among the various states and regions over the years. We shall now attempt to provide a conceptual framework within which the main elements in this growth phenomenon can be described and analyzed.

To begin, let us consider for a moment how our economic system determines what commodities are produced in which locations and in what amounts and who receives income and in what amounts. In our society it is the market mechanism or price system that organizes and directs economic activity. The prices of final products and of production factors in different places, as well as the quantities of final products produced and of production factors employed in these places, are arrived at through a process of mutal determination often referred to as the general equilibrium system. Through its workings, the volume and composition of output and the factor prices in different places are determined. The factor prices—essentially, the prices of labor and capital—together with the pattern of ownership of these factors determine the income of different persons.

The basic data for economic analysis of the workings of this system are data on number, tastes, and location of consumers; quantity and location of all factors of production; technological developments; and institutional influences. As the basic elements change over time, the system generates new solutions to the economic problem which involve changes in the volume and composition of output in different places and in the incomes of persons in these places.

It is not our intention here to attempt a study of the workings of the general equilibrium system in its entirety. Rather, as in any applied research project in economics, we shall seek to identify those variables within its operation that are *of strategic importance* for the particular problem with which we are concerned —the problem of determining relative growth in the volume of economic activity and in per capita incomes or welfare in different places.

Volume and Welfare Aspects of Growth

Growth in total output, we have shown, is not always associated with growth in per capita income. For this reason we shall consider these two kinds of growth phenomena separately in our analysis. Both the volume and welfare aspects of economic development, it is true, depend generally on the same set of forces; but the strategic variables that determine them need not be identical. The forces determining the former—the "volume" forces—are those that affect relative costs of production (both costs of material inputs and labor costs) in the various parts of the country, the relative size of different market centers (both final or consumer and intermediate producer markets), and relative transport costs as between different places. The forces determining the level of per capita income, on the other hand—the "welfare" forces—are those that influence the relation between the rate of increase in population and labor force and the rate of increase in non-human factors of production within given regions and those that differentiate one region from another in the characteristics of the population—in their skills, age, sex, and racial composition.

There is another reason also why the volume and welfare aspects of regional economic growth should be considered separately. Economic efficiency is widely accepted in the United States as a desirable social goal. Technically, economic efficiency means an organization of production and distribution of the national product so that the highest total real value of output is achieved with the resources available. The pertinent point here is that national economic efficiency may require that the volume of economic activity in certain areas grow less rapidly than in others or actually decline.

To illustrate, let us consider the hypothetical instance of an area which produces nothing but a single agricultural commodity under competitive conditions, and which is suitable for no other kind of production. Let us suppose further that, as economic development proceeds, the demand for this commodity declines. If production remains unchanged, the price of this commodity will then fall relative to the prices of other commodities, and the returns to factors of production employed in producing it will fall relative to the returns to identical factors employed in producing other commodities elsewhere. Clearly, this is inefficient from the economic standpoint, since a transfer of labor and capital resources to other areas would increase the national product. If enough labor and capital factors migrate from our hypothetical area to other areas in response to their now lower incomes,[1] the incomes of these factors can be restored to equality with those in other areas and economically efficient production restored. (There may, of course, be important non-economic considerations which would make it desirable to subsidize a situation that is less than optimal from the economic standpoint alone. But under such circumstances it is important to understand just what is involved and what the economic costs actually are.)

In general, then, the failure of the "volume" of economic activity to keep pace with the national average growth in certain areas may be helpful in achieving the socially desirable goal of economic efficiency. Yet this need not imply, as will be shown later, that the incomes of persons in the area affected—either

---

[1] In practice this would be accomplished by a migration of persons and a failure to replace the non-human agents of production as they wear out. To the extent that there are factors such as land which are physically fixed and do not wear out, such inputs would, of course, earn permanently lower incomes.

those who migrate elsewhere or those who remain—need increase any less rapidly than the incomes of persons elsewhere, at least in the long run.

Here we have a truly critical feature of our economic system: every part of the country may not have an equally rapid growth of economic activities, but *persons* in every part of the country, under the proper circumstances (e.g., prejudice aside), *can* enjoy like income for like work.

Economic Growth Theories

Two major theories have been advanced in recent years to explain subnational growth phenomena—or, possibly more accurately put, two major *concepts of* (or *approaches to*) the organization of aggregate data to help explain these phenomena have been proposed. These are the "export-base" concept and the "sector" concept. Both provide highly useful insights, but they are both basically limited in scope.

THE EXPORT-BASE THEORY

This theory, whether used to explain growth of regions or of cities, hypothesizes that the factor initiating growth and determining its extent is the "export-base."[2] Growth in a given unit, it is proposed, is initiated by the response of the industries within this unit to an increase in demand arising outside the unit itself. This results in an expansion of economic activities, particularly local trade and service activities, through a multiplier process similar to the familiar investment-multiplier and foreign-trade multiplier in national income models.[3]

Harold Innis and G. M. Meier,[4] in their studies of the growth of Canada's

[2]See Douglass C. North, "Location Theory and Regional Economic Growth," *Journal of Political Economy*, Vol. 63 (June 1955) pp. 243-58. The main development of the theory has been in terms of urban growth. A rich literature has grown up around what has come to be known as the theory of the Urban Economic Base. See the series of articles by Richard Andrews appearing in *Land Economics* beginning with the issue of May 1953; also articles in this journal and in the *Journal of the American Institute of Planners* by Charles M. Tiebout, John Alexander, Charles Leven, Hans Blumenfeld, Ralph W. Pfouts and others.

[3]Central to the export-base theory is the distinction between export industries and activities and "residentiary" industries and activities. In the development of the theory with specific reference to urban communities, economic activities directly related to the export of goods and services to other areas or in other ways involving the earning of income from outside the area (such as profits from outside investment) have come to be termed "basic" activities and are said to make up the "economic base" of the metropolitan community. Other activities, such as local services and retail trade, are termed "nonbasic" or dependent activities, since their level is set by the income earned through the basic activities.

[4]Harold A. Innis, *Problems of Staple Production in Canada* (Toronto: The Ryerson Press, 1933); *The Cod Fisheries: The History of an International Economy* (New Haven: Yale University Press, 1940); G. M. Meier, "Economic Development and the Transfer Mechanism: Canada, 1895-1913," *The Canadian Journal of Economics and Political Science*, Vol. 19 (February 1953) pp. 1-19.

national and regional economy, and Douglass C. North,[5] writing about regional economic growth in the United States, have stressed the key role of exportable commodities and services. Their position is that capital investment will tend to flow into a region to develop the export industries, including the improvement of production processes and further development of specialized services to the exports. The resulting increase in income will tend to augment demand for secondary products and to induce investment in a variety of other industries. North states:

> "The social overhead benefits that have been created . . . and the development of a trained labor force and indigenous capital make it far easier to develop new exports. Whether such industries were originally residentiary and, by gradually overcoming transfer-cost disadvantages, become export industries, or were originally footloose industries not significantly affected by transfer costs, the result is to broaden the export base. As such a region matures, the staple base will become less distinguishable, since its production will be so varied."[6]

The rate at which a region grows, it is suggested, will depend on the rate at which the export base expands in line with the increase in the demand for the region's exportable commodities and services.

The export-base theory is particularly valuable in bringing to the forefront the fact that the growth of any subnational unit—whether a metropolitan community or a large multi-state region—is directly tied to developments within the national economy and, in some cases, to changes in international trade as well. Because attention is focused mainly on the relationship between a single subnational unit and the "outside world" treated as a whole, the functional ties among regions are hidden from view; however, the changing patterns of national demand and investment receive an appropriately central position in the analysis of regional growth. Aggregation of the industries and activities in a region in terms of export versus local use clearly provides a classification which is meaningful for understanding and measuring certain aspects of growth.

THE SECTOR THEORY

The economic-sector theory flows from the empirical observations of Colin Clark and Allan G. B. Fisher that a rise in per capita incomes in different countries or at different times is generally accompanied by a decline in the proportion of the labor force employed in agriculture and a rise, first in the proportion of employment in secondary activities (principally manufacturing), and then in tertiary or service activities.[7] The main reasons for this shift in the relative importance of the different sectors are different income elasticities

[5]*Op. cit.*

[6]*Ibid.*, p. 256.

[7]Colin Clark, *The Conditions of Economic Progress* (London: Macmillan, 1940); Allan G. B. Fisher, "Capital and the Growth of Knowledge," *Economic Journal*, Vol. 43 (September 1933), pp. 379-89 and "Production, Primary, Secondary and Tertiary," *Economic Record*, Vol. 15 (June 1939), pp. 24-38.

of demand for their products and differential rates of change in labor productivity. For example, demand for food and other agricultural products will normally increase less rapidly than per capita income, and at the same time farm output can be increased with a decreasing proportion of the labor force because of productivity gains through the use of machines, fertilizers, and improved techniques.

Thus, the sector theory focuses on internal rather than external development; economic growth is seen as primarily an internal evolution of specialization and division of labor, although external shifts in demand are not ruled out as of no importance.

As applied to regional economic growth, sector shifts are seen by the proponents of the theory as providing the main dynamic of economic advance both in terms of growth in the volume of economic activities and in terms of improvements in per capita income (although normally the distinction is not clearly made).[8]

The sector theory, joined with suggestions from the theory of the location of economic activities, has given rise to what might be termed a theory of development stages, that is, a theory regarding the "normal" sequence of stages through which regions experience economic growth.[9] It is suggested that the development of most regions will be characterized by the following sequence: (1) a stage of self-sufficient subsistence economy; (2) growth through production specialization in primary activities and interregional trade—which can be expected to accompany improvements in transport; (3) the introduction of "secondary" industries (mining and manufacturing)—which are called for because of the increased pressures from growing population and diminishing returns in the primary activities—as well as of the necessary social overhead facilities and services to support them; (4) a shift from a concentration on processing of farm and forest products and the simpler branches of textile, leather, and clothing industries, as well as on mining and mineral-reduction (usually based on outside capital and enterprise) to more diversified industrialization based on internal industrial linkages and rising incomes; and, finally, (5) at an advanced stage of economic development, specialization in certain tertiary industries for export, including the export of capital, specialized personnel, and services to less advanced regions.

[8]See, for example, *The Economic State of New England*, Report of the Committee of New England of the National Planning Association, Arthur A. Bright, Jr., and George H. Ellis, directors of research and editors (New Haven: Yale University Press, 1954), pp. 3-23. The changing economic structure which has characterized the economic development of the New England states is employed as the frame of reference for the thoroughgoing study of the regional economy.

[9]August Losch, "The Nature of Economic Regions," *Southern Economic Journal*, Vol. 5 (July 1938), pp. 71-78; Edgar M. Hoover, *The Location of Economic Activity* (New York: McGraw-Hill, 1948), pp. 187-96. A valuable description of the stage theory is provided by Edgar M. Hoover and Joseph L. Fisher, "Research in Regional Economic Growth," Universities-National Bureau Committee on Economic Research, *Problems in the Study of Economic Growth* (New York: National Bureau of Economic Research, July 1949), pp. 180-88.

An implication of the theory is that policies and activities of private groups and government can determine the rate at which the economy of a region will evolve from one stage into another; for example, in the building of social overhead facilities such as transport and in the efforts made to attract outside capital.

The tie between the theory of development stages and the sector theory is apparent, and the one can be seen to be an extension of the other. Another extension of the sector theory takes the form of a widely held concept concerning the relationship between regional economic growth and the existence of "growth industries" within a region—that is, industries which have experienced a greater than (national) average increase in employment or in value of product or in earnings per worker over, say, the past decade or two.[10] The most common form in which this concept is expressed is in the presentation of arguments for consciously encouraging the expanding sectors—manufacturing and tertiary activities—as the way of achieving rapid economic growth.[11] A more specific concern with "growth industries" appears in the policy and activities of certain of the state and local "area development" agencies whose function it is to attract industries to a given region. Priority in effort tends to be given to those industries—a favorite is "electronics"—which have expanded relatively rapidly in the recent past.

The sector theory has been found useful by a number of scholars as a frame of reference for the aggregation of data in the field of economic growth. Its focus on industrial and occupational structure, on changes in the pattern of demand (particularly with regard to income elasticity), and on relative changes in productivity has served to point up some significant economic-growth relationships.

LIMITATIONS OF THE EXPORT-BASE AND SECTOR THEORIES

While both the export-base and the sector theories clarify important features of regional growth, their limitations are also apparent. The major limitations in both cases are (1) that they are partial in scope and overlook other equally significant aspects of regional economic growth and (2) that they deal with classifications which, while highly suggestive for general description, are too aggregate for analysis in depth.

The export-base theory does not provide sufficient scope for the internal growth sequences—with the significant economic changes which these invariably involve—and therefore errs in the opposite direction from the sector theory. Residentiary employment does not adapt passively and automatically to the strategic "region-building" or "city-building" industries that have external trade relationships. Nor can all services be viewed as "dependent." Some

[10]See the discussion of "growth industries" in U. S. ·Department of Commerce *Regional Trends in the United States Economy,* A Supplement to the Survey of Current Business (Washington: Government Printing Office, 1951), pp. 5-7.

[11]For a discussion of this point, see Harvey S. Perloff, "Interrelations of State Income and Industrial Structure," *Review of Economics and Statistics,* Vol. 39 (May 1957), pp. 162-63.

provide the essential framework for the production of the export products and in a real sense are "lead" items from the standpoint of economic development. The interrelationships among the various kinds of activities *within* a region, including the complicated "multiplier" effects, are critical in regional economic growth.[12]

It is well to note also that the size of the region chosen for analysis inevitably has a great deal to do with the volume and importance of exports. The size question is particularly significant in the extent to which industry linkages come out as being "internal" or in the export category. And this, of course, greatly influences the view of the region's economic "strength" and its potentialities for growth. The problem arises out of the fact that in the application of the export-base theory, a given region or metropolitan community is analyzed in terms of its relationship to everything "outside." Douglass North has made the useful suggestion that, from the economic standpoint, the very definition of the region might well be in terms of a common export base as providing the unifying force for its development.[13] Such a view provides a useful frame of reference for a region in the earlier stages of development, or for one with quite limited factor endowment, but it runs into serious difficulty when applied to regions which are economically advanced and have a great variety of export industries whose markets range from limited areas to the entire nation or the entire world. To be examined comprehensively, economic growth in any significant area of the nation must be viewed in terms of the total complex of trade and other relationships, including interregional relationships and nodal-center to hinterland relationships, as well as in terms of ties to the national economy as a whole.

The sector theory, unlike the export-base theory, brings "service" activities to the fore as important growth elements and is centrally concerned with internal relationships generally; but, on the other side, it does not provide sufficient scope for the external relationships. It, too, hides from view the significant element of the functional ties between regions as well as the ties to the national economy (aside from the important factors of income elasticity of demand and labor productivity). Additional serious problems result from the grossness of the sectoral aggregates, that is, from the very great differences among the industries which are encompassed by the primary-secondary-tertiary classification with regard to their relationships to regional economic growth. (Still further difficulties attach to the two "extensions" of the sector theory with regard to development stages and "growth" industries. These are discussed in some detail in later sections.)

[12]For a discussion of these and other problems connected with the export-base theory, see Charles M. Tiebout, "Exports and Regional Economic Growth," *Journal of Political Economy*, Vol. 64 (April 1956), pp. 160-64 (also the reply by North in the same issue, pp. 165-68) : and the communications by Harris, Pfouts, and Tiebout on the base theory in the *Journal of the American Institute of Planners*, Vol. 24 (Fall 1958), pp. 233-46.

[13]"It is this that makes it economically unified and ties the fortunes of the area together. This tends to result in the interdependent development within the region of external economies and unified political effort for government assistance or political reform." North, *op. cit.*, p. 257.

It would seem then that neither of these theories offers a really satisfactory framework for the type of broad-scale analysis of regional growth with which we are concerned. Each focuses attention upon some important aspects of the phenomena we study but leaves out other significant aspects of it. However, it is worth stressing that, though partial, these theories are highly useful for the insight they provide into the process of economic growth, and, as the reader will see, we shall try in what follows to show how they fit into the picture of economic growth in the United States.

While we do not attempt in this volume to present a formal general theory of regional economic development, we shall first sketch out what we feel to be the significant features which such a theory should incorporate. In the empirical analysis to follow later, we shall attempt as far as possible at this time to demonstrate how these features have worked themselves out in the past. Such an analysis, we believe, can make a useful contribution to a general theory of regional economic development. Possibly it is only upon a foundation of intensive empirical study that such a theory can be built.

5 / Factors influencing the volume and composition of regional economic activity

The fact that the secular and cyclical forces of the closely knit national economy dominate economic development in every part of the United States might suggest that we could best arrive at an understanding of regional growth by directly tracing to the regions the lines along which national economic growth are recorded. For example, between 1939 and 1954, employment for the nation as a whole increased by about 17%, or by 1.05% per year, and the real value of national output rose by about 92%, or by 4.5% per year. It is conceivable that these rates of growth in employment and output might have been the same for every region and for every industry sector—in fact, for every industry within every region. But, though this would greatly simplify the task of regional analysis, regions have not grown so, any more than have industries. There are wide regional departures from the national norm in both directions. To explain regional growth, therefore, we must explain these departures.

As we see it, to understand economic growth within a particular region, it is necessary (1) to relate the region's development to developments in the nation as a whole; (2) to "weight" its growth in relative terms—that is, in terms of departure from the national norm; (3) to examine the characteristics of its growth pattern; (4) to evaluate its changing position with regard to its ability to hold and attract persons and industries; and, in general, (5) to study how it reacts to changes in the national "parameters" that influence supply and demand conditions for the major industries.

Our analytical framework, therefore, provides for an examination of the following elements:

1. The extent and character of national economic growth during the period that we are reviewing.

2. The impact of change-initiating factors which are central to such growth, particularly (a) technology, (b) natural resources, (c) population and labor force (for example, changes in age structure which lead to more consumer-oriented living), (d) changes in taste, etc., which lead to changes in consumer demand, and (e) strategically important institutional changes, such as those flowing from governmental policy. In short, the analysis is concerned with the

economic impact of the "external parameters" which are key parts in a vast *gestalt* of change through their effect on supply and demand.

3. The relative extent to which the individual regions have *shared* in the national economic growth, and the *shift* in the relative position of the individual regions with regard to the key measures (such as employment within major industries).

4. The major characteristics of the economic growth (or decline) patterns of the individual regions, particularly the extent to which such growth (or decline) is related to industry composition or to within-industry locational changes.

5. The nature of the individual regions, particularly with regard to relative advantages in meeting the input and market requirements of the major industries and with regard to the role of "agglomeration," as in the creation of external economies.

National Forces

The pattern of national economic growth and the forces behind it provide the logical starting point for regional analysis. In our economy, growth in total output is determined in large part by growth in the inputs of resources—labor, natural resources (e.g., land), and reproducible capital—that go into the productive process and by technological and organizational changes that lead to greater output from a given input.[1] Particularly important here are improvements in knowledge, training, skills, etc., of the human resources.

The key national data which need to be drawn on for the various aspects of regional analysis are: (1) growth in population, (2) growth in full-time equivalent workers employed, (3) change in output per man-year. These provide the figures for the change in total output per worker, as well as in the number of consumers. We then want to classify the employment and output (or income) data in terms of the major industries, so that the individual regional growth patterns can be compared with the national norm.

Since so much of the analysis focuses on the developments within specific industries, the national change-initiating forces which are *directly* related to the growth of specific industries come to the forefront. Of these, productivity (on the supply side) and the income elasticities of demand (on the demand side) are particularly important. As population and per capita income grow, the desired composition of total output at given relative prices changes because of differences in the income elasticities of demand for different commodities, resulting from varying physiological needs, changes in taste, introduction of new products, and so on. Such data as we have at our disposal indicate, for example, that the income elasticity of demand for food is much less than one, while that for automobiles is much greater than one. Hence, as per capita income grows we would expect, other things being the same, that relatively more of society's total

[1]For an assessment of the contribution of these two forces to national growth, see Moses Abramovitz, *Resource and Output Trends in the United States Since 1870*, Occasional Paper No. 52 (New York: National Bureau of Economic Research, 1956), pp. 5-23.

resources would be devoted to the production of automobiles and relatively less to the production of food. Likewise, technological change—particularly as it influences productivity—proceeds unevenly.[2] Because of this, the relative prices of different commodities change; consequently, the output of industries in which technological change has been the more rapid tends to increase at above-average rates.

Since the forces which lead to national growth do not affect the demands for all commodities to the same degree, and since regions differ widely in the composition of their output, such changes will stimulate marked growth in some regions while leaving other regions little affected.

Technological change, it should be noted, not only works unevenly among industries at the national level, but may also work unevenly as among regions. With the change in production possibilities made available by changes in technology, the pattern of regional advantage in production may change so that new capacity in an industry may be located in places other than those in which previously existing capacity was located.

Changes in transportation costs, like changes in income elasticities and productivity, have a direct influence on the production and location decisions of individual industries and on their growth patterns. The impact of this factor varies greatly, of course; some industries are little influenced by changes in transportation costs.

While industry shifts are the dominant factor in regional economic growth, some attention must also be devoted to population shifts. The migration of persons in response to income differentials, as well as non-job-oriented population movements, leads to significant changes in the size of markets and in the supply of labor in the various regions.

These, then, are some of the major forces making for differential rates of change in the volume aspects of economic growth among the regions. They are so complex and so interrelated that we cannot directly translate the national parameters into regional growth effects. We find it helpful first to do an "accounting" job—specifically, to compare the growth patterns of the individual regions against the national norm—in order to analyze the relationship of the regional parts to the national whole. We do this mainly in terms of what might be called "share analysis" and "shift analysis." We then examine the national forces making for differential growth among regions specifically in terms of the changing input and market requirements of the major industries, mainly by way of what we call, for convenience, "input-output access" analysis. Here the locational shifts of industries and the reasons behind them are examined in detail. (This is done largely in Part IV.) In this connection we also consider the "agglomeration" patterns, that is, the patterns characterizing the uneven geographic distribution of population and the various industries. These are important in defining markets and, because of the economies and diseconomies which they introduce, in shaping the cost differentials for economic activ-

[2]For estimates of the extent of technological change in different industries see John W. Kendrick, *Productivity Trends: Capital and Labor*, Occasional Paper No. 53 (New York: National Bureau of Economic Research, 1956).

ities in various parts of the country. They are important also because, within broad geographical regions, they lead to local variations in demand and supply. These patterns, together with other specifically regional factors, such as variations in natural resources endowment, climate, amenities, and the like, condition the way in which a specific region can react to a given national change.

We shall take up these various accounting and analytical elements in turn, starting with a discussion of "shares."

Shares of the Whole

It is necessary as a starting point to establish the relationship of the (regional) parts to the (U. S.) whole[3] and to each other. This is so whether the focus is on all parts of the country (as is the case here) or on a single region.

The economy of a region can be usefully characterized in terms of the shares of the U. S. total economy which it contains or contributes, and important insights into economic growth can be obtained by tracing the changes in these shares. The totals and shares to be measured will, of course, depend on the central interest of the analysis; for purposes of growth analysis, interest focuses on the growth indexes—population, income, etc.—and on the industrial structure, particularly as reflected in employment and in production by industrial sectors.

Each part of the country plays a more or less specialized role in the total; it produces and consumes a qualitatively unique share. One part may have basically a "breadbasket" function; another may be a "heavy manufacturing" zone; and a third may have a "playground" function (as is the case for large sections of Nevada and Florida). An analysis of this division of functions is complicated by the large size of the nation—both in area and in terms of markets (so that most products are produced in more than one center)—and by the gradualness of the developmental sequences. And, of course, there are certain ubiquitous functions and activities, such as retailing and local services, which need to be accounted for.

Thus, in addition to recording the quantitative shares, it is necessary to provide qualitative depth by highlighting the unique or specialized elements as compared to the ubiquitous elements in the economic structure of each region.[4] Equally important from the qualitative standpoint are certain relationships among the shares which, in an important sense, characterize the growth patterns

---

[3]The "whole" which is the logical focus of analysis is itself an analytical variable and depends on the nature of the markets and trade patterns which dominate. Thus, study of the U. S. regions in the 18th century would have to relate the regions to the "Atlantic Community"; in the 20th century, the national economy logically serves as the larger framework for regional analysis.

[4]A number of valuable measures of industrial concentration within a given area as compared to the national average have been developed in recent decades. The "coefficient of localization," as developed by P. Sargent Florence has been widely employed. See his treatment of this measure in National Resources Planning Board, *Industrial Location and*

of the various regions. An obvious example is the comparison of a given region's share of the total national population and its share of total income over a period of time. Another example is the connection between a region's share of total employment in the resources industries and its share of the output value of these extractive industries. Thus the following comparison between the Far West and the Southeast provides an important lead for analysis: In 1870, the Far West had 17% of the total national labor force in resource activities and an exactly equal share of the total value of extracted resources; in 1950, its shares were 38% of the labor force and 54% of the value. The comparable figures for the Southeast in 1870 were 40% of the total resources labor force and 25% of the value of extracted resources; and in 1950 they were 38% and 20% of the national totals, respectively. By such a comparison—particularly when the resource industries are broken down into their components (agriculture, fishing, forestry, and various kinds of mining) and the "greater regions" are disaggregated into state units—changes in volume of activities and in relative gains in productivity are brought to the forefront.

The regions must be seen not only in relation to the national totals, but also in relation to each other. It is useful for purposes of analysis to think of the various regions as in competition for shares of the national totals. Thus, it is not enough to know that a particular region currently has a smaller share of the total national employment and production of a given industry, for example steel, as compared to a generation ago; it is important to know also about the regions that gained in shares over the same period. Was their employment gain directly related to their population gain, or was it larger than their population gain? The implications are very different in the two cases. Did they make a productivity gain or only a volume gain? Again, the implications are quite different. Other types of analyses obviously need to be brought to bear on such questions—and these will be discussed in the sections that follow—but here we want to establish the value of share analysis as providing an essential background of information for the understanding of regional economic growth in an appropriate context.

In general, it can be said of share analysis that: (1) it helps to define the regions by relating them quantitatively, and to some extent qualitatively, to the national totals and to each other; (2) it usefully characterizes the economic structure of the various regions, again in relative terms; (3) it highlights the extent to which various aspects of growth are uniform across the entire nation, or large parts of it, and the extent to which they involve shifts from some regions to others; and (4) it helps to characterize the relatively stable and the less stable elements in the national economic structure and in the structures of the individual regions.

National Resources (Washington: Government Printing Office, 1943), pp. 63-84 and 105-24. Also the discussion of a "location quotient" by George Hildebrand and Arthur Mace, Jr., "The Employment Multiplier in an Expanding Industrial Market: Los Angeles County, 1940-47," *Review of Economics and Statistics*, Vol. 32 (August 1950), pp. 241-49; and the discussion of the subject by Otis Dudley Duncan and Associates, *Metropolis and Region* (Baltimore: The Johns Hopkins Press, 1960).

Patterns of Industrial Growth Within Regions

The type of economic change that occurs within a given region depends mainly on two things: (a) the economic activities that are subject to the most significant nation-wide changes and (b) the nature of the given region. In broad terms, then, what has to be done is to trace the regional variations on the major national themes. Let us consider first the influence on regional growth of nation-wide changes in industry growth patterns.

It is often assumed that those regions will grow that have the greatest relative net advantages in attracting the more rapidly growing industries. In an examination of the important sector of manufacturing, however, we found no positive correlation between increases in the proportion of workers within the "growth industries" and relative increases in economic activity in general among the states.

We examined here the relationship between growth in income (total and per capita) and manufacturing employment for the 1939-1954 period. The aspect of structure considered was the percentage of total manufacturing employment in those industries which grew most rapidly for the nation as a whole during these years. The industries selected—nine in all—were all industries in which the relative increases in employment between 1939 and 1954 exceeded the average for all manufacturing; it is worth noting that they accounted for about half the total employment in manufacturing in 1950.[5]

The rank correlation coefficients for both income variables (total and per capita) and manufacturing employment with the percentage of manufacturing employment in these industries were all negative; that is, states which had the largest percentage of manufacturing employment in these more rapidly growing industries tended to have the smallest increases in income, both total and per capita, and in total manufacturing employment. There was a positive but small rank correlation between population increase and percentage of manufacturing employment in these eight industries by states.

The reason for these negative results can be readily seen by examining Figure 18. The states with the highest percentage of manufacturing employment in the rapidly growing industries were generally in the Northeast, where growth was generally less rapid during 1939-1954, while those with the lower proportions in these industries were in the Southeast, where growth in income and total manufacturing employment was generally among the most rapid in relative terms over these years.

Essentially similar results were obtained by comparing the growth measures listed above with the percentage of the *increment* in manufacturing employment

[5]The selection was made by examining trends for the nation as a whole for the 1939-1954 period using Department of Commerce data on wage and salary payments and full-time equivalent employees. The industries were the following: (1) transportation equipment; (2) chemicals; (3) electrical machinery; (4) petroleum and coal products; (5) paper products; (6) machinery except electrical; (7) metals; (8) instruments; and (9) miscellaneous manufacturing. Employment data for states were obtained from the 1950 population census. Also see Table 130.

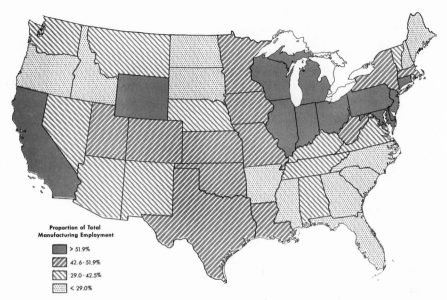

Figure 18. Percentage of Manufacturing Employment in the More Rapidly Growing Industries, by State, 1950.

Source: U. S. Bureau of the Census, *U. S. Census of Population 1950,* Vol. II, State Table 80.

during 1939-1954 that was in these same nine industries, as revealed by data from the manufacturing censuses of these two years. (See Figure 19.)

The, implications of these findings are significant for the understanding of regional economic growth. There are two elements here that seem particularly important. One is that a region may grow through getting an increasingly greater proportion of an industry that as a whole is declining nationally. This would be the case when the remaining portions of a declining industry all cluster into one or two regions, which gain in volume with regard to this industry while all others are losing out. Or a region may grow because it contains the growing parts of a generally declining industry. Since industry categories employed for economic analysis always contain sub-categories (this is highlighted by the Census designation of 1-digit, 2-digit, 3-digit and 4-digit categories),[6] some of the sub-categories will normally be expanding even when the average for the whole group shows a decline; this is the case, for example, with the growing cattle industry in the generally declining over-all industry of agriculture. Conversely, the textile industry is a declining sub-category of the generally growing manufacturing category. When these various possibilities are combined, it can

[6] The higher the number of digits, the more detailed the classification. Thus "mining" is a 1-digit category. (a) Petroleum and natural gas, (b) Nonmetallic mining, (c) Metallic mining, and (d) Coal mining are the 2-digit subcategories. The metallic mining category is further disaggregated into 3-digit classes, including such industries as iron ore, gold and silver, copper, and so on.

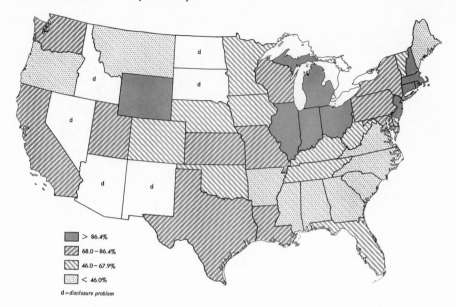

Figure 19. Increase in Manufacturing Employment in the More Rapidly Growing Industries, as a Percentage of the Increase in All Manufacturing Employment, 1939-54.

Source: Appendix Table K.

be seen that a given region may contain, at one extreme, an increasing share of a growing sub-category of a nationally-increasing industry or, at the opposite extreme, a declining share of a declining sub-category of a nationally declining industry, with many combinations in between.[7]

Proportionality and Differential Shifts

Regional economic growth can be understood only when all of this can be clarified, measured, and explained. The statistical technique that we have employed for this purpose is an elaboration of the "shift" technique described in Chapter 3. It is based upon the fact that the shifts in total employment (or in other important economic growth components) observed among the states and regions in relation to the national average are generated by two distinct types of

---

[7]Emphasis on the fact that regional economic growth is not simply a matter of attracting the so-called rapid-growth industries should in no way diminish the significance for economic expansion of the presence of such industries. Clearly, a growing industry within a region is a stimulus to over-all growth. This is so evident that it does not require emphasis. The other side does require emphasis; namely, that a region can enjoy a substantial amount of over-all economic growth by absorbing a larger and larger share of a declining industry or by attracting the growing parts of an industry which is declining on the average. This, as we will note later, will be particularly effective if the industries are of the type which tend to generate a strong multiplier effect.

phenomena. We call the resultant employment shifts "proportionality employ-ment shifts" and "differential employment shifts."[8]

The net differential shift in employment arises out of the fact that some regions are expanding in certain employment sectors (say, in the steel industry or personal services) more rapidly than other regions. The regions that show net upward differential shifts, as we shall see, are those in which over-all access to basic inputs or to markets has been improved relative to other regions engaged in the same activity; they have gained because of their greater locational advantages for the operations of given activities or industries.

Proportionality shifts are distinct from differential shifts. They arise out of the fact that, nation-wide, some of the employment sectors or industries expand more rapidly than others. (That is, here the "growth industry" effect is re-corded.) As a consequence, those regions that tend to specialize in the slow-growth sectors (e.g., agriculture and mining) show net downward proportion-ality shifts in total employment, while those that tend to specialize in the rapid-growth sectors show net upward proportionality shifts.

There are two ways by which the net proportionality shift in total employment can be computed. One way would be to use a complex weighted average based upon the degree of specialization in each sector by each state and the rate of employment growth for each sector. Obviously this is a very time-consuming method. The second way is based on the premise that the net differential shift in total employment and the net proportionality shift in total employment add up to the net total employment shift. Thus we can simply subtract the net differential shift in total employment from the net total employment shift to obtain the net proportionality shift in total employment.[9]

Because of the importance of this analytical tool in the discussion of regional

---

[8]This involves a standardization procedure of the type employed when changes in rates and composition are both of interest. See Frank A. Hanna, "Analysis of Interstate Income Differentials: Theory and Practice," *Regional Income*, National Bureau of Economic Research, Studies in Income and Wealth, Vol. 21 (Princeton: Princeton University Press, 1957), pp. 113-60; also the discussion by Denison, Williams, and Borts, pp. 161-93.

[9]The following may help clarify this point. Let:

E_{ij} = employment in the i-th industry and j-th state in the initial time period
E^*_{ij} = the same in the terminal period
$E_{i.}$ = national employment in the i-th industry = $\Sigma_j E_{ij}$
$E_{.j}$ = total state employment = $\Sigma_i E_{ij}$
$E_{..}$ = total national employment in all industries = $\Sigma_{i,j} E_{ij}$

Then, the total shift for a state is:

$$(1) \quad S_t = E^*_{.j} - (E^*_{..}/E_{..})\ E_{.j}$$

The differential shift for the state is:

$$(2) \quad S_d = \Sigma_i\ [E^*_{ij} - (E^*_{i.}/E_{i.})\ E_{ij}]$$

And,

$$S_t - S_d = [E^*_{.j} - (E^*_{..}/E_{..})\ E_{.j}] - \Sigma_i\ [E^*_{ij} - (E^*_{i.}/E_{i.})\ E_{ij}]$$
$$= \Sigma_i\ (E^*_{i.}/E_{i.})\ E_{ij} - (E^*_{..}/E_{..})\ \Sigma_i\ E_{ij}$$
$$(3) \quad = \Sigma_i\ [\ (E^*_{i.}/E_{i.}) - (E^*_{..}/E_{..})\ ]\ E_{ij}$$

But, (3) is simply the proportionality shift, S_p, a weighted average of the excess of national industry growth rates over that for all industry nationally, where the weights for a given state are its total industry employment in the initial period.

economic growth which follows, it may be well to provide an actual example here. Between 1939 and 1954, California had an increase in total employment of 2,116,282 workers. If its employment had grown at the same percentage rate as for the country as a whole over these years, its increase would have been only some 812,477 workers. Thus, California can be said to have had a net upward shift in employment between 1939 and 1954 of 1,303,805—the difference between the two figures.

If we apply the same technique to each industry, instead of to only the total, we get the following result:

Agriculture	+ 139,333
Mining	+ 3,163
Construction	+ 77,708
Manufacturing	+ 435,374
Transportation and Public Utilities	+ 74,799
Wholesale Trade	+ 12,267
Retail Trade	+ 91,303
Finance, Insurance, and Real Estate	+ 28,860
Service and Miscellaneous	+ 45,615
Government	+ 224,766
Total	+ 1,133,188

In other words, every major industry in California had a greater increase in employment than it would have had if it had grown at the national rate; in manufacturing, the increase was some 435,000 more than "expected." However, the total—1,133,188—is less than the total net shift in employment indicated earlier; less by 170,617. The reason is that, not only did each industry in California grow more than the national average for the industry, but California's industry mix or composition was such that the number of workers employed in "growth industries" exceeded the national average. This effect is reflected in the 170,617 difference noted above, or what we call the "proportionality effect."

The California situation of growth in every department is, of course, only one type of situation observed. Other states have had a different experience. Table 13 shows the differential shifts for Texas, Pennsylvania, and Georgia in addition to California. In deriving the figures presented here, we first computed the net upward or downward shift in each of the various employment sectors. The net differential upward or downward shift in total employment for each state is the algebraic sum of these shifts in the component sectors.

Again we note that California had a net upward differential shift of 1,133,188 wage jobs based upon upward shifts in every component sector. Texas also shows a net upward shift, but the drop in agricultural employment here dampens the total performance. Pennsylvania, by contrast, shows net downward shifts in virtually every sector except agriculture and wholesale trade. Georgia's total net shift is downward in spite of upward shifts for most of the component sectors. The downward shift in agriculture is so large that it overwhelms the gains in the

Table 13. An illustration of the differential shift for selected states, 1939-1954

Major industrial sectors	California	Texas	Pennsylvania	Georgia
Agriculture	+ 139,333	− 64,896	+ 4,734	−171,044
Mining	+ 3,163	+ 80,347	− 86,653	+ 772
Construction	+ 77,708	− 6,911	− 3,742	− 12,471
Manufacturing	+ 435,374	+142,854	−240,017	+ 10,760
Transportation and Public Utilities	+ 74,799	+ 35,060	− 29,609	+ 4,710
Wholesale Trade	+ 12,267	+ 24,166	+ 3,797	+ 14,285
Retail Trade	+ 91,303	+ 54,224	− 64,242	+ 8,232
Finance, Insurance, and Real Estate	+ 28,860	+ 33,328	− 4,483	+ 9,561
Service and Miscellaneous	+ 45,615	+ 33,436	− 22,999	− 7,252
Government	+ 224,766	+ 77,261	−102,696	+ 26,736
Total differential net shift in employment	+1,133,188	+408,869	−545,910	−115,711

SOURCE: Appendix Table H.

other sectors. (An explanation of the behavior of these states and others is offered later in the text.)

Suppose that, by an extraordinary coincidence, none of the component sectors shown in Table 13 had any net upward or downward shift (that is, no change in position as compared to all other areas of the nation). It would follow that the *differential* net shift for each state would be zero. It would not follow, however, that there would be no shift in total employment for these same states because the proportionality effect remains as a source of shifting employment shares.

Table 14 sets down the total net shift in employment for the 1939-1954 period and the total differential net shift from Table 13 for these four states. In no case does the differential net shift match the shift in total employment. It either fails to exhaust the total or is larger than the total. The balance or deficit in each case is attributable to the proportionality effect, which arises out of the fact that, nationwide, some of the *employment sectors* themselves expand more rapidly than others.

While it is only a limited illustration, Table 14 reveals that several kinds of situations can develop. California experiences an upward shift in total employment because both the differential and proportionality effects contributed to it. Texas experiences an upward shift in total employment but only because a very strong upward differential shift is sufficient to offset a significant downward proportionality shift based upon this state's relative specialization in mining and agriculture. Pennsylvania reverses the experience of Texas. This state experiences a downward employment shift because a strong downward differential

Table 14. Illustration of total employment shifts derived from a combination of the differential effect and the proportionality effect for selected states, 1939-1954

Total employment shift	California	Texas	Pennsylvania	Georgia
Net shift in total employment	+1,303,805	+112,286	−276,399	−273,931
Net differential (within industry) shift in total employment	+1,133,188	+408,869	−545,910	−115,711
Net proportionality (industry growth) shift in total employment	+ 170,617	−296,583	+269,511	−158,220

SOURCE: Appendix Table H.

shift is sufficient to offset a significant upward proportionality shift based upon relative specialization in manufacturing, trade, and services.[10] In Georgia, the differential effect and the proportionality effect reinforce each other in generating downward shifts in total employment.

This statistical device provides a useful framework for analysis. Sources of change in the regional structure of the economy are divided into two classes. Each requires a distinctly different type of analysis. The differential effect arises out of the fact that some regions gain, over time, a differential advantage (vis-a-vis other regions) in their access to important markets and inputs for each of one or more specific activities. An understanding of this effect involves an understanding of regional input-output relationships for specific activities and sources of their changing form. One must become deeply involved in location analysis. The proportionality effect arises out of the fact that the various regions start with a different industry mix or composition—that some regions claim a larger (or smaller) proportion of the nation's rapid-growth (or slow-growth) industries. An understanding of this effect involves one in an analysis of the changing total demand and supply relationships for the individual industries, including such elements as income elasticity of demand, changing tastes, technological developments, as well as an analysis of the special advantages of a given region for such rapid-growth or slow-growth industries.

An examination of regional change must clearly take into account both types of phenomena.

[10]New Jersey, in contrast, displays an upward employment shift for the 1939-54 period because the downward differential shift is *not* strong enough to offset a significant upward proportionality shift based upon its relative specialization in rapid-growth sectors.

6 / Location factors

Location theory[1] suggests that growth in a given area's volume of economic activities is directly related to two factors: its access at competitive costs to the inputs of production and its access at competitive costs to markets for the outputs of this production. The quantity and quality of a region's resources are therefore significant for growth; and, because so much of manufacturing involves the fabricating of processed materials, with many stages of value added, the availability of intermediate inputs may be equally or more significant. The size of the regional market and the proximity (in terms of transport costs) of national markets are also important considerations. The regions differ widely in these attributes. To understand the dynamic elements through which these relative regional advantages and disadvantages come into play, it is necessary to appreciate the principles behind location decisions in our economy.

Location Principles

The general principles that govern the location of economic activity are essentially the same as those that govern all of man's efforts to make the most of his economic resources. On the production side, expenditures for inputs reflect an effort to produce the product-mix buyers want most with the smallest possible commitment of economic resources. On the consumption side, expendi-

---

[1] The discussion of location factors in regional economic growth is largely based on materials prepared by Edgar S. Dunn. These factors will be taken up in some detail at a later point.

For valuable discussions of location theory, see Alfred Weber, *Theory of the Location of Industries*, edited by C. J. Friedrich (Chicago: University of Chicago Press, 1920); E. M. Hoover, Jr., *Location Theory and the Shoe and Leather Industries* (Cambridge: Harvard University Press, 1937) and *The Location of Economic Activity* (New York: McGraw-Hill, 1948); Bertil Ohlin, *Interregional and International Trade* (Cambridge: Harvard University Press, 1952); William H. Dean, *The Theory of the Geographic Location of Economic Activities*, (Ann Arbor: Edwards Bros., 1938); National Resources Planning Board, *Industrial Location and National Resources* (Washington, D.C.: Government Printing Office, 1943); Walter Isard, *Location and Space-Economy* (New York: Technology Press of Massachusetts Institute of Technology and John Wiley & Sons, 1956).

tures for products reflect the desire to acquire a market basket of items that will provide the maximum satisfaction possible within the restraints of individual incomes. The complex set of decisions that constitute man's economizing effort are made largely within the framework of the market mechanism.

Both facets of location are discussed here: the location of productive activity and location of consumption activity.

LOCATION OF PRODUCTIVE ACTIVITY[2]

The businessman's principal concern in picking a production site is to select one that will enable him to operate at the most profitable level of output. Production costs and revenues vary from one site to another, depending upon variations in access to the basic inputs and markets that are significant for specific activities. Sometimes input access is dominant in determining the location of an activity, and sometimes market access; sometimes neither is dominant, with the result that an intermediate or indeterminate location develops. This has led writers in the field to characterize production activity as being market-oriented, material-oriented, or oriented to intermediate sites.[3]

This basic grouping of industries with similar location characteristics is a helpful descriptive and analytical device. However, we have found it useful to make two changes in the classification. First, the term "material orientation" is not altogether an appropriate one. It would be better to speak more generally of orientation to input requirements, for there is often orientation to inputs that are distinctly non-material in character. This is true particularly of labor services, which constitute the principal input for most businesses. Second, the classification scheme can usefully be enlarged, as follows:

I. Activities that maximize their total access by orienting primarily to inputs

    A. Resource inputs

[2]Here we are using production in its broadest sense, including all extractive, processing, trade and service occupations that contribute to the economic welfare of the populace.

[3]Market orientation may be of different types. Many market-oriented activities—for example, the production of bakery goods and consumer services—are oriented specifically to final markets. Many others, such as machine shops, are oriented to intermediate markets. A few industries, such as production of fertilizers, tin cans, etc., are oriented essentially to resource activities as markets.

The same diversity can be observed in input orientation. Many input-oriented activities, such as coal-mining, are oriented to resource inputs. Others, such as paper-manufacturing, are oriented to intermediate inputs. And a few, such as scrap and waste collection, are oriented to inputs primarily generated at market sites.

Many activities, such as wholesaling and automobile production, are intermediate to both markets and inputs. Some activities, such as petroleum-refining and some petrochemicals industries, have mixed orientation patterns. Under one combination of markets and inputs, they tend to be market-oriented; another combination may lead to input-orientation. It is important to realize that any given production activity might have a different location orientation at the same time in different regions.

Some activities, such as hosiery production or some branches of electronics, do not have any strong orientation pattern. Such industries may be footloose in varying degrees.

B. Intermediate inputs

C. Market inputs

II. Activities that maximize their total access by orienting primarily to markets

A. Final markets

B. Intermediate markets

C. Resource markets

III. Activities that maximize their total access by selecting locations intermediate to inputs and markets

IV. Mixed location patterns

V. Production activity without specific orientation (footloose)

LOCATION FACTORS

The costs attendant upon the assembly of inputs and the distribution of outputs can vary a great deal from one region to another. And these variations, together with interregional price differences, are the main determinants of the location patterns. Thus transfer relations with input sources and markets are a major factor in explaining the location of various industries.

There are two special situations, however, in which transfer relations are unimportant in determining location. In one, transfer costs may be significant, but the transfer alternatives offer no choice. In the other, transfer alternatives may offer many choices, but transfer costs are insignificant.

The first of these situations is illustrated by the immobile input that is indispensable and for which there is only a single source and/or no substitutes. In such a case the production activity utilizing the input must turn to the single source of supply, and transfer costs become irrelevant in the decision.

The second type of situation often develops in relation to a product or service for which transfer costs are very small relative to the value of the product or service. A hosiery mill's total transport cost on material inputs and products, for example, is less than 1% of its operating costs; and some branches of the electronics industry assemble their materials for less than one-fourth of 1% of their total costs. Obviously, in these cases, a substantial percentage difference in transfer costs could exist between regions without changing the operating costs of the enterprise by as much as one-fourth of 1%. For such enterprises, the location choices are almost unlimited and the final choice is to a considerable degree objectively indeterminate.

Except in these two types of situations, in which location is either fixed or indeterminate, transfer costs can exercise influence on an industry's choice of location. This influence can be operative even in cases where inputs or outputs are immobile if there are substitute sources for the same input or substitute markets for the same output. For example, mining activities are inevitably oriented to the immobile natural site of the resource. However, where there are several alternative sites, that one will be selected that gives the mining firm the greatest total access to the essential resource input and its potential markets.

In situations of this type, the existence of transfer alternatives is a major factor in determining the order in which resource sites may be brought into use and the intensity with which they may be exploited.[4]

For the vast majority of enterprises, production inputs and outputs are mobile and substitutable, and transfer relations are important. These characteristics make every possible site in the economic landscape a potential production site. However, such activities must resolve the transfer costs associated with inputs and outputs favorably. As a result, economies with reference to sources and markets help make specific the location pattern and type of orientation for each enterprise. This potential flexibility of space arrangements presents the opportunity for a host of factors to influence access through transfer costs and hence to influence the location decision.

The ratio of transfer costs on inputs as compared with outputs is of major importance among these influences. In general, a higher rate of transfer costs on inputs relative to outputs over the same distance tends to make the production activity input-oriented. The location pattern of pulp and paper-manufacturing is a good example of this influence. A reverse ratio of transfer costs favors a market-oriented production site. Brick and concrete products are good examples. These transfer costs depend, in turn, upon a number of factors. The relative weight and bulk of the products and the inputs are important. Weight losses (as in beet sugar processing) or weight gains (as in the production of soft drinks) in the production process and differences in transport rates per ton/mile on inputs and outputs strongly influence transfer ratios. The time factor in transfer imposed by perishability or special service requirements is important.[5]

Another set of factors influencing the location of an enterprise is the spatial character of its supply sources and markets. Actually orientation in terms of strict juxtaposition to markets or supply sources can occur only if the market or the supply source is essentially pointform, that is, if it exists only at a single

[4]This process involves three elements. (1) The direct transfer costs in distributing the output of the mine which will give some mine locations an advantage over others. (2) The opportunity costs that arise out of the fact that natural resource deposits vary in quality. (3) Rivalry costs associated with the competition of other firms for scarce resource deposits and for the market. The firm will attempt to minimize the combined costs from all three sources. It is important to note that the rivalry costs have, themselves, a significant space dimension derived from the management decisions of the rival firms. To focus upon the influence of space on the direct transfer costs of one firm would ignore the important indirect influence of space imposed by a rival's choice.

[5]In general the ratio of transport costs on inputs and outputs will result in orientation either to markets or input sources. Intermediate sources face two serious handicaps. 1) An intermediate source will require an additional handling charge because it introduces a transshipment. 2) The graduated rate structure that makes short hauls relatively more expensive than long hauls tends to make prohibitive the combined hauls necessitated by an intermediate site. There are two circumstances, however, that may offset this handicap in specific cases. 1) Breaks in transport (i.e., between rail and water) between the input source and market require a transshipment anyway and often present a feasible intermediate location point. This is a factor that adds considerably to the economic importance of port cities. Sugar refining in Atlantic seaboard ports forms a good example of this influence. 2) Peculiarities in transport rate structure sometimes make intermediate points favorable sites from the point of view of transfer costs. Sometimes this result is accidental

point in space. Markets are seldom pointform for those production enterprises that are oriented to markets associated with final demand.[6] People do not exist at one or even a few points in space; they are areally distributed. Thus, production activities directly serving their wants almost always find their markets areally distributed. Market orientation in such a case is only relative and involves determining an approximate transport center for an areally distributed set of market transfers. Retailers, wholesalers, food processors, and personal service enterprises of all kinds exemplify this situation.

A similar situation often arises with reference to resource supply sources— particularly if the production process is oriented to agricultural inputs. Pulp mills, cotton gins, flour mills, meat-processing plants, and milk-processing plants all must orient their production with reference to areally distributed supply sources. Input orientation involves determining an approximate transport center for an areally distributed set of input transfers.

The general influence of market and supply *areas* is to increase the importance of intermediate sites. Where a production process has a supply area but an essentially pointform market outlet (such as a single firm at one point in space), this circumstance might tend to strengthen the pull of the market. Where a production process has a market area but an essentially pointform supply source, this might tend to strengthen the pull of the important input. Production enterprises that are oriented primarily to intermediate inputs and outputs would have the greatest chance for having pointform markets and supply sources. There would, therefore, be a greater chance for final orientation to markets or inputs in these cases.[7]

The internal scale economies of an individual enterprise are likewise of significance for location patterns. By economies of scale, we refer to the fact that technological production characteristics determine whether, to produce efficiently, an enterprise must produce on a very large, medium, or small scale. Scale economies leading to firms of large size have the effect of reducing the number of feasible input sources (in the case of input orientation) or markets (in the case of market orientation). If a firm is market-oriented, it must have a market large enough to allow for the operation of at least one minimum-sized

or it results from a peculiar combination of "block rates." More often it is deliberate and is a result of an "in transit" privilege in which the carrier grants the "through rate" to an intermediate producer even though there is a transshipment involved. The location of flour mills and soybean mills in the Midwest have evidently been influenced by this factor.

[6]Unless final demand presents itself in the form of a governmental unit or an export demand.

[7]The location character of a production enterprise is also significantly influenced by the number of inputs and/or outputs that are characteristic of its production function in a way similar to the influence of the spatial character of supply sources and markets just discussed. Even in a case where all production inputs are pointform, multiple production inputs will tend, as does a supply area, to encourage location at an intermediate location. There are exceptions (1) when the production inputs are all coincident in space and (2) when one of the inputs is locationally dominant (i.e., its location weight exceeds the combined weight of all other inputs and products). The same generalizations apply to multiple products and their influence upon location.

plant. In the extreme case where one firm (or a few firms) can efficiently produce an output adequate for the national market, production will inevitably be
considerably concentrated in this field. One region may have excellent transfer
relations with reference to inputs and markets and therefore represent an
excellent location point for producing a particular product. If, however, a
producer in another region (likewise with good transfer relations) has pre-
empted the total market, this excellence of site will avail nothing. At the other
extreme, small-scale efficiency relative to market size usually results in wide
dispersion of activities of this type.[8]

Another set of factors that exert an influence upon location patterns are
external scale economies. Once a firm has achieved its minimum efficient size in
terms of its internal technological structure, it may enjoy additional cost savings
originating from sources *external* to itself.

One source of these savings is an increase in efficiency within an industry as
a whole. The growth of an industry (such as the automobile industry) may
enable a specialized supplier to this industry (such as an ignition manufacturer)
to achieve internal scale economies that result in lower costs to the firms in the
base industry. Growth in the number of firms in an industry may permit the
organization of specialized services devoted to that industry (such as the removal or processing of waste materials). Joint research, organized markets for
finished products, specialized brokers, and specialized machinery producers are
all examples of the kinds of economies that may be involved.

Another source of external cost savings is the increase in efficiency that results
when a group of unlike enterprises grow together. Organized raw-material
markets, more favorable freight rates, the generation of a large body of labor
with specialized skill and training, the availability of specialized services for
maintaining business machines, and important community services such as
power and water are all examples of important external economies of this type.

Not all external economies available to firms in an industry require that the
firms be located in an area of concentration. Such things as the advantages of
organized exchange, improvements in machinery resulting from the growth of
an industry, and fundamental or applied research are available to all firms
irrespective of their location. Many of the others, however, are available only to
firms concentrated in an area. Thus, external economies may be mobile or
immobile.[9] Where the economies result from areal concentration, the term
"agglomeration economies" is applied.

---

[8]Production enterprises in the U. S. exhibit great variety in this respect. A plant of
minimal efficient scale producing typewriters can produce up to 30% of the national
industry capacity. By contrast, a cement mill of minimal efficient scale produces less than
1% of the national capacity. For an additional classification of industries in this regard,
see J. S. Bain, "Economies of Scale, Concentration, and the Condition of Entry in Twenty
Manufacturing Industries," *The American Economic Review*, Vol. 44 (March, 1954),
pp. 15-39.

[9]This distinction has been underlined by E. A. G. Robinson, *The Structure of Competi-
tive Industry* (New York: Pitman Publishing Corp., 1959), p. 142. See also John A. Guthrie,
"Economies of Scale and Regional Development," *Papers and Proceedings of the Regional
Science Association*, Vol. 1 (1955), pp. J1-J10.

Agglomeration

It is evident that the restraints imposed by *space* on the movements of inputs and products importantly influence decisions on the location of productive activity. Thus a region's position in the spatial framework of the national economy directly affects its economic growth. In each location decision, considerations of agglomeration and nodality play a role—that is, the size and closeness (essentially in economic terms) of the market and of the input sources are weighed.[10] As a result, the existing distribution of population and economic activities among and within the regions in itself becomes a factor in differential regional growth.

The current agglomeration or spatial configuration of the country, which is essentially the end-result of past growth, is itself a significant influence on future growth. This arises from the fact, discussed earlier, that the existing agglomeration pattern has a great deal to do with decisions currently made by producers as to the appropriate location of new or added production facilities.

Whenever there is development of a given resource or group of resources within a given region in response to external and internal demand, fixed capital is invested; and the rate at which it can be depreciated profitably often makes for its continued use in this region even if opportunities for somewhat higher rates of return to new capital investment develop elsewhere. Once an investment is made in plant and equipment, a firm is likely to find that it pays to continue operations within the existing location for a long period of time.

Location decisions well into the future will be influenced by the fact that a number of economic activities *have located close to each other* at a given period of time because of the circumstances of that time—as, for example, when a large group of iron and steel and linked metal fabricating plants, together with related servicing industries, locate in a given area because of the existing natural resource, transportation, and market situation and the general pattern of prices. The influence arises from many factors but especially from those which have come to be analyzed in terms of agglomeration economies (and diseconomies), which are appropriately viewed as external economies arising from the concen-

---

[10]It should be noted that location decisions are often made in a descending geographic scale. A firm producing for the national market will normally decide first on the broad region which best satisfies its input and output requirements. Often this will mean a decision to locate close to the greatest concentrations of population and industry. At the second level (what is sometimes called "localization") it will decide which specific locality within this region will best serve its requirements. Thus, a firm which wants to supply the vast market of the Manufacturing Belt may decide to locate at some midpoint, perhaps in a city in Ohio, or at the periphery, perhaps in a city in Minnesota or Kentucky or Virginia or New Hampshire. Finally, it will have to decide on a specific site within the locality of its choice (sometimes called "siting.")

The number of location decisions needed may be fewer, however. For example, if a firm is geared specifically to supplying a more limited regional market, rather than a national market, it may only have to make localization and siting decisions. A local trade or service enterprise (such as a retail grocery) will normally have to decide only on the site.

tration of economic activities in a given area. These, as pointed out earlier, are related to the existence within established centers of linked industries, social overhead facilities—particularly transport facilities[11] (and more favorable freight rates), specialized business services, and the like, as well as concentrated pools of labor (particularly skilled labor).

To the extent that regional and community agglomerations can generate *immobile* economies (as against economies which are available to all firms within an industry irrespective of their location), these economies can be a source of interregional cost differences that will have the same type of binding effect upon location as the existence of immobile resources. Where they are recurrent in space, the choice of one of a set of possible agglomerations will depend upon the relative interregional price difference they generate and their position with reference to other mobile inputs and markets. Since these agglomeration economies tend to coincide with high population concentrations (hence markets), their effect often is to strengthen existing tendencies to market orientation—and the piling up of more agglomeration upon existing agglomeration. The tremendous growth of our metropolitan centers can be explained in large part in these terms.

The distribution of people and economic activities which has evolved from the past influences all current location decisions because the overwhelming majority of location decisions must take market, input, and transport factors *as given*. Thus, the decision of the present, or the marginal decision in other words, is based to an important extent on the locational (and price) situation as it has evolved from the past. This is not to suggest that a firm, in making its location or production decision, does not look ahead; rather, the main element is that, at any point in time, the future costs and returns are necessarily estimated in terms of the relatively slowly evolving pattern of agglomeration.

The same general considerations apply in the investment made in a given location by the labor which comes in to help exploit the resource or group of resources. Here the investment may be, in part, in the form of fixed capital in a home and a different type of investment arising from close bonds to friends, children's schools, and the comfort of being among familiar things. There is some analogy here with the situation of fixed capital investment. The older person, like the older firm, will weigh differential opportunities differently than will the younger person with far less investment in the existing location.

Given the considerations behind locational decisions, it is not surprising that regional agglomeration patterns have considerable permanence. For example, in 1900 the Manufacturing Belt contained 49% of the population and 74% of the nation's manufacturing workers; in 1957 it still had 46% of the population and 64% of the manufacturing workers, despite the tremendous growth of the Southeast and the West over these years.

[11]Clearly, the network established by the railroads in the middle of the 19th Century in response to the regional pattern of production and trade of that period gave significant cost advantages to firms locating along the main lines, where other production considerations were equal.

But while the relatively inflexible elements which reflect "sunk" costs must be given adequate consideration, there are also significant elements of flexibility in the economic system. Capital (and particularly "new capital") as well as labor (and, again, particularly "new labor") do tend to seek out new and better opportunities and will move over wide areas of the country to achieve an improved over-all situation. Free trade among the regions can be expected to work strongly towards a geographic equalization of the prices of the factors of production—or, at least, towards a narrowing of a spread in prices—through its effect on the relative demands for the different factors.[12] However, the high degree of flexibility in the economic system is implicit in the entire discussion of input-output access and need not be elaborated here.

Nodality

The role of nodality, or orientation toward a central place or node, should also be touched upon here. Nodality has at least two important features of significance for regional economic growth; first, in relation to agglomeration and, second, in relation to transportation and transport cost.

Nodality helps to provide deeper understanding of the agglomeration concept. In the broadest sense, it suggests the locational relationship of economic activities to each other and to population with a focus on the relative degree of concentration and distance.

The importance of nodality for regional economic growth stems from the hypothesis, for which a number of scholars have presented strong evidence, that *closeness* to population and industry concentrations directly influences the volume, type, and intensity of economic activities.[13] Nodality in this sense can be viewed from three standpoints: first, the position of a given area with respect to the over-all configuration of population nodes or to the national market (thus, for example, locations in the western end of the Manufacturing Belt have become increasingly advantageous with the growth of the West); second, distance from a major population node or metropolitan center (the very use of the term "center" suggests the nodality element and an expected decrease in population and activity as distance from the node increases); and, third, dis-

[12]See Paul Samuelson, "International Trade and the Equalization of Factor Prices," *Economic Journal,* Vol. 58 (June 1948), pp. 163-84 and Svend Laursen, "Production Functions and the Theory of International Trade," *American Economic Review,* Vol. 42 (Sept. 1952), pp. 540-57.

[13]See, for example, T. W. Schultz, *The Economic Organization of Agriculture* (New York: McGraw-Hill, 1953), p. 147. Schultz has suggested that "The existing economic organization works best at or near the center of a particular matrix of economic development." Also, Alexander Melamid, "Some Applications of Thünen's Model in Regional Analysis of Economic Growth," *Papers and Proceedings of the Regional Science Association,* Vol 1 (1955), pp. L1-L5, and John R. P. Friedmann, *The Spatial Structure of Economic Development in the Tennessee Valley* (University of Chicago, Program of Education and Research in Planning, Research Paper No. 1, March 1955).

tance from a number of minor nodes or the extent of urbanization within a given broad area.[14]

Through the use of "nodal indexes" representing the three aspects of nodality, the role of space in the development of the economy can be analyzed in terms of various significant measures of activity within the various economic sectors, such as agriculture, mining, manufacturing, etc. Thus, the intensity of farm and mining activities, for example, and the relative returns to these activities can be measured by way of nodal indexes. To take just one example, measurement of this type reveals that access to markets is conducive to intensive agricultural activity; but it is access to a regional market, or metropolitan center,[15] rather than access to the national market (as measured by population potential) that is chiefly associated with high per-acre values of products sold and of high per-acre values of land and buildings.[16] In general, the use of the nodal measures greatly enriches the concept of agglomeration and provides

---

[14]The first aspect can be examined by way of the measure of "population potential" (Stewart) and of "market potential," (Harris) " . . . an abstract index of the intensity of possible contact with markets." Population potential can be regarded as a summary measure of the distribution of population over the entire nation with reference to a given point in the nation. The value of the potential index reflects not only the density or concentration of population in the local area, but the settlement pattern over the entire United States. Theoretically, the potential of population at a given point is obtained as the sum, over the entire population, of the reciprocal of each person's distance from that point. In practice, of course, the computation is approximate.

The initial concept was developed in relation to population by John Stewart. See "Empirical Mathematical Rules Concerning the Distribution and Equilibrium of Population," *Geographical Review*, Vol. 37 (July 1947), pp. 461-85; and "Demographic Gravitation: Evidence and Applications," *Sociemetry*, Vol. 11 (February-May, 1948), pp. 31-58. More recent models based upon these concepts include Chauncy D. Harris, "The Market as a Factor in the Localization of Industry in the United States," *Annals of the Association of American Geographers*, Vol. 44 (December 1954), pp. 315-48; Edgar S. Dunn, Jr. "The Market Potential Concept and the Analysis of Location," *Papers and Proceedings of the Regional Science Association*, Vol. 2 (1956), pp. 183-94; William Warntz, *The Geography of Price*, unpublished doctoral dissertation, University of Pennsylvania, 1955.

The second facet can be indexed approximately by the linear distance separating an area from its nearest metropolitan center. The degree of proximity to a major population node, of course, influences the area's population potential; but the measures are not redundant. An area of relatively low population potential can be located in the vicinity of a metropolitan center, for that center is only one of many agglomerations of population which jointly determine the area's potential.

An "index of urbanization," a summary measure of the size-of-community distribution of the population residing in the local area, can be used as an indicator of the third facet of position in the spatial framework of the economy. The size-of-place distribution of population in the local area is formally and empirically independent of the area's distance from a metropolitan center and would seem to be a negligible component of the area's population potential.

[15]This is, of course, in keeping with what would be expected on the basis of economic theory; namely, that given the greater competition for land among alternative uses in areas close to metropolitan centers, agricultural uses can compete successfully only if they use the land intensively and yield a substantial net return to the land.

[16]The relationship between distance from a metropolis and value of products sold is such that if, in 1950, a State Economic Area was 130 miles from the nearest metropolis, it could

valuable insights into the role of space in regional economic growth by pointing up specific locational relationships.

The critical element in location, as has already been suggested, is the relative accessibility of the various parts of the country to inputs and markets. Accessibility, however, is less a matter of distance in miles than of relative transportation costs. This phase of the problem has already been touched upon; we need only note here that it tends to reinforce the evolutionary growth features of the economy.

Historically, it was no accident that cities tended to develop in places where transportation by water afforded a relatively cheap means of exchanging commodities. Later, as means of land transportation were developed, these tended to connect areas which already had relatively high concentrations of production and trade. Today, because these areas offer a wide variety of modes of transportation, with favorable freight rates based on volume and special arrangements, they are often favorable sites for the assembly of raw materials or partly fabricated inputs and for the distribution of intermediate or final outputs. It is useful, in this connection, to re-examine the "growth" areas (as discussed in Chapter 2) in terms of their location with regard to the established major transportation routes. Given the role of input-output access, it is of course no surprise to find that areas advantageously located at breaks-in-transport points reveal important advantages for economic growth.[17]

LOCATION OF CONSUMPTION ACTIVITIES

Production activities seeking locations have a two-fold interest in populations and their regional distribution: as a source of labor inputs and as a destination for outputs. Presumably, then, any factor influencing population distribution would also influence the pattern of production activities.

In analyzing regional population distribution, it is convenient to view the household as the decision-making unit that assembles consumption inputs (consumption products and services) and distributes labor outputs. When the household is viewed in this way, it appears in the first instance that the transfer costs in marketing its labor output over any considerable distance exceed those of assembling its consumption inputs. In short, the household is oriented to regional markets for its labor output. It would follow that populations would be distributed essentially on the basis of the regional distribution of economic opportunity. Therefore, the factors that explain the location of production activity would explain the distribution of consumption activity.

be expected to have an average value of product sold per acre of about $15. On the other hand, an area which was 35 miles from the nearest metropolis could be expected to have an average value of product sold per acre of about $32. Of course, there are many SEA's showing marked deviations from the expected value based on the formal measures.

[17]The "nodality" facet of the study has been investigated by Duncan and his associates and the results of their research appear in the volume *Metropolis and Region*.

This does not cover the total picture, however. An important part of our population is not engaged at all in the marketing of labor outputs. Some 8% of the U. S. population is over 65 years of age. Approximately two-thirds of these persons are not working, and many enjoy some form of paid retirement. They are free to seek locations that give them greatest access to the consumption inputs they feel are important. Since many of their basic consumption requirements can be met equally well in all regions, with only minor differences, many of these persons will seek out the more intangible advantages (such as climate and coast) that do vary substantially from region to region.

In addition, many households that do provide labor outputs may find that good transfer relations with reference to consumption inputs are more important than good transfer relations with reference to labor markets. There are families that will choose to move to large urban centers in order to take advantage of better educational and health and welfare facilities, even in the face of uncertainty with regard to job opportunities. The force of consumption considerations is apt to be particularly strong over shorter distances. The movement to the suburbs can be interpreted in part at least in terms of the search of households for more convenient access to certain consumption inputs at the penalty of significantly greater transfer costs in marketing labor outputs. Specialized services often can be supplied over substantial distances, allowing the household to be located in a place that is considered to give it greatest access to its consumption requirements.

Still further, certain firms that are oriented to labor markets tend to be foot loose. In the absence of compelling transfer cost factors affecting production location, these firms may often seek locations that provide favorable access to the kind of consumption requirements that management or some employee consensus may deem important.

It is difficult, given the lack of information on this point, to evaluate the extent to which the location of populations is essentially independent of considerations affecting the location of production. However, while the location of jobs seems clearly to be the critical element, some attention must be given to the role of "independent" household decisions in analyzing regional economic growth, particularly for areas like Florida, California, and parts of the Southwest and Mountain regions. It is not surprising to find that the most rapid economic growth in recent decades has taken place in precisely those areas where both the consumption and production elements are relatively favorable and reinforce each other.

7 / *"Input-output access"*
and multipliers

"Input-output access" is a netting-out of the relative advantages and disadvantages of each region for the economic activities of any given industry or of all industries combined. Because the input and output requirements vary greatly as between industries (as is evident when the requirements for agriculture and for manufacturing are compared), the netting-out must necessarily be selective and related to specific industries rather than in terms of a measurable aggregate quantity or single index.[1]

When we speak of access as the sum of the relative advantages and disadvantages for the production of a particular commodity at some given place, we refer to more than just the resistance, and hence costs, imposed by space on the assembly of inputs and the distribution of outputs. We refer, rather, to all the cost elements inherent in production of the commodity. Transport costs, to be sure, are a significant proportion of total costs in many cases, but they are never the only element in cost. The prices of inputs and final products for

[1]There are a number of reasons why a general index of access cannot at this time be utilized in explaining regional growth and anticipating the growth potential of regions.

(1) Access as an element in economic growth is basically functional and specific. For example, a region might have a low access index relative to the aggregate of basic resources but a very high access to one or two specific resources (say, oil and gas) capable of supporting much activity. In the same way it might have a high access to specific markets.

(2) In a modern economy such as ours, the processing stages have become so subdivided that a region may not need very high access to natural resources and final markets to support significant growth. The important thing may be access to specific intermediate suppliers and markets.

(3) Regions would seem to differ in the degree to which their access potentials are realized. A region with a relatively low over-all access potential that has been only partially realized can be expected to show more growth over a given time period than another region with a higher initial potential already fully exploited.

(4) In a modern economy—where many decisions are consumption-oriented—free resources such as climate are significant to economic growth, and there is no practical way to include these in a general measure of access.

The main point we wish to stress is that, to come to grips with the problem of access, it is necessary to move to a consideration of specific functions in specific regions.

a particular firm or industry at a particular point in space are also influenced by the competition of rival producers or products. Likewise, a "good" opportunity at a given place might not be exploited because of the existence of a better opportunity elsewhere. Therefore, "rivalry" and "opportunity" costs, as well as transport costs, are included in the concept of access.

Returns on New Investment

So far, we have referred only to the relation between price per unit of output and the prices of factors of production, both material and labor, and to technological relationships at the point of production. But when the access concept is used as a framework for studying economic growth, another distinction must be made. One of the critical elements for economic growth in an area is *new* investment, and decisions on new investment are determined by relations *at the margin*—that is, by small increments of change rather than by average relationships. Thus, it is quite possible that an area might have, on the average, favorable conditions for the production of a given commodity and not grow simply because the opportunities for new investment are unfavorable in this area *relative* to other areas.

To illustrate this, let us consider three different regions and summarize the factors affecting the level of investment in a particular industry in these areas by three schedules, one for each region. This we do in Figure 20, on which we plot for each region the marginal return per dollar of capital stock employed in production, r, as a function of the total capital stock, K. Suppose further, for the purposes of this illustration, that there is a level of return, r_e, at which new investment is just profitable and that this rate is the same for all three regions and independent of total capital stock in the region. The total capital stock that each of the three regions will support under the conditions summarized in the schedules of marginal return on capital are K_1, K_2, and K_3, respectively. In equilibrium, defined as a position in which there is no incentive for anyone to make new investments, the total capital stock in the first region would greatly exceed that in either of the other two. Suppose, however, that, at a given point of time, capital stock in Region 1 is K_1 while in Regions 2 and 3 it is K_4. Such a situation would imply that the rate of return on new investment in the latter two regions would be r_1, which exceeds r_e, and hence it would be profitable to add to the capital stock. In Region 1, however, there would be no incentive for anyone to add further to the total capital stock. Hence, the growth possibilities are better for Regions 2 and 3 than for Region 1.

But Figure 20 also illustrates another point. Given that the rate of return on new capital investment in Regions 2 and 3 is the same, it does not necessarily follow that the growth prospects for the two are the same. As the figure indicates, because the schedule for Region 3 is less steep than the one for Region 2, it will take a greater increase in the capital stock in Region 3 to bring the marginal return on new investment down to the point where no further investment is profitable. The slopes of these schedules depend, among other things, upon the extent to which price received per unit of output falls and price paid per unit of material and labor input rises with an increase in the region's output. (Changes in transport costs which might accompany changes in the volume of material input shipped into the region or of output shipped from the region influence the extent to which input and output prices change as the region's output expands.)

One further point. If we are seeking to explain differences in growth over some time period, such as 1939 to 1954, we might interpret Figure 20 as show-

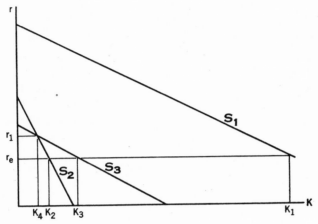

Figure 20.   Returns on Capital in Three Regions.

ing the schedules of marginal return on capital, given the conditions that exist at the beginning of the period. As discussed above, given these conditions, prospects for growth at the beginning of the period depend upon the actual capital stock in relation to the equilibrium capital stock. However, over a rather long time period such as this, these schedules would shift as a result of shifts in demand for the region's output, changes in technology, and shifts in the supply schedules for the inputs used in production in the region. (Shifts in transport costs might lead to shifts in either the demand for output or the supply of one or more material inputs.) Thus, in addition to the factors discussed above, shifts in the schedules in Figure 20 would lead to differential growth rates as among regions.

Consequence of Variations in Access Characteristics

When regions are examined in terms of input-output access (as defined above) with regard to the requirements of specific industries and for all economic activities taken together, the extent to which they vary in their prospects for growth becomes apparent. Conceptually, and in an abstract sense, one might use the variations in access characteristics to identify at least sixteen possible types of regions, as presented in Figure 21. Clearly, the table is an extreme simplification and has only general illustrative meaning. Also, "good" and "poor" are only relative designations and obviously do not represent discrete and separate types. But a classification scheme such as this, though artificial, has the advantage of focusing attention on the wide range of prospects for growth. For example, one cannot think seriously about the basic concept and not see the fallacy of the extreme local economic-development approach which regards every region and community as capable of limitless economic expansion.

To the extent that a region's general access characteristics may be taken as a rough index of its potential for growth, Region 4 in Figure 21 would have little prospect for growth, while Region 13 would have an unsurpassed growth potential.

Other regions fall in between these extremes. Regions 1, 2, 3, 8, 12, and 16 are only a little better off than 4. In these cases, reasonable access to inputs is offset by lack of market access, or vice versa. Thus, for example, one type of region may be developed to the extent that it contains an important mineral resource which is much in demand, but its development may be essentially limited to the exploitation of that particular mineral because of its disadvantage with regard to transporting almost all other products to distant markets. In general, regions 6, 7, 10 and 11 are somewhat better off because they at least have some access to both inputs and markets. Regions 5, 9, 14, and 15 are still better off because they combine good internal access to markets *or* inputs with good external access.

The restraints placed upon the future prospects for these regions also differ. Region 4 would have very dim prospects of evolving into a region type with greater growth potential. Any change in its character must rest upon a doubly fortuitous set of circumstances. Technology, discovery, or institutional changes must bring about an improvement in its access to both inputs and markets. For Region 3, which has good access to inputs in the home region but no external markets, the prognosis is poor but not as hopeless. This region must either (a) overcome the restriction upon its transfer relationships with other regions or (b) exploit its resources through a prolonged series of internal growth sequences. Region 12, with good access to external markets but poor access to input sources, might have a better prospect for breaking out of its dilemma. Discovery, technology, or even the pressure of growing demand might improve its access to basic inputs.

A major advantage of this schematic approach is that it forces attention on the variety of growth experiences that can be found in regions of different types. This is especially true if we consider the direction of growth sequences. As suggested earlier, it is widely assumed that development tends to follow a prescribed sequence, with growth initiated by advances in primary extractive activity. However, this is not always the case for the regions of an economically advanced nation.

		Good access to basic inputs* from external regional and national sources		Poor access to basic inputs* from external regional and national sources	
		Good access to basic inputs in home region	Poor access to basic inputs in home region	Good access to basic inputs in home region	Poor access to basic inputs in home region
Poor access to external regional and national markets	Poor access to markets in home region	#1 II	#2 I	#3 I	#4 0
	Good access to markets in home region	#5 III	#6 II	#7 II	#8 I
Good access to external regional and national markets	Poor access to markets in home region	#9 III	#10 II	#11 II	#12 I
	Good access to markets in home region	#13 IV	#14 III	#15 III	#16 II

*Not only basic resources but important intermediate sources need to be considered.

NOTE: Roman numerals indicate number of "good" access dimensions, and suggest relative over-all locational advantages or disadvantages.

Figure 21. A Schematic Presentation of Types of Regions that Can Exhibit Different Potentials with Respect to Growth.

A region such as type 11 might show a sequence of development completely the reverse of the sequence typically hypothesized. Florida is an example. It has had relatively poor access to home markets (that is, a limited scope for development on the basis of the size of the home market) and to external input sources. The major characteristic of its input access in the home region has been its large fund of coast and climate. Its access to external markets for this resource was good because, in our highly developed economy, population movements often take the form of a quest for amenities rather than economic opportunity. The exploitation of a resource was dominant in this development, but it is a special kind of resource that might be identified as a resource-service. No primary activities in the old sense were associated with its exploitation. Rather the exploitation of this resource required an intense development of tertiary activities servicing population. In 1950, some 66% of all employment in Florida was in tertiary activities. Market-oriented activities dominated.

A stage is developing, however, where the population concentration and the availability of business services are attracting increasing quantities of secondary manufacturing activities. Typical of these are small-scale market-oriented manufacturing such as metal construction products and relatively footloose activities such as electronics. As the wealth and size of the population grows, deficit food supplies make possible the use of agricultural lands that, at an earlier date, could not be considered an economic resource. This calls for an expansion in the primary sector of the economy. In this situation the tertiary-secondary-primary sequence is more logical than the reverse.

Actually it is not at all impossible for a growth sequence to start in what is thought of as typically the "middle" and perhaps go both ways. A region of type 6 or 8 might exhibit this kind of sequence. Sometimes the exhaustion of a resource or the development of a substitute may leave a region "over-developed." If labor is slow in out-migrating, the pool of relatively immobile labor with depressed wages may attract secondary manufacturing activities oriented to cheap labor. The new secondary activity may induce growth sequences that lead to expansion in primary, tertiary, and other secondary activities in the region. If this should happen, the region may regain a level of growth and production commensurate with that of other regions. In short, in an advanced society such as ours, there are many different kinds of regional growth sequences. Growth may begin with primary, secondary, or tertiary activities and it may proceed in several directions.

The variety of growth experience is apparent not only in the different sequences that are possible but also in the variety of functional pathways it might take. For a region (such as 7, for example) with good access to inputs and markets only in the home region, growth is largely restricted to the internal evolution of specialization characteristic of more or less "closed" regions. In another region (such as 11) growth may take the form of interregional specialization in response to external stimuli. In other regions (such as 13) it is more apt to be compounded of elements of both external and internal response.

A region (such as 10) which has poor access to inputs and markets in the home region might sustain considerable growth because of its nodal position with reference to external sources and markets.

Regions vary widely in their capacity to achieve "mature" development. A rationalized, variegated, mature development of economic functions is unlikely in a region that does not have good access to external national markets. All of the functions that are dominated by important external and internal scale economies would be denied to it.

In general, then, interregional differences in access to inputs and markets can be expected to bring about different patterns of regional growth behavior. Conversely, *the various growth patterns displayed can be explained by identifying the relative advantages and disadvantages of the regions with regard to input and output access for the major types of economic activities.*

Multipliers

Regional economic growth (or decline) is not simply a consequence of a discrete set of locational decisions. Every sizable injection of new investment within an area or increase in inputs and outputs, brings in its train a series of related economic effects. The economic impact of such forces upon an area is encompassed within the concept of regional multipliers. A highly complex set of interrelationships are involved. Thus, various autonomous forces can be considered to come into play: new investment; changes in the volume and composition of inputs (particularly labor) ; changes in the volume and composition of output of the area's industries; and, cutting across the latter two, changes in the volume and composition of exports and imports. The economic impact can be viewed in terms of the effect on employment in the area, on income, on household purchases, and also on induced investment.

The dynamics of the multiplier is one of the reasons why regional growth is not simply a matter of the proportion of "growth" industries within a given area or of the ratio of export to residentiary activities. While specific measurement is difficult,[2] the evidence suggests that there is no direct correlation between the rate of growth of a given industry and its multiplier effects in terms

[2]Although highly suggestive approaches to the measurement of regional multipliers have been proposed, the concept is not sufficiently developed nor the data adequate to permit us to work out actual impact measures. Frederick T. Moore and James W. Petersen, employing a modified Leontief interindustry relations model, have attempted to estimate the multiplier effects within a state. "Regional Analysis: An Interindustry Model of Utah," *Review of Economics and Statistics*, Vol. 37 (November 1955), pp. 368-83.

Werner Hirsch has developed an interindustry flow table for metropolitan St. Louis, employing 1955 data from company records, on the basis of which he has worked out estimates of income and employment multipliers. "Interindustry Relations of a Metropolitan Area", *Review of Economics and Statistics*, Vol. 41, August 1959. Thus, he finds, for example, that the income impact of the printing and publishing industry on the St. Louis economy in 1955 was such that a $1 million final demand increase raised the area's income by about $870,000. By contrast, the same amount of increase in final demand in the products-of-coal-and-petroleum industry could be expected to bring about an increase in the area's income by only some $220,000. The extremes in the case of the employment multiplier, Hirsch finds to be Plumbing and Heating Supply and Fabricating Structural Metal Products (an employment gain of 138 workers per $1 million final demand increase) and the Products of Coal and Petroleum (a gain of only 14 workers).

of inducing additional economic growth within the area in which it is established. Also, export industries do not all generate equal amounts of residentiary or service activity. The various types of multipliers are related to different kinds of industry characteristics. It is clear, for example, that a given industry's employment multiplier will be directly related to its own relative labor-intensive character and to the character of its "backward-" and "forward-linked" industries attracted into the region, and of course labor intensity has a logic of its own, not necessarily correlated with "growth" measures.

As a shortcut in dealing with this highly complicated set of phenomena, it is convenient to think of the growth or decline set in motion by any activity change in a region as depending upon what might be called its *activity interaction potential.* This refers to the nature of the input-output ties which an activity has with other activities within the same region and elsewhere. Given an activity change, the kind of growth (or decline) that will follow, and its duration, depend upon the extent to which the new activity is closely tied to (or independent of) the associated processes that precede and follow it. For example, a hosiery mill attracted to a given area by surplus labor and a minimum of community services within this area will, by itself, normally generate little subsequent growth within the area. Its supply sources and markets are such that its input-output ties are almost entirely external. In conjunction with other activities, it might make a modest contribution to regional population growth and add modestly to the demand for community and business services. By contrast, a new steel mill, such as the Fairless plant on the Delaware, may bring with it large population migrations, huge construction expenditures, many associated fabricators and suppliers, and generate multiple rounds of expansions in community and business services and marketing functions.

Multiplier effects are related to the technology and organization of a given industry at a given period of time. The time element is important because technology and organization influencing activity interaction within any given industry is subject to change, and in some industries—such as the chemical industry—rather rapid change.

Multiplier effects also have an over-all component, aside from the individual industries. This is related in an important way to how highly developed or relatively underdeveloped a region happens to be. In a less developed area—where social overhead facilities, such as public utilities, have to be built up and new services have to be brought into being—a given amount of manufacturing growth will generate more economic expansion than it will in a "mature" region which already is well equipped with facilities and services. In the latter case, there is likely to be a certain amount of unused capacity that can be employed to service the needs generated by the manufacturing growth.

As population grows regionally and nationally, some regions will reach a threshold where certain activities become feasible for the first time. Every activity has some minimum-sized market that its scale economies require for efficient production or distribution. Every region has a degree of market concentration and nodality that establishes limits upon the kinds of internal and external economies that are available. In a region where the development of economic activities is relatively undifferentiated, population growth may push that region to successive points where new functions become feasible.

It also follows that these new functions serve as a special stimulant to growth. Regions introducing them would claim a greater advantage in growth relative to (a) regions that had not yet achieved the threshold and (b) regions that would not expect to expand their functions much further. The areas most likely to achieve these successive thresholds are those that (a) have already achieved some minimum degree of accumulation of population and (b) are already serving as foci for a pyramid of regional and metropolitan functions.

This set of factors would seem to be particularly important in explaining the dramatic growth of California and, to a lesser degree, of the other states of the Far West and the Southwest. The multiplier effects here are reinforced by relative isolation from other important national centers of activity. Under such circumstances, activities that possess only marginal efficiency cannot be as easily provided by adjacent regions during early growth periods. This helps to explain why certain of the economically undifferentiated sectors of the country seem to be outrunning the older sectors in relative (and sometimes absolute) growth rates. Henry Bruton puts it this way: "Increasing size of an economy proceeding from a small base results in various kinds of economies of scale, but such economies are finite in quantity and effect. It seems clear that, after an economy has reached a given size, further increases in the size of the system itself will not result in further economies of scale and indeed may create a classical diminishing returns problem."[3]

Multiplier effects are intimately tied to the sequences of economic growth within a region. (This proposition can equally well be put the other way around.) This can be highlighted by an illustration.

Hypothesize the initiation of exploitation of an important new resource deposit in a relatively unpopulated region. (It would not matter whether technology or discovery created this new resource, or whether it was due to a significant change in relative prices.) This might well lead to a series of cumulative changes, somewhat as follows:

(1) Initial investment in resource facilities accompanied by an initial in-migration of workers and their families would take place. (2) Improvements in internal transport facilities and new transport links with other regions would follow. (3) Community facilities and services would be provided, such as housing, water, sewerage, and so on. (4) The new population nucleation would attract some small market-oriented enterprises. (5) The initial resource exploitation would attract suppliers of materials and equipment as well as business services ("backward linkage"). (6) The resource source might also attract some input-oriented processing enterprises. (7) The requirements for new construction and new employment in basic production and related umbilical activities, in community facilities, and in population-oriented activities would involve further expansion in population and new enterprises supplying

[3]Henry J. Bruton, *A Survey of Recent Contributions to the Theory of Economic Growth* (Cambridge: Center for International Studies, Massachusetts Institute of Technology, April 1956), p. 148.

materials and services for the construction activity, so that the initial agglomeration of people and activities grows in size and complexity. (8) It now becomes possible for some activities to move in that are relatively footloose but do require some minimum of community and business services to function efficiently. (9) There is further growth in general and specialized business services. (10) As the population and industry complex continues to grow, the transport relations with other regions are improved and refined, and this elaboration of the inter-regional network may lead to the new community developing some new "nodal" functions in transfer relationships with other regions. It is possible that the change in transport configuration might attract to it some enterprises that are "intermediate oriented." (11) The growing size of the population complex can attract more and more activities whose scale economies require larger market areas. (12) As the region grows, specialized services, market institutions, and financial sources evolve, and the region becomes more and more attractive for enterprises requiring these services. (13) The basic changes in the location of inputs and markets brought about by the development of the region will alter production and consumption relationships in other regions and thus transmit to them elements of its dynamism. (14) Increases in external demand will stimulate production within the industries established in the region. (15) And so on.

Note, however, that though this sequence is logical, it is not necessary. Its form might have been quite different if the new resource had more limited ties with market-oriented input sources and input-oriented markets, if the population movement in response to the new economic opportunity had been blunted by a regional oversupply of labor and only persons already in the region had been absorbed in the resource activity, if the combined multiplier effects did not bring the region to the threshold where scale economies would make feasible a substantial diversification of activities but stopped at the directly linked industries, etc. And of course the whole picture would have been very different if the resource exploitation had been undertaken in a region already highly developed and possessing an extensive complement of services and facilities.

This brings us, round circle, to the initial proposition that regional economic growth can be viewed most effectively in terms of (1) the more important stimuli, particularly as evolving from structural changes within industries and among industry groups in response to major market and technological changes, (2) the characteristics and functional composition of the various regions as potential "carriers" of the changes, and particularly the evolving "quality" of access to inputs and markets and the multiplier potential, and (3) the basic types of growth sequences which are generated. This involves a recognition of the rather wide variations in regional economic growth patterns that can be expected to result from the highly complex characteristics of industrial change and from the basic differences in regional structure.

8 / *Factors influencing per capita incomes*

The index that has come to be generally accepted as the best over-all measure of *national* economic growth is a sustained increase in per capita income. There is a clear logic in this. In the first place, any measure of growth among nations of different sizes, say China and Cuba, can more readily be used when population size is taken into account. In addition, a continuing increase in total population within a nation from year to year and over long periods of time can normally be expected. Given the severe restrictions on international migration, the key "volume" item of population increase can thus be taken for granted. Increase in *total* income, under such circumstances, now has a minimum rate or floor attached to it; psychologically it is hard to regard an increase in the volume of income which is at a lower rate than the increase in total population as "economic growth," although in the volume sense, *growth* is taking place. Thus, it is understandable why, in the case of national economies, increase in *per capita* income should be taken as *the* measure of economic growth.

This now traditional approach to the measurement of economic growth tends to be employed in the study of regions also. But there are significant differences in the case of regions. Continuing population growth cannot be taken as a starting point. Families can migrate freely from one region to another, so that a given region might well experience a decline in population. In such a case, even if total income should remain at the former level, or slightly drop, per capita income can still go up, that is, workers' earnings can go up in the face of declining population. In other words, a divergence between gain in volume and gain in welfare is conceivable—and, as a matter of fact, such divergence has taken place in the United States.

Once it is understood how widely regional growth patterns can vary, it is not surprising to find that changes in the industrial sectors—agriculture, manufacturing, etc.—are associated quite differently with volume changes than they are with welfare changes. In the previous sections, we have discussed the volume forces; here we shall touch upon the welfare forces.

This can be seen by examining the relation of changes in population and total income (the volume measures) as well as in per capita income (the welfare measure) with the changing relative importance of different kinds of employment by states. In Table 15 we have done this for the two periods 1880-1920 and 1920-1950.[1]

[1]The income and population variables used for the comparisons are end-of-period value *as a percentage of* beginning-of-period value. The employment measures are end-of-period

Table 15. Summary of rank correlations: economic growth and changes in employment structure, among the states, 1880-1920 and 1920-1950

Measure	1880-1920	1920-1950
Agriculture		
Volume measures:		
Population	+0.25*	+0.06
Total personal income	+0.04	−0.24
Welfare measure:		
Per capita income	∠ −0.45**	∠ −0.48**
Manufacturing		
Volume measures:		
Population	−0.23	−0.32*
Total personal income	0	+0.09
Welfare measure:		
Per capita income	∠ +0.46**	∠ +0.57**
All Other (Services, etc.)		
Volume measures:		
Population	+0.08	+0.26*
Total personal income	+0.11	+0.28*
Welfare measure:		
Per capita income	+0.27*	+0.07

*Significant at 5% level.   **Significant at 1% level.

During these two periods, there was little relationship between *differential* changes, by states, in population and the volume of economic activities (symbolized by change in total personal income) on the one hand and changes in the employment structure on the other. A close association between changes in "volume" within the states and changes in the relative importance of employment in the various categories (agriculture, manufacturing, services) would be shown by a high rank correlation coefficient. Actually the correlation coefficients are neither high nor consistent as between the two periods examined.[2]

But for both periods there were significant and rather large correlations

employment in the particular category relative to total employment for the state minus the same for the beginning of the period. The comparison was made separately for two time periods, 1880-1920 and 1920-1950; the latter was based upon forty-eight observations, the former on forty-six since income data for 1880 are not available for Oklahoma or separately for the Dakotas. For each period the comparison was made for three separate employment categories: Agriculture, Forestry and Fisheries; Manufacturing; and All Other (Service, Trade, Government, etc.).

[2]Even in the instances in which the observed rank correlation coefficients are large enough to rule out the hypothesis of chance association, they are not large enough to be of much practical import.

between differential changes in per capita income (welfare) and the changes in the relative importance of agricultural and manufacturing employment by states. Where the percentage of labor force employed in agriculture tended to decline most and the percentage in manufacturing to increase most, per capita income increased relatively most. However, no consistent or strong association is seen between differential change in per capita income within the states and relative importance of the All Other category, which includes services, government, trade, etc.

Thus, sectoral change would seem to be significant in regard to the influence of a decline in agriculture and an increase in manufacturing on per capita income (for reasons which will be explained later), but to have little to do with the differential growth in the volume of regional population and activities.

On the "volume" side, these data reinforce our view that growth can be understood only in terms of the varying input and market requirements of specific industries (with the industry disaggregation carried as far as needed to differentiate the critical requirements). At the same time, they suggest that rather significant insights into welfare can be obtained from an examination of even extremely aggregate industrial sector groupings (that is, as aggregate as "agriculture" and "manufacturing"). It would seem that the characteristics of these broad groupings are more general with regard to returns to labor and capital than with regard to their locational and production requirements. We find even further, and not unexpectedly, that the industrial structure of a given region emerges as being even more determining of per capita income levels when structure is disaggregated below the very broad categories employed in Table 15.[3] Thus, the industrial location shifts, which have been of central concern in our discussion of regional growth in volume, can be seen to be highly significant in per worker returns and therefore in regional levels of per capita income. In fact, the most critical factors in differential levels of per capita income among regions appear to be (a) the relative per worker returns of the dominant industries within the various regions on the one side and (b) the relationship between capital inflow and population growth on the other. Before turning to these, it is useful to note certain characteristics of the welfare elements.

Reasons for Differences in Per Capita Income Levels

To introduce the discussion of the forces making for per capita income differences among different places, let us hypothesize a position of long-run competitive equilibrium, defined so as to imply among other things that no producer would have any incentive to change his rate of output or location and no worker would have any incentive to change jobs at a given location or move to a new location. Then, let us ask, would we expect to find equality of per capita incomes as among regions (however the latter are defined)? Such a position might

[3]See Harvey S. Perloff, "Interrelations of State Income and Industrial Structure," *Review of Economics and Statistics*, Vol. 39 (May 1957), pp. 162-71.

never be observed, of course, but it might be considered "ideal" in the sense that if it were achieved, no transfer of resources could increase the national product. Equilibrium in this sense would imply that workers of identical skill would earn the same wages everywhere.

However, even if such were the case, there are many reasons why we might expect to find differences in per capita incomes in different parts of the country.

First, there are several reasons why workers of different groups would receive different real wages in such an equilibrium. These are summarized in the observation that (1) the relative proportion of skilled and unskilled workers can be expected to differ among regions because the employment structures differ, and (2) factors other than the current real wage influence the relative attractiveness for workers of different employments. Hence, if the industrial and/or occupational composition of the labor force differed in different places, one would expect these differences to be reflected in different per capita incomes.

Second, in addition to differences in the price per unit received from the sale of labor services, the incomes of persons in different places depend upon their ownership of non-human factors of production. Their incomes thus reflect the present returns on past capital investments.

Third, populations at different places differ in the proportion employed. Such differences result not only from differences in the proportions of persons not normally in the labor force—the young and old—but also from differences in the proportions of persons of working age in the labor force.

Also, there are several reasons why a given level of per capita income would have different implications for consumer welfare at different places. If the level of money prices of consumer goods were to vary, a given level of money income would command different bundles of real commodities in the market. Likewise, not all goods and services that affect the welfare of consumers are bought and sold on the market. Certain areas have advantages as to climate and other living conditions which might imply that a lower than average level of money income would attract persons to them.

Thus, areal differences in per capita money incomes might well persist even if the economy were in a position of long-run competitive equilibrium. Such income differences need imply neither differences in consumer welfare nor differences in the marginal productivity of labor (as reflected in the level of wages) at different places. Likewise, as economic conditions change over time, the forces discussed above might lead to continued differentials in per capita incomes in different parts of the country.

In the real world, of course, differences in wages of workers of identical skill are actually an important force making for differences in per capita incomes. First, the data available suggest that on the average for the nation, and particularly in the Southeast, the real returns to labor employed in agriculture are below those in other employments. Even under static conditions in which the total population and the total capital stock were to remain unchanged over time, a reshuffling of people from farm to non-farm employments would lead to an increase in the national product and to an increase in per capita incomes, and hence would lead to economic growth.[4] Likewise, it would appear that wages received by workers in a given industry differ regionally and that these differences are too great to attribute to equalizing differences (such as differences in skills, money prices, etc.). Here, too, a reshuffling of resources would lead to economic growth in either the "volume" or "welfare" sense.

Given the fact that wages are relatively low in some or all industries in a particular area, how would we expect this situation to influence the composition of economic activity in that area? Economic analysis would suggest two things: First, in areas in which wages are below the national average, conditions would be especially favorable for location by industries for which labor is a relatively important production factor. Hence, we would expect to find some concentration of the labor-intensive industries there. And, to the extent that the wages of workers of a given skill tend to be below average in an area, firms would have an incentive to use more labor relative to capital and perhaps to materials in the area. Thus, a low wage area would tend to be one with a low capital-labor ratio in all or most industries.

Influence of Population Growth

Here we would introduce a final proposition. The regional level of per capita income and the differential rate of growth in per capita income fundamentally depend on the evolving relationship between the rate of capital input and material input, on the one hand, and the rate of population increase (or decrease), on the other. In other words, the implications of the capital-labor ratio have to be broadened to include the dynamic factors of capital formation and movement among regions and the increase in total population numbers.

A convergence over time in the levels of wages for workers of equivalent skill would tend to bring about a partial convergence of per capita incomes in different places. We say partial because such factors as differences in skills of the population in different places, differences in their ownership of factors of production, and preferences for living in certain areas might result in persistent income differences. But, do differences in wage levels more or less automatically set in motion forces that would result in their eventual elimination? Here the answer has to be *Yes and No*. To the extent that workers migrate over time from low-wage areas to higher-wage areas, wage levels in the different regions will tend to converge. New capital investment in low-wage areas will also tend to equalize wages.

However, there are several reasons for qualifying this answer. First, the adjustments called for are not of the once-and-for-all variety; rather, we can expect that, as economic growth proceeds, adjustments of a continuing nature will have to be made. Take the example of agriculture. On the demand side

---

[4] This statement does not mean that all persons should leave agriculture or that some persons should leave agriculture from all places. Rather, it means that to achieve economic efficiency, some persons should leave agriculture from some places.

for labor, the fact that in our economy the income elasticity of demand for most farm products is less than unity means that, as per capita incomes increase, a smaller proportion of national output will be devoted to farm products (at given relative prices). Likewise, continuing technological advance implies that a given output can be produced with less labor and other factors of production. Hence, it seems likely that growth in income at the national level will call for continued out-migration of labor from agriculture. On the side of capital, the analysis of location factors and input-output access makes it apparent that the level of wages is one but *only one* factor influencing new investment decisions. For certain industries, traditionally characterized as "labor-oriented," wage costs are the most significant factors affecting location. The cotton-textiles industry is perhaps the best example; others are the apparel and shoe industries. In recent years these industries have accounted for a declining share of total national employment. Of course, differences in wage levels might influence the location of new capacity in other industries as well. But for many industries, requirements with regard to natural resources, markets, and transportation are the primary locational considerations. Unless the area could supply these requirements, therefore, a given wage differential might not be sufficient to attract a significant in-migration of capital.[5] Finally, imperfections in the capital market might prevent the location of new industry in low-income areas.

On the side of population, there are well-known institutional and behavioral forces which prevent workers and their families from migrating from low-wage areas at a rate sufficiently rapid to bring about an equalization of wages over relatively short periods of time.

Under certain circumstances, however, the forces making for convergence can and do function with great effectiveness. Regional per capita income levels, taken as a whole, have converged on the national average during the period for which statistics are available—the years since 1880. More telling, however, is the experience of the various (multi-state) regions with relative growth in population and income, an experience which in a few cases is quite dramatic in highlighting the forces for convergence.

The record which we have brought together reveals that the various regions have tended to "fill up" during the periods when labor was scarce in relation to job opportunities and wages were relatively high, as were also returns to capital, and that this "filling up" process tended to continue until wages and per capita income were brought up roughly to the national average and then to slow down or stop. For example, the Plains region's share of total national population rose from 1870 to a peak around 1890 and thereafter fell off quite rapidly. Its share of total personal income reached its peak a decade later, about 1900, and then declined sharply, somewhat more sharply than the popula-

---

[5]The presence of "ghost towns" in the West provides mute testimony on this point. As mines gave out, wages in these areas no doubt fell relative to those in other areas. Since these mining areas offered almost no advantage to other types of production, the solution was for an outmovement of persons. Likewise today, industrial development has helped to alleviate the problems of some low income farming areas, but not all such areas offer sufficient advantage to new industry.

tion share. In the Mountain region, the rate of population growth was higher than that of the nation as a whole throughout the period 1870-1920. It was particularly high during the decades 1870-1890, slackened during the last decade of the century, but picked up again after 1900, though it failed to regain the rate of the eighties. In spite of these fluctuations, the region's share of total population continued to climb and only reached its peak about 1920 (at which time the Mountain region was still the most sparsely populated region in the country). The growth of total income had meanwhile not sufficed to raise the region's share of the national personal income total beyond the level of 1900; in fact, it had declined by some 2% by 1920. Income per capita in the Mountain region, which in the years around 1880-1900 had been among the highest of any region, converged downward rapidly toward the national average after 1910, and after 1920 dipped somewhat below the average, where it remains in spite of some relative recovery after 1930.

While the history of each region has unique features, the continuing play of the forces making for an adjustment between capital and population growth and movements can be noted. However, certain tendencies can be seen which help greatly to explain why the adjustments actually emerging do not provide for full covergence in regional per capita income. One of the most obvious, as well as one of the most powerful, of these tendencies is the greater ease of "filling in" when opportunities for capital and labor are unusually good than "emptying out" when opportunities (and wages) on the whole decline below the national average. The problems of liquidating capital investment once it is made, the difficulties of shifting to new jobs in other parts of the country for older persons, the attachment to home, community, and friends—these and similar factors are deterents to out-migration. The nature of these factors also helps explain why the "emptying out" process is particularly difficult in farm sections. Possibly most important of all, the birth rate is relatively high in low-income farm areas and even a high level of out-migration can be neutralized, at least in part, by a rapid natural increase in population. And yet, of course, farmers have left the soil in great numbers. The problem is essentially one of *rate* of net increase or decrease in population as against the rate of new capital formation in the region.

As long as new investment decisions are based only partly on regional differentials in wage rates, and as long as only certain areas have the necessary advantages in input-output access to attract a large inflow of capital, the critical factor for many of the low-wage low-income areas will remain the rate of out-migration. Any forces which pull industries away from locating in the areas which provide the best over-all situation for their particular requirements can do so only at the expense of the rate of increase in national product and average per capita income for the country as a whole.

9 / Summary

Our examination of the many factors that influence the relative rate of increase in the volume of regional economic activities and per capita income levels has produced a number of quite significant *YES, BUT* propositions. These can be summarized as follows:

1. Economic expansion is in general associated with a relatively high rate of increase in employment in manufacturing and services. Thus, growth of total income and population has been associated in a general way with declines in the relative importance of agricultural employment and increases in the relative importance of manufacturing employment, both for the nation as a whole and for almost every state separately. *BUT* there has been little relation between *differential change*, by states, in total income and population (i.e., in "volume") and the changing relative importance of different industries.

2. "Growth" industries—those that are expanding in employment or value-added at a rate exceeding the average for all industries—favorably influence growth in the volume of economic activities within a region. *BUT* a region may grow by gathering in a greater and greater proportion of the slower-growth industries. Also, industry aggregates include a variety of industrial sub-categories some of which are expanding more than others. Regions may experience growth even when they specialize in those industrial activities (such as agriculture or mining) which may be on the decline on the whole. As a matter of fact, regions can be somewhat like individual firms. Just as some farmers, or coal mining firms, or textile or shoe manufacturing firms tend to make extremely attractive profits and increase their output in situations where competing firms are having serious trouble, so there are farming and mining and textile areas which, by intensive production and the growth of service activities (which grow because of the generally high income levels) can experience growth when other areas with similar kinds of specialization are declining. Regions that are worried about decline can learn some useful lessons from the flourishing firms in generally declining industries.

3. It is true that, no matter how the various industrial groups are aggregated or designated, certain industries are more conducive to regional growth than others. *BUT* not all regions have the relative advantages in regard to input-output access that make it possible for them to attract such industries; many can expect to grow only slowly on the basis of the industries for which they

do have special advantages. (One way of putting this is that not every area can hope to have the nice, clean, and fast-growing electronic and research industries.) Looked at in terms of relative advantages in resources, markets, human skills, amenities, climate, transport facilities and cost, and the rest of it, some areas can hope to grow only by attracting labor-intensive industries; others, by attracting certain kinds of processing industries exploiting relatively unexploited natural resources; some may have special advantages for certain types of assembly operations; still others for relatively intensive recreation activities, and so on. The attraction of industry is a competitive matter. There are many things that a region can do to enhance its locational advantages, particularly with regard to human resources and social overhead facilities. But many features of nature and position within the nation are "givens." Our analysis suggests that a realistic appraisal of a region's relative advantages and disadvantages with regard to input-output access is an essential starting point for an understanding of its growth potential, as well as of its past growth.

4. The growth of export industries within a region—those that tap the national and/or a broad regional market—strongly influence the expansion in the volume of economic activities. *BUT* the multiplier effect varies greatly with different industries, and the expansion of residentiary industries and services is not directly related to the growth of exports; the pattern of expansion of the residentiary industries and services within a given region is itself significant for differential growth as among the various regions. The direct and indirect impact on local income and employment of various export industries covers a full range from very great to relatively little; this is true of both the linked-industry effect (the expansion of business services, the local manufacture of parts and equipment, etc.), and the effect on increased consumer expenditures. Also, the extent of residentiary industries tends to increase with the growth of regional markets. As such markets grow in size with the growth of population and income, more and more industries find that they can achieve adequate scale economies while producing in every part of the country. This would seem to be particularly true of a wide variety of assembly operations and banking and financial activities, but many other types of activities tend to become almost ubiquitous as well, as far as the broad regions are concerned.

5. A high capital-labor ratio (as will be shown in Part V) is necessary in providing a high level of wages within a given region, and different industries at any point in time vary greatly in the average pattern of factor proportions employed, so that wage level differentials are to be expected on this score. *BUT* there does not seem to be any inherent reason why any industry cannot increase the capital-labor ratio when adjustments in relative prices are conducive to such an increase. Thus, for example, certain types of farming have had rapid and large increases in labor productivity and the areas where these types of farming are located enjoy relatively high levels of per capita income.

6. Every region in the country cannot hope to experience rapid increases in the volume of economic activities and in population. *BUT* every region *can* hope to enjoy a high and rising level of per capita income (as long as the nation's output and productivity increases) if it is willing to face up to the

need for a relative "emptying out" when the over-all situation with regard to relative advantages among regions calls for it.

These *YES, BUT* propositions add up to the following: All the regions of the United States are subject to the pervading influence of the national economy. At the same time, they are characterized by tremendous variety—in their physical features, their closeness to national market centers, their existing plant and equipment, their population densities, their industrial structures, and their economic histories. Industries making their locational choices, given their special requirements, will inevitably find certain regions more attractive than others. But these requirements change over time, so that industrial shifts are an integral feature of a dynamic and basically rational economy. Thus, some regional economies will always be expanding more rapidly than others—essentially, on the basis of their relative advantages with regard to input-output access within the total spectrum of industries—old and new. Yet, as pointed out above, while not every region can expect equally rapid growth in the volume of economic activities, each can enjoy a general level of living not far away from the level of the nation as a whole. Policy at both the national and the local levels might well be directed to the achievement of such an objective.

Part

III / *Regional Economic Development*

1870-1950

10 / Regional differentiation in the American economy before 1870

The variety of possible growth sequences in a developing economy is well illustrated by differing regional experiences in the United States after 1870. The modern continent-wide economy has its roots in the small and relatively isolated settlements planted along the Atlantic seaboard by European (mostly British) families and investors during the seventeenth century. For long these thinly populated settlements, clustered around some port community, were largely unconnected with each other but maintained vital ties with northern Europe and the West Indies. Only in the late seventeenth century did their common connections assume any regular or significant pattern.

By 1700 there were perhaps 300,000 people unevenly distributed along the maritime fringe; few had made large fortunes and their collective economic achievements were modest indeed. The great expectations of early investors and landholders had been mostly disappointed and, with minor exceptions, interest in the growth potential of mainland settlements north of the Chesapeake area had sharply declined. But within the next six decades population was to increase fivefold and a notable differentiation of productive activities and levels of well-being was to appear. Relations with the wider Atlantic community probably played a more decisive role in this transformation than those among the mainland communities themselves, but, except for the plantation economies of the Chesapeake and Carolina regions, progress was as much a consequence of local efforts as of aid from outside.[1]

In all the colonial settlements, labor and credit were in short supply; land was the only factor in abundance. From the outset, therefore, development was closely governed by local resource availabilities, and market outlets were necessarily confined within narrow reaches. Where great commercial crops—tobacco, rice, or sugar—could not be produced, where forests did not yield naval stores or furs, primary production remained relatively undifferentiated.

[1] C. Bridenbaugh, *Myths and Realities: Societies of the Colonial South* (Baton Rouge: Louisiana State University Press, 1952); idem. *Cities in the Wilderness: The First Century of Urban Life in America, 1625-1742* (New York: Ronald Press Co., 1938); E. B. Greene and V. D. Harrington, *American Population before the Federal Census of 1790* (New York: Columbia University Press, 1932), p. 4.

By the mid-eighteenth century, to be sure, cattle, wheat, and smaller grains were raised for urban markets by cultivators in both the Middle Atlantic and the Southern colonies; wheat and dairy products were also obtained from the thickly settled river valleys of New England. Manufactures (mostly handicrafts) and trade were likewise based upon local materials extracted from forests, fields, and seas; the New England fisheries and carrying activities were a major source of income for many coastal communities. But the availability of land at this time probably aggravated the shortage of labor and deterred the accumulation of venture capital; numerous immigrants who might have done well as artisans or laborers chose self-employment at a lower level of living on the land rather than work for a master once their terms of indenture had expired.[2] Under such conditions much of the needed social overhead was not forthcoming and the bulk of commerce was restricted to local exchange and the coastal trade. Only credit and the complex geometry of the Caribbean connection enabled the northern colonies to obtain their modest provision of consumer goods from the merchants of Europe. Even at the close of the colonial period the coastal trade was probably no more than a third of the combined ocean trade with Britain and the West Indies in value, although it greatly exceeded the latter in volume.[3]

No doubt the low rate of capital formation was in some small part the outcome of mercantile restriction in the interest of the mother country, but it was also a consequence of the fact that credit was always scarce and borrowing expensive. In any case, the rich endowments of forests, fisheries, and farm lands made for an unquestionable advantage in sectors which required only small fixed investment in tools and equipment. Yet if all colonial communities had depended exclusively on the export of services or natural resources, it is likely that few would have proved viable. As it was, the plantation economy of the South was for almost two centuries the richest section on the mainland; its soil and climate combined with slave labor to give it a marked advantage in the cultivation of certain staples which were in regular, if somewhat erratic, demand throughout the growing Atlantic economy.[4] For reasons of soil and climate, New England was by far the poorest agricultural section, and by the mid-eighteenth century it was already a net importer of certain foods and

---

[2] R. M. Tryon, *Household Manufacturers in the United States, 1640-1860* (Chicago: The University of Chicago Press, 1917) ; R. G. Albion, *Forests and Sea Power: The Timber Problem of Royal Navy, 1652-1862* (Cambridge: Harvard University Press, 1926) ; H. A. Innis, *The Cod Fisheries: The History of an International Economy* (New Haven: Yale University Press, 1940), pp. 160-62; R. B. Morris, *Government and Labor in Early America* (New York: Columbia University Press, 1946).

[3] J. S. Homans, *Historical and Statistical Account of the Foreign Commerce of the United States* (1857), pp. 6-7; R. Pares, *Yankees and Creoles: The Trade Between North America and the West Indies before the American Revolution* (London or New York: Longmans, Green and Co., 1956).

[4] G. D. Ramsay, *English Overseas Trade during the Centuries of Emergence* (London: Macmillan, 1957), pp. 207-39. C. Bridenbaugh, *op. cit.*, p. 14, emphasizes that by 1765 the Chesapeake Tidewater economy faced bankruptcy and that only the new Piedmont lands enjoyed prosperity thereafter.

fibers. Thereafter its growth was assured only by the development of handicrafts, distilleries, shipbuilding (built on forest resources), and other services to maritime commerce, in all of which it came to excel. Resource availabilities in the Middle Colonies had meanwhile made for a better balance between nascent manufactures and husbandry, between the more differentiated activities of town and country, and had fostered a progressive division of labor in support of the rising population.[5] Eventually, the adaptation of water power in the river valleys of the Middle Atlantic and New England colonies permitted local concentrations of mills and furnaces, though here, too, larger-scale investments and operations had to await the growth of closer linkages among the separate settlements and a more intensive exploitation of their common market potential.[6]

The disparity between conditions of life in the Old World and the New excited the comment of observers long before the English colonies entered upon their separate political career and, if anything, the awareness of difference had increased as the nineteenth century progressed. As Tocqueville remarked in 1835, fortune had indeed proferred Americans "an immense booty." Not that this booty was ever there just for the taking; a special kind of *human* resourcefulness was needed in order to realize the bountifulness of nature. It was never enough simply to take up new lands in the West; this may have postponed the need to face the Malthusian challenge, but in itself "land" did not provide an answer. If Americans had simply looked to the land for subsistence, they might have turned into a nation of peasants; as it was, most cultivators, large and small, hoped to raise a sizable crop surplus for market, while growing numbers turned to trade and eventually to manufactures.[7]

Between 1790 and 1810 the number of cities with more than 8,000 inhabitants increased from six to eleven. Communities of 2,500 or over rose by 43% during these two decades. In the decade after 1810, there was a relative decline in urban population owing to the interruption of commerce by the War of 1812 and to the taking up of new land in the West. As late as 1820 only six cities had populations exceeding 20,000. New York and Philadelphia, however, both exceeded 100,000, and Baltimore had expanded to 62,000. None of these urban centers was yet a city of "factories" in the sense of Manchester or Lyons in

[5] By the mid-eighteenth century English producers complained that people in the Middle Colonies were "sliding into the manufactures proper to the mother country."; E. E. Lampard, "History of Cities in the Economically Advanced Areas," *Economic Development and Cultural Change*, Vol. 3 (January 1955), pp. 116-17.

[6] The potential greatness of the American economy was nevertheless apparent by the last quarter of the eighteenth century. Already in 1776 Adam Smith foretold that Americans would create "an extensive empire . . . one of the greatest and most formidable that ever was in the world." He saw America surpassing the wealth of England in little more than a hundred years. *Wealth of Nations*, ed., E. Cannan (New York: Random House, Inc., 1937), pp. 588 and 590. Also, D. M. Potter, *People of Plenty: Economic Abundance and the American Character* (Chicago: The University of Chicago Press, 1954), pp. 78-86.

[7] For the continuing dependence of American expansion on the Atlantic trading area, see Frank Thistlethwaite, "Commercial America," in H. C. Allen and C. P. Hill, eds., *British Essays in American History* (London: Edward Arnold (Publishers) Ltd., 1957), pp. 102-105.

the Old World. The expansion of all, with the possible exception of Philadelphia, was essentially a commercial-service growth due to the swelling of trade as the resources of the interior became available for export. New York had been especially successful in attracting trade from the back country. The completion of the Erie Canal in the middle twenties clinched its supremacy and inaugurated a nation-wide mania for internal improvements.[8]

Among rivals for third place after New York and Philadelphia, Baltimore had grown by nearly 80% in the decade of the second war with England, Boston by little more than 30%. Baltimore's geographical position and mercantile enterprise combined to give it a notable advantage in the growing commerce of the North Atlantic seaboard region. In 1828 its merchants began construction of the Baltimore and Ohio Railroad with which to challenge even the supremacy of New York and Philadelphia. Boston, on the other hand, was losing ground in this clash of urban imperialism. Though its fleet was unmatched and its growth considerable, its geographic location in relation to the main thrust of internal development and the paucity of resources in its own back-country combined to threaten its position as the chief entrepôt north of the Hudson. After 1815 the Boston merchants and their associates set out to corner the entire New England trade, and their success can be measured in the relative decline of most other communities in the region. The Boston merchants, in fact, were forced to create business, and this they did by promoting an industrial revolution in Massachusetts. The impetus to the integration of specialized manufacturing processes in urban factories came not so much from the semi-rural centers of handicrafts in Rhode Island or Massachusetts as from the embattled commercial metropolis.[9] By importing raw material from Southern states and combining it with surplus labor from the countryside at strategic

[8] Robert Albion suggests that New York had more than positional advantage in the struggle for commerce; its business leaders had established a very successful auction system for disposing of imports, had a growing coastwise trade, especially with parts of the South, and had regular and reliable transocean packets; *The Rise of the Port of New York, 1815-1860* (New York: Charles Scribner's Sons, 1939), p. 13. By the early 19th century Philadelphia already had a diversified base of manufactures: textiles, hats, grain and saw mill products, hosiery, paper, printing, sugar, iron foundry and tool-making products, carpets, carriages, stoves, and ships; it was also a center of rationalist thought and scientific inquiry. See E. E. Lampard, *loc. cit.*, p. 117.

[9] The old tradition of semi-rural manufactures in both New England and the Middle Atlantic states had helped "industrialize" a section of the labor force and had nurtured a familiarity with machine processes. Even before 1820 some $600,000 of mercantile capital went into the so-called "Waltham Plan" to finance the improved power loom and to integrate the specialized processes of cotton cloth manufacture in single plants under unified managements, see G. R. Taylor, *The Transportation Revolution, 1815-1860* (New York: Rinehart, 1951), pp. 207-249; C. F. Ware, *The Early New England Cotton Manufacture* (Boston: Houghton Mifflin Co., 1931); V. Shlakman, "Economic History of a Factory Town: A Study of Chicopee, Massachusetts," *Smith College Studies in History*, Vol. 20, (1934-35); R. K. Lamb, "Entrepreneurship and Community Development," *Explorations in Economics . . . contributed in Honor of F. W. Taussig* (New York: McGraw-Hill Book Co., 1936), pp. 526-534.

points along the natural waterways, merchant capitalists of Boston accelerated a social process which lifted southern New England over the initial threshhold to rapid economic growth. Other communities followed suit and the territorial division of labor between town and country and between region and region was thus enabled to exert its beneficent sway.

By 1840, one historian states, "It would have been difficult to find 50 out of the 479 townships in southern New England which did not have at least one manufacturing village clustered around a cotton or a woolen mill, an iron furnace, a chair factory or a carriage shop, or some other representative . . . of manufacturing which had grown up in haphazard fashion in every part of the three states.[10] The same process was also at work by 1840 in parts of the Middle Atlantic region and in the Ohio Valley.[11]

Estimates of per capita income originating in commodity production and commerce by states in 1840 provide some measure of this early differentiation. The nation-wide average per capita income from these sources in that year was around $65. New England, more especially southern New England, had by 1840 surpassed all other states and territories except Louisiana (whose small population dominated the growing trade of the Mississippi system). The highest per capita figure for any state was that of Rhode Island, $118. Louisiana was next with $113; but then came Massachusetts with $107 and Connecticut with $91. Elsewhere in the expanding South only Mississippi ($84), Arkansas ($68), and Florida ($69) exceeded the national average. New Jersey ($83), New York ($80), and Pennsylvania ($75) in the Middle Atlantic region and the Wisconsin Territory ($80) in the Great Lakes region were also well above the national average. Nonagricultural income per worker *excluding commerce* was nearly 122% of the national average of $338.9 in the West South Central states and 102.5% in the Middle Atlantic states; in New England it was almost 138%.[12] (See Table 16.) These estimates give some indication of the extent to which New England was transforming its economic base away from agriculture and commerce before the mid-century.

Only during the second and third decades of the nineteenth century, however, as a result of the impact of technological advances in transportation on the pattern of resource availabilities, did a dynamic system of regional economic

[10]P. W. Bidwell, "The Agricultural Revolution in New England," *American Historical Review*, Vol. 26 (1921), p. 686. In spite of New England's demand for cotton, the value of raw cotton rose from less than 40% in 1821 to nearly 60% of all U. S. exports in 1851.

[11]In 1840 only New England and the Middle Atlantic states had greater concentrations of nonagricultural workers than the nation as a whole, 38.4% and 32.1% of their respective labor forces compared with 20.8% for the nation. Greatest concentrations of agricultural workers were to be found in the labor forces of the East South Central states (92.1%) and the South Atlantic states (89.9%). See Table 16.

[12]R. A. Easterlin, "Interregional Differences in Per Capita Income, Population, and Total Income, U. S., 1840-1950," National Bureau of Economic Research, *Conference on Research in Income and Wealth*, September 4-5, 1957 (mimeo.), Table A-3. Easterlin's estimates are based principally on the 1852 edition of Ezra C. Seaman, *Essays on the Progress of Nations* (New York: Charles Scribner, 1852).

Table 16. Population, labor force, and income originating in commodity production in the United States, by region, 1840

(000's population and current dollars)

Region	Popula-tion	Labor force		Per capita income from commodity production and commerce	Per capita income from commodity production	Agric. income per worker	Non-agric. income per worker	
		Non-agric.	Agric.				incl. commerce	excl. commerce
United States	17,020	1,007	3,828	$64.8	$54.9	$173.3	$436.6	$338.9
New England	2,235	246	394	*83.2*	*70.4*	*181.7*	*465.0*	*465.6*
Middle Atlantic	5,074	416	879	*76.9*	*62.3*	*225.4*	*462.4*	*347.5*
Great Lakes	2,925	132	601	46.1	39.4	147.3	348.4	239.3
Plains*	427	19	107	51.1	42.4	139.5	372.4	227.9
South Atlantic	3,334	110	973	54.6	49.6	148.2	342.8	231.6
East South Central	2,575	65	752	55.1	50.7	155.8	379.6	252.6
West South Central**	450	20	121	*103.6*	*72.2*	*238.0*	*904.4*	*413.4*

Figures in italics are above the national average.

*Iowa and Missouri.

**Arkansas and Louisiana.

SOURCE: R. A. Easterlin, "Interregional Differences in Per Capita Income, Population and Total Income, U. S., 1840-1950," National Bureau of Economic Research, *Conference on Research in Income and Wealth*, Sept. 4-5, 1957 (mimeo), Tables A-2, A-3.

interdependence emerge on the mainland of North America.[13] Corn and salt pork from the Ohio Valley, grain from the prairies of Ohio and Illinois, lumber and cotton from Tennessee and Mississippi, were gathered in from country points by the merchants of Pittsburgh, Cincinnati, Louisville, and St. Louis and shipped aboard river steamboats to New Orleans, there to be transferred to coastal vessels bound for the Atlantic seaboard or to ocean freighters for the ports of western Europe. By the early 1840's the volume of grain shipped east via the Great Lakes exceeded that shipped down the Mississippi; and even though the commerce of New Orleans continued to grow, the Atlantic ports began to dominate the business of the interior.

These were by no means autonomous developments; westward expansion and regional differentiation were closely linked to general expansion of the greater Atlantic trade area, but by the mid-century the rise of the textile industry in New England and the more gradual and diversified growth of manufactures in the Middle Atlantic states marked the beginnings of economic "independence." By that date a quarter of the raw cotton crop was being diverted to meet American needs and, though the balance of international trade remained generally passive until after 1870, dependence on foreign manufactures slowly declined, more rapidly after 1860. The introduction of the high tariff during the Civil War years gave added impetus to industrial development, accelerated differentiation in the Northeast, and led directly to the expansion of the domestic market for American manufactures without depriving the economy of benefits it derived from the export of primary produce.

During the third quarter of the century, therefore, primary producers in the Trans-Appalachian West were adjusting to the demands of two industrial centers: Western Europe *and* the Northeastern states. Some found opportunities even closer at hand and pondered the question whether greater enrichment lay in developing local markets or in reducing the cost of moving surpluses to Southern and Eastern entrepôts. Cotton growers were never wholly reconciled to their dependence on the milltowns of Lancashire and New England; wheat growers and cattlemen took advantage of local outlets, provisioning newcomers, army posts, mining and lumber camps within the radius of a two days' journey. The sequence of early land entries in parts of the Old Northwest indicate that settlers and speculators had an eye for local market potential as well as for the general accessibility or natural properties of an area; town sites and farm lands were often developed together.

The historic predicament of the primary producer in the West arose from the fact that his locality usually failed to grow (i.e., differentiate) at a rate sufficient to absorb incremental outputs made possible by further inputs of

---

[13]To surpass the average levels of material existence achieved in Europe, the U. S. did not require the unified economy or the centralized political institutions of its counterparts across the ocean. Its vast land area, its diversity of natural endowments, the variety of institutions and jurisdictions under which its peoples lived had retarded "nationalizing" tendencies without obvious cost to the general welfare. It was a virtual customs and payments union; so far it had enjoyed the advantages of union without completing the political struggle for unification.

labor and capital on virgin soils, thereby heightening his dependence on extra-local markets and a train of intermediaries in transportation and wholesaling. It was for this reason that the early grain growers of Wisconsin, for example, seized upon the railroad as the sure way to "bring New York to our doors."[14]

Only improved transportation could bring the primary producer closer to his market and at the same time facilitate the growth of more diversified activities nearby. The development of competitive water routes had fostered differentiation in the interior, but all water courses were closely circumscribed by

Table 17. Percentage distribution of United States population in the "West," 1840 and 1860

Region	1840	1860
% in "West" *	37.5	49.2
Great Lakes	17.1	22.0
South Central (west of Appalachians)	17.9	16.5
Plains	2.5	6.9
Southwest	—	2.2
Mountain	—	0.2
Far West	—	1.4

*U. S. total population was 17,020,000 in 1840 and 31,400,000 in 1860.

SOURCE: R. A. Easterlin, *loc. cit.* Tables A-2 and A-3, see Table 16; 17th U. S. Census, 1950, see *supra*, Table 1, note.

the capacity of vessels, handling facilities, and by the highly seasonal character of inland navigation.[15] Nevertheless, the availability of cheaper western food tended to depress food production in the South and Northeast, forcing the one region to intensify its commitment to the cotton staple and the other to commerce and manufactures. Only the iron railroad could at once free western activities from the paralytic grip of winter and emancipate developments in coastal sections from the directions imposed by primary river flow.

[14] " . . . when the railroad penetrates our borders, and gives us at all times access to the Atlantic Seaboard, what more can the farmer ask or need, but well directed industry, to crown his efforts?" Wisconsin State Agric. Society, *Transactions,* (Madison: Beriah Brown, State Printer, 1853), Vol. 2, (1852), p. 104; *ibid.,* Vol. 3, (1853), pp. 115-122.

[15] By 1820 some sixty steamboats had reinforced the flat-boat fleet on the Mississippi system; by 1840 their number exceeded four hundred, and by 1860 it had reached a thousand. Growth of steam navigation on the Great Lakes was somewhat slower, but by 1840 the quantity of grain shipped via the Great Lakes probably exceeded that moving down the Mississippi. In 1820 receipts of Western produce formed 58% of commodities reaching New Orleans, and by 1860 only about 23% of a larger total. See L. C. Hunter, *Steamboats on the Western Rivers* (Cambridge: Harvard University Press, 1949); G. R. Taylor, *op. cit.,* pp. 56-73.

The strongly agrarian character attributed to the westward movement by most historians and the emphasis placed by others on western railway development during the mid-fifties have tended to obscure the influence exerted by a third factor—urbanization. The growth of cities was by no means confined to the more industrialized coastal sections. In every new country the growth of central places is an essential concomitant of economic development, since no efficient *organization* of settlement can proceed very far without creating non-agricultural communities which carry on the vital functions of collecting and distributing articles of trade. From the early nineteenth century, if not before, certain places in the interior—the "valley centers" and "lake centers"—had served as entrepôts for western commerce.[16] Around their mercantile core had grown up a variety of processing and servicing activities such that by 1860, when more than half the total population of thirty-one millions lived west of the Appalachians (Table 17) and more than 14% west of the Mississippi (excluding Louisiana and Arkansas), seven western cities had populations exceeding 50,000 (Table 18), with sizable proportions occupied in manufactures. By this time, also, over 23% of all employment in manufactures was located west of the Appalachian divide, more than half of it in the Great Lakes states.

It is no exaggeration to say that Western promoters had sited, and in some cases developed, their urban real estate almost before the farmers had brought in the first commercial harvest. During the second quarter of the nineteenth century almost every crossroads village in the West had postured as the future "Queen City" of its region, serving the vast primary producing areas around it and eventually surpassing the great centers of the Eastern seaboard. They vied with each other in a fabulous struggle for "internal improvements," to build plankroads to link up rivers with canals and later to join river systems to the Great Lakes with railways. Though on a much smaller scale than the historic rivalry between Boston, New York, Philadelphia, and Baltimore, the feeling was no less intense and the rhetoric no less rotund. The struggle between Milwaukee, Chicago, and St. Louis to dominate the territory where the Great Lakes touch the Mississippi system is but the most famous and best-documented of these urban rivalries; its essence was repeated in microcosm through every section of the interior.[17]

[16]R. C. Wade, "Urban Life in Western America, 1790-1830," *American Historical Review*, Vol. 66, (1958) ; C. E. Reiser, *Pittsburgh's Commercial Development, 1800-1850*, (Harrisburg: Pennsylvania Historical and Museum Commission, 1951).

[17]The creative force of urban development can be traced in the public press and in the reports of local chambers of commerce and city clubs. By the fifties, spokesmen for Western cities had realized that their growth potential was limited so long as it was based exclusively on commerce. The editor of the Cleveland *Leader* declared: ". . . no thinking man with capital will stop here when we have only commerce to sustain us. A manufacturing town gives a man full scope for his ambitions." His paper advocated popular subscriptions to factory enterprise, reductions in the prices of real estate, protection of "home manufactures." A similar stand was taken 1863 by the new Milwaukee Manufacturers' Association, and the city's *Sentinel* insisted: "Commerce alone can never give us permanent prosperity." A decade later the Cleveland paper affirmed on some unstated authority that "a thousand dollars put into manufacturing does more to gather population than a million dollars put into trade." In short, business leaders in many Western cities had

The scale of urban development is registered in the size of city populations. In 1840 only New Orleans of the cities outside the East, exceeded 100,000 population and, strictly speaking, this was a maritime-colonial city like old Boston or Philadelphia rather than a true city of the interior. But by 1860 Cincinnati and St. Louis had populations of over 150,000, and Chicago had passed the 100,000 mark (Table 18). Louisville and San Francisco numbered over 50,000, and half a dozen other cities had grown beyond 20,000. Within the next decade

Table 18. Larger urban centers of the "West" in 1860, ranked in order of population engaged in manufactures

Urban center	Total population	Percentage in manufactures
Cincinnati	161,044	18.3
Louisville	68,033	9.8
Buffalo	81,129	6.9
St. Louis	160,773	5.8
Chicago	109,260	4.9
New Orleans	168,675	3.0
San Francisco	56,802	2.6

SOURCE: 8th U. S. Census, 1860, *Mortality and Miscellaneous Statistics*, p. xviii.

seven cities in the interior had more than 100,000 inhabitants and, with the first trunk railroads linked to New England and New York, the main thrust of urban development had shifted from the Ohio Valley to the Great Lakes' shores. The five Lake cities—Buffalo, Cleveland, Detroit, Chicago, and Milwaukee—had a combined population in 1870 that was sixteen times their combined population in 1840; in the same interval their states had increased their populations only threefold.[18]

When the character of American manufactures in the years before the Civil War is considered, there is every reason why urban-industrial centers should have emerged in the midst of the great resource-producing hinterland. The leading branches of manufacture in 1860 included many processing activities working on primary raw material. Where weight losses were substantial in any process, it was likely that the relatively high level of transfer costs would foster local or regional processing: lumber products, flour and grist-mill prod-

realized what was apparent to their forebears in Boston more than half a century before, that commerce in raw materials was a wasting asset and that future growth "involved substituting the encouragement of manufacturing for an earlier emphasis on trade."

See also W. W. Belcher, *The Economic Rivalry between St. Louis and Chicago, 1850-1880* (New York: Columbia University Press, 1947) and Bayrd Still, *Milwaukee, the History of a City* (Madison: State Historical Society of Wisconsin, 1948).

[18]B. Still, "Patterns of Mid-Nineteenth Century Urbanization in the Middle West," *Mississippi Valley Historical Review*, Vol. 28 (September 1941), pp. 187-206.

ucts, and some types of leather products were eminently adapted for western locations. Taken together they made up a sizable proportion of the total value of manufacturing output, if a somewhat smaller share of value added by manufacture (Table 19).

Table 19. Leading branches of manufacture in the United States, 1860

Item	Employment	Value of product (000's of $)	Value added by manufacture (000's of $)	Rank by value added
1. Flour & meal	27,682	248,580	40,083	4
2. Cotton goods	114,955	107,338	54,671	1
3. Lumber	75,595	104,928	53,570	2
4. Boots & shoes	123,026	91,889	49,161	3
5. Men's clothing	114,800	80,831	36,681	5
6. Iron (cast, forged, rolled, wrought)	48,975	73,175	35,689	6
7. Leather	22,679	67,306	22,786	9
8. Woolen goods	40,597	60,685	25,030	8
9. Liquors	12,706	56,589	21,667	10
10. Machinery	41,223	52,010	32,566	7

SOURCE: 8th U. S. Census, 1860, *Manufactures,* pp. 733-42.

Table 20 highlights the dominant place of the Middle Atlantic and New England regions in the nation's early manufactures, but it also points to the fact that by 1860 processing outside of these two regions was no longer negligible. Particularly it shows the beginnings of a rapid growth in manufactures which, in the period after 1870, would tie the Great Lakes region into the Northeastern industrial belt. Yet, taking the country as a whole, the combined value of three major farm crops (corn, wheat, and hay) in 1860 exceeded the total value added by manufacture, while capital invested in manufactures was less than one-sixth the value of all agricultural land and buildings. As yet there was only a beginning of the enormous industrial transformation that would be experienced more or less in all parts of the country by the post-bellum generation.

Finally, we conclude this brief review by considering possible relationships between differential levels of living and occupational structures toward the end of the period. Table 21 shows how the eight regions ranked in real personal income per capita in 1880 (the first date for these figures) and gives data on the urbanization of their populations and on the distribution of their labor forces among the agricultural, nonagricultural-resources, and manufacturing components of employment. The highest levels of per capita personal income were achieved in the as yet largely underdeveloped Far West and Mountain regions and, the next highest in the urban-industrial New England and Middle

Table 20. Employment in manufactures in the United States, by region, 1850 and 1860

Region	1850	1860
United States	958,079	1,311,246
	100.00%	100.00%
New England	32.64	29.88
Middle Atlantic	43.90	41.66
Great Lakes	9.70	12.09
South (East of Appalachians)	6.28	5.45
South (West of Appalachians)	5.08	4.36
Plains	1.83	2.30
Southwest	.12	.34
Mountain	.01	.03
Far West	.44	3.89

SOURCE: 9th U. S. Census, 1870, Vol. III, Table VIII (A).

Table 21. Rank order of regions by personal income per capita, urbanization of population, and labor force industry components, 1880

Region	Personal income per capita (1929 dollars)	Urban proportion of population	Labor force components		
			% Agri-culture	% Non-agri.* resource	% Mfg.-service
United States	$302.1	28.2%	49.39	2.27	48.34
Far West	638.2	35.9(3)	28.81(5)	14.46(2)	56.73(3)
Mountain	501.5	25.0(5)	24.00(7)	27.35(1)	48.65(4)
New England	425.0	52.4(1)	21.46(8)	1.51(6)	77.03(1)
Middle Atlantic	422.8	49.8(2)	24.02(6)	2.91(3)	73.07(2)
Great Lakes	307.4	27.5(4)	50.75(4)	1.67(4)	47.58(5)
Plains	271.2	18.2(6)	61.36(3)	1.23(7)	37.41(6)
Southwest	182.7	9.2(8)	72.33(2)	1.58(5)	26.09(7)
Southeast	150.6	9.4(7)	75.36(1)	0.64(8)	24.00(8)

Figures in italics are above the national average.
*Forest and logging, mining, and fisheries.
( ) Rank order.

SOURCE: Unpublished data by R. A. Easterlin; 17th U. S. Census, 1950, see *supra*, Table 4, note; and Appendix Tables A1–A7.

Atlantic regions; the lowest were in the rural-agricultural regions of the Southwest and Southeast. In between the higher urban-industrial regions and the lower rural-agricultural regions were situated the Great Lakes and Plains regions (mostly eastern Plains states), with per capita income levels closest to the countrywide average.

Thus, by 1880, there were, broadly speaking, four different regional levels of living in the United States as measured by per capita personal income, and each was associated with a characteristic occupational structure of the regional labor force. In the first group were the sparsely populated nonagricultural-resource regions of the Far West and Mountain regions with high concentrations of their small labor forces employed in mining. The medium concentrations of industrial employment in these two regions were in services rather than manufactures, and both regions had relatively low concentrations of agricultural activities. The second group comprised the two densely populated regions of the North Atlantic seaboard, New England and the Middle Atlantic states. At this time, New England, with the higher concentration of manufacturers, seems to have had a slightly higher average level of per capita income than the Middle Atlantic region, but the difference was probably not significant. In the third group came two rapidly developing regions of industrial and agricultural potential, the Great Lakes and the Plains region, the former already more urban-industrialized and enjoying a higher average level of living than the still largely unsettled Plains. The fourth group, comprising the heavily populated Southeast and the partly settled Southwest, were the most agricultural and the least industrial regions in the country; as a consequence of their relative economic "backwardness," their personal income per capita was little more than half the national average.[19]

Such were the different regional levels of living in the United States at the end of the 1870's. On the face of it, some regions were relatively poorer in 1880 than they had been in 1840 and some were relatively much richer; the range from the poorest to the richest was certainly much greater than it had been at the earlier date. That factors of production could not yet move "freely" throughout all parts of the continental territory, seems implicit in the extent of regional divergence in income which, if anything, had grown over previous decades. The remote undeveloped Mountain and Far West regions had achieved their exceptional levels of per capita income because they were largely unsettled and possessed the bulk of the nation's domestic supply of precious metals; wages in these outlying areas were usually much higher than in other parts of the country. The Plains and Southwest, meanwhile, had considerably larger populations but apparently lacked resource availabilities other than agriculture. On the other hand, the highly developed New England and Middle Atlantic regions had already achieved a rapid rate of urban-industrial growth and were shortly to be joined by the Great Lakes region. The Plains, however, failed to realize its earlier promise and, if it did not revert to the lower levels of the Southeast or Southwest, it had nevertheless declined relative to the urban-industrial regions by the close of the century. A similar fate overtook the Mountain region somewhat later. The changing fortunes of the several regions as they joined in the burgeoning national economy after 1870 are the subject of the next chapter.

[19]There can be little doubt that the degree of Southern "backwardness" was largely the result of Civil War dislocation as well as relative "overpopulation" of the countryside. See Table 16 above for the 1840 figures by contrast.

11 / Changing regional structure of the U.S. economy, 1870-1910:

(1) GROWTH AND SHIFT OF POPULATION

The phase of American economic history dominated by the self-conscious striving of rival seaboard communities to develop the resource potential of the interior ended during the third quarter of the nineteenth century and the period of "national" development was finally well under way. Between 1870 and 1910 the economy was rapidly industrialized, a far-reaching social process which affected not merely manufactures but resource and service activities as well. A growing population, enlarged by millions of immigrants, surged out from the eastern half of the country into the greater West; a trickle of miners came eastward across the Sierras into the Southwest and Mountain regions. Railroads, partly financed by European capital, tied the Atlantic to the Pacific and sent long fingers into remote regions to secure the untapped resources of the continent. Giant business corporations were organized to build up the iron and steel, oil, farm equipment, copper, lumber, transportation, and many other basic industries on a continental scale. During the last quarter of the century all energies were turned to the creation of an industrial society.

The broad outlines of this industrial transformation will be represented by three historical series: 1) a measure of changes in regional populations, 2) a measure of changes in the structure of regional production, and 3) a measure of accompanying changes in regional income and material well-being. The first of the series traces the occupation and settlement of the continental territory, the second shows how the populations of the various regions were employed, and the third presents the outcome of these changes in terms of total and per capita personal income.

Growth and Shift of Population, 1870-1910

Between 1870 and 1910 the population of the United States more than doubled, rising from less than 40 millions to more than 91 millions. This increase was marked by a steady decline in the rate of population growth, although the annual increase averaged one and a third millions down almost to 1920. Migration was pronounced; each decennial census down through World War I reported that more than 20% of native white Americans had moved from the state of their birth.[1] In less than thirty years the vast land area between the frontier line of 1860 and the Pacific was overrun by population and the historic "frontier" line had ceased to exist. But when this fact was first reported in the 11th United States Census, the territory beyond the 95th meridian was by no means closely settled; large pockets of land were not yet put to productive purposes and in some parts good farming land was still available as late as 1910. Even then many areas in the semi-arid West supported only a thin veneer of permanent settlement.

The relative rates of regional population growth for the period 1870-1910 are shown in Table 22. The four regions of the greater West (Mountain, Southwest, Plains, and Far West) were the fastest growing areas of settlement in the period before 1890; and with the exception of the Plains, these same regions continued to grow at a relatively higher rate than the rest of the nation until well into the twentieth century. Meanwhile, the older settled areas of the Southeast and the Northeast had steadily increased their populations, but at a much slower rate than the West; only the Middle Atlantic region here surpassed the national rate of population growth before 1910.

Table 22. Percentage increases in population by census decades, by region, 1870-1910

Region	1870-80	1880-90	1890-1900	1900-10	1870-1910
United States	26.0	25.5	20.7	21.0	131.0
New England	15.0	17.2	19.0	17.2	87.9
Middle Atlantic	19.4	20.3	*20.9*	*23.6*	114.7
Great Lakes	22.8	20.3	18.6	14.2	100.0
Southeast	17.8	17.8	18.3	15.6	89.7
Plains	*59.7*	*45.1*	15.8	12.5	*201.8*
Southwest	*73.1*	*56.6*	*51.6*	*46.4*	*501.4*
Mountain	*151.4*	*113.1*	*43.1*	*53.7*	*1,078.8*
Far West	*64.0*	*64.5*	*27.0*	*73.8*	*495.6*

Figures in italics are above the national average.

SOURCE: 17th U. S. Census 1950, see *supra*, Table 1, note.

States and regions which experienced the most rapid growth were, almost without exception, the least populated parts of the country. Table 23 shows population per square mile of land area in 1870, 1890, and 1910 for the regions

[1] C. J. Galpin and T. B. Manny, *Interstate Migration Among the Native White Population as Indicated by Difference between State of Birth and State of Residence*, U. S. Department of Agriculture, Bureau of Agricultural Economics, Washington: Government Printing Office, 1934), pp. 6-7.

Table 23. Density of population, by region, 1870, 1890, and 1910

(population per square mile of land area)

Region	Area*	1870	1890	1910
United States	2,974,726 sq. mi.	13.4	21.2	30.9
New England	(2.12)	*55.2*	*74.4*	*103.7*
Middle Atlantic	(3.78)	*87.6*	*125.8*	*188.1*
Great Lakes	(8.23)	*37.3*	*55.0*	74.5
Southeast	(17.95)	*21.7*	*30.1*	41.2
Plains	(17.17)	7.6	17.5	22.8
Southwest	(19.08)	1.8	4.8	10.7
Mountain	(17.23)	0.3	1.8	3.9
Far West	(14.44)	1.7	4.5	9.9

*Figures in parentheses show proportion of total U. S. land area 1950. Figures in italics are above the national average.

SOURCE: *Statistical Abstract of the United States, 1954*, Table 4, p. 10; 17th U. S. Census 1950, see *supra*, Table 1, note.

Table 24. Regional distribution of U. S. population, 1870 – 1910

(per cent of total)

Region	1870	1880	1890	1900	1910
United States	39,818,449 100%	50,155,783 100%	62,947,714 100%	75,994,575 100%	91,972,266 100%
New England	8.8	8.0	7.5	7.4	7.1
Middle Atlantic	24.7	23.4	22.5	22.5	23.0
Great Lakes	22.9	22.3	21.4	21.0	19.8
Southeast	29.1	27.3	25.5	25.1	23.9
Plains	9.7	12.3	14.2	13.6	12.7
Southwest	2.5	3.5	4.4	5.5	6.6
Mountain	0.4	0.9	1.4	1.7	2.2
Far West	1.8	2.3	3.1	3.2	4.7

SOURCE: 17th U. S. Census 1950, see *supra*, Table 1, note.

and for the nation as a whole. Except for the Middle Atlantic region after 1890, the regions with population density higher than the national average were those whose rate of population growth was below the national average throughout the period under review. In absolute terms, of course, the Middle Atlantic, Great Lakes, New England, and Southeast regions persistently had the heaviest increases in population, though by 1910 their combined share of national population had fallen almost 14%. The effects of these disparate rates of growth on the percentage distribution of total population among the regions is shown in Table 24. All regions west of the Mississippi increased their shares of national population in each successive decade between 1870 and 1910 except the Plains, which reached its peak in 1890 and declined thereafter. All regions east of the Mississippi experienced declining shares of national population through the same period, except the Middle Atlantic region, which held its position after 1890 and actually increased its share of the national total during the opening decades of the present century.

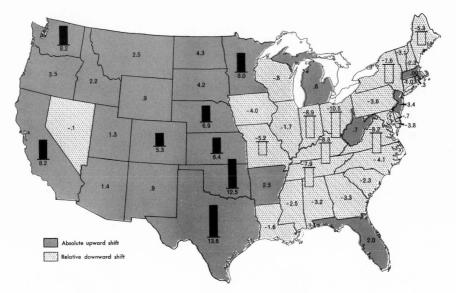

Figure 22. Net Shift in Total Population, 1870-1910.
State figures represent % of total net shift. Total net shift as % of incremental change: 25.4. Total net shift as % of 1870 population: 33.2.

Figure 22 shows the shift of population among the states during the period 1870-1910.[2] The heaviest net upward shifts occurred in the Far West, Southwest, and Plains states, and the heaviest net downward shifts in the Ohio Valley, the New York area, the Upper South, and the older settled Plains states, such as Missouri and Iowa; Maine also experienced a sizable net downward shift. These upward and downward tendencies accord closely with the popular notion of the "westward movement." The principal net shifts are summarized in Table 25.

[2]The state figures are based on net shifts, employing the technique described in Chapter 3; that is, the percentage increase in national population over the 40-year period is applied to each state's population in 1870 to obtain what might be called the *expected change* by 1910 if population had increased at a uniform rate throughout the states and territories, and this *expected* population for each state is then compared with the *actual* population as recorded by the United States census for 1910. The change in relative position is set down as an "upward" or "downward" shift.

A further feature of population changes after 1870 is the marked decline in the proportion of total population living in rural areas and the corresponding increase in urban population. In every decade between 1870 and 1910 all eight regions showed a decline in the rural proportion of their total populations. The rate of increase in urban population was positive at every census during the 40-year period.

Table 25. Principal net shifts in population among states, 1870 – 1910

	Percentage net upward shift		Percentage net downward shift
Texas	13.57	Ohio	10.50
Oklahoma	12.53	Indiana	8.93
Washington	8.22	Kentucky	8.34
California	8.19	Virginia	8.21
Minnesota	8.02	Tennessee	7.92
Nebraska	6.87	New York	7.63
Kansas	6.42	Maine	5.34
Colorado	5.35	Missouri	5.16
N. Dakota	4.32	N. Carolina	4.12
S. Dakota	4.21	Iowa	4.03

SOURCE: See Table 1, note.

Table 26. Urban population as percentage of total population, by region, 1870 and 1910

Region	1870	1910
United States	25.2	45.7
New England	*44.4*	*73.3*
Middle Atlantic	*44.1*	*70.2*
Great Lakes	21.6	*52.7*
Southeast	9.5	19.4
Plains	18.9	33.2
Southwest	6.9	22.5
Mountain	13.9	40.7
Far West	*31.2*	*56.0*

Figures in italics are above the national average.

SOURCE: 17th U. S. Census, 1950, see *supra*, Table 4, note.

The proportion of urban to total population in each of the regions in 1870 and in 1910 is shown in Table 26, and decennial rates of urban increase, by regions, in Table 27. Read in conjunction, the two tables show that the regions with the highest rates of urbanization are the "newer" and the less developed regions.

Table 27. Decennial rates of increase of urban population, by region, 1870 – 1910

Region	1870-80	1880-90	1890-1900	1900-10
United States	41.0	56.5	36.4	39.3
New England	35.7	13.8	32.5	25.3
Middle Atlantic	34.7	39.6	35.0	34.6
Great Lakes	*56.2*	*66.0*	*41.2*	33.2
Southeast	16.2	63.8	37.1	48.3
Plains	*53.1*	*106.2*	27.7	31.3
Southwest	*133.5*	*135.2*	*165.9*	118.3
Mountain	*351.5*	*197.9*	*51.6*	68.6
Far West	*89.1*	*94.1*	37.4	112.1

Figures in italics are above the national average.

SOURCE: 17th U. S. Census 1950, see *supra*, Table 4, note.

The data reveal a tendency for *rates* of urbanization to fall off over the period as a whole in all regions except the Southeast and the Far West. They also reveal a cyclical tendency; decades of relatively rapid urbanization are almost always followed by decades of relatively slower urbanization, with the rate of over-all urban increase slackening in each successive cycle.

Table 28 compares the rates of increase in urban population for the eight regions over the 1870-1880 and 1900-1910 decades and shows the proportion of the nation's total urban population in each region in 1870 and in 1910.

The net shifts in urban population between 1870 and 1910 are shown for the states in Figure 23 and the principal shifts in Table 29. Some parts of the more

Table 28. Rank order of regions by rate of increase in urban population 1870 – 1880 and 1900 – 1910, and regional proportions of U. S. urban population, 1870 and 1910

Region	1870-80 % Rate	1870 Proportion	1900-10 % Rate	1910 Proportion
(1) Mountain	351.5	0.2 (8)	68.6 (3)	2.0 (8)
(2) Southwest	133.5	0.7 (7)	118.3 (1)	3.3 (7)
(3) Far West	89.1	2.2 (6)	112.1 (2)	5.7 (6)
(4) Great Lakes	56.2	19.7 (2)	33.2 (6)	22.9 (2)
(5) Plains	53.1	7.3 (5)	31.3 (7)	9.2 (5)
(6) New England	35.7	15.5 (3)	25.3 (8)	11.4 (3)
(7) Middle Atlantic	34.7	43.4 (1)	34.6 (5)	35.3 (1)
(8) Southeast	16.2	11.0 (4)	48.3 (4)	10.2 (4)

Rank order in parentheses.

SOURCE: 17th U. S. Census 1950, see *supra*, Table 4, note.

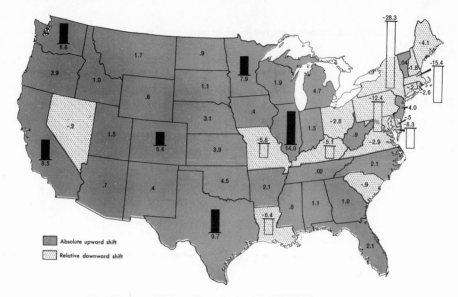

Figure 23. Net Shift in Urban Population, 1870-1910.

State figures represent % of total net shift. Total net shift as % of incremental change: 22.0. Total net shift as % of 1870 urban population: 70.1.

recently settled areas of the country—the Far West states and Texas—are seen to have had sizable upward shifts in urban population over these years. The greatest relative increase in any one state, however, was in Illinois, chiefly in the Chicago metropolitan area. Minnesota and Michigan also show considerable increases which are connected, as in Illinois, with the growth of their dominant metropolitan centers. The greatest downward shifts were in states in the highly

Table 29. Principal net shifts in urban population among states, 1870 – 1910

	Percentage net upward shift		Percentage net downward shift
Illinois	13.97	New York	28.31
Texas	9.73	Massachusetts	15.35
Washington	8.62	Pennsylvania	12.41
California	8.46	Maryland and D. C.	10.74
Minnesota	7.88	Louisiana	6.37
Colorado	5.44	Missouri	5.79
Michigan	4.69	Kentucky	5.09
Oklahoma	4.54	Maine	4.13
New Jersey	3.97	Virginia	2.88
Kansas	3.91	Ohio	2.81

SOURCE: 17th U. S. Census 1950, see *supra*, Table 4, note.

urbanized New England and Middle Atlantic regions. In the Great Lakes region, however, only Ohio shows any noteworthy relative decline in its rate of urban growth.

In *absolute* terms, however, urbanization was most marked in states which developed concentrations of manufactures and related service activities. From the standpoint of social change, these centripetal currents of population were more decisive than the centrifugal currents of "the westward movement." By 1900 only six in every ten people were classified as "rural," and before 1920 less than half the population of 105,000,000 could be credited to the countryside. The United States had become an urban-industrial society; every other American, native-born and immigrant, lived out his life in an urban environment.

12 / Changing regional structure of the U. S. economy, 1870-1910:

(2) SHIFTS IN PRODUCTIVE ACTIVITIES

The continuing growth and redistribution of population within the United States after 1870 was accompanied by changes in the size, occupational structure, and geographical distribution of the labor force.[1] There is perhaps no better single index of changes in the growth and distribution of productive activities, of society's economic base, then the changing pattern of employment through which a population earns its living.

The major categories used for this structural analysis have already been suggested in our description of the economy in 1870; they are three in number, having reference to successive stages in the production process:

1) Resource or Primary Activities, which are concerned with the extraction of raw materials. They embrace such varied occupations as agriculture, forestry and logging, mining, and fishing.

2) Processing or Secondary Activities, which have to do with the transformation of raw materials into finished or semi-finished goods—in short, with manufactures and associated mechanical trades.

3) Servicing or Tertiary Activities, which are essentially the "all other" types of employment engaged in by the residual component of the labor force, i.e., by workers not engaged in either the extraction of materials or the manufacture of products.

Together, these three categories—primary, secondary, and tertiary activities —comprise the total labor force available for production in the nation or any of its regions.

The growth of the national labor force and its principal components in the United States between 1870 and 1910 is shown in Table 30, and its changing regional distribution over these years in Table 31. In size and distribution, as might be expected, the labor force at any time is roughly proportionate to the

---

[1]For present purposes the term "labor force" includes all active workers, ten years old and over, regularly [since 1940, currently at the time of the census] employed in a given occupation.

total population.[2] Thus in 1870, when the westward movement of population was in full swing, the four older regions east of the Mississippi had about 85% of the nation's total population and almost exactly the same percentage of its total labor force. By 1910 their share in the population had dropped to a little over 73% and their share of the labor force to slightly less than 75% of the national total. Most of this decline in the share of the labor force—approximately two-thirds of it—took place before the symbolic closing of "the frontier" in 1890. The shift of some 10% of the greatly expanded labor force west of the Mississippi over the 40-year interval is a cumulative measure of the westward movement in terms of job opportunities.

Table 30.   U. S. labor force, distribution by major industry group, 1870, 1890, and 1910

Year	Labor force	% Resource	% Manufactures	% Services
1870	12,505,923	53.45	21.14	25.41
1890	22,735,661	43.39	24.30	32.31
1910	38,167,336	35.62	27.92	36.46

SOURCE: Appendix Tables A1–A7.

Table 31.   Regional distribution of U. S. labor force, 1870, 1890, and 1910

Region	1870	1890	1910
United States	12,505,923	22,735,661	38,167,336
	100%	100%	100%
New England	10.39	8.82	7.64
Middle Atlantic	25.23	24.30	23.56
Great Lakes	21.90	20.61	19.02
Southeast	28.04	24.09	24.51
Plains	9.24	13.14	11.66
Southwest	2.18	3.51	6.20
Mountain	.57	1.75	2.24
Far West	2.45	3.78	5.19

SOURCE: Appendix Table A-1.

Within the emergent greater West, the growth of the labor force before 1890 was fastest in the Mountain states but largest in the Plains; the Southwest and Far West grew at roughly the same rate and to the same extent (see Table 31).

[2]The proportion of the total population in the labor force, however, was somewhat higher at the end of the period under review than at the beginning—about two-fifths in 1910 as compared to about one-third in 1870.

Between 1890 and 1910, however, the Plains region passed its peak share, and by 1900 was already in relative decline; but the other regions continued to increase their shares of the growing national labor force. The Southwest grew somewhat faster than the Mountain or the Far West regions during these years, and by 1910 had overtaken the Far West as the second largest western region after the Plains.

The westward movement, again, had a differential impact on the relative labor force shares of the four older regions in the East. Between 1870 and 1890, the shares of New England and the Southeast both declined by 14%; in contrast, the decline in the Great Lakes region was only 5% and that in the Middle Atlantic region about 4%. Between 1890 and 1910, the Southeast actually increased its share of the total labor force slightly, but the shares of the other three regions continued in decline.

The differential effects of the redistribution of population and labor force among the regions over the 1870-1910 period as a whole are summarized in Table 32.

Table 32. Percentage change in regional shares of U. S. population and labor force, 1870 – 1910

Region	Population	Labor force
New England	− 18.72	− 26.47
Middle Atlantic	− 7.04	− 6.62
Great Lakes	− 13.44	− 13.15
Southeast	− 17.85	− 12.59
Plains	+ 30.55	+ 26.19
Southwest	+160.63	+184.40
Mountain	+411.63	+292.98
Far West	+158.33	+111.84

SOURCE: 17th U. S. Census, 1950, see *supra*, Table 1, note. Appendix Table A-1.

Resource Activities in the Regions, 1870-1910

There were major shifts in the location of primary resource activities within the national economy between 1870 and 1910.[3] Most striking perhaps was the Northeast's relative decline after about 1890 (Table 33). Its share in the national labor force engaged in resource extraction fell from 44% of the total in 1870 to 36% in 1890 and to only 27% in 1910. All four regions of the greater West had larger shares of the nation's resource activity in 1910 than in 1870. However, in the Plains region, though some net gain took place over the

[3]Moses Abramovitz, *Resource and Output Trends in the United States since 1870*, Occasional Paper 52 (New York: National Bureau of Economic Research, 1956), pp. 5-23.

period as a whole, the share of the total primary labor force was smaller in 1910 than in 1890. The Far West's relative increase was also surprisingly small after 1890.

Table 34 presents a regional breakdown of labor force in resource activity, classified in the four principal sectors: agriculture, mineral extraction, forestry and logging, and fisheries. In agriculture the Northeast was in continuous decline over the entire 1870-1910 period; this decline was especially marked in New England and the Middle Atlantic states. The combined share of the Northeastern regions in the nation's agricultural labor force fell from 43% of the total in 1870 to 34% in 1890 and only 24% in 1910. In contrast, the Southeast's share rose in every decade but one (1890); by 1910 more than 44% of the nation's total agricultural labor force was employed in the Southeast. The expansion here, however, was more than offset by the decline in the Northeast. As a result, the greater West's share of farm labor shows an increase for every decade between 1870 and 1910.[4]

Table 33. Regional distribution of all U. S. resource industries labor force, 1870, 1890, and 1910

Region	1870	1890	1910
United States	6,684,219	9,864,596	13,596,815
	100%	100%	100%
New England	5.43	3.65	2.29
Middle Atlantic	14.85	12.33	9.68
Great Lakes	23.44	20.15	15.05
Southeast	39.71	37.68	42.34
Plains	10.80	16.12	14.07
Southwest	3.02	5.29	10.41
Mountain	.64	1.63	2.45
Far West	2.10	3.15	3.71

SOURCE: Appendix Table A2–A5.

The bulk of the westward shift in agriculture occurred before 1890, as is evidenced by the fact that the agricultural labor force in the greater West already comprised 26% of the national total in 1890 compared with less than 16% in 1870 (and some 30% in 1910). Moreover, all four western regions greatly increased their shares of the agricultural labor force between 1870 and 1890; the impact was felt heavily in the Plains during the seventies and in all the regions during the eighties. The share of the Plains peaked in 1890, as did that of the Far West; but while the Plains continued in decline after 1900, the Far West had more than recovered its 1890 position by 1910. The Mountain

[4]This period, of course, was one in which there were generally increasing amounts of labor used in agriculture.

region increased its share of farm workers over every census decade during this period. But the most striking growth was that in the Southwest, especially in Texas and Oklahoma around the turn of the century. By 1910 the proportion of the agricultural labor force in the Southwest exceeded that of the New England and Middle Atlantic regions combined.

In the second largest resource sector, mining employment, there was considerably less regularity in the changing patterns of regional distribution between 1870 and 1910. Mining developed more rapidly in relative terms than agriculture, but in some of the regions also declined more spectacularly as fixed mineral deposits were used up.

Mining was the most western of all economic activities in 1870. At that time the four regions west of the Mississippi had 43% of the nation's mineral labor force as compared with only about 15% of the total population, about the same percentage of the total labor force, and approximately 16% of the agricultural labor force of the country. About 40% of all mining employment was concentrated in the Mountain and Far West regions. But after 1870, in contrast to the general westward movement, the trend of mining was eastward. During the eighties the Far West's share in mining employment declined by one-half, and by 1890 the greater West had only 30% of the nation's mining workers. By 1910 the proportion had fallen to 26%; almost 74% of the total mining force was now employed in the regions east of the Mississippi. This change suggests the rising importance of coal mining during the last quarter of the century.

The movement of labor in forestry and logging activity after 1870 resembles that both of general population and labor force in its shift to the West. Between 1880 and 1890, however, there was an even more pronounced shift into the Southeast, more nearly resembling that in mining activity. Much of the Southern expansion seems to have stemmed directly from the destruction of the pine forests in the northern Great Lakes states. By 1900, in fact, the entire Northeastern share of logging activity had been greatly reduced. In 1870 the Northeast accounted for almost two-thirds of all forest employment. By 1910 its

Table 34. Regional distribution of each resource industry's labor force, 1870 – 1910

			Agriculture		
Region	1870	1880	1890	1900	1910
United States	6,437,372	8,590,280	9,235,290	11,288,027	12,389,840
	100%	100%	100%	100%	100%
New England	5.32	3.93	3.56	2.78	2.27
Middle Atlantic	14.26	11.70	11.01	8.97	7.54
Great Lakes	23.71	21.36	20.09	17.83	14.74
Southeast	40.93	41.51	39.32	41.73	44.50
Plains	11.07	14.35	16.68	16.32	14.67
Southwest	3.12	4.93	5.52	8.38	11.01
Mountain	.37	.52	1.14	1.40	2.06
Far West	1.22	1.70	2.68	2.59	3.21

Mineral Extraction

Region	1870	1880	1890	1900	1910
United States	186,616	297,784	447,001	694,352	965,169
	100%	100%	100%	100%	100%
New England	2.85	2.44	2.11	1.17	.94
Middle Atlantic	33.36	34.61	35,91	34.49	36.68
Great Lakes	16.54	13.01	21.43	19.56	19.61
Southeast	4.10	4.84	10.07	13.28	16.73
Plains	3.08	6.44	8.64	8.97	8.40
Southwest	.45	2.53	2.03	3.37	4.33
Mountain	10.05	16.65	11.28	11.12	7.49
Far West	29.57	19.48	8.53	8.04	5.82

Forestry and Logging

Region	1870	1880	1890	1900	1910
United States	32,360	55,931	122,143	140,599	173,531
	100%	100%	100%	100%	100%
New England	10.94	6.61	5.63	4.97	5.23
Middle Atlantic	20.61	14.37	17.01	12.41	7.77
Great Lakes	23.66	33.93	26.14	17.80	13.00
Southeast	16.84	14.85	21.31	33.04	35.13
Plains	9.45	9.21	7.96	8.83	7.32
Southwest	1.31	2.83	1.96	3.87	4.93
Mountain	1.83	3.24	3.82	2.71	3.31
Far West	15.36	14.96	16.17	16.37	23.31

Fisheries

Region	1870	1880	1890	1900	1910
United States	27,871	41,352	60,162	68,940	68,275
	100%	100%	100%	100%	100%
New England	40.32	30.78	25.32	18.07	18.23
Middle Atlantic	21.53	25.96	31.25	27.37	21.21
Great Lakes	7.84	6.64	7.37	8.64	11.03
Southeast	24.38	18.53	25.51	30.19	31.71
Plains	1.15	1.16	1.97	2.95	2.30
Southwest	.21	.35	.74	1.10	1.71
Mountain	.04	.07	.11	.08	.22
Far West	4.53	16.51	7.73	11.60	13.59

SOURCE: Appendix Tables A2–A5.

share was only about one-fourth, while the Southeast had more than one-third and the Far West almost one-fourth of the national labor force in this important resource sector.

The data on fisheries employment show a pattern of regional redistribution quite different from that seen in the other primary industries. In 1870 the New England and Middle Atlantic regions together accounted for almost 62% of the nation's fishing activity. In 1890 these two regions still employed more than 56% of the total fisheries labor force. New England's share in fishing employment declined during these two decades, but this decline was partly offset by a rise in the Middle Atlantic fisheries, which reached their peak in 1890. The Southern fisheries and those of the Great Lakes region barely held their own between 1870 and 1890; and in the Far West, rapid growth during the seventies was followed by an almost equally rapid relative decline during the eighties. After 1890, however, the shares of the Southeast and Far West in the fisheries labor force increased considerably, while those of the New England and Middle Atlantic regions continued in gradual relative decline. Elsewhere, only the Great Lakes region showed much incremental activity. Its share rose from around 7% before 1890 to more then 11% by 1910.

Table 35 summarizes changes between 1870 and 1910 in the share of the Northeast, the Southeast, and the West in each of the four major categories of resource employment. The Northeast declined relatively over these years in all categories except mineral extraction. The Southeast gained relatively in all and most notably in mineral extraction, which increased fourfold, and in forest employment, which more than doubled. The West gained relatively in all cate-

Table 35. Percentage distribution of each resource industry's employment, by great region, 1870 and 1910

Region	Industry	Year	
		1870	1910
Northeast	Agriculture	43.29	24.55
	Mineral extraction	52.75	57.23
	Forestry and logging	55.21	26.00
	Fisheries	69.69	50.47
Southeast	Agriculture	40.93	44.50
	Mineral extraction	4.10	16.73
	Forestry and logging	16.84	35.13
	Fisheries	24.38	31.71
West	Agriculture	15.78	30.95
	Mineral extraction	43.15	26.04
	Forestry and logging	27.95	38.87
	Fisheries	5.93	17.82

SOURCE: Appendix Tables A2–A5.

gories except mineral extraction, most notably in fishing and agriculture, which trebled and doubled, respectively; mining activities declined relatively by more than one-third.

Value of Resources Extracted, 1870-1910

When the data on value of resources extracted are examined, the regional shares of the national totals assume somewhat different proportions from those shown by the data on labor force employed in resource activities.[5] The most striking change again is the continuous decline in the shares of the Northeastern regions (Table 36). In 1870 these three regions contributed more than 58%

Table 36. Regional distribution of value of primary U. S. resources extracted, 1870, 1890, and 1910

Region	1870	1890	1910
United States	$2,745,463*	$3,280,974*	$10,512,395*
	100%	100%	100%
New England	6.8	4.7	3.2
Middle Atlantic	23.7	17.3	11.6
Great Lakes	27.7	24.2	20.6
Southeast	25.2	21.7	22.4
Plains	11.1	18.9	24.5
Southwest	1.9	4.1	7.6
Mountain	.5	3.9	4.1
Far West	3.1	5.2	6.0

* (000's of current dollars).

SOURCE: Appendix Table B-1.

of the total primary resource value, but by 1910 their combined share had fallen to little more than 35%. The Southeast also suffered a relative decline although the low point was reached before 1890 and its share recovered somewhat thereafter. The regions of the greater West, on the other hand, improved their relative shares between 1870 and 1890 and again down to 1910. The rate of relative gain, however, was greater in the earlier period (it doubled) than in the later period (less than one-third). A comparison of these value components with

[5]The figure for the value of extracted resources is a rather crude aggregate of the following items culled from official sources: the gross value of farm production; the gross value of mineral production; the gross value of fish at point of sale by fishermen (excluding the whale fishery); and the average value of hardwood and softwood cut for timber plus the value of domestic pulpwood. These figures are not strictly comparable from decade to decade (quite apart from changes in the value of money), but they do provide a fairly accurate geographical cross-section of current values produced at any one time.

Table 37. Distribution of labor force in resource industries, and value of extracted resources, by great region, 1870, 1890, and 1910

Region	1870		1890		1910	
United States	L.F. 100%	Value 100%	L.F. 100%	Value 100%	L.F. 100%	Value 100%
Northeast	43.7	58.2	36.1	46.2	27.0	35.4
Southeast	39.7	25.2	37.7	21.7	42.3	22.4
West	16.6	16.6	26.2	32.1	30.7	42.2

SOURCE: Appendix Tables A2–A5 and B-1.

shares of the primary labor force reveals some striking discrepancies, most notably in the Southeast and the greater West (Table 37).

The Southeast's rising share of the primary labor force after 1890 was in no way matched by a corresponding increase in its share of the value of the nation's extracted resources. From the standpoint of the value of primary resources, this region was relatively worse off in 1910 than at the height of Reconstruction. The West, on the other hand, experienced a large increase in its share of the primary labor force (more than 80%) but an even greater increase in the value of its extracted resources (a rise of more than one and a half times). The Northeast managed to hold its declining proportions of both primary labor force and value of resources in approximate balance.

These divergencies underline the fact that, for a variety of reasons, labor productivity differs markedly among the several resource sectors and that within each sector it varies from region to region. Thus, since the eighties, the strength of resource extraction in the West has lain in the proportion of its high value

Table 38. Regional distribution of value of resources extracted by major resource industry 1870, 1890 and 1910

Agriculture

Region	1870	1890	1910
United States	$2,447,541* 100%	$2,460,003* 100%	$8,494,231* 100%
New England	6.29	4.33	2.89
Middle Atlantic	21.41	14.03	9.13
Great Lakes	28.26	23.07	21.63
Southeast	27.44	25.51	21.83
Plains	11.75	22.18	28.33
Southwest	2.10	4.67	8.04
Mountain	.27	1.23	3.17
Far West	2.48	4.98	4.98

Mineral extraction

Region	1870	1890	1910
United States	$152,596*	$582,133*	$1,238,415*
	100%	100%	100%
New England	3.03	3.86	1.40
Middle Atlantic	56.73	32.46	30.45
Great Lakes	15.44	23.11	19.18
Southeast	3.27	7.30	12.90
Plains	3.13	8.19	10.52
Southwest	.24	2.61	6.15
Mountain	5.07	16.62	11.46
Far West	13.09	5.85	7.94

Forestry and logging

Region	1870	1890	1910
United States	$134,229*	$199,937*	$725,737*
	100%	100%	100%
New England	15.19	6.56	7.78
Middle Atlantic	28.49	9.63	7.36
Great Lakes	32.41	45.51	12.88
Southeast	11.41	16.95	45.48
Plains	8.51	12.60	5.18
Southwest	.52	2.40	4.95
Mountain	.55	.58	2.23
Far West	2.92	5.77	14.14

Fisheries

Region	1870	1890	1910
United States	$11,097*	$38,901*	$54,012*
	100%	100%	100%
New England	72.90	27.16	28.03
Middle Atlantic	7.63	38.40	22.26
Great Lakes	10.67	5.17	9.33
Southeast	4.28	19.43	25.57
Plains	.04	1.07	1.32
Southwest	—	.82	.83
Mountain	.02	.20	—
Far West	4.46	7.75	12.66

* (000's of current dollars).

SOURCE: Appendix Tables B2–B5.

resource activities rather than in the absolute size of its primary labor force. Table 38 shows the value of the four main categories of resources extracted in the regions between 1870 and 1910. The relative decline of the Northeast is apparent in *all* categories, although output of mineral wealth in the Middle Atlantic region and the strength of the Great Lakes region in agriculture, minerals, and forest activities (before 1900) tends to cushion that decline. The relative decline in the Southeast's agricultural values in contrast to agricultural labor force emphasizes the labor-intensive nature of the region's agriculture. Labor force components in mining and fishing in the Southeast also make up a larger proportion of the national totals in these sectors than do the value components that result from labor; the disparity, however, is much less marked than in agriculture. The most favorable aspect of the Southeast's resource economy before 1910 is the strong rise of its forest industries: the share of the forest labor force increased by almost two-thirds between 1890 and 1910, but the relative value of the raw forest product increased by more than 168%.

Among the Western regions at this time, the most spectacular achievement in the Plains was the rise of agriculture in the face of many natural obstacles; the share of the farm labor force between 1870 and 1910 rose by a little more than one-third, but the relative share of farm values more than doubled. Certainly no other Western region contributed as much to the nation's agriculture in these years. On the other hand, *all* Western regions made important contributions to the exploitation of mineral wealth. By 1910 the Mountain and Plains regions had achieved the larger shares, although the former was already in relative decline; but rapid growth in the Southwest (notably Texas) after 1890 and the revival of mineral interest in the Far West (notably California) marked the appearance of new and valuable oil fields in the nation's resource economy. The riches of the Far West (especially the Pacific Northwest) in forest resources also began to make their mark around the turn of the century. This sector was still very labor-intensive as late as 1910, but the share of raw forest values was beginning to rise much more rapidly than the share of the forest labor force. Structural differences in the primary labor force plus differences in labor productivity and product prices help account for the varying contributions of the regions to the nation's resource economy.

Taking the nation's resource economy as a whole during this period, what

Table 39. Percentage distribution of value of all resources extracted, by major resource industry, 1870 and 1910

Resource industry	1870	1910
All resource industries	$2,798,637*	$14,827,073*
	100%	100%
Agriculture	89.15	80.80
Mineral extraction	5.56	11.78
Forestry and logging	4.89	6.90
Fisheries	.40	.52

*(000's of 1929 dollars).

SOURCE: Appendix Tables B2–B5.

changes in the four resource sectors can be linked to the development of resources in the three great regions? Between 1870 and 1910 the real value of resources extracted increased fivefold; the value (in terms of 1929 dollars) was about $2,798,637,000 in 1870 and over $14,827,073,000 by 1910. The contribution of agriculture declined somewhat during this period as a whole, while that of forest activities and especially of mineral activities increased considerably; fisheries made only a slight contribution at all times (Table 39). Actually, the share of agriculture had increased after the recovery from the depression of the early nineties and, *pari passu*, the share of mining had declined after 1890 in spite of the early rise of the petroleum industry. Only forestry, in fact, appears to have improved its relative position throughout the entire period.

These developments marked important geographical shifts in the nation's resource economy. Thus, apart from the Great Lakes states, the recovery of agriculture after the depression of the nineties was confined essentially to the greater West, especially to the Plains and Southwest. Neither the Northeast nor the Southeast raised its relative agricultural contribution after 1890; in all the territory east of the Mississippi, only the Great Lakes region held its own in the

Table 40. Percentage distribution of value of all resources extracted, by major resource industry and great region, 1870, 1890, and 1910

Resource industry	Northeast	Southeast	West	United States
Agriculture				
1870	49.89	24.46	14.80	89.15
1890	31.06	19.13	24.79	74.98
1910	27.19	17.64	35.97	80.80
Mineral extraction				
1870	4.18	.18	1.20	5.56
1890	10.55	1.29	5.90	17.74
1910	6.01	1.52	4.25	11.78
Forestry and logging				
1870	3.72	.56	.61	4.89
1890	3.76	1.03	1.30	6.09
1910	1.93	3.14	1.83	6.90
Fisheries				
1870	.38	.01	.02	.40
1890	.84	.23	.12	1.19
1910	.31	.13	.08	.52

SOURCE: Appendix Tables B2–B5.

agricultural sector. In minerals each of the three great regions of the country contributed to the upsurge in total value between 1870 and 1890, although in absolute terms the Southeast's share was modest in comparison with that of the Northeast or the West. But thereafter the contribution from Northeastern minerals fell off sharply, and even the West experienced a moderate, although temporary, decrease, whereas the Southeast continued its less spectacular growth throughout the entire 40-year period. In the forest sector, the Northeast, the West, and the Southeast all increased their relative shares of *total* resources value between 1870 and 1890 (the strength of the Northeast here, as in agriculture, lay exclusively in the Great Lakes region). After 1890, however, the Northeast went into relative decline; the West continued to grow, and the Southeast by 1910 had more than doubled its relative share (Table 40).

Attention to the multi-state regions alone conceals some significant changes in resource activities among the states within the regions. We shall now examine these changes to determine more precisely where, when, and in what magnitude the pronounced geographical shifts occurred.

AGRICULTURE

The period 1870-1910 was generally one of great instability in agricultural markets; but in spite of a secular decline in most farm prices down until the late nineties, agricultural settlement continued to spread across the entire

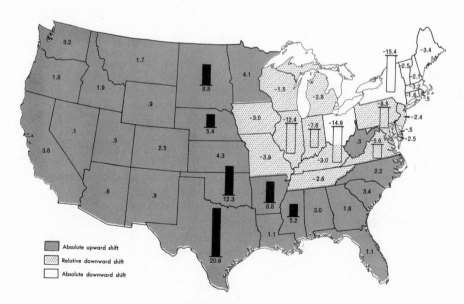

Figure 24. Net Shift in Agricultural Labor Force, 1870-1910.

State figures represent % of total net shift. Total net shift as % of incremental change: 47.7. Total net shift as % of 1870 agricultural labor force: 44.1. Source: Appendix Table C.

country. Figure 24 and Table 41 summarize the principal net upward and downward shifts in the agricultural labor force of the various states over these four decades. More than a third of the total net upward shift of farm workers during these years took place in the Southwest (principally in Texas and, after 1890, also in Oklahoma), and a further 22% in the wheat belt of the western

Table 41. Principal net shifts in agricultural labor force among states, by decade, 1870 – 1910

1870-1880		1880-1890		1890-1900		1900-1910	
Net upward shift							
Tex.	23.45	N. & S. Daks.	16.64	Okla.	26.01	Tex.	15.82
Kans.	17.40	Nebr.	15.76	Tex.	19.64	Okla.	12.65
Ark.	10.92	Minn.	9.77	Ala.	9.36	Ga.	10.49
Nebr.	9.39	Calif.	9.10	Miss.	8.61	Miss.	10.16
Minn.	5.47	Tex.	6.54	Ark.	5.36	Ark.	6.59
La.	5.00	Wash.	5.91	Ga.	4.02	Ala.	6.34
S. C.	4.65	Kans.	5.34	Minn.	3.66	N. C.	5.84
Iowa	4.37	Ark.	5.30	Ky.	3.38	S. C.	4.89
N. & S. Daks.	4.24	Colo.	5.04	N. C.	3.31	N. Dak.	4.53
Calif.	2.70	Wis.	3.38	Tenn.	3.16	Calif.	3.34
Share of 10 leading states in total net upward shift	87.59		82.78		86.51		80.65
Net downward shift							
N. Y.	19.05	Ga.	*14.14*	N. Y.	*17.59*	Ill.	*11.59*
Ohio	18.21	Ill.	*10.43*	Ohio	12.21	Mo.	*9.41*
Ill.	8.93	Ala.	*10.15*	Pa.	9.90	Ohio	*9.13*
Va.	7.54	Ind.	*9.39*	Ill.	9.78	Iowa	*8.58*
Tenn.	6.67	Ohio.	*8.57*	Ind.	7.46	N. Y.	*7.83*
Pa.	5.99	Va.	*8.28*	Mich.	5.05	Ind.	*7.69*
Mass.	*5.36*	Ky.	*6.90*	Kans.	4.84	Pa.	*7.24*
N. J.	*4.35*	N. Y.	*5.60*	Nebr.	3.39	Mich.	*5.52*
Maine	3.85	Pa.	*4.95*	Maine	*3.03*	Kans.	*4.41*
Ky.	3.37	N. C.	*4.50*	Mass.	*3.03*	Ky.	*3.21*
Share of 10 leading states in total net downward shift	83.32		82.91		76.28		74.61

The figures in italics are absolute downward shifts.

SOURCE: Appendix Table A–2.

Plains states and Minnesota (mostly before 1890). The spread of cotton-growing also brought sizable net upward shifts into certain southeastern states, notably Arkansas, Alabama, and Mississippi.

The absolute and relative declines in agricultural employment were heaviest in the more urban-industrial and older agricultural states. The New England, Middle Atlantic, and Great Lakes regions lost relative to other parts of the country at each decennial census; and after 1890 New England's decline became absolute, as did that of several Middle Atlantic and even Great Lakes states after 1900 (New York, Pennsylvania, Illinois, Ohio, Indiana, and Michigan). At various times many Plains and Southeastern states also contributed to the total net downward shift, while at others they experienced growth; relative declines in the Plains were most marked after 1890, those in the Southeast during the eighties. Over the period as a whole, however, Missouri and Iowa were the only states in the Plains region and Virginia, Kentucky, and Tennessee the only states in the Southeast that showed a net downward movement.

Agricultural fortunes in both the Plains and the Southeast were adversely affected during the last quarter of the nineteenth century by severe price fluctuations in the national wheat and cotton markets and by prolonged periods of drought. Urban industrialization, moreover, did not proceed fast enough in these regions to absorb all the labor displaced by mechanization in certain types of farming. A further factor complicating the economic position of farmers in many parts of the country before 1900 was the fact that, in spite of increases in population, demand for farm products grew less rapidly than supply. In 1870 people spent on an average about one-third of their current incomes on agricultural products; by 1890 the proportion had fallen to little more than one-fifth, and it was to fall still further before the upturn about 1897. Only a slackening in the growth of farm population, amounting almost to rural depopulation in some parts of New England, and the concurrent decline in cultivated acreage and in the growth of farm output after about 1897, together with the regional growth of urban population, permitted some gradual amelioration of the staple farmer's economic position before World War I.[6]

MINERAL EXTRACTION

The exploitation of mineral resources has been a vital feature of economic development in the United States. After 1870 the nation's draft on coal, iron, copper, lead, zinc, and other ores increased enormously. Nature had endowed the different regions of the country (except New England perhaps) with an immense variety of minerals, most of which were sooner or later adapted to meet

[6]T. W. Schultz, *Agriculture in an Unstable Economy* (New York: McGraw-Hill, 1945), p. 115; H. U. Faulkner, "The Decline of Laissez-Faire, 1897-1917," in *The Economic History of the United States* (New York: Rinehart and Co., 1951), Vol. 7, pp. 315-65. Before 1897, however, the position of farmers in the dairy and corn belts of the Great Lakes region was only less critical than that of the wheat and cotton producers in the Plains and Southeast.

this growing need of industry for materials and fuels. Given adequate transportation service, there seemed no limit to the potential supply of domestic minerals. Fortunately, the older eastern part of the country had a superb system of natural and artificial inland waterways and, by 1870, had the makings of a first-class railroad network. Precious metals apart, there was no pressing need to develop the mineral resources of the West before railroad transportation had become available in the closing decades of the century. Between 1870 and 1910 the share of minerals in the real value of all extracted resources in the United States more than doubled.

Mining employment rose steadily throughout these four decades, principally as a result of greatly increased coal-mining activity. The importance of coal mining in the resource economy of the late nineteenth century is evidenced by the fact that more than one-third of the total net upward shift in mining employment took place in Pennsylvania and West Virginia (see Figure 25). A

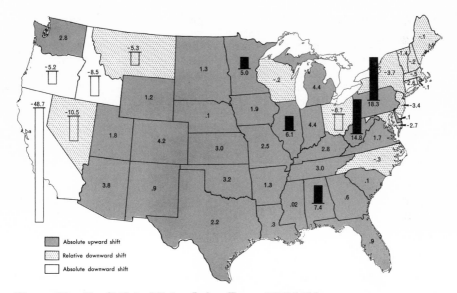

Figure 25. Net Shift in Mining Labor Force, 1870-1910.

State figures represent % of total net shift. Total net shift as % of incremental change: 47.8. Total net shift as % of 1870 mining labor force: 199.5. Source: Appendix Table C.

further 10% was registered in the coal-producing states of the Great Lakes region; Illinois was especially strong during the 1890's although initial developments both here and in Indiana can be seen to go back as far as the seventies. In the Southeast, the coal and iron district of Alabama showed nearly 8% of the total net upward shifts, mostly between 1880 and 1900, and Tennessee about 4%. Altogether, some 50% or more of the nation's total net upward shift in mining employment during the 1870-1910 period was connected with coal developments, and the half-dozen states concerned all lay east of the Mississippi. Nearly two-thirds of the net downward shifts in mining employment over these years occurred in the precious metals producing states of the Far West, in spite of some revival of activities in Nevada after 1900 and in Washington a decade earlier. The principal net upward and downward shifts among the states are summarized for each decade in the 1870-1910 period in Table 42.

Table 42. Principal net shifts in mining labor force among states, by decade, 1870 – 1910

1870-1880		1880-1890		1890-1900		1900-1910	
			Net upward shift				
Colo.	44.40	Ohio	21.94	Wash.	15.18	W. Va.	31.18
Pa.	11.49	Pa.	10.51	W. Va.	13.81	Pa.	19.31
Ariz.	7.49	Mich.	9.81	Ala.	12.12	Minn.	8.67
N. & S. Daks.	6.16	Ala.	7.93	Okla.	9.07	Nev.	5.75
Kans.	4.72	Mo.	7.53	Ill.	6.37	Ky.	5.59
Ill.	3.97	W. Va.	4.74	Tenn.	5.57	Okla.	4.81
Ind.	3.54	Tenn.	4.21	Minn.	5.33	N. Y.	3.65
Mich.	3.19	Mont.	3.78	Ariz.	4.77	Ariz.	3.02
Utah	3.05	Wyo.	3.07	Ore.	3.62	Ind.	2.98
Iowa	2.62	Minn.	3.05	Pa.	3.00	Tex.	2.97
Share of 10 leading states in total net upward shift	90.63		76.57		78.84		87.93
			Net downward shift				
Calif.	30.47	Calif.	*41.77*	Ohio	15.39	Colo.	*21.84*
Ohio	*25.12*	Colo.	*28.61*	Calif.	15.34	Calif.	*13.66*
Nev.	*10.26*	Nev.	*6.49*	N. Y.	*13.45*	Mont.	*10.12*
Mont.	*9.15*	N. J.	*4.43*	Mich.	10.20	Wash.	*9.63*
Idaho	*8.96*	Ariz.	*4.36*	Nev.	*9.39*	Mo.	9.24
N. Y.	3.92	Ore.	*4.01*	Wis.	*5.08*	Idaho	*5.63*
Ore.	*3.91*	N. & S. Daks.	*3.78*	Colo.	4.57	Ore.	*5.58*
Conn.	*2.33*	Idaho	2.50	Md.	4.05	Mich.	3.54
N. J.	1.25	Md.	1.29	Conn.	*3.57*	Iowa	3.52
Md.	1.10	Conn.	.68	Mass.	*2.61*	Ohio	2.60
Share of 10 leading states in total net downward shift	96.47		97.92		83.65		85.36

The figures in italics are absolute downward shifts.

SOURCE: Appendix Table A–3.

Activity in the extraction of basic metal ores, notably iron and copper, was most marked in Michigan (especially in 1870-1880) and Illinois (1880-1910). But the most spectacular fluctuations in this branch of the mineral economy occurred in the Mountain region. On balance, Colorado, Utah, and Wyoming ended up the 1870-1910 period with a net upward shift representing some 7% of the total; Montana and Idaho, on the other hand, registered a combined net downward shift of more than 13%. Certain decennial fluctuations in the Mountain region were quite remarkable. Thus Colorado experienced 44% of the total net upward shift during the 1870's (see Table 42) and almost 29% of the total net downward shift in the following decade. Similarly in the Southwest, Arizona showed a net upward shift for the seventies of more that 7%, a net downward shift of 4% in the eighties, and a further net upward shift of just less than 5% in the last decade of the century.

The appearance of Oklahoma and Texas among states with sizable net upward shifts around the turn of the century signalizes the beginnings of the petroleum industry (also of some coal mining), but the greatest relative net increase in the Southwest before 1910 was in Arizona (almost 4% over the period as a whole), mostly in connection with copper mining.

New England had little to contribute to the nation's mineral economy at any time, and even the modest quarrying activity carried on in some parts was a wasting asset through most of the period.

Those who had dug for precious metals in the Mountain and Far West regions during the third quarter of the nineteenth century had set in motion a chain of events which had led to the opening up of the entire West. But already by 1890 it was evident that much of the more enduring mineral wealth of the nation was still to be extracted from regions east of the Continental Divide.[7]

FOREST ACTIVITIES

Throughout the whole period 1870-1910 agricultural and mineral products together accounted for 90% or more of the gross value of primary resources extracted in the United States. Primary forest products (hardwood and softwood lumber plus pulpwood but excluding wood for fuel) at no time contributed more than 7% of the total, but the share fluctuated less than that of either of the two principal resource sectors. The value of primary forest output in current dollars increased slowly throughout the entire period, and down until 1910 forest employment also showed considerable increases over each census decade.

The regional shifts in forest employment in the late nineteenth and early twentieth centuries were perhaps even more dramatic than those in mining activity. Almost every section of the country was involved at some time or

---

[7]W. J. Trimble, *The Mining Advance into the Inland Empire* (Madison: University of Wisconsin Press, 1914), Isaac Lippincott, *Economic Development of the United States* (New York: D. Appleton & Co., 1921), pp. 326-347, lists Pennsylvania, West Virginia, Illinois and Ohio as much greater producers of mineral wealth than any other states before World War I; next in order came California, Michigan, Arizona, Montana, Oklahoma, Missouri, Colorado, Minnesota, Alabama, Texas, and New Mexico.

Table 43. Principal net shifts in forest labor force among states, by decade, 1870 – 1910

1870-1880		1880-1890		1890-1900		1900-1910	
Net upward shift							
Mich.	58.63	Wash.	22.65	Ark.	15.03	Wash.	37.56
Colo.	5.43	Pa.	21.29	Tenn.	11.48	W. Va.	15.44
Mo.	5.26	N. C.	10.16	Wash.	9.07	Ore.	10.09
Tex.	4.47	Ore.	6.78	Tex.	8.14	La.	9.21
Ore.	2.99	La.	5.78	La.	7.63	Miss.	6.44
S. C.	2.96	Ky.	5.62	Fla.	7.55	Idaho	5.53
Wis.	2.91	W. Va.	5.00	Ga.	6.33	N. C.	3.68
Calif.	2.90	Ark.	4.22	Miss.	6.14	Okla.	3.62
N. Mex.	2.14	Va.	3.59	W. Va.	5.44	Maine	2.86
Mont.	1.83	Mont.	3.25	Minn.	4.29	Tex.	2.17
Share of 10 leading states in total net upward shift	89.52		88.34		81.10		96.60
Net downward shift							
Maine	*19.25*	Mich.	39.88	Mich.	*29.12*	Pa.	*26.79*
Pa.	19.03	Calif.	19.60	Pa.	*21.05*	Mich.	*12.41*
N. Y.	13.29	N. Y.	6.36	Wis.	*14.09*	Ga.	*7.10*
Nev.	*7.09*	Tex.	5.85	Colo.	*5.26*	Wis.	6.12
Ind.	*6.27*	Minn.	4.94	Calif.	4.97	Ark.	*5.23*
La.	4.10	Wis.	4.80	Maine	*4.84*	Ky.	*5.04*
Tenn.	*4.01*	Ill.	3.56	N. Y.	*4.18*	Ill.	*4.99*
Ohio	3.35	N. H.	2.80	Ind.	*3.65*	Ohio	*4.21*
Minn.	3.16	Nev.	2.59	Nev.	*2.24*	Calif.	*3.26*
Ala.	3.05	Iowa	2.03	Mont.	*2.08*	Mo.	*2.81*
Share of 10 leading states in total net downward shift	82.60		92.41		91.48		77.96

The figures in italics are absolute downward shifts.

SOURCE: Appendix Table A–4.

another except the Mountain and Plains regions, where for the most part forest cover was minimal. The heaviest net upward shifts occurred in the Pacific Northwest and the Southeast. Washington and Oregon together accounted for more than 35% of the total upward shift (Figure 26), and West Virginia for

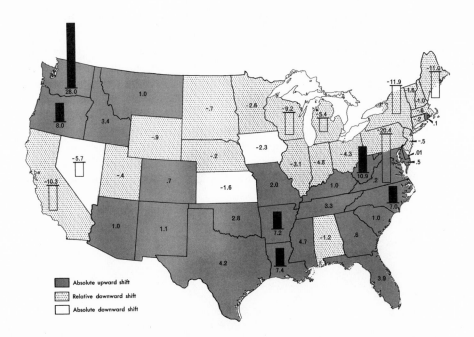

Figure 26. Net Shift in Forest Labor Force, 1870-1910.

State figures represent % of total net shift. Total net shift as % of incremental change: 48.9. Total net shift as % of 1870 forest labor force: 213.2. Source: Appendix Table C.

more than 11% (second only to Washington). There were also sizable upward shifts in Louisiana, Arkansas, Mississippi, Florida, and Virginia in the Southeast. Until 1900 logging activity remained buoyant in some of the Great Lakes states also, but thereafter went into rapid decline. During the nineties, Wisconsin, Michigan, and Minnesota (in the Plains) were the country's leading producers, but by 1910 they were net importers of lumber and their cut-over pinelands were already being abandoned.[8]

The heaviest net downward shift in forest employment came, of course, in the states which had provided the bulk of the nation's lumber for nearly three centuries—the once heavily forested states of the New England and Middle Atlantic regions. Pennsylvania, New York, and Maine accounted for more than 40% of the total net downward shift between 1870 and 1910. There was also a marked decline—nearly 16%—in logging activities in California and Nevada, which had been the earliest sources of softwood supply in the Far West (Table 43).

[8]R. F. Fries, *Empire in Pine: The Story of Lumbering in Wisconsin, 1830-1900* (Madison: State Historical Society of Wisconsin, 1951). Also, Isaac Lippincott, *op. cit.*, pp. 348-359.

FISHING ACTIVITIES

Important as fishing may be locally in a number of coastal areas, its contribution to total resource value has not exceeded 1% since 1900. In several regions, however—the New England, Middle Atlantic, Southeast, and Far West regions—there is an historic concern with fishing, which has provided a modest livelihood for tens of thousands of people. During the present century, moreover, it has supplied a major part of the material on which the growth of the important canning and frozen food industries has been based.

The value of the catch (excluding the whale fishery) rose from around $11,000,000 in 1870 to more than $54,000,000 in 1910.[9] The principal interregional changes in fishing employment over these years (summarized in Figure 27) involved the growth of the Gulf and Far Western fisheries and the relative

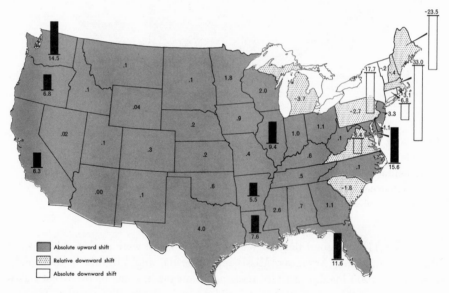

Figure 27. Net Shift in Fishing Labor Force, 1870-1910.
State figures represent % of total net shift. Total net shift as % of incremental change: 55.6. Total net shift as % of 1870 fishing labor force: 80.6. Source: Appendix Table C.

decline of those in New England and, to a lesser extent, the Middle Atlantic region. During the seventies, the largest net increases occurred in Oregon, California, and Maryland. But in the ensuing decade the Far Western states declined relatively and the Chesapeake states of Virginia and Maryland scored the greatest relative gains; smaller net upward shifts also occurred in North Carolina, Florida, and Louisiana during this decade. By the turn of the century,

[9]This figure is based on data provided in the detailed federal census of fisheries made in 1908.

however, the growth of the California and Gulf fisheries and of some of the inland fisheries (notably in Illinois and Arkansas) had produced relative net downward shifts in the Chesapeake area.

Summary

The occupation of the greater West after 1870 greatly enlarged the area of the nation's resource economy. Between 1870 and 1910 the proportion of the primary labor force west of the Mississippi increased by more than 84%, and constituted almost a third of all resource employment in the latter year. By far the largest part of this increase was contributed by agriculture. The essential role of the West in these years was to augment the flow of raw materials into the industrializing Northeast and, in the case of agriculture, to supply international markets as well. Apart from farm produce, the West's most important output was mineral ores, notably copper, lead, zinc, and, later, iron. Around the turn of the century the development of oil resources in California (after 1895), in Texas (after 1898), and in Oklahoma (after 1904) represented a major addition to the nation's fuel economy. Following the rapid destruction of the Great Lakes forests in the late nineteenth century, the Pacific Northwest became an important source for the nation's lumber supply. The growth of coal mining in three of the four Eastern regions and the spectacular rise of lumbering in the Southeast were perhaps the only new developments east of the Mississippi to compare with the contributions of the West.

Manufacturing Activities, 1870-1910

The most striking feature in the history of American manufacturing is the enduring strength of the Northeast. The industrial pre-eminence of the southern New England and Middle Atlantic states, of course, dates back to the beginning of the nineteenth century; and, after 1850, the Northeast's position was reinforced by the spread of manufacturing into the Great Lakes states. By 1870, 80% of the nation's manufacturing employment was concentrated in these three regions. Thereafter, technological change and the growth of the transportation system permitted some wider diffusion of manufacture, notably into the upper Southeast and eastern Plains states and, more recently, into the Far West. But even today the great industrial belt in the Northeast continues to dominate the regional structure of American manufactures much as it did at the beginning of this century.

Table 44 shows the interregional redistribution of the manufacturing labor force between 1870 and 1910. The shares of the New England and Middle Atlantic regions in the nation's manufacturing employment declined over these years, and the shares of all other regions increased. The general diffusion, however, abated somewhat after 1890. The Mountain region's share in 1910 was only slightly greater than in 1890, while that of the Plains region had actually declined. The Southwest and Far West maintained approximately the same rates of relative growth between 1890 and 1910 as between 1870 and 1890.

Only the Southeast showed a significantly greater rate of relative increase after 1890 than before. New England's relative decline was as great in the later of these two periods as in the earlier, but the decline in the Middle Atlantic region relative to other regions was somewhat slower after 1890 than between 1870 and 1890.

Table 44. Regional distribution of the manufacturing labor force, 1870, 1890, and 1910

Region	1870	1890	1910
United States	2,643,417	5,525,692	10,656,545
	100%	100%	100%
New England	21.65	17.38	13.42
Middle Atlantic	38.35	35.84	33.55
Great Lakes	20.36	21.23	22.61
Southeast	9.94	10.42	12.69
Plains	6.52	8.88	8.35
Southwest	.72	1.31	2.74
Mountain	.35	1.44	1.64
Far West	2.11	3.50	5.00

SOURCE: Appendix Table A–6.

Table 45, which extends the data for the three great regions to 1950, shows that surprisingly little redistribution of the manufacturing labor force has taken place since 1890. The Northeast experienced a relative decline in its share of about 9%, the Southeast an increase of some 48% (on a low base), and the West an increase of about 12%. The further growth of manufactures, especially after 1910, has involved no major regional relocation and only the Southeast among the great regions has continued, moderately, to show an uninterrupted improvement in its relative position. In the West, relative declines in the shares of the Plains and Mountain regions have offset the continuing growth of the Southwest and Far West.

Table 45. Distribution of manufacturing labor force, by great region, 1870 – 1950

Region	1870	1890	1910	1930	1950
United States	100%	100%	100%	100%	100%
Northeast	80.36	74.45	69.58	66.38	67.64
Southeast	9.94	10.42	12.69	14.38	15.43
West	9.70	15.13	17.73	19.24	16.93

SOURCE: Appendix Table A–6.

Another useful measure of manufacturing activity is provided by value added by manufacture.[10] Table 46 shows the regional shares of total value added by manufacture for the period 1870-1910. In general, each region's share is roughly proportionate to its share of all manufacturing employment. Indeed, the parallel is much closer than in the case of resources value and employment.

Table 46. Regional distribution of U. S. value added by manufacture, 1870, 1890, and 1910

Region	1870	1890	1910
United States	$1,577,387*	$3,453,518*	$8,188,527*
	100%	100%	100%
New England	23.95	17.48	14.32
Middle Atlantic	42.16	40.05	36.90
Great Lakes	18.07	24.35	25.59
Southeast	6.23	6.83	10.04
Plains	6.68	7.00	6.42
Southwest	.31	.68	1.49
Mountain	.24	.68	1.21
Far West	2.36	2.93	4.03

* (000's of current dollars).

SOURCE: Lee, Miller, Brainerd, and Easterlin (see note for Table 4), Table M-8.

Table 47. Distribution of manufacturing labor force and value added by manufacture, by great region, 1870, 1890, and 1910

Region	1870		1890		1910	
	L.F.	V.A.	L.F.	V.A.	L.F.	V.A.
United States	100%	100%	100%	100%	100%	100%
Northeast	80.36	84.18	74.45	81.88	69.58	76.81
Southeast	9.94	6.23	10.42	6.83	12.69	10.04
West	9.70	9.59	15.13	11.29	17.73	13.15

SOURCE: Appendix Table A-6; Table 46.

[10]Unlike the figure for value of extracted resources, value added by manufacture is a "net" figure, derived by subtracting the cost of raw materials, semi-manufactured parts and components, supplies, fuels, purchased electric energy, and contract work from the value of shipments of manufacturing establishments. This measure avoids duplication in the value of shipments which results from the use of products of some establishments as materials by others. As such, it constitutes the best value measure available for comparing the relative economic importance of manufacturing among industries or regions.

As Table 47 and Figure 28 show, the Northeast achieved a persistently higher proportion of the nation's value added by manufacture than it did of manufacturing employment. This was true of no other great region in the period before 1910. Only after 1890 did the Southeast begin to reduce the disparity between its shares of employment and value added, while between 1870 and 1890 the growth of value added in the West did not keep pace with the growth of manufacturing labor force.

An analysis of shifts in manufacturing employment among the individual states for 1870-1910 shows, not surprisingly, the more urban-industrial states to have sustained the greatest relative losses and many of the more rural-agricultural states to have achieved the greatest relative gains. As late as 1870 the industrial states of the New England and Middle Atlantic regions contained 60% of all manufacturing employment; by 1910 their share had been reduced to about 47%. But, considering the growth of manufacturing in other parts of the country over these years, the astonishing fact is that a state like Pennsylvania, for example, did not show a greater net downward shift—about 4% over the four decades (see Figure 29). (In absolute terms, of course, manufacturing employment in Pennsylvania actually increased from less than 327,000 in 1870 to more than 1,250,000 in 1910.) New Jersey actually experienced a relative net upward shift of more than 4%. The greatest relative losses were in New

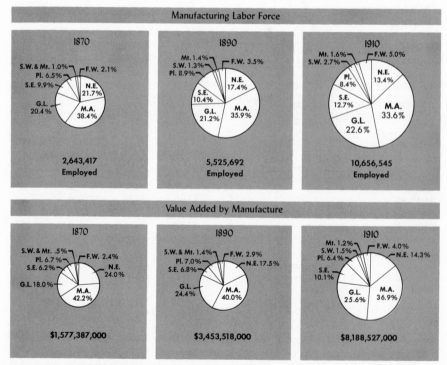

Figure 28. Regional Distribution of U. S. Manufacturing Labor Force and Value Added by Manufacture, 1870, 1890, and 1910.

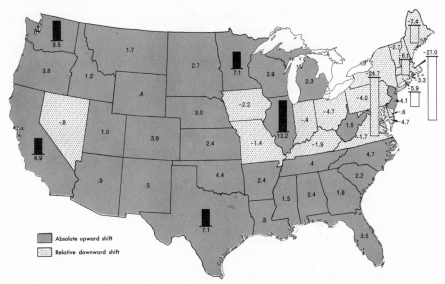

Figure 29. Net Shift in Manufacturing Labor Force, 1870-1910.
State figures represent % of total net shift. Total net shift as % of incremental change: 20.9. Total net shift as % of 1870 manufacturing labor force: 63.3. Source: Appendix Table C.

York and Massachusetts, where the shifts were 24% and 27%, respectively, of the total net downward shift.

Only five states had net increases amounting to more than 5% of the total net upward shift. These were: Illinois (13.2%), Washington (8.5%), Minnesota (7.1%), Texas (7.1%), and California (6.9%). The principal net upward and downward shifts are shown by decades in Table 48.

To give greater definition to these changes in manufacturing employment, the regional shares of employment in ten selected branches of manufactures are summarized in Table 49.[11] The shift analysis has shown, for example that there was a net upward shift of secondary employment in every Southwestern and Mountain state between 1870 and 1910. These same two regions, moreover, show growth in more of the ten selected branches of manufacture than any of the other regions—in eight out of the ten. Nevertheless, the actual numbers employed by 1910 in any of these industries in the Mountain states were still only a minute proportion of national employment in each case. Increases were mostly confined to Colorado, and petroleum refining and lumber

[11]The basis of selection for these ten manufacturing activities is simply that it has been possible to devise fairly consistent and comparable figures on them for the entire period since 1870. They are not necessarily the most important industries either in terms of employment or value. A comprehensive treatment of recent changes in manufactures is given in Part IV of this study.

products were the only industries in which there was any discernible contribution beyond the possible needs of local population. These same two processing industries loomed large in the Southwest at the turn of the century; and in Texas and Oklahoma, at least, petroleum refining had risen to almost 10% of the total employment in that industry by 1910. Moreover, by reason of its relatively large population, Texas also contained most other branches of manu-

Table 48. Principal net shifts in manufacturing labor force among states, 1870 – 1910

1870-1880		1880-1890		1890-1900		1900-1910	
Net upward shift							
Pa.	10.24	Ill.	15.37	Ill.	17.37	Wash.	13.76
Calif.	9.31	Wash.	10.93	N. C.	10.47	Calif.	12.35
Ill.	9.17	Nebr.	10.76	S. C.	7.99	Tex.	10.35
N. J.	9.00	Minn.	10.63	Ind.	7.88	Okla.	8.64
Colo.	8.88	Tex.	5.69	N. J.	7.09	Ore.	6.43
Minn.	8.33	Colo.	4.89	Okla.	5.91	La.	5.64
Wis.	6.65	Wis.	4.17	Ala.	4.96	Mich.	5.00
Nebr.	6.15	Ala.	3.32	Ohio	4.68	Fla.	4.50
Kans.	5.01	Ga.	3.26	Wis.	3.96	Ill.	4.40
Tex.	4.56	Ore.	3.10	Ga.	3.82	Miss.	2.86
Share of 10 leading states in total net upward shift	77.30		72.12		74.13		73.93
Net downward shift							
Mass.	24.90	N. Y.	26.41	Mass.	20.70	Mass.	26.23
N. Y.	23.98	Mass.	18.65	N. Y.	11.16	N. Y.	18.22
Ohio	13.31	Pa.	9.05	Nebr.	*10.24*	Pa.	12.76
Maine	7.93	Conn.	6.51	Maine	8.72	Conn.	5.27
N. H.	4.70	Maine	5.73	N. H.	7.11	N. H.	5.24
Vt.	3.33	Ind.	4.91	Md.	5.22	Iowa	5.08
La.	3.21	R. I.	4.70	Calif.	5.06	R. I.	4.20
Md.	3.01	N. H.	4.10	Conn.	4.98	Md.	4.07
Va.	3.00	Md.	3.97	Ky.	3.65	Mo.	3.84
Tenn.	2.74	Ohio	3.96	Colo.	3.50	Maine	3.71
Share of 10 leading states in total net downward shift	90.11		87.99		80.34		88.62

The figures in italics are absolute downward shifts.

SOURCE: Appendix Table A–6.

facture, the close association with population being most evident in the case of printing and publishing.

The Far West, also a growth region, showed development in seven of the ten manufacturing categories (in this case, nine categories, as the region has virtually no cotton textile industry). Most of the general expansion between 1870 and 1910 was in California where, of course, the population increase was also greatest; the modest proportion of manufacturing development before 1910 suggests that here, as in other regions of the West, industries served local or regional markets rather than the nation as a whole. Their growth was the result of geographical remoteness from the national centers of manufacturing in the Northeast, and they demonstrate the important historical fact that the Far West, and California in particular, developed a manufacturing economy stemming in no small part from its particular geographic position.

There is one likely exception to this tendency. The largest single concentration of manufacturing employment in the Far West before 1910 was in lumber and lumber products; the region had 11.4% of the total national employment in the industry. More than half of this regional proportion, moreover, was located in the state of Washington, where this industry provided the major manufacturing export of the region. By 1910 also, more than 23% of the nation's primary employment in forestry and logging was located in this region, and since 1880 Washington had been the principal contributor to the region's forest labor force (see Table 43).

The contribution of the Far West, Southwest, and Mountain regions to the growth of the American economy before 1910 appears to have been confined almost wholly to the resource sector, notably forests and minerals, together with a few departments of agriculture; with the exception of lumber products, the local manufacture or processing of these primary materials had so far assumed only minor importance in the nation's economy.

The Great Lakes region, which experienced increases in seven of the ten industries, was clearly the most important manufacturing growth area to emerge in the period after the Civil War. In 1870, for example, Ohio was already one of the leading manufacturing states, and by 1900 it had been joined by Illinois. By 1910 the Great Lakes region contributed more than 20% of national employment in half of our selected industries. Its furniture and fixtures industries, located principally in Michigan and Illinois and based on the region's rich lumber supply, employed 47% of the nation's total workers in this category by 1910. Iron and steel production had also become a major activity, especially in Ohio and Illinois, and the share of the five Great Lakes states was almost one-third of national employment in this basic industry. The region's share of employment in paper products and in printing and publishing by 1910 was about one-fourth of the national total; Ohio, Wisconsin, and Illinois were the leading states in these categories. Not surprisingly, petroleum-refining and lumber products were both smaller proportions of the national total by 1910 in the Great Lakes region than in 1870, but even in these two fields actual employment had risen markedly. Of least significance at any time in this region were the basic textile industries. There was an absolute decline in woolen and worsted

Table 49. Regional distribution of employment in ten selected manufacturing industries, 1870, 1910, and 1954

Region	Woolen & worsted goods			Cotton & cotton goods		
	1870	1910	1954	1870	1910	1954
United States	92,973	175,176	93,285	135,763	387,771	495,829
	(per cent)					
New England	55.17	63.08	49.82	70.00	49.75	11.53
Middle Atlantic	29.90	29.64	21.92	21.45	10.21	6.14
Great Lakes	8.59	3.35	6.11	0.78	0.98	0.62
Southeast	3.00	2.99	19.59	7.28	38.49	79.77
Plains	2.20	0.38	0.55	0.27	0.15	0.21
Southwest	0.13	0.03	0.12	0.21	0.42	1.65
Mountain	0.11	0.06	0.09	0.01	—	0.02
Far West	0.90	0.47	1.80	—	—	0.06

Region	Iron & steel products			Petroleum refining		
	1870	1910	1954	1870	1910	1954
United States	141,003	952,527	987,419	1,747	16,640	153,072
	(per cent)					
New England	10.99	13.11	3.79	8.01	—	0.71
Middle Atlantic	57.60	42.88	35.41	53.18	56.65	20.22
Great Lakes	18.92	32.72	42.56	31.08	17.65	18.18
Southeast	8.68	5.40	7.85	6.36	2.69	10.91
Plains	3.05	3.18	2.71	0.80	3.46	4.18
Southwest	0.02	0.50	1.77	0.17	9.97	30.66
Mountain	0.02	0.45	1.40	—	2.69	3.34
Far West	0.72	1.76	4.51	0.40	6.89	11.80

Region	Leather & leather goods			Lumber & lumber products		
	1870	1910	1954	1870	1910	1954
United States	177,963	295,973	356,578	163,637	784,989	645,936
	(per cent)					
New England	42.06	42.17	30.87	12.75	6.10	5.69
Middle Atlantic	34.71	26.82	30.27	24.33	10.21	6.75
Great Lakes	13.88	17.90	16.51	35.28	15.85	10.22
Southeast	4.87	3.58	7.82	14.42	44.77	38.18
Plains	2.97	8.09	10.98	7.66	5.86	3.71
Southwest	0.16	0.06	1.07	1.12	4.10	4.23
Mountain	0.16	0.18	0.58	0.73	1.70	3.44
Far West	1.19	1.20	1.90	3.71	11.41	27.78

Region	Furniture and fixtures			Paper and paper products		
	1870	1910	1954	1870	1910	1954
United States	57,091	144,140	340,694	18,779	147,808	530,210
	(per cent)					
New England	24.65	7.60	5.86	38.82	30.12	13.27
Middle Atlantic	33.89	26.82	21.82	42.33	37.34	25.89
Great Lakes	29.29	46.83	29.98	14.85	25.21	26.05
Southeast	4.59	10.31	26.40	2.79	2.88	18.91
Plains	6.44	5.36	4.06	0.96	2.74	5.84
Southwest	0.25	0.60	3.49	—	0.21	1.65
Mountain	0.18	0.20	0.39	0.04	0.07	0.36
Far West	0.71	2.28	8.00	0.21	1.43	8.03

Region	Printing & publishing			Tobacco products		
	1870	1910	1954	1870	1910	1954
United States	30,924	388,466	804,386	47,848	197,637	96,240
	(per cent)					
New England	15.38	8.97	7.46	4.49	3.82	1.32
Middle Atlantic	44.04	37.79	34.48	39.71	44.96	22.95
Great Lakes	19.26	24.29	27.11	19.30	20.96	3.85
Southeast	7.72	7.78	8.76	24.03	21.70	69.75
Plains	9.81	11.43	8.73	8.45	6.24	1.24
Southwest	0.59	2.82	3.92	0.12	0.28	0.52
Mountain	0.22	1.88	1.35	—	0.56	—
Far West	2.98	5.04	8.19	3.90	1.48	0.37

SOURCE: 9th U.S. Census, 1870, Vol. III, *Statistics of Wealth and Industry,* Table VIII (c) ; 13th U.S. Census, 1910, Vol. X, *Manufactures,* "Reports for Principal Industries," *passim;* U.S. Census of Manufactures, 1954, Vol. II, Pts. 1 and 2.

goods manufacture after 1870, while the region's share of employment in cotton goods rose only from about 0.7% to 0.9% of the national total between 1870 and 1910. Thus throughout this period the Great Lakes states were not only processing their indigenous supplies of natural resources but, in iron ore and wood pulp, were already drawing upon the materials of other regions, such as the Southeast and the Plains. Their proportions of national employment, moreover, in certain crucial branches of manufacture indicate that they were already supplying a much larger share of the national market than that contained within their own borders.

Two regions, the Plains and the Southeast, experienced moderate manufacturing growth during the period 1870-1910. They more or less broke even in their shares of the ten selected industries; both show relative increases in five categories and relative decreases in the other five. Only two of the expanding manufactures in the Plains, however, amounted to any considerable proportion of national employment by 1910. Leather and leather products, centered chiefly in Missouri and to a lesser extent in Minnesota, accounted for more than 8% and printing and publishing for 11.4% of total employment in these categories. Much smaller shares were registered by iron and steel products (again chiefly in Missouri and Minnesota) and petroleum refining (mostly in Kansas). Our ten industries, however, do not include one of the major manufacturing developments of the Plains during this period, namely flour and grist mill products. Here the eastern Plains states achieved a remarkable expansion as the major wheat belts of the country shifted to the westward out of the Great Lakes states. By 1910 the Plains region employed more than 27% of all workers in the milling industry and was rapidly becoming the major source of the nation's supply of flour and grist mill products.

The leading edge of growth in the Southeast, even before the end of Reconstruction, was provided by lumber products and, to a lesser extent, by cotton textiles. By 1910 this region accounted for nearly 45% of total employment in lumber products and almost 39% of all cotton textiles employment. All Southeastern states seem to have participated in the development of lumber products, but cotton textile growth was centered almost exclusively in the Carolinas, Georgia, and Alabama. The furniture and fixtures industry, mostly in North Carolina and Tennessee, also contributed to the growth of Southern manufactures; the region had more than 10% of national employment in this industry by 1910. Minor advances in petroleum-refining had been made in Louisiana by 1910 also and in paper products in Virginia and West Virginia. In spite of a sizable development in iron and steel products in Alabama, Tennessee, and Kentucky during this period, however, the Southeast contributed a somewhat smaller share of all employment in this crucial sector by 1910 than it had during the height of the Reconstruction period. In other words, actual development of the iron and steel industry in the Southeast had not kept pace with developments elsewhere in the nation.[12] More suggestive, if not more significant, perhaps, is the fact that printing and publishing remained a relatively static industry in one of the most thickly populated regions of the country.

Turning, finally, to what in the late nineteenth century was still the heartland of American manufactures—the New England and Middle Atlantic regions—we find more of the ten selected industries in relative decline than in relative growth. New England registered declines in seven and growth in three of these industries between 1870 and 1910, and the Middle Atlantic region declined in eight and grew in only two. Though this conforms to the analysis of shifts in all manufacturing employment shown in Figure 29, there were actually only two cases of absolute decline among the ten manufactures and both occurred in New England: petroleum-refining had disappeared, or at least did not warrant inclusion in the Census of Manufactures, and furniture and fixtures production had

[12] C. Vann Woodward, *Origins of the New South, 1877-1913*, Vol. 9 of *A History of the South* (Baton Rouge: Louisiana State University Press, 1951), pp. 291-320; H. L. Herring, *Southern Industry and Regional Development* (Chapel Hill: University of North Carolina Press, 1940), pp. 31-5.

declined absolutely in every New England state except Vermont. New England's three growth industries during this period were woolen and worsted goods in Massachusetts and Rhode Island, iron and steel products in Massachusetts and Connecticut, and leather products, more especially the boot and shoe manufactures of Massachusetts. In all three of these categories, however, the region was not merely processing indigenous materials but by 1890 was already importing much of the raw product from other parts of the country.

In the Middle Atlantic region there were, of course, absolute increases in numbers employed in each of the ten selected branches of manufactures; but growth, i.e., relative increase in the region's share of national employment, was confined to petroleum-refining (chiefly in New Jersey and Pennsylvania) and tobacco products (chiefly in Pennsylvania and New York). Pennsylvania, of course, had been the birthplace of the great petroleum industry, while New Jersey had acquired its later prominence owing to its seaboard location and its proximity to the most densely populated urban centers in the country. The tobacco industry, however, is a somewhat special case. Before the widespread adoption of cigarette smoking and the consequent mechanization of tobacco manufactures, employment in this industry was closely associated with population, not unlike printing and publishing or the major food industries. By 1910 the Middle Atlantic region was by far the largest employer, accounting for nearly 45% of all tobacco employment, while the Southeast's share had fallen from 24% to 21% since 1870. Within the Southeast, Florida employed a considerably larger number of tobacco workers than either North Carolina or Virginia, owing to the concentration of cigar-making in the Tampa area. The growth of cigarette smoking and the mechanization of cigarette manufacture was by 1950 to restore all but 30% of tobacco employment to the Southeast and largely concentrate it in North Carolina, Virginia, and Kentucky.

Service Activities in the Regions, 1870-1910

The tertiary or service sector of the economy has often been regarded as itself a key measure of economic development and material progress. As technical and organizational advances in the primary (resource) and secondary (manufacturing) sectors have augmented labor productivity, a growing proportion of the labor force has been freed from resource extraction and manufactures to engage in so-called "services" to business and consumers, e.g., in transportation and communications, wholesale and retail trade, finance, recreation, amusements, the professions, and other services to individuals. There is, moreover, some evidence that when personal incomes rise, persons tend to purchase larger proportions of service items than when their personal incomes are lower; that is, most tertiary items have higher income elasticity of demand than most primary or secondary items. There is, likewise, some correlation between the growth of service activities and the degree of urbanization of a population.[13]

[13]E. E. Lampard, "History of Cities in the Economically-Advanced Areas," *Economic Development and Cultural Change*, Vol. 3, (January 1955), pp. 99-102; Colin Clark "The Economic Functions of a City in Relation to its Size," *Econometrica*, Vol. 13, (April 1945), pp. 97-8.

When the service sector of the economy is defined as "all other activities"—i.e., as the total labor force less the workers engaged in primary and secondary activities—so many different types of activities are involved that it does not seem wise to generalize too freely about their character and significance.[14] But with this reservation in mind, let us examine the distribution of tertiary employment much as we have previously examined the other two labor force groupings. Table 50 shows the changing proportions of all service activities in the eight regions and three greater regions of the United States between 1870 and 1910. The principal features of these regional changes are the relative stability of the

Table 50. Regional distribution of services labor force, 1870, 1890, and 1910

Region	1870	1890	1910
United States	3,178,287	7,345,373	13,913,976
	100%	100%	100%
New England	11.45	9.34	8.43
Middle Atlantic	36.14	31.69	29.48
Great Lakes	19.95	20.77	20.15
Southeast	18.55	16.13	16.13
Plains	8.25	12.34	11.84
Southwest	1.61	2.76	4.72
Mountain	.58	2.14	2.48
Far West	3.47	4.83	6.77
Northeast	67.54	61.80	58.06
Southeast	18.55	16.13	16.13
West	13.91	22.07	25.81

SOURCE: Appendix Table A–7.

Southeast and some partial reversal in the relative positions of the Northeast and the West. (These tendencies, as we shall see later, continue to operate in the subsequent period, 1910-1950.) At first the relative losses of the two Northeastern seaboard regions were recouped by the central portion of the country, notably the Great Lakes and Plains regions, but even before 1910 the Plains had failed to sustain its relative growth and the gradual westward shift of tertiary activities had continued into the Far West and Southwest.

Table 51 compares percentage changes in regional shares of the nation's total tertiary employment with percentage changes in total labor force and total population shares between 1870 and 1910. During these years, which saw the flood tide of the westward movement of population, the Great Lakes region was the only region east of the Mississippi that increased its share of service employment. In contrast, *all* regions west of the Mississippi increased theirs. The Plains, Mountain, and Southwest regions actually increased their shares of

[14]See G. J. Stigler, *Trends in Employment in the Service Industries* (Princeton: Princeton University Press, 1956).

Table 51. Percentage change in regional shares of population, total labor force, and services labor force, 1870 – 1910

Region	Population	Labor force	Services labor force
New England	−18.72	−26.47	−26.38
Middle Atlantic	−7.04	−6.62	−18.43
Great Lakes	−13.44	−13.15	+1.00
Southeast	−17.85	−12.59	−13.05
Plains	+30.55	+26.19	+43.52
Southwest	+160.63	+184.40	+193.17
Mountain	+411.63	+292.98	+327.59
Far West	+158.33	+111.84	+95.10

SOURCE: 17th U. S. Census, 1950, see *supra*, Table 1, note; Appendix Tables A–1, A–7.

service employment considerably more than their shares of total labor force. The Far West, on the other hand, had a smaller relative increase in service employment than in labor force. This disparity is accounted for in part by the importance of transport and communications in the three "corridor" regions.

No two regions in the eastern half of the country show like patterns of change. In the Great Lakes region, service employment increased relatively, though slightly, while both population and labor force shares declined considerably. In the Middle Atlantic region, there was a greater relative decline in the service sector than in either labor force or population. In the Southeast, the relative loss was greater for population than for labor force or service employment. In New England, it was greater for labor force and service employment than for population.

In view of the gross character of our service sector, an analysis of these shifts

Table 52. Principal net shifts in services labor force among states, 1870 – 1910

Net upward shift		Net downward shift	
Texas	11.27	New York	20.38
Washington	10.32	Pennsylvania	11.76
Illinois	9.86	Maryland	8.64
Minnesota	9.86	Virginia	7.35
Oklahoma	7.51	Kentucky	6.51
California	7.17	Massachusetts	6.47
Colorado	5.84	Maine	5.89
Dakotas	5.42	Ohio	5.00
Nebraska	5.20	Louisiana	4.59
Kansas	4.81	Michigan	4.14

SOURCE: Appendix Table A–7.

in the detail of particular decades would have little or no significance. Accordingly, we shall show only the principal net upward and downward shifts in service employment over the 1870-1910 period as a whole (Table 52). The figures for the states bear a close resemblance to the broad regional changes outlined above. Net downward shifts in services are registered chiefly in the eastern half of the country and relative net upward shifts in all of the Western states except Missouri and Nevada. The westward shifts in services, as in population, were generally greater during decades of prosperity than of depression, and reached their greatest volume after 1900. As early as 1880, however, there was a relative net upward shift into parts of the Southeast, principally into Florida, which, except for West Virginia, was the only Southern state that had a net upward shift in service employment over every decade of the 1870-1910 period. Considering the high proportion of all service employment made up at this time of transportation, trading, and domestic services (our service sector also includes construction workers), it is clear that the opening up of the West was the dominant factor influencing the redistribution of tertiary employment. In this respect, the tertiary sector is not very different from either the resource or the manufacturing sectors; but in the degree of redistribution, it is affected much more profoundly than manufactures. There was less diffusion of manufactures than of services; hence there was less disparity among the regions in services by 1910.

It would seem that in a growing economy like that of the United States, regions do not have to develop any particular stage or level of manufactures in order to obtain a fairly wide range of service employments. Services are not necessarily dependent on an economic base in manufactures and may indeed contribute a large part of a locality's base on their own account—e.g., wholesale trade in the Far West or transportation in the Mountain and Plains regions. Nevertheless, the fact that Texas, Washington, and California were the leading growth states in services west of the Mississippi before 1910 suggests that the development of *some* services is probably contingent on the growth of some

Table 53. Percentage growth in total labor force, services labor force, and labor force in four selected service industries, 1870–1910

	% *1870–1910*
All labor force	+205.19
All service labor force	+337.78
Transport and communications	+506.84
Trade and finance	+377.73
Professional services	+385.93
Personal and domestic service	+67.73

SOURCE: 9th U.S. Census, 1870, Vol. I; 13th U.S. Census, 1910, Vol. IV, *Occupational Statistics.* Appendix Tables A–1, A–7.

types of manufactures. The fact that the principal net downward shifts in service employment occurred in states with already high levels of manufacturing and other business activity does not seem to affect the point one way or the other. The Middle Atlantic states alone contributed more than 40% of the total net downward shift in services in this period and only 34% of the total net downward shift in manufacturing employment.

Up to this point we have treated changes in the tertiary sector as a whole without attempting any close analysis of their significance because of the heterogeneous nature of the sector. It is doubtful that anything certain can be said about so diverse an occupational grouping as a whole.[15] But some definition can be given to the changes in this sector by examining certain of the major service activities separately. We have selected the four following service activities for such an examination for the 1870-1910 period: transportation and communications, trade and finance, professional services, and personal and domestic services. As Table 53 shows, the first three of these follow the general tendency of service employment to rise faster than the labor force as a whole. The fourth— personal and domestic services—shows a different pattern. Indeed, after 1910, the numbers in this category go into absolute decline.[16].

Transportation and communications showed the fastest growth between 1870 and 1910. The rates of growth for trade and finance and professional services closely paralleled each other during this period. There was marked regional differentiation, however, in both the direction and extent of these changes (see Table 54). Broadly speaking, the growth in the West was at the expense of the

Table 54. Regional distribution of labor force in four selected service industries, 1870 and 1910

	Transport and communications		Trade and finance		Professional services		Personal and domestic service	
Region	1870	1910	1870	1910	1870	1910	1870	1910
United States	100%	100%	100%	100%	100%	100%	100%	100%
Northeast	15.26	7.17	12.60	8.58	12.12	8.48	9.58	8.28
Middle Atlantic	35.68	27.07	38.60	29.66	28.89	26.44	33.95	29.03
Great Lakes	20.98	20.92	20.54	21.27	24.59	21.10	20.64	17.61
Southeast	12.71	15.33	14.09	13.78	18.31	14.67	22.11	22.20
Plains	9.99	13.19	8.84	12.75	10.92	13.98	8.08	10.08
Southwest	1.14	5.10	1.34	4.94	2.01	5.41	1.68	4.75
Mountain	.82	3.45	.60	2.21	.36	2.79	.50	2.09
Far West	3.42	7.77	3.39	6.81	2.80	7.13	3.46	5.96

SOURCE: See Table 53.

[15]To give only a few examples, it includes transportation workers, dentists, army officers, civil servants, housemaids, shopkeepers, real estate brokers, traveling salesmen, many types of construction workers, fortune-tellers, Indian guides, and scavengers.

[16]It is personal services *inside* rather than *outside* the home that contribute to the decline.

relative position of the Northeast and, to a lesser extent, of the Southeast. The Southeast actually increased its relative strength in transport and communications and retained an unchanging share of personal and domestic services, but it lost ground relatively in trade and finance and in professional services. In the Northeast, New England suffered the greatest relative declines except in personal and domestic services. Its share of transport and communications was reduced by one-half, and its share of both trade and professional services by about one-third. Considering the relative size of the Middle Atlantic region in 1870 (it had more than a third of all employment in each category except professional services), its losses were fairly moderate. The Great Lakes region actually held its own in the transport and trade categories, although it declined relatively in the other two. In the period before 1910 the West advanced substantially in *all* categories; in its least buoyant category, personal and domestic services, it gained more than 67%. The Southwest and Mountain regions, the least developed regions in 1870, made the greatest relative gains; but in absolute terms, of course, the development of the Plains and the Far West was more remarkable.

Table 55 shows the percentage of the labor force that each of these service categories comprised in the eight regions and in the nation as a whole in 1870, 1910, and 1950. All of them except personal and domestic services formed a larger proportion of each region's labor force in 1950 than in 1870. The same, of course, was true for the nation as a whole; economic growth from 1870 to 1910 was accompanied by a significant rise in certain types of services, more especially services to commerce and industry. That the growth of such services was geographically uneven is attested by the fact that two regions, the Southeast and Southwest, were *below* the national average in all four categories both at the beginning and at the end of the period. In this sense, these two regions may be said to have been "underserviced" by the national standards of the day. Two other regions, the Middle Atlantic and the Far West, were *above* the national average in the four selected categories in 1910, as earlier in 1870.

Table 56 summarizes the percentage growth or decline of each of the four service categories as proportions of their total regional labor forces and compares regional changes in this regard with those for the nation as a whole. As already noted, three of the categories were generally growing during this period and only one was generally in decline. It is significant that transportation and communications services were the most buoyant. Even in the two Northeastern seaboard regions, where transport services failed to grow at as fast a rate as in the nation as a whole, these services formed a larger part of the regional labor forces in 1910 than in 1870. Trade and finance likewise increased their shares of the labor forces in every region during this period, although in four of the regions the increase was less than that for the nation. All regions also increased the professional services contingent in their labor forces; three regions grew faster than the nation but of these only the Mountain and Far West regions exceeded the national rate of growth in any notable degree. Finally in the one declining category, personal and domestic services, four regions declined at a

Table 55. Labor force in four selected service industries as a percentage of total labor force, by region, 1870, 1910, and 1950

Region	1870				1910				1950			
	Transport & comm.	Trade & fin.	Prof.	Domestic & pers.	Transport & comm.	Trade & fin.	Prof.	Domestic & pers.	Transport & comm.	Trade & fin.	Prof.	Domestic & pers.
United States	3.48	6.05	2.74	17.98	6.91	9.47	4.36	9.88	7.26	20.70	7.77	5.80
New England	*5.10*	*7.34*	*3.19*	16.59	6.48	*10.64*	*4.84*	*10.71*	5.96	20.36	*8.68*	*4.92*
Middle Atlantic	*4.92*	*9.26*	*3.13*	*24.20*	*7.94*	*11.92*	*4.89*	*12.17*	*8.04*	*22.25*	*8.20*	5.69
Great Lakes	3.33	5.67	*3.07*	16.94	*7.60*	*10.59*	*4.84*	9.15	*7.41*	20.32	7.44	4.61
Southeast	1.58	3.04	1.79	14.18	4.32	5.33	2.61	8.95	5.95	17.24	6.61	*7.49*
Plains	*3.75*	5.78	*3.24*	15.71	*7.82*	*10.36*	*5.23*	8.55	*7.97*	*21.58*	*8.29*	4.59
Southwest	1.81	3.71	2.53	13.84	5.69	7.56	3.81	7.58	7.42	*22.26*	7.70	*7.29*
Mountain	*5.06*	*6.37*	1.74	15.82	*10.67*	9.36	*5.44*	9.22	*9.16*	21.26	*8.97*	5.08
Far West	*4.86*	*8.38*	*3.13*	*25.47*	*10.36*	*12.43*	*6.00*	*11.36*	7.46	*23.23*	*8.52*	5.74

Figures in italics are above the national average.

SOURCE: See Table 53, 17th U. S. Census, 1950, Vol. II, State Volumes.

Table 56. Percentage change in regional distribution of labor force in four selected service industries, 1870 – 1910

Region	Transp. and communication	Trade and finance	Professional	Personal and domestic
	%	%	%	%
United States	+ 98.56	+ 56.53	+ 59.12	− 45.05
New England	+ 27.06	+ 44.96	+ 51.72	− 35.44
Middle Atlantic	+ 61.38	+ 28.72	+ 56.23	− *49.71*
Great Lakes	+*128.23*	+ *86.77*	+ 57.65	− *45.98*
Southeast	+*173.42*	+ *75.33*	+ 45.81	− 36.88
Plains	+*108.53*	+ *79.24*	+ *61.42*	− *45.58*
Southwest	+*214.36*	+*103.77*	+ 50.59	− 45.23
Mountain	+*110.87*	+ 46.94	+*212.64*	− 41.72
Far West	+*113.17*	+ 48.33	+ *91.69*	− *55.40*

Figures in italics are above the national average.

Source: See Table 55.

rate faster than the national rate, but of these only the Far West greatly exceeded the national rate of decline.

These trends in the growth and redistribution of service activity during the late nineteenth century were an important feature of the nation's economic growth. They underline the fact that, in order to develop the full resource potential of the greater West and integrate Western materials into the nation's resource economy, it was necessary to organize a nation-wide system of transportation and communications together with a whole edifice of related services to trade and finance. These services, in turn, help account for the surprisingly high levels of urbanization obtaining in some of the Western states before 1910 without a corresponding growth in local manufactures. Specialized organizational functions, therefore, are not merely a way of absorbing excess manpower released from more "fundamental" primary and secondary production through the introduction of labor-saving techniques; they are an essential concomitant of efforts to control and utilize raw materials over wider expanses of continental territory. Without these services and facilities, which provided a major outlet for new investment at the time, the natural resources of the West could not have been made available to the industrializing areas at home and abroad. They are evidence of structural changes in the labor force which accompanied the "nationalizing" of the American economy.

Industrialization of the labor force after 1870 did not mean that a majority of the gainfully employed became manufacturing wage-earners. Of the total labor force of some 38,167,000 in 1910, all categories of skilled, semi-skilled, and unskilled workers outside agriculture comprised little more than 39% of the total. Farm proprietors (6,000,000), dealers in wholesale and retail trade (2,600,000), and other owners, managers, or officials of business enterprises comprised almost 23% of the labor force. There were at least 5,500,000 farm laborers and an additional 8,000,000 workers in clerical jobs and in services of a personal or professional nature.[17] And as the twentieth century progressed, manufacturing workers formed an even smaller share of the total labor force.

[17]In 1910 nearly 2 million children 15 years old or under held jobs, compared to only 750,000 in 1870. The number of employed women more than doubled between 1890 and 1910, exceeding 8 millions (21.2% of the labor force in 1910: about 30% were in domestic service).

13 / Changing regional structure of the U. S. economy, 1870-1910:

(3) REGIONAL INDUSTRIAL STRUCTURES AND INCOME

The great advances in industrialization that occurred in the closing decades of the nineteenth century profoundly affected economic developments in the various parts of the country. Between 1890 and 1910 the economic boundaries came to coincide more exactly with the political boundaries of the country than at any time since 1803. The completion of the railroad network, the construction of oil pipelines, the development of "instantaneous communication" by telegraph and telephone, and the beginnings of automobile transportation now linked all outlying regions with the historical growth centers of the economy. Henceforth, major economic decisions must be taken in the light of truly nation-wide opportunities. The full resource potential of every region was now at the disposal of a national system of production and could be utilized to meet the growing demand of a nation-wide system of distribution and markets.[1]

The consequences of the nation's economic growth for regional development can best be understood by comparing regional economic structures with the economic structure of the nation as a whole. The changing structure of productive activities reflected in the national labor force between 1870 and 1910 is shown in Table 57. The proportions of various activities in the national labor force serve as a yardstick against which to measure particular developments in the regions. For example, in Figure 30, the proportion which the agricultural component comprises of each region's labor force is compared with that of the national labor force for the 1870-1910 period. The Southeast, Southwest, and Plains regions have greater concentrations of agricultural labor than the nation

---

[1] In 1914, before the outbreak of the World War, G. B. Hotchkiss points out, "the whole conception of the domestic market had changed. It was no longer a definite place, but people. The manufacturer was able to consider as his market all potential customers, wherever located, since he had a means of reaching them with his products and with information about his products." See *Milestones of Marketing* (New York: The Macmillan Co., 1938), pp. 220-21. The growth of nation-wide advertising dates from about 1890.

as a whole throughout this period and may be identified as agricultural regions. The Great Lakes region begins the period as a predominantly agricultural region, but by 1890 other activities have assumed greater importance and the region rapidly becomes less agricultural than the nation as a whole. In the New England, Middle Atlantic, Mountain, and Far West regions the concentrations of agriculture are persistently below the national average over these years.

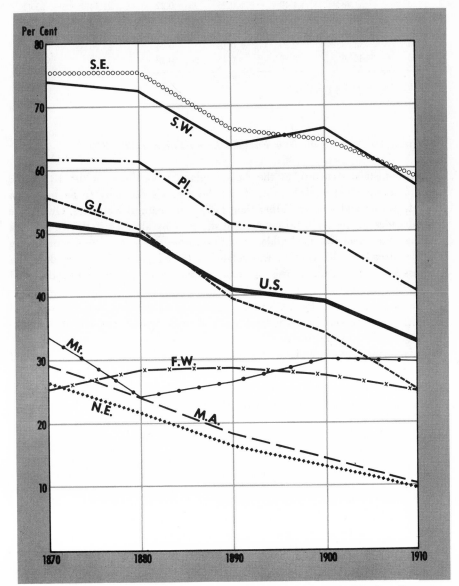

Figure 30. Change in the Regional and National Agricultural Labor Force as Percentage of Total Labor Force, 1870-1910.

Source: Appendix Tables A-1 and A-2.

Table 57. U. S. labor force, distribution by industry, 1870 – 1910

(per cent of total)

Year	Agri-culture	Mining	Forestry	Fisheries	Manu-facturing	Services
1870	51.48	1.49	0.26	0.22	21.14	25.41
1880	49.39	1.71	0.32	0.24	22.09	26.25
1890	40.62	1.97	0.54	0.26	24.30	32.31
1900	38.83	2.39	0.48	0.24	24.76	33.30
1910	32.46	2.53	0.45	0.18	27.92	36.46

SOURCE: Appendix Tables A1–A7.

Industrial Structure of the New England Labor Force, 1870–1910

The industrial structure of the New England labor force in the 1870-1910 period, summarized in Table 58, shows the region's economy to be based on manufacturing and services rather than indigenous natural resources. Over these four decades the agricultural component declined by almost two-thirds, and the mining component was negligible. The upsurge in the forest component during the first decade of this century was related to the adoption of new woodpulping processes which permitted use of some of the region's remaining stands of timber in outlying places (notably in Maine). The fisheries, though more concentrated here than in the nation at large, were a declining share of the total regional labor force. New England was the most heavily concentrated manufacturing region in the American economy during this period. Unlike the other manufacturing regions, its labor force in services was a smaller share of the total

Table 58. Distribution by industry of New England region labor force, 1870–1910

(per cent of total)

Year	Agri-culture	Mining	Forestry	Fisheries	Manu-facturing	Services
1870	26.38	0.41	*0.27*	*0.87*	*44.05*	28.02
1880	21.46	0.46	0.23	*0.81*	*47.98*	29.06
1890	16.37	0.47	0.34	*0.76*	*47.87*	34.19
1900	13.18	0.34	0.29	*0.53*	*48.16*	37.50
1910	9.65	0.31	0.31	*0.43*	*49.05*	40.25

Figures in italics are above the national average.

SOURCE: Appendix Tables A1–A7.

than the labor force in manufactures. The growth of services after 1880, how-ever, proceeded at a faster rate than the growth of manufactures, and the earlier disparity between the two sectors was much reduced by 1900.

The differentiation among the states that compose a region are sometimes no less marked than the regional differentiation of production activities within the national economy. The northern New England states—Vermont, New Hamp-shire, and Maine—differ sharply from the southern New England states—Mas-sachusetts, Rhode Island, and Connecticut—in their economic structure. The extreme case here is Vermont which, over the 1870-1910 period, was always more agricultural than the nation as a whole. During the eighties, moreover, quarrying in Vermont brought the mining component of its labor force into parity with that of the nation as a whole. New Hampshire had a larger propor-tion of manufacturing employment throughout these years than either of its northern neighbors; it was also somewhat less agricultural and much less of a services state. In southern New England, Rhode Island was (and, in fact, still is) the most heavily concentrated manufacturing state in the nation. Connecti-cut was more agricultural than either Rhode Island or Massachusetts. After 1900, however, it developed a heavier concentration of manufactures than Massachusetts. But Massachusetts had a larger proportion of its labor force in service occupations than either Connecticut or Rhode Island.

Industrial Structure of the Middle Atlantic Labor Force, 1870-1910

The industrial structure of the labor force in the Middle Atlantic states, sum-marized in Table 59, shows a regional economy based on manufactures and services with an increasing segment of the labor force engaged in mining activ-ities. The mining activities, however, in spite of their vital contribution to the region's industrial fuel supply, are not large enough for the region *as a whole* to be identified with mining. Nevertheless, Pennsylvania is one of the great mining

Table 59. Distribution by industry of Middle Atlantic region labor force, 1870-1910

(per cent of total)

Year	Agri-culture	Mining	Forestry	Fisheries	Manu-facturing	Services
1870	29.09	*1.97*	0.21	0.19	*32.13*	*36.41*
1880	24.02	*2.47*	0.19	*0.26*	*34.87*	*38.19*
1890	18.39	*2.91*	0.38	*0.34*	*35.84*	*42.14*
1900	14.76	*3.49*	0.25	*0.28*	*37.28*	*43.94*
1910	10.39	*3.94*	0.15	0.16	*39.75*	*45.61*

Figures in italics are above the national average.

SOURCE: Appendix Tables A1–A7.

states of the American economy: miners comprised almost 5% of its labor force in 1870, 7.27% in 1890, and nearly 10.5% in 1910. Maryland is the only other state in this region with any significant amount of mining employment.

The region's agricultural labor force declined by almost two-thirds between 1870 and 1910, and forestry accounted for an even smaller proportion of total employment than the fisheries, which were important locally in some of the seaboard states. The concentration of employment in service activities, in excess of manufacturing employment, is due in part to the fact that many financial and business services, located in New York, New Jersey, and Pennsylvania, actually service wide areas of the economy outside the Middle Atlantic region itself. The region also includes the District of Columbia, where the service component is very large. Service employment in most of the other Middle Atlantic states also was a greater proportion of total employment than in the states in other manufacturing regions (except perhaps Massachusetts in New England and Illinois in the Great Lakes regions). Delaware was the most agricultural of the Middle Atlantic states throughout the 1870-1910 period, though it failed to reach the national proportion in this sector. New Jersey was the least agricultural, and Delaware and New York had the least mining. Maryland had heavy local concentrations of fisheries and Pennsylvania the greatest forest activity. New Jersey, New York, and Pennsylvania, of course, had the greatest concentrations in manufactures.

Industrial Structure of the Labor Force in the Great Lakes Region, 1870-1910

The industrial structure of the Great Lakes region in the 1870-1910 period is shown in Table 60. During these years this region experienced the full impact of the industrial revolution, although Ohio had already developed a major concentration of manufactures before 1870. During the nineties the region also began to show its potential strength in service activities; here, Illinois was the

Table 60. Distribution by industry of Great Lakes region labor force, 1870-1910

(per cent of total)

Year	Agriculture	Mining	Forestry	Fisheries	Manufacturing	Services
1870	*55.72*	1.13	*0.28*	0.08	19.65	23.14
1880	*50.75*	1.07	*0.52*	0.07	22.01	25.58
1890	39.59	*2.04*	*0.68*	0.10	*25.04*	*32.55*
1900	34.18	2.31	0.43	0.10	*27.28*	*35.70*
1910	25.16	*2.61*	0.31	0.10	*33.19*	*38.63*

Figures in italics are above the national average.

SOURCE: Appendix Tables A1–A7.

largest contributor both in relative and absolute terms. Until the nineties, however, the Great Lakes region was primarily an agricultural region. It was only
after 1900 that the manufacturing component actually surpassed the agricultural
component of the labor force. Indiana and Wisconsin remained the most agricultural states in this region; as late as 1910, one-third of their workers were in
agricultural pursuits.

After 1880 the great mineral wealth of the region (in coal, iron, and copper)
made a crucial contribution to its development. Mining employment in the
region as a whole exceeded the national average both in 1890 and in 1910 and fell
only slightly under it in 1900. Except during the depression in the late seventies,
Ohio always exceeded the national proportion, as did Michigan and Illinois
after 1890. No Great Lakes state, however, achieved the level of mining concentration that developed farther east in Pennsylvania or West Virginia. The
largest concentration occurred in Michigan, which had 3.28% of its labor force
engaged in mining around 1910. The region's employment in forestry and
logging activity surpassed the national level from the mid-seventies until about
1890, when it reached its peak. At this time Michigan had one of the heaviest
concentrations of forest labor anywhere in the nation, and Wisconsin also
ranked high. Finally, though the region's stake in fisheries was a minor one,
Michigan's lake fishing corresponded closely with the national level of fishing
activity until 1880.

Clearly, the Great Lakes region was one of the greatest resource regions in the
American economy. Its mines, fields, and forests made a key contribution to
national economic growth in the late nineteenth century. Its natural abundance
not only provided a firm foundation for its own burgeoning manufactures and
commerce, but also gave new strength to the continuing thrust of industry
elsewhere in the greater Northeast. By the end of the century it was already
drawing in natural resources from adjacent states in the Southeast and Plains
regions.

Industrial Structure of the Labor Force in the Southeast, 1870-1910

The industrial structure of the Southeast's labor force in the 1870-1910 period,
shown in Table 61, contrasts sharply with that of the Great Lakes region.
Although the Southeast had begun to develop its abundant natural resources and
diversify its economic base by 1890, the progress made was inadequate in view
of the large population in this region. As a result, the Southeast fell behind
the rest of the country in many important respects. For example, the share of
agricultural employment in its labor force declined only 22% during these years
as compared with 37% in the nation as a whole and 55% in the Great Lakes
region. The character and organization of farming through much of the Southeast at this time suggests that there was severe under-employment in agriculture.

Somewhat paradoxically, the share of manufacturing in the labor force
increased faster in the Southeast than in any other region over these years; the
growth of industry in the "New South" during the eighties, in fact, had become

Table 61. Distribution by industry of Southeast region labor force, 1870-1910

(per cent of total)

Year	Agri-culture	Mining	Forestry	Fisheries	Manu-facturing	Services
1870	*75.13*	0.22	0.16	0.19	7.49	16.81
1880	*75.35*	0.31	0.18	0.16	7.81	16.19
1890	*66.28*	0.82	0.48	*0.28*	10.51	21.63
1900	*64.95*	1.27	*0.64*	*0.29*	11.34	21.51
1910	*58.93*	1.73	*0.65*	*0.23*	14.46	24.00

Figures in italics are above the national average.

SOURCE: Appendix Tables A1–A7.

a matter for comment and satisfaction. But the South had a long way to go; and it did not go far enough or fast enough in view of the size and density of the population on the land. Thus in 1910 the Southeast was still the least industrialized of all the regions in the sense that the manufacturing-services component of its labor force remained the lowest in the nation.

It was only in forest and logging activity that the region as a whole began to achieve a superior position relative to the rest of the nation. Florida, and later West Virginia, developed heavy concentrations of loggers and, reinforced by developments in Arkansas and Louisiana, brought lumbering in the Southeast rapidly up above the national level of forest activities. After 1890 the influx of logging activity stemmed directly from the exhaustion of the pinelands in the northern Great Lakes states.[2] By 1910 the proportion of loggers and other forest workers in the Southeast's labor force had reached a peak not to be surpassed much before 1940.

In absolute terms, miners outnumbered woodsmen and loggers in the Southeast during the 1870-1910 period. The proportion of miners in the regional labor force, however, was less than that in the national labor force. But West Virginia was among the great mining states. Even before 1870 it exceeded the national average in mining employment, and by 1910 only two states—Arizona and Nevada—had a greater proportion of their labor forces occupied in mining than West Virginia. By 1900 Alabama also exceeded the national average. Kentucky, Tennessee, and Virginia, on the other hand, failed to achieve the national level of mining employment over these years.

The absolute size of the Southeastern fisheries was small throughout the period under review. But after 1880 the region had a much greater relative concentration of fishing employment than the nation as a whole. Virginia, Florida, and Louisiana were among the leading fishing states; before 1890 they were joined by North Carolina and shortly thereafter by Arkansas, which had

[2] F. W. Kollmeyer, "Northern Pine Lumbermen: A Study in Origins and Migration," *Journal of Economic History*, Vol. 16 (1956), pp. 529-38.

developed important river fisheries.

Throughout the 40-year period Mississippi had the greatest concentration of agricultural workers (85% in 1870 and 76% in 1910) and the lowest concentration of manufactures (3% in 1870 and only 7.5% in 1910). Elsewhere in the Southeast the structure of the state labor forces changed rapidly from decade to decade. At the beginning of the period in 1870 West Virginia had the greatest concentration of manufactures (14%) and Louisiana was the least agricultural of the Southeastern states (61% in agriculture). By 1890, Virginia was most heavily concentrated in manufactures (15.26%) and also the least in agriculture (51%). By 1910, however, Florida had developed the greatest concentration in manufactures (22.8%) and West Virginia had the smallest proportion of its labor force in agriculture (35.6%). In absolute terms, Virginia had the largest manufacturing contingent in 1910, almost 162,000 workers.

The Southeast had started late down the road to industrialism; there was a chronic scarcity of skilled labor and liquid capital. The region had begun first-stage processing of its bulkier materials, but apart from the furniture and fixtures industry in North Carolina and a few textile centers, it was as yet rare for the Southeast to produce finished products for the rest of the nation. Recent students of Southern industry differ as to the precise reasons for this prolonged backwardness. But they are in general agreement that the region was still a tributary raw-material economy dominated by absentee owners and suffering the penalties attendant on "backwardness": low wages, lack of opportunity, and general poverty.[3]

Industrial Structure of the Labor Force in the Plains Region, 1870-1910

In some respects the Plains region resembles the Southeast more than any other part of the country in its industrial character (Table 62). It differs, however, in that it supports a much smaller population and is culturally more akin to the western Great Lakes states than to the Southeast. It is primarily a region of agricultural staples, although Missouri, Kansas, and Minnesota have or have had major deposits of important minerals such as coal, oil, and iron ore. The region's slight forest cover was rapidly depleted in the course of settlement, and its fisheries are negligible. Manufacturing has been confined mainly to processing activities in a relatively few urban-industrial centers. Service employment has been at a much higher level than in the Southeast; in most years, close to the national average. The farm lands of Iowa and adjacent states are among the best in the country, but beyond the Missouri Valley the Plains merge into the "Great American Desert" and agriculture becomes a hazardous business for the small cultivator.

[3]H. L. Herring, *Southern Industry and Regional Development* (Chapel Hill: University of North Carolina Press, 1940), pp. 31-5; C. Vann Woodward, *Origins of the New South, 1877-1913* (Baton Rouge: Louisiana State University Press, 1951), pp. 291-320; W. H. Joubert, *Southern Freight Rates in Transition* (Gainesville: University of Florida Press, 1949), pp. 1-134; and C. B. Hoover and B. U. Ratchford, *Economic Resources and Policies of the South* (New York: Macmillan, 1951), pp. 65-88.

Table 62. Distribution by industry of Plains region labor force, 1870-1910

(per cent of total)

Year	Agriculture	Mining	Forestry	Fisheries	Manu-facturing	Services
1870	*61.63*	0.50	0.26	0.03	14.91	22.67
1880	*61.35*	0.95	0.26	0.02	14.34	23.08
1890	*51.57*	1.29	0.33	0.04	16.42	30.35
1900	*49.87*	1.69	0.34	0.06	16.75	31.29
1910	*40.85*	1.82	0.29	0.04	19.99	*37.01*

Figures in italics are above the national average.

SOURCE: Appendix Tables A1–A7.

As late as the 1880's the western reaches of the Plains were still undergoing settlement and, while the agricultural sector of the labor force in Minnesota, Iowa, and Missouri was already in decline, that of the Dakotas, Nebraska, and Kansas were still growing. By 1890 agricultural employment was shrinking relatively in every part of the Plains except the Dakotas and continued to decline thereafter. By 1910 it made up less than half of total employment in every state except North and South Dakota, and in Minnesota and Missouri it was barely one-third of the total.

Mining surged forward rapidly in this region in the 1870's owing to the fervid search for precious metals in the Dakotas. In 1880 mining employed 7.3% of the territorial labor force, but by 1890 the proportion of South Dakota's labor force employed in mining had declined to 2.3%. Less spectacular digging had raised Missouri's mining contingent over these years to 1.8% of its total labor force, by 1890 and that of Kansas and Iowa to almost 1.5% each. Before the close of the century mining employment had risen to 2.3% of total employment in Missouri and 2.2% in Kansas; it had declined to 2.1% of the total in South Dakota. By 1910 the focus of concentration in mining in the region had turned northward to the iron fields of Minnesota (2.3%), the oil and coal fields of Kansas (2.2%), and the coal fields of Missouri (2.08%). Only North Dakota and Nebraska, in fact, then had a negligible proportion of miners in their labor forces.

Forest employment accounted for from 1% to 1.2% of total employment in Minnesota. Elsewhere in the Plains the forestry sector made little contribution to employment, although for a brief period around 1870 the small labor force of the Dakotas contained a logging contingent of about 2.28%, probably as an adjunct to mining activity.

The early promise of the Plains region was based on its rich agricultural lands and the occasional outcrops of mineral wealth. Yet as early as 1870 its industrial component—manufactures and services—amounted to more than 37% of the regional labor force and by 1910 to 57%. It was in services, however, rather

than manufactures that the greatest advances were made and where parity with
the nation was achieved after the slump of the seventies. Missouri and Minnesota were always the region's leading manufacturing states. After 1890 they
had from 19% to 24% of their labor forces in manufacturing, whereas the
Dakotas did not have 10% of their workers in manufactures before the end of
the century. Minnesota and Missouri were likewise the leading centers of service
employment, though the extension of railroads and expansion of trade in
Nebraska, Kansas, and Iowa slowly increased the concern of these states with
services as well. The Plains region, therefore, like the Southeast was primarily
a resource region during this period, with little manufacturing except in the
larger metropolitan centers of Missouri and Minnesota. But, unlike the Southeast, its population densities were relatively low; this permitted it to achieve a
considerably higher level of personal income per capita than the Southeast.

Industrial Structure of the Labor Force in the Southwest, 1870-1910

The industrial structure of the labor force in the Southwest, shown in Table
63, characterizes this region also as essentially a resource region. The growth of
its manufactures before 1910 was at least as unimpressive as that of the Southeast. By 1910, however, its proportion of employment in manufactures and
services combined was running ahead of the Southeast's by almost 2 percentage

Table 63. Distribution by industry of Southwest region labor force, 1870-1910

(per cent of total)

Year	Agriculture	Mining	Forestry	Fisheries	Manu-facturing	Services
1870	*73.67*	0.31	0.16	0.02	7.04	18.80
1880	*72.33*	1.29	0.27	0.02	6.41	19.68
1890	*63.94*	1.14	0.30	0.06	9.11	25.45
1900	*66.71*	1.65	0.38	0.05	8.35	22.86
1910	*57.67*	1.77	0.36	0.05	12.37	27.78

Figures in italics are above the national average.

SOURCE: Appendix Tables A1–A7.

points. In area, the Southwest is one of the largest of all the eight regions,
covering nearly 20% of the continental United States, but it has one of the
lowest population densities. Hence it represents a very different type of resource
economy from that of either the Southeast or the Plains.

Until well into the present century the Southwest, apart from Texas, was a
political dependency of the federal government. Oklahoma achieved statehood
in 1907, Arizona and New Mexico only in 1912. The census provides very little
data on Oklahoma before 1890, since it was mostly a separate Indian territory.

The region as a whole was overwhelmingly agricultural. Yet as early as 1870, because of work on the railroads, the Arizona Territory had more than twice as many workers in transportation, trade, and manufactures as in agriculture. Mining developments were also under way. Although the preponderance of the manufacturing-services component in Arizona endured into the nineties, miners comprised more than one-fourth of the territorial labor force by 1880, and as late as 1910 mining provided nearly 18% of all employment. Meanwhile, developments in Texas and the later opening of farm lands in Oklahoma had begun to affect the industrial structure of the region as a whole. By the early nineties, agricultural workers comprised about two-thirds of the labor force in these two areas and more than half the labor force of the neighboring territory of New Mexico. The Southwest, in fact, like the Mountain and Far West regions, was increasingly agricultural down into the opening years of this century. Arizona's labor force also contained the largest proportion of workers in forestry and logging, although Texas had the largest numbers involved, Texas likewise contained a vast majority of the region's fishery workers.

The contribution of the Southwest to the growth of the national economy in these years was made primarily through its mineral resources—at first copper, and later oil. Only the Mountain and Far West regions ever achieved greater concentrations of mine workers than the Southwest; and only individual states like Pennsylvania and West Virginia developed comparable concentrations of miners east of the Mississippi (though actual numbers of mine workers in the great coal-producing states of the East, of course, greatly exceeded the concentrations of the West). Arizona and, to a lesser extent, New Mexico, were the chief mining territories of the Southwest, but after 1900 both Texas and Oklahoma increased their contribution to mineral wealth through the medium of oil development. The economic development of Texas was also a major factor in the growth of the entire Southwest in both the argricultural and the industrial sectors.

Industrial Structure of the Mountain Region's Labor Force between 1870-1910

The structure of the Mountain region's labor force between 1870 and 1910 is shown in Table 64. The proportion of the regional labor force in agriculture was below the national average throughout these years. Unlike the Southwest and the Far West, the Mountain region was not settled primarily by agriculturalists. Mining and services provided the principal means of subsistence until the early seventies, and in both sectors the region was an "exporter" in the sense that even its services were in large part used in facilitating the development of regions around it.

In 1870 miners outnumbered the combined totals of farm and service workers in Idaho and Montana, while in Colorado they almost equalled the numbers in manufactures. The Mormon commonwealth of Utah was at once the largest agricultural and the largest manufacturing territory in the region; the thinly

Table 64. Distribution by industry of Mountain region labor force, 1870-1910

(per cent of total)

Year	Agriculture	Mining	Forestry	Fisheries	Manu-facturing	Services
1870	33.59	*26.54*	*0.84*	0.02	12.94	*26.07*
1880	24.00	*26.37*	*0.97*	0.02	18.02	*30.62*
1890	26.53	*12.71*	*1.18*	0.02	19.99	*39.57*
1900	30.12	*14.72*	*0.73*	0.01	18.68	*35.74*
1910	29.93	*8.47*	*0.67*	0.02	20.48	*40.43*

Figures in italics are above the national average.

SOURCE: Appendix Tables A1–A7.

populated Wyoming territory had a striking concentration in tertiary employ-ment, chiefly transportation workers.

By 1890 Colorado had acquired the greatest concentration of manufactures, and Idaho had the greatest concentration in agriculture. All states had large volumes of service employment, ranging from 27% in Idaho to 42.4% in Colorado. Utah had the smallest stake in mining (6.5%); in its neighboring states, mining activities ranged upward from 11.7% in Wyoming to more than 17% in Idaho and Montana.

By 1910, all states in the region except Idaho (32.8%) had about 40% of their working force in services; all except Idaho, once more, had from one-third to one-fourth of their labor forces in agriculture; Idaho had 42%. The greatest concentrations in manufactures were in Utah (23%) and Colorado (22%); Wyoming had the least (15%). The largest mining contingents were in Mon-tana and Wyoming (just over 10% each); the smallest was in Idaho (about 5%). Idaho and Montana had the largest proportions of forest workers; in Idaho they constituted more than 2% of the labor force in 1910. These two states had, in fact, dominated the region's small forest economy since the decline of Wyoming a decade or so before.

Thus the semi-arid Mountain region was another of the great resource regions of the United States in the 1870-1910 period. The development of its material wealth during this period indicates that it contributed much to the growth of the industrial economy in other parts of the country. As a consequence, its own modest manufactures largely took the form of first-stage processing in prepara-tion for later processing and finishing in other regions, e.g., copper smelting. Much of the necessary fuel supply could be found locally in one or other of the Mountain states, but before 1910 little effort was made to exploit the region's known oil potential.

Like the Southwest, the Mountain region was also an important "corridor" between the East and Far West. For this reason it developed important trans-portation and communications services which helped bind the national economy together. Yet nature had placed both the Mountain and Southwestern regions in the heart of an arid and semi-arid expanse. That the desert might be turned into a garden had been proved long before 1870 by the Mormon pioneers in Utah; what they and their successors had not proved, however, was the capacity of the region to support vastly increased numbers of people at higher levels of living.

Industrial Structure of the Labor Force in the Far West, 1870-1910

The industrial structure of the Far West's labor force is shown in Table 65. The enormous contribution in resources which this region made to American

Table 65. Distribution by industry of Far West region labor force, 1870-1910

(per cent of total)

Year	Agriculture	Mining	Forestry	Fisheries	Manu-facturing	Services
1870	25.73	*18.03*	*1.63*	*0.41*	18.20	*36.00*
1880	28.81	*11.46*	*1.65*	*1.35*	20.45	*36.28*
1890	28.85	*4.44*	*2.30*	*0.54*	22.55	*41.32*
1900	27.65	5.27	*2.17*	*0.76*	22.06	*42.09*
1910	20.10	2.84	*2.04*	*0.47*	26.95	*47.60*

Figures in italics are above the national average.

SOURCE: Appendix Tables A1–A7.

growth during the 1870-1910 period can be judged from the fact that it had higher concentrations than the national average in three of the four resource sectors: mining, forestry, and fisheries.

But the strength of the Far West during the period here under review was by no means confined to the resource sectors of the economy. This can be seen by comparing the combined manufacturing and services component of its labor force with that of each of the three most industrialized regions—the New England, Middle Atlantic, and Great Lakes regions (Table 66). Though less industrialized, in this sense, than either the New England or the Middle Atlantic regions, the Far West was nevertheless more industrialized than the dynamic Great Lakes region. Its strength, however, was in services rather than manufactures.

The remoteness of the Far West from the industrial center of the Northeast meant that it had to develop certain manufactures which it could not secure from the rest of the economy except at almost prohibitive cost. By 1870, therefore, it had achieved the greatest concentration of manufacturing-service activities outside the Northeastern industrial belt. The fact of distance, measured in terms of costs of the long haul to the Coast by land or sea, had the effect of placing a "protective tariff" around some forms of Far Western manufactures.

Thus the economy of the region developed somewhat as an empire apart from the rest of the nation.

California was more industrialized than any of its neighboring states, or indeed than the United States as a whole, during this period.[4] But by 1890 Washington had emerged as a second industrial state, with sizable shares of employment in both manufactures and services; and after 1900 Oregon's proportion of manufacturing-services workers also exceeded the national average. By 1910 the three Pacific Coast states were among the nation's leading industrial areas. Nevada's small labor force contained a larger proportion of miners than the labor force of any other state in the nation (21.9%).

Table 66. Combined manufacturing-services components of labor force of Far West, New England, Middle Atlantic, and Great Lakes regions, 1870, 1890, and 1910

(per cent of total)

Year	Far West	New England	Middle Atlantic	Great Lakes
1870	54.20	72.07	68.54	42.79
1890	63.87	82.06	77.98	57.59
1910	74.55	89.30	85.36	71.82

SOURCE: Appendix Tables A1, A6, and A7.

At various times during the 1870-1910 period all states in the region made large contributions to the nation's lumber supply. By the end of the nineteenth century, however, the preponderance of forest activities had passed to Washington and Oregon. During the present century, in fact, forest industry products have regularly yielded a large proportion of the income of these two states. The same two states usually had the region's largest concentrations of fishing employment (including the lucrative salmon fisheries) and at all times had large numbers employed in various specialized branches of agriculture. By 1910, Oregon had the largest proportion of farm workers of any state in the region. Needless to add, California was also one of the great fishing, forest, and farming states, but its rapidly growing shares of employment in manufactures and services tended to reduce the relative significance of its numbers in the resource sector even before the turn of the century.

In celebrating the great material endowment of the Far West, it is well to conclude by stressing at least one major disadvantage. With practically no commercial supply of coal, the Far Western states were for long without an adequate or assured fuel base for their growing industries and communications

[4]See R. G. Cleland and Osgood Hardy, *March of Industry* in J. R. McCarthy, ed., *California* (Los Angeles, Calif.: Powell Publishing Co., 1929), on early industrial development in California.

systems. Before the close of the century, however, California's oil potential was already being developed; production soared from 4,000,000 barrels in 1900 to 55,000,000 barrels in 1910. Natural gas also soon came to be a major source of domestic heat in the region's burgeoning urban-industrial centers. Oregon and Washington also lacked ample coal for industrial purposes and the deficiency had to be made up by importing coal from British Columbia and oil from California. The abundant rainfall and strong river currents also combined to make the Far West (especially the Northwest) a great potential producer of hydro-electric power. The development of this resource, however, lies outside the period which ended in 1910.

Income Changes, 1880-1920

Changes in total personal income and per capita personal income provide a rough guide to changes in the regional volume of activities and levels of living; and these, in turn, are related to the structural changes in population and labor force which we have described. We shall now turn to a consideration of some of these relationships during the period 1880-1920.[5]

Data on the regional distribution of total income over these years are shown in Table 67. The over-all trend in the regions clearly reflects the growth of total personal income in the nation as a whole. The rate of growth was, in general, greater between 1900 and 1920 than between 1880 and 1900. Among the more populated regions, the agricultural Plains probably experienced the fastest relative growth in income before 1900, surpassing both New England and the Southeast, in absolute terms, by 1900. Thereafter, however, it slowed considerably, and by 1920 its share in the total national income was somewhat smaller than in 1880. The Southeast, like the Plains, had a smaller share in 1920 than in 1880; its decline, however, occurred entirely within the earlier half of the period. New England's relative share declined throughout these years. Among the newer Western regions, the Far West and Southwest increased their relative shares both between 1880 and 1900 and between 1900 and 1920; their gains were especially marked after 1900. The Mountain region, like the Plains, rose between 1880 and 1900 and dropped back after 1900. Its decline, however, in the second of these periods was by no means as great as that of the Plains, and its relative share in 1920, though lower than in 1900, was higher than in 1880.

---

[5]Unfortunately, for the first half of our period, the years for which income data by states are available do not coincide exactly with the years for which population and labor force data can be obtained. Thus, figures of state income payments, devised by Richard Easterlin, begin with 1880 and proceed at two-decade intervals until 1920; thereafter figures become available by decades and after 1929, in fact, on an annual basis in the Commerce series.

See E. S. Lee, A. R. Miller, C. P. Brainerd, and R. A. Easterlin, *Population Redistribution and Economic Growth, United States, 1870-1950* (Philadelphia: American Philosophical Society, 1957), pp. 703-45; C. F. Schwartz and R. E. Graham, Jr., *Personal Income by States since 1929*, a supplement to the Survey of Current Business, Office of Business Economics, U. S. Department of Commerce (Washington: Government Printing Office, 1956).

Table 67. Regional distribution of total personal income in the United States, 1880, 1900, and 1920

(U. S. income in millions)

Region	1880	1900	1920*
United States	$8,743	$15,391	$69,276
	100%	100%	100%
New England	11.30	9.86	8.75
Middle Atlantic	32.60	30.80	30.20
Great Lakes	22.84	22.45	22.21
Southeast	13.66	12.02	13.02
Plains	11.07	13.27	10.27
Southwest	2.11	3.76	5.69
Mountain	1.43	2.53	2.47
Far West	4.99	5.31	7.39

*1919-21 average.

SOURCE: Lee, Miller, Brainerd and Easterlin, Table Y-1. (See note to Table 8.)

The Middle Atlantic and Great Lakes regions grew as the nation grew throughout the entire period. Their combined share of the nation's total income in 1880 was 55%; and in 1920, after four decades of rapid growth and redistribution of economic activity, it still exceeded 52%. In absolute terms, these two regions enjoyed the largest total personal income throughout the 40-year period.

Table 68, which shows the principal net upward and downward shifts among the states during this period, highlights the more striking changes. Almost half of the net upward shift (relative growth) occurred in four states in the South-

Table 68. Principal net shifts in total personal income among states, 1880-1920

Percentage net upward shift		Percentage net downward shift	
Texas	16.15	Pennsylvania	13.20
Oklahoma	13.02	Iowa	10.37
Washington	11.48	Missouri	9.11
California	9.34	Indiana	8.25
Dakotas	5.60	Massachusetts	8.20
Michigan	4.61	New York	7.97
W. Virginia	4.00	Kentucky	5.43
Illinois	3.89	Ohio	5.38
New Jersey	3.68	Maine	3.82
Minnesota	3.61	Louisiana	3.35

SOURCE: Same as Table 67.

west and Far West—29.17% of it in Texas and Oklahoma and 20.82% in California and Washington. These same four states also accounted for almost 43% of the total population shifts during the 1870-1910 period. Altogether, five of the ten states with the greatest relative income growth between 1880 and 1920 were also among the ten with the greatest relative population growth between 1870 and 1910. And seven of the ten states with the greatest relative declines in total personal income between 1880 and 1920 were among the ten with the greatest relative declines in population in the 1870-1910 period.

The weakness of personal income growth in the Plains region after 1900 was somewhat localized, as the figures in Table 68 show; it stemmed from the relative decline in the key states of Iowa and Missouri, which together contributed almost 20% of the total net downward shift in personal income among the states during the 1880-1920 period. Similarly, in the Great Lakes region, the relative strength of Michigan and Illinois did not entirely offset the relative downward shifts in Indiana and Ohio (Figure 31). In the Southeast, also, there

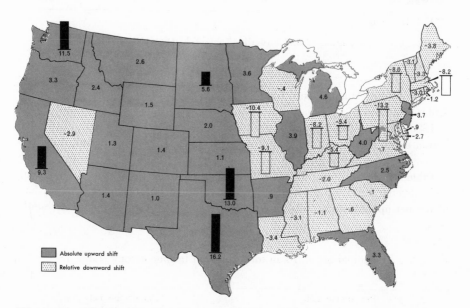

Figure 31. Net Shift in Total Personal Income, 1880-1920.

State figures represent % of total net shift. Total net shift as % of incremental change: 29.2. Total net shift as % of 1880 personal income: 90.1.

were a number of income growth states between 1880 and 1920—West Virginia, Florida, North Carolina, and Arkansas in that order—but their combined upward shift of 10.62% did not offset the relative declines registered by the other states in that region. Relative decline in income was in some respects even more pronounced in the two seaboard regions of the Northeast. New Jersey was the only state among ten which did not experience a net downward shift in personal income; Pennsylvania, Massachusetts, and New York, in fact, contributed more than 29% of the total net downward shifts in income among the states during this period.

The relation between the relative growth in total population and in total income within a state or region, as shown in the figures for personal income *per capita,* provides a valuable, if rough, measure of changes in the levels of living. Table 69 shows how the regions ranked in terms of real income per capita as compared with the national average during the 1880-1920 period. The Far West, Mountain, New England, Middle Atlantic, and Great Lakes regions exceeded the national average throughout these years. The Plains, Southeast, and Southwest regions consistently fell below.

In the above-average group, the greatest relative gains were made by the urban-industrial regions of the Northeasten seaboard, and more especially by the heavily populated Middle Atlantic region. By 1900 the increasingly urban-industrialized Great Lakes region was also making rapid gains in personal income per capita, but the sparsely populated rural-mining Mountain region was already in absolute decline. The Far West was the only one of the newer Western regions that maintained its position in the above-average group; and its greatest growth occurred after 1900, by which time it too had developed a labor force structure resembling the urban-industrial pattern of the Northeast.

In the below-average group, the Plains region came closest to the national average. Around 1900 its per capita income reached 97% of the average for the nation as a whole; by 1920, however, it had fallen to less than 90%. The Southwest and Southeast, in contrast to the Plains, did somewhat better after 1900 than before. The Southwest, to be sure, was closing the gap between its per capita income level and the national level throughout the period 1880-1920, but the Southeast began to converge on the national average only around the

Table 69. Rank order of regions by personal income per capita,* 1880, 1900, and 1920

(1929 dollars)

1880		1900		1920	
Far West	638.2	Far West	674.6	Far West	780.6
Mountain	501.5	Mountain	601.0	Middle Atlantic	772.5
New England	425.0	Middle Atlantic	570.2	New England	719.3
Middle Atlantic	422.8	New England	551.7	Great Lakes	623.5
Great Lakes	307.4	Great Lakes	439.6	Mountain	590.7
United States	**302.1**	**United States**	**414.0**	**United States**	**578.0**
Plains	271.2	Plains	401.5	Plains	501.0
Southwest	182.7	Southwest	283.2	Southwest	466.2
Southeast	150.6	Southeast	197.7	Southeast	326.2

*Weighted averages of state incomes per capita.

SOURCE: Unpublished data by R. A. Easterlin.

turn of the century. In spite of impressive growth in total personal income, the depressing effect of population in the Southeast held the per capita figure far below the national average in both relative and absolute terms.

We turn finally to a consideration of certain relationships between demographic patterns, occupational structure of the labor force, and levels of per capita personal income as they have emerged in our survey of economic changes. The associations between urban-industrial structure and levels of living in 1920 are set out in Table 70. There is evident the close relationship between the degree of urbanization and the industrialization of the labor force and, to a lesser extent, between the degree of urbanization and the quantitative decline in agricultural employment. The Far West, however, deviates somewhat here from the rest of the country. There is also evident a close association between urban-industrial structure and high levels of personal income per capita and, by the same token, between rural-agricultural structure and relatively lower levels of per capita personal income. There is, however, no apparent association between the non-agricultural resource sector (mining, fisheries, forestry and logging) and urban-industrial structure or personal income per capita. But, read in conjunction with certain other occupational-structural and demographic features, the data on the non-agricultural resource sector may throw some light on the income performance of the Far Western and Mountain regions.

The Far West is of special interest with regard to these relationships. As it was only the third most urban-industrialized region in the period under review, it might be expected to rank below the top in average personal income. But it

Table 70. Rank order of regions by personal income per capita, urbanization of population, and labor force industry components, 1920

Region	Personal income per capita (1929 dollars)	Urban proportion of population	Labor force components		
			% Agric.	% Non-agric.* resource	% Mfg. & Services
United States	$578.0	51.2%	25.63	3.27	71.10
Far West	*780.6*	*61.6*(3)	*18.33*(6)	*3.99*(2)	*77.68*(4)
Middle Atlantic	*772.5*	*74.7*(2)	7.38(7)	*3.69*(4)	*88.93*(2)
New England	*719.3*	*75.9*(1)	6.93(8)	1.12(8)	*91.95*(1)
Great Lakes	*623.5*	*60.8*(4)	*18.72*(5)	3.00(6)	*78.28*(3)
Mountain	*590.7*	39.7(5)	*32.85*(4)	*7.73*(1)	59.42(6)
Plains	501.0	37.7(6)	*36.35*(3)	2.08(7)	61.57(5)
Southwest	466.2	30.3(7)	*44.88*(2)	*3.81*(3)	51.31(7)
Southeast	326.2	23.9(8)	*49.50*(1)	*3.59*(5)	46.91(8)

Figures in italics are above the national average.
*Forestry and logging, mining, and fisheries.
Rank order in parentheses.

SOURCE: Unpublished data by R. A. Easterlin; 17th U. S. Census, 1950, see *supra*, Table 4, note; and Appendix Tables A1–A7.

ranks first. An explanation of this, we believe, is to be found in a combination of historical and geographical circumstances peculiar to this region. Economic development of the Far West got under way during the third quarter of the last century after the initial discovery of precious metals, but it did not gather great momentum before the completion of railroad connections with the East around 1870. At this time, the Far West's share of total population and its level of population density were lower than those of any other region except the Mountain; these same relative conditions still obtained during the second decade of the twentieth century. Thus crowding on land, which has been an income-depressing factor in other regions, did not occur in the Far West. The region was also rich in minerals, forest, and agricultural land ("desert" was widespread only in the sparsely populated state of Nevada and in parts of southern California). This fortunate combination of low population and abundance of resources lifted the Far West, and to a lesser extent the Mountain region, to the highest per capita income levels anywhere in the United States between 1880 and the end of the century.[6]

The urban-industrial regions of the Northeast, and especially the Middle Atlantic region, had drawn upon their own and other regions' resources to raise their much larger populations to average levels of personal income not so very far below those obtaining in the Mountain or Far West regions. Before 1910, in fact, the Middle Atlantic and New England regions had surpassed the per capita income levels obtaining in the Mountain region, and before the close of the next decade the Middle Atlantic region was challenging the Far West for first place. By 1920 again, the rapidly industrializing Great Lakes region had also surpassed the income levels of the Mountain region and had climbed into fourth place behind the Far West, Middle Atlantic, and New England regions.

The relative decline of the Mountain region and the accelerated growth of the Far West after 1900 are reflected in the occupational structure of their respective labor forces (see Table 71). Between 1900 and 1920 the Far West maintained its development along urban-industrial lines, whereas the Mountain region experienced only a modest increase in the industrial-services sector, and that increase was primarily in services rather than in manufactures. After oil was developed in California and transportation had been facilitated by the completion of the isthmian canal, the Far West could realize its industrial potential; but the Mountain region remained relatively inaccessible and was handicapped by the partial exhaustion of some important mineral resources. Yet, compared with other predominantly non-industrial regions (Table 70), the Mountain region continued to enjoy relatively high levels of per capita income at least until 1920. Its labor force structure was clearly not following the typical pattern of the older urban-industrial regions, but neither was it settling down into the pattern of the older rural-agricultural regions. As long as this region would maintain its rich non-agricultural resource sector and hold its population increase in bounds, it might hope to go on enjoying higher average levels of

[6]No doubt, the high average levels of personal income obtaining in Far West and Mountain states also reflect the high prices which prevailed in these relatively inaccessible parts of the country.

Table 71. Resource and non-resource components of the labor force in the Mountain and Far West regions, 1900 and 1920

(per cent of total)

Region	1900		1920	
	Resource	Other	Resource	Other
Mountain	45.58	54.42	40.58	59.42
Far West	35.85	64.15	22.32	77.68

SOURCE: Appendix Tables A1–A7.

personal income than the more heavily populated, rural-agricultural regions, such as the Plains, Southwest, and Southeast.

These suggestive associations between the industrial structure of a region and its level of per capita income raise many questions concerning the human, material, and institutional forces that underlie the development of a given industrial structure. Certain of these questions are probed in some detail in later sections of this book. Here it will suffice to say that, with one exception, no region that was significantly below the national average in urban-industrialization was able to exceed the national average in per capita income level. The exception was the Mountain region, much the most sparsely populated part of the country and a region, moreover, in which the non-agricultural resource component of the labor force as late as 1920 was more than twice the relative size of the non-agricultural resource component of any other region. Between 1900 and 1920, however, the Mountain region was the least buoyant of the eight regions. As the relative size of its agricultural labor force grew, its level of per capita personal income fell. It had a larger share of the nation's population in 1920 than in 1900, but it was the only region that had a relatively larger agricultural labor force in 1920 than in 1900 and it was the only region to experience a falling average level of per capita income. After 1910, the relative size of its manufacturing labor force also declined. Thus, between 1910 and 1920, the Mountain region was unique in that its manufacturing was already in relative decline while its agriculture continued in relative growth.

14 / Nationalizing the American economy, 1870-1910:

THE PLAY OF TECHNOLOGY ON RESOURCES

We have traced the growth and redistribution of population, productive activities, and personal income that attended the evolution of the continental economy in the United States between 1870 and 1910. We shall now consider the role of natural resources, and especially the resources of the West, in the general economic history of these years.

For practical purposes, the joining of the Union and Central Pacific railroads in Utah on May 10, 1869, may be said to symbolize the beginnings of a truly nation-wide economy.[1] Subsequent preoccupation with the vast resource potential made accessible by the completion of the railroad network did not mean, of course, that the country severed its close ties with the Atlantic economy. On the contrary, the movements of population, capital, and goods across the Atlantic reached unprecedented levels during the late nineteenth century. The pace and character of American growth, however, were no longer determined so largely by the size and kinds of overseas demand. Exports rose in volume throughout the rest of the century, but they were an increasingly smaller portion of total American output. More significant, though the United States remained the world's largest debtor, its economic development was now less dependent upon continuing imports of European capital. Billions of dollars flowed into the economy concurrently with millions of immigrants, but indigenous capital formation seldom comprised less than 95% of investment increase in any one year. Industrial Europe, meanwhile, became more and more dependent on supplies of American farm staples. Technical developments over these years enabled the United States to meet its mounting foreign obligations with a declining proportion of its greatly enlarged output.

[1] A transcontinental telegraph was opened in October 1861. Before that time it required at least three weeks for mails to reach San Francisco from the Mississippi Valley by the Overland Mail or from the Atlantic seaboard via the Pacific Mail and Panama route. The "Pony Express," inaugurated in 1860, could carry urgent communications in about eight days, but heavy duty freight movements from coast to coast were impossible except by long ocean passage.

The forces of population growth and of technical and economic progress that had been operative in the crucial political-economic decision of the sixties were now free to shape the continental framework of the nation's economic growth.[2] On average, net national product per capita increased over 10% per decade over the years 1870-1910. After 1890, when the so-called "frontier of settlement" finally disappeared, the advertising of numerous products was undertaken on a nation-wide scale, and by the early years of the 20th century the domestic market embraced all the population.

Some historians have suggested that in the years after 1860 the urban-industrial Northeast imposed its way of life upon a defenseless rural America. But this essentially "political" point of view exaggerates the consensus among Northeastern manufacturers in regard to such issues as tariff and monetary policy; the interests of New England textiles and Pennsylvania iron in these issues, for example, were by no means identical. Moreover, a national banking system, land grants to transcontinentals, and the easing of state incorporation laws were not so much examples of "sectional imperialism" as of belated and, on the whole, successful efforts to create institutions by means of which productive activities could be organized on a continental scale. If sectional conflicts persisted, and for a while at least they were aggravated by agrarian politics, they were nevertheless a waning influence, complicating administration and policy, but always giving way before the surge of industrial growth. By the early years of this century modern urban-industrial America had been achieved: a powerful continental economy made up of a complex of differentiated regions that could offer families in every part of the country a more abundant material life.

This enormous transformation was not, of course, effected merely by the impersonal forces of industrial revolution. It was also the lifework of millions of men and women whose motivations and mores were moulded in turn by the social process they helped forward. No period of American history has produced a more dramatic human spectacle than the decades following the Civil War; at no other time perhaps did "economic" man so completely dominate the American scene. But the heroes of this "age of enterprise" were no longer provincial merchants gathering in a material surplus for trade beyond the seas; they were the promoters of continental empires in transportation, finance, natural resources, and manufactures. The Astors were no longer an exceptional breed;

---

[2]At the turn of the century the *Final Report* of the U. S. Industrial Commission (Washington: Government Printing Office, 1902), Vol. 19, p. 1, concluded that the country had been occupied and that remaining "areas of unsettled country" were chiefly (1) mountainous regions unsuited to agriculture or inaccessible to markets; (2) swamp and lake regions; (3) timber lands; and (4) arid lands. In fact, more land was taken up under terms of the Homestead Act and its successors after 1890 than ever before. As late as 1913 the Secretary of Agriculture reported that less than 60% of arable land was under cultivation and that, of this, not more than 12% was yielding "reasonable full returns." See D. F. Houston, *Eight Years with Wilson's Cabinet* (New York: Doubleday Page and Co., 1926), p. 200; L. P. Jorgenson, "Agricultural Expansion into the Semiarid Lands of the West North Central States During the First World War," *Agricultural History*, Vol. 23 (January 1949), pp. 30-40.

they were followed by a generation of energetic and ruthless "national business-men" who made an indelible impression on the course of American development. The Havemeyers in sugar, the Dukes in tobacco, the Weyerhaeusers in lumber, the Armours and Swifts in meat-packing, the Carnegies and Fricks in steel, the Harrimans and Hills in transportation, the Cookes and Morgans in finance, the Rockefellers in oil, became the effective arbiters of national growth. For a period, at least, they acquired for themselves and their corporate dynasties huge portions of the land, resources, and wealth of the nation. They managed its democratic politics in the interest of bounties, franchises, tariffs, and immu-nities from taxes or public regulation. If their formal residences were usually on the Northeastern seaboard, their creative energies were oriented away from the harbors and shipping lanes towards the railroads and freightyards of the in-terior. Such men thought and acted in continental terms, for the entire country had become a stage on which to play out the continuing drama of their quest for wealth.

To focus only on the achievements of the star performers would be as serious a distortion as to neglect the human factor altogether. On every hand were a host of lesser lights, smaller figures whose profit horizons were limited to the region or locality in which they lived, yet whose strength lay in association or com-petition with others of their kind. They were no mere local chorus echoing the grand themes of acquisition stated by the principals; they spoke their own lines and originated private roles within the continuity of the general plot. They also served in opening up the new territories and reaped rich harvests on their per-sonal account; their modest capital or credit went into small companies and partnerships, into the plant and machinery which heightened the play of tech-nology on resources. Then, too, there were the vast majority who made up the crowd scenes, both participants and spectators, producers and consumers, who took their cues from the main actors or from the contagion around them. As they moved west with the surge of population and industry, their expectations rose and their efforts were redoubled. Like Tocqueville a half century before, Lord Bryce found them in the greater West of the eighties "reaching forward to and grasping at the future."[3]

What had occurred since the relatively calm midcentury to release this flood of energies in continental development? Did productive possibilities in the West of the late nineteenth century differ in any important respect from productive possibilities in the West of earlier years? Judged by the type and volume of activities, the answer must be that, with few exceptions, it offered little that was essentially new; grazing lands, copper ores, petroleum deposits, and great stands of timber were by this time hardly novelties. The absolute volume of resource inputs, of course, was greatly expanded as a consequence of Western develop-

[3]All the passionate eagerness of people in the West was directed towards the development of their country: "to open the greatest number of mines . . . to scatter cattle over a thousand hills, to turn the flower-spangled prairies of the Northwest into wheat fields, to cover the sunny slopes of the Southwest with vines and olives: this is the end and aim of their lives, this is their daily and nightly thought . . ." J. Bryce, *The American Common-wealth,* Vol II (London: Macmillan and Co., 2nd edition revised, 1891), p. 700.

ment. But the greatest gains in output were obtained not from increased quantities of materials but from the reorganization of production functions along
capital-intensive lines—that is, by industrialization. Industrialization was a
process that involved and affected all regions. Multiplication and differentiation
of areas and activities within the continental system widened and deepened technological influences in every aspect of American life; all areas were made accessible to each other through increasingly refined networks of transportation and
communications; agriculture was reorganized into specialized "type of farming"
areas; remote sources of minerals and lumber were made available in order to
sustain the growth of industrial manufactures. Thus it was the extension of
industrial technique and organization, not only to manufacture and distribution,
but to agriculture, mining, and forestry as well, that made Western resources
economically significant at this point in the nation's history. These resources
eased the course of industrialization in all parts of the country. But they did
not determine its pace or its direction; this was a function of demand.

In early phases of industrialism, the character of demand is usually shaped
by the requirements of industrialization itself, by the need to accumulate stocks
of capital goods—plant, machinery, materials, and various forms of "social
overhead" such as transport services, urban housing, and utilities. In the
American case, however, many authorities have pointed to the unprecedented
demands of war after 1860 as imparting a momentum to economic growth that
sufficed to industrialize the Northeast and carry industrial influences across the
continent. No doubt, the task of supplying the Union armies with food, clothing,
and munitions did create opportunities in agriculture, mining, and heavy manufactures; mechanization of some branches of agriculture and some sections of
the men's garment industry was accelerated. The outcome of the war removed
certain political obstacles to completion of the transcontinentals and liberalized
the conditions of public support for important economic interests. Nevertheless,
even before the war, industrialization had already taken hold in both the New
England and the Middle Atlantic states and the process of regional differentiation had gone far. It was probably railroad construction and operation, both
East and West, that after 1850 gave greatest impetus to economic development
and set in motion new patterns of resource utilization.

Technology and Resources: the Role of the Railroads

The first construction of railroads into the older West had begun as early as
1853 and, if anything, the prosperity of the later war years attracted capital
away from what had already proved to be a risky venture. Little new construction was attempted during the war years beyond the double-tracking of routes
into the coal and ore producing districts of the Middle Atlantic states. But the
manufacture of iron rails alone absorbed almost two-thirds of the increased pig
iron output during the years 1860-64; and by the end of the war, the total railway use of iron exceeded 42% of the nation's output. Half the incremental coal
product of the war years likewise went into fuel supply for rail manufacture or

was consumed by the locomotives themselves. *It was railroad building on this scale which quickly revealed critical limits to the industrial raw material potential of the Middle Atlantic and New England states.* By the end of the war some 13% of all iron was being derived from ores extracted in the Great Lakes region; smaller inroads were also being made upon the forests and bituminous coal fields of this region in order to meet the demands of industry in the rapidly developing Northeast.[4]

The most spectacular surge of railroad construction was reserved for the post-war period, when cheaper rails made from Bessemer steel were introduced. In 1866, rails absorbed less than 1% of the nation's minute steel output and steel rails were twice as expensive as iron rails; but in little more than a decade, nearly 70% of the greatly enlarged steel output went into rails and steel rails cost only one third more than their iron counterpart. Meanwhile their superior strength and quality had permitted the development of larger and heavier locomotives and had raised the freight potential of the emergent railroad network. By the late seventies, also, railroad construction and operation were absorbing from 12 to 15% of all coal output and around 10% of the annual lumber cut. At the end of the century, when for all practical purposes the great continental rail net had been completed, more than 20% of the pig-iron total was being rolled into railroad bars.[5]

Railroad construction generated unprecedented demands for capital, land, and labor; larger lines such as the Central Pacific, Union Pacific, and Illinois Central employed upwards of 10,000 men each in their peak years of construction. One authority estimates that the national figure for railroad construction workers probably reached a maximum of 200,000 during the eighties. By that time the census reported employment in railroad transportation service in excess of a quarter of a million. Similarly, the mobilization of funds for railroad investment had become the major concern of financiers on two continents and enforced a wholesale adaptation of financial institutions and techniques. Experience with railway finance trained a key generation of specialists in the business of manipulating huge aggregations of mobile capital. Up to World War I, in fact, railroads remained the second largest consumer of capital, second only to the construction of buildings for residence and business.[6] Thus, in Leland Jenks' words, "the initial impetus of investment in railway construction led in widening arcs to increments of economic activity over the entire American domain, far exceeding in their total volume the original inputs of investment capital."[7]

These increments of activity across the nation are the essential contribution of the railroad to the dynamics of regional growth. The railroad carried the

[4]P. H. Cootner, *Transport Innovation and Economic Development: The Case of the U. S. Steam Railroad,* unpublished Ph.D. Thesis, M.I.T., (June 1953), Chap. V, pp. 13-14.

[5]*Ibid,* Chap. VI, pp. 10a and 12.

[6]T. C. Cochran, *The American Business System: A Historical Perspective, 1900-1955* (Cambridge, Mass.: Harvard University Press, 1957), pp. 29, 32-35.

[7]L. H. Jenks, "Railroads As An Economic Force in American Development," *Journal of Economic History,* Vol. 14 (May 1944), p. 7.

industrial revolution into every part of the continental interior. Historians have stressed the role of the railroad in reducing the cost of freight and speeding the flow of goods, but from the present standpoint at least three other features are of equal significance. First, the railroad liberated the course of economic growth from the relatively fixed and narrow channels of the coastal and inland waterways systems. The import of this "emancipation" had been evident in some areas during the era of sectional rivalry before the war, but in the years after 1870 its influence was paramount everywhere. Second, the penetration of the railroad into the trans-Mississippi West brought a heavy-duty, high-capacity transport service into regions of untold resource potential which otherwise could have acquired little economic significance. Finally, the physical task of building railroads across boundless plains and high mountain passes from the Great Lakes to the Gulf and Pacific coasts fostered a growth of heavy manufactures and a consequent demand for raw materials beyond the capacity of older resource regions to supply. Railroad building in the Plains and Western Great Lakes states, for example, necessitated some tapping of the ore, fuel, and forest resources of these areas concurrently with their agricultural settlement.

Railroad mileage in operation during the calendar years 1870, 1880, 1890, 1900, and 1910 in each of the eight regions is shown in Table 72, together with

Table 72. Railroad mileage in operation during calendar years and percentage increases by decades, by region, 1870-1910

	1870	1880	1890	1900	1910
Region	Mileage	Mileage & % increase	Mileage & % increase	Mileage & % increase	Mileage & % increase
United States	52,922	93,267 (76)	163,596 (75)	193,348 (18)	240,438 (24)
New England	4,494	5,982 (33)	6,718 (12)	7,521 (12)	7,921 (5)
Middle Atlantic	10,577	15,147 (43)	19,745 (30)	22,464 (14)	23,777 (6)
Great Lakes	14,701	25,109 (71)	36,924 (47)	41,007 (11)	44,928 (10)
Southeast	11,843	16,328 (38)	31,785 (95)	41,134 (29)	55,932 (36)
Plains	8,046	19,094 (137)	38,354 (101)	42,988 (12)	49,730 (16)
Southwest	711	4,640 (553)	12,248 (164)	15,302 (25)	25,391 (66)
Mountain	873	3,236 (271)	9,330 (188)	11,634 (25)	15,550 (34)
Far West	1,677	3,731 (122)	8,492 (128)	11,298 (33)	17,209 (52)

Figures in italics are above the national average.

SOURCE: *Poor's Railroad Manual;* Interstate Commerce Commission, *Statistics of Railways in the U. S.*

percentage increases in track over each intervening decade. After 1880 the bulk of the nation's increased facilities appears to have been constructed in the South and trans-Mississippi West, although increases in the Great Lakes states remain sizable down through 1890. After 1890, however, railroad building falls off relatively in the Great Lakes region and also in the Plains. In all Western regions the penetration of the railroad seems closely associated with agricultural settlement; but in the Mountain and Southwest regions, changes in the rate of mileage increase also follow the general increase or decrease in mining employment; changes in the general level of business activity seem to have had a greater influence on Western railroad building in the nineties than in the seventies. By 1900, except in the Mountain region, probably few farms were more than ten miles or so from a railroad. Meanwhile, the nation was already entering the automobile age.

Differentiation in Agriculture

The new accessibility of the trans-Mississippi West, together with the growth of foreign and domestic markets for farm produce, effected a radical transformation in the location of agricultural activities over the decades following the Civil War. Already by 1860 the Plains region was contributing about 9% of all wheat threshed in the United States, but the heart of the wheatlands still lay in Wisconsin and Illinois. A decade later the Plains region's share of wheat threshed had risen to 23% and by 1890 reached 37% (see Table 73). Its share of the corn harvested for grain in the United States rose from 21% of the total in 1870 to more than 48% two decades later. In 1870 very little milk was sold from farms in the Plains, but by 1890 that region (mostly Minnesota and Iowa) contributed one-fifth of the greatly expanded national milk supply. Cattle had likewise become a major concern in some Plains states by 1870, but by 1890 the region had more than doubled its share of all cattle population and had over 27% of the national total. The cattle industry of the Southwest had meanwhile received a comparable stimulus as the railroad penetrated further into Texas. Over the first half of the decade 1870-80 Texas had also risen to second place after Mississippi among the nation's cotton producers, with Arkansas ranked third. The spread of the cotton culture into Texas was almost wholly a consequence of railroad development, since most of the fertile cotton lands were far removed from the Gulf coast.[8]

A microcosm of this prolonged agricultural transformation can be found in the history of Wisconsin and the adjacent territories. Until the second quarter of the nineteenth century, the fertile and partially forested lands between Lake Michigan and the Mississippi River had remained isolated and undeveloped. Prior to that time their only economic significance had lain in an abundance of

[8]On the relation of transport developments to increased farm production and regional marketing problems, see U. S. Industrial Commission, *Report on Agriculture and Agricultural Labor*, Vol. 10 (Washington: Government Printing Office, 1901), pp. X-XV, and relevant testimony.

Table 73. Regional distribution of selected farm products, 1870–1950

Wheat (threshed)

(000's bushels)

Region	1870	1890	1910	1930	1950
United States	287,746	468,374	683,379	800,649	1,006,559
	100%	100%	100%	100%	100%
New England	0.35	0.07	0.01	—	—
Middle Atlantic	14.19	8.87	5.98	4.18	3.84
Great Lakes	44.35	31.33	17.74	12.64	16.50
Southeast	10.30	8.06	4.61	2.44	2.42
Plains	23.40	37.28	56.18	46.83	38.30
Southwest	0.27	1.01	2.54	12.49	15.86
Mountain	0.37	1.30	4.16	12.00	14.02
Far West	6.77	12.08	8.78	9.42	9.06

Corn (harvested for grain)

(000's bushels)

Region	1870	1890	1910	1930	1950
United States	760,945	2,122,328	2,552,190	2,130,752*	2,778,190*
	100%	100%	100%	100%	100%
New England	0.97	0.29	0.32	0.07	0.03
Middle Atlantic	9.81	3.96	3.62	2.94	2.98
Great Lakes	36.49	27.10	33.12	25.09	35.75
Southeast	28.49	16.91	16.87	18.01	14.63
Plains	21.24	48.23	39.04	47.39	43.73
Southwest	2.79	3.30	6.71	5.40	2.34
Mountain	0.04	0.08	0.23	0.98	0.46
Far West	0.17	0.13	0.09	0.12	0.08

*excluding silage corn.

All cattle

Region	1870	1890	1910	1930	1950
United States	23,820,608	57,648,792	61,803,866	63,895,826	76,762,461
	100%	100%	100%	100%	100%
New England	5.71	2.45	2.18	1.98	1.42
Middle Atlantic	16.17	7.58	7.41	6.69	5.69
Great Lakes	22.75	15.67	15.89	16.63	15.87
Southeast	23.93	15.56	16.61	13.95	17.51
Plains	12.32	27.00	28.54	31.12	28.88
Southwest	14.94	20.24	17.46	16.35	15.99
Mountain	0.70	7.00	5.99	7.26	7.92
Far West	3.48	4.50	5.92	6.02	6.72
	37.51	28.64	27.71	32.08	27.66

Whole milk (sold from farms)

(000's lbs.)

Region	1870	1900*	1910	1930	1950
United States	2,025,305	18,359,540	16,660,400	38,318,493	68,529,441
	100%	100%	100%	100%	100%
New England	13.19	10.04	9.05	6.74	5.00
Middle Atlantic	67.07	32.47	39.99	26.94	20.21
Great Lakes	15.63	28.84	34.13	37.54	37.32
Southeast	1.49	2.18	2.69	6.08	9.01
Plains	.86	20.57	7.46	7.35	11.80
Southwest	.03	0.61	0.87	2.80	3.42
Mountain	.07	1.40	1.33	2.61	2.73
Far West	1.66	3.89	4.48	9.94	10.51

*1890 figure not comparable.

SOURCE: U. S. Department of Commerce, *U. S. Census of Agriculture: 1950*, Vol. II, (Washington: Government Printing Office, 1952), pp. 401, 403, 404, 410, 540, 549, and 558.

peltries traded by Indians and in lead deposits recently opened up on some scale along Wisconsin's southwestern border with Illinois. Permanent agricultural settlement had only begun in the years 1834-40, when lands in southern Wisconsin were first surveyed and offered for sale.

Under the existing "frontier" conditions the farmers needed a commercial crop within one or two seasons if they were to sustain themselves and their families on the new land; and the only staple crop in this part of the country was wheat. With great difficulty they sold wheat to the nearby miners and woodsmen, to other settlers, to the villages along the lakeshore; much was shipped down the Mississippi towards St. Louis and in the early forties exports commenced from Milwaukee, then a small town of 2,000 inhabitants. Between 1849 and 1855 the Wisconsin wheat crop doubled, and by 1860 it had trebled again. In 1855 the Milwaukee Board of Trade reported a crop of more than 8,000,000 bushels and in 1860 a crop exceeding 27,000,000 bushels. The bulk of the wheat surplus, moreover, was now shipped to the East.

The spread of wheat culture across Wisconsin closely paralleled the frontier of farm settlement and both were a function of improved communications, by river, by plank roads, and finally by the railroad itself. Improvements in farm implements during the forties and fifties almost made up for deficiencies in farming technique and succeeded for a while in masking the limitation of the soil. Meanwhile, the railroads heightened competition from newer wheatlands further west, and the combination of price fluctuations and declining yields in the late fifties caused serious doubts in older settled sections about the viability of an extensive wheat culture.

Civil War prosperity brought a resurgence of wheat-growing throughout the settled parts of the state, though a few of the more enterprising cultivators took

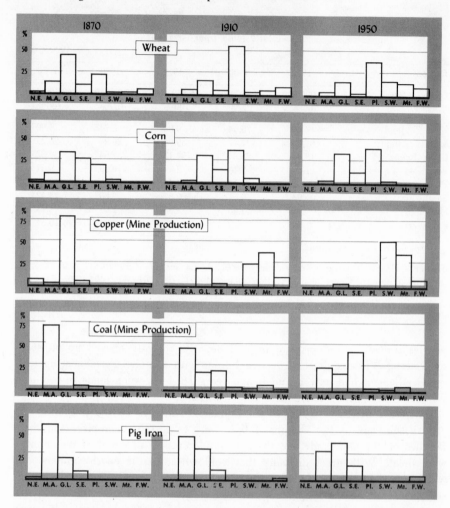

Figure 32. Regional Shares of Production 1870, 1910, 1950.

advantage of good times to experiment with other crops, including hops, flax, tobacco, and even sorghum. But once the war boom had passed most farmers discovered that diversification did not pay. A growing appreciation of the state's natural advantages led many to try livestock farming. The first adjustment was toward sheep-raising which offered most of the remedial, "land-restoring" features of a grass-grain husbandry at only a fraction of the cost involved in a shift into beef or dairying. Further south, in Illinois, resources were shifted into the more profitable corn-hog and beef complexes.

There followed a series of institutional changes, however, under the auspices of newly founded regional and state dairymen's associations, which speeded the transition to a more complex pattern of animal husbandry after 1870. By adopting the "associated dairy system," growing numbers of small farmers in northern Illinois and southern Wisconsin found it possible to transfer their limited resources into milk production and thereby secure a higher return; they pooled the milk from herds of improved "native" and Shorthorn cattle to produce larger amounts of cheese and butter for the local and regional provision trade.

After 1872 remarkable business leadership was provided by the Wisconsin State Dairymen's Association, which urged a rejection of "Granger" politics and proposed intensive specialization as the more certain road to economic survival. Factory cheesemaking was developed, after the earlier pattern of New York, as a means of exploiting the special skills of a few expert cheesemakers; but equally important vital connections were pioneered in profitable dairy markets at home and abroad. While wheat-growing still flourished on the newer lands of the western Wisconsin counties and in the newly settled parts of Minnesota, the Dairymen's Association sponsored dairy boards of trade and promoted reform of farm and factory management in the eastern and southern portions of the state in order to enhance Wisconsin's competitive position in the great produce markets of Chicago and New York.

The introduction of fast-freight service and refrigerated cars at this juncture facilitated the movement of dairy products over longer distances; a series of triumphs at national dairy shows soon secured the state a reputation for prime produce. Not all branches of the emerging dairy industry, of course, were equally specialized at this time. Farmers who did not yet have cheese factories in their vicinity were advised to make butter and since this was a relatively simple process there was less need for skilled operatives or factory organization. As a consequence, Wisconsin buttermaking remained a domestic chore until well into the eighties when technical advances in cream separation combined with price changes in regional dairy markets to foster a rapid growth of creameries. Since Wisconsin had large pre-empted leadership in cheesemaking, dairymen in the adjacent states of Minnesota and Iowa concentrated their first efforts on buttermaking. Meanwhile in Illinois the expansion of the Chicago milk shed caused many farmers to direct their output into the more profitable market for fluid milk.

Thus the revolution in dairy organization, technique, and markets gradually disrupted the older modes of production and enlarged the element of skill in the new. Under a double compulsion to preserve the fertility of the soil and raise the return on its use, dairy farmers of Wisconsin and adjacent areas concentrated on the improvement of feeds and breeds in order to achieve an increased flow of milk at lower costs per unit. This was accomplished between 1870 and 1890 by a more balanced crop program and by extending lactation through the winter months. Ensilage (silos) provided the long-sought solution to winter dairying problems while research, at the State University and in other parts of the country, related the cow's yield of milk to her intake of digestible nutrients. Further experiment, based on German examples, resulted in the development of a "balanced dairy ration" which combined the several feed components in the correct proportions required by the flow of milk. Finally in 1890 the celebrated Babcock fat-test provided at once the first cheap, accurate measure of milk quality and a more equitable basis for making payments for milk at the factory; it compelled even closer attention to scientific breeding and better feeding practices.[9]

The continuing revolution in dairy farm management led, in turn, to more numerous and larger manufacturing establishments. A series of technical and scientific developments permitted even greater control over manufacturing processes. By the nineties, improvements in milk sanitation and pasteurization helped reduce the hazards of fluid milk consumption, condenseries had obtained a foothold in northern Illinois and southeastern Wisconsin, and hence a growing share of the regional milk supply was being diverted to lucrative market milk outlets in midwestern cities. Milk sold as whole milk or cream to city milk dealers (or condenseries) generally displaced milk manufacturing (cheese and butter) in areas close to large urban populations, where land values and most other cost factors (except transportation) were usually high. Cheese and butter manufactures slowly relocated in belts beyond the market milk zones. In Wisconsin, climatic conditions and resultant crop programs usually gave milk sold for cheese an edge over milk sold for butter, but in southwestern parts of the state and in adjacent sections of Iowa and Minnesota, butter-making in conjunction with hog-raising and corn-growing proved more viable.[10] Thus competition for milk among the different branches of dairying gradually enforced a pattern of local specialization within the dairy belt of the Great Lakes and Plains regions as it had done somewhat earlier in the more populous Middle Atlantic and New England regions.[11]

Table 74 highlights the continuing relocation of agricultural production in the late nineteenth and early twentieth centuries. The wheat belt gradually moved further west, eventually settling in the western Plains, Southwest, and Mountain states and becoming increasingly dissociated from the corn belt. Meanwhile livestock activities concentrated more intensively in the rich corn belts and grasslands of the Great Lakes and eastern Plains states. The corn-hog-cattle complex, for example, located in southern parts of these regions where growing seasons are notably longer, while the grass-cattle-dairy complex tended to concentrate north of the corn-belt. Local adjustments within this over-all pattern have occurred from time to time during the present century but they do not appear related to the expanding transportation system or, for that matter,

[9]Henceforth cows were tested for their individual yields and herds were slowly up-graded. By 1900, Holstein and Channel Islands' breeds were preferred above all others; public and private efforts were joined to eliminate the scourge of bovine tuberculosis from Wisconsin herds; the interrelation of technical and economic forces in the growth of dairying is discussed at length in the forthcoming volume, E. E. Lampard, *The Rise of the Dairy Industry: A Study of Agricultural Change in the Midwest, 1820-1920*, (Wisconsin State Historical Society, Madison, Wis.).

[10]Skim milk from creameries, or separated on the farm, provided an important supplement to hog feed. Corn quickly became the staple animal feed, hence beef cattle were also well-suited to states in which corn was the principal grain. Corn-hog-beef production at this time was usually more profitable than dairy farming, but its geographical spread was limited by the exacting climatic requirements of corn culture.

[11]E. Brunger, "Dairying and Urban Development in New York State, 1850-1900," *Agricultural History*, Vol. 29 (October 1955), pp. 169-74.

Table 74. Leading states in the production of whole milk sold from farms, wheat threshed, and all cattle, 1870-1950, as a percentage of U. S. total

Whole milk

1870		1900*		1910		1930		1950	
N. Y.	57.65	N. Y.	20.85	N. Y.	27.06	Wis.	18.93	Wis.	18.47
Ohio	9.46	Wis.	11.82	Wis.	15.34	N. Y.	15.32	N. Y.	10.92
Mass.	6.49	Iowa	10.03	Pa.	8.75	Pa.	8.23	Cal.	7.64
Pa.	6.12	Ill.	8.74	Ill.	8.16	Cal.	6.67	Pa.	6.30
Ill.	3.93	Pa.	8.01	Ohio	5.13	Ill.	5.35	Minn.	5.61
Conn.	2.66	Minn.	4.86	Mich.	3.82	Ohio	5.09	Ohio	5.26

Wheat threshed

1870		1890		1910		1930		1950	
Ill.	10.47	Minn.	11.17	N. D.	17.08	Kans.	18.55	Kans.	14.47
Iowa	10.23	Cal.	8.73	Kans.	11.34	N. D.	11.94	N. D.	10.49
Ohio	9.69	Ill.	7.98	Minn.	8.34	Neb.	6.73	Okla.	7.82
Ind.	9.64	Ind.	7.97	Neb.	6.98	Okla.	6.39	Tex.	7.48
Wis.	8.90	Ohio	7.59	S. D.	6.89	Tex.	5.51	Wash.	5.73
Pa.	6.84	Kans.	6.49	Wash.	5.99	Wash.	5.32	Ohio	5.27

All cattle

1870		1890		1910		1930		1950	
Tex.	14.68	Tex.	14.83	Tex.	11.22	Tex.	10.33	Tex.	10.20
N. Y.	8.59	Iowa	8.49	Iowa	7.20	Iowa	6.48	Iowa	5.92
Ill.	7.20	Kans.	5.50	Kans.	4.98	Wis.	5.54	Wis.	4.88
Ohio	6.03	Ill.	5.31	Neb.	4.74	Kans.	5.05	Neb.	4.73
Pa.	5.64	Mo.	5.15	Wis.	4.34	Minn.	4.94	Kans.	4.57
Mo.	4.84	Neb.	3.72	Mo.	4.14	Neb.	4.93	Mo.	4.27

*Figures for 1890 not available.

SOURCE: *U. S. Census of Agriculture, 1950*, Vol. II, pp. 401, 410, 549, 558.

to the taking-up of new land. They have more to do with changes in demand, wartime needs for food and fibers, and government policies for agriculture. Nevertheless, some adjustments have stemmed from improvements in technique —the introduction of new breeds of cattle (important in the South), the development of hybrid corn (important in areas with short growing seasons), and the extension of irrigation (important in semi-arid areas of the Southwest and Far West).[12]

[12]L. Haystead and G. C. Fite, *The Agricultural Regions of the United States* (Norman: University of Oklahoma Press, 1955); E. S. Dunn, Jr., *The Location of Agricultural Production* (Gainesville: University of Florida Press, 1954).

Differentiation in Mining Activities

Regional developments in mining activities in the late nineteenth century were, perhaps, even more spectacular than those in agriculture. At the close of the Civil War, for example, the Great Lakes region was providing about 13% of the nation's iron and a somewhat larger proportion of its iron ore. By 1870 some 30% of the iron ore total originated in this region, and by 1890 the proportion had risen to 48%.

Over the same period the mining of Alabama-Tennessee ores raised the Southeast's share of national ore production from 2% to almost 20%. It was no coincidence that this great expansion in Southern mining, like that in the Great Lakes states, accompanied two decades of rapid railroad building both regionally and nationally. In the Southeast, moreover, it was a genuine regional expansion in the sense that, although much of the enterprise and capital came from outside, much of the demand for iron products originated in the region itself. For a period, at least, the Southern iron manufacture benefited from its low-cost production, which ranged as much as 26% below Pittsburgh. The ores were not suited to the Bessemer process of steelmaking, yet their proximity to cheap coal and improved access to growing markets for foundry iron sufficed to insure their lively development.

In contrast to the Great Lakes and Southern iron fields, the great ore reserves of the northern Plains were largely unaffected by the national demand for iron and steel products. As late as 1890 the entire Plains region supplied less than 8% of the nation's ore requirements. There were, to be sure, certain processing problems connected with the soft and crumbly hematite of Minnesota which probably retarded Plains development; on the other hand, the ore was admirably suited to the newer stripping and steam shovel techniques used in selective mining. It required only the linking of the local Mesabi mine railways to the Great Northern system in the late nineties to release this ferric treasure for American industry.[13] Unlike the earlier exploitations of iron ore in the Middle Atlantic, Great Lakes, and Southeast regions, however, the rapid development of the Minnesota ores did not result in any great upsurge of local pig-iron production. The proximity of the mines to cheap water routes on the Great Lakes made these new fields a tributary to the iron and steel manufacture of the Great Lakes and Middle Atlantic states.[14]

Lead mining was perhaps even more profoundly affected by railroad development than iron. In 1870 about 60% of the lead produced in the United States

[13]J. W. Thompson, "The Genesis of the Great Northern's Mesabi Ore Traffic" *Journal of Economic History*, Vol. 16, (December 1956), pp. 551-57. In 1906 James J. Hill claimed that "never in the whole world has the same amount of track moved the same tonnage, or approached it." Between 1896 and 1900 shipments of iron ore from Lake Superior ports doubled, from 9,600,000 tons to 18,600,000 tons: 80 per cent of this ore was received by ten ports on the lower shores of Lake Erie; Industrial Commission, Vol. 19, *op. cit.*, pp. 472-74.

[14]The opening of the Lake Superior ore district appears to have coincided with the abandonment of the high-cost production of the Appalachian range. Experts of the U. S. Geological Survey estimated that, at the prevailing rate of output of the early 1900's, produc-

came from the Great Lakes region and about 34% from newer developments in
the Plains. At this time no significant amounts of lead were reported from the
Mountain region. But a decade or so later, after branch lines from the mines
had linked up with major systems, Colorado, Utah, and Nevada supplied more

Table 75. Domestic mine production of recoverable lead,* by region, 1870-
1950

(1870 = current dollar value; short tons thereafter)

Region	1870	1890†	1910	1930	1950
United States	$736,004	181,141	386,899	556,948	430,678
	100%	100%	100%	100%	100%
New England	.41	—	—	—	—
Middle Atlantic	1.02	—	—	.50	.34
Great Lakes	60.10	1.02	1.21	.32	.76
Southeast	3.94	.16	.05	1.03	.80
Plains	34.26	26.62	41.35	38.16	33.46
Southwest	—	4.37	1.63	6.80	11.93
Mountain	—	66.70	54.61	50.70	44.44
Far West	.27	1.13	1.15	2.49	8.27

*Less zinc residues.

†181,141 short tons is a combined total of production of lead-bearing ores in Rocky
Mountain states and the lead recovered in other states. The total recovered lead reported
in the *Mineral Industries* section of 1890 U. S. Census, pp. 163-173, is 182,967 short tons.

SOURCE: 9th U. S. Census, 1870, Vol. III, p. 768; Compendium of the *11th U. S. Census:
1890*, Pt. 2, pp. 479-80; *Mineral Resources, 1910*, Pt. I, p. 234; *Mineral Resources,
1930*, p. 489; *Minerals Yearbook, 1951*, p. 742.

than 66% of the enlarged national lead requirements.[15] Meanwhile production
of recoverable lead in the Great Lakes region had declined to a trickle. In the
Plains region, on the other hand, Missouri has continued as a major producer of
lead down to the present; and since 1910 Far Western production has assumed a
modest importance as older regions have declined.

That the "new accessibility" was not the whole story of Western mineral
development in the late nineteenth century, however, is well illustrated by the
history of copper mining. Penetration of new territory by the railroad did not
at once guarantee the exploitation of its mineral wealth. Thus the fact that
"lake copper" from Michigan adequately met requirements before the eighties
delayed the construction of feeder lines into the Montana and Arizona copper

tion would reach a maximum in the next thirty years and begin to decline; National
Conservation Commission, *Report*, (3 vols., Washington: Government Printing Office, 1909),
Vol. I, pp. 95-110; Vol. III, pp. 483-520. If anything, their concern for the coal supply at
the time was even greater, since, unlike the iron, fuel could only be used once; *ibid*, Vol.
III, pp. 426-446.

[15] U. S. Industrial Commission, Vol. 19, *op. cit.*, pp. 229, 242-46; W. R. Ingalls, *Lead and
Zinc in the United States*, (New York: Hill Publishing Co., 1908).

lands, though their potential was publicized by seekers after the precious metals in the 1860's. It was an important shift in the utilization of copper following the rise of the electrical industries which revealed the essentially inelastic conditions of supply in older mining areas and compelled recourse to the new.[16] During the eighties the market price of copper fell off somewhat, but smelter production increased by more than 300%; both changes can be attributed to the impact of ores from the Mountain and Southwest regions.[17]

But if improved transportation and shifts in demand combined to make Western ores available to meet national requirements, many technical problems had to be solved before the mineral resources of newer regions could be fully developed. The mining of ores under the wide range of geological conditions prevalent in the greater West taxed the accumulated experience and ingenuity of mining engineers and metal processors in two continents. New and deeper understanding of ore genesis and location stemmed directly from the work of the United States Geological Survey (1879) and later from such private ventures as the Anaconda Geological Department (1898). In turn, this intelligence led to more careful planning and preliminary development, while new and complicated machines gave added power to the grossly inadequate supply of skilled labor. The introduction of improved tools and better explosives and the perfection of mechanized pumping, drilling, hoisting, and handling equipment required the massing of great funds of mobile capital for Western mining enterprise in much the same fashion as for the railroad.[18]

Copper, once more, provides impressive evidence of the creative interplay of technology on resources. The rich "native" ores from the Great Lakes region were notably free from impurities, and comparatively simple concentration processes sufficed to yield high-grade metal suitable for all existing uses of copper and its principal alloys. Likewise, the first ores extracted from the Butte mines in Montana were so rich that they required no exacting concentration.

[16]Copper had long been used for sheathing ships but steel was substituted for this purpose during the nineties; it had also been used for roofing and gutters as well as for domestic and laboratory utensils (brass). "The great development of electricity in recent years . . . has added very largely to the demand for copper, chiefly on account of its conductivity, and it is not likely that any cheaper material can be substituted with satisfaction." U. S. Industrial Commission, Vol. 19, *op. cit.*, pp. 230-32. This source also has an interesting commentary on the differences in mining laws between Michigan and Montana.

[17]The same decade significantly saw the beginnings of local coal mining in the Mountain region, chiefly in Colorado and Wyoming. Coal mines were also developed in Utah. In competition with Wyoming mines, Colorado and Utah produced for the railroads and for local smelters. Some producers also attempted to sell anthracite in California but ran into stiff competition from sea-borne coal carried as ship's ballast; U. S. Industrial Commission, *Report on Capital and Labor Employed in the Mining Industry*, Vol. 12 (Washington: Government Printing Office, 1901), p. VII.

[18]A summary of technical advances in the mining industries and metal extraction during this period is given in U. S. Industrial Commission, Vol. 19, *op. cit.*, pp. 235-50; also C. Kirchoff, "A Decade of Progress in Reducing Costs," in American Institute of Mining Engineers, *Transactions*, Vol. 29 (1899), pp. 352-71; and C. C. Spence, "When the Pound Sterling Went West: British Investments and the American Mineral Frontier," *Journal of Economic History*, Vol. 16 (December 1956), pp. 482-92.

But within a few years recourse to deeper sulphide ores, averaging less than 6% copper, rendered older crushing and gravity concentration methods increasingly impractical.[19] Some electrolytic refining was also introduced during the nineties and produced an excellent Western copper at relatively low cost. But the great changes became necessary after 1905 with the shift from the mainly oxidized ores to so-called "porphyry" sulphide deposits assaying between 2.5% and 0.75% copper. Their development was facilitated in part by the adaptation of selective mining techniques from the Mesabi iron range but in much greater part by the "oil flotation" method of concentration which gave greater recovery from the same grade of ore than the old fashioned gravity method. Selective flotation made it possible to concentrate practically all Western ores and even tailings, although the variety of local conditions still imposed special process features on particular operations.[20] Already before World War I, the combined output of six large porphyry mines in the West made up nearly 30% of the nation's copper supply.

The significance of these technological advances which (with the possible exception of the leaching of oxidized ores) were all in general use by the second decade of this century, can be seen in a comparison of the declining yields from various United States ores. During the heyday of the Calumet and Hecla Mining Company in Michigan before 1880, native ore had once run as high as 20% copper. But in the years 1887-1905, the average yield of "lake ore" was only 2.96%, somewhat below the country-wide average of about 3% during the nineties. By 1906 the national average yield had declined to 2.5% and by 1915 to 1.66%. A decade later the figure was 1.54%, and by the midcentury it had dropped to 0.91 percent.[21]

The advent of deeper mining and the growing capital requirements for both

---

[19]Steam stamping proved very wasteful and was quickly replaced by a staged crushing and rolling treatment with concentration at each successive stage in order to remove the bulk of copper and other concentrates as they broke away from the gangue and were reduced to slimes. The finer copper matte was then smelted in blast and, to obtain still higher yields, in reverberatory furnaces or modified Bessemer Converters (blister copper).

[20]By oil flotation methods, the ore, after some preliminary milling, is treated in a mixture of water and chemicals (chiefly oils) through which air is driven to carry the heavier minerals to the surface in bubbles. The resulting froth is then removed and the oils separated from the metal concentrate by heat.

[21]U. S. Department of the Interior, Bureau of Mines, *Materials Survey—Copper*, (1952), p. VI-41. Mine sources of U. S. copper production in 1950 are shown in the following table, *ibid*, p. II-25:

	Ore (short tons)	Per cent yield	Per cent of total copper
Concentrating ores: Native (Mich.)	4,386,474	0.58	2.9
Sulphides and oxides	85,819,695	0.89	86.5
Smelting ores	624,261	3.37	2.4
Leaching ores	3,755,362	0.88	3.7
Copper from precipitates	—	—	4.5
			100.00

the extracting and smelting phases of copper production tended to increase the size of the major producers. For example, through large investments of New England capital, Calumet and Hecla had acquired a dominant position in Michigan mining before the Civil War, and in the highly competitive period following the introduction of Western ores, economies of large-scale operations proved decisive in both the old areas and the new (Table 76).[22] The same tendency was

Table 76. Domestic copper mine production, by region 1870-1950

(1870 = current dollars; short tons thereafter)

Region	1870	1890	1910	1930	1950
United States	$5,201,312	111,715	541,998	688,748	909,337
	100%	100%	100%	100%	100%
New England	6.90	.03	—	—	—
Middle Atlantic	1.52	—	.08	.21	—
Great Lakes	82.90	39.46	20.54	12.29	2.82
Southeast	7.96	.01	1.57	—	—
Plains	—	—	—	.01	.33
Southwest	.14	15.79	27.87	46.57	51.64
Mountain	—	44.63	39.49	28.34	37.21
Far West	.58	.08	10.44	10.01	6.41
Unallocated	—	—	.01	2.57*	1.59†

*Figure given is for North Carolina, Tennessee, and Vermont.
†Covers Pennsylvania, Tennessee, and Vermont.

SOURCE: 9th U. S. Census, 1870, Vol. III, p. 767; *Mineral Resources 1910*; Pt. I, pp. 172, 170 (Mine Returns); *Mineral Resources 1930*, Pt. I, p. 706; *Minerals Yearbook 1950*, p. 473.

soon apparent in the West as one or another large corporation came to dominate its locality; eventually both mining and smelting processes were integrated under single managements. Of the four or five giant mining companies of the present century, however, only Anaconda moved very far into the fabricating side of the industry through its subsidiary, American Brass, leaving American Smelting and Refining, not a mining company, to take the lead in refining phases of the industry.

Not only did the development of mining corporations and mineral technology facilitate the opening up of new fields in the West, but the special geological features of each area prompted innovation in technique and additions to scientific knowledge. L. D. Graton has summarized this interaction between experi-

[22]W. B. Gates, *Michigan Copper and Boston Dollars: An Economic History of the Michigan Copper Industry* (Cambridge: Harvard University Press, 1951); R. G. Raymer, *A History of Copper Mining in Montana* (Chicago: The Lewis Publishing Co., 1930); U. S. Industrial Commission, *op. cit.*, (1901), p. 606; *ibid.*, Vol. 19, *op. cit.*, pp. 232-35, for the formation and operations of the Amalgamated Copper Company.

ence and understanding through which, one by one, the mining districts "yielded up specific, fundamental secrets" as follows: Leadville (1882), replacement and certain aspects of structural control; Marquette (1893), structural barriers for descending solutions; Butte (1896), secondary sulphide enrichment; Seven Devils (1899), contact-metamorphic ores; Rico (1901), structural barriers for ascending solutions; Coeur d'Alene (1908), pre-ore faulting of vain structures; Goldfield (1909), alunitic alteration. . . .[23]

Differentiation in Iron and Steel Production: the Dominance of Fuels

The dynamic influences of science and technology were not, of course, confined to the processes of mining and smelting ore; they pervaded almost every branch of productive activity. The record of iron and steel, thought by many observers of the late nineteenth century to be the epitome of economic progress, reveals the influence of technology on processing and fabricating to be at least as significant as on the extraction and treatment of ores. If the development of the Minnesota iron ranges marked a profound shift in the regional pattern of ore supplies, changes in the location of iron and steel production were affected by other forces, more especially by developments in metallurgical science and fuel supply. Compared with either lead or copper, iron production was not critically dependent on the provision of new railroads.[24] Thus, as Table 77 shows, the regional pattern of iron manufacture, apart from expansion in the South, was not drastically changed down to World War I (or, for that matter, thereafter). Regardless of shifts in ore production, the Middle Atlantic and Great Lakes regions dominated pig-iron production throughout the period 1870-1910 and have declined only moderately since, notwithstanding the recovery of the South and more recent developments in the Mountain and Far Western regions. The impact of Mesabi ores after 1890 was felt not in the Plains or even the western Great Lake states, but in Ohio and other manufacturing centers linked to the ports along the southern shores of Lake Erie.

In steelmaking the growing ascendancy of the Great Lakes region within the larger Northeastern industrial belt was already apparent before 1910, though its rise to dominance was delayed until the interwar years. The attraction of the cheap water route from Minnesota was no doubt a factor in the decisions of steel

[23]L. D. Graton, "Seventy-five Years of Progress in Mining Geology," *Seventy-five Years of Progress in the Mineral Industry 1871-1946*, (New York: The American Institute of Mining and Metallurgical Engineers, 1947, p. 10. Also, C. R. Hall, *History of American Industrial Science* (New York: Library Publishers, 1954), pp. 185-216.

[24]Iron ore moved over some 200 miles of railroad, in addition to its voyage on the Lakes, to reach the furnaces of the manufacturing belt. Coal, limestone, ore, and pig loomed large in the bulk of railroad freight in the Great Lakes region. Until 1860 Pennsylvania was the largest iron ore producer, but by 1902 it had fallen to sixth place among the states. Iron manufactures in the Atlantic coastal states benefited from their seaboard location, and ore imports rose rapidly in the late nineteenth century. By 1913 they exceeded 2,500,000 tons, most of which came from Cuba and Chile. Isaac Lippincott, *Economic Development of the United States* (New York: D. Appleton and Co., 1921), pp. 176, 330-32.

Table 77. Pig iron production, by region, 1870-1950.

(long tons)

Region	1870	1890	1910	1930	1950
United States	1,832,878[a]	9,202,703[a]	27,303,567[a]	31,752,169[a]	57,666,937
	100%	100%	100%	100%	100%
New England	1.68	.28	.06	—	—
Middle Atlantic[b]	66.53	54.89	50.55	39.42	34.90
Great Lakes[c]	25.44	27.13	36.57	44.36	43.94
Southeast[d]	6.35	17.35	11.25	13.69	17.05
Mountain[e]	—	.23	—	2.53	—
Far West[f]	—	.12	1.57	—	4.11

[a] Includes ferro-alloys.

[b] Includes Massachusetts after 1910.

[c] Includes Missouri in 1890, Minnesota in 1910 and 1950.

[d] Includes Texas after 1870 and Maryland in 1950.

[e] Includes Wisconsin, Minnesota and Iowa in 1930.

[f] Includes small amounts in Missouri and Colorado in 1910, and Colorado and Utah in 1950.

SOURCE: U. S. Census 1870, Vol. III, p. 603; American Iron and Steel Association, *Annual Statistical Reports, 1890,* p. 62 and *1910,* p. 95; American Iron and Steel Institute, *Annual Statistical Reports, 1930,* p. 4 and *1950,* p. 18.

men to move the Lackawanna plant from Scranton to Buffalo (1901) and to locate the new Gary works in Indiana, as it was in the still earlier proliferation of Bessemer plants around Chicago. However, more potent factors can be found in the superior access of Lake sites to the westward-moving steel market (Buffalo also provided cheaper access to some Eastern markets) and in the growing complications of the fuel supply. The persistence of an iron and steel complex in southern Illinois and eastern Missouri after the virtual impoverishment of local ores is further testimony to the importance of fuel and market considerations in the steel geography of the period before 1910.

Over the decades 1870-1890 larger and more efficient blast furnaces raised average furnace output sixfold, while the Bessemer converters multiplied in areas with access to non-phosphoric ores. But already in the seventies the industry was confronted with the critical inadequacy of its principal charcoal and anthracite fuels. Uncoked bituminous coals had been used in Pennsylvania during the 1840's and many new furnaces in the eastern Great Lakes states had also adopted this fuel, but conversion to coke (often in conjunction with anthracite) was not common until the Civil War decade. By 1871 about 30% of the total iron output was produced with so-called "beehive" coke, and within the next few years the proportion produced with coke fuel surpassed the combined proportion produced with anthracite and charcoal.[25]

[25]Charcoal had remained the principal American smelting fuel until about 1855 and the persistence of "obsolescent" technique is underlined by the fact that as late as 1917 some

After 1859 Connellsville coke and Lake ores provided the material bases for the rise of western Pennsylvania, and notably Allegheny county, to leadership in the American iron industry. From the mid-90's, coke from "by product" ovens began to displace the beehive coke; nevertheless, it was not before World War I that the steel industry converted to by-product fuel on any large scale.[26] By 1919 by-product ovens provided 57% of all coke, and the output of the beehive variety went into steady decline. In view, therefore, of the appreciably greater weight of fuel than ore required in the manufacture of steel ingots before 1910, it is not surprising that major blast furnaces were located near sources of coking coal.[27] Without improvements in fuel technology, which between 1879 and 1954 reduced the fuel consumption per ton of pig by 40%, it is unlikely that iron and steelmaking would have been released from its century-long tie to coal.[28]

If the volume of iron and steel output was ultimately dependent on the availability of ore, fuels (Table 78), and alloy ingredients, the actual yield might vary with the process of manufacture. Around 1870, for example, only about 80,000 net tons of steel ingots were produced in the entire country, of which almost 45% was obtained by antiquated crucible, puddled iron, and other processes.[29] Not before the eighties did the improved Bessemer process begin to make its

376,525 tons of pig were made in 18 blast furnaces using charcoal fuel. American Iron & Steel Institute, *Annual Statistical Report, 1917*, p. 21.

[26]The utilization of coal-chemical by-products (ammonia, coal tar, and benzol) made an important addition to revenues of the iron and steel industry, especially after the outbreak of war in 1914 had closed off German sources of supply.

[27]Approximate consumption of coke per ton of pig-iron produced in the United States, 1879-1954:

	Coke*	(tons) Coal Equivalent
1879	1.47	2.10
1889	1.29	1.85
1899	1.20	1.72
1909	1.13	1.62
1919	1.07	1.53
1929	.91	1.31
1939	.88	1.27
1954	.87	1.24

*Coal-Coke conversion factor = 70%.

SOURCE: Walter Isard, "Some Locational Factors in the Iron and Steel Industry since the early 19th Century," *Journal of Political Economy*, Vol. 56 (1948), p. 205; American Iron and Steel Institute, *Annual Statistical Report, 1940*, p. 11, *1956*, p. 46.

[28]Control of apparently minor difference in fuel input, air infiltration, and draft regulation, mostly introduced since 1910, have been the principal factors in reducing fuel consumption from upwards of 6 million B.T.U. per ton of ingots to between 3-4 million B.T.U. characteristic of the best recent practice: C. D. King, "Seventy-five Years of Progress in Iron and Steel," *Seventy-Five Years of Progress in the Mineral Industry, 1871-1946* (New York: The American Institute of Mining & Metallurgical Engineers, 1947), p. 188.

[29]Some 45,000 net tons of ingots were made in six Bessemer plants located in the Middle Atlantic and Great Lakes regions (3 in Pennsylvania, and 1 each in Michigan, Ohio, and Illinois); 2,000 net tons were made by the one open-hearth plant located in New Jersey. (*Ibid.*, pp. 174-82.)

weight felt in American steel production after the incorporation of the improved Thomas-Gilchrist "basic" acid lining (1878). By 1890 the Bessemer processes contributed about 80% of the 5,000,000 net tons of steel ingots made in the United States.[30]

Table 78(a). Coke production, by region, 1880–1950

(net short tons of beehive and by-produce oven coke)

Region	1880	1890	1910	1930	1950
United States	3,338,300	11,508,000	41,709,000	47,972,000	72,718,000
	100%	100%	100%	100%	100%
New England	—	—	1.08	2.85	2.02
Middle Atlantic	84.51	74.38	66.06	42.69	42.33
Great Lakes	3.39	.96	5.79	37.13	35.09
Southeast	11.16	22.03	21.50	13.41	14.13
Plains	.09	.16	.74	2.38	1.99
Southwest	.05	.08	1.21	—	.94
Mountain	.80	2.34	3.47	1.44	2.79
Far West	—	.05	.14	.10	.71

SOURCE: *Mineral Resources, 1920*, Part II, folder inserted in back of book; *Mineral Resources, 1931*, Part II, pp. 382-83; *Minerals Yearbook, 1950*, p. 410.

Meanwhile the somewhat cheaper, though slower, open-hearth (Siemens-Martin) process had been introduced from Europe and, with improved linings, had shown itself suited to all grades and types of ore.[31] Its slowness, moreover, was soon recognized as an advantage over the Bessemer process since it facilitated much greater qualitative control over the final steel product. A second great advantage of the open-hearth is its ability to take scrap metal as part of its charge, a factor which told increasingly in its favor during the twentieth century. Finally the open-hearth is a much smaller operation than the Bessemer, and the surge of small plants towards the close of the century was mostly a consequence

[30]The core of Bessemer technique involved blowing air through the molten metal in the converter, thereby oxidizing part of the iron and most of the manganese, silicon, and carbon contents. Sulphur and phosphorus, however, were unaffected by the oxygen and adoption of the process was largely dependent on the availability of low phosphoric ores. The Thomas-Gilchrist basic lining absorbed most of the residual phosphorus in the converter and made possible the wider use of phosphoric ores. The first use of an improved magnesium limestone base in the place of the acid bottom came in 1884 but, according to C. D. King, the most important "single development in steel," came after 1889 when "the hot metal mixer came into general use (and) the Bessemer became firmly established on a large scale." *Ibid.*, p. 181.

[31]The Lakeside plant of the Otis Company in Cleveland is said to be the first establishment designed for the exclusive manufacture of open-hearth steel in the United States (1874) and it was here in 1886 that the first basic open-hearth operation was conducted with magnesite imported from Austria.

Table 78(b). Coal production, by region, 1870-1950

(short tons of bituminous, lignite, and anthracite coal)

Region	1870	1890	1910	1930	1950
United States	33,035,580	157,770,963	501,596,378	536,911,000	559,976,000
	100%	100%	100%	100%	100%
New England	—	—	—	—	—
Middle Atlantic	76.53	58.39	47.89	36.52	26.90
Great Lakes	17.01	19.12	19.95	17.40	20.35
Southeast	3.02	11.27	21.56	38.34	46.60
Plains	2.78	5.73	3.23	2.22	1.84
Southwest	—	.91	1.61	1.05	.61
Mountain	.18	3.67	4.97	4.01	3.53
Far West	.48	.91	.79	.43	.16
Unallocated	—	.01	—	.03	.01

SOURCE: *Mineral Resources, 1921*, Part II, Back Folder; *Mineral Resources, 1931*, Part II, p. 430; *Minerals Yearbook, 1951*, p. 312.

of the comparatively small capital involved. Not before 1908, however, did annual open-hearth output surpass the Bessemer but by the early 1950's; the Bessemer process had declined to about 3% of all steel output.

A third major process, the electro-metallurgical technique, was first introduced on a large scale in the United States during the winter of 1909-10 at the South works of Illinois Steel. World War I demonstrated the superiority of the electric technique over the crucible in meeting new demands for alloy-steel ingots and castings, and the increasing capacities of electric furnaces, in common with most others since that time, has brought their product for some purposes into competition with the open-hearth.[32]

The growth of an immense iron and steel making complex in the Northeast

[32]Bessemer production was surpassed in quantity by electro-metallurgical steel during World War II. Nevertheless, in the early 1950's, the open-hearth still contributed about 90% of all United States Steel production which passed 120,000,000 net tons in 1954; the electric furnaces made up only 7%, while Bessemer's remaining 3% has increasingly gone into dephosphorized steel which has been found to possess the good welding and free-machining qualities of original Bessemer. According to some industry sources the most important recent adaptation of Bessemer has been in the production of seamless pipe. For that matter, the enlarged market for all steel products during this century has been a consequence of improvements in rolling and finishing practices which make steel not only the primary metal for all heavy manufacture and construction but also for a wide variety of consumer goods formerly made of wood.

American Iron and Steel Institute, *Annual Statistical Report*, 1956, p. 9-11. Among purely manufacturing categories, iron and steel continued to be the principal consumer of capital during most of this century, although it was only fifth among all categories. After 1900 most new capital in iron and steel went into the conversion from Bessemer to open-hearth in order to take fuller advantage of Superior ores. After 1920 the continuous strip rolling mill producing thin standard sheets for the automobile industry became the largest capital-consuming innovation; T. C. Cochran, *op. cit.*, pp. 30, 45-6.

was clearly rooted historically in ready access to major deposits of coking coal and in the availability of local ore, as well as in access to the major markets of the nation. The bog iron of the Atlantic seaboard had been used up in the eighteenth century and the coal mines of eastern Virginia, whose development Hamilton had wanted to stimulate by an import duty, were abandoned soon thereafter. Before another century had passed, the iron resources of the Appalachian range had gone into decline and the anthracite coals of eastern Pennsylvania could be worked only at steadily increasing cost.[33] By the late 1890's a pronounced drift of the iron and steel complex into the Great Lakes states was evident, following the large-scale development of Minnesota iron, but the force of this attraction was diminished by the greater weight of fuel requirements in treating Mesabi ores.[34] Within the next two decades, however, advances in fuel technology reduced the bondage to fuel supplies, and various market factors had begun to exert a more decisive influence. The subsequent drift of steelmaking within the Northeast, therefore, reflects a locational force stemming from countrywide markets, notably the variety of demands for structural steel and the rise of the automobile industry. Nevertheless, the major iron and steel markets have coincided historically with fuel sites in general and coal sites in particular. When coal was the paramount locational factor, most other heavy industry and processing trades oriented to iron and steel converged on the coal sites. Because so many manufacturing activities were themselves heavy users of coal (either as coke or electricity, the classic locational pattern of industrial revolution was set in the Northeast.[35] In the absence of primary markets outside the more urban-

[33]P. Roberts, *The Anthracite Coal Industry* (New York: Macmillan Co., 1901), chap. I–IV and XI. The waste of coal fuel in the late 19th century was prodigious. The waste in mining was computed at from 40 to 60%; steam engines utilized about 8% of the coal they burned and not 10% of the fuel burned in power plants was converted into energy. Electricity generating stations were said to utilize less than 1% of the coal consumed; K. Coman, *The Industrial History of the United States* (New York: The Macmillan Co., new and revised edition, 1918), p. 385.

[34]The effect of Mesabi ore on the coke consumption rate at blast furnaces became clear during the first decade of this century. In 1902 when the proportion of Mesabi ore in burden was 43.8%, the coke rate (lbs. per net ton of iron) was 2,155; by 1907 when the proportion of Mesabi ore had risen to 68.7%, the coke rate was 2,362. This temporary reversal of declining fuel consumption was due primarily to an inability to control the channeling of gases and general irregular working; H. S. Brassert, "Modern American Blast Furnace Practice," in American Iron & Steel Institute, *Yearbook, 1914*, p. 40.

[35]W. Isard, "Some Locational Factors in the Iron and Steel Industry since the Early Nineteenth Century," *Journal of Political Economy*, Vol. LVI (1948), pp. 203-17. Since transfer costs are generally minimized by moving the heaviest goods the shortest distance, the mass of heavy industry can still be most efficiently located in terms of the energy costs of transporting primary fuels and ore. Under modern conditions, however, the availability of cheaper fuels for processing and fabrication by maritime transport or low-cost pipeline, and differentials in space-heating costs due to climatic variation, may make a geographically distant point more economical than one within a few miles of a coal field. The critical factor, therefore, is total energy cost and not simply distance; F. Cottrell, *Energy and Society; The Relation between Energy, Social Change, and Economic Development* (New York: McGraw-Hill Book Co., 1955), pp. 296-98. The enduring strength of the Northeastern industrial belt and the selective migration of manufactures to other regions since 1910, detailed earlier, provides documentation of this view.

industrialized areas, the external economies of local concentration combined with the immense capital commitment in existing facilities to impose profound restraints on any wholesale relocation of heavy industry.[36]

Differentiation in Lumber Production

For a long period after the Civil War, the almost universal material for construction and fabrication was not iron and steel, but wood. The homes, mills, vehicles, and much of the mechanical equipment and fuel with which the West was initially developed had their origins in the great forests. The period 1870-1910, therefore, witnessed the peak of lumber production and the beginnings and rapid ascent of pulp and paper manufacture; it also produced the first significant impact of the conservation movement as the public awoke to the danger of forest depletion.[37] Already before 1870, production centers of the lumber industry were shifting from the New England and Middle Atlantic regions into the Great Lakes states, where the commercial practices of the great lumber companies proved even more destructive than the broad ax of the pioneer. By the 1890's much of the best timber had been cut away from the upper Mississippi Valley (white pine) and heavy demands were being made upon the pine barrens of the Gulf states. The forests which had for long sheltered the sugar plantations and citrus groves were also being laid low. Before 1910 more than a fifth of the great Carolina forests had been removed and structural timbers were being shipped the width of the continent from Oregon to Maine. The nation's insatiable appetite for lumber, in fact, had compelled migration from the cutover sections of the Great Lakes and Plains regions into the Far West, where hitherto only timbers close to rivers had been heavily felled.[38]

[36]The steel capacities of other regions, even in the age of "foot-loose" industry, are severely limited by the size and character of local demand. Before World War II the only fully integrated steel plant in the Mountain or Far West regions was at Pueblo, Colorado. Those in Utah, California, and the Pacific N. W. were small- and medium-scale mills operating mostly on scrap. Western expansion, under government auspices, has raised the capacity of these two regions to nearly 6% of the national, but a recent study indicates that the existing market in those parts is closer to 10% of the national; C. L. White, "Is the West Making the Grade in the Steel Industry?" *Business Research Series No. 8* (Stanford: Stanford University Graduate School of Business, 1956).

[37]As late as 1940 woodpulp had probably not yet displaced fuel as the second largest consumer of the forests, although the peak of fuel-wood consumption was reached around 1890. Indeed, only after that date did lumber sawed exceed the lumber equivalent burned. In the entire eastern half of the country and the Plains, wood burned was probably a greater commodity drain than the entire product of the saw mills. Much of this wood, of course, was not suited to lumber use and the drain was in any case much reduced before the assault began upon the softwood forests of the interior and the Pacific N. W.; R. V. Reynolds and A. H. Pierson, "Fuel Wood Used in the United States, 1630-1930," U.S.D.A. *Circular No. 641.* (February 1942), pp. 14-15.

[38]U. S. National Conservation Commission, *Report* (Washington: Government Printing Office, 1909), Vol. 1, pp. 51-73; Vol. 2, pp. 179-269, 547-80, 498-511, and 748-58. The Commission reported that since 1900 the cost of white pine lumber had increased 53%, oak 54%, hemlock 56%, Douglas fir 63%, yellow pine 65%, and poplar 78%. About two-thirds of timber felled never reached the market.

In 1910, therefore, the forest economy of the United States was a nationwide organization with major sources of supply located far from the chief centers of consumption. It is testimony once more to the thrust of technology that the period of the lumber industry's greatest efflorescence was also the final stage in the transition to the age of iron and steel.

The "free land" that drew the covered wagons westward and helped build the transcontinental railroad was no less attractive to the lumberman than to the farmer or the dealer in railway real-estate. The forest story is an integral part of the epic of the public lands.[39] The westward movement of the lumbermen after the destruction of the Appalachian forest cover was initially not unlike the parallel migration of the farmers. Unlike mining development, the forests were not at that period dominated by a handful of great corporations but by "a profusion of partnerships and coalitions of partnerships amid a general environment of intense competition."[40] Nevertheless, before the close of the century the lumber industry had also responded to the institutional tendencies of the day, increasing its investment, expanding its facilities, and organizing against frantic competition. Regional and nationwide trade associations had emerged, sometimes in rivalry, as when Great Lakes groups tried to close the market to Southern pine, and at other times in co-operation, as in efforts to stabilize prices.[41] The main impulse to expansion and association had its roots in the problem of securing countrywide distribution from regional production centers and in the need to concentrate large holdings of virgin timber in a few hands in order to forestall competitive cutting. Important, if not spectacular, changes in technique slowly reinforced these market pressures.[42]

The development of techniques for making paper from woodpulp had pro-

---

[39]Of the four principal land acts passed during the 1870's, at least three were directly concerned with Western timberlands and met the needs of special interests operating there: the Timber Culture Act of 1873, the Timber and Stone Act of 1878, and the Timber Cutting Act of the same year. These measures, subject to flagrant abuse, remained in force until Cleveland's General Revision Act of 1891 which remedied some of the worst defects in public lands disposition and authorized the establishment of forest preserves, the first step in the national conservation movement; R. G. Lillard, *The Great Forest* (New York: Alfred A. Knopf, 1947), pp. 233-76; R. K. Winters, ed., *Fifty Years of Forestry in the U.S.A.* (Washington, D. C.; Society of American Foresters, 1950), pp. 1-29; R. F. Fries, *Empire in Pine: The Story of Lumbering in Wisconsin, 1830-1900* (Madison: State Historical Society of Wisconsin, 1951), pp. 161-203; W. A. Rowlands, "The Great Lakes Cutover Region," in M. Jensen, ed., *Regionalism in America*, pp. 331-46.

[40]F. W. Kohlmeyer, "Northern Pine Lumbermen: A Study in Origins and Migrations," *Journal of Economic History*, Vol. 16 (December, 1956), pp. 529-38.

[41]R. C. Bryant, *Lumber, Its Manufacture and Distribution* (2nd ed., New York: John Wiley and Sons, 1938), pp. 309-45; W. B. Greeley, *Forestry and Men* (Garden City, N. Y.: Doubleday and Co., 1951), pp. 30-63.

[42]P. L. Buttrick, *Forest Economics and Finance* (New York: John Wiley and Sons, Inc., 1943), pp. 217-18, lists the following among principal advances in logging and saw mill practice before World War I: Construction of railways deep into the woods permitted the cutting of timber formerly too remote from streams for river driving; this facilitated year-round logging and the movement of hardwoods not buoyant when green. Powered loaders and skidders cheapened and accelerated the removal of logs from forests to the mills. Within the mills, band-saws and other automatic machinery increased labor productivity.

found repercussions on the regional distribution of forest activities. The Tilghman experiments with effects of various acids on wood had commenced about 1867; sulphurous acid was found to dissolve the ligneous elements readily and to leave a residue of cellulose fibers. Improvements in this first sulphite process were carried out in Europe and incorporated into the first American pulping plants before 1880. A variety of other processes were perfected before the end of the century, the most significant of which were the sulphate (1884) and caustic soda methods. For most types of paper only the cellulose fibers can be employed but in the production of newsprint almost the entire fibrous matter can be used and hence a cheaper, purely mechanical, grinding process will suffice to convert wood into pulp, provided small quantities of sulphite pulp are added to give the paper body.[43] By no means all species of wood are adaptable for pulping, and for a long time only spruce and hemlock could be utilized. Small supplies of these species were available near some of the New England and New York paper mills which were already oriented to the existing source of materials (straw, rags, waste paper, and manila stock) readily obtainable near the industry's larger urban markets. But as late as 1910 the larger and apparently more viable paper mills were still locating in areas where pulpwood was either scarce or non-existent; by this time the most accessible forests where the desired species were still abundant were situated in Maine and Wisconsin.[44]

Exhaustion of the remaining pulpwood stands in the New England and Middle Atlantic states before World War I was accelerated by a brief revival of lumbering in these regions. The shift of lumbering into the Plains and western Great Lakes states three or four decades earlier had tended to raise the price of lumber in leading Eastern markets and, as a consequence of the construction boom after 1900, it became economical once more to start cutting in previously inaccessible reaches of the Eastern forests. This belated invasion, moreover, was facilitated by the recent introduction of compact and highly mobile saw mills. But from the standpoint of the pulp mills, this last spasm of lumbering proved an unmitigated calamity. Since the preferred white pine had already been cut out, the main weight of the new assault fell on the spruce and hemlock, leaving the pulp industry dependent for supplies on wood from abroad or from other more remote regions of the United States.[45] Paper users, especially the newsprint industry, immediately sought and obtained some reduction of tariffs; as a result, after 1913 the position of Eastern newsprint producers was further undermined by rising imports from Canada.[46]

[43]The quantity of fibrous material which needs to be separated from wood constituents varies with the end product sought. The U. S. Tariff Commission, *Report to the United States Senate on Wood Pulp and Pulpwood*, Report No. 126, 2nd Series (Washington: Government Printing Office, 1938), pp. 38-43, gives a clear account of pulping processes; also C. R. Hall, *op. cit.*, pp. 274-79.

[44]More than 50 of the 135 pulp mills in operation or under construction in 1882 had closed by 1899; H. Hunter, "Innovation, Competition, and Locational Changes in the Pulp and Paper Industry: 1880-1950," *Land Economics*, Vol. 31 (1955), pp. 317-18.

[45]*Ibid.*, pp. 318-19.

[46]J. A. Guthrie, *The Newsprint Paper Industry, An Economic Analysis* (Cambridge: Harvard University Press, 1941).

The force of foreign competition was felt even in the Great Lakes region, and the locus of new pulping activity shifted closer to its wood supply in the Pacific Northwest or the South. Meanwhile, surviving paper manufacturers on the Eastern seaboard could stay in business only by closing their newsprint and low-grade papermaking plants and concentrating their facilities on high-grade papers, such as book stock and special printing, writing, and tissue paper. After World War I it became more economical to ship the processed woodpulp rather than the raw pulpwood and the possibility of cheap water transport *via* the newly opened Panama Canal now gave the stranded paper industry of the North-east a further lease on life. Improvements in the sulphate process proved a special boom to makers of crude wrapping or "Kraft" papers in the South; owing to the belated adoption of improved forestry practices, producers here could henceforth compete favorably with their rivals in the Pacific Northwest. This heightening of interregional competition gradually forced the paper indus-try as a whole to move closer to the sources of pulp in the Southeast and Far West, while down to World War II at least, the more expensive high-grade papers maintained their hold in the older Northeast.[47]

Mass Production for National Markets

By the opening decade of the twentieth century the economy of the United States was effectively nationalized. Both resource and processing activities were slowly and selectively adjusting to the conditions of a nationwide market. The railroad network extended to every part of the continental territory and in some regions was supplemented by a somewhat dilapidated system of inland water-ways. Coastal shipping had recently witnessed a notable revival, and the early efforts of Standard Oil to prevent the growth of a system of oil pipelines in competition with their captive railroads had failed.[48] Already the promise of the automobile was stimulating interest in the long-neglected public highways

[47]By 1930 more than half the pulpwood used in Pennsylvania and New York was im-ported from Canada and Sweden and by 1940 the proportion of imported wood used in the paper states of the Lakes region, Michigan and Wisconsin, approximated one-quarter; H. Hunter, *loc. cit.,* pp. 322-23; J. A. Guthrie, *The Economics of Pulp and Paper* (Pullman, Wash: The State College of Washington Press, 1950), pp. 81, 143-64.

[48]G. R. Taylor and I. D. Neu, *The American Railroad Network, 1861-1890* (Cambridge: Harvard University Press, 1956); A. M. Johnson, *The Development of American Petroleum Pipelines: A Study in Private Enterprise and Public Policy, 1862-1906* (Ithaca, N. Y.: Cornell University Press for The American Historical Association, 1956); Inland Water-ways Commission, *Preliminary Report (Senate Document No. 325,* 60th Congress, 1st Session [Washington: Government Printing Office, 1908]), pp. 177-312; U. S. Commissioner of Corporations, *Transportation by Water in the United States: Report* (Washington: Government Printing Office, 1909), Vol. I, pp. 149-380 and Vol. II, pp. 249-80. The ex-tension of coastwise shipping regulations to Alaska, Hawaii, and the Philippines helped raise the Pacific registered tonnage 120%, 1897-1909. Total coastwise tonnage, including Lakes and Western river vessels, in 1909 was 6,500,000 or eight times the tonnage registered for ocean trade. Also, H. U. Faulkner, "The Decline of Laissez-Faire, 1897-1917" in *The Economic History of the United States* (New York: Rinehart and Co., 1951), Vol 7, pp. 220-48.

and would shortly result in a burst of construction in and between the major metropolitan centers. Of course, spatial frictions had not been eliminated; but all parts of the country were now accessible—at a price.

Institutional or "artificial" distances had acquired a greater economic significance than the actual physical distances they were designed to reflect. After 1887 the Interstate Commerce Commission had given legal sanction to railway-association rates and classifications which, in effect, had divided the country into four or five "rate territories". There was a so-called "Official Territory" that corresponded almost exactly with the greater Northeastern industrial belt; its boundaries ran along the Mississippi River in the west, then east along the Ohio and Potomac, and finally southeast to the Atlantic coast in Virginia. There was also a "Southern Territory," which included the states that comprise our Southeast except Virginia, Arkansas, and Louisiana, and a "Southwestern Territory" made up of Arkansas, Louisiana, Texas, and parts of New Mexico. The rest of the greater West was eventually divided into two further territories. Low rates for raw materials moving into the "Official Territory" and high rates for manufactured items produced outside it undoubtedly discouraged and retarded the diffusion of manufactures into outlying regions where they might have derived some cost advantage from proximity to their raw materials.[49] Undoubtedly, throughout this period, the "natural" and "artificial" costs of moving heavy freight were a formidable "imperfection" in the working of the American market system. But by 1910, increasing competition among the different transport media, together with more effective public regulation, was beginning to effect a greater equality of net per ton mile rates.[50]

The reduction of interregional freight differentials at this time paralleled a convergence in the levels of per capita personal income in the various regions. Differences in personal income were relatively greater before 1880 than at the end of World War I. While the rich mineral and forest resources of the Mountain and Far West regions helped to raise the personal income levels of their

[49]For a description of freight traffic movements by class of commodity originating on the lines of reporting railroads, see Industrial Commission, Vol. 19, *Final Report, op. cit.*, pp. 264-66. The consequences of discrimination were later described as follows: "For nearly three generations . . . the country has been accepting influences and conditions which have made a workshop region of one section . . . , with the other sections, as marked off by the present territorial rate boundaries, being largely in a position of contributors of raw materials and semifinished products to the industrialized region." J. H. Alldredge, *The Interterritorial Freight Rate Problem of the United States, House Document No. 264*, 75th Congress, 1st Session (Washington: Government Printing Office, 1937), p. 51.

[50]But as recently as 1938 it was estimated that, on average, shippers of classified goods in the Official Territory paid 75% less for the same railroad services than shippers in the Southwestern Territory, 71% less than those in the Western Trunkline Territory, and 35% less than shippers in the Southern Territory. Five years later these differentials had been still further reduced, but it was affirmed in a *Report on Interterritorial Freight Rates* that "territorial differences in the levels of first-class rates . . . are large, but the trend during the past 25 or 30 years has been towards reducing the spreads." *House Document No. 303*, 78th Congress, 1st Session, pp. 21 and 55-57. Also, *Regional Freight Rates: Barrier to National Productiveness, ibid., No. 137.* By no means all of these differentials, of course, can be attributed to "discriminations."

small populations far above the national average, the rapidly industrializing Middle Atlantic and Great Lakes regions had also achieved a substantial advance. For a period, only the war-devastated Southeast appeared unaffected by the surge of national income. But as population continued to pour into the regions of the newer West, per capita incomes everywhere settled closer to the national average. This tendency toward convergence did not, of course, obliterate sizable absolute differences, but it did bring about a situation where families in every section of the country were extending the range of goods and services they wanted and could afford to acquire. Even farm families, except in the South, were enjoying unprecedented prosperity and could expect much the same attention from manufacturers and distributors as their neighbors in the city. The United States had, in fact, become a vast national "free trade" market.[51]

Unlike the national markets of many smaller European countries, the American market was essentially a mass market. It demanded and obtained large quantities of cheap low-to-medium quality goods with comparatively little variation from one part of the country to another. Where products could be standardized, as was already evident in a few instances at the time of the Civil War, the logic of growth required that production be mechanized.[52] The essential condition for an economical system of mass production was its complement, a mass market; this condition and a number of other preconditions had already been met by 1910.[53] In volume, the production of durable goods for capital equipment rose at an average annual rate of 5% between 1901 and 1913 as against 2.6% for goods intended for human consumption, though in value terms the capital goods sector probably amounted to not more than 20% of total goods production even in the peak years. Significantly, this great surge in industrial production, which according to one index more than doubled over the years 1899-1919, "was due largely to the development of our mineral resources and to the increasing volume of fabricated goods into which raw mineral products enter."[54]

Hardly less significant for the shaping of the economy than the growth of mass production and marketing was the fact that most of the primary sources of materials—the mines, fields, and forests—were located within the same ter-

[51]G. B. Hotchkiss, *Milestones of Marketing* (New York: The Macmillan Co., 1938), p. 220.

[52]The shortage of skilled labor outside of the mechanical trades and the ability to import European products on increasingly favorable terms (subject to the tax of the tariff) meant that the relatively small American "quality" markets could be supplied by imports or by the small-scale operations conducted by immigrants steeped in the tradition of old-world craftsmanship.

[53]These preconditions include the capacity for making very fine heavy-duty machine tools (which had recently been enhanced by the perfection of a new high-speed carbon steel during the years 1900-06 by F. W. Taylor and J. M. White), as well as the ability to mobilize adequate capital through a specialized capital market over and beyond the usual profits plowed back into expansion.

[54]F. C. Mills, *Economic Tendencies in the United States* (New York: National Bureau of Economic Research, 1932), pp. 13, 21-23. According to Mills the average annual rate of increase in the physical volume of non-durable goods (raw and processed) production was 2.5% over the years 1901-13, that of semidurable (mostly textile and leather) production

ritorial-political boundaries. Unlike the manufacturing nations of Europe, the economy of the United States was for most material and market purposes "self-sufficient." Whereas England and Germany must bring increasingly large volumes of materials from abroad, "the industrial progress of the United States was the result of carrying labor to raw materials."[55] Though abundant, these materials were irregularly distributed throughout the continental territory and hence the comparatively unskilled, if highly mechanized, labor force had to be able and willing to move on to primitive conditions of successive frontiers. The existence of these unused resources did not, however, guarantee industrial progress. Only by harnessing the power of machines and by deploying capital in corporate array could the outlying regions be organized to render up their growth-sustaining material to the corpus of national economy. This involved a restructuring of the labor force among extractive, processing, and servicing activities, and the redistribution of these activities among regions across the continental territory. This marks the real distinction between the earlier period of loose-knit economic sectionalism and the later period of integrated national economy. Whereas the pioneer in the ante-bellum West was on the frontier of an essentially mercantile-colonial economy, his children and grandchildren, whether farmers, miners, loggers, or urban workers, were increasingly full participants in the industrialization of the entire nation. It was the dynamic interplay of technology on the natural resources of both the more and the less developed regions, joined with human ingenuity and industrial organization, that in the period 1870-1910 brought about a continental system of exchange and, with it, the most affluent level of living in recorded history.

2.6%, and that of durable goods production 4.6%. The industrial production index referred to is that of Day and Thomas which stood at 100 in 1899, 159 in 1909, and 214 in 1919; E. E. Day and W. Thomas, *The Growth of Manufactures, 1899-1923 (Census Monographs VII, 1928)*, Washington, D. C.: Government Printing Office, pp. 32-4.

[55]V. S. Clark, *History of Manufactures in the United States* (3 Vols., New York: McGraw-Hill Book Co., 1929), Vol. II, p. 2. By 1900 American per capita consumption of manufactured goods was almost half as much again as that of Britain and double that of Germany and France; S. Rezneck, "Mass Production since the War between the States," in H. F. Williamson, ed., *The Growth of American Economy* (New York: Prentice-Hall, Inc., 1946), p. 498.

15 / Regional adjustments within the national economy, 1910-1950:

(1) POPULATION SHIFTS

In the first half of the nineteenth century the urban-industrial form of economic development was a highly localized phenomenon grounded in the original patterns of settlement and local advantage obtained under the technology-resource potentials of the time. During the second half of the century urban-industrialization became generalized as resource depletion in the more advanced areas, the rapid progress of technology, and the growth and migration of population necessitated both the diversification and extension of the economy's material base. By the first decade of the twentieth century, some narrowing of the differentials among regions in industrial structure and in levels of living was apparent in spite of different conditions and different stages of development. In this sense, the American economy was effectively nationalized. Subsequent growth and adjustment turned on further refinement in the system of *interdependence* among the regions for the greater benefit of the whole.

By 1910 the dominant regional patterns with which we are today familiar had already taken shape. Thus, for example, in spite of many technical advances in the important light-metals and alloy-steel industries and shifts in the composition of the industrial fuel supply, manufacturing is still almost as much the specialized concern of the Northeastern industrial belt as it was in 1910. Yet the apparent fixity of the twentieth century regional structure can be overstated. It is no small matter that petroleum reginning and related industries, certain phases of the lumber products industry, and more recently the aircraft and electronics industries have taken root in parts of the Southeast, Southwest, and Far West regions rather than in the Northeast. Nor can the fact be lightly dismissed that, within the Northeastern industrial belt itself, the bulk of growth in the twentieth century has taken place in the Great Lakes region rather than in the Middle Atlantic or New England states. There has, moreover, been some general diffusion in manufacturing activity in close association with movements of population. But far more striking than these changes have been shifts in resource activity and concomitant regional growth.

Developments in the twentieth century, it is clear, have been characterized far less by the gross, nation-building sweeps of movement than those of the previous century. Throughout the nation, regional economies have become more complex, and significant internal (intraregional) changes as well as powerful exogenous changes have to be reckoned with. Within the national framework, for example, growth has been increasingly affected by the drawing force of regional markets and changing concentrations of populations within metropolitan areas.

Because of the growing complexity and refinements of the sub-national economy, a full understanding of regional economic developments of the recent past calls for analysis in substantial detail. This is undertaken in Parts IV and V of this book. Here, we shall sketch only in broad outline the changes in the regional structure of the U. S. economy after 1910 as revealed by the same key indices that we have employed in describing the period 1870-1910, that is, regional changes in population, productive activities, and income.

Growth and Shift in Population, 1910-1950

Between 1910 and 1950 the rate of population growth in the United States slackened: in the 40-year period from 1870 to 1910, population numbers had risen by more than 130%; in the ensuing 40-year period they rose by less than 64%.

Table 79. Percentage increases in population by census decades, by region, 1910-1950

Region	1910-20	1920-30	1930-40	1940-50	1910-50
United States	14.9	16.1	7.2	14.5	63.8
New England	12.9	10.3	3.3	10.4	42.1
Middle Atlantic	*15.3*	*17.4*	5.8	11.0	59.0
Great Lakes	*17.7*	*17.8*	5.3	14.2	*66.6*
Southeast	10.5	12.2	*10.6*	12.0	53.5
Plains	7.8	6.0	1.7	4.0	20.8
Southwest	*21.4*	*22.9*	7.7	*16.3*	*86.9*
Mountain	*26.9*	7.3	*9.3*	*15.8*	*72.5*
Far West	*32.1*	*46.8*	*18.8*	*48.8*	*242.7*

Figures in italics are above the national average.

SOURCE: 17th U. S. Census 1950, see *supra*, Table 1, note.

Regional populations generally reflected the broad inclinations of the national movements: prosperity, depression, and war are mirrored in the decennial fluctuations of population growth. After World War I, however, the trend in most regions was in closer conformity with the national trend than it had been before 1910, and only the Far Western states bordering the Pacific experienced rapid growth comparable with that in the earlier period (Table 79). By 1930 the Southwest had already fallen into closer step with countrywide development, while the surge of population into the Mountain region had ended a decade before. Among Western regions, however, only the Plains failed to maintain the national rate of growth; it continued in a phase of relative decline which had set in after 1890. By 1930, in fact, Minnesota, Nebraska, and Kansas (like Iowa and Missouri earlier in the century) had fewer in-migrants than out-migrants, and between 1930 and 1940 the western Plains states experienced an absolute decrease in numbers.

The urban-industrial regions of the Northeast reveal some significant contrasts with the earlier period. New England fails to maintain the national rate of population growth but, for a while, the Middle Atlantic and Great Lakes regions are the beneficiaries of an "eastward" movement.[1] The Middle Atlantic region had, to be sure, been growing at a faster rate than the nation since 1890, but after 1910 the Great Lakes region had a comparable rise; both regions con-

Table 80. Density of population, by region, 1910, 1930, and 1950

(population per square mile of land area)

Region	Area*	1910	1930	1950
United States	2,974,726 sq. mi.	30.9	41.3	50.7
New England	(2.12)	*103.7*	*129.3*	*147.5*
Middle Atlantic	(3.78)	*188.1*	*254.5*	*299.1*
Great Lakes	(8.23)	*74.5*	*103.3*	*124.1*
Southeast	(17.95)	*41.2*	*51.1*	*63.3*
Plains	(17.17)	22.8	26.0	27.5
Southwest	(19.08)	10.7	16.0	20.0
Mountain	(17.23)	3.9	5.4	6.8
Far West	(14.44)	9.9	19.3	34.1

Figures in italics are above the national average.
*Figures in parentheses show proportion of total U. S. land area 1950.

SOURCE: *Statistical Abstract of the United States*, 1954, Table 4, p. 10; 17th U. S. Census, 1950; see *supra*, Table 1, note.

tinued in the ascendent until the onset of depression in 1930. Only after the outbreak of World War II was there any notable recovery in the general westward movement, and it was somewhat more selectively directed now towards parts of the Far West, Southwest, and southern Mountain states. Throughout the years between 1870 and 1930 the Southeast lost relatively, but between 1930 and

[1] C. Goodrich, et al., *Migration and Economic Opportunity* (Philadelphia: University of Pennsylvania Press, 1936), pp. 675-83; George Soule, "Prosperity Decade; From War to Depression, 1917-29" in *The Economic History of the United States* (New York: Rinehart and Co., 1947), Vol. 8, pp. 208-15.

1940 the situation was reversed. In that decade its population grew faster than that of the nation and relatively faster than that of any other region except the Far West. The effect of these disparate rates of growth on regional densities of population are summarized in Table 80.

The effect of the differential rates of growth on regional shares of national population after 1910 is clearly much slighter than in the years between 1870 and 1910 (Table 81). The combined share of the four Eastern regions (New England, Middle Atlantic, Great Lakes, and Southeast) in 1870 was 85.5%; in 1910 it was 73.8% and by 1950 it had declined only to 71.1%. New England, of course, has continued in slow relative decline over the whole of the period

Table 81. Regional distribution of U. S. population, 1910-1950

(per cent of total)

Region	1910	1920	1930	1940	1950
United States	91,972,266	105,710,620	122,775,046	131,669,275	150,697,361
	100%	100%	100%	100%	100%
New England	7.1	7.0	6.7	6.4	6.2
Middle Atlantic	23.0	23.1	23.3	23.0	22.3
Great Lakes	19.8	20.3	20.6	20.2	20.2
Southeast	23.9	23.0	22.2	22.9	22.4
Plains	12.7	11.9	10.8	10.3	9.3
Southwest	6.6	7.0	7.4	7.4	7.6
Mountain	2.2	2.4	2.2	2.3	2.3
Far West	4.7	5.3	6.8	7.5	9.7

SOURCE: 17th U. S. Census, 1950, see *supra*, Table 1, note.

Table 82. Principal net shifts in population among states, 1910-1950

Percentage net upward shift		Percentage net downward shift	
California	44.72	Pennsylvania	13.78
Michigan	11.81	Missouri	9.64
Florida	10.28	Iowa	6.85
Texas	8.87	Virginia	6.40
New Jersey	4.53	Kansas	5.78
Washington	3.39	Georgia	5.55
Maryland-D. C.	3.21	Massachusetts	5.52
N. Carolina	2.98	Kentucky	5.40
Oregon	2.80	Mississippi	5.12
Arizona	2.77	Arkansas	4.48

SOURCE: 17th U. S. Census 1950, see *supra*, Table 1, note.

since 1870, but the relative stability of the other two Northeastern regions, since 1890 at least, is quite remarkable. Even the Southeast has lost relatively little in respect of its population share since 1910.

The growth of the West is merely the reverse of the decline in the East, but not all regions shared equally in this growth. The Plains region has been in relative decline since the 1890's, and the Mountain region has barely held its own since 1920. The Southwest, on the other hand, raised its share of total population 13% between 1910 and 1950, and the Far West by a spectacular 106%.

Table 82 and Figure 33 show the results of our shift analysis of net upward and downward movement across state lines (the extent to which states exceed or fall short of the percentage national growth of population) between 1910 and 1950. The most startling development of this period took place in California, which accounted for 44% of the total net upward shift. Both Washington and Oregon, among Far Western states, also registered considerable relative growth.

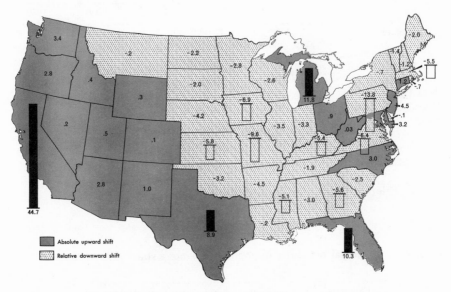

Figure 33. Net Shift in Total Population, 1910-50.

State figures represent % of total net shift. Total net shift as % of incremental change: 25.5. Total net shift as % of 1910 population: 16.3.

In the Southwest, growth after 1910 was chiefly confined to Texas, although Arizona also contributed sizably to the region's advance. Oklahoma, however, experienced a relative net downward shift of more than 3%, in contrast to its relative growth in years before 1910. All of the Plains states contributed to the total net downward shift; Missouri, Iowa, Kansas, and Nebraska were among the greatest net losers of population, with a combined relative net downward shift of 26%.

In the eastern half of the nation, eight states increased relative to the national average, almost offsetting the total relative downward shift of the remaining states. In the Great Lakes region, Michigan's relative net influx of almost 12% compensated for relative declines in Illinois, Indiana, and Wisconsin; as a result, this region held its own over-all. Maryland and New Jersey contributed combined upward shifts of more than 6% to the Middle Atlantic region but failed to offset the marked net downward shifts in Pennsylvania; New York, however, almost held its own. Among the New England states, Connecticut's 1.21% of net upward shift was the only symptom of relative growth; other states declined quite heavily; Massachusetts registered a net downward shift of more than 5%. Three states in the Southeast—Florida, North Carolina, and West Virginia—had relative net upward shifts, but only the first two did much to counter the effect of sizable downward shifts from the balance of the region.

One further feature of demographic changes which deserves special attention is the continued growth of cities. Table 83 shows the urban proportions of regional population in 1910 and in 1950. Every region except New England and the Middle Atlantic states experienced considerable urbanization after 1910

Table 83. Urban population as percentage of total population, by region, 1910 and 1950

Region	1910	1950*
United States	45.7	59.0
New England	*73.3*	*74.3*
Middle Atlantic	*70.2*	*74.0*
Great Lakes	*52.7*	*65.7*
Southeast	19.4	38.0
Plains	33.2	49.9
Southwest	22.5	55.5
Mountain	40.7	51.8
Far West	*56.0*	*62.7*

Figures in italics are above the national average.
*Old Census definition.

SOURCE: 17th U. S. Census, 1950, see *supra*, Table 4, note.

(Table 84), but only in the Southwest and Southeast was the over-all increase greater in the later period than in the earlier one.[2] Since 1920, however, not only has the rate of urbanization declined in many parts of the country, but the character of urban settlement has changed. Population generally has become more urban, but it has been shifting out from the congested older city centers

[2]Nevertheless the trend had everywhere gone so far by 1950 that the Census Bureau's definition of "urban" was found to understate the true size of city populations and a new definition was introduced.

into the suburbs and metropolitan areas around. If country people continued to drift in towards the major centers of population, city people themselves have spread out into the perimeters of urban areas or to small satellite communities in their vicinity.[3] The most rapidly growing metropolitan areas since 1910 have been in the west; the lowest rates of growth in the Northeast. According to Amos Hawley's findings, metropolitan areas in the West have had the most widely scattered urban population in every census year since 1910, and deconcentration has been endemic there since the beginning of this century. Deconcentration from city centers into surrounding areas did not become the dominant trend until after 1920 in the Northeast and after 1930 in the Southeast.[4]

As of 1950, the Far West had moved into the fourth position in the nation with regard to proportion of total U. S. urban population, while the limited population growth of New England had reduced this region to sixth place as compared to third place in 1910 (Table 85).

The results of applying "shift" analysis to urban population growth among the states, 1910-50, are summarized in Table 86 (see also Figure 34). Once more California is the leading contributor of new urban growth, accounting for more than 30% of the entire upward shift in the years since 1910. New upward shifts in Texas, Michigan, and Florida also parallel the net upward movements

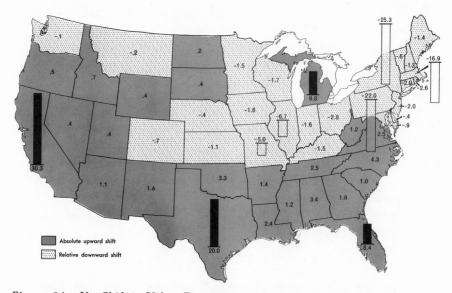

Figure 34. Net Shift in Urban Population, 1910-50.

State figures represent % of total net shift. Total net shift as % of incremental change: 28.1. Total net shift as % of 1910 urban population: 31.3.

Source: Table 4, note.

[3]A. H. Hawley, *The Changing Shape of Metropolitan America: Deconcentration Since 1920* (Glencoe, Ill.: Free Press, 1956), pp. 12-23.
[4]*Ibid.*, pp. 146-60.

Table 84. Decennial rates of increase of urban population, by regions, 1910-1950

Region	1910-20	1920-30	1930-40	1940-50
United States	29.0	27.3	7.9	19.5
New England	17.0	12.3	1.7	7.8
Middle Atlantic	22.7	20.7	4.8	8.0
Great Lakes	*35.7*	*28.7*	3.9	14.5
Southeast	*36.0*	*39.3*	*18.6*	*33.5*
Plains	22.2	17.6	7.9	17.1
Southwest	*63.6*	*55.0*	*19.4*	*52.3*
Mountain	23.8	14.7	*18.1*	*31.0*
Far West	*45.1*	*60.3*	*14.9*	*43.6*

Figures in italics are above the national average.

Source: 17th U. S. Census, 1950, see *supra*, Table 4, note.

Table 85. Rank order of regions by rate of increase in urban population, 1900–1910 and 1940–1950, and regional proportions of U. S. urban population, 1910 and 1950

Region	1900-10 % rate	1910 proportion	1940-50 % rate	1950 proportion
(1) Southwest	118.3	3.3 (7)	52.3 (1)	7.1 (7)
(2) Far West	112.1	5.7 (6)	43.6 (2)	10.3 (4)
(3) Mountain	68.6	2.0 (8)	31.0 (4)	2.0 (8)
(4) Southeast	48.3	10.2 (4)	33.5 (3)	14.4 (3)
(5) Middle Atlantic	34.6	35.3 (1)	8.0 (7)	28.0 (1)
(6) Great Lakes	33.2	22.9 (2)	14.5 (6)	22.5 (2)
(7) Plains	31.3	9.2 (5)	17.1 (5)	7.9 (5)
(8) New England	25.3	11.4 (3)	7.8 (8)	7.8 (6)

Rank order in parentheses.

Source: 17th U. S. Census, 1950, see *supra*, Table 4, note.

of all population (see Table 82), though urbanization is proceeding faster in Texas than in either of the two other states. The growth of Detroit and other urban areas in southern Michigan has enabled that state to become the most rapidly urbanizing area east of the Mississippi. Another important development since 1910 is the sharp increase in urbanization in many parts of the Southeast, a region of relatively declining population. Altogether *six* Southeastern states number among the ten most urbanizing states in the nation, 1910-50, whereas only *two* appear in the list of ten achieving greatest relative upward shifts in all

Table 86. Principal net shifts in urban population among states, 1910-1950

Percentage net upward shift		Percentage net downward shift	
California	30.31	New York	25.30
Texas	19.95	Pennsylvania	22.01
Michigan	9.79	Massachusetts	16.87
Florida	8.38	Illinois	6.70
N. Carolina	4.28	Missouri	5.02
Alabama	3.37	Ohio	2.81
Oklahoma	3.28	Rhode Island	2.62
Tennessee	2.51	Connecticut	2.00
Virginia	2.48	New Jersey	1.95
Louisiana	2.37	Wisconsin	1.67

SOURCE: 17th U. S. Census, 1950, see *supra*, Table 4, note.

population.[5] (See Table 82.) Over the entire 80-year period since 1870, the rate of relative urban decline has been greatest in most highly urbanized parts of the country—in the Middle Atlantic and New England and, after 1910, in the Great Lakes region (except Michigan) and some of the Plains states. It is to be expected that highly urbanized states like New York, Pennsylvania, and Massachusetts, which have long histories of urban-industrial concentration, cannot maintain the same percentage rate of city growth as in former times.

We have already noted that, from the standpoint of size distribution, urban-industrial concentration in the more developed regions assumes the pattern of "urban hierarchy." By 1910, the New England, Middle Atlantic, and Great Lakes regions had developed veritable pyramids of cities, ranging upward from a broad base of small centers with populations of from 50,000 to 100,000 to an apex of large metropolitan centers with three-quarters of a million or more inhabitants. By 1950 the metropolitan pattern of urban hierarchy had become even more wide-spread across the country, extending, though in truncated form, into the more accessible populated parts of the Southeast and Mountain regions (see Table 87). Eleven cities had populations exceeding three-quarters of a million in 1950, and every region but the Mountain region had at least one center with a half-million or more inhabitants.

By 1950 almost half of the nation's growing number of standard metropolitan areas had begun to merge into some eighteen larger "urban-regions," having a total population in excess of 60,000,000. Many cities and their surrounding satellite areas, formerly demarcated on the map into separate metropolitan areas, now tended to overlap in vast complexes of homes, factories, and commerce.[6]

[5] No Southeastern state appears in the list of ten experiencing greatest relative downward shifts in urban population, whereas *five* are listed among the ten registering greatest relative downward shifts in *all* population after 1910 (Table 82). See R. B. Vance and N. J. Demareth, *The Urban South* (Chapel Hill: University of North Carolina Press, 1954), pp. 6-107.

[6] The relaxation of urban concentration since 1910 is chiefly attributable to the centrifugal forces of automobile transportation and cheap transmission of electric power.

Table 87. Regional distribution of cities in the United States with 50,000 or more inhabitants, by size group, 1950

(000's population)

Region	50-100	100-250	250-500	500-1,000	1,000+
New England	17	11	0	1	0
Middle Atlantic	23	13	3	4	2
Great Lakes	31	10	4	3	2
Southeast	23	15	4	1	0
Plains	9	4	3	2	0
Southwest	10	6	3	1	0
Mountain	2	1	1	0	0
Far West	11	5	5	1	1

SOURCE: *Statistical Abstract of the United States, 1955,* Table 14, pp. 22-23.

Six of the eighteen urban-regions each contained more than three million inhabitants and two others already exceeded one million. Of these eight giant conurbations, five were located in the Northeast and three on the Pacific Coast. A single urban-region on the Atlantic coast stretched southward from Haverhill, Massachusetts, to the far tip of Fairfax County, Virginia, in an almost unbroken succession of cities, towns, and suburbs linked together by expressways and turnpikes. In 1950 it had a population of 27,500,000, and an estimate for 1957 credited it with almost 32,000,000 inhabitants.[7] Only five of the eighteen great urban-regions had developed in regions other than the Northeast and Far West: two in North Carolina, two in Texas, and one in Missouri (which, in many respects, was merely the westernmost extremity of the Northeastern industrial belt). But there were 65 standard metropolitan areas outside the Northeast and Far West: 36 were located in the Southeast, 13 in the Southwest, 12 in the Plains, and 4 in the Mountain region.

Clearly, the growth of metropolitan areas was the characteristic pattern of urban settlement in all parts of the United States at the mid-century and, in the more industrialized sections, metropolitan areas were already merging into urban-regions. In 1950 the urban-regions might embrace only 45% of the nation's standard metropolitan areas, but more significant, they already contained 71% of all metropolitan population. Such were the main demographic patterns exhibited in the United States at the close of our period. The westward movement of population was now confined largely to the Far West and selected localities in the Southwest. The great agricultural heartland of the interior was losing population relatively both to the Far West and to the urban-regions of the Northeast. Rural population generally was still declining as people moved toward the city, but the city itself was rapidly extending its boundaries out into the surrounding countryside. In the more developed regions, the Northeast and the Far West, the cities were beginning to assimilate one another.

[7]*New York Times,* January 27, 1957, pp. 1 and 72.

The growth of urban-regions also had important implications for the character of the American market. The same forces of technology and organization that created these vast conurbations have also been directed towards meeting the consumption demands of the increasingly urbanized population. The pattern of these demands became set during the prosperous twenties, when urban consumers changed the disposition of their expenditures in the direction of the new mass-produced durable goods, processed foods, and services. While there have been fluctuations in consumer outlays for durables, non-durables, and services, the broad proportions of each have not changed much since the late twenties. As a consequence, regional divergences in patterns of personal consumption at given levels of income have also been reduced. Such differences as do endure, between urban and rural consumers or between rural-farm populations in the South and in other parts of the country, for example, are less than they were even a quarter of a century ago.[8] It goes without saying, moreover, that the construction and servicing of urbanized communities during the present century has provided a major impetus to economic growth regionally and nationally. Between 1900 and 1930 the investment in urban power and light installations alone was as large as that of the previous century in railroads. But the strategic invention at the heart of the modern metropolitan complex was the automobile. The upsurge of automobile production betweeen 1914 and 1929 directly stimulated the output of oil, steel, rubber, glass, lacquers, and many other items. Indirectly, the automobile was responsible for the massive investment in highways, bridges, service stations, motels, and for the enormous expansion of suburbs.[9] It was the style of life emerging in these urbanized regions during the second quarter of this century that, on the demand side at least, was shaping the character of productive activities in the nation as a whole.[10]

---

[8] U. S. Department of Commerce, *Historical and Descriptive Supplement to Economic Indicators, 1955* (Washington: Government Printing Office, 1955), pp. 10-11; also M. T. Copeland, "Marketing," *Recent Economic Changes in the United States* (New York: McGraw-Hill Book Co., 1929), Vol I, pp. 321-424. On the equalization of per capita disposable incomes among the states, see C. F. Schwarz and R. E. Graham, Jr., *Personal Income by States since 1929*, a supplement to the Survey of Current Business, Office of Business Economics, U. S. Department of Commerce (Washington: Government Printing Office, 1956), Table XV, p. 48.

[9] "No one," writes Thomas C. Cochran, "can reliably estimate the vast size of capital investment in reshaping society to fit the automobile." The direct and indirect capital investment involved "was probably the major factor in the boom of the 1920's." *The American Business System: A Historical Perspective, 1900-1955* (Cambridge, Mass.: Harvard University Press, 1957), pp. 35-45.

[10] The 1954 Census of Business showed that the four superior per capita income regions had more than 68% of wholesale trade receipts and almost 64% of retail trade receipts. By the early 1950's regional shares of national population coincided almost exactly with shares of total receipts from retail trade. In six of the eight regions the correspondence was within 2 percentage points. The two exceptions were the Southeast and the Far West, the regions of lowest and highest per capita personal incomes respectively. The Southeast's share of population was 22.4%, its share of retail trade receipts only 16.6%; the Far West's share of population was only 9.7%, but its share of retail trade receipts was 12.2%. Wholesaling, of course, had a somewhat lower association with population than retailing.

16 / Regional adjustments within the national economy, 1910-1950:

(2) SHIFTS IN PRODUCTIVE ACTIVITIES

The main trends in employment structure that were evident before 1910 continued unchanged well into the second quarter of the present century. Resource activities (agriculture, mining, fisheries, forestry and logging) absorbed a progressively smaller share of the working population (Table 88). The manufacturing sector continued to grow through part of the period, but before 1950 its share in total employment, like that of the resource sector, shows relative decline. Service activities, however, grew rapidly throughout the 1910-1950 period.

Character of the Labor Force

In absolute numbers, the labor force grew from some 38 million in 1910 to more than 60 million in 1950. A striking development of these years is the increase in the number of women regularly employed. In 1950 there were some 16½ million women in the labor force, as compared with 5,000,000 in 1910. Almost 27% of all females 10 years old and over were gainfully employed in 1950; two out of five of these workers were married women. Children, on the other hand, were a much smaller proportion of the labor force at the midcentury than in the decade after 1900. Before 1910 some 20% of all children between the ages of 10 and 15 in the United States were gainfully employed, but by 1930 the proportion had already fallen to less than 6%. The percentage of older workers has also fallen; in 1900 almost 40% of all persons 65 years old and over were gainfully employed, but in 1950 the proportion was less than 25%.[1]

[1]Lee, Miller, Brainerd, and Easterlin, *Population Redistribution and Economic Growth, United States, 1870-1950* (Philadelphia: American Philosophical Society, 1957), pp. 598-99. In 1950 slightly higher proportions of females 10 years old and over were employed in the textile states of New England and the Southeast than in the rest of the country; Rhode Island with 33% was the highest; the lowest was West Virginia with only 17.7%. Opportunities for female employment created by the offices of the Federal Government can be seen in the District of Columbia, where the proportion reached as high as 46%.

Table 88. U. S. labor force, distribution by major industry group, 1910, 1930, and 1950

Year	Labor force	% Resource	% Manufactures	% Services
1910	38,167,336	35.62	27.92	36.46
1930	48,829,920	23.97	28.90	47.13
1950	60,200,847	13.59	23.92	62.49

SOURCE: Appendix Tables A1–A7.

Economic opportunities for Negroes after 1910 accelerated migration out of both the rural and the urban Southeast, mainly into the cities of the Middle Atlantic and Great Lakes regions. Over the decade 1910-1920 Negro migration to the Northeast and West showed a net gain for these regions of 334,000.[2] At the beginning of the century more than 86% of all gainfully occupied Negroes were employed in agriculture or personal and domestic service. By 1920, that proportion had fallen to 67%, and almost one-third of all working Negroes were engaged in manufactures, trade, and transportation, though mostly in the lower-paid jobs requiring little skill.[3] Even more substantial opportunities for Negro workers opened up in the urban-industrial centers of the Northeast and Far West in the decade after 1940.

The growth of opportunities for both women and Negroes during and after World War I undoubtedly reflected not only the rise of service industries but also the decline in immigration from Europe, which had contributed so much to the labor force in prewar years. The Census of 1910 showed that the proportion of the foreign born in the total population was about 14%, whereas in the labor force it was 20%. Immigrants comprised about 45% of the labor force in mining, 36% in manufactures, and 25% in the transportation industries in 1910. About 70% of all garment workers were foreign born, as were over half of all workers in the iron and steel mills, oil refineries, slaughtering and meat-packing plants, furniture factories, leather tanneries, and textile mills. In the important transportation industries half the longshoremen and laborers on the electric and steam railroads were foreign born.[4] About half of the gainfully employed foreign-born women in 1910 were engaged in personal and domestic service and about one-fourth in manufactures.

[2] U. S. Department of Commerce, Bureau of the Census, *14th Census of the United States, 1920: Population,* Vol. II (Washington: Government Printing Office, 1922), Table 9, p. 616.

[3] L. V. Kennedy, *The Negro Peasant Turns Cityward* (New York: Columbia University Press, 1930), pp. 32-33; E. J. Scott, *Negro Migration During the War* (New York: Oxford University Press, 1920), pp. 13-18; L. J. Greene and C. G. Woodson, *The Negro Wage Earner* (Washington, D. C.: The Association for the Study of Negro Life and History, Inc., 1930), pp. 339-44.

[4] W. M. Leiserson, *Adjusting Immigrant and Industry* (New York: Harper and Brothers, 1924), pp. 7-14; J. Jenks and W. J. Lauck, *The Immigration Problem* (New York: Funk and Wagnalls Co., 1922), pp. 148-52.

The majority of these immigrants and their children lived in urban-industrial centers; 71% of the entire foreign white stock made up almost half—48%—of the nation's urban population. In 1920 immigrants comprised over 25% of the total population in New England, 22% in the Middle Atlantic region, and 15% in the Great Lakes region. Together with their children (foreign white stock) they made up 61%, 54%, and 42%, respectively, of the populations in these three regions. In the Far West 20% of the population was foreign born and 44% of foreign white stock. The comparable figures for the Great Lakes region were 15% and 42% and for the Mountain region 14% and 36%. In the Plains region only 11% of the population were of foreign birth, but 37% were of foreign white stock, and these were more concentrated in rural areas than the

Table 89. Rank order of states with greatest relative concentration of foreign born white and of foreign white stock, 1920 and 1950

(proportion in the white population of the U. S. = 100)

Foreign born				Foreign white stock			
1920		1950		1920		1950	
R. I.	202	N. Y.	239	N. D.	196	R. I.	202
Mass.	196	Mass.	206	Minn.	186	Conn.	195
Conn.	192	Conn.	203	Wis.	176	Mass.	193
N. Y.	189	R. I.	194	R. I.	174	N. D.	181
Ariz.	185	N. J.	186	Mass.	164	N. Y.	177
N. J.	168	N. H.	145	Conn.	164	N. J.	175
Nev.	145	Mich.	135	S. D.	154	Minn.	157
Calif.	144	Calif.	132	N. Y.	153	N. H.	144
N. H.	143	Ill.	129	N. J.	149	Wis.	142
N. D.	142	Wash.	110	Mich.	140	Ill.	135

SOURCE: 17th U. S. Census, 1950, Vol. IV, *Special Reports*, Pt. 3, Chap. A., Tables 13 and 12; E. P. Hutchinson, *Immigrants and Their Children, 1850-1950* (New York: John Wiley and Sons, 1956), p. 29.

foreign stock in any other part of the country. The Southeast and Southwest had been least affected by the flood of European immigration, but proximity to the Mexican border had raised the Southwest's proportion of foreign white stock to more than 11%. In 1920, in fact, Arizona had the highest relative concentration of foreign-born residents outside the Middle Atlantic and New England states.[5]

Between 1920 and 1950 the proportion of foreign born in the total population fell from 14% to 7.5% and the proportion of foreign white stock from 24% to 14.4%. Table 89 shows the concentration of these two groups relative to total

[5] N. Carpenter, *Immigrants and Their Children, 1920*, Census Monographs VII (Washington: Government Printing Office, 1927), pp. 308-9; E. P. Hutchinson, *Immigrants and Their Children, 1850-1950* (New York: John Wiley and Sons, 1956), pp. 22-62.

white population in various states during this period. The foreign born are chiefly concentrated in the New England and Middle Atlantic states in both 1920 and 1950 and to a lesser extent in the Far West.

The situation on the foreign white stock is somewhat different. In 1920 the highest relative concentration of immigrants and their native-born children was in the Plains states of North Dakota and Minnesota. By 1950 the relative concentration of foreign white stock is understandably highest in New England, where most foreign-born parents had concentrated in the twenties. Meanwhile the Middle Atlantic states of New York and New Jersey have tended to achieve greater concentrations than the Plains states, and the lowest concentrations among leading states are in Wisconsin and Illinois. It follows, of course, that immigrants and their children are a much less important part of the labor force during the decade of World War II than during the decade of World War I. Nevertheless, with the exception of the Plains region, immigrants and their children remained concentrated in manufacturing and service occupations, which proliferate in the more urban-industrial regions of the country.[6]

Regional Distribution of the Labor Force

The rate of movement of the labor force to the regions west of the Mississippi River has been less than half as great in the period since 1910 as before 1910. Also, the westward movement of the labor force, like that of population generally, has become more highly selective as among the four western regions. Table 94 shows that the Mountain and Plains regions declined relatively over the period 1910-50 and the Southwest had only a moderate increase, while the Far West almost doubled its share of the national labor force. In the Northeast,

Table 90. Regional distribution of U. S. labor force, 1910, 1930, and 1950

Region	1910	1930	1950
United States	38,167,337	48,829,920	60,200,847
	100%	100%	100%
New England	7.64	7.03	6.47
Middle Atlantic	23.56	24.52	23.46
Great Lakes	19.02	20.70	20.70
Southeast	24.51	21.01	20.74
Plains	11.66	10.35	9.22
Southwest	6.19	6.84	7.12
Mountain	2.24	2.14	2.21
Far West	5.18	7.41	10.08

SOURCE: Appendix Table A-1.

[6] E. P. Hutchinson, *op. cit.*, pp. 197-218; Lee, Miller, Brainerd, and Easterlin; *op. cit.*, pp. 349-60.

New England continued its gradual relative decline throughout these years. But the Middle Atlantic and the Great Lakes regions increased their shares until 1930, and the Great Lakes managed to hold its own after 1930. Their combined share of the national labor force was greater in 1950 than in 1910. Read in conjunction with the relative declines of the Southeast, Mountain, and Plains regions since 1910, the remarkable buoyancy of the Great Lakes and Middle Atlantic regions is evidence of some northward and eastward movement of the working population, though the trend has been relatively more into the Great Lakes region than the seaboard region. Thus in the period since 1910 only the Far West, Southwest, and Great Lakes regions have achieved positive rates of increase in both population and labor force (Table 91). But whereas

Table 91. Percentage change in regional shares of U. S. population and labor force, 1910-1950

Region	Population	Labor force
New England	− 13.20	−15.31
Middle Atlantic	− 2.91	− 0.42
Great Lakes	+ 1.66	+ 8.83
Southeast	− 6.31	−15.38
Plains	− 26.24	−20.93
Southwest	+ 14.05	+15.02
Mountain	+ 5.00	− 1.34
Far West	+109.03	+94.59

SOURCE: 17th U. S. Census, 1950, see *supra*, Table 1, note; Appendix Table A-1.

the Far West increased its share of population more than its share of the labor force, the Great Lakes region increased its share of the labor force considerably more than its share of total population. The Southwest's increase was about the same in both.

Resource Activities in the Regions, 1910-1950

The share of resource activities in the total labor force of the United States declined by 61% between 1910 and 1950, compared with a decline of 33% in the 1870-1910 period. Nevertheless, the country's natural resources still provide the basic materials for all other economic activities, and it is only recently that dependence on foreign materials for strategic purposes has become a matter of public concern. The declining share of resource activities is the logical outcome of rising labor productivity in all the major resource sectors and, during the present century at least, it also reflects a decreasing use of materials per unit of manufactured output.

Within this secular decline of primary activities countrywide, there have been significant regional variations, reflecting in part the differential experience of the four component resource sectors: agriculture, mining, fisheries, forestry and logging (Table 92). Between 1910 and 1950 the combined share of the three Northeastern regions in all primary employment fell by 10%, as did the share of the Southeast also; at the same time, the combined share of the four Western regions rose by 23%. The Southeast's relative decline over these years, however, was only in agriculture. In the other resource sectors it has greatly expanded its share of resource employment since 1910, and in the mining and forest sectors, in particular, its growth has been much more striking than that of the greater West. Within the West, moreover, it is the Far West that has contributed most of the expansion; with the significant exception of agriculture, the shares of the Plains and Mountain regions have generally declined.

Table 92. Regional distribution of all U. S. resource industries labor force, 1910, 1930, and 1950

Region	1910	1930	1950
United States	13,596,815	11,706,790	8,184,509
	100%	100%	100%
New England	2.29	2.06	1.86
Middle Atlantic	9.68	8.73	8.12
Great Lakes	15.05	13.85	14.26
Southeast	42.34	39.95	38.06
Plains	14.07	15.05	16.87
Southwest	10.41	11.55	10.39
Mountain	2.45	3.32	3.53
Far West	3.71	5.49	6.91

SOURCE: Appendix Table A2–A5.

Table 93. Regional distribution of each resource industry's labor force, 1910-1950

			Agriculture		
Region	1910	1920	1930	1940	1950
United States	12,389,840	10,665,812	10,471,998	8,700,376	6,962,779
	100%	100%	100%	100%	100%
New England	2.27	2.10	2.03	1.76	1.76
Middle Atlantic	7.54	7.03	6.54	6.27	6.27
Great Lakes	14.74	14.95	13.86	14.49	14.95
Southeast	44.50	41.93	41.36	40.80	38.28
Plains	14.67	15.64	16.20	17.10	19.00
Southwest	11.01	11.17	11.89	11.36	9.86
Mountain	2.06	2.97	3.09	2.98	3.39
Far West	3.21	4.21	5.03	5.24	6.49

Mineral Extraction

Region	1910	1920	1930	1940	1950
United States	965,169	1,090,223	984,323	913,000	929,421
	100%	100%	100%	100%	100%
New England	.94	.45	.67	.51	.52
Middle Atlantic	36.68	32.17	32.22	26.47	22.46
Great Lakes	19.61	19.84	14.71	12.43	11.61
Southeast	16.73	22.53	26.22	30.26	34.87
Plains	8.40	6.80	5.40	5.08	5.16
Southwest	4.33	8.49	9.86	12.89	16.24
Mountain	7.49	5.88	5.57	5.75	4.92
Far West	5.82	3.84	5.35	6.61	4.22

Forestry and Logging

Region	1910	1920	1930	1940	1950
United States	173,531	217,378	177,189	186,688	215,432
	100%	100%	100%	100%	100%
New England	5.23	10.29	6.08	7.53	6.17
Middle Atlantic	7.77	7.16	5.36	4.43	4.70
Great Lakes	13.00	16.10	11.05	6.88	6.12
Southeast	35.13	27.90	32.73	43.91	44.15
Plains	7.32	9.27	5.25	3.83	3.61
Southwest	4.93	3.63	5.09	5.03	4.38
Mountain	3.31	4.74	5.76	3.38	3.11
Far West	23.31	20.91	28.68	25.01	27.76

Fisheries

Region	1910	1920	1930	1940	1950
United States	68,275	52,836	73,280	60,027	76,877
	100%	100%	100%	100%	100%
New England	18.23	17.15	15.35	14.87	15.80
Middle Atlantic	21.21	17.02	14.27	13.57	12.36
Great Lakes	11.03	8.33	8.34	7.33	6.06
Southeast	31.71	33.93	39.67	41.55	39.75
Plains	2.30	2.42	2.55	1.66	1.93
Southwest	1.71	1.27	2.12	3.38	4.37
Mountain	.22	.17	.24	.50	.68
Far West	13.59	19.71	17.46	17.14	19.05

Source: Appendix Tables A2–A5.

In the agriculture sector, both the Northeast and the Southeast declined relative to the West after 1910 (Table 93). But the Southeast's share fell off by about 11%, and that of the Northeast by only 6%. In terms of labor force, at least, the agricultural strength of the Northeast lay in the Great Lakes rather than in the other two regions. The reverse side of this relative agricultural decline in the East is, of course, the rising share of agricultural activities in the greater West: the Plains, Far West, and Mountain regions each contributed to the over-all increase in employment shares of about one-quarter between 1910 and 1950.

In the minerals sector the Northeast's decline is very marked, its relative share falling off by almost 40% over the four decades. The decline in coal mining affected the Middle Atlantic region somewhat more than the Great Lakes region, but both had substantially smaller shares in 1950 than in 1910. The West increased its share of mining employment by about one-sixth over these years; most of this increment accrues to the Southwest, since other Western regions had smaller shares of the nation's mining activity in 1950 than in 1910. In contrast, the share of the Southeast in the nation's mining sector more than doubled, with much of the increase taking place in the late thirties and forties.

The Northeast's share of forest and logging employment declined relatively by more than one-third between 1910 and 1950. The West's share remained relatively unchanged, the decline of forest activities in the Plains states being just about offset by the rise in the Pacific Northwest. Almost all of the relative gain in forest activities in this period, therefore, was achieved in the Southeast which increased its share of forest employment by almost one-fourth. In 1950 more than 44% of all forest and logging activity in the United States was located in the Southeast.

In the nation's fisheries, also, the Northeast suffered relative decline in the period from 1910 to 1950, its employment falling off relative to the rest of the nation by almost one-third. New England, however, made a larger *relative* contribution to national employment in the fisheries than in any other resource sector. The Southeast raised its share of fishing employment during these years by about one-fourth, and the West its share by almost 47%. Most of the West's gain came in the coastal states of the Far West, but a not insignificant share was contributed by fishermen of the Southwest sailing from ports on the Gulf Coast of Texas.

The application of "shift analysis" to resource employment in the states enables us to determine more precisely which parts of the country contributed to growth in the various resource sectors and conversely which suffered greatest relative declines.

AGRICULTURE

After 1910 the most notable trend in agricultural employment is *absolute* decline: from 10,471,998 in 1910 to 6,962,779 in 1950. Though several states achieved absolute increases in farm employment during particular decades, only five states had absolute net increases over the 40-year period as a whole (Table 94). Four of these have actually experienced absolute decline since 1930, although their 1950 total still represented a net increase over 1910; one, Montana, has been in absolute decline since 1920. The other five among the ten states with the greatest net upward shifts all have had absolute declines since

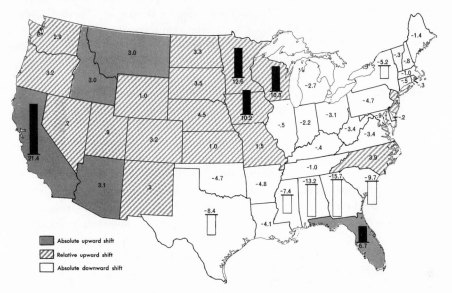

Figure 35. Net Shift in Agricultural Labor Force, 1910-50.

State figures represent % of total net shift. Total net shift as % of incremental change: 15.2. Total net shift as % of 1910 agricultural labor force: 6.7. Source: Appendix Table D.

Table 94. Principal net shifts in agricultural labor force among states, 1910-1950

	Percentage net upward shift		Percentage net downward shift
California	21.40	Georgia	15.74
Florida	6.69	Alabama	13.17
Arizona	3.11	S. Carolina	9.73
Montana	3.04	Texas	8.36
Idaho	3.01	Mississippi	7.39
Minnesota	*12.60*	New York	5.15
Wisconsin	*10.28*	Arkansas	4.77
Iowa	*10.19*	Pennsylvania	4.71
Nebraska	*4.49*	Oklahoma	4.69
N. Carolina	*3.88*	Louisiana	4.12

States in italics experienced relative net increases only.

SOURCE: Appendix Table A-2.

1910; but because their rate of decline in each case was slower than for the nation as a whole, they appear in 1950 with relative net increases for the 40-year interval. Twenty-six states experienced *absolute* declines in farm employment, and all but five of the remaining twenty-two had only *relative* increases.

In the East, Florida was the only state with absolute increase in farm employment during the years 1910-50, but three others—Wisconsin, North Carolina, and New Jersey—ended the period with relative increases.[7] All New England states showed absolute declines, although their combined declines accounted for only 4.3% of the total for the nation.

The heaviest downward shift occurred in the Southeast, especially in South Carolina and westward to Arkansas and Louisiana, reflecting the decline of cotton and other labor-intensive types of row-cropping as well as the effects of farm mechanization. Much of this net downward shift in the Southeast, incidentally, took place after 1930, although some of it occurred during World War I. Texas and Oklahoma in the Southwest together accounted for more than 13% of the nation's total net downward shift; the causes here were much the same as in the Southeast. However, owing to the expansion of truck farming and certain field crops, Arizona was third only to California and Florida among states registering absolute net increases over the period. Montana and Idaho in the Mountain region, the other two states with absolute net upward shifts, seem to owe their rising level of farm activities to the westward encroachment of the wheat belt during World War I.

MINING

Unlike agriculture, mineral production taken as a whole, and for the whole period 1910–1950, has been a more or less stabilized sector of resource employment (see Table 93). There have been, however, a number of ups and downs in employment. There was some falling-off in mining activities between the two

Table 95. Principal net shifts in mining labor force among states, 1910-1950

	Percentage net upward shift		Percentage net downward shift
Texas	28.01	Pennsylvania	42.16
West Virginia	24.66	Ohio	7.51
Kentucky	16.87	Illinois	7.40
Oklahoma	9.78	Michigan	6.75
Louisiana	7.83	Colorado	5.83
Virginia	5.55	Missouri	5.58
New Mexico	1.58	Iowa	4.05
Mississippi	1.21	Montana	3.21
Utah	.83	Indiana	2.78
Arkansas	.70	Washington	2.42

SOURCE: Appendix Table A-3.

[7] Relative increases of the agricultural labor force in North Carolina and New Jersey are probably accounted for by increases in tobacco and vegetable production, respectively. Wisconsin's relative increase reflects the stability of labor requirements in dairying.

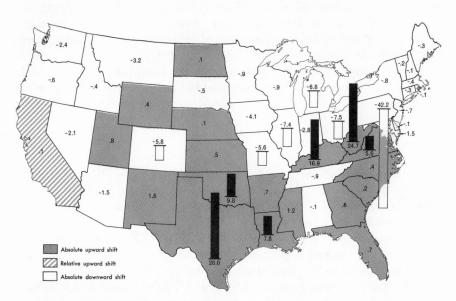

Figure 36. Net Shift in Mining Labor Force, 1910-50.

State figures represent % of total net shift. Total net shift as % of incremental change: 818.8. Total net shift as % of 1910 mining labor force: 30.3. Source: Appendix Table D.

World Wars and the trend was not reversed until after 1940. Between 1940 and 1950 mineral employment rose by a little more than 1%.[8]

The period 1910-1950 as a whole is marked by the rise of mineral fuels to dominance in the nation's mining activity. By 1950 about three-quarters of all mining employment originated in either coal or petroleum; metallic and other non-metallic mining had decreased correspondingly. Developments in a few Southeastern and Southwestern states, moreover, account for nearly 93% of the total net upward shift in all mining employment since 1910 (Table 95). Minor upward shifts, all accounting for less than 1% of the total, also occurred in three western Plains states (mostly in Kansas) and in two Mountain states (Wyoming and Utah). Absolute net downward shifts were registered by all the Northeastern states (more than 42% of the nation's total in Pennsylvania alone) and by all the Far Western states except California, where the upsurge of petroleum activities between 1920 and 1940 offset the sharp decline in metal mining. The two great mining states of the Mountain region, Montana and Colorado, also experienced sizable absolute net downward shifts in mining labor force, amounting to more than 9% of the national total over the 40-year period.

[8] A more recent figure from the *Census of Manufactures 1954*, however, suggests that the number of production workers, at least, is again in decline—nearly 9 per cent since the 1939 *Census of Manufactures*.

For practical purposes, therefore, the growth of petroleum, natural gas, and coal in Texas, Louisiana, West Virginia, Kentucky, and Virginia is the sum of the growth in mining employment achieved in recent decades, though World War II brought a revival to the Minnesota iron fields after three successive decades of steady decline. On the other hand, the decline of coal mining in the Middle Atlantic and Great Lakes states is the most important factor in the downward shift.

FORESTRY AND LOGGING

The record of employment in forestry and logging in the 1910-1950 period resembles that of mining, but recovery in this sector between 1940 and 1950 was much more substantial, amounting to more than 15%. In the past four decades, logging activities have been increasingly concentrated in the Far West (almost exclusively in Oregon) and the Southeast (Table 96). Eight of the ten principal growth states are located in the Southeast; these states contributed almost 55% of the total upward shift in logging activities between 1910 and 1950.

World War I brought a revival of logging activities in some of the northern New England states, New York, and states bordering Lake Superior, but thereafter the camps moved off to the Pacific Northwest, the Southeast, and the

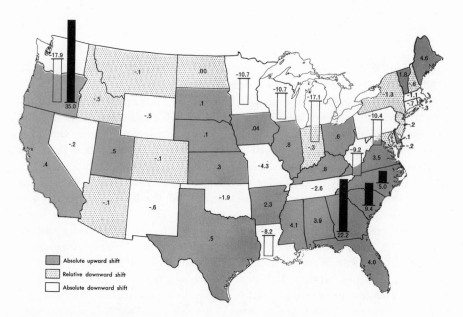

Figure 37. Net Shift in Forest Labor Force, 1910-50.

State figures represent % of total net shift. Total net shift as % of incremental change: 132.0. Total net shift as % of 1910 forest labor force: 31.9. Source: Appendix Table D.

Southwest. During the depression decade more than 68% of the entire net upward shift in logging activity took place in Georgia and Florida, but by World War II employment shifted back again to Oregon and California in the Far West and to the Carolinas and Mississippi.[9] During this century the forest industries have been profoundly affected, on the demand side, by the greatly increased domestic pulpwood requirements and, on the supply side, by policies

Table 96. Principal net shifts in forest labor force among states, 1910-1950

Percentage net upward shift		Percentage net downward shift	
Oregon	35.02	Washington	17.87
Georgia	22.21	Michigan	17.12
S. Carolina	9.37	Minnesota	10.74
N. Carolina	5.04	Wisconsin	10.67
Maine	4.59	Pennsylvania	10.44
Mississippi	4.10	West Virginia	9.23
Florida	3.96	Louisiana	8.15
Alabama	3.89	Missouri	4.26
Virginia	3.50	Tennessee	2.63
Arkansas	2.33	Oklahoma	1.91

SOURCE: Appendix Table A-4.

of conservation and reforestation. Much of the enduring strength of the Southeast and the northern New England states can be attributed to conservation policies supported by government and industry. Unfortunately, recognition of the economic advantages of sustained yield practices came too late to arrest the devastation of the great forests of Michigan, Wisconsin, and Minnesota. These three states, as a consequence, accounted for more than 38% of the total net downward shift in logging activities between 1910 and 1950; most of their decline occurred in the years after 1920.

[9] There has been, in fact, a curious cycle in logging activity over the years since 1910: many of the states which experience the largest net upward shifts during one decade often experience the largest net downward shifts during the ensuing decade and vice versa. Thus the largest net upward shifts 1910-20 occurred in Maine, Minnesota, Wisconsin, and New York; the largest net downward shifts from Washington, Pennsylvania, West Virginia and Louisiana. Over the decade 1920–30 the largest net upward shifts were registered in Oregon, Washington, Florida, and Mississippi; the largest downward shifts from Minnesota, Wisconsin, Maine, and Michigan. During 1930–40 the largest upward shifts took place in Georgia, Florida, Alabama, and South Carolina; the largest downward shifts from Washington, Michigan, Idaho, and Minnesota. 1940–50 saw the largest net upward shifts in Oregon, California, North and South Carolina, the largest net downward shifts from Florida, Washington, Georgia, and New Hampshire.

FISHERIES

Most of the trends evident in fishing employment during the late nineteenth century have intensified since 1910. The heaviest net downward shifts during the 1910-1950 period have been in the New England and Middle Atlantic regions and Chesapeake Bay areas, heavy net upward shifts into Far Western and in certain Gulf states (Table 97). Since the 1930's, downward shifts in the Great Lakes fisheries, especially in Illinois, have also contributed to the relative

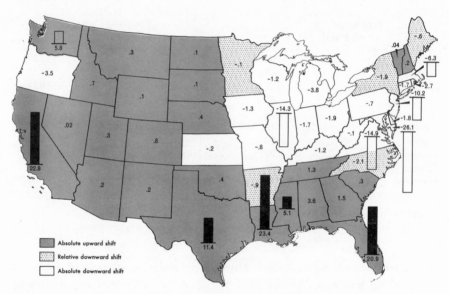

Figure 38. Net Shift in Fishing Labor Force, 1910-50.

State figures represent % of total net shift. Total net shift as % of incremental change: 194.0. Total net shift as % of 1910 fishing labor force: 24.4. Source: Appendix Table D.

Table 97. Principal net shifts in fishing labor force among states, 1910-1950

Percentage net upward shift		Percentage net downward shift	
Louisiana	23.40	Maryland	26.12
California	22.84	Virginia	14.85
Florida	20.94	Illinois	14.31
Texas	11.41	New Jersey	10.18
Washington	5.80	Massachusetts	6.33
Mississippi	5.10	Michigan	3.82

Source: Appendix Table A-5.

decline in the Northeast. The greatest gains were achieved during this period by Louisiana, California, Florida, and Texas; together they accounted for more than 78% of the total net upward shift over these years. Far Western and Gulf fisheries have been providing about half the total value of the fishing catch in recent years, which indicates that canned and frozen seafoods, together with menhaden and other meal-oil species, have become a much more lucrative sector of the industry than the market fish brought into ports along the North Atlantic and Great Lakes shores. The revival of the Maine fisheries in New England after 1940 was also probably connected with the development of new processing facilities in that state.

The Value of Extracted Resources

In terms of the gross value of resources extracted in the various regions, the most striking change has been the almost complete reversal in the positions of the Northeast and greater West between 1870 and 1950. In 1870 the three Northeastern regions contributed 58.2% to the gross value of the nation's extracted resources. By 1950 that proportion had fallen to 25.5%. The share of the four Western regions rose during these years from 16.6% in 1870 to 54.4% in 1950. The relative share of the Southeast has remained almost unchanged since the 1880's.

Since 1910, however, the rate of redistribution between the Northeast and the West has slowed markedly. Between 1870 and 1910 the Northeast's share in total resources value declined by more than 39%; but since 1910 the decline has been less than 28%. And the share of the West rose by more than 153% between 1870 and 1910, but by only 29% after 1910.

In the earlier period the Southeast's share declined by more than 11%, but after 1910 the decline slowed to 10%.

Table 98. Regional distribution of value of primary resources extracted, 1910, 1930, and 1950

Region	1910	1930	1950
United States	$10,512,395* 100%	$17,426,866* 100%	$35,030,981* 100%
New England	3.2	2.6	2.1
Middle Atlantic	11.6	11.8	8.5
Great Lakes	20.6	15.0	14.9
Southeast	22.4	21.0	20.1
Plains	24.5	18.7	18.6
Southwest	7.6	13.9	16.9
Mountain	4.1	5.6	5.6
Far West	6.0	11.4	13.3

*000's of current dollars.

SOURCE: Appendix Table B-1.

Table 98 reveals that New England's decline in resources value continued throughout the 1910-1950 period. The Great Lakes region, on the other hand, declined by one-fourth between 1910 and 1930, but thereafter retained an almost constant share of the greatly increased total value of extracted resources. In the years down to 1930 the Middle Atlantic region contributed stability to the share of the Northeast, but thereafter it too went into relative decline. Among the Western regions, the Far West and Southwest contributed most to the growth of extracted resources value; between 1910 and 1950 both these regions more than doubled their shares, while the Mountain region leveled off after 1930 and the Plains region continued its decline from the peak reached in

Table 99. Percentage distribution of value of all resources extracted, by major resource industry and great region, 1910, 1930, and 1950

Resource industry	1910	1950
All resource industries	$14,827,073* 100%	$20,667,245* 100%
Agriculture	80.80	62.95
Mineral extraction	11.78	30.20
Forestry & logging	6.90	5.96
Fisheries	.52	.89

	Great region			
	Northeast	Southeast	West	United States
Agriculture				
1910	27.19	17.64	35.97	80.80
1930	17.64	13.54	32.01	63.19
1950	17.74	11.09	34.12	62.95
Mineral extraction				
1910	6.01	1.52	4.25	11.78
1930	10.44	4.46	14.74	29.64
1950	6.70	6.83	16.67	30.20
Forestry and logging				
1910	1.93	3.14	1.83	6.90
1930	1.02	2.82	2.69	6.53
1950	.71	2.00	3.25	5.96
Fisheries				
1910	.31	.13	.08	.52
1930	.32	.16	.17	.65
1950	.31	.23	.35	.89

*000's of 1929 dollars.

Source: Appendix Tables B1–B5.

Table 100. Regional distribution of value of resources extracted, by major resource industry, 1910, 1930, and 1950

Agriculture

Region	1910	1930	1950
United States	$8,494,231*	$11,011,329*	$22,052,255*
	100%	100%	100%
New England	2.89	2.86	2.41
Middle Atlantic	9.13	8.26	7.44
Great Lakes	21.63	16.81	18.34
Southeast	21.83	21.42	17.62
Plains	28.33	25.83	25.80
Southwest	8.04	10.59	11.71
Mountain	3.17	5.35	5.62
Far West	4.98	8.88	11.06

Mineral Extraction

Region	1910	1930	1950
United States	$1,238,415*	$5,164,968*	$10,579,973*
	100%	100%	100%
New England	1.40	.95	.41
Middle Atlantic	30.45	21.18	11.66
Great Lakes	19.18	13.09	10.11
Southeast	12.90	15.03	22.62
Plains	10.52	7.61	7.46
Southwest	6.15	23.38	30.67
Mountain	11.46	6.73	5.96
Far West	7.94	12.03	11.11

*000's of current dollars.

Forestry and Logging

Region	1910	1930	1950
United States	$725,737*	$1,137,180*	$2,086,249*
	100%	100%	100%
New England	7.78	4.48	4.24
Middle Atlantic	7.36	3.55	3.47
Great Lakes	12.88	7.56	4.14
Southeast	45.48	43.18	33.56
Plains	5.18	2.12	2.13
Southwest	4.95	4.74	3.86
Mountain	2.23	3.25	3.98
Far West	14.14	31.12	44.62

Table 100. Regional distribution of value of resources extracted, by major resource industry, 1910, 1930, and 1950 (continued)

Fisheries

Region	1910	1930	1950
United States	$54,012* 100%	$113,389* 100%	$312,504* 100%
New England	28.03	25.64	19.38
Middle Atlantic	22.26	16.63	12.58
Great Lakes	9.33	7.36	3.33
Southeast	25.57	24.04	25.66
Plains	1.32	3.32	.82
Southwest	.83	.93	3.72
Mountain	—	—	—
Far West	12.66	22.08	34.51

*000's of current dollars.

SOURCE: Appendix Tables B1–B5.

Table 101. Distribution of labor force in resource industries and value of extracted resources, by great region, 1910, 1930, and 1950

Region	1910		1930		1950	
	Labor force	Value	Labor force	Value	Labor force	Value
United States	100%	100%	100%	100%	100%	100%
Northeast	27.0	35.4	24.6	29.4	24.2	25.5
Southeast	42.3	22.4	40.0	21.0	38.1	20.1
West	30.7	42.2	35.4	49.6	37.7	54.4

SOURCE: Appendix Tables A-1, B-1.

1910. It is evident that the relative eclipse of agriculture and the rising output of liquid fuels (oil and natural gas) underlies this continuing regional transformation (Tables 99 and 100).

The comparison of regional shares of total resource value with shares in primary employment shown in Table 101 throws further light on changes in the resource sector since 1910. Thus the Southeast's limited decline in its resource employment share can be seen to have been accompanied by a proportionate decline in its share of the gross value of extracted resources. The greater Northeast suffered a much greater relative loss in resource value, with only a small decline in labor force. On the other hand, the moderately rising share of the

West in all primary employment was accompanied, as in the period before 1910, by a much more than proportionate increase in its share of extracted resources value. In recent decades, however, it is the Far West and Southwest rather than the Plains or the Mountain regions which have made the greatest contributions to the value of resources extracted in the greater West. In short, labor productivity in the four primary resource sectors has continued to diverge, and within each sector some activities result in high values per unit of labor input, others in low. Recently, the Southwest and Far West have been developing resources which require relatively low labor inputs for high-value outputs, while the reverse has been true of the Southeast. Moreover, during the present century at least, the Plains and Mountain regions have been moving more toward the pattern of the Southeast and have been unable to develop the more lucrative types of resource activity characteristic of the Southwest and Far West.

Manufacturing Activities in the Regions 1910–1950

As in the earlier period, the most striking feature of American manufacturing developments after 1910 was the enduring strength of the urban-industrial Northeast. In spite of the decline in the Northeast's natural riches, the combined share of the Middle Atlantic, New England, and Great Lakes regions in manufacturing employment declined by only 2.8% between 1910 and 1950. In the forty years before 1910, their combined share had declined by more than 13%. It has been the Great Lakes region rather than the New England and Middle Atlantic regions, however, which has given the manufacturing Belt its strength; between 1910 and 1950 the share of the Great Lakes region in all manufacturing employment rose by almost 28%.

Outside the Northeast the most notable relative gains have been registered in the Far West and Southeast during these years (Table 102). The Southwest gained until 1930 but had dropped again by 1950. In the Plains and Mountain regions, manufacturing has, with certain exceptions, been in relative decline. Taken as a whole, the greater West, like the Northeast, has a slightly smaller share of country-wide employment in manufactures than it had in 1910.

Thus, after more than eighty years of continuing industrial transformation, more than two-thirds of the nation's manufacturing employment is *still* located in the Northeastern industrial belt stretching from southern New England south to the Potomac and west to the Mississippi. Manufacturing, therefore, remains in 1950 much more localized than either resource or service activities.

Another instructive measure of manufacturing activity is "value-added by manufacture." Unlike the category "value of extracted resources," value-added by manufacture is a *net* figure which enables us to determine precisely how much of the final value of a product is attributable to the manufacturing process as distinct from materials, containers, power, etc. Table 103 presents the regional shares of all value-added by manufacture in the nation as a whole. In general, changes in each region's share of total value-added by manufacture

Table 102. Regional distribution of manufacturing labor force, 1910, 1930, and 1950

Region	1910	1930	1950
United States	10,656,545	14,110,652	14,398,854
	100%	100%	100%
New England	13.42	10.48	9.59
Middle Atlantic	33.55	30.31	29.11
Great Lakes	22.61	25.59	28.94
Southeast	12.69	14.38	15.43
Plains	8.35	7.11	5.68
Southwest	2.74	4.13	3.28
Mountain	1.64	1.34	.87
Far West	5.00	6.66	7.10

SOURCE: Appendix Table A-6.

Table 103. Regional distribution of value added by manufacture, 1910, 1930, and 1950

Region	1910	1930	1950 (47)
United States	$8,188,527*	$30,693,709*	$74,353,602*
	100%	100%	100%
New England	14.32	10.35	9.16
Middle Atlantic	36.90	33.75	29.87
Great Lakes	25.59	31.63	31.57
Southeast	10.04	9.86	12.49
Plains	6.42	5.74	5.54
Southwest	1.49	2.00	3.00
Mountain	1.21	.95	.88
Far West	4.03	5.72	7.49

* 000's of current dollars.

SOURCE: Same as Table 46.

parallel changes in its share of total manufacturing employment and, as in the earlier period, the parallel is closer than that between changes in the shares of extracted resources value and in the shares of primary employment. By the late 1940's, however, two regions still deviate somewhat from the close parallel existing in the other six: the Southeast has a considerably larger share of manufacturing employment than of value-added, while the Great Lakes region has a larger share of value-added than of manufacturing employment. It is significant perhaps that before 1930 the Middle Atlantic region also had a larger share of

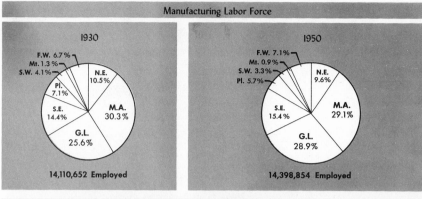

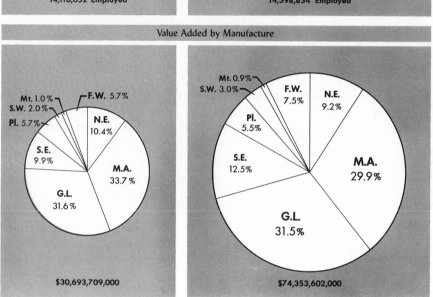

Figure 39. Regional Distribution of U. S. Manufacturing Labor Force and Value Added by Manufacture, 1930 and 1950.

Table 104. Distribution of manufacturing labor force and value added by manufacture, by great region, 1910, 1930, and 1950

Region	1910		1930		1950	
	Labor force	Value added	Labor force	Value added	Labor force	Value added
United States	100%	100%	100%	100%	100%	100%
Northeast	69.58	76.81	66.38	75.73	67.64	70.60
Southeast	12.69	10.04	14.38	9.86	15.43	12.49
West	17.73	13.15	19.24	14.41	16.93	16.91

Source: Appendix Table A-6; Table 103.

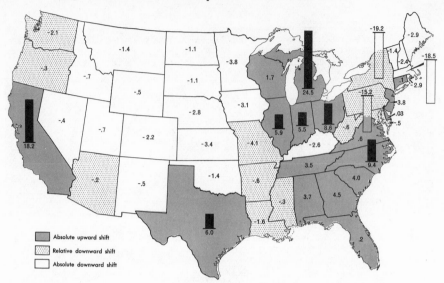

Figure 40. Net Shift in Manufacturing Labor Force, 1910-50.

State figures represent % of total net shift. Total net shift as % of incremental change: 52.7. Total net shift as % of 1910 manufacturing labor force: 18.5. Source: Appendix Table D.

value-added than of manufacturing employment. The implication of these developments, therefore, is that the Great Lakes region is now the nation's most productive manufacturing region (in terms of value-added per worker) and that the Southeast is relatively the least productive among those in which manufactures are still concentrating. The stress on the relative character of these comparisons is particularly important because of the marked increase in labor productivity in manufacturing throughout the entire country.

A comparison of the ratio of manufacturing employment to value-added in the three great regions suggests that the disparity between the two is somewhat less general today than in 1910 (Table 104). The tendency towards convergence is particularly striking if we examine the trend of the two categories in each of the regions over the years of depression and war since 1930. Since 1930 only the Southeast and Far West have had their shares of value-added rising at a faster rate than their shares of manufacturing employment and, what amounts to the same thing, only the Plains and Mountain regions have had their shares of employment falling at a faster rate than their shares of value-added by manufacture. Broadly speaking, each of these four regions is somewhat more productive relatively (value-added per worker in manufactures) in 1950 than at the onset of depression in 1930. On the other hand, the New England and Middle Atlantic regions' shares of the nation's value-added has fallen at a faster rate than their corresponding shares of manufacturing employment. In the Great Lakes region the share of value-added has remained almost stationary since 1930, but the share of the manufacturing labor force has increased. Broadly speaking, therefore, these last three regions are proportionately somewhat less

Table 105. Principal net shifts in manufacturing labor force among states, 1910-1950

	Percentage net upward shift		Percentage net downward shift
Michigan	24.53	New York	*19.24*
California	18.15	Massachusetts	18.45
N. Carolina	9.36	Pennsylvania	*15.17*
Ohio	8.61	Missouri	*4.09*
Texas	5.96	Minnesota	3.76
Illinois	5.86	Kansas	3.38
Indiana	5.45	Iowa	3.14
Georgia	4.50	Rhode Island	2.93
S. Carolina	3.95	Maine	2.87
New Jersey	3.76	Nebraska	2.77

The figures in italics are relative downward shifts only.

SOURCE: Appendix Table A-6.

productive in 1950 than in 1930.[10] From an historical standpoint, however, it is too early to regard these tendencies as marking any genuine turning point in the regional distribution of American manufactures. In the perspective of the entire period since 1910 such minor convergence among the regions does not appear to have produced any noteworthy redistribution either of manufacturing employment or value-added.

When the developments within particular states in the period 1910-1950 are examined, it is evident that there is a tendency for the older urban-industrial areas to sustain the greatest relative losses in manufacturing employment (Table 105 and Figure 40). Nevertheless, it is no longer true that the more rural-agricultural states necessarily experience the greatest net upward shifts. Except for several Southeastern states, most of the relative net increases occurred in such states as Michigan, California, Ohio, Indiana, and New Jersey, which were already substantial urban-industrial areas before World War I. As a matter of fact, apart from California, Texas, and the three Southeastern states—the Carolinas and Georgia—the balance of upward shift was almost wholly confined to the Great Lakes region, every one of whose member states registered a net upward shift. By 1950 the Great Lakes region was almost level with the Middle Atlantic region in its share of the nation's manufacturing employment.

[10] Average value-added per production worker (or per worker employed in manufactures) varies from region to region with: 1) the proportion of the manufacturing labor force in high, medium, or low value-added industries, and 2) the variation from region to region in value-added per worker in the same industry group. A recent Department of Commerce study indicates that for a combination of these reasons the Southeast and New England rank below the countrywide average value-added per production worker in 1939 and 1947. The Far West ranks highest above the national average. U. S. Dept. of Commerce, *Regional Trends in the United States Economy,* (Washington: Government Printing Office, 1951), pp. 83-87.

Table 106. Principal net shifts in manufacturing labor force among states, by decade, 1910-1950

1910-20		1920-30		1930-40		1940-50	
Percentage net upward shift							
Mich.	32.38	Calif.	22.93	Mich.	17.36	Calif.	32.54
Ohio	20.23	Mich.	14.85	N. C.	15.92	Texas	14.42
Calif.	13.76	Texas	12.73	Conn.	10.17	Ind.	8.85
Texas	8.22	Ill.	10.05	N. J.	9.42	Wis.	7.54
N. J.	6.52	N. C.	8.24	Ill.	8.42	Ohio	6.79
Ala.	3.72	Tenn.	5.04	Ohio	7.60	Minn.	4.83
N. C.	3.64	Ga.	4.67	S. C.	5.85	Iowa	2.75
Okla.	2.75	Fla.	4.38	Ga.	4.21	Kan.	2.75
Fla.	2.14	S. C.	3.81	Va.	3.96	Mich.	2.48
Ga.	1.86	Okla.	3.47	Ind.	3.76	Ore.	2.39
Share of ten leading states in total net upward shift	95.22		90.17		86.67		85.34
Percentage net downward shift							
N. Y.	27.82	Mass.	*28.79*	Texas	*12.08*	N. Y.	17.38
Pa.	13.91	Pa.	*21.72*	Calif.	*9.07*	Mass.	16.56
Mass.	7.70	N. Y.	9.57	Okla.	*8.32*	Pa.	14.79
Mo.	6.13	Ohio	9.14	Kan.	*6.79*	Conn.	9.66
Ill.	5.55	Conn.	5.76	Minn.	*6.02*	N. J.	8.71
Ky.	*5.48*	R. I.	*3.78*	Fla.	*4.74*	N. C.	7.33
Minn.	4.54	Iowa	*2.99*	Neb.	*4.61*	R. I.	5.80
Maine	3.37	N. H.	*2.83*	Wash.	*4.55*	Md.	4.54
Colo.	*3.01*	Minn.	2.60	Iowa	*4.52*	Va.	3.91
Kan.	2.96	Maine	2.59	N. Y.	3.76	Maine	3.19
Share of ten leading states in total net upward shift	80.47		89.77		64.46		91.87

Figures in italics are absolute net downward shifts.

SOURCE: Appendix Table A-6.

Service Activities in the Regions, 1910-1950

Services have been the most rapidly growing sector of the labor force during the twentieth century. Resource employment, the bulk of which is still agricul-

tural, has declined absolutely and relatively since 1910; manufacturing employment has declined relatively since 1920, and since 1930 has barely held its own
in absolute terms. In contrast, employment in services grew from around 14
million to over 37 million between 1910 and 1950. The share of this sector in
the total labor force rose by 71% over these years. In 1910 service activities
employed about one-third of a total labor force of 38 million; in 1950, they
employed nearly two-thirds of a total labor force of over 60 million.

Changes in the regional distribution of the services labor force between 1910
and 1930 appear to have been very slight, but since 1930 both the Southeast and
the West have grown at the expense of the urban-industrial Northeast (Table
107). In the West, all regions except the Plains have increased their shares

Table 107. Regional distribution of services labor force, 1910, 1930, and 1950

Region	1910	1930	1950
United States	13,913,976	23,012,448	37,617,484
	100%	100%	100%
New England	8.43	7.44	6.27
Middle Atlantic	29.48	29.00	24.63
Great Lakes	20.15	21.19	18.95
Southeast	16.13	15.45	19.00
Plains	11.84	9.94	8.91
Southwest	4.72	6.11	7.89
Mountain	2.48	2.03	2.44
Far West	6.77	8.84	11.91
Northeast	58.06	57.63	49.85
Southeast	16.13	15.45	19.00
West	25.81	26.92	31.15

SOURCE: Appendix Table A-7.

since 1930, but only the Far West and the Southwest have improved their relative positions as compared with 1910. In the Northeast, the shares of the
Middle Atlantic and Great Lakes regions have declined only since 1930, but
New England has been losing relative to other regions since before the turn of
the century.

Table 108 compares the percentage growth in regional shares of all the
United States service employments with the percentage growth in regional shares
of all labor force and population since 1910. Because of the great rise in service
employment in the Southeast, Southwest, and Far West, services as a proportion
of the national total have declined more sharply than either labor force or

population in all the Northeastern regions. Indeed, the Great Lakes region has registered increases in both total labor force and population but has nevertheless shown decline in services. The Southeast, on the other hand, has had a very marked increase in service employment in contrast to its shrinking shares of labor force and population. Within the West, the Plains region has declined

Table 108. Percentage change in regional shares of population, total labor force, and services labor force, 1910-1950

Region	Population	Labor force	Services labor force
New England	− 13.20	−15.31	−25.62
Middle Atlantic	− 2.91	− 0.42	−16.45
Great Lakes	+ 1.66	+ 8.83	− 5.96
Southeast	− 6.31	−15.38	+17.79
Plains	− 26.24	−20.92	−24.75
Southwest	+ 14.05	+15.02	+67.16
Mountain	+ 5.00	− 1.34	− 1.61
Far West	+109.03	+94.59	+75.92

SOURCE: 17th U. S. Census, 1950, see *supra*, Table 1, note; Appendix Tables A-1, A-7.

very sharply in all three categories, but more sharply in population and services than in total labor force. The Mountain region has declined moderately in labor force and service employments but has gained in population. Only the Southwest and Far West have gained in all three categories. But whereas the Southwest gained least in population and labor force and most in service employment, the Far West gained most in population and least in services.

Considering the gross character of our tertiary sector (all non-resource and non-manufacturing employment), this analysis cannot be pressed too far, but it is instructive to conclude the discussion of employment shifts with a brief look at the shifts in service employment among the states. Table 109 summarizes the principal net upward and downward shifts among the states over the period 1910-1950. The gains of the Far West were chiefly registered in California, involving more than 37% of the total net upward shift in the country. The Southwest gained mostly in Texas, but a further 6% of the total also accrued to Arizona, Oklahoma, and New Mexico. Florida is the great service state of the Southeast, but sizable net upward shifts also occurred in North Carolina and Virginia. Net downward shifts were most marked in the three great manufacturing states of the Atlantic seaboard—New York, Pennsylvania, and Massachusetts. The relative decline of the Plains states and of all the Great Lakes states except Michigan is no less remarkable. Michigan, in fact, is the only state in the urban-industrial Northeast to show any sizable balance of net upward shift of service employments over the last four decades.

Table 109. Principal net shifts in services labor force among states, 1910-1950

	Percentage net upward shift		Percentage net downward shift
California	37.29	New York	22.09
Texas	18.73	Pennsylvania	16.42
Florida	11.05	Massachusetts	12.30
Michigan	7.51	Illinois	9.60
N. Carolina	6.28	Missouri	7.87
Virginia	3.35	Iowa	4.52
Arizona	2.30	Minnesota	3.87
Oklahoma	1.85	Ohio	3.13
New Mexico	1.65	Kansas	2.37
Oregon	1.25	Indiana	2.30

SOURCE: Appendix Table A-7.

These tendencies can be given clearer definition by considering certain major service components separately; namely, employment in transport and communications, in trade and finance, in professional activities, and in personal and domestic service (Table 110). In the period before 1910, the first three of these service categories rose at a faster rate than service employments as a whole; but only two of the four have maintained this distinction in the years since 1910, namely, trade and finance and professional employment. Transport and communications, which had run so far ahead of the others during the heyday of the westward movement, fell back into third place over ensuing decades. Personal and domestic services were unique in that, after 1910, they declined absolutely.

There were, of course, regional differences in the distribution of these four categories after 1910, although the rate of redistribution for all regions was

Table 110. Percentage growth in total labor force, services labor force, and labor force in four selected service industries, 1910-1950

ALL LABOR FORCE	+ 57.75
ALL SERVICE LABOR FORCE	+170.36
Transport and Communications	+ 65.61
Trade and Finance	+244.84
Professional Services	+180.99
Personal and Domestic Services	− 8.58

SOURCE: Appendix Tables A1 and A7; 13th U. S. Census, 1910, Vol. IV, *Occupational Statistics*; 17th U. S. Census, 1950, Vol. II, State Volumes.

lower than in the earlier period. Only three regions increased their shares of the total employment in all four categories: the Southeast, Southwest, and Far West (Table 111).[11] Apart from these three, the Great lakes region increased its share of transportation and communication workers, and the Mountain region gained very slightly in trade and finance. But both these regions declined relatively in the other three categories. The Middle Atlantic region lost relatively in all categories, but most heavily in personal and domestic services. New

Table 111. Regional distribution of labor force in four selected service industries, 1910 and 1950

Region	Transport and communications		Trade and finance		Professional services		Personal and domestic services	
	1910	1950	1910	1950	1910	1950	1910	1950
United States	100%	100%	100%	100%	100%	100%	100%	100%
New England	7.17	5.31	8.58	6.36	8.48	7.23	8.28	5.49
Middle Atlantic	27.07	25.98	29.66	25.21	26.44	24.77	29.03	23.05
Great Lakes	20.92	21.14	21.27	20.31	21.10	19.83	17.61	16.48
Southeast	15.33	17.00	13.78	17.26	14.67	17.64	22.20	26.80
Plains	13.19	10.13	12.75	9.61	13.98	9.85	10.08	7.31
Southwest	5.10	7.29	4.94	7.66	5.41	7.06	4.75	8.96
Mountain	3.45	2.79	2.21	2.27	2.79	2.55	2.09	1.93
Far West	7.77	10.36	6.81	11.32	7.13	11.07	5.96	9.98

SOURCE: 13th U. S. Census, 1910, Vol. IV, *Occupational Statistics;* 17th U.S. Census, 1950, Vol. II, State Volumes.

England had proportionately greater declines than the Middle Atlantic region in all four categories but its greatest losses were also in personal and domestic service. The Plains suffered quite heavy losses in all four categories; the greatest being in professional services. It is interesting that, since 1910, the three service "growth" regions—the Southeast, the Southwest, and the Far West— have all increased their shares of the generally declining personal and domestic services category.

The percentage of the total labor force employed in each of the four selected service categories is shown in Table 112 for the eight regions and the nation as a whole. All of these categories except personal and domestic services were a larger proportion of the national labor force in 1950 than in 1910. In every region, the share of personal and domestic services in the regional labor force declined over these years, and the share of transportation and communication

---

[11] The Southwest and Far West, incidentally, were the only regions that increased their shares in all four categories over the entire period 1870-1950; New England and the Middle Atlantic were the only regions to experience relative losses in all four categories over the entire period.

workers was smaller in 1950 than in 1910 in four regions—the New England, Great Lakes, Mountain, and Far West regions.[12]

The uneven regional redistribution of these services is attested by the fact that by 1950 no region was above the national level for all four categories, while in 1910 both the Middle Atlantic region and the Far West exceeded the national level. The New England and Great Lakes regions both exceeded the national level in three categories in 1910 but in only one category in 1950. The Southeast and the Southwest fell short of the national level in all four categories in 1910; by 1950, the Southeast was still below the national level in three categories, but the Southwest exceeded it in all but one category. The Southeast was the only region in the country which fell short of the national level in trade and finance by any appreciable amount in 1950. It was in this category, moreover, that the rate of increase was greatest, both nationally and regionally, in the present century.

Table 112. Labor force in four selected service industries as a percentage of the total labor force, by region, 1910 and 1950

	1910				1950			
Region	Trans-port & Comm.	Trade & Fin.	Prof.	Pers. & Dom.	Trans-port & Comm.	Trade & Fin.	Prof.	Pers. & Dom.
United States	6.91	9.47	4.36	9.88	7.26	20.70	7.77	5.80
New England	6.48	*10.64*	*4.84*	*10.71*	5.96	20.36	*8.68*	4.92
Middle Atlantic	*7.94*	*11.92*	*4.89*	*12.17*	*8.04*	*22.25*	*8.20*	5.69
Great Lakes	*7.60*	*10.59*	*4.84*	9.15	*7.41*	20.32	7.44	4.61
Southeast	4.32	5.33	2.61	8.95	5.95	17.24	6.61	7.49
Plains	*7.82*	*10.36*	*5.23*	8.55	*7.97*	*21.58*	*8.29*	4.59
Southwest	5.69	7.56	3.81	7.58	*7.42*	*22.26*	7.70	7.29
Mountain	*10.67*	9.36	*5.44*	9.22	*9.16*	*21.26*	*8.97*	5.08
Far West	*10.36*	*12.43*	*6.00*	*11.36*	*7.46*	*23.23*	*8.52*	5.74

Figures in italics are above the national average.

SOURCE: 13th U. S. Census, 1910, Vol. IV, *Occupational Statistics*; 17th U. S. Census, 1950, Vol. II; State Volumes.

The measure of the Southeast's backwardness in this most rapidly expanding service sector can be seen in the fact that, although its share of trade and finance expanded far more than that of any other region—or, indeed, than that of the nation as a whole—it was still the furthest below the national level in 1950 (Table 112). It is in this crucial trade and financial category, and to a lesser

[12] Of these four regions, however, only New England's proportion of transport and communications workers was smaller than the national proportion. On the other hand, the Southeast, which had enlarged its regional proportion in this category, was still below the national proportion in 1950.

Table 113. Percentage change in trade and finance shares of regional and total labor forces, 1910-1950

United States +118.6	Northeast +91.4	Middle Atlantic +86.7	Great Lakes +91.9
Southeast *+223.4*	Plains *+108.3*	Southwest *+194.5*	Mountain *+127.1*	Far West +86.9

Figures in italics are above the national average.

Source: Same as Table 112.

extent in professional employment, that the expanding service sector is most likely to grow in the immediate future. All regions of the country can expect to participate in the development, and the greatest relative gains will probably occur in the Southeast and Southwest.

In view of the prolonged relative decline in resource activity and the more recent relative decline in manufacturing, the changing structure of service employments, has from the standpoint of expanding population and labor force, become of crucial importance. Productivity per worker in services does not generally increase at rates comparable to those in the resource and manufacturing sectors; hence services are likely to continue for some time as the principal sector for labor force growth on the national level and in most of the regions.

Within the service sector, moreover, shifts among the major categories of employment provide a revealing index to recent social-economic change. Since World War I, for example, the two categories of trade and finance and professional services have overtaken transport and communications as leading forms of service growth. Completion of the railroad network before 1910 and changing modes of transportation in the inter-war years help account for the slackening in this important category.[13] On the other hand, the increasing significance of consumption, reflected in the growth of nation-wide marketing, the proliferation of retail services, and the rise of insurance, savings, and credit services explains much of the buoyancy in trade and finance. In this same connection, the absolute decline in personal and domestic services registers the shrinking of the labor force available for domestic work, for there is every indication that personal services outside the home have greatly expanded during the last forty years. Finally, the upsurge in professional activity since World War I is the understandable concomitant of further developments in the urban-industrial organization of society, with its dependence on scientific, technical, and organizational "expertese."

[13] Part of the change, however, is explained by the difficulty of meaningful classification within the service sector. Should not the large numbers employed in servicing automobiles and their drivers, for example, be classified as transportation workers?

17 / Regional adjustments within the national economy, 1910-1950:

(3) REGIONAL INDUSTRIAL STRUCTURES AND INCOME

The changes that have occurred since 1910 in the structure and geographical distribution of productive activities within the national framework have had effects on the structure of activities in the regions themselves, which we shall now consider. By the early twentieth century, as we have seen, the farthest reaches of the United States had been brought into the national economy, and continued growth no longer involved the settlement and development of "empty" territories. For practical purposes, all parts of the country were accessible to one another. The completion of the Panama Canal and the introduction of truck-hauling services effectively reduced the transport costs that had for so long retarded the full development of the greater West. The resource potential of every region was finally at the disposal of a truly nation-wide system of production and marketing. The gradual decline of regional interests and wage differentials during the present century reflects this greater effective mobility of capital and labor.

Thus, by 1910, the stage was set for a period of intensive interregional competition in which every type of productive activity must sooner or later meet the test of higher outputs at lower unit cost.[1] Changes in the industrial structures of the eight regions since 1910 reflect both this heightening of inter-regional competition and, more variously, the secular movement of labor out of resource activities and manufacture into services.

The effects of the long-run secular change in the national labor force are summarized once again in Table 114. The period 1910-1950 was one in which all types of production except services declined in their shares of the total labor

---

[1] The progressive reduction of the freight factor in total costs of production, especially in regard to movements of raw materials, has enlarged the geographical area in which production is potentially located. While production has become more "foot-loose" in this sense, competition among sites for a given activity has generally been heightened.

force. Agriculture had reached its peak share, of course, long before 1870 and the onset of nation-wide industrialization; fisheries had peaked about 1890 and forestry and logging at roughly the same time. Mining and manufactures achieved their largest relative shares of the labor force in 1920. Only the tertiary or services sector represented a larger share of the total labor force of the nation in 1950 than in 1910 (and there is no reason to suppose that, if current classifications are maintained, it will not continue to increase for a considerable time to come). These changing proportions of the national labor force provide a yardstick with which to measure and compare the levels of productive activities in the various regions.

Table 114. Labor force, distribution by industry, 1910-1950.

(per cent of total)

Year	Agriculture	Mining	Forestry	Fisheries	Manufacturing	Services
1910	32.46	2.53	0.45	0.18	27.92	36.46
1920	25.63	2.62	0.52	0.13	30.90	40.20
1930	21.44	2.02	0.36	0.15	28.90	47.13
1940	17.53	1.84	0.38	0.12	21.01	59.12
1950	11.56	1.54	0.36	0.13	23.92	62.49

SOURCE: Appendix Table A1-A7.

Industrial Structure of the New England Labor Force, 1910–1950

The industrial structure of New England's labor force is shown in Table 115. The resource sectors as a whole have continued to decline in importance since 1910. Mining, mostly quarrying, now employs only one-tenth of 1% of the regional labor force, and agriculture upwards of 3%. New England, in fact,

Table 115. Distribution by industry of New England region labor force, 1910-1950.

(per cent of total)

Year	Agriculture	Mining	Forestry	Fisheries	Manufacturing	Services
1910	9.65	0.31	0.31	*0.43*	*49.05*	*40.25*
1920	6.93	0.15	*0.69*	*0.28*	*50.63*	*41.32*
1930	6.20	0.19	0.31	*0.33*	*43.10*	*49.87*
1940	4.52	0.14	*0.42*	*0.25*	*34.24*	*60.43*
1950	3.15	0.13	0.34	*0.31*	*35.46*	60.61

Figures in italics are above the national average.

SOURCE: Appendix Tables A1-A7.

has very little activity left in the resources sector. It is worthy of note, however, that its proportion of workers in fisheries, though smaller in 1950 than in 1910, was above the national level throughout this period, as was the proportion in forestry during two of the decades under review.

In spite of relative decline in most of its basic industries in recent years, New England is still a heavily concentrated manufacturing region. By 1930, however, its expanding service sector had surpassed its declining manufacturing sector.

The differences between the industrial structures of northern and southern New England were somewhat less marked in 1950 than in the years before 1910. Although Connecticut and Rhode Island were still the most concentrated manufacturing states in the region in 1950, New Hampshire had surpassed Massachusetts and risen to third place. Massachusetts, however, retained its priority in the service sector and in fisheries. Vermont was still by far the most agricultural state in the region in 1950, with more than 17% of its workers on farms; Maine had the second highest relative concentration of loggers in the country, being surpassed only by Oregon.

Industrial Structure of the Middle Atlantic Labor Force, 1910–1950

Table 116 shows the industrial structure of the Middle Atlantic labor force in the recent period. In 1950 this region had the highest concentration of the nation's services. The growth of commerce and finance in the metropolitan areas and the enormous expansion of government and related activities in

Table 116. Distribution by industry of Middle Atlantic region labor force, 1910-1950.

(per cent of total)

Year	Agriculture	Mining	Forestry	Fisheries	Manufacturing	Services
1910	10.39	*3.94*	0.15	0.16	*39.75*	*45.61*
1920	7.38	*3.45*	0.15	0.09	*40.43*	*48.50*
1930	5.72	*2.65*	0.08	0.09	*35.72*	*55.74*
1940	4.44	*1.97*	0.07	0.07	*26.32*	*67.13*
1950	3.09	1.48	0.07	0.07	*29.68*	*65.61*

Figures in italics are above the national average.

SOURCE: Appendix Tables A1-A7.

and around the District of Columbia have reinforced the tendency for the tertiary activities to expand at a more rapid rate than the primary and secondary sectors. The Middle Atlantic region, in fact, has become the least agricultural region in the country. In all other resource activities, also, it has grown considerably less important, notwithstanding the great concentration of coal miners in Pennsylvania. Like New England, and indeed like advanced manufacturing areas elsewhere in the world, the Middle Atlantic region depends increasingly on the material resources of other less developed regions for its economic progress.

As in 1910, New Jersey had the heaviest concentration of manufactures in this region in 1950 and Delaware the heaviest concentration of agricultural labor. Pennsylvania, of course, had the largest proportion of mine workers, and Maryland (together with the District of Columbia) the heaviest concentration of service workers, having recently surpassed New York.

Industrial Structure of the Labor Force in the Great Lakes Region, 1910–1950

The Great Lakes region's industrial structure is shown in Table 121. During the present century, the growth of its labor force has been based on manufactures and services rather than resources; its resources have been in sharp decline since about 1930. Indeed, the Great Lakes region is unique among the more advanced industrial regions in having a slightly heavier concentration of manufactures in 1950 than in 1910, though manufacturing here has not regained its pre-depression peak and may even now be in relative decline. Michigan and Ohio have the greatest concentration of manufacturing labor in the region; Wisconsin and Illinois have the lowest, yet both exceed the national level of manufactures by a very considerable margin.

Table 117. Distribution by industry of Great Lakes region labor force, 1910-1950

(per cent of total)

Year	Agriculture	Mining	Forestry	Fisheries	Manufacturing	Services
1910	25.16	*2.61*	0.31	0.10	*33.19*	*38.63*
1920	18.72	2.54	0.41	0.05	*37.36*	*40.92*
1930	14.36	1.43	0.19	0.06	*35.72*	*48.24*
1940	12.51	1.13	0.13	0.04	28.88	57.31
1950	8.36	0.87	0.10	0.04	*33.43*	57.20

Figures in italics are above the national average.

SOURCE: Appendix Tables A1-A7.

Until the 1930's, the Great Lakes region had a substantial agricultural sector, but since 1940 this has undergone a sharp relative decline, and by 1950 agricultural workers comprised little more than 8% of the regional labor force. Wisconsin, however, had the heaviest concentration of farm labor in the entire urban-industrial Northeast in 1950 (17.9%), and Indiana had the third largest (11%).

The decline of mining in the region has been due mainly to the relative eclipse of iron and copper mining in Michigan. Though much of the fuel supply is still obtained locally, some of the mining areas must be included among the relatively depressed parts of the country. The forests of the region have also become a wasting asset; even Wisconsin is now well below the national level of forest employment. More surprising, the proportion of the regional labor force in service employment has also slipped below the national level in recent years; in 1950 Illinois had the region's largest concentration of service workers—61.7%—but remained just below the national proportion of 62.5%. Except for Michigan, services have grown at a lower rate than in the nation as a whole. It is in manufactures, therefore, that the Great Lakes region has shown the greatest relative strength in the 1910-1950 period.[2]

Industrial Structure of the Labor Force in the Southeast, 1910-1950

As recently as 1930 the President of the United States referred to the Southeast as "the Nation's No. 1 economic problem." At that time, while the region had only 9% of the national income, it had 21% of the nation's population and

Table 118. Distribution by industry of Southeast region labor force, 1910–1950

(per cent of total)

Year	Agriculture	Mining	Forestry	Fisheries	Manufacturing	Services
1910	*58.93*	1.73	*0.65*	*0.23*	14.46	24.00
1920	*49.49*	2.72	*0.67*	*0.20*	18.38	28.54
1930	*42.21*	2.52	*0.57*	*0.28*	19.78	34.64
1940	*33.41*	2.60	*0.77*	*0.23*	15.40	47.59
1950	*21.35*	2.60	*0.76*	*0.24*	17.79	57.26

Figures in italics are above the national average.

SOURCE: Appendix Tables A1-A7.

the highest birth rate in the country.[3] Table 118 shows the changing industrial structure of the Southeast since 1910. Compared with the earlier period, there has been a significant industrial expansion over the last four decades. However, manufactures have risen only very slowly, though the Southeast is the only

[2] In the late nineteenth century the Great Lakes region became the largest producer of silage corn and whole milk. It is still rich in coal and oil resources and formerly had the greatest regional production of iron and copper ore. The region has the cheapest and most efficient system of natural inland waterways; it produces more automobiles, processes more rubber, makes more farm equipment and, along with the Plains region, packs more meat than any other part of the country.

[3] R. B. Vance, *The South's Place in the Nation*, (Public Affairs Pamphlet, No. 6, Revised 1941), pp. 8, 14; H. W. Odum, *Southern Regions of the United States* (Chapel Hill: University of North Carolina Press, 1936), p. 51.

region except the Great Lakes to have a higher proportion of its labor force in manufactures in 1950 than in 1910. In 1950, however, Southeastern manufacturing had not regained the structural importance it had achieved in 1930. It is perhaps too early to judge whether this crucial sector is now in relative decline, as it appears to be everywhere else in the country.

It is clear that the Southeast is still a major resource region: it is the only region in the country to be above the national level in all four primary resource sectors. The manpower in agriculture has shown a steady decline, especially since 1930, while mining has gathered strength. Between 1940 and 1950 the Southeast displaced the Middle Atlantic region as the third most concentrated mining region in the country. Its forests and fisheries are major suppliers for the nation, and employment in both sectors appears buoyant.

Within the region itself, the range of industrial structures exhibited by the states is very great, yet no single state presents a structural profile which resembles that of the nation as a whole. The Carolinas and Georgia, for example, come closest to the national proportion of manufacturing employment, but their agricultural sectors still comprise from one-fifth to one-quarter of their entire labor forces. In 1950, eight states in the Southeast had larger agricultural than manufacturing sectors. Mississippi was at the top of the list with 40.8% of its labor force in agriculture and only 10.6% in manufactures; its service sector, 46.6%, was the lowest in the region and in the nation.

Five Southeastern states—West Virginia, Kentucky, Louisiana, Alabama, and Virginia—are above the national level in mining employment. West Virginia, in fact, has the greatest concentration of mining employment of any state in the Union, 20.3%; its closest rivals are Wyoming with 7.2% and, in the Southeast, Kentucky with 6.8%. West Virginia has a greater share of its total labor force in mining than in either agriculture (9.4%) or manufactures (17.2%). In view of the secular decline in coal mining, this is by no means a favorable situation.

Georgia, Arkansas, and Mississippi have the largest concentrations of logging employment, ranging from 1.2% to 1.3% of their respective labor forces, while Kentucky has the lowest, 0.3%. Louisiana and Florida have the largest proportions in fisheries, 0.8% and 0.6%, and West Virginia the lowest, only one-tenth of 1%. Florida has by far the largest concentration of service employment, 77.7%, a proportion which is exceeded in only one other state, Nevada, and the District of Columbia.

Industrial Structure of the Labor Force in the Plains Region, 1910–1950

The Plains region presents a somewhat different kind of economic growth problem. Its population density is rising very slowly, for its decennial increases in population have been the lowest in the nation since 1890; its share of national population has declined by more than 26% since 1910 and its share of the labor force by 20%. This is a great farming region. By 1950 the Plains region had an even higher concentration of agricultural workers in its labor force than the Southeast (Table 119).

The region's contribution to the nation's iron ore supply since the 1890's has been monumental, but employment in mining (chiefly in Minnesota) has, with minor interruption, been in relative decline since 1920. Meanwhile employment in forests and fisheries has also gone into eclipse. Manufactures reached their peak share of the regional labor force in 1920 and declined by almost one-half during the depression decade. There has been partial recovery since 1940 in

Table 119. Distribution by industry of Plains region labor force, 1910-1950

(per cent of total)

Year	Agriculture	Mining	Forestry	Fisheries	Manufacturing	Services
1910	*40.85*	1.82	0.29	0.04	19.99	37.07
1920	*36.35*	1.62	0.44	0.03	21.04	40.52
1930	*33.59*	1.05	0.18	0.04	19.85	45.29
1940	*30.46*	0.95	0.15	0.02	11.26	57.16
1950	*23.84*	0.86	0.14	0.03	14.75	60.38

Figures in italics are above the national average.

SOURCE: Appendix Tables A1-A7.

some of the eastern Plains states, but it has not been adequate to bring the region much closer to parity in manufacturing employment with the rest of the nation. Since 1920, in fact, the Southeast has made a much better showing in manufactures than the Plains region and has experienced a greater percentage increase in its service sector.

By 1950 Missouri was the only Plains state which almost approached the national proportion of manufacturing employment, and the only one with a manufacturing concentration greater than its agricultural concentration. North Dakota has the lowest proportion of manufacturing employment in the nation (2.8%); South Dakota, the third lowest (4.6%). North Dakota has the nation's greatest concentration of agricultural labor—43.2%; and South Dakota, with 39%, has the third highest, following Mississippi in the Southeast. Minnesota, with one-third of 1% of its labor force in logging is the leading forest employer in the region. And Minnesota with 1.3% and South Dakota with 1.08%, have the largest proportions of mining employment; Nebraska with only two-tenths of 1% is the lowest. Kansas and Nebraska have the highest concentrations of service employment, 64.1% and 62.3% respectively, while North Dakota has the lowest, 53.6%. Clearly, the saving grace of the Plains region is the fact that its population growth is slight. It has escaped the threat of relative impoverishment through the willingness of its people to follow employment opportunities to other parts of the country. Relative net downward population shifts in the seven Plains states between 1910 and 1950 amounted to more than one-third of the total net downward shift for the nation.[4]

[4] Missouri, Iowa, and Kansas alone accounted for 22.27% of the total net downward shift in population between 1910 and 1950 (See Table 82).

Industrial Structure of the Labor Force in the Southwest, 1910-1950

Table 120 shows the industrial structure of the Southwest's labor force since 1910. The region has remained primarily a resource region with important segments of the nation's agriculture, mining, and, to a lesser extent, forestry

Table 120. Distribution by industry of Southwest region labor force, 1910-1950

(per cent of total)

Year	Agriculture	Mining	Forestry	Fisheries	Manufacturing	Services
1910	*57.67*	1.77	0.36	0.05	12.37	27.78
1920	*44.88*	*3.49*	0.30	0.03	15.62	35.68
1930	*37.24*	*2.90*	0.27	0.05	17.45	42.09
1940	*29.15*	*3.47*	0.28	0.06	8.11	58.93
1950	*16.01*	*3.52*	0.22	0.08	11.01	*69.16*

Figures in italics are above the national average.

SOURCE: Appendix Tables A1-A7.

carried on within its bounds. Its fishing resources are as yet very slight, but the Gulf ports of Texas are contributing more to the nation's fisheries each decade. Since 1930, the region has rapidly increased the relative size of its service sector, and by 1950 only the Far West had a proportionately larger body of service workers. Manufactures, which were still growing relatively through 1930, declined sharply in the depression years, but their relative importance has increased again since 1940. Nevertheless, the Southwest had the second lowest concentration of manufactures in the country in 1950.

The heaviest manufacturing concentration in this region has been achieved in recent decades by Texas, which had about 12% of its labor force in manufactures by 1950.[5] New Mexico is now the least affected by industrialism, with only 5.1% in manufactures. Oklahoma has the highest proportion of farm labor in the region—19.6%—and Arizona the lowest—14.1%. Oklahoma also has the highest relative concentration of workers engaged in mineral extraction—almost 5% in 1950—while Texas, somewhat surprisingly, has the lowest—3%. The regions' forest resources are very small. Arizona has the largest proportion of forest labor, but that amounts to only three-tenths of 1%. All four Southwestern states have high proportions of service employment, ranging from 73.8% in Arizona to 66.1% in Oklahoma. In absolute terms, of course, Texas dominates the Southwest, and its enormous endowments of agricultural and mineral wealth have served to enrich not only the region but the entire nation.

[5] In 1910 Arizona had the highest proportion of manufacturing, 20.8%, and Texas the lowest, 11.8%.

Industrial Structure of the Labor Force in the Mountain Region 1910-1950

The industrial structure of productive activities in the Mountain region between 1910 and 1950 is presented in Table 121. This region also remains primarily a resource region. Throughout most of the period it had the heaviest relative concentration of mineral workers in the country; by 1950, however, it was surpassed in this respect by the more populous Southwest. Since 1920 its proportion of agricultural employment has been above the national average. In

Table 121. Distribution by industry of Mountain region labor force, 1910-1950

(per cent of total)

Year	Agriculture	Mining	Forestry	Fisheries	Manufacturing	Services
1910	29.93	*8.47*	*0.67*	0.02	20.48	40.43
1920	*32.85*	*6.65*	*1.07*	0.01	18.72	*40.70*
1930	*30.95*	5.25	*0.98*	0.02	18.12	44.68
1940	25.12	5.10	*0.61*	0.03	7.64	*61.50*
1950	17.72	3.44	*0.50*	0.04	9.46	*68.84*

Figures in italics are above the national average.

SOURCE: Appendix Tables A1-A7.

logging employment, the peak share of the national total was reached in 1930, but the peak share in the regional labor force had been reached a decade before this. Its manufacturing employment reached a peak in 1910, somewhat earlier than in other new regions of the West. After 1930, the most rapidly growing employment sector was services, which surpassed the national level throughout most of the period.

Utah and Colorado have the heaviest concentrations of manufactures in the region (about 11% each) and Wyoming the lowest (5.2%). Idaho has remained the most agricultural state in the region (25.6%), closely followed by Montana (23.7%); Utah is now the least agricultural (11.8%). In mineral employment, Wyoming leads the region with 7.2% and Colorado is in the lowest position with only 2.0%. In forestry employment, Idaho has the heaviest concentration, amounting in 1950 to 1.4%; Montana is in second place with 0.8%. Utah and Colorado lead in services activities, their service employments in 1950 amounting to 71.6% and 72.3% of their respective labor forces. Idaho has the lowest regional share of services, 62.9%. The economic structure of this region suggests a rather unique resources-services base of economic activities whose progress is closely tied to developments in the major industrial centers of the country and to federal government policy.

Industrial Structure of the Labor Force in the Far West, 1910-1950

The promise for growth shown before 1910 by this great "empire apart" has, on the whole, been fulfilled in the intervening years. With every decade since 1910 the Far West has absorbed a greater share of the nation's population. Its only rival has been the Southwest, where the rate of population increase has nevertheless been much smaller. The resulting density is still much below that of the urban-industrial Northeast or the largely rural-agricultural Southeast, but since 1940 it has exceeded that of the Plains by a growing margin. In the single decade 1940-50 the population of the Far West increased by almost 30%.

Table 122. Distribution by industry of Far West region labor force, 1910-1950

(per cent of total)

Year	Agriculture	Mining	Forestry	Fisheries	Manufacturing	Services
1910	20.10	*2.84*	*2.04*	*0.47*	26.95	*47.60*
1920	18.33	1.71	*1.85*	*0.42*	28.89	*48.80*
1930	14.56	1.45	*1.41*	*0.35*	25.99	*56.24*
1940	11.51	1.52	*1.18*	*0.26*	14.83	*70.70*
1950	7.44	0.65	*0.99*	*0.24*	16.85	*73.83*

Figures in italics are above the national average.

Source: Appendix Tables A1-A7.

Table 122 shows the changing industrial structure of this rapid growth region. The Far West has the smallest proportion of agricultural workers in its labor force anywhere outside the New England and Middle Atlantic regions; and its concentration of mineral activities has been below the national level since 1910. Its proportion of fishing employment still exceeded the national level in 1950, but it had fallen throughout the period. Forestry is the only primary resource sector in which the Far West retained national priority.[6]

Between 1930 and 1950 the Far West's labor force grew from about 3,500,000 to 6,000,000 or from about 7.4% of the national labor force to 10%. During the same two decades the combined resource sector fell from 17.8% to 9.3%, and the combined manufacturing-service component rose from 82.2% to 90.7%. It was services, however, more than manufactures, that accounted for this rise in the industrial component. Over these years the proportion of the total regional labor force employed in services increased from 56.2% to 73.8%. Services, therefore, absorbed not only the bulk of the displaced primary workers

[6] Annual cut still exceeds growth; though this holds true for most logging areas, it is especially pronounced in the Far West, which contains the greatest share of the nation's forest resources. The immense construction needs of the region in recent decades and the availability of new timber have resulted in the virtual destruction of whole forests.

but secondary workers as well, and no doubt the larger portion of in-migrants.

The somewhat faster rate of increase in the region's population than in its labor force during this period reflects the large proportion of persons under and over employment age. Thus the rising numbers of service workers were partly employed in serving a population which was not itself fully employed. Such important activities as trade and finance, the professions, education, recreation and entertainment, and, not least, construction, experienced considerable impetus from the investment of capital which had been accumulated outside the Far West itself.

The small absolute decline in resource employment between 1930 and 1950, and a somewhat larger absolute decline in manufacturing employment, appear as very large relative declines in these sectors since 1930 (Table 122) when set against the absolute growth of the Far Western labor force in general and the service sector in particular. Whether this rate of growth in the service sector can be sustained is quite another matter; whether it is something peculiar to the spectacular growth of the Far West during the historical period 1930-1950 is something which can only be determined by future developments.[7]

In 1950 California had much the heaviest concentration of manufacturing employment within the Far West, 17%, and Nevada the lightest, only 4.6%. Oregon had the heaviest local concentrations of both agricultural and forest employment, 11.4% and 4.5% respectively. In fact, by 1950, Oregon had the heaviest relative concentration of loggers and woodsmen of any state in the country and the largest in absolute terms as well. Because of the very small size of its labor force, Nevada had the largest proportion of miners of any Far Western state—4.7%—but in absolute terms, of course, they numbered less than one-tenth the mineral labor force in California. For the same reason, Nevada also had the heaviest concentration of service activities in the nation, 81.5%—exceeded only by the special case of the District of Columbia; yet, compared with California or any other Far Western state, the actual number of service workers in Nevada was always insignificant. In relative terms, priority in the region's fisheries had by 1950 passed to Washington (0.54% compared with California's 0.18%), but in absolute terms the 8,000 fishermen of California outnumbered those of Washington or any other state in the Union.

The enormous growth of the California labor force is one of the most striking phenomena in recent economic history. In 1910 California was only tenth among the states in the number of its workers; in 1950 it was surpassed only by New York itself. From less than a quarter of a million workers in 1870 it had risen to almost four and a half millions at the mid-century.

[7] In many ways the Far West is the most favored region in the country. Rainfall reaches 60 inches in some localities, while in arid areas irrigation projects permit a growing season up to 8 months. It is a region of profitable agricultural specialties, though water supply may prove to be a critical limitation. It is the largest lumber producer and has the richest fisheries; it is the leading gold producer and, more important, the second largest oil region after Texas-Oklahoma. Industrialization is based on its oil and water power resources. The region has recently become a center for ships, aircraft, aluminum, and scientific research. The rapidly growing population makes the region a major market for utilities and consumption goods.

Income Changes, 1920–1950

The structural adjustments in population and labor force described above were accompanied by significant changes in personal income payments among the various regions. These are analyzed in some detail in Part V of this book. However, to round off the descriptive picture of regional economic development in recent decades, we here present summary data on income changes during the period 1920-1950.

Changes in the relative position of regions with regard to total personal income have characterized the entire period. Between 1920 and 1930, for example, a significant relative decline in total personal income occurred in four regions: the Mountain, Southeast, Southwest, and Plains regions, i.e. in the regions with the highest relative proportions of their labor forces in agriculture. In the Far West and Middle Atlantic regions, on the other hand, total personal income was higher in 1930 than in 1920. Over the depression decade, 1930-40, an essentially reverse change took place. During this interval, all of the agricultural regions except the Plains improved their relative positions, while two of the urban-industrial regions, the Middle Atlantic and New England, experienced some decline. A similar pattern obtained for the period 1940-1950. Because of the unusual agricultural prosperity in 1950, all of the farm regions had a better income standing in this year than in 1940.

Table 123 shows the effect of these varying regional rates of change on the shares of total personal income.

The net shifts in total personal income among the states over the 1920-1950 period as a whole are shown in Figure 41, and the principal upward and downward shifts are summarized in Table 124. In the Far West, every state registered

Table 123. Regional distribution of total personal income in the United States, 1920-1950

(U. S. income in millions)

Region	1920*	1930	1940	1950
United States	$69,276	$76,780	$78,522	$225,473
	100%	100%	100%	100%
New England	8.75	8.58	8.15	6.73
Middle Atlantic**	30.20	33.32	30.50	26.37
Great Lakes	22.21	22.57	22.69	22.51
Southeast	13.02	11.15	13.23	15.16
Plains	10.27	8.86	8.30	8.81
Southwest	5.69	4.75	5.21	6.50
Mountain	2.47	1.93	2.03	2.22
Far West	7.39	8.84	9.89	11.70

* 1919-21 average.

** 1920—D.C. omitted; 1930-50—D.C. included.

SOURCE: Same as Table 8.

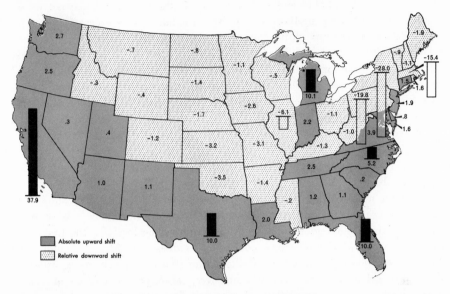

Figure 41. Net Shift in Total Personal Income, 1920-50.

State figures represent % of total net shift. Total net shift as % of incremental change: 14.7. Total net shift as % of 1920 personal income: 32.7.

some net upward shift of personal income, and California alone accounted for more than a third of the national upward shift. In the Southeast, Florida, North Carolina, and Virginia made the greatest relative gains, with Tennessee, Louisiana, and Alabama showing less sizable increases. Michigan was the only state in the Great Lakes region that made any notable relative gain; indeed in

Table 124. Principal net shifts in total personal income among states, 1920-1950

	Percentage net upward shift		Percentage net downward shift
California	37.85	New York	28.04
Michigan	10.09	Pennsylvania	19.76
Florida	9.99	Massachusetts	15.36
Texas	9.97	Illinois	6.08
N. Carolina	5.20	Oklahoma	3.48
Virginia	3.93	Kansas	3.15
Washington	2.70	Missouri	3.14
Oregon	2.50	Iowa	2.56
Tennessee	2.48	Maine	1.84
Indiana	2.19	Nebraska	1.68

SOURCE: Same as Table 8.

all the other Great Lakes states except Indiana there were relative net downward shifts, especially in Illinois. All New England states except Connecticut had relative downward shifts but only Massachusetts showed very serious relative decline. In the Middle Atlantic region, New York and Pennsylvania together contributed more than 47% of the total net downward shift in personal income; New Jersey, Maryland, and Delaware all registered net upward shifts. The Plains region was the only region in which every state suffered relative losses; the total for the region was 13.9%. In the Mountain region, only Utah registered a slight relative net upward shift; all other Mountain states underwent relative decline.

Table 125 compares real personal income per capita in the eight regions for the years between 1920 and 1950 with the national average for these years. Throughout most of this period four urban-industrial regions rank above the national average and four rural-agricultural regions rank below. After 1920, when the Mountain region falls below the countryside level for the first time, the rank order of the relatively poorer states does not change, though after 1930 all converge upwards toward the national average. The rank order of the richer urban-industrial regions, however, is subject to change in almost every decade, though after 1930 all converge downwards toward the national average.

Table 125. Rank order of regions by personal income per capita,* 1920-1950

(1929 dollars)

1920		1930		1940		1950	
F.W.	780.6	M.A.	912.9	M.A.	965.8	F.W.	1,279.4
M.A.	772.5	F.W.	837.0	F.W.	959.7	M.A.	1,255.2
N.E.	719.3	N.E.	826.7	N.E.	925.4	G.L.	1,183.9
G. L.	623.5	G.L.	701.6	G.L.	815.4	N.E.	1,160.4
Mt.	590.7	U. S.	**640.0**	U. S.	**727.4**	U. S.	**1,062.7**
U. S.	**578.0**	Mt.	551.8	Mt.	649.2	Mt.	1,017.8
Pl.	501.0	Pl.	523.1	Pl.	590.5	Pl.	1,003.6
S.W.	466.2	S.W.	411.3	S.W.	511.0	S.W.	916.6
S.E.	326.2	S.E.	321.0	S.E.	419.3	S.E.	719.2

* Weighted averages of state incomes per capita.

SOURCE: Same as Table 9.

Relationship of Personal Income and Population

A comparison of regional income shares with regional population shares for the years between 1870 and 1950 throws some light on changing levels of living in the various parts of the country during the period of rapid national growth after 1870. Table 126 shows the year in which each region reached its *peak* share of the nation's total population and the year in which it reached its *peak* share of total personal income. It also describes the trend of per capita personal income in each region relative to the national average level since 1870. The significant feature of this trend is the great rise in real per capita income throughout the nation and the reduction in the disparity between regional average levels of living. Since 1920, the convergence in per capita income has become even more marked than in the period before that date, in spite of the transformations brought about by alternations of prosperity and depression.

Some interesting connections between the growth of population and total personal income are reflected in the changing levels of per capita income in the various regions. Three of the eight regions reach their peak shares of both total population and personal income before the beginning of our period in 1870: the New England, Middle Atlantic, and Southeast regions.[8] As these three regions had all been settled and partly developed during the eighteenth and first half of the nineteenth centuries, the development of newer regions to the west could be expected to be at the expense of their relative shares. The five other regions, however, reach or approach their peak shares of total population and personal income after 1870 in the following order: the Great Lakes, the Plains, the Mountain, the Southwest, and the Far West. The last two, in fact, appeared to be still enlarging their shares of the two national totals at the expense of the rest of the country as recently as 1950. It follows from what we have already noted about convergence in regional levels of per capita personal income that the redistribution of population and total personal income has proceeded at a much slower pace since World War I than before.

The experience of the four Western regions (and of the Great Lakes region also) indicates that both population and total personal income shares grow very rapidly during the initial phases of settlement but that the rate of growth tends to slacken after a certain period has elapsed. As a result of this rapid initial growth, per capita personal income levels in the four Western regions were converging towards the national average by 1900. Unusually rapid population growth would seem to cease in each case at about the time when per capita personal income comes closest to the national average level—in other words, when total personal income ceases to maintain its earlier rapid rate of growth or when population has been increasing at a more rapid rate than total income.

The Great Lakes region's share of national population peaked around 1870; over the ensuing decades the rate of population growth and the share of total population slowly declined. The share of total personal income continued to

---

[8] The fact that the Southeast has recently surpassed its 1880 share of total personal income once again does not belie the fact that its shares of both income and population peaked before the Civil War. There is reason to believe that the Southeast's share of total personal income had fallen drastically from pre-war proportions by 1880; see R. A. Easterlin, "Interregional Differences in Per Capita Income, Population, and Total Income, United States, 1840-1950," National Bureau of Economic Research, *Conference on Research in Income and Wealth*, Sept. 4-5, 1957 (mimeo).

Table 126. Regional peaks of population and total personal income shares, and trend of regional relative to national per capita income in the United States since 1870

Region	Peak year for population relative to that of the nation	Peak year for total personal income relative to that of the nation	Trend of per capita income relative to that of the nation
New England	before 1870	before 1880	Always *above* U. S. Rising before 1880 but converging slowly downward toward U.S. thereafter.
Middle Atlantic	before 1870	before 1880	Always *above* U.S. but converging downward toward national level after 1900.
Great Lakes	ca. 1870	ca. 1880	Converges from *below* U.S. level about 1880, diverges *above* thereafter until about 1930.
Southeast	before 1870	Only since 1940 has it risen above 1880 relative level	*Below* U.S. always, but converges upward slightly after 1900. Diverges downward again after 1920 until late 1930's when it converges once more.
Plains	ca. 1890	ca. 1900	Always *below* U.S. but converges from below before 1900. Diverging downward thereafter until about 1940.
Southwest	1950 still rising	1950 still rising	Always *below* U.S. but converging slowly until 1920; diverging downward until 1930, converging upward since 1940.
Mountain	ca. 1920	ca. 1900	*Above* U.S. before 1920 but converging downward sharply. Diverges *below* U.S. until 1930's, converging upward again after 1940.
Far West	1950 still rising	1950 still rising	Always *above* U.S., but converging slowly downward to national level throughout period, except for rapid upward divergence during 1930's.

grow, however, and the level of per capita income surpassed the national average in all the years for which there are income data. In or around 1880, the share of total personal income was at its peak; thereafter it also declined, although more slowly than the share of total population. For this reason per capita personal income in the Great Lakes region continued to rise as compared with the national average. Between 1900 and 1920 the region moved into fourth rank order of regional per capita income, behind the other three leading urban-industrial regions.

The Plains region reached its peak share of national population around 1890; its rate of population growth and its share of total population then fell off quite rapidly. Total personal income reached its peak share a decade later, about 1900, and thereafter sharply declined, somewhat more sharply in fact than the population share. As a consequence, per capita personal income in the Plains region came into closest convergence with the country-wide average in 1900, after which it continued to fall through 1920.[9]

In contrast, in the more sparsely populated agricultural Southwest, there was a gradual convergence on the national level throughout the 1870-1950 period. The rate of population growth began to slacken as early as 1880, but it nevertheless continued to be higher than the rate for the nation as a whole; hence the share of total population also continued to grow, although at a markedly slower pace after 1910. The region's share of total personal income also rose down through 1920 and, although the rate of increase was slower after 1900 than before, it stayed ahead of population growth at all times. Thus, the level of per capita income in the Southwest had a greater relative rise than that of the Plains region, even though in absolute terms it remained somewhat below the Plains level.

The experience of the Mountain region differs somewhat from that of any other region although the main trend broadly parallels that of the Plains. As in the Southwest, however, the rate of population growth, despite some fluctuations, was somewhat higher than the national average rate throughout the years from 1870 to 1920. The region reached its peak share in the national population around 1920, at which time it was still the most sparsely populated area in the country. The growth of total personal income, however, had meanwhile not sufficed to raise the share of the national total beyond the level of 1900; in fact, the share had declined some 2% by 1920. Hence, while the population share increased after 1900, the personal income share fell somewhat, and the effect on per capita personal income was decline. Personal income per capita in the Mountain region had been among the highest in the nation around 1880-1900. After 1910 it converged rapidly downward toward the national average, and after 1920 it was below the national average for the rest of the period.

The Far West alone among the newer Western regions maintained a very high level of per capita income throughout the entire 1870-1950 period. Though not by Eastern standards a densely populated region, the Far West is heavily populated. From 1870 to 1890 it had a heavy rate of population increase, which slackened only during the depression years of the nineties; and after 1900, its decennial rate of increase was, without exception, considerably greater than that of any other region. But through most of the period since 1900 its total personal income has maintained a fast rate of growth. Hence, despite its sustained population growth, the Far West has had the highest

[9]The Plains did not arrest its relative decline in per capita personal income much before 1940.

level of per capita income of any region in the country during the present century except for a brief interval in the inter-World War years when it was surpassed by the Middle Atlantic region. Nevertheless, its per capita income level has been slowly converging toward the national level in recent years.

The share of New England in the nation's population declined steadily throughout the 1870-1950 period. But that of the Middle Atlantic region, though it declined between 1870 and 1890, turned upward again after 1900 and continued to grow through 1940. In both these regions, it is likely that per capita income levels rose high above the national average over the third quarter of the nineteenth century.[10] After 1880, however, they gravitated slowly downward toward the national level. But the growth of total income in the Middle Atlantic region was such that the fall in its share of the national total was very slight, and after 1900 almost negligible. As a result, this region rose from fourth to third place in rank order of regional per capita income between 1880 and 1900 and from third to second place between 1900 and 1920. From the late twenties until after 1940, it ranked first among the regions in per capita income (Table 125). In New England, on the other hand, the shares both of population and of total personal income declined continuously after 1900. The rate of decline was always greater, however, for population than for income, while both were greater in the period before 1900 than in the years between 1900 and 1920. Between 1880 and 1900 New England fell from third to fourth place in rank order of regional per capita income. Between 1900 and 1920 it rose again to third place owing to the rapid decline of the Mountain region. But by 1950 it had been surpassed by the Great Lakes region and was once more fourth in rank.

Developments in the Southeast differ from those in any other region. The trends here are complicated somewhat by the fact that, during the period under review, the states in the western part of the region were growing while those on the South Atlantic seaboard were in continuous decline. On balance, however, the Southeast's share of total personal income declined between 1880 and 1900, but much of the lost ground was recovered before 1920 by gains in individual states. The population share declined at about the same rate in both periods. The declining population share, accompanied by a rising share in total personal income after 1900, brought the Southeast's level of per capita personal income back towards the average for the nation as a whole. In absolute levels of per capita income, the region was only slightly better off in 1920 than in 1880; the rise over these years was from 50% to 56% of the national average. Between 1920 and 1950, however, the Southeast's share rose significantly to 68% of the national average.

Thus, with minor qualifications, per capita incomes everywhere seem to have converged towards the national level during the opening decades of the twentieth century. And with the possible exception of the Southeast, this trend continued through the entire period 1880-1950. The newer Western regions and the Great Lakes region reveal strikingly similar patterns of association

[10]R. A. Easterlin, "Interregional Differences in Per Capita Income, Population, and Total Income, United States, 1840-1950," *loc. cit., passim.*

between population and total personal income; in all these regions the rapid growth of population and total personal income shares is accompanied by a marked convergence of per capita personal income levels towards the national average. When the rate of growth in regional income shares begins to slacken, as it always does sooner or later, the trend towards parity in regional levels of per capita income is also gradually arrested. The more urban-industrial regions seem to hold their levels of per capita income above the national average, while the more agricultural, less urban-industrial regions seem to settle at below-average levels. In either case, rapid growth apparently ceases at or around the time when per capita personal income levels approach close to the national average. Moreover, if per capita income levels are moving down toward the national average, as for example in the Mountain region, the share of total personal income appears, not unexpectedly, to have ceased its rapid growth phase somewhat before population growth has slowed down. On the other hand, if convergence is upward from below the national average, as in the Great Lakes region around 1870 or the Plains around 1890, it seems likely that rapid growth in the regional share of total population has ceased somewhat before rapid growth in the total income share.

Income and Industrial Structure

We turn finally to some further consideration of the possible relationships among demographic patterns, industrial structure, and levels of per capita personal incomes. The associations between urban-industrial structure and levels of living in 1920 were presented in Table 70. Those existing in 1950 are shown in Table 127.

By 1920, there was a fairly close correlation between the degrees of urbanization and industrialization of the labor force and levels of personal income per capita; a high degree of urban-industrialism meant, without exception, a high level of per capita income in a region. What was true of 1910-1920 had not been true of 1870-1880, when the highest levels of per capita personal income had obtained in the sparsely populated rural-mining regions of the Far West and Mountain states. On the other hand, the association between rural-agricultural structure and low levels of per capita income held consistently in both periods for regions of high and low population density. In 1950 the associations of 1910-1920 still hold in a general way, in spite of the continuing convergence of occupational structures and levels of per capita personal income; urban-industrial regions rank above the national averages as they did in 1910-1920, rural-agricultural regions rank below. The close identity of rank orders among the various categories, however, is no longer so sure.

As regional levels of living and occupational structures have converged on national levels and structures in recent decades, deviations from the earlier identity of rank orders have increased somewhat. The Far West, for example, which again ranked first in per capita income by 1950, ranked fourth in urbanization, third in industrialization (manufacturing-services), and had the

Table 127. Rank order of regions, by personal income per capita, urbanization of population, and labor force industry components, 1950

Region	Personal income per capita (1929 dollars)	Urban proportion of population	Labor force components		
			% Agric.	% Non-agric.* resource	% Mfg.-service
United States	$1,062.7	59.0%**	11.57	2.03	86.40
Far West	*1,279.4*	*62.7* (4)	7.44 (6)	1.87 (4)	*90.69* (3)
Middle Atlantic	*1,255.2*	*74.0* (2)	3.09 (8)	1.62 (5)	*95.29* (2)
Great Lakes	*1,183.9*	*65.7* (3)	8.36 (5)	1.01 (7)	*90.63* (4)
New England	*1,160.4*	*74.3* (1)	3.15 (7)	0.78 (8)	*96.07* (1)
Mountain	1,017.8	51.8 (6)	*17.71* (3)	*3.98* (1)	78.31 (6)
Plains	1,003.6	49.9 (7)	*23.84* (1)	1.03 (6)	75.13 (7)
Southwest	916.6	55.5 (5)	*16.01* (4)	*3.82* (2)	80.17 (5)
Southeast	719.2	38.0 (8)	*21.35* (2)	*3.60* (3)	75.05 (8)

Figures in italics are above the national average.

*Forestry and logging, mining, and fisheries.

**Old Census definition of urban; under new definition the proportion of urban population would be somewhat higher in most cases but would not affect the rank order; under new definition U. S. proportion is 64% in 1950.

Rank order in parentheses.

SOURCE: C. F. Schwartz and R. E. Graham, Jr., *Personal Income by States Since 1929,* Table 1; see Table 8, note; *17th U. S. Census 1950,* see *supra,* Table 4, note; and Appendix Tables A1–A7.

third smallest agricultural component. The Middle Atlantic region ranked second in per capita income, second in urbanization and industrialization, but had the smallest agricultural component of any region. The Great Lakes region ranked third in per capita income, third in urbanization, fourth in industrialization (actually only .06 of a percentage point below the Far West), and had the largest agricultural component of any of the higher income regions. Finally, the small and densely populated New England region in 1950 ranked fourth in per capita income but first in urbanization and industrialization and had the second smallest agricultural component. The rank order of urban-industrial regions in per capita income, incidentally, has not had any apparent connection with the size of their non-agricultural resource components (mining, forestry, and fisheries), at least in the period since 1900.

The fact that occupational structures and levels of living do not have a simple or too-obvious relationship in the more advanced stages of industrial growth is highlighted by the position among the relatively poorer regions. The Plains, for example, with its second lowest level of labor force industrialization, highest agricultural component, and second lowest level of urbanization "ought" to exhibit a lower level of living than the Southwest. As recently as 1950, however, this was not the case. It is noteworthy, nevertheless, that these poorer, less urbanized regions not only still have the largest agricultural labor force components but, with the important exception of the Plains, the largest non-agricultural resource components as well. The Mountain, Southwest, and Southeast regions, in fact, have a higher ratio of non-agricultural resource activity to manufactures than any of the other regions. If their further industrialization turns on the development of the earlier stages of raw materials processing, this kind of activity usually offers relatively low value-added per worker and is not likely, therefore, to cause any sudden improvement in their relative income positions. Now that the convergence of income levels has proceeded so far, further changes in relative income positions will depend on the kinds of activities carried on, i.e. whether low or high value-added per worker, and on adjustments in regional population shares.

But here we are entering on the analysis of what lies behind the more recent expansion of productive activities in various regions and behind the varying rates of growth in income, the subjects of Parts IV and V which follow. In Part III, we have sought only to detail the long-run structural changes in the American economy as background for the economic analysis of more recent regional adjustments.

18 / Resource activities and regional economic growth since 1870:

A RETROSPECT

Since 1870 the people of the United States have experienced an unprecedented rise in their average level of material well-being. Over the first half of this century alone, while population doubled, real national output increased fivefold and output per capita increased two and a half times. But the actual human effort expended—as measured by total man-hours of labor input—increased by only 80%.[1] In the same period real personal income per capita rose by more than 150%, reflecting the fast-growing productive efficiency of the economy as a whole. Economic progress in the United States, has, of course, been interrupted by recurrent, and occasionally extreme, cyclical fluctuations; nevertheless, the long-run upward trend over the last eight decades is unmistakable.

While sharing in the nation's economic progress, the various states and regions have experienced diverse rates of growth, and there has been a continuing tendency for population, productive activities, and personal income to be redistributed across the continental territory. The share of the nation's population residing west of the Mississippi, for example, almost doubled in the years 1870-1950. The share of total personal income payments received west of the Mississippi rose by about half in the years 1880-1950. Personal income per capita has risen in every part of the country and, more significant, differences in average income levels among all of the regions have been reduced, especially in the last quarter of a century. Certain tendencies in the structure of the nation's labor force have also been evident in the changing structure of the regional labor forces. Since 1910, for example, though not before, the agricultural sectors have steadily fallen and the service sectors have risen except in the Mountain region. And since the 1920's, even the Mountain region has conformed to these nationwide trends. From the standpoint of employment, the service sector has provided the bulk of growth. Finally, every region has

---

[1] F. C. Mills, *Productivity and Economic Progress*, Occasional Paper 38 (New York: National Bureau of Economic Research, 1952), pp. 2-5.

become more highly urbanized than it was half a century ago and, though the shape of metropolitan areas has changed since 1920, there seems little likelihood that the urban tide will soon ebb.

The fact that rates of urbanization or of growth in per capita income are usually higher in regions that were still "undeveloped" in the late nineteenth century means that the economic growth of the nation has reduced disparities in levels of living among the regions. Judged by the convergence of personal income per capita, however, the movements of productive resources to and from the more affluent regions have not yet left any of the less affluent regions at a permanent disadvantage. There have been currents of demand and counter-flows of capital, for example, which have served to increase production in many of the less developed parts and have helped raise average levels of well-being. All regions, therefore, contribute something of importance to the continental commonwealth and in turn share in the general gain.

If this convergence of demographic, labor force, and income structures among the regions represents the principal finding of the historical section of this

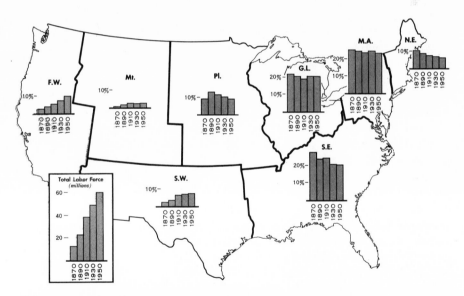

Figure 42. The Changing Regional Structure of the Labor Force, 1870-1950. Source: Appendix Table A-1.

study, it is of almost equal significance that regional differentials have not been entirely eliminated (see Figure 42). Regional differentials (and within regions, state differentials) in the structures of productive activities, in per capita output and income, and in salary-wage rates remain, in spite of the over-all tendency to convergence.

Were it not for the relatively high average levels of personal income that prevailed in the Far West and Mountain regions during the closing decades of the last century, it would appear that the more urban-industrialized parts of the country have been "better-off" than the rural-agricultural regions over the entire period since 1870. Indeed, they have been "better off," for the Far West and Mountain regions at that time were not so much an exception to the rule regarding differentials between urban and rural regions as a distinctive type of region not covered by the urban-rural rubric. Thus the agricultural components of the labor forces in the two regions were far below the agricultural component of the national labor force; they were not rural-agricultural regions of the same type as the Southeast, the Plains, or even the Great Lakes. Nor were they, on the other hand, manufacturing regions such as the New England or Middle Atlantic regions. Rather were they remote, sparsely populated areas with large proportions of their relatively small labor forces engaged in service occupations (especially transportation) and resource activities other than agriculture (mostly mining and lumbering). Already in 1870 the Far West was the third most urbanized region in the country; and some of the Mountain states, Colorado, for example, were urbanized to a surprising degree.

Since 1900 the substantially higher levels of per capita personal income achieved in the more urban-industrial regions have tended to raise the average level for the nation. The differential experience of the Far West and Mountain regions during the decades 1900-1930 underlines this fact. After 1920 the Mountain region fell below the country-wide average, this decline coinciding with the years in which its agricultural labor force component reached an all-time high. Though the Mountain region's per capita income levels have been converging upwards again since 1940, its fortunes have more closely paralleled those of the agricultural Plains rather than those of the more diversified Far West. The rising levels of per capita personal income in all of the agricultural regions in recent decades may stem as much from the fact that they have become more highly specialized parts of the greater industrial economy of the nation as from their higher local concentrations of urban-industrial population. Broadly speaking, urban-industrialization appears to have been the dynamic ecological pattern assumed by growing populations, regionally and nationally, as they have organized to control, utilize, and enjoy a greater volume and variety of material goods and services.[2]

Certainly, the economic and social transformation implicit in the redistribution and restructuring of the labor force and productive activities among the regions after 1870 was a product of rapid industrialization, a process which had already gathered momentum in the Northeastern part of the country during the second quarter of the nineteenth century. Continued industrialization eventually required the mobilization of resources on a continental scale, thereby heightening territorial specialization and regional interdependence across the entire nation. Under the technological and organizational conditions of manufacture prevailing at that time, urban concentration was, so to speak, the

[2]In this regard, see the suggestive hypotheses of J. P. Gibbs and W. T. Martin, "Urbanization and Natural Resources: A Study in Organizational Ecology," *American Sociological Review*, Vol. 23, (June 1958), pp. 266-77.

demographic corollary of rapid economic growth. Apart from the increase in population itself, the crucial variables in the industrial process were technology and organization. Technology, of course, means the practical arts, the physical and intellectual capital accumulated by a resourceful population in order to achieve its higher levels of living: the technologies of transportation, of rapid communications, of manufactures, and, not least, of resource extraction, notably the technologies of agriculture and mineral development. The distinctive role of organization, however, should not be underestimated even though it defies close measurement. It signifies the complex institutional arrangements, the modes of conducting business, the forms of community structure that arise among populations differentiated, functionally and spatially, in the performance of their more specialized and routinized tasks.[3] Organizational functions (for example, the proliferation of independent "middlemen" and formalized bureaucracy) have become major contributors to the growth of service activities; they systematize the wider market and give direction and coherence to the expanding social economy.

In addition to population, technology, and organization, a fourth variable is required to round out the analytic framework of regional economic growth, namely, environment. Natural resources are a special feature of the environment; but, in the broadest sense, the term refers to the total milieu in which a population subsists—all the external forces affecting life, including habitat or dwelling-space and other populations. We have been primarily concerned with the resource potentials of different regional environments but have argued that natural resources do not acquire significance for economic growth until they are confronted by a highly motivated population equipped with technology and organization to develop them. The interdependence among the four variables is implicit in our use of the metaphor "the play of technology on resources." This interplay accounts for both the wider and the more efficient use of resources. Americans organized and applied technology in myriad ways to make the resources of nature useable and available. Whether or not such resources were used at any given time was largely determined, of course, by conditions of the market. Thus the longrun impetus to the development of the agricultural, mineral, and forest potentials of the greater Southeast and West was the expansion of the urban-industrial economies of Western Europe and the Northeastern United States during the nineteenth century; capital and population were exported from both these "advanced" regions in order to render the hitherto untapped resources of undeveloped regions accessible and available to world markets.

The territorial expansion of the American economy, therefore, cannot be understood without recognizing the interplay of technology and environment in meeting the growing demands of urban-industrial populations. The growth of that economy, moreover, cannot be explained historically without considering

---

[3] K. E. Boulding, *The Organizational Revolution* (New York: Harper and Bros., 1953), pp. xvi-xxiv, 202-221. Also, T. W. Schultz, *The Economic Organization of Agriculture* (New York, McGraw-Hill, 1953), which places emphasis on the relation between urban centers and economic development.

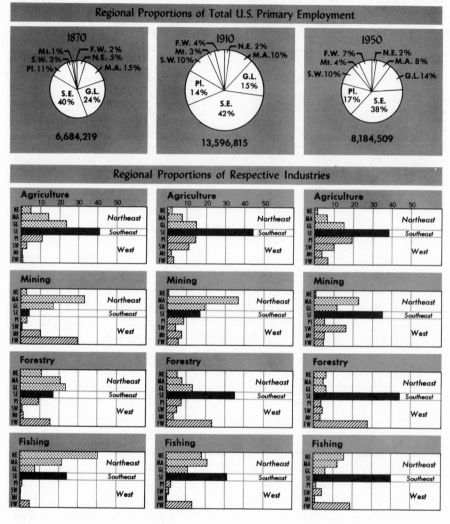

Figure 43. National and Regional Employment in the Primary Industries, 1870, 1910, and 1950.

Source: Appendix Tables A2–A5.

the geographical extension of its effective boundaries and the incorporation of "new" regions into the system of national and international markets. These two features of the period 1870-1910 were, of course, a continuation of a process dating back to the original settlement and development of the maritime sections of North America during the seventeenth and eighteenth centuries. The "triangle trade" of the colonial period, the swelling currents of exchange between the grain producing "Northwest," the cotton-producing "South," and the industrializing "Northeast" during the early nineteenth century, climaxed

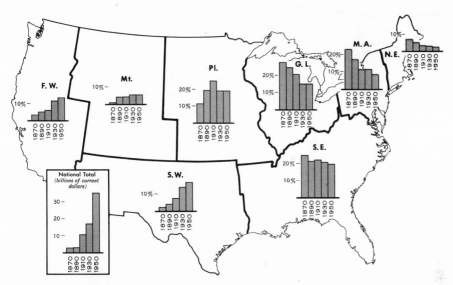

Figure 44. Regional Proportions of Value of Primary Resources Extracted, 1870-1950.
Source: Appendix Table B-1.

in a system of multi-lateral regional interdependence by the close of the century. The continuing extension of accessibility has been a critical factor in the growth of the economy. The exploitation of the contiguous land mass of the interior was always dependent on great improvements in transportation and communications. Before 1840 the economy was for all practical purposes coterminous with the capacities of coastal and inland waterways. Prior to the completion of an integrated railroad network during the last quarter of the nineteenth century, the full resource potential of expanses situated between the Mississippi system and the Pacific coastal fringe could not be made available for economic growth. No doubt, the possibility of occupying and developing the vast Western territory provided a powerful incentive to individual and corporate enterprise at home and abroad. Eventually the greater West was to augment the quantity and variety of resource availabilities; nevertheless, failing the requisite technique and organization to integrate the "new" resource regions into the older Atlantic economy, demand for such resources would have been ineffective and their development retarded.

Throughout the period under review, there has been a substantial redistribution of resource activities across the nation (Figures 43 and 44). This is only to be expected, since many older sources of materials have been depleted, new ones have been developed, and the whole resource economy has been transformed by technological advances which have given rise to new resource uses or have reduced the volume of resource inputs in a given manufactured output. The redistribution of activities was somewhat greater in the first half of the period. The consumption of many raw materials per unit of gross national product has generally declined during the present century,[4] and the location of manufactures has in general become less oriented towards raw materials and more towards markets. All but three of the eight regions—the Plains, the Mountain, and the Far West—have smaller shares of the nation's total resource employment than they had before 1910. Only two regions, moreover, show sizable increases in the proportions of the labor forces employed in major resource activities: the Southeast shows an increase in the relative size of its labor force in both forestry and logging and mineral extraction, the Southwest has a larger proportion in mineral extraction alone (see Figure 43).

Compared with the period before 1910, the redistribution of agricultural activities has been slight: a relatively minor decrease in the Southeast and a somewhat larger concentration in the greater West outside of the Southwest. The major belts of farm staples are unchanged except at their perimeters; high-value crops have continued to locate close to the major urban markets or in a few select localities with special climatic advantages; the more spectacular increases in farm productivity have been largely confined to these same localities.[5] Forestry and logging activities have declined relatively in the Northeast, outside of New England, and have remained relatively stationary in the greater West; the share of the Southeast meanwhile has risen by about the same proportion as that of the Northeast has declined. Mineral activities reveal the greatest redistribution since 1910. The Northeast has declined relatively by almost 40%, the greater West has risen by about 17%, mostly in the Southwest, while the Southeast has more than doubled its share of mineral activities.

Most of the redistribution in mineral activity can be attributed to the change in the relative position of coal and oil products in the nation's fuel economy, to the growth of the Southeast and Southwest, and to the relative decline of coal mining in the Middle Atlantic region. The principal sources of petroleum and natural gas since World War I have been located outside the Northeastern manufacturing belt, notably in the Southwest, the Far West, and Gulf areas of the Southeast. Coal, on the other hand, is still obtained in large quantities in the Middle Atlantic and Great Lakes regions and in adjacent parts of the Southeast, chiefly West Virginia. Coal and coke remain the major sources of heat-energy in two of the nation's most industrialized regions, hence the most powerful stimulus to petroleum consumption so far has not been industrial manufactures but the automobile.

To the extent that resource activities have contributed to the convergence of per capita personal income among the regions in recent decades, the growth of petroleum activities and declines in staple agriculture have probably made the greatest contributions.

[4]According to indexes of consumption of select materials per unit of G.N.P. made by E. Vera Eliasburg, Resources for the Future, Inc., only oil and gas and non-ferrous metals among major resource categories show any sizable increase since 1900.

[5]*U. S. Census of Agriculture, 1950*, Vol. V, Special Reports, Pt. 6, *Agriculture 1950—A Graphic Summary* (Washington: Government Printing Office, 1952), 69-102.

Regional resource activities within the growing national economy since 1870 may be summarized as follows. The initial contributions of the relatively undeveloped Southeastern and Western regions (mostly agricultural staples and metallic ores) helped sustain growth already achieved in the more advanced urban-industrial regions on the basis of their indigenous endowments of mineral, agricultural, and forest resources. By the close of the last century, resource depletion in the more developed Northeast, the progress of technology and, of course, the continuing growth and migration of population required that the material base of the national economy be extended over a wider area. By that time the area of economy more or less coincided with the political boundaries of the nation and henceforth growth has turned on the organization of production and distribution on a truly national scale; that is, on the further refinement of the system of interdependence among *all* the regions. Though there are still differential advantages for production and consumption to be had within the national framework, the progressive equalization of per capita income among the regions at higher levels, not excluding the Southeast, is proof that the national economy as a whole is potentially greater than any of its parts, provided the parts are differentiated along lines of comparative advantage. All regions have eventually come to share in the larger abundance.

If the play of technology on resources has been a primary factor in the growth and redistribution of the nation's wealth, a necessary condition has been the opportunity for labor and capital to flow freely throughout the commonwealth, seeking their most profitable employment in resource development, manufacture, or servicing, as the case may be. In the course of this general amelioration some regions, New England for example, have made painful adjustments; wide areas of the country have been ruthlessly and in some cases, perhaps, needlessly denuded of their natural endowment. Coal mines have been exhausted, rich ores depleted, forests cut down, and the soil impoverished. Yet, on balance, the American economy, if sometimes terribly wasteful, is not simply a predatory system. In one sense, resources unused are no better than resources abused. Public and private interests have become aware that, having used up the riches of one area, they can no longer expect to return that area to nature and move on to "new frontiers" elsewhere. The frontiers of tomorrow must be found in their own backyard.

The same thrusts of technology and the same, if more civilized, instincts which urged population out across the continent in search of higher returns have also reduced the quantities of resource inputs required for a given production: new and more economical methods of extraction, precision control over the processing of materials, and a nationwide organization of production and distribution have continually yielded higher returns to effort. Public and private programs for conservation over the last half-century have, in the long run, contributed to the same end. In recent years, however, the American economy has drawn increasingly on the natural resources of countries which do not immediately share in the full prosperity of the American system. It cannot be known how critical this dependence is likely to become. The nation's own regional experience, however, indicates that, in spite of technological economies at home, the newer interdependence reaching across national boundaries is likely to be more rather than less important in the years ahead. It is in the resource sector above all that the need for interdependence is likely to be felt by the United States. Whether Americans can apply the institutional lessons of their own good fortune in their economic relations with others is a question that in all probability will be answered not too far in the future.

Part

IV / *The Regional Distribution of*

Economic Activities in the

United States, 1939-1954

19 / An approach to the study of changes in the regional distribution of economic activities

The broad regional changes in economic activity between 1870 and 1950 that we have described bear out the observation with which our study opened—that, although the United States has grown steadily in population and per capita income, the various regions within the national economy have not all shared equally in this growth. Some have shown a rate of development exceeding the average for the nation as a whole; others have fallen below the national standards.

To arrive at an understanding of this phenomenon, we shall now inquire more deeply into the principles governing regional distribution of economic activity. We are primarily concerned at this point with the regional distribution of the *volume* of economic activity (rather than interregional differences in welfare). The best over-all view of this distribution is provided by employment data, for they enable us to study in detail what has been taking place in specific sectors of economic activity. Most of our attention here is addressed, therefore, to analyzing the meaning of employment structure and employment shifts in terms of differential regional growth. In our examination of these data we limit our inquiry to the years 1939-1954, both because this period is more specifically relevant to an understanding of present regional positions and because it permits us to use more detailed techniques and reach deeper levels of analysis of the phenomenon with which we are concerned.[1]

[1]Although employment does not reflect all of the factors determining the comparative economic importance of industries, it provides the only *uniform* basis for measuring and comparing the distribution of all types of economic activities. Furthermore, in some ways employment is a better measure of relative activity than either "value of products" or "value added," which are available for manufacturing only. The former includes the value of raw materials; and for both, comparisons between different periods would be distorted if changes in the price level took place. (It should be noted, however, that this could be corrected for.) While employment alone is far from a perfect measure of relative changes in volume of activities, it would seem to be the best measure, and employment changes are also significant in and of themselves.

Employment changes are particularly useful as an indication of changes in the volume of economic activities because of the close tie between employment and population. The rank correlation between total population distribution by states and total employment by states is .991; clearly the association is ex-

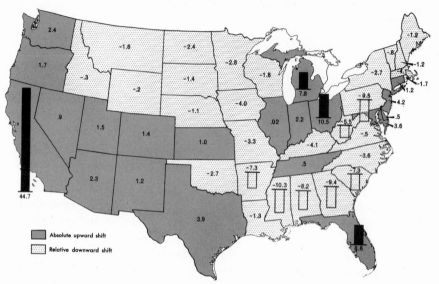

Figure 45. Net Shift in Total Employment, 1939-54.

State figures represent % of total net shift. Total net shift as % of incremental change: 18.5. Total net shift as % of 1939 employment: 7.1. Source: Appendix Table H.

tremely close. Figure 45 shows the net shifts in total employment by states from 1939 to 1954. When this is compared with Figure 10, showing the net population shifts for the same period, the similarity of configuration is evident. In all but five states,[2] the relative shifts in population and in employment take the same direction.

[2]Kansas, Louisiana, Virginia, Illinois, and Tennessee. However, it should be noted that while the correlation between population and employment is very high, individual variations can be significant. There are thirteen states where employment share deviates from population share by as much as 10% or more. There are many reasons why this is so. (1) In some cases there is significant data distortion. Employment data are subject to some bias because of interregional variation in business cycle performance. There is also reporting bias. In heavily agricultural states, employment share is inclined to be overstated because of the tendency to report as employed farm workers who are, in the words of Rudyard Kipling, "scrutiating idle." (2) In other cases the discrepancy between employment share and population share is a result of the influence of amenities. Many households can locate independent of the requirements of economic opportunity. This appears to be clearly the case for Florida and Arizona, for example. In spite of the fact that these states had low shares of income and employment relative to population, they continued during 1939-1954

Changes in Regional Activity Revealed by Total Employment

We have already presented in Figure 45 a summary picture of the net shift in total employment among the states between 1939 and 1954.[3] Table 128 shows the relative importance of the shifts over these years in the ten broad industry sectors or 1-digit components of total employment. The shifts amounted to a significant proportion of the absolute changes in employment in each of the major employment sectors, averaging 18.5% for all, (Col. 8). However, only in three sectors—agriculture, mining, and finance-insurance-real estate—were the employment changes among some of the states greatly removed from the national average for the sector. And only in mining was the change in position among the states really great compared to the national average absolute change. In terms of the size of the net shifts as a percentage of the number of persons employed in the category in 1939, construction is in the "large shift" class also (Col. 9).

We shall now turn to the employment shifts shown in Figure 45 to see whether some useful generalizations can be derived from them. But this examination will be much more revealing if we recognize the distinction that we have previously made between the "differential" shifts and the "proportionality" shifts that together make up the total employment shifts. By way of re-

to augment their population shares at a more rapid rate than their shares of employment. (3) In still other cases the discrepancy may be a symptom of a lag in adjustment to economic opportunity. In any case, if the reader wishes at some point to apply the demonstrations that follow concerning structure and change in employment to an understanding of the distribution and shifts in population, he will do well to recognize the existence of and reasons for these discrepancies.

[3]Throughout Part IV we shall place considerable emphasis upon shifts in employment patterns as evidence of the changes taking place in the regional structure of the American economy. Our repeated use of this device, however, should not lead the reader to overlook two very important facts. First, when we concentrate upon the "shift" pattern, we are focusing attention upon the *marginal increment of change* in a regional economy. Often this is only a small part of the total absolute increment demonstrated by the dimension being examined. For example: In the case of employment over the period 1939-54, the total net shift in position among the states was slightly less than 3,000,000 wage jobs. This was only 18% of the total increase in employment during this period, and only 7% of the total 1939 employment. These are significant shifts, to be sure, and well worth examining. But the use of these data has consequences that need to be kept in mind.

(a) Constant attention to these incremental changes may give an exaggerated notion of the quantitative significance of regional shifts. The truth is that the American economy demonstrates enormous stability in the face of change. At the same rate it would take 200 years for employment shifts across state boundaries to equal total 1939 employment. At the present time, two-thirds of the nation's labor force is employed in the states east of the Mississippi that make up only one-third of the total land area. The states in the manufacturing belt, with less than 15% of the nation's land area, contain roughly 45% of its population and employment. The shifts we describe here are not apt to change these proportions significantly within the short-run future.

(b) Focusing attention upon net shifts magnifies the possibility of error resulting from imperfect data. It is possible, therefore, that some of the shifts we describe have a spurious origin. This is more likely when a state can claim only a very small portion of

view, the differential shift is the shift which a region shows relative to the national average in employment in the broad industry components (the so-called 1-digit categories) of total employment.[4] In other words, it is the *intra-industry effect* among regions. Thus the principal "growth" regions may show their net upward shifts because, for a variety of reasons, they are outstripping the rest of the nation in their rate of increase in the components of total employment. The proportionality shift, on the other hand, is the effect of a region's *industrial composition* in terms of the employment sectors that, for the nation as a whole, have expanded more rapidly or less rapidly than others. The "growth" region then may be one that has a proportionately larger share of the rapidly expanding sectors of employment. The total net shift in employment shown in Figure 45 is the sum of these two types of shifts.

There are statistical counterparts to these concepts. If we compute the net shifts for each of the ten 1-digit components of total employment, we find that the sum of the differential net shifts displayed by each component for a single state rarely exhausts the total net shift in employment. The balance, then, is the proportionality net shift. In Figures 46 and 47 we divide the total net shift presented in Figure 45 into its differential and proportionality components.[5] It works out in this case that about half of the total shift is generated by the proportionality effect and about half by the differential effect.

Figures 46 and 47 reveal how widely these two types of net shifts differ in their regional effect. About 92% of the total proportionality net upward shift has occurred in the Manufacturing Belt states. Outside this area, only five states—Maine, New Hampshire, Florida, California, and Washington—exhibit net upward proportionality shifts; and of these, only California can claim a sizeable net gain from the proportionality effect. In contrast only Michigan, Indiana, and Ohio in the Manufacturing Belt show net growth from the differential effect. The net differential upward shift is concentrated in the part of the nation west of the Mississippi, except for a few of the Plains and northern

the total net shift. Generally, however, this type of error can be avoided by careful attention to other data and types of knowledge.

It is also well to note with regard to the use of the shift analysis that, as the gains or losses in employment shares are based upon relative rates of change, it is quite possible for a state with a "net downward shift" (i.e., a below-average rate of increase) to have a larger incremental increase in employment than one experiencing a "net upward shift." This is a function of the differences in the absolute size of the economic base. The focus on relative changes as against a national standard is appropriate for the principal questions being examined here. There are, however, a number of questions for which a knowledge of *absolute* elements might be more relevant.

[4] The breakdown employed here covers: agriculture; mining; construction; manufacturing; transportation and public utilities; wholesale trade; retail trade; finance, insurance, and real estate; service and miscellaneous; and government.

[5] The reader should be aware that the statistical dimensions of the proportionality and differential shifts (or total net shift for that matter) are not independent of the arbitrary decisions concerning the way and the frequency with which we slice a given employment universe. If we select a different classification of ten components we will get different shift dimensions. If we increase the number of components to 20 we will get different shift dimensions. We point this out to emphasize that such measures can be interpreted only in terms of the specific classifications upon which they are based.

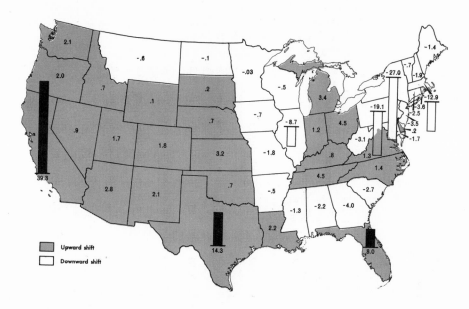

Figure 46. Differential Net Shift in Total Employment, 1939-54.

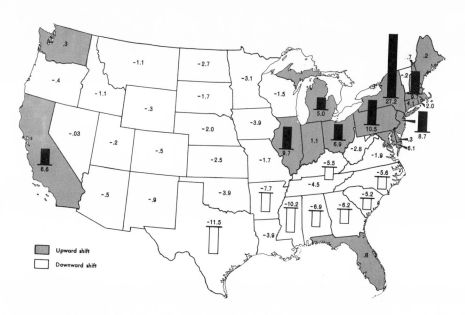

Figure 47. Proportionality Net Shift in Total Employment, 1939-54.
Source: Table 157.

Table 128. Relative importance of employment shifts, within the major employment sectors, 1939-1954.

1-Digit employment sectors	(1) 1939	(2) %	(3) 1954	(4) %	(5) Absolute chg. 1939-54	(6) % Increase col. 5 as % of col. 1	(7) Total net shift 1939-54	(8) Col. 7 as % of col. 5	(9) Col. 7 as % of col. 1
			Employment						
Total employment	40,908,238	100%	56,689,380	100%	15,781,142	38.6	±2,916,061	18.5	7.1
Agriculture	11,250,252	27.5	9,597,316	16.9	− 1,652,909	− 14.7	± 572,908	− 34.7	5.1
Mining	827,410	2.0	754,238	1.3	− 73,172	− 8.8	± 165,390	−226.0	20.0
Construction	1,177,000	2.9	2,617,600	4.6	1,435,600	122.0	± 261,790	18.2	22.2
Manufacturing	9,622,923	23.5	15,683,317	27.7	6,060,394	63.0	± 986,398	16.3	10.3
Transportation and public utilities	2,912,000	7.1	4,039,600	7.1	1,127,600	38.7	± 223,180	19.8	7.7
Wholesale trade	1,605,347	3.9	2,581,007	4.6	975,660	60.8	± 179,178	18.4	11.2
Retail trade	4,821,806	11.8	7,121,351	12.6	2,299,525	47.7	± 373,323	16.2	7.7
Finance, insurance and real estate	1,364,700	3.3	2,118,400	3.7	753,700	55.2	± 227,941	30.2	16.7
Services & misc.	3,339,700	8.2	5,430,000	9.6	2,090,300	62.6	± 249,480	11.9	7.5
Government	3,987,100	9.8	6,746,600	11.9	2,759,500	69.2	± 563,774	20.4	14.1

Source: Appendix Tables F1, F2, and H.

border states. The upper Southeastern states, however, share this effect. California, Texas, and Florida led the nation in differential rates of growth during the period under review.

Table 129 shows how the total shift for each state is divided between the proportionality and differential effect. There is considerable variety of performance. For example, Florida, the Far Western states, the southern Mountain states (Colorado and Utah), and Arizona demonstrate net upward shifts almost entirely because their important employment sectors are growing at a rate that exceeds the national average for these sectors. Maine and New Hampshire exemplify the reverse of this situation; they show net downward shifts because their important employment sectors have declined or have failed to keep pace with the rate of increase for these sectors in the nation as a whole.

In contrast, specialization in employment sectors that were growing at a faster rate than the average for all industries largely accounts for Maryland's net upward shift in total employment. And specialization in employment sectors that were declining nationally or growing at a below-average rate for the nation as a whole is the major factor in the net downward shifts shown by Minnesota, Iowa, North and South Dakota in the Plains region, by Wisconsin in the Great Lakes region, and by Kentucky, Arkansas, Mississippi, Alabama, and South Carolina in the Southeast.

In all the other states the total employment shift significantly reflects *both* the proportionality and the differential effect. In some cases (Michigan, for

Table 129 Total, differential, and proportionality net shifts in employment, by state, 1939-1954

State	Absolute shift			% of state total	
	(1)	(2)	(3)	(4)	(5)
	Total	Differential	Proportionality	Differential	Proportionality
New England					
Maine	− 34,687	− 40,091	5,404	−115.6	15.6
New Hampshire	− 36,155	− 55,248	19,093	−152.8	52.8
Vermont	− 24,371	− 18,778	− 5,593	− 77.1	− 22.9
Massachusetts	−119,129	−368,577	249,448	−309.4	209.4
Rhode Island	− 50,832	−101,772	50,940	−200.2	100.2
Connecticut	35,728	− 70,713	106,441	−197.9	297.9
Middle Atlantic					
New York	− 79,626	−777,501	697,875	−976.4	876.4
New Jersey	123,322	−100,699	224,021	− 81.7	181.7
Pennsylvania	−276,399	−545,910	269,511	−197.5	97.5
Delaware	14,919	5,943	8,976	39.8	60.2
Maryland & D.C.	105,893	− 49,567	155,460	− 46.8	146.8

Table 129—continued

State	(1)	(2)	(3)	(4)	(5)
Great Lakes					
Ohio	304,790	128,436	176,354	42.1	57.9
Indiana	63,052	35,339	27,713	56.0	44.0
Illinois	498	−249,193	249,691	−50,039	50,139
Michigan	227,725	98,019	129,706	43.0	57.0
Wisconsin	− 52,577	− 14,966	− 37,611	− 28.5	− 71.5
Southeast					
Virginia	− 13,591	36,141	− 49,732	265.9	−365.9
W. Virginia	−159,903	− 88,733	− 71,170	− 55.5	− 44.5
North Carolina	−103,806	41,250	−145,056	39.7	−139.7
South Carolina	−211,282	− 78,006	−133,276	− 36.9	− 63.1
Georgia	−273,931	−115,711	−158,220	− 42.2	− 57.8
Florida	250,586	230,706	19,880	92.1	7.9
Kentucky	−118,309	23,258	−141,567	19.7	−119.7
Tennessee	14,034	129,041	−115,007	919.5	−819.5
Alabama	−239,053	− 62,175	−176,878	− 26.0	− 74.0
Mississippi	−299,100	− 36,903	−262,197	− 12.3	− 87.7
Arkansas	−211,474	− 13,987	−197,487	− 6.6	− 93.4
Plains					
Minnesota	− 80,226	− 1,054	− 79,172	− 1.3	− 98.7
Iowa	−117,559	− 18,593	− 98,966	− 15.8	− 84.2
Missouri	− 97,364	− 53,463	− 43,901	− 55.5	− 44.5
North Dakota	− 71,289	− 2,393	− 68,896	− 3.4	− 96.6
South Dakota	− 39,548	4,520	− 44,068	11.4	−111.4
Nebraska	− 30,847	21,314	− 52,161	69.1	−169.1
Kansas	28,708	92,037	− 63,329	320.6	−220.6
Southwest					
Oklahoma	− 79,746	19,168	− 98,914	24.0	−124.0
Texas	112,286	408,869	−296,583	364.1	−264.1
New Mexico	36,201	59,403	− 23,202	164.1	− 64.1
Arizona	68,058	81,238	− 13,180	119.4	− 19.4
Louisiana	− 36,947	63,854	−100,801	172.8	−272.8
Mountain					
Montana	− 45,079	− 17,927	− 27,152	− 39.8	− 60.2
Idaho	− 8,246	20,045	− 28,291	243.1	−343.1
Wyoming	− 4,986	3,892	− 8,878	78.1	−178.1
Colorado	39,695	51,779	− 12,084	130.5	− 30.5
Utah	43,631	48,968	− 5,337	112.2	− 12.2
Far West					
Washington	68,812	60,810	− 8,002	88.4	11.6
Oregon	48,839	58,317	− 9,478	197.5	− 97.5
California	1,303,805	1,133,188	170,617	86.9	13.1
Nevada	25,478	26,290	− 812	103.2	− 3.2

Source: Table 157.

example) both effects contribute to a net upward shift. In other cases (West Virginia, for example) both contribute to a net downward shift. In still other cases (Illinois, for example) the proportionality and differential effects tend to offset each other and the total net shift depends upon which effect is the stronger.

Interpretation of Observed Regional Behavior

Table 130 compares the percentage change in employment in each of the ten broad industry sectors with the rate of change in the nation's total employment between 1939 and 1954. Mining and agriculture alone fall below the national average for these years. In each of the remaining eight sectors the rate of increase exceeds the average rate for the nation's employment as a whole. It should follow that the states which specialize in mining and agriculture would show net downward proportionality shifts.

This is precisely the case. Table 131 shows the distribution of each state's total employment in 1939 between the industry sectors with an above-average rate of growth and those with a below-average rate. Without exception, the states that have a large proportion of their total employment in the slow-growth sectors—agriculture and mining—correspond exactly to those that are shown to have net downward proportionality shifts in Figure 47. Mississippi, which has a large net downward proportionality shift, devoted nearly 75% of its employment to agriculture and mining in 1939, as compared with 29% for the nation as a whole. In West Virginia, which also shows a net downward proportionality shift, almost 21% of the total employment was in mining as compared with a national average of only 2%. In contrast, New York, which shows a large net upward proportionality shift, devoted 93% of its total employment in 1939 to the rapid-growth sectors of employment, as compared

Table 130. Percentage change in employment in the United States, by industry, 1939-1954

Construction	+122.0%
Government	+ 69.2
Manufacturing	+ 63.0
Service and Miscellaneous	+ 62.6
Wholesale Trade	+ 60.8
Finance, Insurance and Real Estate	+ 55.2
Retail Trade	+ 47.7
Transportation and Public Utilities	+ 38.7
TOTAL ALL EMPLOYMENT	+ 38.5
Mining	− 8.8
Agriculture	− 14.7

SOURCE: Appendix Table G.

Table 131. Relative employment in rapid-growth and slow-growth industries*
in the United States, by state, 1939

State	Slow-growth	Rapid-growth
	%	%
United States	29.5	70.5
New England		
Maine	27.4	72.6
New Hampshire	15.9	84.1
Vermont	36.6	63.4
Massachusetts	5.2	94.8
Rhode Island	2.8	97.2
Connecticut	7.6	92.4
Middle Atlantic		
New York	7.3	92.7
New Jersey	6.0	94.0
Pennsylvania	17.5	82.5
Delaware	17.7	82.3
Maryland and D. C.	9.8	90.2
Great Lakes		
Ohio	18.1	81.9
Indiana	25.8	74.2
Illinois	15.0	85.0
Michigan	19.5	80.5
Wisconsin	34.7	65.3
Plains		
Minnesota	40.9	59.1
Iowa	46.4	53.6
Missouri	33.6	66.4
North Dakota	68.8	31.2
South Dakota	59.0	41.0
Nebraska	46.2	53.8
Kansas	45.5	54.5
Southeast		
Virginia	38.4	61.6
W. Virginia	49.0	51.0
North Carolina	47.1	52.9
South Carolina	56.5	43.5
Georgia	50.8	49.2
Florida	24.7	75.3
Kentucky	56.3	43.7
Tennessee	47.7	52.3
Alabama	57.8	42.2
Mississippi	73.4	25.6
Arkansas	71.1	28.9
Southwest		
Oklahoma	52.1	47.9
Texas	49.5	50.5
New Mexico	51.7	48.3
Arizona	42.2	57.8
Louisiana	48.1	51.9

State	Slow-growth	Rapid-growth
	%	%
Mountain		
Montana	48.6	51.4
Idaho	52.1	47.9
Wyoming	43.8	56.2
Colorado	34.6	65.4
Utah	33.4	66.6
Far West		
Washington	27.7	72.3
Oregon	31.8	68.2
California	18.2	81.8
Nevada	32.8	67.2

*Above or below "All Employment" in Table 130.

SOURCE: Appendix Table F1.

with 70% for the nation as a whole. Michigan, Massachusetts, New Jersey, and Connecticut derived most of their net upward proportionality shifts from a specialization in manufacturing, which accounted for 40% or more of their employment, as compared with a national average of 23.5%.[6]

This, of course, constitutes only a superficial explanation of the proportionality effect. All we have done here is to identify the employment sectors in each state that are statistically associated with the proportionality effect. In order to arrive at more fundamental explanations we need to seek the answers to two questions.

First, *why have some sectors of the economy grown more rapidly than others?* In finding answers to this question we must concern ourselves with national demand and supply trends affecting the major employment sectors. And these must be analyzed in terms of important changes in basic economic determinants —population, resources, technology, and institutions. Second, *where are the rapid-growth and slow-growth sectors located and why?* Here we are brought to a consideration of the nature of the region and the principles governing the regional distribution of economic activity. It is evident that to answer these questions, more detailed sectors of the economy must be examined.

Consider next the differential effect and the kinds of factors that are relevant to an explanation of it. A region that shows a differential net upward or downward shift does so because its expansion rate for specific component activities is greater than, or less than, the average *for the same activities* in other regions. This presents a significant contrast with the proportionality effect. The proportionality effect raised this key question: *Why do some employment sectors of the national economy expand more than others?* The differential effect raises another key question: *Why does the same employment sector expand*

[6]The reader interested in viewing in greater detail the employment sectors in each state most responsible for the observed shifts can refer to Appendix Tables F1 and F2.

more rapidly in some regions than in others? An answer to this question requires some knowledge of the reasons why one region may, for a particular activity, have access to inputs and markets superior to that of another region. It requires some knowledge of the significance of these spatial input-output relationships for multiplier effects of the sort discussed earlier.

There are, necessarily, important differences in focus when the research design is applied to the differential effect as contrasted with the proportionality effect. In connection with the proportionality effect a region may experience a net downward shift because its relative access to markets has declined. The reason, however, is associated with the fact that *the total market for its specialized sectors has declined relative to other sectors* so that its share of the total market for all products and services has declined. At the first level the analysis concerns itself with the national trends in supply and demand. In connection with the differential effect, a region may likewise experience a net downward shift because its relative access to markets has declined. The reason in this case derives from the fact that its *market access for a specific activity has declined relative to that exhibited by other regions engaged in the same activity.*

This makes it evident that much useful analysis of the proportionality effect can be accomplished through an investigation into *national* demand and supply factors and trends without consideration of the nature of regions other than to identify the locations of rapid-growth and slow-growth industries. However, little or no useful analysis of the differential effect is possible without taking into account modifications in regional input-output associations that represent changes in access for *specific activities* in *specific regions.* Such an analysis must aim at an understanding of the nature of regions on a basis that disaggregates space as well as employment activities. This is what we attempt to do for the years 1939-1954 in the chapters that follow. Our hope is that, through an analysis of specific economic activities in specific regions, we can clarify the working of the forces that are critical in influencing shifts in the relative volume of regional economic activities.[7]

[7]However, the reader should be cautioned not to expect too much. Properly applied, this research design should be undertaken for a series to time periods. Our resources allow us only a glance at a single period—1939-54. As a consequence, we can do very little in analyzing and generalizing about growth sequences and multiplier effects. All of the input and market ties that are important in defining the dominant access characteristics of specific activities in each region should also be analyzed. We will make a few gestures in this direction, but, even if adequate materials for doing this were readily available, the job is too monumental for more than partial realization here. We do, however, provide case materials that will be of value to persons concerned with problems of regional economic growth and we also present and illustrate a research design which we feel has considerable potential for regional research.

20 / *Regional distribution of mining activity*[1]

Mining is the smallest of the ten broad industry sectors, accounting in 1939 for only 2% of total national employment. However, its significance for regional analysis is greater than its share in total employment would imply, for it provides a large part of the basic material inputs and thus is an origin for many complex sequences of production. For another reason, also, it has great significance for regional analysis. Probably no other economic activity is more unequally distributed geographically. Thus, in spite of its relatively small place in the national employment figures, mining can be most important in explaining the economic behavior of *specific* regions, and even more of specific localities.

Mining employment in 1954 amounted to 754,238 persons as compared to 827,410 in 1939—a decline of 8.8%. The net shifts over these years amounted to ±165,390 workers, or 20% of the 1939 mining employment figure. In other words, while there was relatively little change in total employment over the period, there was a significant change in position among the states. In fact, the net shifts in mining employment were a larger proportion of the absolute changes than in any other of the major employment sectors.

Table 132 gives a rough indication of how widely the major categories of mining departed from the national norms. The experience of the individual states in metal-mining employment, for example, was very different from the change in metal-mining employment for the nation as a whole (a mere .2% between 1939 and 1954). By contrast, while total employment in coal-mining declined by one-third over this period, the net shift was fairly small, amounting to only 12% of the absolute change. The largest net shift in terms of numbers involved was in the petroleum industry (Col. 9).

[1]The term "mining" is employed in the sense in which it appears in the *Standard Industrial Classification Manual* of the Bureau of the Budget (1957), p. 21: "Mining is here used in the broad sense to include the extraction of minerals occurring naturally: solids, such as coal and ore; liquids, such as crude petroleum; and gases, such as natural gas. [It] is also used in the broad sense to include quarrying, well operation, milling (crushing, screening, washing, flotation, etc.), and other preparation needed to render the material marketable. Exploration and development of mineral properties are included. Services performed on a contract, fee, or other basis in the development of mineral properties are classified separately but within this division."

Wherever the term "mining" is used in this chapter, it may be taken to have this meaning except where the context clearly indicates a more restricted sense of the word.

Table 132. Relative importance of net employment shifts in mining, 1939–1954

2-digit mining categories	(1) Employment 1939	(2) %	(3) 1954	(4) %	(5) Absolute chg. 1939-54	(6) % Incr. col. 5 as % of col. 1	(7) Total net shift 1939-54	(8) Col. 7 as % of col. 5	(9) Col. 7 as % of col. 1
All mining employment	827,410	100.0	754,238	100.0	− 73,172	− 8.8	±165,390	226.0	20.0
Metal mining	(95,767)	11.6	97,858	13.0	2,091	.2	± 17,978	859.8	18.8
Coal mining	483,567	58.5	251,421	33.3	−232,146	−48.0	± 28,480	12.3	5.9
Crude petroleum and natural gas	151,939	18.4	292,387	38.8	140,448	92.4	± 63,894	45.5	42.1
Nonmetallic minerals	(95,184)	11.5	112,572	14.9	17,388	18.3	± 18,154	104.4	19.1

Note: Parentheses indicate estimates.

Source: Appendix Tables H and I.

Over-all Proportionality Effect

Fifteen states showed a net downward shift because of their specialization in mining. Table 133 lists these states and indicates the proportion of total employment in each absorbed by mining.[2]

The key fact here is that basic mineral inputs have declined in relative importance when measured against the aggregate of all primary and intermediate inputs. The effect on employment is compounded by the substantial increases in productivity per man-hour, due mainly to mechanization, which have taken place in almost all mining industries in recent decades. Also, with the increasing specialization of functions, some functions that formerly belonged to the mining

Table 133. Mining employment as percentage of total employment, 1939, for states with net downward proportionality shifts in total employment, 1939-1954*, because of specialization in mining.

State	1939 %
United States average	2.0
West Virginia	20.9
Nevada	13.7
Wyoming	7.8
Kentucky	7.5
Arizona	7.4
Utah	7.2
Montana	6.2
New Mexico	5.7
Oklahoma	5.3
Colorado	4.6
Alabama	3.2
Idaho	3.0
Kansas	2.7
Texas	2.6
Virginia	2.5

*This is the total proportionality effect based upon 1-digit components shown in Figure 47.

SOURCE: Appendix Table F1.

industry have been split away. Specialized engineering and financial services, formerly provided by the mining industry, have now been absorbed by the business services sector of the economy. Some beneficiation processes formerly

[2]In addition to the states shown in Table 133, Pennsylvania (which had 7% of its employed labor force in mining in 1939) experienced a downward proportionality effect from mining, but over-all had a net upward proportionality shift for the period 1939-1954 because it specialized mostly in rapid-growth sectors.

included in mining have been segmented to the point that they are now classified as manufacturing.

Until the decade preceding 1920 the rate of growth in the physical volume of mineral production exceeded the rate for the gross national product. Since that time, however, it has been well below the gross national product rate. And the growth that has occurred, as well as the major share of the increase in productivity, has been largely contributed by oil and gas. Except in oil and gas, changes in mining output and productivity have been moderate, resembling the changes in agriculture more closely than those in manufacturing. Borenstein[3] suggests that the reversal in the ratio of mineral production to national product is due, in part, to the predominance of mineral-saving over mineral-demanding developments in technology since World War I. Other factors have also contributed to the decline in the demand for minerals. For example, the more extended processing and fabrication which minerals undergo before reaching the final consumer generally adds to aggregate output without a commensurate increase in mineral input. There has also been an increasing use of scrap metals and of substitutes for minerals, such as plastics, rubber products, and laminated beams.

In short, because of significant long-term trends in supply and demand factors affecting minerals as a whole, the relative importance of the minerals sector of the economy has declined. As a result, the mining specialization states display net downward proportionality shifts in total employment (based upon 1-digit components).

There may be two factors at work, however, which can mitigate this influence: (1) A state may combine good access to mineral resources with good access to markets and basic intermediate inputs. In Pennsylvania, for example, these offsetting factors generated a net upward proportionality shift for the period 1939-1954. (2) A region's access to mineral resources may be so good and/or may have improved so much relative to that of other regions that this may serve as the basis for net upward differential shifts in employment. In such a case, mineral resources may be a net stimulus to regional growth.

Regional Influence of Mining Reflected in the Total Differential Effect

In Figure 46 it was shown that some three-fourths of the differential net shift in total employment occurred west of the Mississippi. Here we are interested in examining the contribution of mining to the total picture. Figure 48 shows the net shift in mining employment between 1939 and 1954. The states west of the Mississippi, it will be seen, contributed some 90% of the net upward shift; all but five of these Western states participated in this rela-

---

[3]For detailed documentation see Israel Borenstein, *Capital and Output Trends in Mining Industries 1870–1948*, Occasional Paper No. 45, (New York: National Bureau of Economic Research, 1954), pp. 10-28. Also, Barger & Schurr, *The Mining Industries, 1899–1939: A Study of Output, Employment and Productivity* (New York: National Bureau of Economic Research, 1944), pp. 3-58.

tive gain. Apparently the general regional picture for mining is roughly consistent with the dominant westward shift of total employment.

Four other general observations of special significance emerge from a more
detailed examination of the shifts. (1) The broad correlation alluded to above
is subject to many individual exceptions. In about one-third of the states, the
mining shift ran counter to the prevailing net differential shift at the 1-digit
level for example, in Indiana, Ohio, Kentucky, Mississippi, and New York. (2)
It cannot be claimed that, over-all, the shift in mining employment has been
an important part of the total differential net shift in employment. There were
only eleven states in which it amounted to more than 5% of the aggregate

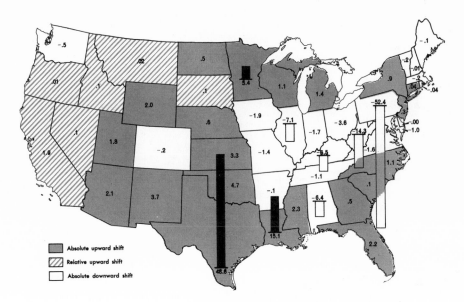

Figure 48. Net Shift in Mining Employment, 1939-54.
State figures represent % of total net shift. Total net shift as % of
incremental change: 226.0. Total net shift as % of 1939 mining employment:
20.0. Source: Appendix Table H.

shift (both upward and downward) recorded by all ten industry sectors for
the state. These eleven states are identified in Table 134. The principal influence of mining upon the total employment shift is restricted to these states.
For them, however, mining tells an important part of the story. As a matter
of fact, the total shift in mining employment was about 20% of the total 1939
mining employment. Thus, in relative terms, the shifts across state lines for
mining were almost three times as important as for total employment. (3) Of
these eleven states, those west of the Mississippi show absolute net upward
shifts and those in the East—the Appalachian states—show absolute net downward shifts. This results, of course, from the substantial effect of the substitu-

tion of oil for coal. Two-thirds of the net upward shift occurred in Texas and Louisiana and almost three-fourths of the net downward shift in Pennsylvania, West Virginia, and Kentucky. (4) A comparison of the mining shifts with the

Table 134. States with relatively largest net differential shifts in mining employment, 1939-1954.

State	Mining shift in state as % of total shift (without regard to sign) of 1-digit employment categories for the state*
Louisiana	36.3%
West Virginia	24.4
Wyoming	21.9
Pennsylvania	15.4
Kentucky	14.5
Texas	14.5
Oklahoma	10.9
New Mexico	10.4
Alabama	6.3
Minnesota	6.3
Utah	6.1

*To make any fair comparison, it is necessary to sum these without regard to sign because the total net differential shift (i.e., the sum with regard to sign) balances out so that mining as a percentage of the net might be an extremely large figure in one or two states.

SOURCE: Table 157.

total net differential shift (Figure 46) reveals that the net upward shifts in mining employment support those in total employment west of the Mississippi. In the East, however, the Upper South and the western end of the Manufacturing Belt show net upward total differential shifts *in spite of* absolute downward shifts in mining employment. This is especially surprising in the case of Kentucky, as mining was an important part of the changing picture for that state.

1-Digit Proportionality and Differential Effect in Mining Employment Based upon 2-Digit Components

Table 135 shows the changes taking place in the four components of mining employment—coal, petroleum and natural gas, metallic minerals, and nonmetallic minerals (other than organic fuels). At this level of aggregation the same proportionality and differential effects can be observed as in the shifts in total employment. The sum of the net shifts in the component sectors of mining rarely exhausts for a state the total net shift in mining employment displayed in Figure 48. The balance is a proportionality shift resulting from the fact that some states specialize more than others in the rapid-growth or slow-growth sectors of mining. The proportionality and differential effects of the mining shift are presented in Figures 49 and 50.

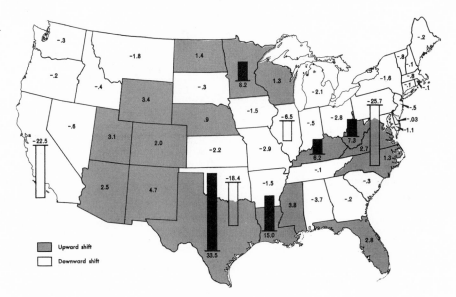

Figure 49. Differential Net Shift in All Mining Employment, 1939-54.

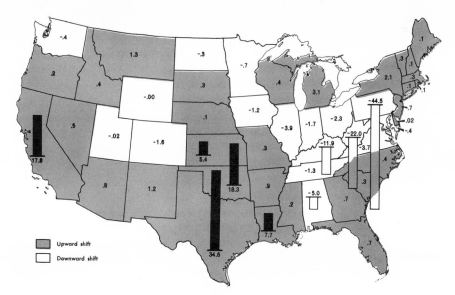

Figure 50. Proportionality Net Shift in All Mining Employment, 1939-54.

The proportionality effect is a more important part of the shift in mining (roughly 60%) than in total employment (roughly 50%). As Figure 50 shows, the proportionality net downward shift is confined to sixteen states. As a matter of fact, more than 90% of this shift occurred in the states along the Appalachian chain. Coal is, of course, the principal factor; employment in coal-mining declined sharply between 1939 and 1954. The three leading coal states—Pennsylvania, West Virginia, and Kentucky—account for 78.4% of the net downward proportionality shift. The dramatic growth of petroleum and natural gas is reflected in the fact that four leading petroleum states—California, Oklahoma, Texas, and Louisiana—account for 78.4% of the net upward proportionality shift.

Table 135. Percentage change in mining employment in the United States by 2-digit industry group, 1939-1954.

Petroleum and natural gas	+92.44%
Non-metallic mining	+18.27
Metallic mining	+ 2.18
ALL MINING EMPLOYMENT	− 8.84
Coal mining	−48.01

SOURCE: Appendix Table G.

The number of states showing net upward shifts because of a truly differential effect is much smaller. Twenty-seven states experienced net upward shifts in total mining employment. Seventeen of these displayed for their mining specialties a rate of growth that exceeded the national average for those categories. These states fell into four groups—the Upper South, the Southwestern states (except Oklahoma), the easternmost Mountain states, and the northern Plains states. Two states, Texas and Louisiana, dominated the net upward differential shift during the period 1939-1954. Three states—California, Oklahoma, and Pennsylvania—dominated the net downward shift. An explanation of these shifts must be sought in the behavior of the individual mining segments.

Analysis of the Differential Effect in Mining

In analyzing the differential effect, we are automatically concerned with the factors that lead the same industry sector of the economy to develop at different rates in different regions. Here the question of access to inputs and markets is of major importance.

Mineral "inputs" are immobile inputs, and it goes without saying that mining activity can take place only where the minerals exist. In fact, no sector of economic activity shows a greater degree of concentration and localization.

Table 136 offers indication of the degree of concentration in mining activity.[4] Mining employment has a significantly smaller geographical association with population than any other major employment sector. The areas of mining specialization fall into three groups—the Mountain states, the Southwest states, and the middle Appalachian states; in addition, three individual states have significant mining activities—Minnesota, Alabama, and South Dakota. In 1954 these states employed 75% of the total mining labor force and contained less than 30% of the total population of the country.

It is obvious that resource access must be an important, if not dominant,

Table 136. Rank correlations of each state's share of employment in selected industries with each state's share of population, 1954.

Total employment .991			
Retail trade employment	.979	Transportation and public utility employment	.957
Service & miscellaneous employment	.972	Finance, insurance & real estate employment	.957
Wholesale trade employment	.970	Manufacturing employment	.936
Government employment	.970	Agricultural employment	.649
Construction employment	.960	Mining employment	.406

SOURCE: See Table 1, note and Appendix Table F-2.

factor in explaining the behavior of the mining sector of the economy. But there are significant variations on this central fact. The extent to which specific resource deposits can establish dominance in the geographic pattern of economic activities is considerably modified by the existence of numerous substitution possibilities.[5]

The range of possibilities is great. At one extreme—admittedly hypothetical—is the resource for which there are no substitutes at all, either in terms of alternate sources or in terms of production technology. In such a case, extrac-

[4]Although this table is presented here in the mining section and alluded to only briefly at this point, it is a general reference table that we will refer to on a number of occasions as we develop this analysis.

[5]The term "substitution" is used here in its most general sense—the process of replacing one form of an input with another because of relative price relationships. At a more particular level several types of substitution effects can be identified: *important here are "source" substitutions in which a multiple-source commodity from a source developing lower "mill" prices will replace one from a source with higher prices.* There are "technological" substitutions in which an input of different technical characteristics may replace an existing input when relative prices of the two differing inputs makes such a change advantageous. A recent example is the production and marketing of an aluminum "tin" can in competition with the traditional terne plate (coated steel) "tin" can. The phenomenon of "factor" substitution is well known; for example, the extent to which an industry will substitute labor-saving machinery for labor inputs depends on interest rate-wage rate relations.

tive activity would be unequivocally wedded to one location—the site of the single deposit. At the other extreme there are the resource deposits that are ubiquitous—for example, the mining of construction sand can utilize supply sources found in every region and almost every locality. In such cases market access rather than resource access is likely to determine the location of extractive activity; the ubiquity of resource deposits offers virtually an infinite range of choices.

Most situations are obviously intermediate. For example, there is a fairly wide geographic distribution of coal and iron ore deposits in the United States and thus a range of possible sites for extractive activity. In such cases, locational decisions will be based upon the relative quality of these deposits and their accessibility as reflected in interregional price differences. These price differences, arising out of interregional differences in costs of extraction and of transport, will be the allocating factor determining (1) which of a series of resource deposits will be exploited, (2) the extent or intensity of its exploitation, and (3) the sequence in which competing sources will be brought into use.[6]

Sites of substitute resources offer a second set of substitution possibilities (for example, hematite *vs.* taconite *vs.* jasper; or coal *vs.* oil). In such cases the choice of location must admit the interregional price ratios of unlike, or substitute, resources as well as like resources.

This series of choices between sites, both of like and unlike resources, determines the geographic location of mining activities.

In short, to undertake analysis of shifts in mining employment requires as much attention to *all the factors influencing market and input access* as the analysis of any other sector of economic activity. In the following section we want to examine the performance of the component sectors of mining employment with this framework in mind.

Regional Influence of Mining

The mineral fuels (coal, crude oil, and natural gas) dominate the minerals resources picture. They account for roughly three-fourths of mining employment and about three-fourths of the value of all mineral products.

COAL MINING

Influence of Coal-Mining in the 1-Digit Proportionality Effect Exhibited by all Mining Employment: In 1939, coal-mining comprised almost 60% of all mining employment; by 1954 its share had dropped to only one-third, and oil and natural gas had taken over a large part of the potential as well as the

---

[6]Further elements of the location choice arise out of the competition of uses for the same resource deposits. In such cases, interregional price differences have the effect of allocating favored sites to the uses that can pay the highest price. This competition of uses determines a fourth regional (and local) dimension—the distribution of resources to different uses and, therefore, the geographical distribution of these different uses. This is not an important element if the picture of extraction always forms an independent production stage. However, in cases where extraction is incidental to a resource-oriented processing stage, this can be important. It is also important in the distribution of site land and agricultural land.

conventional markets of coal. Over these years, the share of coal in meeting the nation's total energy requirements dropped from 51.4% to 29.3% (of total BTU's). At the same time the share of petroleum and natural gas increased from 44.9% to 66.8%. In many uses this economical energy source was a direct substitute for coal. For example, the dieselization of locomotives reduced the railway's use of coal from 120 million tons to 17 million tons between 1945 and 1955. Oil and natural gas have also claimed a large share of the heating market and the electric utility market. While the absolute amount of coal used in generating electric power increased substantially during the period, the share of coal in this important market dropped from 81.7% in 1945 to 65.6% in 1955 (and down to 55% in 1957).

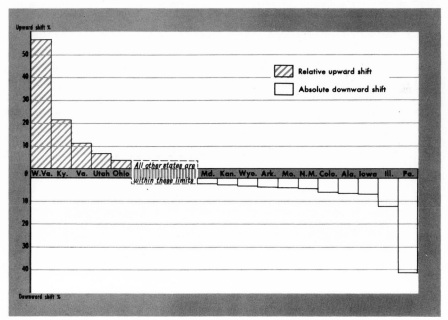

Figure 51.   Net Shift in Coal Mining Employment, 1939-54.
    State figures represent % of total net shift. Total net shift as % of incremental change: 12.3. Total net shift as % of 1939 coal mining employment : 5.9. Source: Appendix Table I.

    Another important reason for the relative decline of coal in the energy market is that oil (and the new oil technology) generated new energy sources and energy markets (notably the internal combustion engine) in which coal was not a reasonable technological substitute. Some of the factors leading to a relative decline in the importance of the mining sector of the economy as a whole might also have a differential effect upon coal-mining. For example, the tendency in recent years for mineral-saving developments to predominate over mineral-demanding developments in technology seems to have been especially important in coal technology. The average amount of coal burned to produce one kilowatt-hour of electrical energy in the United States was 6.4 pounds in 1902, 3.0 pounds in 1920, and 1.2 pounds in 1950.[7]

Influence of Coal-Mining in the 1-Digit Differential Effect Exhibited by all Mining Employment: The important role played by coal in the proportionality effect in the shift in mining employment does not mean that differential shifts between regions in coal-mining have not been an important element in the shift picture. In Figure 49, seventeen states were identified as having had net differential upward shifts in mining employment. The extent to which coal contributed to these shifts is shown in Figure 51. The net upward differential shift shown by the mid-Appalachian states in Figure 49 is plainly due in large part to a relatively strong net upward shift in coal-mining employment for those states. As a matter of fact, Kentucky, West Virginia, and Virginia account for almost 90% of the net relative upward shift.[8] Utah also gains at least a part of its differential strength from coal-mining. On the other hand, Pennsylvania, Illinois, and Alabama obviously derive an important part of their differential net downward shift in mining employment from a net downward shift in their share of coal-mining employment.

A relatively small number of states are involved in these shifts because of the high degree of regional concentration of coal production. While some coal reserves are found in thirty-three states and some coal production takes place in twenty-six, the major portion of mining activity is heavily concentrated. The Appalachian field, extending from northwestern Pennsylvania to Alabama, dominates American coal production. Three states in this area—Pennsylvania, West Virginia, and Kentucky—produce 75% of the output. Elsewhere, only southern Illinois and the mid-Mountain states have any significant degree of concentration.

The shifts noted above would seem to have come about through the workings of a number of forces. In a study based on an examination of 94 State Economic Areas[9] producing coal, Beverly Duncan has reviewed the general access characteristics of the coal industry.[10] In this study she established that the inferior deposits, taken as a group, show a marked tendency to be exploited more intensively in areas of high market accessibility. She also took production as a ratio of available reserves and correlated it with population potential (i.e., closeness to the major centers of population) as an index of market access for the 94 coal-producing State Economic Areas. The coefficient was .65 and the correlation was significant at the .01 level.

She concludes that population potential explains slightly more than two-fifths of the variation in the "index of resource exploitation." This finding, of

---

[7]Petroleum technology made some efficiency gains to be sure but these were concentrated more in the field of motor fuels where coal is non-competitive.

[8]In this case, "upward" shift means that the absolute losses in this area were less than elsewhere.

[9]These are groups of contiguous counties with similar economic and social characteristics.

[10]Reported in Beverly Duncan, *Population Distribution and Economic Activity: The Non-metropolitan United States in 1950*, Ph.D. Dissertation, University of Chicago, 1957 (microfilm), Chapter 3. See also O. D. Duncan, *et al, Metropolis and Region, op. cit.,* Chapter 8.

course, is completely consistent with the hypothesis that the intensity with which coal resources are exploited increases as accessibility of the resource site to the national market increases. It should be pointed out here that the reserves of higher-grade coal tend to be concentrated in or toward the relatively high potential areas. Insofar as the higher ranks are preferred for reasons other than or in addition to their heat content (which has been allowed for here through the use of BTU equivalents), the direct relationship between intensity of production and population potential is strengthened by the areal distribution of mineral resources. In other words, the relatively high potential areas occupy a favorable position both from the standpoint of the quality of their deposits and their proximity to market.

Figure 52 gives some idea of the extent to which the heavy concentrations of industry and population in the northeastern part of the country affect intensity of coal production. While some of the most extensive coal reserves are located in the Mountain states, (particularly Montana, Wyoming, Utah, and Colorado), these states, with few exceptions, have subareas falling in the lowest quintal of the production-to-reserve ratio. The intensity of exploitation of coal reserves is highest in the Appalachian Coal Plateau region, with some State Economic Areas in southern Illinois and the western parts of Kentucky also showing a high rate of exploitation. No SEA west of the Mississippi River falls in the highest quintals of the production-to-reserve ratio.[11]

Small-area data are available on the value received or charged for coal f.o.b. the mine, including the selling cost.[12] An analysis of these data reveals no significant relationship between f.o.b. value per BTU produced and population potential, a summary measure of access to the national market; there is only a

---

[11]Estimates of coal resources by rank (lignitic, sub-bituminous bituminous, and semi-anthracitic) at the state level have been prepared and published by the U. S. Geological Survey; these resources were distributed among SEA's. The estimates are not altogether comparable on an inter-state basis; and, of course, the allocation of state reserves to SEA's was quite arbitrary in some cases. Nonetheless, a quantitative indicator (tonnage) of remaining coal resources by rank is available for each SEA. To obtain a single quantitative indicator of all remaining coal resources for each SEA, the tonnage for each rank of coal was converted to British thermal unit (BTU) equivalents, and the respective equivalents then aggregated into a single statistic. The conversion factors employed assume 26.0 million BTU's per ton of bituminous coal, 25.4 per ton of anthracite, 19.0 per ton of sub-bituminous coal, and 13.4 per ton of lignite. See *Coal Resources of the United States*, by Paul Averitt, Louise R. Berryhill, & Dorothy A. Taylor, Geological Survey Circular 293, (Washington, 1953), pp. 6-12.

Small-area statistics on coal production are available on an annual basis from the *Minerals Yearbook*, prepared by the U. S. Bureau of Mines. Production is reported separately for lignite, bituminous coal, and anthracite. For the analysis, the tonnage of bituminous coal produced was divided into sub-bituminous and bituminous coal in proportion to reserves. This is a highly arbitrary procedure, but at a maximum it affects only the 16 SEA's in which reserves of both sub-bituminous and bituminous coal occur.

[12]The producer's estimate of the value of coal not sold but used by him also is included. The value figures, then, do not include charges incurred in transporting the coal from the producer to the purchaser. [U. S. Bureau of Mines, *Minerals Yearbook 1950* (Washington: Government Printing Office, 1953, p. 322.] Perhaps the most conventional "value" indicator is value per ton produced; but areal variation in value per ton is likely to reflect

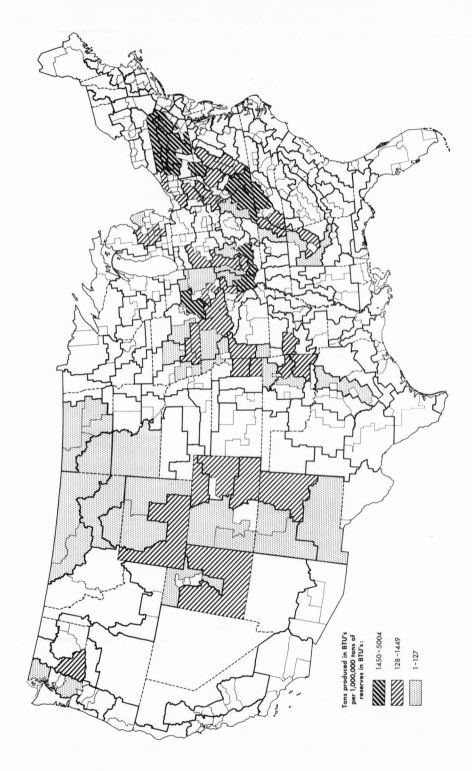

Tons produced in BTU's
per 1,000,000 tons of
reserves in BTU's:

1450–5004

128–1449

1–127

tenuous inverse relationship between f.o.b. value per BTU and population potential $(r = -.10)$.

Cursory inspection of statistics on bituminous coal and lignite distribution suggests that the absence of any positive association between f.o.b. value per BTU and population potential may "explain" in part the relatively low "index of resource exploitation" values observed in the "low-potential" areas. This proposition is, however, sheerly speculative, for no rigorous analysis can be undertaken with the data available. However, the destination of shipments of coal produced in the "low-potential" areas, insofar as it is known, was generally within the area near the site of production. For example, 94% of the coal produced in Colorado was shipped within the Mountain area (Census Division) in which Colorado lies; 60% of the coal produced in Utah was shipped within the Mountain Division in which it lies and 39% to the adjacent Pacific Division. All shipments of the lignite produced in North and South Dakota were within the West North Central Division of which these states form a part.[13] The statistics also show that these divisions were the destination of relatively few shipments from other areas; in other words, it appears that divisional production at the present level is sufficient to meet most divisional needs. With respect to the "national" market, the areas of low population potential clearly have a disadvantageous competitive position, for the costs they incur in transporting coal to the "national" market are greater than those incurred for coal produced in "high potential" areas. In the absence of a differential f.o.b. value favoring the "low potential" areas, their production seemingly must be geared to "local" or "regional" needs. Insofar as f.o.b. value per BTU and the "index of resource exploitation" are independent of one another on an area-by-area basis $(r = .05)$, it is suggested, speculatively to be sure, that intensity of production is associated with population potential, or ease of access to the national market, through differential transport costs.[14]

Here we have an industry in which immobile resource inputs make resource

in large part simply areal variation in the rank of coal produced. Furthermore, any attempt to evaluate value per ton in relation to population potential is especially difficult, for anthracitic and bituminous coal reserves tend to be concentrated in or toward the high-potential areas whereas the reserves of sub-bituminous and lignitic coal tend to be concentrated in the low-potential areas. Consequently, an alternative "value" indicator which has a built-in, rough control on the "quality" of coal produced—value per BTU produced—was employed.

[13]U. S. Department of Commerce, Bureau of the Census, "Bituminous Coal and Lignite Distribution," *1954 Census of Mineral Industries*, Vol. I (Washington: Government Printing Office, 1958), Section 12B.

[14]The analyses reported above are of an exploratory character. The dearth of small-area statistics on mining activity and mineral resources hampers any investigation of the patterns of areal variation in mining. To some extent, the forthcoming release of the detailed results of the 1954 Census of Mineral Industries should permit a more thorough investigation of the relationships discerned here.

Figure 52—opposite. Tons of Coal Produced per Million Tons of Reserves, Measured in British Thermal Units, 1949, by State Economic Areas.

Source: An unpublished series of data for state economic areas prepared by Donald J. Bogue and Calvin L. Beale.

access a major factor in the regional distribution of activity. On the other hand, there are sufficient alternative sources of the same input to make market access an important consideration in the distribution of the industry. Further, the existence of a major substitute product can modify the dimensions of market access considerably.

The interregional shifts shown in Figure 51 are directly tied to changes in these access factors during the period under examination.

Consider, first, factors that may have changed the conditions of input access. Resource depletion has undoubtedly exerted some influence. The shift out of Pennsylvania into the mid-Appalachian fields has arisen in part from the fact that many of the most productive seams have been exploited to the point where mid-Appalachian seams formerly of lower quality have become competitive.[15]

Mechanization of coal mining has also had an important influence. The production economies that have resulted from mechanization in the areas that are adaptable to it[16] have depressed many other coal-mining regions below the margin of feasible economic exploitation. This seems to be an important factor in the major increase in the share of production in the mid-Appalachian fields and the decline in importance of most of the areas outside. Mechanization has altered the comparative advantage of coal deposits in such a way that many deposits, in effect, have been redefined out of existence as an economic resource, given present demand and technology; and for many other deposits, profitable levels of exploitation have been sharply modified.

A third factor may have been important. Labor represents 76% of the purchased inputs for the coal industry. It is possible that institutional factors, such as strong unionization of the coal miners, may have contributed to a change in relative regional access to inputs in the sense that rising labor costs may, in some fields, have submerged production below the margin of economic exploitation. This could be a contributing factor leading to a maximizing of production in those fields where output per man-hour tends to be the greatest.

The combined influence of these factors affecting resource access seems to have increased the importance of the mid-Appalachian states relative to other coal-producing regions.

In a similar way interregional changes in relative access to markets has

[15]This might imply either lower physical quality and equal market accessibility or it might mean equal physical quality with unequal access to the prime markets or both.

Empirical studies indicates that the decline of coal mining in Pennsylvania might have been even more excessive had not open-pit and augur mining methods been substituted for underground mining. In 1940, only about 3 per cent of the state's soft coal production was mined by surface methods; by 1953, over 21 per cent was so mined. Total reserves of bituminous coal in Pennsylvania however, are still extensive. See especially: George F. Deasy and Phyllis R. Griess, "Geographical Significance of Recent Changes in Mining the Bituminous Coal Fields of Pennsylvania." *Economic Geography*. Vol. 33 (October 1957), pp. 283-98.

[16]Effective use of both underground and surface mining equipment requires seams without too many faults. Moreover, underground mining requires seams that ideally are 4-6 feet thick (although lesser and greater thicknesses are exploited); and surface mining requires seams at comparatively shallow depths. The western fields, in particular, in many instances tend to be marginal from the point of view of both thickness of seams and access to markets.

influenced the shifts we observe. The extent to which the substitution of oil for coal in the power market has been regionally concentrated is shown in Figure 53. In general, oil dominates the power market west of the Mississippi and coal east of the Mississippi. Thus coal has succeeded in holding this market in the areas with greatest access to prime coal sources and has lost out in the areas with greatest access to oil. The fact that the substitution of oil for coal is

Figure 53. Relative Use of Coal and of Oil or Natural Gas by Steam Electric Plants, 1955, by State.

Source: National Coal Association, Department of Coal Economics.

not equally feasible in every region is another element serving to explain the relative gains of coal production in the mid-Appalachian area. This region was in the strongest competitive position for retaining a larger share of the declining coal market.[17]

The eastern coal areas were less vulnerable to market loss through substitution for another reason also. This is the area where the nation's manufacturing is concentrated, and it is in the manufacturing sectors that coal seems to have had the greatest success in retaining its market.[18] The portion of total output that goes to manufacturing is about three times greater for coal than for oil and gas.

[17]The loss of markets in home-heating and transportation has exhibited a similar regional differentiation with similar effect.

[18]There is considerable logic to this. The 100% weight-losing characteristic of fuel can exert much more influence in manufacturing than in the other major coal markets. Households do not move to fuel to realize economies in heating; and the economics of power transmission require that electric utilities be close to markets, not fuel sources. Manu-

Table 137. Relative use of coal and coke and of oil and natural gas in manufacturing in Pennsylvania, West Virginia, and Texas, by industry, 1947

(per cent)

2-digit manufacturing categories	Coal and coke			Oil and natural gas		
	W. Va.	Penna.	Texas	W. Va.	Penna.	Texas
Food & kindred products	99.2	83.5	59.8	.8	16.5	39.4
Tobacco manufacturing	—	69.8	—	—	30.2	—
Textile mill products	99.7	77.2	29.3	.3	22.8	70.6
Apparel & related	99.8	79.3	—	.1	20.7	99.6
Lumber & products	82.7	74.7	28.2	17.3	25.1	70.9
Furniture & fixtures	100.00	89.8	68.9	—	10.5	31.4
Paper & allied products	100.00	90.6	—	—	9.4	99.3
Printing & publishing	87.3	82.2	55.5	12.6	18.2	43.4
Chemical & allied products	99.8	82.7	19.6	.2	17.3	79.9
Petroleum & coal products	95.9	86.8	—	3.2	11.7	99.7
Rubber products	—	13.4	—	—	17.3	—
Leather & leather products	100.0	95.5	—	—	4.5	99.5
Stone, clay, & glass	96.9	91.0	31.5	3.1	4.7	68.3
Primary metals products	91.7	89.6	82.2	8.1	10.3	17.8
Fabricated metals products	99.3	75.9	44.5	.7	24.0	55.1
Machinery (exc. elec.)	93.7	82.2	98.0	6.3	23.8	1.9
Electric machinery	99.9	93.0	97.4	—	7.0	2.2
Transportation equipment	—	51.4	2.1	—	12.4	97.7
Instruments & related	—	74.2	—	—	23.4	99.1
Miscellaneous manufacturing	97.8	79.6	67.5	2.2	19.1	32.4

SOURCE: Leland W. McCloud, *Comparative Costs of Competitive Fuels, A Study of Fuel Consumption by Manufacturing Industries in the United States, 1947*, West Virginia University, Business and Economic Studies, Volume 1, June 1951, Tables 4 and 5.

Table 137 indicates the considerable degree to which coal is successful in retaining its markets in manufacturing even in areas where its competitive position is weakest.[19] In Texas twelve of the twenty 2-digit manufacturing

facturing industries have greater freedom in seeking and utilizing the cheapest fuel sources. In many instances this turns out to be coal. Moreover, the technology of manufacturing in many industries may not allow for easy substitution of oil for coal.

Coal became the established industrial fuel before oil and gas came on the scene. It is no accident that the major manufacturing belt is located close to the nation's choicest coal sources. And agglomeration economies and market concentration have kept the manufacturing belt's share of employment and output from diminishing to any significant extent. Since most of the nation's manufacturing is conducted in this belt, close to coal's strongest competitive position, it is not too surprising that coal has succeeded in holding an important portion of this market, in spite of improved transportation, improved fuel techniques, and the alternative of oil.

[19]Since the 2-digit groups are still gross aggregates, we are aware that this state-to-state comparison might be misleading because of differences in the composition of the industries making up these aggregates. The general picture, however, can be considered as valid.

groups used coal and coke for 20% or more of their energy requirements (and nine for more than 50%). In contrast, oil completely failed to penetrate the manufacturing markets in West Virginia and showed only moderate penetration in Pennsylvania despite the fact that pipe lines and ocean transport give Pennsylvania favorable access to oil and gas fuels. Primary metals and machinery rely almost entirely on coal even in the heart of oil's competitive stronghold.[20] Miscellaneous manufacturing and food products also continue to be strong coal users.

One further change in the market has had an important effect on the regional changes in coal production and employment. A sizable part of the output of the coal industry goes to export (12.5% in 1947). Between 1939 and 1954 these exports tripled. The fact that the coal fields with most favorable access to ocean shipping are located in West Virginia, helps to explain the strong relative showing of that state.

We have described here an industry seriously affected by loss of markets and have shown some of the regional consequences. At this point, a note of caution might be appropriate against any assumption that the regional and national trends exhibited will necessarily continue. Energy is one of the fastest growing segments of the economy and the price trends of gas and oil are now starting to favor coal after working against it for thirty years. (Indeed public utility markets in New England, the Southeast, and the big metropolitan markets of New York City and Philadelphia have already started to return to coal.) Add to this the prospects that may develop out of hydrogenation, carbonization and gas synthesis, coal pipelines, etc., and it is possible that the prospects for coal in the years to come may improve.

PETROLEUM AND NATURAL GAS PRODUCTION

The degree of regional concentration and specialization in petroleum and natural gas production is not greatly different in general from that observed for coal. While twenty-four states produce some oil and gas, five states—Texas, Oklahoma, Louisiana, Kansas and California—employ about 78% of the national working force and produce 85% of the national output. The degree of population association (see Table 138, *infra*) is approximately the same as for coal.

The regional distribution, of course, differs markedly. The Appalachian coal area, where oil and gas were first discovered now supplies less than 5% of the total output. Instead, most production comes from the Southwest states plus Kansas and California.

Petroleum and natural gas production have had a marked influence on the 1-digit proportionality shifts exhibited by all mining employment. As pointed

[20]Coal's retention of a major part of the market in primary metals, machinery, etc., helps explain the experience of Utah and Oklahoma in Figure 51. As population and economic activity have expanded in the West and Southwest, there has been an expansion in those manufacturing activities that maintain their allegiance to coal. Utah's strength in coal can probably be explained to a considerable degree by the establishment and expansion of steel facilities at Provo, Utah, and in Southern California.

out earlier, four leading petroleum states (California, Oklahoma, Texas, and Louisiana), accounted for 78.4% of the net upward proportionality shift (Table 50). This important proportionality effect arises from the fact that, alone among mining industries, the petroleum and natural gas industry can claim to be a "growth" industry.

But shifts among the states in total mining employment has also risen from the fact that some "oil" states have made out better than other "oil" states; that is, there has been a differential effect as well as a proportionality, or industry-mix, effect. If we examine once again the seventeen states that showed a net upward differential shift for all mining employment (Figure 49) and compare that with the net shifts in crude petroleum and natural gas employment, we find that 9 of the 17 states receive an important boost from upward shifts of

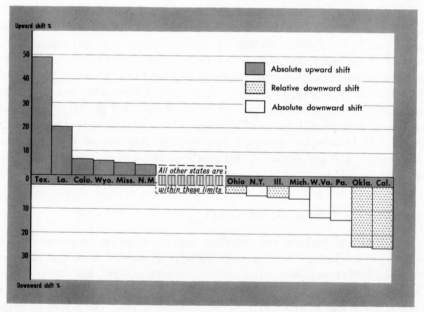

Figure 54. Net Shift in Employment in Crude Petroleum and Natural Gas Production, 1939-54.

State figures represent % of total net shift. Total net shift as % of incremental change: 45.5. Total net shift as % of 1939 crude petroleum and natural gas employment: 42.1. Source: Appendix Table I.

oil and gas employment.[21] In all of these except Utah petroleum dominates the shift in total mining employment. (Utah also gained from coal, as we saw in the previous section.) Figure 54 shows the states at the ends of the shift spectrum.

[21]Mississippi, Louisiana, Texas, New Mexico, Colorado, Utah, Wyoming, North Dakota, and Nebraska.

In some of the states the net downward differential shift in total mining employment has been due to relative losses in petroleum employment. The three states that show almost two-thirds of the net downward shift in total mining employment—California, Oklahoma, and Pennsylvania—also show two-thirds of the net downward shift in oil and gas employment.

Informed opinion holds that the changes in regional positions here are tied to resource depletion and discovery and that markets and non-resource inputs are relatively unimportant in these shifts.[22] In general, the earliest discoveries were in the Northeast; the Oklahoma and Texas fields were brought in at an intermediate period, and the most recent additions to resource capacity have been in Louisiana, Texas and the eastern Mountain states.[23] The Northeastern reserves have been worked for so long that depletion has forced absolute declines in employment and production. California and Oklahoma are not suffering from depletion in the sense that there have been any absolute declines in production. However, their relative position has declined because of their failure to discover new reserves at a rate commensurate with that of Louisiana, Texas, and the eastern Mountain states.

Oil and gas production, therefore, is unique among mining activities in that significant additions to reserves and well capacity have been made during the period under examination.[24] This factor, rather than changes in markets and in production and marketing technology, would seem to have dominated the regional shifts observed.[25]

METALLIC MINERAL MINING

Employment in metal-mining showed a 2% increase between 1939 and 1954 as compared with an 8.8% decrease for mining as a whole. Thus, while specialization in metal-mining had the effect of generating net upward proportionality shifts in mining employment, the tendency to do so was not very strong.

However, it does serve to explain the net upward proportionality shift for all mining in those states that have important metal-mining activities. Production and employment are largely concentrated in the Mountain states and the glacial shield in the Great Lakes region. Elsewhere, only Alabama and the

[22]This is a consensus gleaned from the general literature and discussions with the oil and gas specialists at the Bureau of Mines and at Resources for the Future.

[23]There has been considerable overlapping of time periods, of course.

[24]To a considerable degree, new "additions" to reserves in this period may reflect (a) differences in reserve "bookkeeping" between coal and oil, and (b) differences in the nature of oil and coal "discovery."

[25]However, while the role of changing markets, technology, and institutions do not seem to have been *central* to the regional changes in the industry, it may well be that the location of drilling activity and rates of exploitation have been somewhat influenced by these factors. It may also be that institutional factors such as an increasing trend to vertical integration have encouraged new drilling in marginal areas. At this point we are not in a position to evaluate the relative importance of these factors but, clearly, they deserve further study if a comprehensive picture of all the forces that have been affecting the location of mining activities for mineral fuels is to be achieved.

Ozark plateau show specialization. There are twenty states with little or no metal-mining activity, while the Mountain states, together with Minnesota and Michigan, account for about three-fourths of the activity.

Figure 55 gives some idea of the contribution of metal-mining to the net differential shifts in mining employment. Since total employment in this mining sector remained so nearly stable, the shifts are represented as *absolute* upward shifts or *absolute* downward shifts. For the most part, the states east of the 95th meridian show absolute gains in their shares of employment and the states west of it absolute losses. The major gains were made in the glacial shield region—Minnesota, Michigan, New York—and in Arizona. The biggest losses were in California, Oklahoma, and Alabama.

The access characteristics of the regions engaged in metal-mining suggest some of the reasons for these developments. Metal-mining, more than any other mining activity, exploits an immobile input for which there are relatively few alternative sources within the United States. Thus, in general, a fruitful domestic source will tend to be exploited irrespective of market access considerations, as Table 138 suggests. The association with population and population-centered activities seems to be slighter in metal-mining than in any other of the economic activities we survey (resource or otherwise). Thus we can concentrate our analysis of the regional access changes upon metal resource discovery

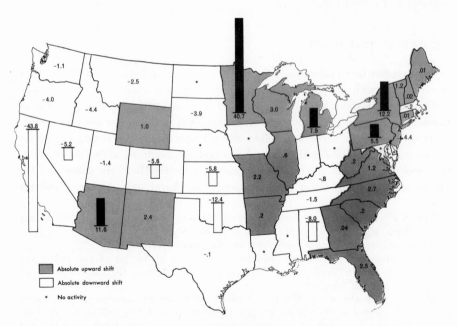

Figure 55. Net Shift in Metal Mining Employment, 1939-54.

State figures represent % of total net shift. Total net shift as % of incremental change: 859.8. Total net shift as % of 1939 metal mining employment: 18.8. Source: Appendix Table I.

Table 138. Rank correlations of each state's share of employment in selected mining activities with each state's share of population, 1954

Total mining employment	.406
Metal mining employment	.001
Coal mining employment	.197
Crude petroleum and natural gas employment	.226
Other non-metallic mineral employment	.828

SOURCE: U. S. Bureau of the Census, *Census of Mineral Industries, 1954* Preliminary Report, Series MI-14-3 (Washington: Government Printing Office, 1956); U. S. Bureau of the Census, *Current Population Reports: Population Estimates*, Series P-25, No. 145 (Washington: Government Printing Office, 1956), Table 2, Page 6.

and depletion and technological changes affecting the cost conditions of supply.[26]

The most obvious starting point for assessing total metal-mining employment is iron ore production, which is responsible for 44% of the total if precious metals are excluded. The importance of iron ore in the metals complex, together with the fact that the nation's industrial growth has made greater demands on it than on any other metal, provides the principal first-level explanation of the eastward shift in metal-mining employment and the dominance of the glacial shield areas.[27] Minnesota, which shows 41% of the net upward shift in mining employment, shows 39% of the net upward shift in iron ore production. New York, Pennsylvania, and New Jersey show another 12% of the net upward shift. While Michigan and Wisconsin did not increase their share of production, their absolute increases were such that they show 11% of the net upward shift of total metal mining employment. Alabama, which shows 8% of the net downward shift for total metal mining, shows 31% of the net downward shift in iron ore production.

Known iron reserves in the United States have not changed in our period, and up to 1954 depletion had not caused any serious curtailment of production (although it is now beginning to do so). The principal change in access therefore, must be associated with changes in the market for iron ore over these years. The most significant change here was the change in the size of

[26] A complicating element derives from the fact that metal mining is not a relatively homogeneous activity like coal mining or petroleum and natural gas production. It embraces the mining activity of some twenty or thirty metals. A part of the shift in metal mining employment should be analyzed, therefore, in terms of the proportionality effect of its component activities. This is not a complicated job, but at the time these materials were being brought together, the relevant minerals statistics for the terminal year of our period were not available. Because of the large number of different metals involved, comprehensive analysis of the regional modifications of access to metallic mineral inputs and markets is also beyond our scope. The best we can do here is to "explain" the shifts in metal mining employment at a superficial level by decomposing this change into the major metal constituents that make it up. We will go beneath this to the access characteristics only to the extent that we may be able to give broad hints.

[27] The production of iron ore during our period increased by 189% as compared with a 76% increase for all metallic minerals.

the total market. The production of pig iron, and therefore the production of iron ore, roughly tripled during the period. Because of the regional concentration of iron ore deposits, the net effect of the expansion in total demand was to establish the dominance of the Great Lakes states in total metal-mining during the 1939-54 period.

There are some other regional effects of interest that the *total* metal-mining picture disguises. (1) The decline in metal-mining employment and iron ore production in Alabama is directly related to a decline in that state's share of pig iron production. (2) Because metal-mining other than iron ore is so important in the West, the data for total metal-mining employment (shown in Figure 55) give no hint that California, Utah, and Texas account for 42% of the net upward shift in *iron ore mining* between 1939 and 1954. This is directly related to the fact that the "undistributed" category in the Minerals Yearbook—California, Colorado, Utah, Texas, Massachusetts, Minnesota, West Virginia and Tennessee—accounts for 80% of the net upward shift in blast furnace output. Of these states California, Texas, and Utah dominate the increase. We make no serious attempt here to go deeper and identify those changes in access that have, in turn, resulted in this shift in blast furnace output. It seems evident, however, that the increases in population and industrial activity in the West and Southwest constitute an important market shift that tells an important part of the story.

For the rest, let us make a quick run-down of the principal factors associated with the major shifts in metal-mining employment. California supplied 44% of the net downward shift in metal-mining during our period. This was due largely to the decline in production of gold and silver.[28] Here is a place where resource depletion seems to be a major element in the change in access. This has been an important element in the whole picture of the eastward shift of metal-mining employment. Among the states west of the 95th meridian, only Utah showed an absolute increase in gold and silver production—largely a by-product of copper mining. The rest recorded steep declines, led by California.

Since almost 90% of Arizona's mining activity is associated with copper and Arizona produces 43% of all copper ores in the United States, its unique performance in the West can be tied directly to copper. During the 1939-54 period Arizona claimed 50% of the total net upward shift in copper-ore mining. The major factors affecting the regional picture in copper-mining seem to be a mixture of technological change and resource discovery. In recent times prospecting has added significantly to the known copper reserves in Arizona, New Mexico, and Utah. During the post-depression period huge new machines for open-pit mining have been developed. This has significantly altered the comparative cost advantage of open-pit mines as compared with shaft mines. Both of these factors have favored Arizona at the expense of the older shaft mines in Michigan and Montana.

The large net downward shift exhibited by Oklahoma and Kansas is tied to

---

[28]Actually, California had increases in many other metal activities including tungsten, chromite, iron ore, lead and zinc. These were not sufficiently important in the total to affect the impact of gold and silver upon the total.

declines in the output of lead and zinc in the Ozark plateau area. The wide-spread net upward shift in metal-mining employment in the eastern states outside the Great Lakes region is associated with a wide variety of lesser minerals that are growing in importance in a metallurgical world: bauxite and manganese in Arkansas; titanium, zirconium, and uranium from phosphate ores in Florida; lithium and a new tungsten mine in North Carolina; and titanium, lithium, and manganese in Virginia are some of the growing metal mining activities in the East.

NON-METALLIC MINERAL MINING

Non-metallic mineral mining has exerted a stronger influence than metal-mining upon the proportionality effect exhibited by mining employment as a whole. Both, of course, are definitely subordinate to the mineral fuels in this respect. Since the area of greatest specialization in non-metallic minerals has been the East, it is here that it has made its greatest contribution to the net proportionality shift in total mining employment.

Figure 56 suggests the contribution made by non-metallic minerals to the differential net shift in total mining employment.[29] On the whole, states west of the 90th meridian experienced net upward shifts, and states east of this line experienced net downward shifts.

Non-metallic mineral mining employment has a closer association with population and its associated activities than any other resource activity (Table 138).[30] The minerals that comprise this group provide an excellent example of the extreme case of substitutability mentioned earlier in the chapter. Deposits for many of these minerals are so ubiquitous that it is possible to exploit those with the most favorable access to markets. This is particularly true of minerals in the stone-clay-sand-gravel category and these make up almost two-thirds of the value of the output of all non-metallic minerals. Two-thirds of the output of these sand and gravel type minerals goes to construction and final demand. As a consequence, the dominant change in access explaining the shifts in non-metallic mining is the westward shift in the market. This shift has been revealed for population but is even more marked for construction. The change in regional access to markets seems to have prompted a more intensive exploitation of the resource deposits near the expanding market areas.

The changes in population and associated markets, however, cannot explain the direction and dimension of all of these shifts. Individual minerals with relatively concentrated deposits are often an important element in the explana-

[29]When we try to explain the shifts in non-metallic mineral mining, however, we run into the same complicating element presented by the analysis of metallic minerals. There are some 60 different minerals which are brought together in this group. This lack of homogeneity makes a thorough analysis far beyond the scope of this study.

[30]This high correlation may be deceiving to a degree because of the fact that non-metallic minerals is a family group made up of so many different minerals. Some of these have highly concentrated markets as well as highly concentrated inputs (like potash and phosphate). However, the fact that there are so many of these activities has the result that they tend to average out spatially and strengthen the correlation rather than weaken it.

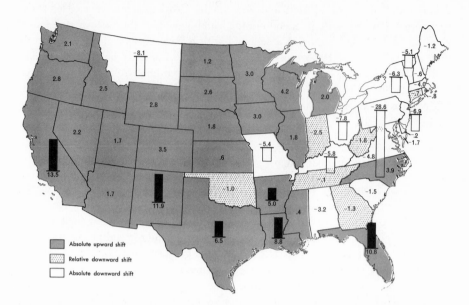

Figure 56. Net Shift in Non-Metallic (other than fuels) Mining Employment, 1939-54.

State figures represent % of total net shift. Total net shift as % of incremental change: 104.4. Total net shift as % of 1939 non-metallic mining employment: 19.1. Source: Appendix Table I.

tion. While California records a large net upward shift (13.5%) in part because of sizeable increases in the construction minerals, other factors are (1) that it has major deposits of borates, which is a "rapid-growth" mineral, and (2) that it has expanded its share of the output of both salt and gypsum. The large increase in New Mexico arises primarily from the fact that it supplies 90% of the nation's potash output, and potash has been a growth mineral. Further, Texas has increased its salt output four times as much as the rest of the nation. Arkansas shows up strong because of an important discovery of a new bauxite deposit which has made it the leading producer of this mineral. Florida's performance stems in part from the fact that it produces three-fourths of the nation's phosphate—still another growth mineral. We cannot attempt to evaluate the changes leading to these shifts.

REGIONAL IMPACT OF MINING ACTIVITY

The general regional influences reviewed here have touched a large number of states that have some mining activity. It should be recognized, however, that in only a few of these states have the shifts in mining employment been sufficiently important to make an impact upon total employment. There were only eleven states (Table 134) in which the shifts accounted for more than

5% of the total differential effect; in all but three of these states the shifts in mining employment took the same direction as the shifts in total employment.[31]

Most striking is the fact that the performance of mining employment explains the behavior of one of the major growth regions and one of the major relative decline regions.

Of the states which have shown the greatest growth in total employment, the Southwest in general and Texas and Louisiana in particular seem to have owed a major part of their growth to the mineral sector of the economy. Texas and Louisiana, which had two-thirds of the net upward shift in mining employment, were the only states where the share of mining and employment increased significantly more than the share of population. This would suggest the possibility of mineral resources being an important lead factor in the growth of these areas. Oil and gas and their geological associates—sulphur and salt— were chiefly responsible for this performance.

The Appalachian states comprised one of the major areas of relative decline, with a marked downward shift in coal-mining employment. Pennsylvania, West Virginia, and Kentucky account for about 75% of the net downward shift in total mining employment. The proportionality effect was dominant here. As a matter of fact, Kentucky and West Virginia strengthened their *relative* position in coal-mining and displayed a net upward differential shift for that industry. However, this effect was slight compared to the large losses associated with the proportionality effect. There was also a downward differential shift in petroleum and natural gas and, though less important, in non-metallic minerals in these states.

A review of the regional influence of mining activity based upon the materials in this chapter cannot provide a complete picture, however. California is a case in point. It exhibited the greatest over-all growth in the nation for the 1939-1954 period but showed only a modest relative upward shift in mining employment. This shift was based almost entirely upon the proportionality effect; the only differential upward shift was in non-metallic minerals. This does not mean, however, that mineral activities have not made important contributions to the growth of California. California shows an amazing diversity of output in both metallic and non-metallic minerals and produces about 10% of the total oil and gas output for the nation. This diversified resource base has undoubtedly contributed to the state's economic growth. Furthermore, the shift picture can be deceptive. For example, the relative net downward shifts recorded for petroleum and natural gas are still consistent with sizable absolute increases. If petroleum and natural gas have any important multiplier relationships with other activities, these increases could support growth that would be reflected in other dimensions.

If we could examine these cumulative factors more adequately there are a number of questions concerning the regional influence of mining activity for which we might wish to seek answers. (1) Does the considerable importance

---

[31]The upward shifts in mining employment displayed by Louisiana, Minnesota, and Wyoming ran counter to, and were overshadowed by, the general shifts in other employment sectors in those states.

of substitute sources and substitute products plus the possibility of exhaustion place regions which are mining specialists in a more vulnerable position than other regions? Is it possible that their growth behavior tends to be more erratic and less predictable than other types of regions? (2) Since mining regions are usually subject to important external as well as internal stimuli, does this have any special significance for the growth performance of mining regions? (3) Since mineral inputs often exhibit significant weight-loss when processed and since most of these inputs go to intermediate processing activities rather than final demand, do mineral specializing regions tend to have a higher multiplier effect working for them than some others (like agricultural regions, for example)? (As we proceed to an examination of the components of manufacturing activity in Texas we may gather some evidence of this.) (4) There seems to be a trend underway that displays an expanding number of substitution possibilities in the minerals industries. Discovery and technology are enlarging the range of mineral product substitutes. Technology often has the effect of making feasible alternative mineral sources that were previously non-economic. Does this mean that the mold for economic activity imposed by the distribution of natural mineral resources is becoming more flexible? Is the spatial influence of these resource sectors becoming less important, and what does this imply for the regional dimensions of future growth?

Topics such as these require volumes rather than chapters.

21 / Regional distribution of

agricultural activity:

(1) FARMING IN GENERAL

In terms of employment numbers, agriculture was the largest of the ten broad industry components of total employment in 1939; and in 1954 it was exceeded only by the manufacturing sector.[1] But, as in mining both the absolute and the relative importance of agriculture in the nation's total employment is declining. In this chapter we shall consider the factors that are operative in this development and the regional consequences of it.

[1] An examination of unpublished long-term resource output and employment indices compiled by Neal Potter and Francis T. Christy, Jr., at Resources for the Future, Inc., reveals that the years 1939 and 1954 were reasonably "normal" *for purposes of comparison, with respect to output and employment.*

Sector	A O 1939	B O 1954	C
	Av O 1937-41	Av O 1952-56	(B–A)
	O = Output in physical terms, selected major components		
All agriculture	97.6	98.5	.9
All crops	94.3	97.5	3.2
Wheat	88.4	91.0	2.6
Corn	100.2	94.1	− 6.1
Cotton	89.5	93.4	3.9
Livestock			
Dairy products	99.3	101.3	2.0
Hogs	108.8	97.3	−11.5
Cattle	100.3	101.6	1.3

As indicated in Columns A and B of the table above, output in major agricultural sectors tended to be somewhat lower for the years 1939 and 1954 than for the average of neighboring years.

Column C represents the difference between the ratios in Columns A and B. If there is little difference in the ratios, one can assume that conclusions resulting from comparison of the 1939 and 1954 figures are not substantially impaired by the fact that these years were somewhat atypical. Where the difference is positive, the conclusions may be overstated with

*Regional Influence of Agriculture Reflected in
the Proportionality Effect*

Between 1939 and 1954 thirty-one states experienced a net downward proportionality shift in total employment as a consequence of their specialization in
sectors of economic activity that have grown more slowly than others or have
actually declined for the nation as a whole over these years (Figure 47). Mining
specialization, as we have seen, contributed to this downward shift in about half
of these states, but it was the major cause of the proportionality effect in only
two of them—Nevada and Utah. In twenty-nine of the thirty-one states the net
downward proportionality shift was attributable primarily to specialization in
agriculture. Table 139 shows agriculture's share of total employment in each
of these states in 1939 and in 1954.

The agricultural labor force of the nation declined by 14.7% over these years.
But the decline in agricultural employment does not have its origin in the current period; it goes back over several generations. Since 1870 the share of
agriculture in the nation's total labor force has fallen off by more than two-
thirds,, and its share in total income by more than a half.

Several long-term trends in supply and demand help to explain these developments. On the supply side, the major trends may be summarized as follows:

(1) There has been a pronounced long-run trend for agriculture to cover
fewer economic activities than formerly. This has been a function largely of
technological advances and the increased specialization that characterizes an
advancing society. To a considerable extent, activities that once belonged to
agriculture have been taken over by the manufacturing and the trade and service
sectors of the economy. The relative importance of agricultural employment has
declined significantly as a result.[2]

(2) The value-added factor also helps to explain the *relative* decline of agriculture. The more extended fabrication that agricultural products undergo

respect to the period—where negative, understated. Thus, for all agriculture, both years
are slightly subnormal and the slight degree of difference suggests that comparative conclusions for the period are not seriously compromised. Major departures are apparent with
respect to corn and hog output, but the differences being negative, comparisons involving
these two products during the period 1939-1954 would tend to be understated.

Potter-Christy agricultural employment data tend to support the assumption of normalcy
for these years:

	A E 1939 E1937-1941	B E 1954 E1952-1956	C (B–A)
All Agriculture			
Employment	100.7	97.8	− 2.9
Manhours	100.4	99.3	− 1.1

[2]Cf. John H. Davis and R. A. Goldberg, *A Concept of Agribusiness* (Boston: Harvard
University Press, 1957). Ronald Mighell has estimated that employment in agriculture and
its associated pre-farm and post-farm activities amounted to about twice that of agriculture
alone in 1950. See Ronald L. Mighell, *American Agriculture: Its Structure and Place in
the Economy*, A Volume in the Census Monograph Series, (New York: John Wiley and
Sons, 1955), p. 11.

Table 139. Agricultural employment as percentage of total employment, 1939 and 1954, for states with net downward proportionality shifts in total employment, 1939-1954, because of specialization in agriculture

State	1939 %	1954 %
United States Average	27.5	16.9
Mississippi	74.3	59.2
Arkansas	70.1	54.9
North Dakota	68.3	55.4
South Dakota	57.6	50.5
South Carolina	56.3	31.8
Alabama	54.6	32.1
Georgia	50.4	23.4
Idaho	49.1	39.5
Kentucky	48.8	34.5
North Carolina	46.9	34.8
Texas	46.9	25.4
Oklahoma	46.8	31.2
Louisiana	46.5	29.6
Tennessee	46.2	33.2
Nebraska	46.1	35.1
New Mexico	46.0	27.5
Iowa	45.6	35.9
Kansas	42.8	27.7
Montana	42.4	29.5
Minnesota	40.0	28.4
Wyoming	36.0	23.2
Virginia	35.9	22.2
Vermont	35.1	24.5
Arizona	34.8	22.7
Wisconsin	34.5	23.6
Missouri	32.7	21.8
Oregon	31.4	19.8
Colorado	30.0	19.5
West Virginia	28.1	17.6

SOURCE: Appendix Tables F1 and F2.

before reaching the final consumer generally adds to aggregate output without a commensurate increase in agricultural output.

(3) Great increases in worker productivity have helped bring about a relative decline in the importance of agricultural employment.[3] There have been enormous increases in efficiency through mechanization and other technological improvements. Agricultural land and labor could be made to go further for

[3]This increase in worker productivity, however, would not explain the relative decline in agricultural employment if all sectors of economic activity improved worker productivity by an equal amount. Manufacturing has similarly improved worker productivity. The services and trades, however, have lagged behind agriculture in this respect. Since agriculture has experienced a more rapid technological development than the services and trades, we expect this sector to lose labor over time to the services and trade sectors.

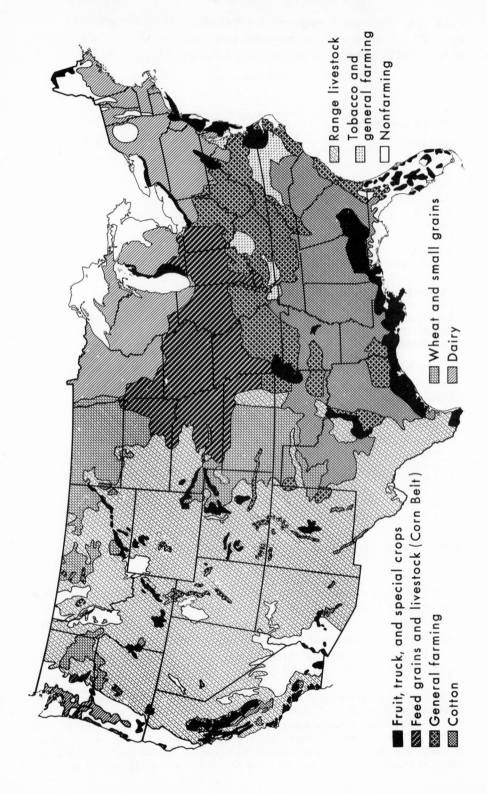

another reason: tractors don't eat hay. Between 1918 and 1953, substitution of tractor power for horse and mule power released about 70 million acres of land formerly used to produce feed for draft animals. The release of agricultural labor was similarly impressive.

Long-term trends operating on the demand side of the market have also contributed to the relative decline of agricultural employment. Three of these are worth special mention.

(1) Consumption of farm products as a whole is not very responsive to changes in income; income elasticities are relatively small. This is seen most readily in the case of food products. Expenditures for food at retail stores and restaurants have been increasing at a rate which is more or less in proportion to increases in income. But these expenditures include many services of processing and distribution. And it is these services that have been increasing with rising per capita income rather than the consumption of farm products. The quantity of food consumed per person increases very little as incomes rise. Agriculture's *share* of total demand declines progressively as incomes and total demand grow.

Recent studies of per capita expenditures for food in relation to income (both in real terms) covering the periods 1929-41 and 1948-56 suggest an income elasticity of demand for food of .44; a 10% increase in real per capita income has resulted in an average increase of around 4½% in food expenditure per person. However, this total is made up of two parts; the bill for processing and marketing and the farm share (with some two-thirds of the total currently going to processing and marketing). For the dates studied, the income elasticity for the service part was found to be .775 (the "quantity" of services increased by about 7¾% with a 10% increase in income), while the income elasticity of demand for food *at the farm level* was less than .15 (a 10% increase in real consumer income per person resulted in a gain of only 1½% in per capita expenditures for food). The very low income elasticity of demand for farm products at the farm level has resulted in a long-run decline in the farmers' share of total expenditures, and even of expenditures for farm products as such.[4]

Not only has the income elasticity of demand for farm products been low in recent decades, but it has been falling. Thus data for market value of all food in relation to disposable money income suggest the following income elasticities of demand:[5]

1929-41	1948-57	Spring 1955	(cross section
.68	.38	.25	data)

[4]Rex F. Daly, "Demand for Farm Products at Retail and the Farm Level: Some Empirical Measurements and Related Problems," *Journal of the American Statistical Association*, Vol. 53 (September 1958) pp. 665-68; and "The Long-Run Demand for Farm Products," *Agricultural Economics Research*, Vol. 8 (July 1956), pp. 73-91.

[5]Marguerite C. Burk, "Some Analyses of Income-Food Relationships," *Journal of the American Statistical Association*, Vol. 53 (December 1958), pp. 905-27.

Figure 57—opposite.   Major Types of Farming in the United States.
Source: U. S. Department of Agriculture, Agricultural Research Service.

While estimates of this type involve all sorts of statistical problems, the general magnitudes are highly suggestive and help to explain developments in the farm sector of the economy.[6]

There is an obvious physiological limit to per capita consumption of food, whether considered in terms of weight, calories, or other constituents. The population of the United States has probably come closer to reaching this limit than any other group in history, although it must be recognized that many Americans lack an adequate diet. Also, of course, changes in eating habits influence food purchases.

(2) There has been a long-run decline in agriculture's share of American exports. This can be traced to a number of things such as the tariff policy of the United States,[7] agricultural protection abroad and modifications in comparative advantage and the terms of trade to favor manufactured products. This declining trend has been interrupted occasionally by abnormal war demands but has been a fairly consistent long-run element in agricultural demand over a number of decades.

(3) Lastly, for a number of agricultural products, there has been sharp competition from synthetic and natural substitutes of non-agricultural origin. The case of the synthetic fibers is a good example.

In short, significant long-term trends in supply and demand have reduced the relative importance of the agricultural sector of the economy. As a consequence, the regions that have depended largely on agriculture have tended to lose out relative to regions with better access to manufacturing markets and basic intermediate inputs.[8] In spite of this generally depressing effect of agricultural specialization, *some regions received significant assistance from agriculture in generating net upward shifts in total employment.* This is so because there were significant interregional *differential* shifts in agricultural activity.

[6]See also James P. Cavin, "Projections in Agriculture," *Long-Range Economic Projection. Studies in Income and Wealth,* Vol. 16 (Princeton: Princeton University Press, 1954), pp. 107-30; U.S. Dept. of Agriculture, *Food Consumption of Households in the United States; Northeast; North Central Region; South; and West.* Household Food Consumption Survey 1955 Reports 1 to 5, (Washington: U.S. Dept. of Agriculture, 1956). University of Pennsylvania, *Study of Consumer Expenditures, Incomes and Savings,* 1956. (1950 food data in volumes III and XII, Spring 1951 food data in Vol. XII.)

[7]Since the first half of the 1939-54 period was dominated by World War II and the succeeding international adjustments, agricultural products constituted an abnormally low proportion of total exports (an eight year average of 20%). When compared to the latter half of the period (an eight year average of 25%), it is apparent that during this period agricultural products constituted a rising proportion of total exports.

However, the long run trend is one of declining proportion. During the five years following World War I (1919-23) the average proportion of agricultural exports was 46%, while during the similar period following World War II (1946-50) the proportion was 28%. U.S. Department of Agriculture, *Agricultural Statistics, 1957* (Washington: Government Printing Office, 1958), Table 808, p. 702.

[8]It should be noted that the multi-state regions used for analytical purposes in this study do not always correspond well with the generalized agricultural regions (See Figure 57). If one were focusing essentially on the major features of the agricultural sector of the national economy and seeking to understand the factors that have given shape to the economic geography of American agriculture, this would be a serious shortcoming. The purpose of

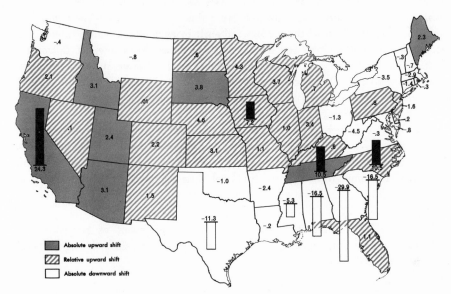

Figure 58. Net Shift in Agricultural Employment, 1939-54.

State figures represent % of total net shift. Total net shift as % of incremental change: 34.7. Total net shift as % of 1939 agricultural employment: 5.1. Source: Appendix Table H.

Regional Influence of Agriculture Reflected in the Differential Effect

Figure 58 shows the net shifts in agricultural employment, by states, between 1939 and 1954.[9] It is clear, when this figure is compared with Figure 46, that

this study is somewhat different, however; it seeks to understand differential regional development in terms of the array of economic activities and their changes. Agriculture is but a part of this total picture, and our concern is with its role in the total pattern of regional economic development. Thus, it is this kind of "vertical" analysis that requires that the geographical regions be held constant throughout.

For a finer "grain" of analysis, we have focused on shift phenomena at the state level. A glance at the maps portraying the nature and direction of the shifts in activity allows the reader to aggregate by states visually in any manner of interest to him. Thus, in Figure 58 one could conclude that the Corn Belt states generally enjoyed a modest net upward shift in agricultural employment during the period 1939-54, while the Cotton Belt states suffered a modest-to-extensive net downward shift during the same period.

[9]In evaluating the figures that are presented on agriculture, it should be kept in mind that agricultural employment differs from most other employment. In most activities, persons are considered employed only when actually working for wages or directing such workers. In agriculture, many "workers" are essentially persons not working elsewhere. Farming conceals much unemployment and underemployment and their extent is not constant from period to period. Thus agricultural "employment" data must be viewed with this consideration in mind.

agriculture has played a significant part in the differential net shifts in *total* employment. Of the twenty-six states with net upward differential shifts in total employment, nineteen show relative gains in agriculture; these nineteen states account for 77% of the net upward shift in agricultural employment. The correlation is not so high for the twenty-two states that show net downward shifts in total employment. However, in over half of these states, agriculture contributed to the relative decline; 83% of the net downward shift in agricultural employment occurred in states which also show a net downward differential shift in total employment.

Additional evidence supports the impression that agricultural employment shifts have been an important part of the observed total differential shifts. Table 140 identifies twenty-six states in each of which the agricultural shift accounted for more than 10% of the total shift (computed without regard to

Table 140. Differential shifts in agricultural employment as percentage of total employment for states with largest net differential shifts in agricultural employment, 1939-1954

State	Agricultural shift in state as % of total shift (without regard to sign) of 1-digit employment categories.
South Carolina	70.1%
Georgia	64.3
Alabama	56.8
Idaho	54.6
South Dakota	49.1
Tennessee	45.3
Mississippi	36.2
Nebraska	35.9
North Carolina	30.1
Iowa	29.6
Utah	28.0
West Virginia	26.7
Arkansas	25.3
Indiana	22.9
Arizona	22.0
Wisconsin	21.9
Colorado	20.9
Oregon	20.7
Maine	19.9
Minnesota	17.3
Montana	16.1
Kansas	14.3
New Mexico	14.1
North Dakota	12.6
California	12.3
Texas	11.7

SOURCE: Table 157.

sign) of the 1-digit employment components for that state. The states most significantly affected by the performance of agriculture are concentrated in the Southeast, Plains, and Mountain regions.

There are no usable figures for the 1939-54 period on employment in the component segments of agriculture, such as we used in our examination of mining employment. In order to present a more detailed analysis, therefore, we have used data on the value of agricultural products sold in each of the main agricultural categories. These data are presented in Table 141. The net shifts in value, or the over-all departure of states from the national norm, have been significant in each of the main categories. Departures from the national average change have been greatest in vegetables and poultry and products and smallest in dairy products.

The state-by-state shifts in the value of all farm products sold are shown in Figure 59. Like the data on agricultural employment, these data support the general picture of a westward shift in agriculture. The states in the East on the whole display downward shifts, and those in the West predominately upward shifts. Further, 86% of the net upward shift in the value of farm products sold took place in states that also displayed upward shifts in agricultural employment.

There are, however, marked discrepancies between the shifts in the value of farm products sold and the shifts in agricultural employment. Several Mountain, Plains, and Great Lakes states that show net upward employment shifts show net downward shifts in value of farm products sold. Just the reverse is

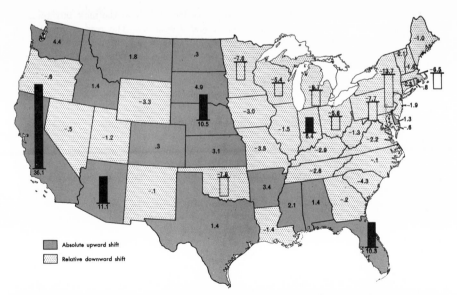

Figure 59.   Net Shift in Value of All Agricultural Products Sold, 1940-54.
State figures represent % of total net shift. Total net shift as % of incremental change; 9.2. Total net shift as % of 1940 value of all agricultural products sold: 24.7. Source: Appendix Table J.

true for some of the Southeastern states. The most marked contrast is the sharp upward shift in agricultural employment in Tennessee and North Carolina in the face of relative downward shifts in the value of farm products sold.

There can be many reasons for these discrepancies. (1) Some labor-intensive agricultural commodities may have made relatively limited gains in agricultural values over the period. (This seems to be the case for dairy products, which may help explain the discrepancy in the Great Lakes states.) (2) There are substantial regional differencies in part-time farming and opportunities for off-farm employment that might serve to explain some of these differences. (3) Mechanization has proceeded more rapidly during this period for some agricultural products than for others. (4) Interregional differences in farm tenancy and other institutional and cultural patterns may have some influence. (5) Historical factors arising out of farm adjustments in previous periods and the differences in timing of the same adjustment in different regions may play an important role. (6) A whole host of "accidental" factors that are more or less peculiar to a specific region may exert their influence.

We cannot undertake here the complex job of translating value phenomena into employment phenomena.[10] We proceed, however, to examine in greater detail the shifts displayed by the value of farm products sold for two reasons. First, there is no better alternative for providing disaggregated detail within the practical time limits with which we are faced. Second, the within-component changes reveal many things of direct value in arriving at an understanding of the shifts in agricultural employment.

---

[10]To highlight the types of problems involved, let us look briefly at the most intriguing of these discrepancies, displayed by North Carolina and Tennessee. The reader should keep in mind that the base for the shift is the average performance for the nation and this net upward shift is primarily evidence of a less rapid decline in farm employment in these states. (Even Tennessee's evidence of an absolute upward shift is unimportant. Less than 4% of the net upward shift for this state was generated by an absolute increase.) With this in mind we should recognize that North Carolina and Tennessee made an earlier adjustment in their farm economy than the Deep South. Thus, in the current period their decline in agricultural employment was less marked and became recorded as a net upward shift. We have examined several sets of statistical data that support this conclusion. Further, Tennessee and North Carolina have had fewer farm tenants than the Deep South, and farm tenants tend to leave the soil more readily than farm owners. Secondly, there is some evidence that the set-back in manufacturing employment that occurred in the Manufacturing Belt in 1954 may have sent a number of transient industrial workers back to their hill farms in time to be counted in the census. Third, Tennessee and North Carolina are the most industrialized of the Southeastern states and present more off-farm employment opportunities that encourage part-time farming. This tends to keep up agricultural employment without equal support to farm production. Fourth, dairy and poultry are reasonably concentrated activities in these states and they tend to be labor intensive although they have not made the gains in value that other agricultural products have. Fifth, much bottom land in these two states was in production at the beginning of our period that was inundated and out of production by 1954. Much of this production was in high value vegetable crops. This could help explain the relatively depressed character of value of farm products relative to farm employment.

One can see that a wide variety of factors can serve to explain the discrepancy in each case.

Table 141. Relative importance of net shifts in value of agricultural products sold, 1940-1954

Categories	Value of agricultural products sold				Absolute change 1940-54 (million dollars)	Percentage increase (col. 5 as per cent of col. 1)	Total net shift, 1940-54 (million dollars)	Col. 7 as % of col. 5	Col. 7 as % of col. 1
	1940		1954						
	Dollars (million)	Per cent	Dollars (million)	Per cent					
	(1)	(2)	(3)	(4)	(5)	(6)	(7)	(8)	(9)
All agric. products sold	6,682	100.0	24,642	100.0	17,960	268.8	±1,649.2	9.2	24.7
Field crops	2,471	37.0	9,922	40.3	7,451	301.6	±1,204.9	16.2	48.8
Vegetables	200	3.0	645	2.6	446	223.3	± 122.7	27.5	61.5
Fruits & nuts	295	4.4	1,199	4.9	903	305.8	± 146.3	16.2	49.5
Horticultural spec.	129	1.9	454	1.8	324	250.8	± 53.1	16.4	41.1
Dairy products	1,118	16.7	3,334	13.5	2,216	198.2	± 260.8	11.8	23.3
Poultry & products	555	8.3	1,917	7.8	1,361	245.1	± 324.6	23.8	58.4
Livestock & products	1,874	28.1	7,041	28.6	5,167	275.7	± 778.5	15.1	41.5
Farm forest products	39	.6	130	.5	91	233.1	± 33.3	36.6	85.4

Source: Appendix Table J.

Table 142. Percentage change in value of agricultural products sold for 2-digit agricultural sectors, 1940-1954

Fruits and nuts	305.8%
Field crops	301.6
Livestock and products	275.7
ALL AGRICULTURAL PRODUCTS	268.8
Horticultural specialties	250.8
Poultry and products	245.1
Farm forest products	233.1
Vegetables	223.3
Dairy products	198.2

SOURCE: *U. S. Census of Agriculture 1940*, Vol. III, T. 8, pp. 905-11; *U. S. Census of Agriculture 1954*, Vol. II, General Report, Chap. 9, "Value of Farm Products."

1-Digit Proportionality and Differential Effects in the Value of Farm Products Sold Based Upon 2-Digit Components

In Figure 59 we have shown the net shift in value of all agricultural products sold. In order to introduce further detail into our picture of structure and change in American agriculture, we shall now subdivide this total value into its eight major components—field crops, fruits and nuts, horticultural specialities, dairy products, poultry and products, livestock products, and farm forest products. By computing a shift pattern for each of these components and summing them for each state, we arrive at the total differential net shift in the value of farm products sold. Since this figure does not typically exhaust the total shift portrayed in Figure 59, the balance represents the proportionality effect. The proportionality shift is presented in Figure 60 and the differential shift in Figure 61.

The proportionality effect contributes only about 20% of the total shift in the value of farm products sold. However, it assumes significant proportions in specific regions. The net downward proportionality shift is concentrated in the Northeast—the New England, Middle Atlantic, and Great Lakes states. Two states, Wisconsin and New York, account for 43% of it, and Pennsylvania for 12%.

Table 142 points out the reasons for this effect: dairy products, poultry products, vegetables, horticultural specialities, and farm forest products are the principal slow-growth sectors of agriculture when measured by the value of agricultural products sold. Table 143 shows that these are also the sectors with the greatest association with markets. It is no surprise then, to find the net downward proportionality shift concentrated in the highly populous market centers of the Northeast. Since dairy products create well over half of the total value of these slow-growth commodities, they tend to dominate the net downward proportionality shift. It is also no surprise to see the concentration in

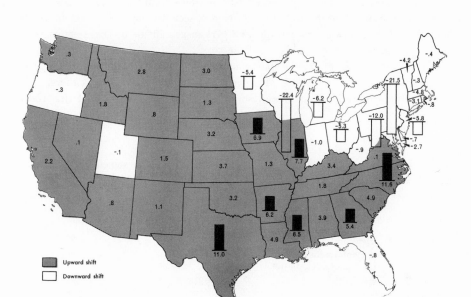

Figure 60. Total Proportionality Net Shift in Value of Agricultural Products Sold, 1940-54.

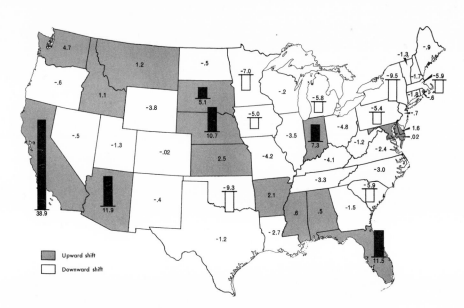

Figure 61. Total Differential Net Shift in Value of Agricultural Products Sold, 1940-54.

Wisconsin and New York. These are the nation's dominant dairy states. The largest net upward proportionality shifts are seen to have occurred in North Carolina, Texas, Iowa, Mississippi, and Arkansas; in all of these states there is specialization in the rapid-growth sectors.

An understanding of this proportionality effect requires some knowledge of the reasons why some sectors of agriculture expand more than others. The modifications of total demand and supply factors that bring about this result are legion.

Table 143. Rank correlations of each state's share of selected agricultural activities with each state's share of population, 1939 and 1954

Agricultural activity	1939	1954
Total value of agricultural products sold		.666
Total agricultural employment	.708	.649
Value of agricultural products sold in*		
Horticultural specialities	.816	.859
Dairy products	.736	.762
Poultry products	.754	.751
Vegetables	.759	.694
Fruits and nuts	.723	.641
Field crops	.544	.383
Other livestock products	.368	.324

*Figures for 2-digit components of "Value of Agricultural Products Sold" are for 1940.
Source: See Sources for Appendix Tables F1, F2, H and J.

One factor is, again, income elasticity of demand.[11] It is true that for agricultural products as a whole, the income elasticity of demand is less than one. However, there can be significant variations among agricultural products. Fruits and nuts and livestock products tend to show relatively high income elasticities. This may be an important factor in explaining the growth performance of these sectors. On the other hand, vegetables and dairy products also tend to have a higher income elasticity than field crops, so some other factors must play a role.

One aspect of the observed rates of growth may be explained by an important substitution. For some uses, vegetable oils have proved to be a potent substitute for dairy products. During our period the repeal of restrictive legislation on oleomargarine and the stimulus provided by the war undoubtedly created a significant adjustment. Since vegetable oils are classed under field crops, this development could be an important factor in explaining the relatively poor performance of dairy products vis-a-vis field crops.

The large increases in farm productivity that have accompanied mechanization may also be a factor. In general, field crops have been far more suscepti-

[11] See Theodore W. Schultz, *The Economic Organization of Agriculture*, (New York: McGraw-Hill Book Co., 1953), pp. 175-94.

ble to mechanization than animal livestock activities. Dairying in particular has shared less in the productivity increases that have accompanied farm mechanization. We also know that the farm price-support program has not been applied uniformly to all agricultural commodities. For example, storable commodities are easier to subsidize than non-storable commodities. Perhaps field crops were nudged into the rapid-growth category by the role of farm price-supports. It is also possible that short-run distortions in farm output were caused by the changes in agricultural demand that accompanied the war.

When we turn our attention to the differential net shift, we can see clear evidence of the point already made—the differential effect dominates the net shift in the value of farm products sold. The configurations in Figure 61 match very closely those in Figure 59. Only Texas, Colorado, and North Dakota experienced upward shifts that were created because of their specialization in rapid-growth products alone. It can also be easily established that the states showing the greatest upward and downward shifts in the value of farm products sold also show the greatest upward and downward differential shifts. The explanation of these shifts must lie in the differential regional behavior of the components of agricultural activity.

Access Characteristics of Agricultural Activities

As a resource activity, agriculture must be located at the site of the immobile resource attributes it exploits. The range of substitution possibilities in cultivation is so great, however, that these immobile attributes exercise only moderate influence upon the specific location of agricultural activity. Other factors can exert considerable influence. There are several reasons why this is so.

(1) The resource that agriculture exploits is land—land and all of its attributes of fertility, topography, water-holding capacity, and its associated precipitation and temperature patterns. However, arable land in the United States is nearly ubiquitous from a regional point of view. True, arable land is not all of the same quality. When we consider specific agricultural functions and/or small areas, the amount of land specifically suitable may be much less ubiquitous. The general picture, however, is one of a wide range of substitute input sources.

(2) The fact that labor and capital can be substituted for land resources to a considerable degree enlarges the range of substitution possibilities. The appropriate temperature conditions can be provided by hot houses, the moisture conditions by irrigation, and the fertility conditions by chemical fertilizers in areas where the natural attributes are found wanting. Such factors as these can open the way for a larger influence upon location by non-resource attributes.

(3) Another attribute of agriculture is that it is based on a *renewable* resource. It is true that large land areas have been depleted of much of their productive capacity and that important regional shifts have been associated with this depletion. In the main, however, advantage is taken of the replenishible characteristic of agricultural land with two consequences of significance

for regional analysis. First, regions that specialize in agriculture need not be in as serious danger as mining areas of economic stagnation due to resource exhaustion. Second, there is a choice between rational husbandry and an essentially "mining" type of activity. The former, which is increasingly the choice, means that purchased inputs become more important in agriculture than in other resource activities. Thus, the range of substitution possibilities on the supply side are greater, and this is another factor contributing to greater locational flexibility for agriculture.

(4) More than almost any other activity, agriculture is subject to important external substitution alternatives. By its very nature, it cannot be as concentrated an activity as mining or manufacturing. This extensive use of land surface in agriculture makes this activity more liable than most to the influence of "rivalry" costs. All agricultural activities cannot locate at the same point. Competition for the most central sites bids up land rents. Producers of certain agricultural products need a central location more than others and will be able to pay a higher rent. These functions appropriate the most favorable locations and, by imposing upon them an undesirable external cost element, displace other activities to peripheral areas. (This relationship applies not only to alternative agricultural uses but to alternative urban household and industrial uses as well.) Thus, the location of agricultural production is modified in its detail by these important competitive relationships influencing the relative availability of land inputs on the supply side. An understanding of the regional access characteristics of an agricultural activity, therefore, involves considerable understanding of the characteristics of rival agricultural systems.

Certain of the special characteristics of agriculture may be seen by comparing the inputs into agriculture with the inputs of mining, the other major resource sector. Such a comparison is made in Table 144. The mining inputs support an almost classical view of a resource activity. Some 85% of the purchased inputs come from the final demand sector, which is primarily labor.[12] Another 15% is split between manufacturing and service. This is not far removed from the simple picture of labor being applied to natural resources to create value —the traditional view of resource exploitation. In agriculture, the contrast is marked. Labor inputs are significant, but they account for less than half of the total.[13] Significant purchases are made from manufacturing, the services (especially transportation), and agriculture itself.

Consider these inputs further. Purchases from the manufacturing and service sectors account for half of the non-labor farm expenses. As short a time as thirty years ago, agriculture purchased only from 20% to 30% of its non-labor farm inputs.

Less than a century ago the farmer not only produced food and fiber but also created most of his own production supplies, provided his own storage, and

---

[12]The final demand sector includes tax payments to governments as well as payments to labor. Labor payments in this case are just under 80 per cent.

[13]The data on this point in the BLS table represent rough estimates at best. There are serious difficulties involved in measuring the labor inputs of self-employed farmers and partially employed workers.

Table 144. Percentage distribution of inputs and outputs for major industry groups, 1947

a. Distribution of Inputs

Input source	Output				
	Agricul-ture	Mining	Manufac-turing	Services and trade	Final demand
Agriculture	25.7	0.0	9.9	.8	3.1
Mining	0.1	1.0	3.4	1.1	0.3
Manufacturing	10.2	8.7	39.4	15.3	27.9
Services and trade	14.6	6.2	8.8	19.9	44.4
Final demand (mainly labor)	49.3	85.8	38.2	63.0	24.6
TOTAL	100.0	100.0	100.0	100.0	100.0

b. Distribution of Outputs

Output Distribution	Industry				
	Agricul-ture	Mining	Manufac-turing	Services and trade	Final demand
Agriculture	25.7	.5	2.1	3.0	6.7
Mining	0.0	1.0	0.4	0.3	2.6
Manufacturing	47.9	73.4	39.4	8.8	25.0
Services and trade	3.7	24.1	15.3	19.9	41.2
Final demand	22.7	0.9	42.7	67.8	24.6
TOTAL	100.0	100.0	100.0	100.0	100.0

Note: Final demand includes, among other items, government and households.

Note: Final demand output for mining is abnormally low because domestic consumption of coal was arbitrarily assigned to real estate and rentals in the service group.

SOURCE: Bureau of Labor Statistics, *Interindustry Flow of Goods and Services by Industry of Origins and Destination, 1947* (200-Sector Inter-Industry Table).

did most of his own selling.[14] These functions are now largely performed by other segments of the economy; and the sources of these off-farm inputs must have an effect upon agricultural location and thus dilute the influence of the immobile resource attributes.

It is true that agriculture still produces 50% of its non-labor inputs, but even here significant functional changes are taking place. Within agriculture,

[14]See John H. Davis, "From Agriculture to Agribusiness" *Harvard Business Review*, Vol. 34, (Jan.-Feb., 1956), pp. 107-9.

functions are growing less generalized and independent and becoming more specialized and dependent. The farmer in the Northeast buys his concentrates from the farmer in the Midwest. The Western rancher buys cottonseed from a Southern farmer.

Similar changes in the destination of agricultural outputs have occurred. Not more than two generations ago, the typical farm unit consumed most of its output. The limited and occasional surpluses were carted to a commodity market and usually distributed locally. Currently, something like 26% of agricultural output goes directly to services and final demand,[15] and another 48% directly to manufacturing and processing operations that usually service final markets directly. Thus final markets are apt to have a much stronger influence on agriculture than on mining, where the outputs that go to manufacturing are usually absorbed into an extensive intermediate series of operations. This is made all the more likely when we recall the greater flexibility of agriculture on the input side. Further, since intra-industry transfers are important in agriculture and not in mining, the influence of extra-industry markets is understated for agriculture.

In general, then, the more purely resource attributes of agriculture are probably less dominant in explaining its regional distribution than in the case of mining. It is true that agriculture is bound to the land and some sort of natural resource endowment is a necessary condition for agricultural production. However, it seems plain that this resource endowment is not a *sufficient* condition for agricultural production. Substantial leeway exists for other factors to influence the regional distribution of agricultural activity. It must follow that market access places a definite stamp on the regional distribution of agricultural production, not only because it will make some land or capital substitution possibilities more attractive, but also because (through the competition of urban uses, etc.) it may make some of these substitution possibilities less attractive.

Several separate bits of evidence tend to confirm this view. First, as Table 143 showed, the rank correlation between each state's share of agricultural employment and its share of population is .649. (The value of agricultural products sold has a slightly higher coefficient—.666). This compares with a correlation of .406 for mining. The distribution of the market (as measured by population distribution) therefore apparently has some significance for the location of agricultural production—much more so than for mining. This is particularly true when we observe that, excluding non-metallic minerals, no sector of mining displayed a coefficient much over .200 (see Table 140). Still the coefficient for agriculture is low enough to imply a significant role for resource inputs.

Second, only 19 states show any form of mining specialization. By contrast, only 17 of the 48 states fail to show some form of agricultural specialization.[16]

These two points, however, could be merely a manifestation of the non-local-

---

[15]Final demand includes the purchases of government and net exports.

[16]I.e., those states whose share of agricultural employment exceeds their share of population, or whose percentage of total employment exceeded the U. S. average. If we include those states whose share of farm products sold exceeds their share of population, only 12 states fail to show some form of specialization.

ized character of agricultural resources rather than an indication of the importance of non-resource factors; so we shall examine two additional bits of evidence.

To make some comparisons, we have used a crude measure of the regional distribution of "good" agricultural land.[17] It was determined that 21 states had a larger share of good agricultural land than of superior market situations—as measured by population distribution. Only four of them, however, showed a share of agricultural employment or of value of farm products sold that exceeded their share of the good farm land. Most of the concentrations of agricultural employment (and/or value of farm products sold) relative to share of good farm land came in states where the good farm land was in short supply relative to the market as measured by population distribution. Further, the 21 states that had a concentration of good farm land accounted for only slightly more than half of the agricultural employment and the value of farm products sold.

This point is also highlighted by a detailed examination, applying multiple regression techniques to sample data drawn from State Economic Areas by Beverly Duncan, prepared for this study. An effort was made to explain interregional variations in such items as per-acre value of products sold and rural farm population density using three types of explanatory variables—(1) market accesses measured by an index of population potential, (2) resource access as measured by an index of soil quality, and (3) the effect upon agriculture of "rivalry cost" imposed by competition for the land by urban uses, etc., as measured by the distance to metropolis and local urbanization.

The results of this study demonstrate that market access exerts considerable influence upon the regional distribution of agricultural activity. The simple correlations reveal that the per-acre value of products sold varies inversely with distance from a metropolitan center and directly with population potential (or closeness to the major centers of population). Inter-area differences in this measure of intensity appear to be largely independent of inter-SEA variations in the quality of the soil. For the sample of SEA's, 27% of the variance in per-acre value of products sold is accounted for by differences in distance from a metropolitan center and 16% by differences in population potential.

Further, such an analysis reveals that the *rural-farm density* is also directly related to population potential. About 29% of the variance in rural farm density is accounted for by population potential. Farm population density is, on the average, highest in areas of high population potential. Population density in

[17]The National Resources Planning Board allocated the total acreage of each state to one of five land productivity classes. These were developed by considering ". . . the principal physical conditions influencing productivity, such as soil type, topography, rainfall and temperature . . ." and assuming ". . . the input of labor and capital will be that most nearly capable of maintaining the natural level of productivity, but without irrigation, additional drainage, or the addition of lime fertilizer or other amendments except nitrogen fixing legumes." For our purpose we have lumped together the "excellent," "good" and "fair" grades in contrast to "poor" and "non-tillable." Obviously, there are many limitations to our treatment. See National Resources Planning Board, *Industrial Location and National Resources* (Washington: Government Printing Office, 1943) pp. 36-39.

the rural-farm sector is, on the average, highest in areas where the physical environment is not particularly well suited for agricultural activity. The inverse relationship between population potential and soil rating suggests that, on the average, the areas with high accessibility to the national market have relatively poor natural resources for agricultural production, but nevertheless these areas have more persons and more production than would be expected if soil fertility was the dominant factor in farming.

Clearly, modern agriculture is inseparable from the economic functions that supply much of its inputs and market much of its outputs. Although a resource activity, it enjoys a wide range of substitution possibilities arising out of the relative ubiquity of its resource attributes, the alternatives provided by an advancing technology, and the external restraints imposed by alternative land uses. These substitution possibilities tend to create a fairly wide range of location choices for an industry that makes use of necessary resource inputs. Reference to a group of gross indicators has tended to underline this fact.

We have to recognize, however, that indicators of this type are not fully adequate tools for explaining the detailed structure and shifts that characterize American agriculture. Changes in market access or input access for specific agricultural activities (generated by forces such as changes in demand and technology) have stimulated shifts in agricultural activity. The relative flexibility of agriculture as a resource activity would seem to be reflected in the fact that 80% of the net shift in the value of agricultural products sold is generated by differential shifts characteristic of 2-digit agricultural groups. While we cannot hope to make an adequate statement of the regional changes in access for specific agricultural commodities, it is useful to examine these 2-digit sectors in some detail. They can make a contribution to our understanding. The next chapter will address itself to this task against the background of generalizations touched upon in this chapter.

22 / Regional distribution of agricultural activity:

(2) THE MAJOR COMPONENTS

For a deeper understanding of the differential shifts among the states that we have observed in agricultural employment, we shall now examine each of the major 2-digit components of agricultural activity—field crops, vegetables, fruits and nuts, horticultural specialties, dairy products, poultry and products, and forest products. We shall also examine at this point the regional influence of commercial fishing on the theory that this activity resembles agriculture in its general characteristics more than any other resource or processing activity.

Field Crops

The field crops sector of agriculture is, without a doubt, the most important in explaining the observed changes in agricultural activity. As measured by the value of farm products sold, it is the largest of the sectors, accounting for 40% of the total value in 1954. It is also an important source of inputs for the livestock sectors of agriculture and therefore exerts influence on the second largest component of agricultural production.

In addition to its relatively large size, two factors establish the contribution of this sector to the proportionality effect upon the regional shift in the value of farm products sold in the 1939-1954 period: (1) the rate of growth in value for field crops was second only to that for fruits and nuts over this period; (2) the areas that specialize in field crop production are almost identical with those that show proportionality upward shifts in the total value of agricultural products sold between 1939 and 1954. Twenty-seven states showed net upward proportionality shifts in total value of farm products sold during this period (Figure 60). Of this number, all but four exhibited one or both of the following indices of field crop specialization: first, each had a larger share of the nation's total field crop production than of the total population; second, each had a larger proportion of its total agricultural production in field crops than the average for the nation as a whole.[1] The four states that failed to conform to this pattern—California, Nevada, Wyoming, and Virginia—were all except California, states whose shares in the total proportionality effect were extremely small. The states with the largest shares of the total net upward proportionality effect—the Southeast, Southwest, and Plains states—[2] were also the states that showed the most marked specialization in field crops.

While field crops include a widely diversified set of crop activities, some generalizations about the locational characteristics of these activities are possible.

(1) Close direct access to final markets, in relative terms, is not an important consideration for field crops as a whole. The 200-sector B.L.S. input-output table publishes data for four important field crop sectors: food grains and feed, cotton, tobacco, and oil crops. In none of these did the combined output going to households, eating and drinking places, and government exceed 3%. The tie-in with final markets is almost exclusively through the medium of intermediate processors. Furthermore, in the case of food grains and feed crops, 72% of the output is absorbed *within* agriculture. This can be an important factor in strengthening ties with important inputs—particularly the resource inputs.

(2) These resource inputs exert a strong effect in their own right. The same input-output table records for these field crop activities a higher proportion of total expenditures on land than in the case of any of the other agricultural functions reported. These activities are the most land-extensive. Furthermore, field crops are the "bread-basket" items in agriculture. They are the basic staple commodities that have traditionally made the most stringent demands upon the fertility and productive attributes of the soil. Large-scale and effective production requires resource inputs of good quality. In this connection it is worth noting that the states with the highest concentrations of good farm land are in the very regions that show the most concentrated specialization in field crop activity.

(3) Per unit of land area, field crops tend to have a comparatively low-value yield. They are less able, therefore, to pay the higher land rents that are generated by other uses nearer the final market concentrations. At the same time, these products are highly transportable and incur a relatively small penalty from distance.

The combined effect of these factors tends to bring about a concentration of field crop activity in areas with poorer market access but favorable resource attributes.

The importance of resource inputs, unencumbered by significant rivalry costs, helps to explain which regions can be expected to gain because of the contribution made by field crops to the proportionality effect in American agriculture. It also suggests that changes in the access relationship between field

[1] The data on which the identification of these states is based are presented in Appendix Tables H, and J.

[2] For a discussion of recent changes in the relative importance among crops grown in the Plains and Great Lakes states, see John C. Weaver, "Changing Patterns of Cropland Use in the Middle West," *Economic Geography*, Vol. 30, January 1954, pp. 1-17.

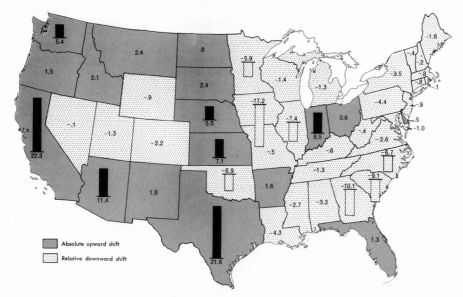

Figure 62. Net Shift in Value of Field Crops Sold, 1940-54.

State figures represent % of total net shift. Total net shift as % of incremental change: 16.2. Total net shift as % of 1940 value of field crops sold: 48.8. Source: Appendix Table J.

crop activities and their resource inputs may be dominant factors determining the major differential shifts.[3]

Figure 62 shows the shift in the value of field crops sold in the 1939-54 period. The net upward and downward shifts seen here closely parallel the total differential shifts shown in Figure 61. Twelve of the fifteen states with net upward differential shifts in the total value of farm products show significant upward shifts in field crops. And twenty-nine of the thirty-three states with downward shifts in the total have downward shifts in the field crops sector.

The task of analyzing the contribution of each field crop to the shifts in the total goes beyond the scope of our study. "Field crops" is an umbrella term that covers a wide range of crop activities. The census lists over *sixty* categories. The most that we can do here with so heterogeneous a classification is to point to a few important examples.

The small grains have, in general, grown in value at a more rapid rate than the national average for all crops, and these find their greatest concentration west of the 95th meridian. Wheat, oats, and barley all show an above-average increase, as does the legume alfalfa; much of this increase has been stimulated by military and economic needs during and since World War II. For soybeans, the increase has been three times greater than the average; this has undoubtedly

[3]In evaluating these factors, however, due weight must be given to the fact that this is the largest segment of agriculture in which price has been supported by governmental action.

influenced the upward shifts shown by Indiana and Ohio. Grain sorghums have shown extremely large increases that must have had a considerable effect on the upward shift in Texas, New Mexico, and perhaps some of the Plains states. And the increase for rice, at twice the national average rate for all crops, must have influenced the shift shown by Arkansas.

On the other hand, some important products have shown below-average rates of increase in value. Corn is one of these. This fact must account in large part for the declines in the Corn Belt vis-à-vis the Western states and, to an important extent, for the downward shift in the Southeast. Peanuts, sweet potatoes, and sugar cane, in all of which the Southeast tends to specialize, have also failed to maintain the average rate of increase. So have sugar beets and Irish potatoes, which may be a factor in the downward shifts in the mid-Mountain states.

Developments in cotton and in the food and feed grains deserve particular attention.

COTTON

The over-all field crop shift out of the Southeast and into the Southwest has been dominated by cotton.[4] Cotton follows the typical field crop pattern. All of its output goes to textiles or foreign trade. Transport costs relative to its value have never been sufficient, however, to influence significantly the location of cotton culture or of the textile industry that uses its output. It must follow that the shift out of the Southeast has taken place because of a change in that region's access to important resource inputs for cotton culture relative to the Southwest and California. The story of this change is one of the most dramatic in American economic history.

The Southeast was settled to open up new cotton and tobacco lands because these crops were highly profitable and because the foreign credits earned through their export were important to a young debtor nation. The consequence of this was a high degree of crop specialization at an early period that did not become characteristic of other agricultural functions until quite modern times. Early in history the Southeastern farmer had to develop intimate input-output relationships with off-farm functions—again a relationship that developed in other farming systems and regions only recently. This system of specialization and off-farm ties created four significant institutional patterns. First, cotton was very labor-intensive, requiring enormous amounts of hand cultivation. This was a serious restraint against its production in a young labor-hungry country. The consequence was slavery. Second, with the break-up of the plantation system, the labor-intensive character of cotton culture forced a fragmentation of land holdings into small units. Third, because cotton could not be pilfered for food and was worth little until ginned, its cultivation lent

[4]The farming system is heavily oriented to the resource characteristics of the land and climate. Cotton production requires 200 frost free days (which limits it to the areas south of the 36th parallel) and makes rather specific requirements upon soil, topography and moisture.

itself to absentee ownership and created a region addicted to share-cropping. Fourth, this fact, combined with the importance of off-farm input and market sources, created a dominant role in Southeastern agriculture for the merchant-banker as well as the absentee owner.

Add to these cultural and institutional relationships the fact that resource exhaustion became important. Cotton in certain circumstances not only exhausts soil nutrients but vitiates humus. In the Southeast, at best, this resulted in enormous increases in fertilizer applications and, therefore, farm costs. At worst, it created wholesale erosion and farm abandonment.[5]

Most of these factors came to have a special significance with the advent of mechanization.[6] Because mechanization requires even topography and rock-free soil, large land holdings, and capital in large amounts, its introduction altered the character of the inputs essential to cotton culture.

In short, a number of changes reduced the Southeast's comparative advantage in cotton production and augmented that of the West. (1) Significant soil exhaustion had taken place in many parts of the Southeast. (2) Uneven topography and small land-holdings denied the gains of mechanization to many Southeastern cotton-producing areas. (3) The history of cotton culture in the Southeast explains why the Southeast had relatively limited access to the necessary capital inputs. (4) The spread of irrigation increased the West's access to some extraordinarily fertile cotton lands.[7]

The significance of cotton to regional economic growth, however, merits consideration in terms beyond those involved when the focus is on changing access and consequent shifts in field crops. The economic conditions which created the cotton culture of the Southeast, and the institutional arrangements that evolved to facilitate it, have created a regional maladjustment so great that it affects the growth prospects for the whole Southeastern portion of the nation.[8] The phenomenon of erosion and the westward shift of cotton culture are making imperative a new form of agricultural production, particularly a new form of grass, grain, and livestock culture. This, however, calls for increased mechanization and larger land holdings. Unfortunately, the institutional

[5]The crop was intertilled year after year on hilly uplands that were particularly susceptible to erosion. In addition, in most instances no winter cover crop protected the land after the crop was removed. Little or no organic matter was returned to the soil as plant residues or animal manure.

[6]If cotton was one of the first farming systems to become specialized, it was one of the last to become mechanized. The peculiar nature of the cotton plant and the specialized labor requirements it makes during the growing season created mechanical and technical problems not found in wheat or corn. Currently most of these problems have been solved and a wave of mechanization has set in.

[7]Another factor has been the boll weevil, which reached the height of its destructiveness in 1921, ruining at least one-third of the cotton harvest in that year. The famed sea-island cotton industry along the Atlantic Coast never fully recovered from damage inflicted by this insect, which is particularly effective in moist climates. In contrast, the drier climates of northwestern Texas, western Oklahoma, and southern California tend to repel the insect.

[8]Cotton has been significantly aided in this bit of mischief by tobacco which has most of the same characteristics outlined above. It will not serve our purpose, however, to expand this discussion further.

arrangements evolving from a century of cash cropping inhibit the needed transition. The southern farmer owns little capital, while the southern merchant-banker, habituated to the security of a staple commodity, hesitates to risk new credit and tenant arrangements. As a result, many of the southern farmers have not been able to finance the drastic changes which effective adjustment of the Southern economy would require. The instability of cotton prices over generations and the cost-price squeeze growing out of the aforementioned factors have been hard on the man on the land. The resultant human erosion has been more serious than that of the land.

Although rational adjustment has been slow in coming to the Southeast, it has been taking place and the mere fact of adjustment, even if limited, is creating new problems related to the Southeast's growth. Cotton and tobacco are very labor-intensive operations. The new, more rational farm systems require much larger holdings and much less labor. This creates, in effect an area with a large surplus labor supply and significant underemployment. A population adjusted to an outdated cotton culture is now too large for its land resource base. This creates a situation where people must either move out or alternative employment move in. Both these movements have been taking place, but not fast enough to offset regional inequities in welfare.

FOOD AND FEED GRAINS

Food and feed grains share the field crop characteristic that little output goes to final demand and land costs represent a relatively large part of total inputs. They share therefore the general feature of being oriented to the resource characteristic of the land. In fact, this orientation is probably strengthened by the fact that three-fourths of the output of these grains is absorbed by agriculture itself—principally by the livestock sectors.

Corn and its livestock ties explain an important part of the shifts shown in Figure 62. Corn is grown successfully in almost every part of the United States. It really flourishes, however, in the region between the 98th meridian and the Appalachians above the Ohio River. The long hot summer days and hot nights, combined with top grade soils, have created an historic dominance here for this crop. Mechanization, new fertilization techniques, hybrid corn, and other technological advances have only seemed to accentuate the relative land-resource advantage of this area.

Why, then, has this area displayed a net downward shift in field crops? Iowa shows the most marked downward shift of any state and certainly it is *the* corn state. Here the data—i.e., using the *value* of farm products sold as a measure—turn out to be somewhat misleading. Actually in *physical* terms, these Midwestern states would be included in the upward shift category, as compared to the rest of the country. The answer lies in the fact that most corn is not sold but is converted into prime beef and pork. During the 1939-54 period a higher proportion was used directly for feed rather than sold. This shows up in Figure 62 as a net downward shift.

This factor also helps to explain the upward shifts exhibited by Indiana and

Ohio. Here just the reverse has happened. Less feed grain was fed and more sold. The reason for this is the significant industrial expansion that has taken place in these states. Large numbers of farms in these areas have become part-time, with the operator working off the farm. Under these circumstances he can raise the grain for sale but he cannot administer a feeding program.

Wheat and grain sorghums played an important part in the West's relative gain in field crops during the period under review.[9] Two factors have been favorable to its position in wheat:

(1) Changes in technology, such as techniques of dryland farming and the development of drought-resistant strains of wheat, as well as the development of large machinery, seem to have favored the West; and (2) factors favoring the expansion of corn culture in the Midwest have resulted in some displacement of wheat in the transition area between the two cultures. (This is a good example of rivalry costs transmitting the influence of change in one crop culture to another.) Add to this development in wheat the advent of grain sorghums, which have shown a marked expansion in the West, and much of the shift configuration observed is explained.

The upward shift shown by Indiana and Ohio is attributable in part to soybeans, which have tended in these states to replace crops with a smaller output per acre.[10] Soybeans have also been responsible for the relative decline of competing oil crops, such as peanuts.

Livestock Products

Livestock products constitute the second most important sector of the agricultural economy. In 1954 they accounted for almost 29% of the total value of farm products sold. Like field crops, they are in the rapid-growth category. It is not surprising, then, that the states specializing in their production—the Mountain and Plains states and some of the Great Lakes states—show an upward proportionality shift in the value of farm products sold (see Figure 60).

Three generalizations can be made about the locational factors that determine the distribution of livestock production: (1) The largest single input tie for the livestock products sector is with other agricultural sectors; over 50% of its inputs come from agriculture—particularly the feed grains and forage sectors. Access to high-quality land resources is not directly important as in field crops. But access to the feed sectors is an important locational determinant unless offset by the influence of some other factor, such as market access. (2) Less than 10% of the meat output goes to final demand; 81% goes to intermediate processors, chiefly packing houses. Since this intermediate processing involves con-

[9] The proportionality shifts recorded came about because of the change in relative values stemming from the war-inspired increase in demand and the politically inspired postwar price support program. Wheat output declined steadily from 1919 to 1939. With the war came good prices and a concerted effort to increase production. Wheat benefited from the increase in demand more than most agricultural products.

[10] This has been less true in Iowa and the western end of the corn-soy belt because there it has tended to replace corn as a result of the federal acreage-control program.

siderable weight loss, the tendency is for the packing houses to locate near the livestock sources, thus increasing the significance of access to basic feed inputs. (3) There is another factor that might be expected to offset this tendency to a degree. Livestock products are high-value products and are relatively expensive to transport either dressed or on the hoof. Ordinarily this would incline an industry to a location toward the market. However, this factor has not been able to overcome the importance of feed inputs and the weight-loss characteristic of intermediate processing. But it has been sufficiently important to bring about some degree of regional specialization in feeder-stock and finish-feeding, with finish-feeding done as close as possible to the source of high-grade finishing feeds and to the packers.

Actually, the whole activity of livestock products production looks somewhat more like a manufacturing activity than a resource activity. The animal, in effect, is a biological machine that takes purchased and farm-raised inputs and produces a marketable product. As a matter of fact, often (as in dry-lot feeding) the significance of land as an input rests more upon its situs than its resource characteristics. The most economical position for the animal depends upon the relative costs of assembling inputs and marketing outputs. In this case, the input sources dominate the location scheme. It is interesting to note in this connection that the correlation between livestock products and population is very slight (Table 144).

Figure 63 shows the net shifts in the value of livestock products sold during

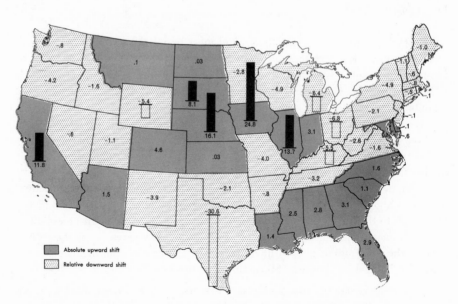

Figure 63. Net Shift in Value of Livestock Products Sold, 1940-54.

State figures represent % of total net shift. Total net shift as % of incremental change: 15.1. Total net shift as % of 1940 value of livestock products sold: 41.5. Source: Appendix Table J.

the 1939-54 period. The major upward shifts over these years were in the Corn Belt states, California, and the Southeast. This configuration suggests that live-stock products are quite an important factor in the total differenial shifts shown in Figure 61. Of the fifteen states that show net upward differential shifts in the value of farm products, twelve also show net upward shifts in the value of livestock products sold. It is important to note, however, that the center of the Corn Belt and certain of the Southeastern states show downward shifts in agri-cultural products as a whole despite upward shifts in livestock products.

The principal locational factors that have prompted the differential shifts in the production of livestock products appear to be associated with regional changes in access to feed. This is certainly the dominant factor behind the largest net upward shifts—those in the corn-soy belt. Hybrid corn has been influential in expanding the productivity of this region. So also has been the increasing practice of finish-feeding, which places a premium on access to finish-feeds such as corn.

The Southeast's upward shift is also associated with a relative increase in its access to feed sources. This is another part of the story of adjustment in this region away from the row-cropping systems that have debilitated the soil. Rational adjustments in the Southeast call for an extension of cover-cropping, and this expansion of potential livestock feed encourages an expansion of livestock activities.[11]

Most of the Southwestern and Mountain states display net downward shifts.[12] These states are livestock specialists. They appear, however, to have suffered *relative* losses in input access. The factors here are as follows: (1) These states are predominantly feeder-stock areas and the increased practice of finish-feeding means that they lose out relatively in a measure based upon agricultural values. (2) Much of the mid-Mountain region has been overgrazed, and this practice is leading to a deterioration in access to feeds. (3) Competitive land uses may have occasioned some loss of access to feeds in Texas and New Mexico. Cotton and grain sorghums, for example, have made striking gains in acreage in these states.

The significant upward shift in California is of particular interest because the principal reasons for this gain seem to have been a large increase in the regional market. The remoteness of the Far West region tends to place it outside the dominant national transfer patterns for livestock products. As a result, the regional market exerts a stronger modifying influence than is usual for the nation as a whole.

---

[11]Technology has aided this shift also by introducing new pesticides and strains of stock (the Brahmin) that are better adapted to warmer climates. The adjustment is going slowly because it requires heavy capital investments. Also the intermediate processing units are not as readily available in the Southeast, and the institutional factors mentioned earlier act as restraints. However, there seems to be a definite adjustment under way.

[12]In the case of Texas, it is particularly striking and serves to explain the discrepancy between the strong upward shifts in field crop activity in the face of a downward shift in the total value of farm products. It should be noted that Texas cattle sales were unusually low in 1954, due to a drought. The trends discussed above are basically secular, however.

Dairy Products

Dairy products in 1954 accounted for 13.5% of the total value of farm products sold. The rate of increase for this sector between 1939 and 1954 was smaller than for any other sector of agricultural activity. As a result, the states specializing in dairy products correspond closely with those shown in Figure 60 as having experienced net downward proportionality shifts over these years. Twenty-eight states show a specialization in dairy products as measured by one or both of the following indices: (1) a larger share of the nation's dairy products production than of its population; (2) a larger proportion of their total agricultural production in dairy products than the average for the nation as a whole.[13] Of these twenty-eight states, only nine fail to show downward proportionality shifts in the total. The areas of specialization are in the New England and Middle Atlantic regions, the northernmost Lakes and Plains states, and the Far West states plus Utah and Idaho.

In the production of dairy products, as in livestock production, the animal is essentially a biological factory, and the most economical location for it depends upon the relative costs of assembling inputs and marketing outputs. With 43% of the inputs coming from feed sources and 58% of the outputs going to final markets, one can see that the dairy culture might be torn between its affinity for feed sources and its affinity for markets. This is precisely the dominant locational fact about this production system.[14]

The distribution of dairy products specialization reveals a split in production orientation along these lines. The area of concentration in New England, the Middle Atlantic states, and the Far West is essentially explained in terms of markets. The big concentration in the Great Lakes States, however, is hard to rationalize on the basis of market proximity. The production statistics show that the densely populated New England and Middle Atlantic areas market fluid milk, with almost 100% going to final demand, while the Great Lakes region markets fluid milk and cream primarily to processors to be transformed into cheese, butter, and condensed and dehydrated products.

The reasons for this split are fairly logical. Fluid milk for comsumption is a highly perishable product that loses no weight in processing and requires special handling. Food concentrates can be shipped at low rates to supplement local feeds so that they can be grown on relatively inferior lands. In contrast, the production activity in the Great Lakes region is oriented to the resource characteristics of the land. The area is too far north for the best corn culture and too hilly to make good crop land. On the other hand, grass and forage crops thrive almost better than any place else in the United States. It is a favorable low-cost area for inputs. If the outputs are transformed into less perishable and more transportable products, this favorable resource advantage can be exploited.

[13]The data on which the identification of these states is based are presented in Appendix Tables H and J.

[14]Production and distribution are influenced by trade barriers in the form of "health" restrictions, but it is difficult to evaluate this factor in the present context.

Figure 64 shows the shifts that occurred between 1939 and 1954 as measured by value. The Southeast and three other states—Wisconsin, Pennsylvania, and California—made the greatest relative gains.

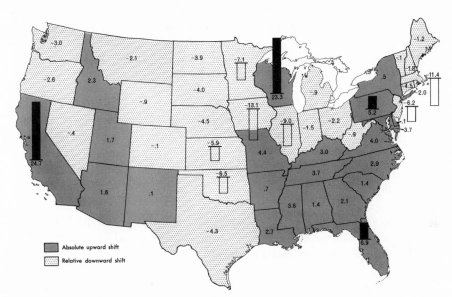

Figure 64. Net Shift in Value of Dairy Products Sold, 1940-54.

State figures represent % of total net shift. Total net shift as % of incremental change: 11.8. Total net shift as % of 1940 value of dairy products sold: 23.3. Source: Appendix Table J.

The dairy products shifts tend to run counter to the total differential shifts. Out of twenty-two states showing upward shifts in dairy products, only eight also show upward shifts in total value. This can be partly accounted for by the proportionality effect just discussed. The gain shown in the Middle Atlantic states is a consequence of the use of the value measure; it seems to result primarily from the fact that the fluid-milk areas were less affected than the milk-processing areas by the drop in the price of butter. The decline in the Great Lakes states, with the exception of Wisconsin, seems to be tied in part to the declining price of butter and in part to the rivalry costs imposed by an expanding corn-soy culture. The fact that the technology of dairy raising increases the economy of larger units tends most to favor Wisconsin, where the ecological factors are the most favorable. The decline in the Plains states may be tied to the price of wheat, which gives the farmers in that area a more favorable alternative economic opportunity.

The growth in dairying in California seems to be most closely tied to the growth of the market. Milk production here is oriented more to direct marketing than to processing, and the share in the nation's dairying activity has increased less than the share in total population.

The shift in production into the Southeast seems to be related to consiaera-tions of both market and resource access. The Southeast has always been a deficit supply area for milk. Further, per capita consumption in the Southeast has always been low. With rising incomes, there is an expanded use of milk products here. On the supply side, the expansion of dairying is closely tied to the decline of cotton and other crops in the Southeast. This expansion has been called for in part because it represents a favorable income alternative to a declining system. It has also been called for because the grasslands that are associated with dairying are the only sensible alternative to abandonment of many of the more eroded and overworked lands.

Poultry Products

Poultry products, which accounted for about 8% of the total value of farm products sold in 1954, show a proportionality effect closely resembling that of dairy products.

The conflict between the pull of the market and the pull of feed sources is seen here also; 78% of the output goes to final demand and 76% of the inputs come from agriculture. Measuring specialization for this sector in the same way as in the earlier sectors examined, we find three separate areas of speciali-zation—(1) the Northeast (including New England and the Middle Atlantic states), (2) the Far West and Utah, and (3) a few of the Southeastern and Plains states. The first two areas appear to be closely associated with market concentrations and the last appears to be more closely associated with good feed access. The first two, it is also interesting to note, tend to specialize in fresh poultry meat and the last in eggs and canned poultry.

Figure 65 shows the shifts that occurred between 1939 and 1954 in the value of poultry products sold. The major upward shifts have been in the Southeast, the Atlantic Coast states, and California.

Basic to all of these shifts is the development over the last 15 years or so of the broiler industry as a separate producing activity. Previously, poultry raising was a by-product of joint-cost operation carried on with other agricultural activities. The technology of poultry raising has advanced so strikingly that now the most economical method of production is a fairly large-scale specialized operation.[15] This technological revolution in the poultry industry has had two consequences. (1) The industry now relies more heavily on prepared feeds and is better adapted to large-scale dressing and processing. This has tended to strengthen the relative importance of market access. (In this connection, note the gains in California and the Northeast.) (2) Under the new system, poultry raising becomes more labor-intensive. Access to adequate cheap labor appears to have assumed some importance. The expansion in Maine seems to be associ-ated in part with the market but mainly with the need for an alternative outlet

[15]The technological advance has proceeded side-by-side with vertical integration of the industry, which has resulted in increased capital availability and risk reductions to the farmer.

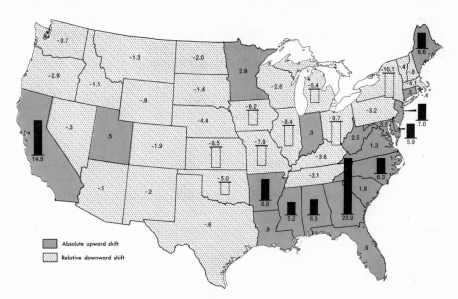

Figure 65. Net Shift in Value of Poultry Products Sold, 1940-54.
State figures represent % of total net shift. Total net shift as % of incremental change: 23.8. Total net shift as % of 1940 value of poultry products sold: 58.4. Source: Appendix Table J.

for part-time fishing employment. This has been particularly feasible because fish and poultry are usually marketed through the same channels. The great expansion in the Southeast is also partly motivated by the needs for labor outlets and partly by the increasing levels of living.

Fruits and Nuts, Vegetables, and Horticultural Specialties

These three sectors of agricultural activity combined account for about 11% of the total value of farm products. The first of them—fruits and nuts—is a rapid growth sector; the other two are slow-growth sectors. All together, however, they comprise such a small part of the total that their proportionality effect is not likely to be very significant. Measuring specialization by the same techniques as before,[16] we see that these agricultural activities all show the same areas of concentration—(1) the highly populated Northeast (particularly the Atlantic coast and the Great Lakes states), (2) Florida, and (3) the Pacific coast states.

These states also display similar input-output structures that contrast with those displayed by field crops and animal products. Nearly three-fourths of the

[16]Utilizing the data in Appendix Tables H and J, we identify all of the states that have a larger share of these products than population and those states for which these products as a percentage of total agricultural production for the state exceeded the national average.

output goes to final demand categories and only one-fourth to processing operations. Practically none is traded within agriculture itself. Labor is the major input item. The expenditures for other items are so widely distributed that these inputs probably have no significance as locational factors. The products are in general high-yield and high-value products that bear heavy transfer costs.

As might be expected, then, these activities are highly associated with centers of market activity. This is especially true for horticultural specialties.[17] Of all agricultural activities this sector reveals the highest rank correlation with population (see Table 143). Not only are these activities seen to have been highly associated with population in the 1939-54 period, but the shift pattern they exhibit is highly associated with the shifts in population over these years.[18]

The fruits and nuts sector and the vegetables sector, however, are considerably further down the scale of rank correlations with population. Figures 66 and 67 show the shift picture for these two sectors. Although this pattern does not correspond closely with the *total* differential shift (Figure 61), these sectors were unquestionably influential in generating the total differential shifts in Washington, California, Arizona, and Florida.

FRUITS AND NUTS

Some 88% of the net upward shift in fruits and nuts production was claimed by the three states—Florida, California, and Washington; in the main market areas, fruit production barely held its own in terms of the national average. A number of factors would seem to be operative here: (1) Citrus is the rapid-growth component of this sector, and none of the main market areas can meet the major resource requirement of citrus production—a frost-free climate. (2) Fruit production in general has always favored moderate climates. The problem of perishability, however, in the past gave overwhelming advantage to good market access. But improvements in the technology of storage and transport have offset the market advantage and permitted production to seek a greater resource advantage. Frozen foods and concentrates offer methods of food preservation with fresh fruit quality. Air transport has been successfully used in marketing prime-grade fruits and vegetables, though not yet in significant volume. (3) Florida has for some time been showing gains relative to California. Its production is cheaper and it is closer to major markets. In recent years also California output has been hurt by the fact that many of the good citrus-producing areas in Los Angeles county were being forced out of production by the competition of urban and suburban uses for the land.

VEGETABLES

Except for Delaware, which showed a small relative gain in vegetable production, all of the areas closely allied with the major markets suffered significant

[17]Horticultural specialties consist of such things as nursery products, cut flowers, vegetables grown under glass, etc.

[18]See Appendix Tables H and J.

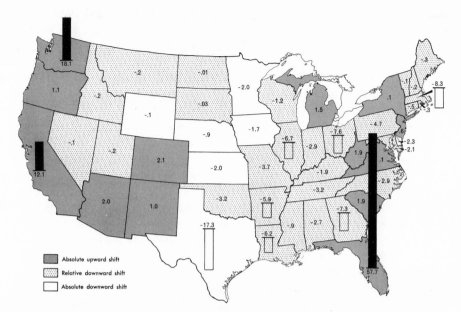

Figure 66. Net Shift in Value of Fruits and Nuts Sold, 1940-54.
State figures represent % of total net shift. Total net shift as % of
incremental change: 16.2. Total net shift as % of 1940 value of
fruits and nuts sold: 49.5. Source: Appendix Table J.

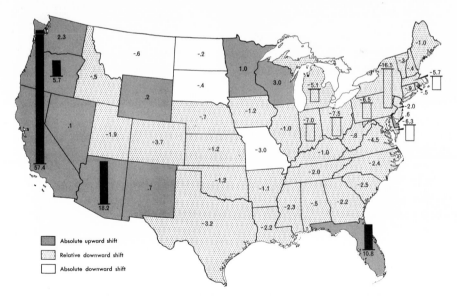

Figure 67. Net Shift in Value of Vegetables Sold, 1940-54.
State figures represent % of total net shift. Total net shift as % of
incremental change: 27.5. Total net shift as % of 1940 value of
vegetables sold: 61.5. Source: Appendix Table J.

relative losses between 1939 and 1954. Florida, California, and Arizona in particular and the West in general had the major gains. Wisconsin and Minnesota also showed upward shifts, based on an increased production of vegetables for canning. The factors responsible for the shifts in vegetable production are, in the main, similar to those accounting for the shifts in production of fruits and nuts. One factor that has been of special importance, however, is irrigation. Effective moisture control has been a great relative advantage to the states that show the greatest upward shifts—Florida, California, and Arizona, Storage and transport innovations have made the exploitation of these advantages feasible.

One comment of general import deserves comment in this connection. Greater latitude is found in the use of immobile agents when existing techniques allow for mobile substitutes in the form of capital. We find an example of this in the case of horticultural specialties. They tend to be grown close to markets irrespective of land resource attributes. This is made possible by substituting capital (in the form of greenhouses, etc.) for land. It is important to realize, however, that the substitution of mobile capital for land may *increase* the immobility. In some cases the purpose of the capital expenditure is to release an important latent land resource rather than minimize the importance of land in the production complex. Such is the case with irrigation. Those lands that were irrigated first are those that could release the maximum potential land productivity. The consequence is that vegetable culture, which benefits particularly from irrigation, is becoming less population-oriented, not more so (see Table 143).

Regional Influence of Forest Activity

One of the 2-digit components of the value of farm products is farm forest products. We have chosen, however, not to discuss the influence of forest activity in that context for two reasons. (1) This is one farm activity where an important part of the output for the sector as a whole comes from off-farm sources. To concentrate upon farm forests would present a distorted picture of the total. (2) This is a sector for which we have quite good data on employment and it is not necessary to limit ourselves to value data. We discuss here the influence of *total* forest activity—both farm and off-farm. Logging employment is our major focus.

In terms of employment, logging and forest activities account for only about a third of 1% of total employment in the nation. Its growth, as measured by employment increases, is about par with the average national increase in employment; the proportionality effect, therefore, is not significant. As with certain other activities, however, forest products become especially important for understanding the performance of *particular* regions.

Forest activity, like agriculture, is ubiquitous in the sense that there is some activity in every state. Only three areas, however, have sufficient production potential to be classified as surplus supply areas—the Far West, the Southeast, and Upper New England.[19]

[19]In an earlier period, the Great Lakes states would have belonged in this array. But declines in production and increases in population bring them now to the point where their

Logging activity, like mining, must take place where substantial reserves are found. Market access does not play a very important role regionally in its location. In the first place, three-fourths of the total output of logging goes to the mills that produce pulp, lumber, veneer, and plywood. Because of the weight loss associated with processing logs, these manufacturing activities are located close to forest reserves.

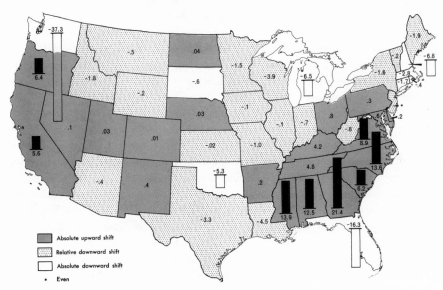

Figure 68. Net Shift in Logging Employment, 1940-50.

State figures represent % of total net shift. Total net shift as % of incremental change: 51.4. Total net shift as % of 1940 logging employment: 17.8. Source: U. S. Bureau of the Census, *U. S. Census of Population 1940*, Vol. III, labor force data in State Table 11; and *U. S. Census of Population 1950*, Vol. II, labor force data in State Table 73.

share of production is less than their share of the population. There is an interesting kind of specialization among these regions. The Southeast tends to specialize in pulpwood and the Far West in sawlogs for lumber. This is due mainly to differences in the sizes of standing timber. The old-growth timber in the Southeast which has been cut over decades ago for sawlogs has been replaced by rapidly growing but lower quality second-growth pines and hardwoods of smaller sizes, primarily valuable for pulp-making. In the West, the remaining extensive areas of large old-growth timber can be converted more efficiently and profitably into high-value lumber. Nevertheless, in terms of the volume produced, Southern pine lumber is next in importance to Douglas fir of the West. Another factor, institutional in nature, will probably strongly influence the future trends in sizes and disposition of timber produced by both regions. In the Southeast, and to a lesser degree in New England and the Great Lakes states, timber holdings are quite small on the average and vested in individual proprietors. In the Far West large national forests and corporation holdings are more common. It is a rare individual owner with small holdings that has the knowledge and capital resources to place into effect the long rotations necessary for sawlogs.

This does not prove, of course, that the market could not influence the whole complex of logging and processing activities. Historically such an influence has been important because historically forest reserves were large relative to current requirements and logging was conducted as an essentially mining type operation. Virgin forest reserves were exploited first in New England, and forest activities then moved westward to the Great Lakes states, southward to the Southern states, and finally to the Far West. This sequence of movement was influenced to a considerable degree by access to the major eastern markets. In our current period, however, these market considerations do not exert much influence upon the location of logging activities. There are no longer any new bodies of timber that are not being exploited because of distance from the market. All of the principal submarginal (costwise) forest lands of yesterday have now passed into use and timber resources are in short supply everywhere. Currently timber is exploited where it can be found.[20]

It follows, therefore, that most regional shifts in forest activity must result primarily from changes in access to forest resources. Figure 68 records the shifts in logging employment from 1940 to 1950.[21] Several major changes in the pattern of activity are apparent. (1) In the Far West, Washington has experienced a marked absolute decline and accounts for almost 38% of the total net downward shift. A shift out of Washington and into Oregon and California is evident. (2) There is a marked upward shift in the Southeast. These states combined account for 85% of the total net upward shift (Florida is a striking exception.) (3) New England and the Great Lakes states show slight absolute and relative downward shifts in activity.

The changes in access to forest resources to which these shifts bear witness stem from a number of factors. Perhaps the most basic of these is resource exhaustion. This is central to the current as well as the historic declines in New England and the Great Lakes states. It is almost the total explanation of the big declines in Florida and Washington; the forest reserves here have been cut out to the point where they will no longer support the previous level of production. These declines forced expansion in the only areas where under-utilization of reserves existed. Northern California and Oregon have the last remaining stands of virgin timber. At the same time, second-growth timber has been coming back in volume in the Southeast.

Closely associated with this phenomenon of exhaustion has been a change of emphasis in forest activities. There has been a perceptible shift away from a

---

[20]Of the non-resource inputs, labor accounts for about 75% of the total and the balance is spread between manufacturing and services without any concentration upon a specific input. There is a special provision in the minimum wage act that exempts logging crews of twelve men or less. This has led, in the Southeast, to the widespread use of contract loggers utilizing small crews which are recruited in a surplus labor market at very low wage rates. This has tended to give the Southeast an advantage in cost. It does not appear, however, that this has been a major factor in determining the regional distribution of activity.

[21]Data for logging activities that coincide with our period (1939-1954) are not available. This information is as close as we can come and is based upon occupation data in the census of population.

mining type of activity toward something approaching silviculture and a hus-
banding of the forest reserves. This means that timber cut will be brought
more and more into line with realizable growth.[22]

A number of additional factors have contributed to the over-all picture. A
change in the composition of demand for forest products has played a role.
From 1939 to 1954 the demand for pulp and paper products increased by about
twice as much as the demand for lumber and lumber products. This factor
favored expansion in the Southeast, which is heavily oriented to the production
of pulp logs. Technological change has aided this shift. The development of the
sulphate process for producing paper pulp brought the resinous Southern pines
into use for this purpose.

Of the growth states, only California and Oregon gained any support from
forest activities during the 1939-54 period. In the major decline states, the
falling-off in forest activity intensified the total downward tendency. The exceptions are the states in the Southeast. Here expanding forest activities seem to
be aiding the necessary adjustments in the agricultural sector of the economy.
However, they do not provide a very high income alternative, nor is the employment alternative sufficient to go very far in absorbing the agricultural surplus.[23]

Regional Influence of Commercial Fishing

Commercial fishing plays a relatively small part in regional growth. By the
most liberal employment estimates, that include casual as well as full-time
workers, there are less than 150,000 wage jobs involved. The shifts that have
occurred in this industry, however, are almost as complex as those in any other
field of activity.

The coastal states claim 90% of the total fishing employment; most of the

---

[22]*The Timber Resource Review* has this to say: "A comparison of realizable growth and
1952 timber cut by sections . . . shows that the current distribution of the timber industries
is not related to timber growing capacity. The West, which is supplying 46 per cent of the
timber cut, has only 29 per cent of the realizable growth. On the other hand, the Southeast,
which is producing 40 per cent of the timber cut has 45 per cent of the realizable growth.
The North contributes only 14 per cent of the timber cut, but has 25 per cent of the realizable growth . . . in the long run, output by regions will tend to become adjusted more
closely to realizable growth than is the case today. This will mean a reversal of recent trends
and a shift of a larger proportion of the timber cut from West to East." See C. E. Behre and
S. B. Hutchison, "Timber Supply and Quality of Domestic Timber," *Timber Resource
Review* (Washington: U. S. Department of Agriculture, Forest Service, 1955), Chap. 7, p. 6.

[23]Something can be said about future prospects for this industry. In the Far West,
California and Oregon may soon join Washington in decline. The timber cut in these
areas is considerably beyond realizable growth as the last virgin stands in the country are
being exploited. This area will suffer both an absolute and relative decline until it arrives
at an adjustment with its long-run sustainable yields. The activity in the Southeast will
probably make a small additional gain in absolute terms and a much larger one in relative
terms. The Great Lakes and upper New England states appear to be in for a reversal of
trend. Low current timber cut relative to realizable growth, and a new semichemical process
that allows low grade hardwoods to be used for pulp seem to indicate a revival of forest
activity in these areas.

remaining 10% is centered in the Great Lakes states. These coastal states, however, do not share in fishing production and employment in proportion to their access to open water. The sea, no less than the land, has its fertile and its barren regions. Commercial fisheries are all narrowly localized and depend upon a favorable combination of oceanographic factors. As a consequence, four major fishing regions can be identified—coastal New England, the Chesapeake area, the Gulf states, and the Pacific Coast states.

Figure 69 shows the principal shifts that have taken place within the fishing industry during the 1940-50 period. Maine, California, and the Gulf states (particularly Texas and Florida) have experienced the major expansions over these years, and Virginia, Maryland, Michigan, and Mississippi, the major declines.[24]

Changes in access to markets and to non-resource inputs do not appear to have been a significant factor in these shifts. Over 50% of the total catch finds a market in the form of meal and oil, and that market is not influenced by the regional shifts of population that have taken place. Most of the balance is canned or frozen at the port of entry. The marketing of fresh fish, where market access really becomes important, is a very small and declining segment of the total activity. On the input side, the labor inputs and capital in the form of boats and nets do not appear to exert any regional influence. It follows that the shifts result primarily from changes in access to the fishing resource.

A number of factors have played a role in changing regional access to fishing resources. Resource exhaustion is important here as in other resource activities. It is particularly important in explaining the decline in Washington and Oregon. The salmon fisheries do not yield as large a catch as formerly.[25] Resource exhaustion has also been an important factor in explaining the declines in the Great Lakes and Mississippi fisheries. In the Great Lakes region the most direct cause has been an increasing infestation with lamprey which prey on the commercial fish. In the Mississippi area resource exhaustion results from stream pollution and overfishing. The decline in Massachusetts is also directly tied to a decline in the groundfish catch that has been the mainstay of its fleet.

At the same time, Maine, the Gulf states, and California have had an increase in their access to fishing resources. A combination of circumstances is respon-

---

[24]The shift data indicate a major decline for the Chesapeake area. This decline appears to be spurious, however. Similar data supplied by the Fish and Wildlife Service of the Department of the Interior show this area to be holding its own in employment and a further check against production figures fails to substantiate this downward shift. The Fish and Wildlife figures appear to be consistent with the rest of the picture. The difference here appears to be due to statistical discrepancy in the reporting process. We have not had an opportunity to track down the exact source of this discrepancy. We have not used the Fish and Wildlife data because their collection is based upon regional fisheries and it is not easy to get them on a comparable basis over time by states.

[25]This may be due to overfishing but this is hard to establish conclusively. Salmon seems to be particularly susceptible to natural fluctuations in numbers, partly because floods or freezing on the spawning grounds and changes in ocean temperatures affecting feeding supplies can bring about large variations in yield. Whatever the cause, the period in question has been a poor one.

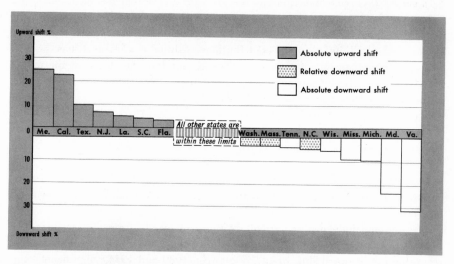

Figure 69. Net Shift in Fishing Employment, 1940-50.

State figures represent % of total net shift. Total net shift as % of incremental change: 36.9. Total net shift as % of 1940 fishing employment: 8.0. Source: U. S. Bureau of the Census, *U. S. Census of Population 1940.* Vol. III, labor force data in State Table 11; and *U. S. Census of Population 1950,* Vol. II, labor force data in State Table 73.

sible for this. In California there has been an expansion in the tuna catch, stimulated in part by favorable marine phenomena and in part by increased demand.

The Gulf states have been influenced mainly by developments in shrimp and menhaden. Menhaden are used exclusively for the production of meal and oil. During the period under review here, the demand for this product was enormously expanded by the increased use of fish meal as a supplement in livestock feed. Most of the expansion in response to this demand has taken place in the Gulf states.

The expansion in shrimp has resulted from three factors: the very great growth in its popularity as a food product; the fact that the frozen food process has reduced the risks and costs associated with serving the market; and the discovery of several major new beds in the Tortugas area off the coasts of Florida and Texas.

The Maine fisheries have shown a large expansion because the ocean has been giving up record quantities of lobster and herring—both of which are restricted largely to the northern New England beds. It is hard to establish a reason for this expansion in resource supply. Many of these fisheries go through natural fluctuations that are not fully understood. It is thought, however, that the area is now beginning to reap the benefits of the size limitations on catch established some years ago.

In short, resource exhaustion and discovery, resource replenishment, changing techniques for preserving and transporting, and changes in the composition of demand all combine to bring about the shifts observed.

However small its absolute contributions, fishing employment has been a factor in the expansion of California, Texas, and Florida—three of the major growth states. The expansion in activity in upper New England runs counter to the general decline recorded for this area.[26]

Review of the Regional Influence of Agriculture

In the last two chapters we have examined many facets of the shifts in agricultural activity. A review of the major characteristics of these changes may be in order.

The regional influence of agriculture stems primarily from the fact that it is the major slow-growth activity among the ten 1-digit employment sectors, recording a downward shift of 14.7% between 1939 and 1954. Significant long-term trends in supply and demand have reduced the relative importance of this sector of the economy over the years. Advancing technology has transformed many of the traditional agricultural functions into manufacturing and trade functions. It has also fostered more extended fabrication of agricultural products and has greatly increased worker productivity. At the same time, competition from synthetic and foreign substitutes has increased, and agricultural products as a whole do not have a high income elasticity of demand. These have been major factors in the net downward shifts observed in the Southeast, Plains, and northern Mountain regions (Figure 45).

But although agricultural activity in the *aggregate* has not contributed to positive growth in the volume of economic activities, it has made important contributions to the growth of specific regions. In the Far West and southern Mountain states and in Kansas and Indiana, the net gain in agricultural employment was a significant element in the upward shifts in total employment displayed by these states. Similarly, the differential shifts in agricultural employment, added to the proportionality effect, contributed significantly to the net decline in the states of the Deep South and in Montana.[27] Other states also experienced significant shifts in agricultural employment that ran counter to the general trend established by the other components of employment. In these cases it had the effect of dampening the total shift effect generated by the other sectors.

We have seen that the differential shifts in agriculture come primarily from changes in field crop and livestock activities. Advancing agricultural technology associated with soybeans, hybrid corn, drought-resistant wheats, new feed sorghums, and cotton have all combined to generate a shift in field crop activity out of the Southeast and into the western states. The same was generally true of

---

[26]The expansion in fishing in this area is coupled with an expansion in poultry raising that also set the performance in agriculture squarely against the trend for this area.

[27]In this connection, compare Table 141 with Figures 58 and 45.

the production of livestock products. The important exception here is that the Southeast gained significantly from an expansion of these products. However, since this shift into the Southeast was a part of the adustment away from labor intensive row-cropping, it was consistent with—and indeed, contributed to—the downward shift in farm employment in this region.

We have also seen that each region's access to the inputs and markets that were significant for each of these agricultural systems was modified by many different types of influences. Changes both in the size and in the composition of total demand have changed the relative advantage of regions. As near as we can determine, this proportionality effect may have assisted the field crop and livestock areas vis-a-vis the dairy, poultry, and general farming areas. Institutional factors—both regional and national—have played a part; for example, the effect of price supports and the repeal of the oleomargarine tax. Changes in technology have modified the land resource requirements, resulting in shifts based upon the new requirements. Resource exhaustion has been an important factor, as have rivalry costs. We have seen that changes in one production system, by altering the competitive conditions of land use, have altered the location and character of otherwise independent production systems.

We shall now briefly summarize the influence of agriculture in the growth behavior of specific regions, considering first the major growth areas. Agriculture contributed significantly to the growth performance of California and Arizona. It accounted for 12% of the differential shift in total employment in California and for 22% in Arizona. California claimed 24% of the nation's net upward shift in agricultural employment and 36% of the upward shift in the value of farm products sold. In the various sectors of agricultural activity, its share in the upward shifts was as follows: field crops—22%, fruits and nuts—12%, vegetables—57%, dairy products—25%, poultry products—15%, livestock products—12%, logging—6%, and fishing—20%.

These changes have been associated with important changes in access. Increases in relative market access have been particularly important for meat, poultry, and dairy products and, to a lesser degree, for vegetables.[28]

Modifications in input access also played a role in this performance. Many of these agricultural activities experienced changes that could not be explained on the basis of over-all shifts in markets. Resource exhaustion played a part. The decline of virgin timber reserves in the Pacific Northwest brought about a relative increase in California's access to valuable resource inputs. Innovations in mechanization and irrigation significantly augmented its access to the kinds of inputs that are significant in cotton culture. Improvements in transportation, storage, and processing of fruits, vegetables, and horticultural specialties have

---

[28]Haystead and Fite point out: "For a generation or so, Pacific Coast farmers had a very slim time of it from the cash angle because they were so far away from the major consuming centers. Then World War II sent millions of people to the Coast industries. Suddenly there appeared to be an almost unlimited market right at the back door of Coast farmers." *The Agricultural Regions of the United States* (Norman: University of Oklahoma Press, 1955), pp. 13-14. A significant part of the recent expansion has grown out of increased shipments of California products to the East as a result of increasing demand.

had the effect of increasing the importance of its valuable resource attributes in producing these products.

The experience of Arizona was essentially the same. If anything, considering its size, it received even greater support from agricultural growth.

The area that includes Texas and extends up through the mid-Mountain states is, generally, a growth area. In this area, however, the influence of agriculture tended to run counter to the growth performance of the region during the period under review. Wyoming and Nevada showed very little strength in any sector of agriculture. Utah showed some strength in dairying, oriented to the expanding West Coast market, but in little else. Colorado made some gains in livestock but little else. Texas and New Mexico made some gains in field crops, but Texas, in particular, lost out significantly in practically every other sector. All of these states experienced relative losses or only marginal gains in the value of farm products sold. All except Colorado, Utah, and New Mexico showed employment losses or very marginal relative gains. In terms of employment, the downward shift for Texas was so marked that it was an important counter to the growth trend for that state.

Florida was a major growth state in the 1939-1954 period and an examination of the agricultural sectors might incline one to claim for agriculture an important part of the growth performance. This state claimed over 10% of the total net upward shift in the value of farm products sold. It experienced an absolute upward shift in the value of farm products sold in every farm sector. This included 58% of the total shift for fruits and nuts, 11% of the total in vegetables, and 7% of the total in dairy products. Although the state's relative gains in product value were marked, upward shifts in agricultural employment accounted for only 2.7% of the state's total relative gains in all employment. At least in terms of employment, agriculture has played a less important part in the growth performance of that state than many are inclined to think.

Of the states in the Great Lakes region showing growth, only Indiana received significant help from agriculture. Some 23% of its total shift was contributed by a net upward shift in agricultural employment. This seems to grow out of favorable input attributes in relation to the corn-soy-hog culture and the important innovations that have taken place in this agricultural sector during our period.

All of the major areas of relative decline received an important impetus to decline from agricultural activities. In the Deep South, absolute downward shifts in agricultural employment accounted for 57% of the total employment shift between 1939 and 1954 in Alabama, 25% in Arkansas, 64% in Georgia, 36% in Mississippi, and 70% in South Carolina. A part of this is a proportionality effect. In 1939 agricultural workers comprised the following percentages of the total labor forces of these states: Alabama—55%, Arkansas—70%, Georgia—51%, Mississippi—74%, and South Carolina—56%. Add to this, important differential downward shifts in field crops, vegetables, and fruits. Upward shifts in meat, poultry, dairy products, and forest products generated some upward shifts in the value of farm products in these states, but they did not provide an alternative for the labor-intensive forms of farm employment they replaced.

Certain of the Lakes, Plains, and northern Mountain states showed relative upward shifts in agricultural employment, supported for the most part by relative gains in field crops and livestock.[29] It should be pointed out, however, that these upward shifts were only relative. These states were agricultural specialists and, hence, received the full effect of the proportionality effect generated by a declining industry.

In the Appalachian states the downward shifts in employment were dominated by other sectors of the economy. Except for West Virigina (which had an adjustment much like that in the Deep South), agriculture did not contribute more than 5% of the total shift performance displayed by any of these states. In general, however, the direction of the agricultural shifts was consistent with that displayed by the states in this region.

[29]Also dairy products in the case of Wisconsin and vegetables and eggs in Minnesota.

23 / Regional influence of

manufacturing activity:

(1) MANUFACTURING IN GENERAL

The relative intensity of manufacturing concentration in different parts of the country is shown in Figure 70, highlighting the familiar pattern of concentrations in the New England, Middle Atlantic, and Great Lakes regions in the Northeast—the "Manufacturing Belt" of the nation—and in the Piedmont area of the Southeast and the coastal states of the Far West. A further view in terms of the broad categories of manufacturing specialization in different parts of the country is presented in Figure 71. Here, manufacturing is broken down into "processing" and "fabricating" types of activity, the distinction being based upon the nature of the inputs—whether mainly raw materials or materials that have already been through an initial processing change in the flow of productive activity.[1] It can be seen at a glance that fabricating activities are highly local-

---

[1]The classification is based on an analysis of the 1947 input-output table, resulting in the following categorization of industries on a 3-digit code basis: primary resource extractors, first-stage resource users, and other manufacturing industries. Industries classified as "processing" are those having a significant proportion of their labor force in industry groups identified as first-stage resource users on the 3-digit basis. All other manufacturing industries have been classified as fabricating industries. The following were classified as "processing" industries. The titles in parentheses are those of the main first-stage resource users included in the industry group:

Furniture, and lumber and wood products (Sawmills, planing, and veneer mills; Plywood)
Primary metal industries (Blast furnaces; Primary copper; Primary zinc; Primary metals, not elsewhere classified)
Food and kindred products (Meat packing and whole poultry; Processed dairy products; Canning, preserving, and freezing; Grain mill products; Sugar; Miscellaneous food

---

Figure 70—opposite. % Employed Labor Force in Manufacturing, 1950, State Economic Areas.

Source: An unpublished series of data for state economic areas prepared by Donald J. Bogue and Calvin L. Beale.

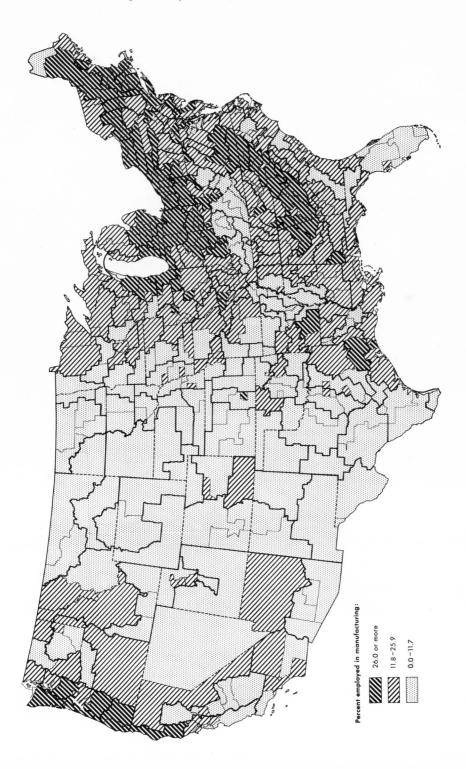

Percent employed in manufacturing:

26.0 or more

11.8 – 25.9

0.0 – 11.7

ized in the Manufacturing Belt and that processing activities predominate in the Southeast, the West, and northern New England.

In addition to these two very broad categories of industrial specialization, there is considerable regional specialization in terms of specific manufacturing activities. Each one of the major industry groups tends to be more or less localized in certain parts of the country.

The reasons behind the existing locational pattern are developed in the following sections through an examination of the shifts in manufacturing employment that have taken place in recent years.

Preliminary View of the Net Shifts in Total Manufacturing Employment

In 1954 manufacturing employed 28% of the nation's total labor force as compared with 18% for all of the resource categories—agriculture, mining, forestry, and fisheries. The manufacturing sector is not only large, but is also as a whole a dynamic, rapid-growth sector of the economy; shifts in manufacturing accounted for almost one-third of the total net shift in employment between 1939 and 1954.[2]

The net shifts in total manufacturing employment over the 1939-1954 period are shown in Figure 72. As in so much of our data, the general westward movement is in effect here; California shows 44% of the total net upward shift, Texas 14.5%, and Kansas 5.6%. The rest of the upward shift is rather widely and evenly distributed. Roughly 91% of the total net downward shift occurs in the

---

products)

Textile mill products (Spinning, weaving, and dyeing)

"Other nondurable" goods (Tobacco manufacture; Pulp mills; Petroleum products; Coke and by-products)

Each of these groups, of course, includes industries which are not first-stage resource users. For example, "furniture, and lumber and wood products" includes "furniture and fixtures," which is a fabricating industry; it also includes "logging," which is a primary resource extractor. Its classification here as a "processing" industry means only that an appreciable proportion of the employment in the industry group is in component industries classified as first-stage resource users. A detailed analysis of the location of these various types of manufacturing industries is presented in the study of Otis Dudley Duncan and Associates, *Metropolis and Region.*

[2]Further, manufacturing is the basic link between the resource sectors and the consuming sectors of the economy. It probably has greater latitude for response to changing economic environment than either of these sectors. This does not mean that manufacturing activity is free from immobilities. However, these immobilities are not created directly by natural forces as in the case of the resource sectors of the economy; nor are the costs and benefits, which are the raw materials for decision-making, as subjective as they would seem to be in the case of households.

Figure 71—opposite. Type of Manufacturing Specialization, 1950, State Economic Areas.

Source: An unpublished series of data for state economic areas prepared by Donald J. Bogue and Calvin L. Beale.

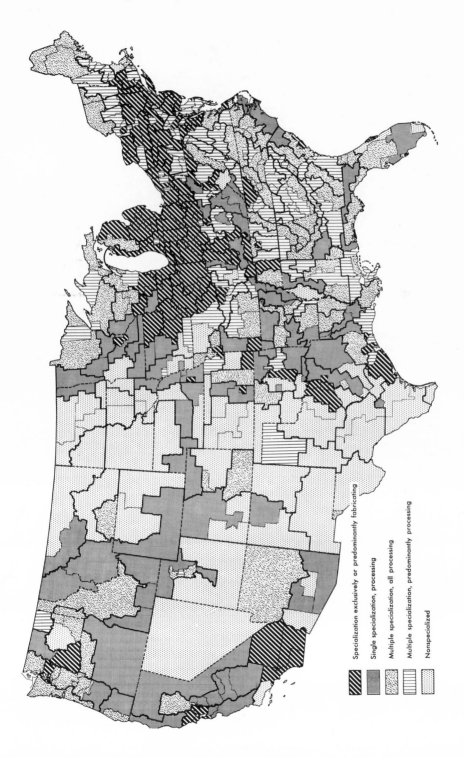

Specialization exclusively or predominantly fabricating

Single specialization, processing

Multiple specialization, all processing

Multiple specialization, predominantly processing

Nonspecialized

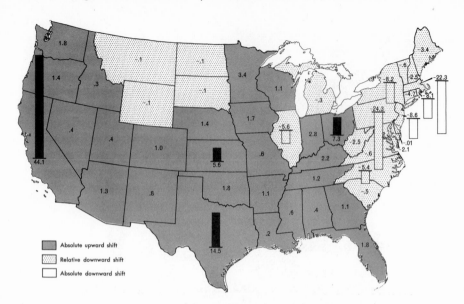

Figure 72. Net Shift in Total Manufacturing Employment, 1939-54.

State figures represent % of total net shift. Total net shift as % of incremental change: 16.3. Total net shift as % of 1939 manufacturing employment: 10.3. Source: Appendix Table H.

states touching on the Atlantic coast; elsewhere, Illinois is the only state with a significant relative decline in manufacturing employment.[3] Except for Rhode Island, which shows an *absolute* decline in manufacturing employment, the net downward shift is entirely relative in character. The Middle Atlantic states and New England account for three-fourths of the total.

The interregional in manufacturing employment have clearly been a very important factor in total employment shifts. This is evidenced by the fact that, of the nineteen states shown to have had upward shifts in *total* employment between 1939 and 1954 (see Figure 45), all but five[4] have also had upward shifts in manufacturing, accounting for 85% of the manufacturing shift. There is an important discrepancy, however. Most of the Southeastern and western Plains states that show significant downward shifts in total employment show modest but perceptible upward shifts in manufacturing employment.

[3]There are some interesting intra-period variations between 1939 and 1954. During the war years the western end of the manufacturing zone showed great strength—probably because of its concentrations of heavy manufacturing. At the same time the Southeast showed relative upward shifts. In the postwar period the Great Lakes states showed relative and absolute downward shifts as they made the adjustment to peacetime activity. At the same time the Southeast commenced to show strength again. Data on the Great Lakes states for the period since 1954 suggest that the postwar adjustment in this area is complete and that this end of the manufacturing belt is continuing to experience net upward shifts.

[4]Four Atlantic seaboard states and Michigan.

Regional Influence of Manufacturing Reflected in
the Total Proportionality Effect

Manufacturing has played a dominant role in generating the net proportionality shifts in total employment.[5] Its rate of growth has been exceeded only by that of construction and government activities, and the number of workers in manufacturing is over twice as great as in any of the other major rapid-growth sectors of employment.[6] Further, when we identify the states that made a contribution to the net upward proportionality shift in total employment because of their specialization in manufacturing, we see that twelve of the seventeen states showing upward proportionality shifts in total employment are manufacturing specialists (Table 145). As a matter of fact, only three of the manufacturing specialists (i.e., states with a higher than average proportion of workers in manufacturing)—North Carolina, South Carolina, and Wisconsin—fail to show an upward proportionality shift in total employment. However, it should be noted that five of the seventeen—Washington, California, Florida, Maine, and Maryland—require the assistance of some of the other rapid-growth sectors to establish their upward proportionality shifts in total employment.

Manufacturing has been expanding its share of total economic activity over a long period of time. For example, between 1870 to 1954, its share of total income payments more than doubled; factory employment increased more rapidly than total employment over these years, and factory output more rapidly than the gross national product. The factors explaining this development are essentially the reverse of the factors that explained the resource sector's declining share. Several of the more important elements require special attention:

(1) The income elasticity of demand for manufactured products has, in general, been considerably in excess of one. In an expanding economy, increments to income are increasingly devoted to more highly processed products.[7]

The attractiveness of manufacturing goods has resulted, in part, from the ability of this sector to increase quality at a rapid pace and/or lower, or limit, relative price rises for a given basket of goods. The manufacturing sector has built enormous gains in production and productivity around the factory system, which feeds its efficiency upon standardization and volume. The resource and

---

[5]This proportionality effect based upon the ten 1-digit components of total employment was presented in Figure 47. We made two observations concerning this picture. (1) About 90% of this upward proportionality shift was concentrated in the Manufacturing Belt states. In addition to these states—where the proportionality effect is dominant—Florida, California, and Washington displayed some upward proportionality shifts. (2) These states are the ones that specialize in the rapid-growth sectors of employment identified in table 130.

[6]Employment data, such as we use here, actually tend to understate the rate of growth of the manufacturing sector because manufacturing has probably made more rapid gains in labor productivity than any other sector.

[7]The service industries have also enjoyed a favorable income elasticity of demand. Apparently, however, they did not progress rapidly enough to cause the proportion of income expended on manufactured consumers goods to decline during the period under investigation.

Table 145. Manufacturing employment as percentage of total employment in states experiencing net upward proportionality shifts mainly because of specialization in manufacturing, 1939 and 1954

State	1939 %	1954 %
United States average	23.5	27.7
Rhode Island	51.5	43.0
Connecticut	46.6	47.4
New Jersey	42.6	42.2
Massachusetts	40.0	37.9
New Hampshire	38.3	40.5
Michigan	38.0	40.5
Ohio	34.9	39.4
Pennsylvania	34.5	37.3
Indiana	31.9	37.8
Illinois	30.2	33.9
Delaware	28.3	29.5
New York	28.0	32.1

SOURCE: Appendix Tables F-1 and F-2.

service sectors of the economy, in contrast, have attributes that limit the application of this basic technique. (a) Both resources and final markets (to which most service sectors are oriented) are widely distributed geographically. It follows that agricultural production and personal services, for example, cannot in most instances create sufficient volume in one place to take as much advantage as manufacturing can of the economics of large-scale organization. (b) These resource and service sectors deal in products and services that are quite heterogeneous in character and often have quality variations that make standardization difficult.

(2) There would seem to be greater opportunity for introducing innovations and creating new products in the processing sectors of the economy than in other sectors. The significance of this lies in the fact that, in their initial stages of exploitation, new products tend to be rapid-growth products. Thus, the innovating sector tends to be the most rapidly expanding sector.

(3) Innovations and new products in the manufacturing sector create a powerful influence that might be called sector substitution. Manufacturing has taken over numerous activities formerly performed by resource and service sectors (although it has also given up many activities to the services sector). Synthetic products, such as rubber, tend to expand manufacturing relative to resource sectors. In producing tractors, agricultural machinery, gasoline and oil, manufacturing has taken over a number of tasks formerly performed on the farm.

Sector substitution is also to be observed in the shift away from the farm to factory slaughter of meat animals and factory production of butter. There had been a similar shift from domestic to factory production—particularly in the soft-goods items. More recently trends are developing toward substituting factory production for on-site construction, and manufacturing is producing a wide range of supplies designed to improve the efficiency of the service sectors.

(4) Exports have played an important role in the relative expansion of manufacturing. It has become more profitable for the United States to devote an increasing proportion of its energies to manufacturing and a declining proportion to the resource sectors—to export less wheat and cotton and more automobiles and machinery. As a consequence, the proportion of manufactured goods in the U. S. export total rose from about 42% in 1870 to roughly 75% in 1954.[8]

In short, significant long-term trends in supply and demand have increased the relative importance of the manufacturing sector of the economy. Thus the regions that have favorable access to the essential inputs and markets for specialization in manufacturing gain, on the whole, relative to the regions that lack these access characteristics. In spite of this generally stimulating effect to manufacturing specialization, in some regions manufacturing activities generated a differential tendency towards relative decline. In others, the gains shown were far out of porportion to the degree of manufacturing specialization. These effects were due to significant interregional differential shifts in manufacturing activity.

Regional Influence of Manufacturing Reflected
in the Total Differential Effect

The data show that manufacturing has played a significant part in the differential net shifts in total employment. (Compare Figures 72 and 46.) In three-fourths of the states, the shifts in manufacturing employment correspond in direction with shifts in total employment. Of the twenty-six states showing upward differential shifts in total employment, twenty show upward shifts in manufacturing employment, accounting for 91% of the total. Of the twenty-two states showing downward differential shifts in total employment fifteen show downward shifts in manufacturing employment, accounting for 94.4% of the total.

There is further evidence of the importance of the manufacturing employment shifts in accounting for the observed total differential shift. Table 146 identifies 31 states in which the manufacturing shift was more than 10% of the state's total employment shift (computed without regard to sign). This means that manufacturing was a major factor in the employment shifts displayed by the great majority of the states.

[8]But while this factor has had an important historical effect, it is not very important during our current period. The war and the acute dollar shortage that followed it stopped this expanding export share, at least temporarily.

Table 146. Differential shifts in manufacturing employment as percentage of total shifts in employment, 1939-1954

State	Manufacturing shift in state as % of total shift (without regard to sign) of 1-digit employment categories
Rhode Island	76.8%
Massachusetts	59.8
New Jersey	53.4
Connecticut	53.3
Maine	49.4
Kansas	44.8
Pennsylvania	42.6
New Hampshire	42.1
Ohio	41.1
California	38.4
Indiana	32.3
Vermont	29.7
Kentucky	29.1
North Carolina	26.3
Texas	25.9
West Virginia	25.3
Oklahoma	24.2
Minnesota	23.9
Oregon	23.4
Washington	19.6
Arkansas	19.3
Maryland and D. C.	19.0
Nebraska	18.0
Illinois	17.9
Colorado	16.8
Arizona	15.5
New Mexico	13.8
Nevada	13.3
Iowa	12.1
Wisconsin	11.5
New York	10.3

SOURCE: Table 157.

1-Digit Proportionality and Differential Effects in Manufacturing Employment Based Upon 2-Digit Components

Figure 73 shows the total differential net shift in manufacturing employment, by states, over the 1939-1954 period. The figures here were arrived at by subdividing total manufacturing employment into the twenty 2-digit components utilized by the census, computing a shift pattern for each of these components,

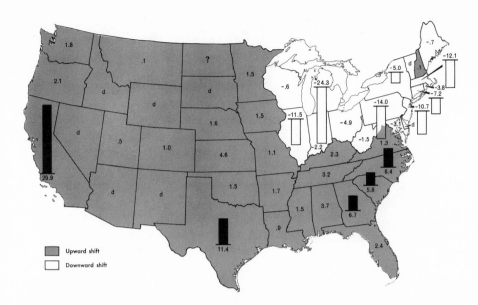

Figure 73. Total Differential Net Shift in All Manufacturing
Employment, 1939-54.

Disclosure problems made it difficult to measure this dimension accurately
for those states marked "d"; the direction of shift was ascertainable,
however, in all states but North Dakota. The % figures are
rough indications of dimension only.

and summing them for each state. As usual, the amount of the differential shift
does not exhaust the total shift for each state shown in Figure 72. The balance
represents the proportionality shift. This is shown in Figure 74.[9]

The proportionality effect, which accounted for some 30% to 35% of the total
shift, is not as important a factor here as the differential effect. Even so, it is
significant, especially in explaining the behavior of particular regions. The net
upward proportionality shift is restricted almost entirely to the Manufacturing
Belt and California; Michigan, Illinois, and Ohio account for 70% of it. North
and South Carolina account for a third of the downward porportionality shift.

Table 147 helps to explain the reasons for this proportionality effect. The
twenty 2-digit manufacturing components are divided here into rapid-growth

[9]In handling this manufacturing data, we are faced with a new problem. For the first
time, we find important data suppressed because of the disclosure rule. This means that
the sum of the shifts for each state does not exactly represent the total differential shift.
This has two consequences. (1) The percentage figures recorded for each state in figures
73 and 74 are approximations and should not be considered exact. (2) Some states have
had a "d" recorded instead of a percentage figure. These states are the ones for which the
disclosure problem is especially acute. In each of these cases, however, we have been able
to determine the probable direction of the proportionality and differential shift—as is
indicated by the appropriate shading.

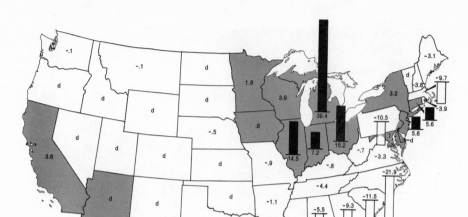

Figure 74. Total Proportionality Net Shift in All Manufacturing
Employment, 1939-54.

Disclosure problems made it difficult to measure this dimension accurately
for those states marked "d"; the direction of shift was ascertainable,
however. The % figures should be taken as rough indications of
dimension only.

and slow-growth sectors. The slow-growth sectors are made up primarily of soft-
goods industries, many of which are first-stage resource users.[10] The rapid-
growth sectors are predominantly hard-goods industries, and their ties with the
resource sectors are less close. Not only do the slow-growth sectors have more
important links with resource sectors, but they are also often more sensitive to
interregional differences in the cost of labor. These tend to be concentrated in
the states outside the principal Manufacturing Belt.[11] The rapid-growth sectors,
on the other hand, are concentrated in the Manufacturing Belt states plus Iowa,
Minnesota, Arizona, and California. It is interesting to note that Pennsylvania,
which displays a downward proportionality shift, has a smaller proportion of its
manufacturing in the rapid-growth sectors than any other state in the Manufacturing Belt (26.9% as compared with a national average of 35.6% in 1939).
It is also interesting to note that the five states with the strongest net upward
proportionality shifts—Michigan, Ohio, Indiana, Illinois, and Wisconsin— show
the strongest degrees of specialization in these rapid-growth sectors (75% in the
case of Michigan, and none below 42%).

[10]That is, the industries receiving an important part of their inputs from the primary or
resource extracting sectors of the economy.

[11]This tendency can be verified by referring to Appendix Table K.

Table 147. Percentage change in manufacturing production worker employment for 2-digit manufacturing sectors, 1939–1954

S.I.C. code	Industry sector	% Change	% of total 1939 employment	% of total 1954 employment
36	Electrical machinery	+191.39	3.2	5.8
37	Transportation equipment	+143.70	7.0	10.7
38	Instruments & rel. prod.	+130.48	1.1	1.6
39	Miscellaneous mfg.	+129.91	3.1	4.5
35	Machinery (except elect.)	+118.50	6.9	9.5
34	Fabricated metal prod.	+ 82.04	5.8	6.6
28	Chemical & allied prod.	+ 81.84	3.5	4.1
30	Rubber prod.	+ 62.53	1.5	1.6
26	Paper & allied prod.	+ 61.24	3.5	3.5
	TOTAL MANUFACTURING EMPLOYMENT	+ 58.46	100.0	100.0
32	Stone, clay & glass prod.	+ 54.26	3.4	3.3
27	Printing & publishing	+ 54.04	4.2	4.0
29	Petroleum & coal prod.	+ 52.11	1.4	1.3
25	Furniture & fixt.	+ 51.36	2.4	2.3
23	Apparel & rel. prod.	+ 42.10	9.6	8.7
20	Food & kindred prod.	+ 41.90	10.3	9.2
33	Primary metal industries	+ 39.57	8.6	7.6
24	Lumber & prod.	+ 21.47	5.4	4.6
31	Leather & leather prod.	− 1.84	4.2	2.6
22	Textile mill prod.	− 12.41	13.8	7.7
21	Tobacco manufactures	− 19.78	1.1	0.6

SOURCE: Appendix Table K.

An understanding of this proportionality effect requires some knowledge of why certain sectors of manufacturing are able to expand more rapidly than others. The demand and supply factors bringing about these results are very numerous, of course. They tend to fall into certain types of influences, however, and we may mention a few with which we have already gained some familiarity.

(1) Income elasticity is important at this level of analysis, as elsewhere. The slow-growth sectors are, generally, the processed food and basic resource-using sectors whose products display low income elasticities of demand compared to the more highly fabricated products of manufacturing activity. The only rapid-growth sectors that can be classed as resource-using sectors (rubber, paper, and chemicals) are the ones most likely to enjoy a high income elasticity of demand for their products because they supply important intermediate inputs for the most rapidly growing industries in the economy.

(2) Sector substitution is an important part of the explanation in many cases. One of the reasons, for example, why forest products industries are in the slow-growth group is that substitutions of metals and plastics have resulted in other manufacturing sectors taking over some production jobs formerly performed

by these sectors. This kind of sector substitution has been partly responsible for the rapid growth of the miscellaneous manufacturing sector, among others.

(3) We have noted that the manufacturing sector of the economy has tended to gain a larger share of the nation's exports relative to the resource sectors. It is also generally true that the more highly finished manufactured goods have gained relatively over such goods as food, textiles, and apparel in the manufacturing export total.

(4) Gains in labor productivity at given price and income elasticity levels have been greater in some manufacturing sectors than in others. For example, the substantial decline in employment in tobacco manufactures arises from the fact that this industry, in the face of inelastic demand, made one of the greatest increases in wage-earner efficiency. In general, when the employment measure is used, this factor tends to make the rapid-growth industries appear to be less rapid growing and the slow-growth industries more slow growing than when growth is measured by indices other than employment. Actually, the industries that we class here as rapid-growth industries have generally made the greatest gains in labor productivity.[12]

(5) Changes in the composition of the consuming sectors of the economy have been important. During the 1939-54 period, for example, there was a large increase in collective consumption. The government absorbed a much larger share of the output than formerly—particularly in the area of military defense. The sectors most apt to benefit from this shift in demand composition are obviously those producing such products as electrical machinery, transport equipment, and so on. Other changes in consumption demand have arisen from changes in the age distribution of the population and in the rate of new household formation.

These factors suggest the types of influences at work in generating the rapid-growth sectors that account for the proportionality effect. But we also need to know where these rapid-growth sectors are located and what determines the locational choice. This involves, of course, a consideration of the kinds of access that are important to each of these sectors. In other words, it involves an understanding of the effects arising out of interregional differences in access phenomena.

We have already mentioned that the differential effect accounts for 65-70% of the total shift in manufacturing employment. A comparison of Figures 72 and 73 underscores the significance of this. Only three out of twenty-seven states displaying upward shifts in total manufacturing employment between 1939 and 1954 failed to show upward differential shifts in manufacturing employment as well.

The general regional picture presented by the differential effect is almost the reverse of that presented by the proportionality effect. The states in the Manufacturing Belt are the ones that display the downward differential shifts. All of the rest show upward differential shifts, with California and Texas leading. In general, in the Manufacturing Belt the downward differential shift outweighed

---

[12]See Solomon Fabricant, *Employment in Manufacturing, 1899-1939* (New York: National Bureau of Economic Research, 1942), pp. 37-42.

the upward proportionality shift—another indication that it was the more important effect during this period. Ohio and Indiana were the exceptions; their proportionality effect was sufficiently strong to create an upward shift in total manufacturing employment. On the other hand in Virginia, North and South Carolina, the upper Mountain states, and the Plains states, the reverse of this situation occurred. The degree of specialization in the slow-growth sectors was so great in these states that there were downward shifts in total employment despite moderate upward differential shifts.

These differential shifts must arise from the fact that each of these sectors of manufacturing activity has expanded more rapidly in some regions than in others. This means that we must break down the total differential shift into that displayed by each of the twenty 2-digit components upon which its measurement was based. Before we do this, however, we shall touch upon a few generalizations that will be of use in analyzing the differential effect in manufacturing.

Some Access Characteristics of Manufacturing Industries

Because manufacturing is a basic link between the resource sectors and the consuming sectors of the economy, it is exposed directly to sources of change on both sides of the market. The input-output data presented in Table 144 documents this fact and lends emphasis to three areas of interindustry relationship.

First, of all the broad categories presented in the simple input-output table, manufacturing uses the largest share of inputs coming from resource sectors (except for the agricultural output that is recycled into agriculture). This suggests that basic regional changes in resource availability might explain some of the major regional shifts in manufacturing.

Such measurement as can be made on a purely aggregative basis, however, does not support the hypothesis that resources have been dominant in shaping structure and change in the manufacturing sector. Consider the cross-section picture. Table 148 shows the rank correlation between several resource and resource-using groups. Employment in the first-stage resource-using group of industries is seen to have a high degree of association with population. Its association with resource employment is much slighter. The second-stage resource users show an even higher degree of association with population and a lesser degree with resource employment. As the major part of manufacturing activity is even further removed from resource association than these groups, natural resources do not appear to bind manufacturing very closely in location in any over-all sense.

These aggregative data should not be interpreted to mean that natural resources cannot play an important role in the location of manufacturing activites. As important inputs of considerable weight and volume, and frequently with weight-losing characteristics, they influence in important ways the location of many *specific* processing activities. In some cases, in fact, the influence may be fairly widespread; thus, for example, the availability of oil in the Southwest

Table 148. Rank correlations of selected resource and resource-using manufacturing groups, 1954

Correlated sectors	Coefficient
(1) Employment in 1st stage resource users with resource employment	.677
(2) Employment in 2nd stage resource users with resource employment	.583
(3) Population with resource employment	.666
(4) Employment in 1st stage resource users with population	.915
(5) Employment in 2nd stage resource users with population	.935

Note: These groups were based upon input-output relationships. The industries classified as 1st stage resource users were those sectors in the 200-industry BLS table that received more than 10% of their inputs (by value) from the resource sectors. The 2nd stage resource users received little directly from the resource sectors but received more than 10% of their inputs from the 1st stage resource users. These two groups combined accounted for slightly less than half of the total manufacturing employment. The 10% dividing line was an arbitrary choice (but was based on what seemed to be in both cases a logical division in terms of the nature of the basic productive processes involved).

Source: Appendix Tables H, I, J and K.

has undoubtedly been an important lead factor in the growth of manufacturing in that region. Yet it remains true that when manufacturing is examined in broad categories, the tie to resources has not been dominant.

We have also seen (Table 144) that 58% of the total output of manufacturing goes to essentially terminal outlets—final demand and services. This is not as large a proportion as for the terminal activities themselves, but it does lend emphasis to the importance for manufacturing of terminal markets. We have seen, too, that manufacturing employment has a much greater association with population than with resource employment—even for the first-stage resource users (Table 148).

Further, the shifts in final markets (as revealed by shifts in population) have been closely associated with major shifts in manufacturing employment. A comparison of Figure 72 with the data of relative state gains in population reveals that California, Texas, and the states in the western end of the Manufacturing Belt have all demonstrated significant gains in manufacturing employment as well as in population. The West, the Southwest, and Florida all exhibit the same association to a lesser degree. Of the major growth regions, only the Middle Atlantic seaboard states show a uniform net downward shift in manufacturing employment., A group of states in the Plains and the Southeast show gains in manufacturing in the face of absolute and relative losses in population. Previous discussion has already revealed that these states have a tendency to resource specialization and/or population pressure. One might suppose, therefore, that manufacturing growth in these areas might be heavily weighted towards processes oriented to labor and resource inputs rather than markets. As we proceed to an examination of the manufacturing sector, we shall note the extent to which the evidence supports this hypothesis.

Intra-industry absorption is perhaps the most significant of the input-output relationships for manufacturing; almost 40% of manufacturing output is absorbed as inputs within manufacturing itself. This intra-industry absorption is greater for manufacturing than for any other category, and has an important influence on the location of manufacturing activities.

Table 149 highlights the fact that primary and secondary metals, metal-fabricating, rubber products, and chemicals all have especially strong ties on both the input and output side with other manufacturing industries. Locations close to manufacturing in general are likely to be quite important for them. It is not suprising, then, that all of these chemicals are concentrated in areas that give them maximum access to all manufacturing. Around 80% of the total output of these sectors is concentrated in the Manufacturing Belt states. This is about twice the concentration of population in these states and half again the rate of general manufacturing concentration in these states.

There are various reasons for the regional concentration of manufacturing activities—particularly those for which the intra-industry absorption is important. The fact of this intra-industry absorption means that rather straight-forward ties with intermediate manufacturing inputs or intermediate manufacturing markets are likely to be important. These industries characteristically assemble their inputs and distribute their outputs to a large number of intermediate sources.[13]

This has two consequences: (a) It vastly strengthens the tendency to choose locations intermediate to sources and markets. Since sources and markets are in this case both groups of manufacturing industries, a clustering of activities is likely to result. (b) This type of situation usually leads to important external economies that can be generated by an agglomeration of functions. Just the problem of maintaining effective communication with a variety of sources and markets is very important, and this type of regional "nesting" can permit greater degrees of industrial specialization that generate economies in which all can share.

These complex interrelationships combine with market organization phenomena in generating large urban-metropolitan regions with agglomerated sets of consumption, service, and manufacturing activities. This, in turn, tends to make these urban regions attractive to other manufacturing activities that are essentially oriented to final markets but find that internal scale economies require some market concentration to realize the most effective level of operation.

Since producing capital tends to become fixed in intermediate periods and since labor acquires some of that fixity through the intermediary of economic opportunity, these agglomerated urban metropolitan regions tend to take on a degree of immobility. More important, the interrelated character of these space

---

[13]For example, in the fabricated metal products group the boiler products industry assembled inputs from 73 of the 140 industries published in the input-output table (200 sector BLS, 1947) and distributed outputs to 65.

structures gives the whole an immobility that exceeds the time duration of any one of its immobile parts. Capital becoming mobile through depreciation or depletion may re-invest in the same urban complex because of intricate ties with it. Thus, the urban metropolitan region tends to develop magnet-like attributes. The polarity that it introduces into the nation's economic structure serves to explain why the Manufacturing Belt has remained dominant over a long period. All of the current structure of economic activity and all of the prospects for and pathways to economic development are conditioned, therefore, by the existence of these relatively immobile urban agglomerations. Manufacturing, because of its important intra-industry absorption, has played an important role in creating these phenomena. An important part of the explanation of the regional influence of manufacturing must, therefore, be related to them.

A second line of thought stems from a recognition of the importance of intra-

Table 149. Per cent of inputs coming from manufacturing and per cent of outputs going to manufacturing for selected 2-digit manufacturing categories, 1947

2-digit manufacturing categories	% Inputs	% Outputs
Food products	25.4	18.8
Textiles	24.5	*70.2*
Apparel	*44.2*	18.3
Wood and paper products	38.4	*47.0*
Chemicals	*43.0*	*60.6*
Petroleum products	13.1	20.8
Coke and coal products	20.2	*56.7*
Rubber products	*45.5*	*41.9*
Glass and other non-metals	23.0	*42.4*
Primary metals	*46.0*	*84.0*
Secondary metals	*47.4*	*89.7*
Metal fabricating	*48.8*	*44.4*
Machinery	*44.2*	36.2
Electrical apparatus	*44.9*	36.6
Transportation equipment	*62.5*	24.8
Miscellaneous manufacturing	*42.2*	24.4
National average for all manufacturing	39.4	39.4

Figures in italics are above the average.

SOURCE: 200 Sector BLS Inter-Industry Table—1947.

industry absorption in manufacturing. It seems to follow that changes in manufacturing in themselves create further changes—that the manufacturing shifts have a very important cumulative effect. One wonders to what extent the expansion in Indiana and Ohio, for example, is a cumulative product of earlier expansions that created important intermediate sources and markets. Certainly many activities that desire the agglomeration economies of the Manufacturing Belt but still find significance in maximizing their access to national markets have increasingly discovered that the western end of the Manufacturing Belt is a region that has been gaining *relative* access to these important inputs and markets. This cumulative aspect also makes it important to have some concept of significant thresholds. Is it not possible, for example, that California's dramatic showing is partly accounted for by the fact that it had arrived at a point in its development where important intermediate supply and market functions make some operations feasible which were formerly not economic?

In conclusion, we have observed the importance for manufacturing as a whole of access to final markets. We have also recognized the importance of access to intermediate inputs for those manufacturing activities in which there is a significant degree of intra-industry absorption. Lastly, we have considered the significance of resource access, but have concluded that this factor is not of dominant importance for manufacturing as a whole. However, the fact that the correlation coefficient between manufacturing employment and population, though high, is smaller than for any other non-resource sector (Table 138) suggests that resource access and, to some extent, access to intermediate manufacturing agglomerations may exert an important pull in opposition to that set up by the market.[14]

This is further suggested by the correlations for the components of manufacturing shown in Table 150. The sectors with the highest association are the ones that, in general, have the closest ties to final markets. Some of these find resource inputs important but—as in the stone, clay, and glass products industries—the resource inputs they exploit are found in every region. The middle range of coefficients is dominated by the sectors for which intra-industry absorption is important. For these, access to intermediate inputs and markets has offset to a degree the influence of final markets. Their coefficients are not the lowest, however, because there is some degree of association between population and the major urban complexes. At the bottom of the scale are industries for which immobile resource or labor inputs must clearly be important. The range of the coefficients shows that the resource and agglomeration elements exert a greater

[14]Here and throughout the text we have been using such rank correlations to give a rough indication of the degree of concentration or dispersion of activity relative to population. We would like to point out that these indexes can reflect many things such as the influence of market pulls or input pulls, the frequency with which the activity occurs, the degree of cluster it exhibits, etc. All of these things can cause the coefficient to be different if the size of the geographical unit upon which it is based is different. (The use of state data has disadvantages for this analysis, but the use of smaller-unit data had to be foregone because of the magnitude of the task.) We are suggesting that an accurate interpretation of the meaning of these coefficients is difficult and *we have used them only for purposes of description and analytical suggestion.* We would like to call the reader's attention to the fact that there are other ways that have been devised for measuring special association that have in some respects superior attributes to the one used here. If interested in this problem of measurement and the techniques that are available, one might look at Wilbur R. Thompson, *The Measurement of Industry Location Patterns* (Unpublished Doctoral Dissertation, University of Michigan). See also Edgar M. Hoover, "The Measurement of Industrial Localization," *The Review of Economic Statistics,* Vol. 18 (Nov. 1936), pp. 162-71.

Table 150. Rank correlations with population of manufacturing employment in selected 2-digit groups, 1954, based upon state data

S.I.C. code	Industry	Coefficient
	(Total manufacturing	.936)
27	Printing and publishing	.931
25	Furniture and fixtures	.924
20	Food and kindred products	.914
32	Stone, clay and glass products	.901
23	Apparel and related products	.898
28	Chemicals and allied products	.893
34	Fabricated metal products	.881
37	Transportation equipment	.839
26	Paper and allied products	.830
36	Electrical machinery	.784
35	Machinery except electrical	.776
39	Miscellaneous manufacturing	.743
33	Primary metal industries	.741
21	Tobacco manufacturing	.722
30	Rubber products	.709
29	Petroleum and coal products	.691
38	Instruments and related products	.687
31	Leather and leather products	.658
22	Textile miscellaneous products	.627
24	Lumber products	.576

Source: Appendix Tables H and K.

effect upon manufacturing than is apparent from the more aggregated phenomena.

This broad sketch of the role of manufacturing in regional growth is, of course, drawn at a very aggregated level. No other aggregate disguises such a diversity of individual functions. There are literally hundreds of industries and thousands of products included in the manufacturing group. It is necessary, therefore, to go beneath these aggregates and examine something of the internal structure of the manufacturing sector and of the changes that have occurred within the various components of manufacturing during the period under review. In the chapters that follow, we shall attempt such an examination, centering it in large part on the differential and proportionality shifts in manufacturing employment. The key data on these shifts are presented in Table 151.

Table 151. 1-digit total, differential, and proportionality net shifts in manufacturing employment and the 2-digit components of the 1-digit differential effect for each state, 1939-1954

State		1-Digit total manufacturing shift	1-Digit differential mfg. shift	1-Digit proportionality mfg. shift	Components of 1-digit differential manufacturing shift							
					20 Food	21 Tobacco	22 Textiles	23 Apparel	24 Lumber	25 Furniture	26 Paper	27 Printing
New England												
Maine	ABS shift	— 26,231	— 7,135	— 19,096	— 803	(Est.) 21	— 1,846	1,112	1,641	26	— 3,872	371
	% shift*		27.2	72.8	4.2	(Est.) 0.1	9.7	5.8	8.6	0.1	20.4	2.0
New Hampshire	ABS shift	— 21,853	729	— 22,582	— 126	(Est.) 62	— 1,140	343	640	217	— 1,717	314
	% shift*		3.1	96.9	0.9	(Est.) 0.5	8.6	2.6	4.8	1.6	12.9	2.4
Vermont†	ABS shift	— 2,552	— 907	— 1,645	— 375		— 1,938	— 1,192	193	714	508	.9
Massachusetts	ABS shift	— 189,872	— 129,451	— 60,421	— 8,165	73	— 44,446	1,340	1,114	1,233	— 8,899	5,011
	% shift*		68.2	31.8	6.0		32.7	1.0	0.8	0.9	6.5	3.7
Rhode Island	ABS shift	— 64,307	— 40,193	— 24,114	— 288	18	— 19,917	310	94	4	— 440	274
	% shift*		62.5	37.5	0.6		43.0	0.7	0.2		0.9	0.6
Connecticut	ABS shift	— 42,360	— 77,110	— 34,750	— 320	188	— 8,986	— 11,784	104	273	— 706	128
	% shift*		68.9	31.1	0.2	0.1	6.6	8.7	0.1	0.2	0.5	0.1
Middle Atlantic												
New York	ABS shift	— 34,206	— 53,892	19,686	— 13,015	(Est.) 771	— 10,047	— 23,628	1,930	315	— 11,865	5,933
	% shift*		73.2	26.8	8.9	(Est.) 0.5	6.9	16.1	1.3	0.2	8.1	4.0
New Jersey	ABS shift	— 78,747	— 113,850	— 35,103	325	4,670	— 9,647	— 20,534	37	668	— 1,019	610
	% shift*		76.4	23.6	0.2	3.6	7.6	16.1		0.5	0.8	0.5
Pennsylvania	ABS shift	— 214,996	— 149,631	— 65,365	— 9,089	1,399	— 33,417	— 13,573	1,828	901	— 4,080	3,869
	% shift*		69.6	30.4	4.7	0.7	17.4	7.0	1.0	0.5	2.1	2.0
Delaware†	ABS shift	— 426	— 105	— 321	1,170	(Est.) 65	157	140	346	(Est.) 3	554	238

Table 151—continued

State		1-Digit total manufacturing shift	1-Digit differential mfg. shift	1-Digit proportional mfg. shift	Components of 1-digit differential manufacturing shift—(continued)							
					20 Food	21 Tobacco	22 Textiles	23 Apparel	24 Lumber	25 Furniture	26 Paper	27 Printing
Maryland (D. C. omitted)	ABS shift	— 27,399	— 32,562	5,163	— 1,268	(Est.) 15	— 1,614	— 12,469	643	529	626	909
	% shift*		86.3	13.7	2.6	—	3.3	25.2	1.3	1.1	1.3	1.8
Great Lakes												
Ohio	ABS shift	42,631	— 52,005	94,636	— 7,067	(Est.) 1,559	— 2,229	— 14,184	741	11	— 2,038	482
	% shift*		35.5	64.5	4.9	(Est.) 1.1	1.5	9.8	0.5	—	1.4	0.3
Indiana	ABS shift	21,774	— 23,171	44,945	— 4,301	202	— 5,500	— 10,843	965	3,082	1,531	
	% shift*		34.0	66.0		1.1	10.7	21.0	1.9	6.0	3.0	
Illinois	ABS shift	— 32,697	— 122,773	90,076	— 1,170	166	— 2,115	— 28,788	— 2,267	— 8,368	— 2,582	9,147
	% shift*		57.7	42.3	8.4	0.4		21.0	1.6	6.1	1.9	6.7
Michigan	ABS shift	— 14,929	— 260,021	245,092	— 13,647	166	— 1,577	— 1,994	— 1,399	— 4,261	— 6,268	160
	% shift*		51.5	48.5	10.0	0.1	1.2	0.5	0.4	1.1	1.6	—
Wisconsin	ABS shift	17,531	— 6,862	24,393	8,092	(Est.) 637	— 1,986	— 174	1,277	1,641	701	1,638
	% shift*		22.0	78.0	12.3	(Est.) 1.0	8.0	0.3	1.9	2.5	1.1	2.5
Southeast												
Virginia	ABS shift	— 6,652	13,807	— 20,459	6,335	1,423	8,997	4,471	1,643	472	1,086	798
	% shift*		40.3	59.7	17.1	3.8	24.3	12.1	4.4	1.3	2.9	2.2
West Virginia	ABS shift	— 20,588	— 16,142	— 4,446	186	351	887	1,094	921	477	(Est.) 209	115
	% shift*		78.4	21.6	0.7	1.4	8.4	4.3	3.6		(Est.) 0.8	—
North Carolina	ABS shift	— 46,541	89,531	— 136,072	6,109	1,839	51,171	10,648	3,442	1,975	2,601	1,392
	% shift*		39.7	60.3	6.4	1.9	53.2	11.1	3.6	2.0	2.7	1.4
South Carolina	ABS shift	— 10,185	61,601	— 71,786	694	(Est.) 1,049	39,004	14,512	1,744	382	1,280	325
	% shift*		46.2	53.8	1.0	(Est.) 1.6	59.1	22.0	2.6	—	1.9	0.5
Georgia	ABS shift	13,093	71,184	— 58,091	7,824	(Est.) 324	27,177	9,402	7,331	1,428	6,095	1,156
	% shift*		55.1	44.9	9.3	(Est.) 0.4	32.4	11.2	8.7	1.7	7.3	1.4

State	Stat	Total	1	2	3	4	5	6	7	8	9	10
Florida	ABS shift	16,288	— 25,431	— 9,143	7,253	(Est.) 458	169	4,205	— 10,007	2,553	5,663	1,847
	% shift*		73.6	26.4	16.0	(Est.) 1.0	0.4	9.2	22.0	5.6	12.5	4.1
Kentucky	ABS shift	20,212	— 24,929	— 4,717	5,411	(Est.) 3,333	316	6,126	360	1,713	191	764
	% shift*		84.1	15.9	14.4	(Est.) 8.9	0.8	16.3	1.0	4.6	0.5	2.1
Tennessee	ABS shift	6,409	— 33,921	— 27,512	2,377	(Est.) 108	1,518	5,582	855	1,808	2,516	778
	% shift*		55.2	44.8	6.3	(Est.) 0.3	4.0	14.7	2.2	4.8	6.6	2.0
Alabama	ABS shift	5,081	— 39,415	— 34,334	3,445	(Est.) 685	9,324	12,175	1,806	1,062	2,461	1,025
	% shift*		53.4	46.6	7.0	(Est.) 1.4	18.8	24.6	3.6	2.1	5.0	2.1
Mississippi	ABS shift	7,118	— 15,646	— 8,533	1,244		621	8,547	7,356	2,515	2,954	320
	% shift*		64.7	35.3	3.7		1.8	25.2	21.7	7.4	8.7	0.9
Arkansas†	ABS shift	10,956	— 17,852	— 6,896	4,066		d	2,791	4,297	747	1,000	371
Plains												
Minnesota	ABS shift	27,498	— 16,043	— 11,455	929	(Est.) 30	597	938	604	481	3,323	77
	% shift*		58.3	41.7	3.7	(Est.) 0.1	2.4	3.8	2.4	1.9	13.3	0.3
Iowa	ABS shift	20,125	— 16,393	— 3,732	1,416	(Est.) 14	457	613	660	18	613	231
	% shift*		81.5	18.5	6.4	(Est.) 0.1	2.1	2.8	3.0	0.1	2.8	1.0
Missouri	ABS shift	6,518	— 12,123	— 5,605	2,385	(Est.) 756	721	7,362	723	563	757	47
	% shift*		62.7	37.3	4.7	(Est.) 1.5	1.4	14.6	(Est.) 1.4	1.1	1.5	—
North Dakota†	ABS shift	— 215	215		490		d	d	(Est.) 157	d	d	104
South Dakota†	ABS shift	— 176	176	790	212		212	(Est.) 31	45	(Est.) 23	d	106
Nebraska	ABS shift	14,249	d	d	17,117	2,868	5,177	692	418	137	d	64
	% shift*		d	d	85.6	14.4	29.9	4.0	2.4	0.8	d	0.4
Kansas	ABS shift	49,168	49,168	(Est.) 293	48,749	419	4,561	1,314	302	111	267	1,461
	% shift*		d	(Est.) 0.5	99.1	0.9	7.4	2.1	0.5	0.2	0.4	2.4
Southwest												
Louisiana	ABS shift	2,739	— 9,601	— 6,862	5,072	(Est.) 286	d	544	8,917	877	3,051	161

Table 151—continued

| State | Measure | 1-Digit total manufacturing shift | 1-Digit differential mfg. shift | 1-Digit proportional mfg. shift | Components of 1-digit differential manufacturing shift—(continued) | | | | | | | |
					20 Food	21 Tobacco	22 Textiles	23 Apparel	24 Lumber	25 Furniture	26 Paper	27 Printing
Oklahoma	% shift*	—	58.3	41.7	12.4	(Est.) 0.7	d	1.3	21.8	2.1	7.4	0.4
	ABS shift	16,771	16,021	750	—1,422	—	d	1,865	—1,430	671	101	204
	% shift*	—	95.5	4.5	6.0		d	7.8	6.0	2.8	0.4	0.8
Texas	ABS shift	115,683	122,110	6,427	8,431	(Est.) 101	1,804	11,499	6,876	4,203	3,884	3,836
New Mexico†	% shift*	—	95.0	5.0	6.2	(Est.) 0.1	1.3	8.5	5.1	3.1	2.8	2.8
	ABS shift	4,279	3,992	287	594			d	67	60		205
Arizona†	ABS shift	10,910	6,295	4,615	732			708	677	188	d	708
Mountain												
Montana	ABS shift	730	1,337	607	—439			d	1,911	(Est.) 109	(Est.) 36	7
	% shift*	—	68.8	31.2	15.0				65.3	(Est.) 3.7	(Est.) 1.2	0.2
Idaho†	ABS shift	4,652	5,606	954	1,424			d	3,834	(Est.) 25	d	107
Wyoming†	ABS shift	—723	431	1,154	375		(Est.) 293	(Est.) 11	—217	d	(Est.) 36	46
Colorado†	ABS shift	10,881	10,755	126	373	(Est.) 120	(Est.) 293	252	958	181	312	970
Utah	ABS shift	4,383	5,662	1,279	—1,299	(Est.) 120	151	545	299	89	d	76
	% shift*	—	81.6	18.4	14.8	(Est.) 1.4	1.7	6.2	3.4	1.0	d	0.9
Far West												
Washington	ABS shift	18,410	19,102	692	101		135	332	—11,296	49	564	119
	% shift*	—	96.5	3.5	0.2		0.3	0.8	26.7	0.1	1.3	0.3

(continued from preceding page)

State											
Oregon ABS shift	23,371	22,957	414	−38	120 (Est.)	590	137	17,580	−2,190	197	250
% shift*	98.2	98.2	1.8	0.1	0.4	2.1	0.5	62.8	7.8	0.7	0.9
California ABS shift	341,915	319,295	22,620	1,639	392 (Est.)	485	17,296	14,848	3,805	7,849	6,186
% shift*	93.4	93.4	6.6	0.5	0.1	0.2	5.4	4.6	1.2 (Est.)	2.4	1.9
Nevada† ABS shift	2,802	1,467	1,335	68			d	363	22 (Est.)		230

Components of 1-digit differential manufacturing shift—(continued)

State	28 Chemicals	29 Petroleum & coal prod.	30 Rubber	31 Leather	32 Stone, clay & glass	33 Primary metals	34 Fabricated metals	35 Machinery	36 Electrical machinery	37 Transportation equipment	38 Instruments	39 Miscellaneous
New England												
Maine ABS	−64	d (Est.)	62 (Est.)	1,619	−400	30	365	−3,432	d	−3,041	265 (Est.)	−11 (Est.)
%	0.3	d	0.3	8.5	2.1	0.2	1.9	18.1	d	16.0	1.4 (Est.)	—
New Hampshire ABS	−143	15 (Est.)	422	−1,369	41	191	85	165	4,683	188 (Est.)	488	978
%	1.1	0.1 (Est.)	3.2	10.3	0.3	1.4	0.6	1.2	35.1	1.4 (Est.)	3.7	7.3
Vermont† ABS	16	d	d	−97	226	41	106	100	d	d	d	578
Massachusetts ABS	−3,928	−1,350	−3,529	−5,943	280	98	−6,817	−15,797	1,473	−6,277	−7,336	−12,870
%	2.9	1.0	2.6	4.4	0.2	0.1	5.0	11.6	1.1	4.6	5.4	9.5
Rhode Island ABS	−272	d	−2,011	210	781	1,647	−2,273	−5,807	−4,033	129	882	6,957
%	0.6	d	4.3	0.4	1.7	3.6	4.9	12.5	8.7	0.3 (Est.)	1.9	15.0 (Est.)
Connecticut ABS	−806	27	−2,502	−366	153	−9,984	−20,297	−17,998	−15,260	−27,885	−8,748	−9,097
%	0.6		1.8	0.3	0.1	7.3	15.0	13.2	11.3	20.6	6.4	6.7

Table 151—continued

State		28 Chemicals	29 Petroleum & coal prod.	30 Rubber	31 Leather	32 Stone, clay & glass	33 Primary metals	34 Fabricated metals	35 Machinery	36 Electrical machinery	37 Transportation equipment	38 Instruments	39 Miscellaneous
Middle Atlantic													
New York	ABS	− 12,092	− 1,938	− 2,586	− 2,621	− 1,830	− 5,032	− 2,482	− 3,288	− 5,626	− 27,416	− 11,454	− 2,479
	%	8.3	1.3	1.8	1.8	1.2	3.4	1.7	2.2	3.8	18.7	7.8	1.7
New Jersey	ABS	− 11,499	− 1,466	− 5,604	71	− 1,901	− 7,615	184	− 1,566	− 22,413	− 20,324	− 4,798	− 12,711
	%	9.0	1.1	4.4		1.5	6.0	0.1	1.2	17.6	15.9	3.8	10.8
Pennsylvania	ABS	− 10,705	− 2,522	− 3,041	630	− 10,103	− 48,368	− 4,379	− 1,822	− 10,454	− 23,653	− 4,185	− 4,357
	%	5.6	1.3	1.6	0.3	5.2	25.1	2.3	0.9	5.4	12.3	2.2	2.3
Delaware†	ABS	490	8	d	859	188	6	107	223	d	544 (Est.)	d	1,043 (Est.)
Maryland	ABS	− 12,989	272	2,126	952	912	943	3,826	790	2,385	5,619	437	616
	%	26.3	0.6	4.3	1.9	1.8	1.9	6.7	1.6	4.8	11.4	0.9	1.2
Great Lakes													
Ohio	ABS	− 536	608	5,259	6,773	7,083	4,509	11,789	19,233	17,595	41,083	566	836
	%	0.4	0.4	3.6	4.7	4.9	3.1	8.1	13.3	12.2	28.5	0.4	0.6
Indiana	ABS	5,543	1,498	1,128	509	898	69	1,809	5,116	1,014	3,854	1,236	2,397
	%	10.8	2.9	2.2	1.0	1.7	0.1	3.5	9.9	2.0	7.5	2.4	4.6
Illinois	ABS	2,591	33	948	5,026	798	2,911	2,966	23,005	7,442	3,565	986	19,934
	%	1.9		0.7	3.7	0.6	2.1	2.2	16.8	5.4	2.6	0.1	14.6
Michigan	ABS	2,532	197	2,798	568	790	15,774	5,677	32,621	389	− 302,992	5,163	2,694
	%	0.6		0.7	0.1	0.2	4.0	1.4	8.4	0.1	77.6	1.3	0.7
Wisconsin	ABS	1,842	230	1,345	1,286	d	5,705	3,320	9,136	7,412	14,562	4,100	644
	%	2.8	0.3	2.0	2.0	d	8.7	5.0	13.9	11.3	22.2	6.2	1.0
Southeast													
Virginia	ABS	− 2,545	82 (Est.)	47	102	119	3	1,352	200	d	− 7,124	d	164
	%	6.9	0.2 (Est.)	0.1	0.3	0.3		3.6	0.5	d	19.3	d	0.4

West Virginia	ABS	— 106	265	d	— 663	— 6,705	— 5,025	— 4,572	324	1,811	— 489	d	— 1,376
	%	0.4	1.0	d	2.6	26.2	19.6	17.9	1.3	7.1	1.9	d	5.4
North Carolina	ABS	— 3,177	d	d	157	731	9	2,657	2,029	7,120	— 118	600	(Est.) 346
	%	3.3	d	d	0.2	0.8		2.8	2.1	7.4	0.1	0.6	0.4
South Carolina	ABS	3,306	— 20	d	(Est.) 45	651	238	(Est.) 332	948	d	— 65	d	(Est.) 1,428
	%	5.0		d	(Est.) 0.1	1.0	0.4	0.5	1.4	d	0.1	d	2.2
Georgia	ABS	— 5,886	— 55	d	— 51	997	— 384	798	1,094	1,148	12,793		(Est.) — 7
	%	7.0	0.1	d	0.1	1.2	0.4	1.0	1.3	1.4	15.2		
Florida	ABS	2,522	d	d	d	2,133	510	5,003	1,391	654	752	d	325
	%	5.5	d	d	d	4.7	1.1	11.0	3.1	1.4	1.6	d	0.7
Kentucky	ABS	4,509	— 231	d	211	— 450	— 2,675	1,644	5,315	1,241	— 1,260	d	(Est.) 1,837
	%	12.0	0.6	d	0.6	1.2	7.1	4.4	14.1	3.3	3.4	d	(Est.) 4.9
Tennessee	ABS	3,277	d	1,218	4,813	— 258	623	— 1,705	2,438	2,923	1,521	d	3,529
	%	8.6	d	3.2	12.7	0.7	1.6	4.5	6.4	**7.7**	**4.0**	**d**	**9.3**
Alabama	ABS	— 1,831	188	2,457	d	1,490	— 1,414	675	2,411	1,740	4,183	d	1,145
	%	3.7	0.4	5.0	d	3.0	2.8	1.4	4.9	3.5	8.4	d	2.3
Mississippi	ABS	— 1,796	190	d	d	689	d	1,427	879	d	4,953	(Est.) 225	234
	%	5.3	0.6	d	d	2.0	d	4.2	2.6	d	14.6	(Est.) 0.7	0.7
Arkansas†	ABS	1,015	91	d	(Est.) 3,463	657	1,772	1,049	212	1,468	287	(Est.) 1,924	(Est.) 1,236
Plains													
Minnesota	ABS	1,009	195	129	185	— 963	1,067	1,041	1,197	2,578	2,152	(Est.) — 1,460	6,008
	%	4.0	0.8	0.5	0.7	3.8	4.3	4.2	4.8	10.3	8.6	(Est.) 5.8	24.1
Iowa	ABS	2,080	49	2,357	— 9	— 188	2,752	— 850	1,138	4,515	2,804	918	329
	%	9.4	0.2	10.7		0.8	12.5	3.9	5.2	20.5	12.7	4.2	1.5
Missouri	ABS	137	550	— 1,240	2,642	— 436	289	171	4,750	— 6,288	13,036	154	7,590
	%	0.3	1.1	2.4	5.2	0.9	0.6	0.3	9.4	12.4	25.8	0.3	15.0
North Dakota†	ABS	d	d	(Est.) 10		138	d	— 21	d	d	d		102
				(Est.)							(Est.)		

Table 151—continued

State		Components of 1-digit differential manufacturing shift—(continued)											
		28	29	30	31	32	33	34	35	36	37	38	39
		Chemicals	Petroleum & coal prod.	Rubber	Leather	Stone, clay & glass	Primary metals	Fabricated metals	Machinery	Electrical machinery	Transportation equipment	Instruments	Miscellaneous
South Dakota†	ABS	d	d	10		—	d	125	d	d	100	d	3
Nebraska	ABS	464	(Est.) 99	d	(Est.) 272	99	325	354	991	1,660	948	2,145	(Est.) 3,470
	%	2.7	(Est.) 0.6	d	(Est.) 1.6	0.6	1.9	2.0	5.7	9.6	5.5	12.4	20.0
Kansas	ABS	3,471	−1,349	d	d	2,173	309	2,067	3,819	(Est.) 679	38,333	d	900
	%	5.6	2.2	d	d	3.5	0.5	3.4	6.2	(Est.) 1.1	62.4	d	1.5
Southwest													
Louisiana	ABS	5,783	4,261	(Est.) 10		1,515	2,872	1,072	155	d	4,920	d	(Est.) 1,497
	%	−14.1	10.4	10		3.7	7.0	2.6	0.4	d	12.0	d	(Est.) 3.6
Oklahoma	ABS	−614	−464	d	d	1,503	1,017	1,980	3,767	d	8,410	342	91
	%	2.6	1.9	d	d	6.3	4.2	8.3	15.8	d	35.2	1.4	0.4
Texas	ABS	13,303	2,866	d	2,481	3,629	14,999	7,157	6,255	2,336	35,163	1,397	5,642
	%	9.8	2.1	d	1.8	2.7	11.0	5.3	4.6	1.7	25.9	1.0	4.2
New Mexico†	ABS	2,535	d		d	51	d	d	d	(Est.) 46	d	d	434
Arizona†	ABS	422	(Est.) 30	(Est.) 10	d	410	987	d	982	(Est.) 193	d	d	253
Mountain													
Montana	ABS	(Est.) 118	−(Est.) 135			25	(Est.) 10	32	70		26	d	234
	%	−4.0	4.6			0.8	(Est.) 0.3	1.1	2.4		0.9	d	0.2
Idaho†	ABS	d	d		(Est.) 20	91	(Est.) 3	252	18	(Est.) 46	d	d	d
		(Est.)											(Est.)

Wyoming†	ABS	26	325	d	—	19			183	d	d	214	d
Colorado†	ABS	1,044	91	d	(Est.) 1,436	420	568	635	932	629	349	332	1,100
Utah	ABS	348	845	(Est.) 290	396	2,912	937	405	d	d	d	d	90
	%	4.0	9.6	(Est.) 3.3	4.5	33.1	10.6	4.6	d	d	d	d	1.0
Far West													
Washington	ABS	4,792	40	d	220	333	7,107	558	70	136	16,090	235	55
	%	11.3	0.1	d	0.5	0.8	16.8	1.3	0.2	0.3	38.1	0.6	0.1
Oregon	ABS	485	234	—	27	233	1,876	1,885	233	574	987	d	345
	%	1.7	0.8	—	0.1	0.8	6.7	6.7	0.8	2.0	3.5	d	1.2
California	ABS	2,918	114	2,818	10,267	14,523	22,811	23,610	26,213	133,287	d	6,589	24,429
	%	0.9	0.8	0.9	3.2	4.5	7.0	7.4	8.2	41.6	d	2.0	7.6
Nevada†	ABS	d		d	524	d	d	d	(Est.) 46	d	d	(Est.) 214	d

*The % figures are not based upon the algebraic total but the total without regard to sign. This avoids astronomical %s where the shifts tend to cancel and provides a uniform basis for comparison.

†The disclosure problem for these states is too severe to establish an accurate total as a base for the %s. The recorded dimensions of the differential and proportionality shifts may also be suspect. In the case of Arizona, Delaware and North Dakota the direction of the differential and proportionality shift may be in error.

d—Disclosure problem.

SOURCE: Appendix Tables P and R.

24 / Regional influence of
manufacturing activity:

(2) THE MAJOR COMPONENTS

We turn now to an examination of the role that the various major components of manufacturing activity have played in the differential shifts across state lines that we have observed in total manufacturing employment. Table 152 shows the absolute employment changes between 1939 and 1954 within each of these components and the relative importance of the total net shifts. In no case are the net shifts insignificant in volume, and in some industries (as in textile mill products, leather, lumber, tobacco, and transportation equipment) the departures of the various states from the national norm for the industry during 1939-54 have been very wide indeed (Col. 8).

Food and Kindred Products

As measured by employment, the food products sector of manufacturing is exceeded in size only by the transportation equipment and machinery sectors. It accounts for almost 10% of total manufacturing employment.

CONTRIBUTION TO 1-DIGIT PROPORTIONALITY EFFECT

The food products industry significantly influences the 1-digit proportionality effect upon regional shifts in total manufacturing employment (see Figure 73). As Table 147 has shown, this is one of the slow-growth sectors of manufacturing activity. Of the thirty-four states that show downward proportionality shifts in total manufacturing employment for the 1939-54 period, twenty-four are food products specialists.[1] The contribution of this specialization to the proportionality effect was probably greatest during these years in the Mountain and northern Plains states and in Louisiana and Florida; in all of these states the proportion of total employment devoted to food products was more than twice the national average. Only the states in the Manufacturing Belt and a few in the

[1]On this, see Appendix Table K and Table 151.

2-digit manufacturing categories	(1) Mfg. production worker employment 1939	(2) %	(3) 1954	(4) %	(5) Abso-lute chg. 1939-54	(6) % incr. col. 5 as % of col. 1	(7) Total net shift 1939-54	(8) Col. 7 as % of col. 5	(9) Col. 7 as % of col. 1
Total mfg. prod. wkrs.	7,808,205	100	12,372,748	100	4,564,543	58.5	± 836,084	18.3	10.7
Food & kindred prod.	802,133	10.3	1,138,239	9.2	336,106	41.9	± 75,908	22.6	9.5
Tobacco mfg.	87,525	1.1	70,216	0.57	− 17,309	− 19.8	± 11,158	− 64.5	12.7
Textile mill prod.	1,081,710	13.8	947,502	7.7	− 134,208	− 12.4	± 145,782	−108.6	13.5
Apparel & rel. prod.	752,829	9.6	1,069,733	8.6	316,904	42.1	± 133,076	42.0	17.8
Lumber prod. (exc. furn.)	422,947	5.4	518,749	4.2	95,802	22.7	± 63,614	66.4	15.0
Furniture & fixtures	189,382	2.4	286,649	2.3	97,267	51.4	± 25,608	26.3	13.5
Paper & allied prod.	270,239	3.5	435,727	3.5	165,488	61.2	± 47,326	28.6	17.5
Printing & publishing	324,371	4.2	499,666	4.0	175,295	54.0	± 27,204	15.5	8.4
Chemicals & allied prod.	275,669	3.5	501,272	4.1	225,603	81.8	± 67,800	30.1	24.6
Petroleum & coal prod.	107,695	1.4	163,811	1.3	56,116	52.1	± 11,474	20.4	10.7
Rubber prod.	120,740	1.5	196,238	1.6	75,498	62.5	± 20,574	27.3	17.0
Leather & leather prod.	327,189	4.2	321,161	2.6	− 6,028	− 1.8	± 24,257	−402.4	7.4
Stone, clay & glass prod.	267,094	3.4	412,031	3.3	144,937	54.3	± 32,628	22.5	12.2
Primary metal indus.	672,438	8.6	938,511	7.6	266,073	40.0	± 83,571	31.4	12.4
Fabricated metal prod.	451,087	5.8	821,172	6.6	370,085	82.0	± 64,539	17.4	14.3
Machinery (exc. electrical)	536,082	6.9	1,171,323	9.5	635,241	118.5	±102,950	16.2	19.2
Electrical machinery	247,930	3.2	722,443	5.8	474,513	191.4	± 82,180	17.3	33.1
Transportation equipt.	544,553	7.0	1,327,078	10.7	782,525	143.7	±385,698	49.3	70.8
Instruments & rel. prod.	84,867	1.1	195,597	1.6	110,730	130.5	± 32,980	29.8	38.9
Miscellaneous mfg.	241,725	3.1	555,746	4.5	314,021	129.9	± 64,672	20.6	26.8
Disclosure omission			79,884	0.65					

Note: Detailed state data are scanty in several 2-digit categories because they have been withheld for disclosure reasons. Because of this, total upward and total downward net shifts can vary widely. The means are shown in Col. 7 above. The widest differences:

	Upward shift	Downward shift
Rubber & products	13,327	− 27,822
Electrical machinery	382,019	− 389,378
Miscellaneous manufacturing	70,183	− 59,161

SOURCE: Appendix Table K.

Southeast failed to exhibit some degree of specialization in food products.

As a generalization, the distribution of food products specialization looks much like that of agricultural specialization, with the Manufacturing Belt the principal area of below-average levels. There are two exceptions to this general association: (1) In the Southeast, the degree of specialization in food products is much less than would be expected on the basis of the degree of agricultural concentration. This is probably due in part to an historic agricultural specialization in fibers rather than food. (2) In the Pacific Coast states, the degree of specialization in food products tends to exceed the degree of agricultural specialization. This is probably a reflection of agricultural specialization in products that require more extensive manufacturing processing. It may also be a reflection of the importance and the quasi-isolated character of the West Coast market.

The importance of resource inputs for the food products industry is exceeded only by that for petroleum refining. Over 40% of the total inputs come from agriculture; in addition, 17% originate in the food industry itself, and 6% of the industry's output is recycled to agriculture. This suggests the importance of access to agricultural inputs in determining which states are food specialists.

But the market must also play an important role in the location of food product activities. Three-fourths of the total output goes directly to terminal market sectors, and the industry ranks near the top of all manufacturing industries in the correlation with population.[2] The food industry thus appears as a direct intermediary between the consuming and resource sectors of the economy. This characteristic not only adds to our understanding of the proportionality effect, but serves notice that the differential shifts that we observe most probably will be explained in terms of changes in regional access to agricultural inputs or to final markets.

CONTRIBUTION TO THE 1-DIGIT DIFFERENTIAL EFFECT

Figure 75 shows the net shifts in food products employment between 1939 and 1954. The food sector contributed to the upward shifts in total manufacturing employment in the Southeast, the Southwest, and some Plains states. The greatest upward shift was in the Southeast. These states accounted for almost two-thirds of the total net upward shift during these years. Texas, Wisconsin, and Nebraska also had large upward shifts. The relative net downward shift occurred principally in the states in the Manufacturing Belt. There is a rough consistency here with the differential shifts in total manufacturing employment shown in Figure 74. However, there were quite a number of states in which the shift in food products ran against the trend for manufacturing as a whole.

In seventeen states food products accounted for more than 10% of the total differential shift in manufacturing employment.[3] It is interesting to note that

[2]This high-rank correlation, however, may overstate the importance of the market. It could be consistent with lower associations with population for most of the components of the 2-digit food products sectors.

[3]New Mexico, Arizona, Utah, Idaho, Wyoming, Montana, North Dakota, South Dakota, Nebraska, Wisconsin, Illinois, Arkansas, Louisiana, Florida, Kentucky, Virginia, and Delaware.

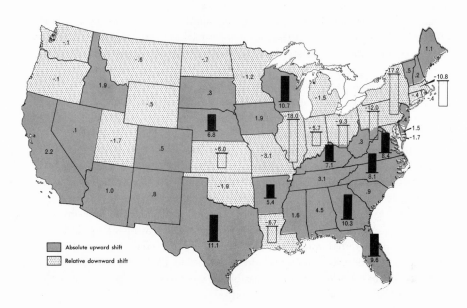

Figure 75. Net Shift in Food and Kindred Products Employment, 1939-54.

State figures represent % of total net shift. Total net shift as % of incremental change: 22.6. Total net shift as % of 1939 food and kindred products employment: 9.5. Source: Appendix Table K.

in Texas and most of the Deep South, where the major portion of the upward differential shifts in food products employment took place, these shifts turned out not to be a major element in the total manufacturing shift.

To understand these differential shifts, we must move to a less aggregated view and consider both the proportionality and the differential effects of specific types of specialization within the over-all food products sector of manufacturing.

The rapid-growth industries of the food products sector are meat products, grain mill products, beverages, and miscellaneous food products. Only the Plains states appeared to receive a significant contribution to an upward shift from specialization in these products. The Southeast in general did not—except for Georgia, Arkansas, and Tennessee. Specialization in the slow growth industries (bakery products, confectionery, sugar, canning and preserving) appears to have been in part responsible for the downward shifts in the Manufacturing Belt states—particularly the Middle Atlantic states and Illinois and Missouri. However, it is the differential effect that has been most significant in this instance.

Further explanation of the differential effect must lie with the differential shifts of specific food-producing sectors. Let us examine a few of these sectors.

Meat Products: Meat-packing, the largest of the food products industries, gets some 76% of its inputs from agriculture and distributes 90% of its outputs to terminal markets. Both supply and market forces, therefore, exert a strong influence upon its location. In general the supply sources have been dominant. The major livestock area and the major meat-packing area coincide in certain of the Plains and Great Lakes states, while the major markets are further east.

There are several reasons why the meat-packing operation tends to locate near supply areas. The cost of shipping meat animals alive to stockyards and providing their care en route establishes an economic limit on the distance they can be shipped. The heavy weight-loss in processing—as much as 50%—has also been a major locational factor.[4]

But although these input factors are very important, meat-packing is by no means *coincident* with the animal supply. The supply sources are not pointform but areally distributed, and packing centers tend to draw from sizeable areas. Thus, while there may be considerable coincidence between processing and animal-raising in broad regions, there may be considerable concentration of packing at the state and local level to minimize costs of transfer to markets.

Several institutional and technological factors in effect during our period have favored a certain amount of decentralization of meat-packing. Improved refrigeration has made markets accessible to more remote supply areas. During the years 1947—1956, the cost of shipping livestock by rail went up 84% —an increase not matched by the rates on finished products. These factors have had the effect of increasing the relative access to markets of more remote animal supply areas. The greater use of trucks has also favored smaller decentralized markets as compared to rail shipment to larger centralized markets. Added to this is the influence of unionization and high labor costs in the large meat-packing cities. In our period, therefore, additions to capacity were being built closer to the cow and pig. But, at the same time, cattle-raising has expanded where there were expanding markets to be tapped. Thus the market influence has been powerful—although in a roundabout fashion.

Meat products obviously go a long way toward explaining the relative rise of food products employment in the Southeast. Some 75% of the net upward shift in meat products employment was in these states. Probably the most important direct explanation for this shift is the fact that the region has significantly increased its access to inputs. It had marked upward shifts in general livestock between 1939 and 1954 (see Figure 63) and accounted for around two-thirds of the net upward shift in poultry over these years (Figure 65). But this, in turn, was attributable at least in part to the growth of the Southeastern market for meat products.[5]

Texas showed a significant upward shift in meat-packing operations in the face of a sizeable net relative downward shift in livestock production. The ex-

[4]This has had an important effect upon the historical movement of meat packing. In response to the westward movement of agriculture, Cincinnati became the country's leading packing center in 1800. By 1850 Chicago became paramount. By 1870 Chicago had to share its dominance with St. Paul, Sioux City, St. Louis and Kansas City.

[5]The eating habits and low incomes prevalent in the Southeast had left much room for an expansion of meat products in the Southeast's food basket. We have not documented this, but the rising level of incomes plus the influence of military service upon diet suggests an important regional influence.

planation appears to lie in two factors: (1) The regional market expanded greatly relative to the national market (with substantial increases in both population and income); and (2) the technological and institutional changes favoring decentralization and location close to supply sources had a favorable effect here. Texas has always been a sizeable livestock producer but heretofore had relied on the major processing centers for its pack; thus processing could increase even though livestock production declined in relative terms.

The meat-producing area of the Plains and Great Lakes had an opposite experience. This area as a whole experienced a net relative downward shift in meat packing at the same time that it showed two-thirds of the net upward shift in livestock employment (Figure 63). While there had been a moderate relative decline in the regional market, this does not appear to be the key factor. This is the area that has long dominated meat-packing in this country. In the face of the institutional and technological factors favoring decentralization of the industry, it is losing its competitive position. The fringe states of the area (Indiana, Wisconsin, and Nebraska) seem to benefit from this decentralization, but the major producing states lose heavily in their *relative* position. In this connection it is interesting to note that Chicago, in its heyday, handled 20% of the nation's hogs and 25% of the nation's cattle. Today it is down to 5% and 7% respectively.

California has had a significant net upward shift in meat packing prompted mainly by expanding markets and by expanding livestock sources which are, in turn, largely a response to the growing markets.

Dairy Products: Unfortunately the definitions used as a basis for collecting data in the dairy industry have been changed twice by the census in the period here under review. As a consequence it is impossible to present an over-all picture for the industry based upon comparable data. But a good deal can be inferred about probable shifts from the available information. The regional growth of dairy-processing units and their location have historically followed the regional trend in milk production.[6] The reasons for this are fairly obvious. It takes about 21 pounds of milk to produce one pound of butter, 10 pounds for one pound of cheese, and 2.2 pounds for one pound of concentrate. In addition, the by-products (skim milk and whey) can be returned to the farm and used in livestock feeding. Thus, we would expect that dairy manufacturing would expand in the Southeast since this region has claimed almost 40% of the net upward shift of farm dairy products. Wisconsin and California are also likely areas of expansion because their relative access to supplies has increased appreciably.

Canning, Preserving, and Freezing: Because the processing of fruits and vegetables involves considerable loss in weight and bulk and because the fresh commodity is highly perishable, the canning, preserving, and freezing industries are heavily oriented to their agricultural inputs. The strong upward shift shown by Florida between 1939 and 1954—a relative gain of 24%—is therefore not hard to explain. Florida also had 58% of the net upward shift in agricultural

---

[6]See Raymond P. Christensen, *The Effect of Agriculture on the Location of Industry*, National Resources Planning Board, June, 1942, pp. 27-376.

fruit products and 11% of the net upward shift in vegetables over these years (see Figures 66 and 67). California, in contrast, experienced a net downward shift in canning and freezing. It had 58% of the net upward shift in vegetables, however, and 12% of the net upward shift in fruits and nuts.

There are two possible explanations for this development. (1) Florida's big increase was in fruits and California's in vegetables. The fruit expansion in Florida was a response to national markets, while the vegetable expansion in California was stimulated more by an expansion in the regional market; a large portion of production for local markets can be marketed fresh. (2) California early built a large canning industry. In recent years, freezing techniques have to a degree been substituted for canning. Since freezing reduces the weight-loss and requires expensive refrigeration, this tends to favor sources closer to the market when contrasted with canning. This could also explain the expansions in the Southeast and the Middle Atlantic states in the face of relative declines in agricultural output. A larger portion of the output may now be going to frozen pack, thus accounting for net upward shifts.[7]

Grain Mill Products: In the food products industries so far discussed, the inputs come very largely from agriculture and the outputs go very largely to terminal markets. The agricultural inputs seem to exert the greater locational influence, and we would say that these activities are oriented primarily to resource inputs.

Grain mill products show a slight departure from this locational pattern. Though the major portion of its inputs also come from agriculture, the share of its output going to terminal markets is much smaller (34%). A large part of the total output (43%) is returned to agriculture, mostly in the form of feed preparations for livestock.

In effect this industry is made up of two segments with basically different characteristics. The first is flour-milling. Its characteristics are almost identical with those of meat-packing. The big wheat areas are in the West, the big market areas in the East. The mills tend to locate near inputs as it takes 196 pounds of wheat to make 70 pounds of flour. At the same time, market influence is strong and the industry tends to locate on the eastern edge of supply areas.

The second segment of the industry is engaged in feed preparation. Its input sources are agriculture and the by-products of other grain-milling activities. Its output goes mainly to that portion of agriculture engaged in livestock production. This segment of the industry is oriented both to resource inputs and resource markets. Since the process does not involve significant weight losses, the resource markets exert more influence upon location in feed preparation than in flour-milling.

The major upward shifts in grain mill products have been in the Southeast, the Southwest, and the Plains and Great Lakes states. These shifts closely parallel the upward shifts for food products as a whole shown in Figure 75. They seem to be best explained in terms of changing regional access to markets

[7]This is not a satisfactory account, of course. These are generalizations based upon logic and superficial observation. A more careful study is required to provide a more complete answer.

for grain feeds.[8] The Southeast has had strong net upward shifts in dairying and livestock products, including two-thirds of the upward shift for poultry, which makes the most intensive use of processed feeds of all agriculture. The Plains and Great Lakes states claimed over half of the net upward shift in livestock products (excluding poultry and dairying). California likewise has had a big increase in these markets for processed feeds. The factors responsible for the shifts in feed markets have already been discussed in an earlier chapter.[9]

Beverages, Bakery, and Confectionery Products: In their pattern of spatial orientation, these industries differ markedly from the food products industries so far discussed. They are generally not first-stage but second-stage resource users. Instead of drawing their inputs from an areally distributed supply source, they assemble them from a limited number of pointform sources. At the same time, their output goes to areally distributed markets. This situation creates a tendency to market orientation. A second attribute (usually associated with second-stage resource users) is that the resource inputs have already undergone decreases in weight and volume and increases in value. This significantly reduces the pull to supply sources. In addition, the final products are frequently perishable and are bulky relative to their value; these characteristics increase the tendency for the industry to be strongly market-oriented.

The employment shifts in this segment of the food products sector of manufacturing seem to be highly associated with the shifts in population as a representation of final markets.[10]

Tobacco Manufacturing:[11] The shift picture for tobacco manufacturing employment is in general one of widespread retrenchment, with most of the upward shifts being relative in the face of a general decline in employment.[12] The major cigarette manufacturing states—North Carolina, Virginia, Kentucky, and Tennessee—strengthened their relative positions with net upward shifts. This is primarily a result of a 2-digit proportionality effect. During the 1939-54 period there was a marked shift in the composition of the demand for tobacco products

[8]A change in relative regional access to resource inputs may also be important in explaining some of these shifts. Further study is required to pin these things down with precision.

[9] Only Texas is difficult to explain on this basis. Rice-cleaning and -polishing is important in Texas and there has been an expansion in corn products. These things, together with some possible expansion in milling, might account for this experience.

[10]There are exceptions to this generalization. The Middle Atlantic region shows some gain apparently due to economies of scale and distribution in national markets for some confectionery products firms. Kentucky makes a strong showing in beverages because of its specialization in hard liquors—a dominance that is buried in history and tradition and scale economies.

Certain problems of comparability make it impossible to compute shifts for bakery products. Disclosure problems also make it impossible for us to analyze the shifts that have taken place in sugar production.

[11]This sector is traditionally classed as a 2-digit industry by the Census. For our purpose, it fits logically as a sub-category. It accounts for only one-half of 1% of total employment. See Appendix Table K for details.

[12]We pointed out previously that the big decline in employment was principally a result of mechanization creating significant increases in labor productivity.

away from cigars to cigarettes. Of the twenty-seven cigar-manufacturing states, only Florida and Pennsylvania show upward shifts—largely attributable to increasing mechanization in an industry where traditional handicraft methods have elsewhere persisted.

Summary: Our review of food-processing developments has been incomplete, to be sure. It does enable us, however, to give a more satisfactory account of the shifts seen in Figure 75.

The large expansion in food production in the Southeast seems to be supported by almost every broad type of food-processing activity. The meat and dairy products segments of employment were perhaps most important, with shifts in response to the greater accessibility of farm livestock products aided by the fact that the Southeast is a deficit supply area for many of these products. This is a reflection of the continuing shift away from an agriculture dominated by cotton and tobacco. In addition, there were important gains in the Southeast— especially in Florida and Virginia—in canning, preserving, and freezing. In the Deep South, grain mill products and confectionery and beverages contributed to an expansion in food products production. Tobacco products made an important contribution to the net gains in the upper South. These developments were the result of a combination of market factors and input factors. Georgia appears to be the leader in this region because of its central position in serving regional markets and assembling regional supplies.

California shows a somewhat smaller net upward shift in food products than might be expected on the basis of its considerable expansion in both markets and resource supplies. The only explanation our data reveal is the relative loss in canning, preserving, and freezing, which seems to grow out of a change in California's competitive position with the advent of frozen foods and concentrates.

Wisconsin's strength in food products stems primarily from meat products, grain mill products, and beverages. In Nebraska, which shows up strongly, the gain is largely explained in terms of a large net upward shift in grain mill products together with a more modest relative increase in meat packing. These states have benefited from the significant increase in the market for prepared feeds in the Plains and Great Lakes states and from the trend toward decentralization in the meat-packing industry.

Other areas of interest to the reader can be examined by way of the additional data presented in the Appendix.

Textile Products

Textile products have also had an important influence on the regional changes in manufacturing activity. In 1954 textiles employment was 8% of total manufacturing employment as compared with 14% in 1939, and the shifts across state lines exceeded in dimension the decline that took place over these years.

CONTRIBUTION TO 1-DIGIT PROPORTIONALITY EFFECT

This sector of manufacturing activity is especially important in explaining the 1-digit proportionality effect upon regional shifts in total manufacturing employment shown in Figure 74. It is one of the principal slow-growth sectors; its decline in employment between 1939 and 1954 (12.4%) was exceeded only by that in tobacco manufacture (see Table 147). Thus the states that specialize in textiles production have been significantly influenced by this effect.

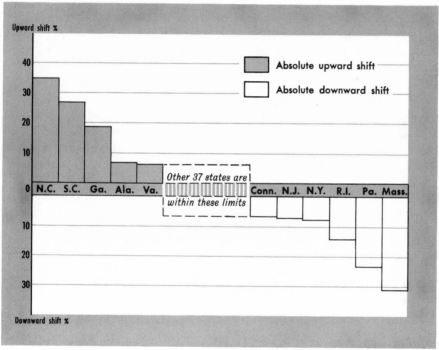

Figure 76. Net Shift in Textile Mill Employment, 1939-54.

Total net shift as % of incremental change: 108.6 Total net shift as % of 1939 textile mill employment: 13.5. Source: Appendix Table K.

Eleven states accounted for almost 90% of total employment in textiles in 1954.[13] The Southeast had roughly two-thirds of this total and the New England and Middle Atlantic states roughly one-third. Three Southeastern states— Georgia, North Carolina, and South Carolina—had 45% of all textiles employment. Some idea of the important role that textiles must play in the total net

[13]Maine, New Hampshire, Massachusetts, Rhode Island, Pennsylvania, Virginia, North Carolina, South Carolina, Georgia, Alabama, and Tennessee. See Appendix Table K for details.

downward proportionality shift in manufacturing employment can be gained from the fact that these eleven states accounted for 87% of this total; Georgia, North Carolina, and South Carolina accounted for 44% of it.

One principal reason why textiles is a slow-growth industry is that some segments of it are characterized by a relatively low income elasticity of demand; another is that the industry's share of exports has declined steadily. Further explanation of the regional distribution of textiles employment will unfold as we discuss the differential effect.

CONTRIBUTION TO 1-DIGIT DIFFERENTIAL EFFECT

Not only did the Southeast dominate the textile industry in 1954; it dominated the shifts in employment between 1939 and 1954. Five Southeastern states— North and South Carolina, Georgia, Alabama, and Virginia—accounted for 93% of the absolute net upward shift in textiles employment during this period. Over 90% of the absolute net downward shift occurred in the New England and Middle Atlantic states. (See Figure 76 and Table 153.)

The shift in textiles employment comprised more than 10% of the total differential shift in manufacturing employment in eleven states over these years.[14] In North and South Carolina it was more than half of the total and in Georgia, Massachusetts, Rhode Island, and Vermont more than one-third.

Table 153. Net shift in textile manufacturing employment, selected regions, 1939–1954

Region	Upward shifts		Downward shifts	
	Absolute	Relative	Absolute	Relative
New England			53.85%	
Middle Atlantic		0.11%	36.54%	
Great Lakes	1.53%		7.70%	
Southeast	93.91%	1.26%	.61%	

SOURCE: Appendix Table K.

In explaining these shifts in textile employment we can observe, as usual, two effects. There is in operation a proportionality effect based upon the 3-digit components of the industry. In general, this proportionality effect has tended to accentuate the relative shift in total textile employment out of the New England and Middle Atlantic states and into the Southeast. The slow-growth sectors of the textile industry are knitting mills, woolen and worsted manufacturing, and hats. The most intensive specialization in these sectors is in the Middle Atlantic and New England regions.

[14]Alabama, Georgia, Indiana, Maine, Massachusetts, North Carolina, Pennsylvania, Rhode Island, South Carolina, Vermont and Virginia. (Employment in New Hampshire, New Jersey, New York and Connecticut was influenced by changes in textiles, though overshadowed in the total by other sectors.)

More important, however, has been the differential interregional shift. Around the middle of the nineteenth century textile manufacturing was located entirely in New England and the Middle Atlantic states; by 1954 the Southeast dominated the industry. The shift has affected every branch of textiles production, without exception.

Certain characteristics of the industry might suggest that material inputs have played a large role in this development. Most of the textile industry's non-labor inputs come from agriculture (primarily cotton). About 70% of its outputs go to intermediate markets, with 43% going to apparel manufacturing. From the fact that there is here a single major resource input and a variety of intermediate outlets, it might be concluded that the resource inputs have been the controlling locational factor. And the observed shift of the industry to the Southeast—a major source of cotton—would give considerable support to such a conclusion. Indeed, it has often been claimed that the textile industry moved to cotton.

In fact, however, the industry did not move to cotton; it moved to cheap labor.[15] Baled cotton has a very high value per unit of weight and undergoes little weight-loss in processing. Thus, interregional differences in transfer costs on both inputs and products are very small compared to the interregional differences in labor costs. The dramatic shift in location is, therefore, a result of a change in each region's access to labor inputs. Over the years New England has grown into a relatively advanced industrial region. Accompanying this evolution have been increased demands upon the labor force, increased needs for special labor skills, and widespread unionization. All of these things have tended to raise the level of wages. Over most of the period, the labor-intensive cotton-tobacco economy in the Southeast built up a large population. As this agricultural system broke down, a large supply of "low-wage" relatively immobile labor was created. Since the interregional wage differences were sizeable and labor costs are important in the textile industry, the resulting movement into the Southeast is not surprising.[16]

Some segments of the textile industry have been less strongly attracted to

---

[15]This fact has been documented by a number of studies, one of the best of which is that of William H. Meirnyk. He concludes from his survey of textile companies: "Most of the firms studied have southern mills. They were attracted to their locations, primarily, by the availability of an ample supply of low cost labor. Other elements of cost were mentioned, but in the absence of labor-cost differentials such items as power costs, and taxes, are not sufficiently important to cause the relocation of a cotton mill. Cotton mills that continue to operate in high labor cost areas do so in spite of their competitive disadvantage." See *Labor Costs and Labor Supply as Determinants of Industrial Location* (Unpublished Doctoral Dissertation, Harvard University, 1952), p. 163.

[16]The long-run prospects for a supply of low-cost unskilled or little-skilled labor may have been an important motivation. Education and tradition enable many New Englanders to move rather readily up to the semi-skilled and skilled category, and demand for such workers in New England remains at a relatively high level. Just the opposite is true in much of the South. At present there are relatively few industries that use semi-skilled and highly skilled laborers in the Southeast. This situation will tend to continue for some time. There is not as much of a chance for a worker in the Southeast to move up, therefore, and thus pull up wages. From management's point of view, this means *longer* relatively low wages for unskilled workers in the Southeast.

Southeastern labor than others and have responded less rapidly. This is true of the rayon mills. Rayon production is more capital-intensive than cotton production; as a consequence, the interregional differences in labor costs did not loom as large. Until recently, also, rayon has had an expanding market, and above average earnings have tended to forestall the shift to the Southeast. Further, rayon had established a strong foothold in New England as a substitute for cotton, which was moving to the Southeast. The period of rapid market expansion now seems to be over, however, and the labor cost differentials still persist for this branch of the industry. Thus, the Southeastern shift is now in evidence here as well.

Woolen and worsted mills also held out against the trend for many years. The Southeast still claims only a fifth of the total employment in this segment of the textile industry. Historical accident is largely responsible for the location of woolen mills in New England and hence the establishment of the wool market in Boston. Once established, however, compelling forces kept the pattern reasonably inflexible. Greasy wool, which is largely imported and distributed through the Boston market, is a weight-losing material. About 60% of its weight is lost in scouring. These initial operations are heavily oriented to the wool market—a sort of resource-input orientation. In addition to this supply factor, the mills found New England a favorable location for three reasons: (1) The atmosphere was better suited to working the looms and jennies without breakage and stoppage. (2) Since many of the fabrics are styled in the looms, there is some advantage in being close to the New York market to provide quick delivery on special orders. (3) Most important, prior to 1947 there was virtually no competition from low-wage regions. The industry was relatively static and no segment had moved to the Southeast to claim labor cost advantages. The advent of air-conditioning for moisture control has increased the Southeast's access to proper climate factors (at a price of course). Competition from synthetic fibers has brought the woolen industry out of its period of static adjustment and increased the importance of labor-cost savings. Finally, for many years the freight rate structure favored the movement of raw materials into the old industrial areas and the movement of finished products from those areas to the market. This advantage has been gradually removed. The consequence of these factors and the persistence of interregional differentials in labor costs have at last started the woolen industry along the path established by cotton textiles many years ago.

Apparel Manufacture

Apparel manufacture is one of the four largest sectors of manufacturing and also one of the most important in explaining the regional influence of manufacturing activity. In this sector, the interstate shifts between 1939 and 1954 were equal to almost one-fifth of the 1939 employment.

CONTRIBUTION TO THE 1-DIGIT PROPORTIONALITY EFFECT

Like textile manufacture, apparel manufacture is one of the slow-growth industries (see Table 147). Its contribution to the total proportionality effect shown in Figure 74, however, has not been nearly so strong as that of the textiles sector. This contribution is limited principally to fourteen states in the Middle Atlantic and Southeast regions that specialize in this activity.[17] The geographical

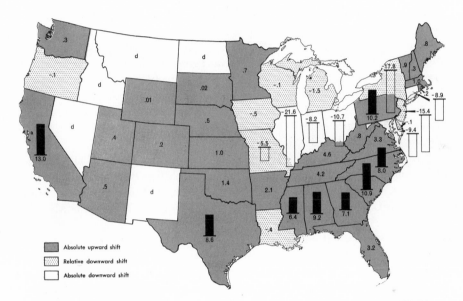

Figure 77. Net Shift in Apparel and Related Products Employment, 1939-54.
State figures represent % of total net shift. Total net shift as % of incremental change: 42.0. Total net shift as % of 1939 apparel and related products employment: 17.7. (d = not available because of disclosure problem.) Source: Appendix Table K.

pattern here is remarkably similar to that for textile products. There are marked differences in detail, however. The Southeastern states account for three and a half times as much employment in textiles as in apparel; the Middle Atlantic states have about twc and a half times as much employment in apparel as in textiles. The textile industry tends to concentrate in small towns and cities, while the apparel industry shows a strong affinity for big cities—especially New York City. In 1950, New York City employed almost 35% of the total for the industry.

The proportionality effect established by these characteristics tended to reinforce the downward proportionality shifts in total manufacturing employment

[17]Massachusetts, New York, Pennsylvania, New Jersey, Delaware, Maryland, Virginia, Kentucky, Missouri, Tennessee, Mississippi, Alabama, Georgia, and South Carolina.

in the Southeast, and it ran counter to the upward proportionality shift in the Middle Atlantic states. We have suggested that this influence was moderate. An indication of this is the fact that Mississippi and New York, the two states with the highest apparel specialization, did not show significant downward proportionality shifts.

CONTRIBUTION TO 1-DIGIT DIFFERENTIAL EFFECT

Apparel manufacture has greater significance in explaining the differential shift in total manufacturing. The shifts in this sector between 1939 and 1954 are shown in Figure 77. Four areas are seen to have had absolute net upward shifts over these years. The Southeastern states all had gains that, combined, account for 60% of the total upward shift. Pennsylvania had an important net upward shift, in striking contrast to the other apparel-manufacturing states in the Middle Atlantic region, and there were small net upward shifts in some of the New England states. California and Texas accounted for almost one-fourth of the total upward shift. The major downward shifts were in the Middle Atlantic and Great Lakes states.

A comparison of these shifts with the differential net shifts in all manufacturing employment (Figure 73) leads to the conclusion that the apparel sector must have made an important contribution to the upward shifts in the Southeast and in California and Texas, and to the downward shifts in the Manufacturing Belt. As a check on this we identify seventeen states in which the shift in apparel employment amounted to more than 10% of the state's total differential shift in employment.[18] This conclusion is borne out except that the shifts in apparel employment semed to be overshadowed by other factors in explaining the upward differential shifts into California and the Southwest (except Arizona).

In examining these shifts in apparel employment we can observe, as usual, two effects. There is a proportionality effect based upon the 3-digit components of the industry. The principal slow-growth components are men's and boys' furnishings and suits and coats. The areas that specialize most in these are in the Southeast, while the areas that specialize most in the rapid-growth sectors are in the Middle Atlantic states. In short, the 3-digit proportionality effect tends to run counter to the exhibited shift in apparel employment. It follows that the differential shift has been the more important in explaining changes in apparel employment. Let us, therefore, examine the important access characteristics of the industry.[19]

[18]Alabama, Arizona, Arkansas, Georgia, Illinois, Indiana, Kentucky, Maryland, Mississippi, Missouri, New Jersey, New York, North Carolina, South Carolina, Tennessee, Vermont and Virginia.

[19]Gunnar Alexandersson presents a very succinct statement of the rationale of location for this industry: "Apparel manufacturing, from a locational point of view, has two main characteristics. It is a big-city industry and it is a low-wage industry. These two seemingly incompatible features can be derived from the dominant influence of style on the industry. Big cities are style-setting centers. As the industry is so dominantly influenced by rapidly shifting fashions, it has not been mechanized in a way comparable with other manufacturing

Basically, there are in this industry two conflicting sets of forces—the dispersing effect of the industry's trend towards low wage areas and the concentrating force exerted by fashion centers.

All of the evidence from the current period seems to suggest that the concentrating force exerted by the fashion centers is being over-balanced by the dispersing force of cheap labor.[20] The Southeast has made the major gains as the apparel industry has tended to shift to cheap labor. And its major gains have been in products for which the style factor was least important. In men's and boys' furnishings (primarily shirts, ties, and separate slacks), for example, 80% of the total net upward shift was in the Southeast. Similarly, the Southeast accounted for almost two-thirds of the net upward employment shift in women's and children's underwear. While there were also net upward shifts for women's and misses' outerwear and for men's and boys' suits and coats, they were much less spectacular. Here the importance of style seems to help the older production centers to retain their dominance. Three Middle Atlantic states, New York, New Jersey and Pennsylvania (and primarily New York City) still account for two-thirds of the total employment in these categories as contrasted with only one-fourth of the total for men's and boys' furnishings.

The strength demonstrated by Pennsylvania would seem to stem from a convenient compromise here between the pull of cheap labor and the pull of the fashion market in New York City. Production in this area has overnight train or truck service to New York City and can take advantage of the depressed

industries. Labor cost is thus a very important cost item. As the biggest item of cost, the fabric, tends to be the same for all firms, . . . labor cost is the most important competitive factor. Low wage districts—cities with predominant male industries and the Southern states —exert a strong pull, especially on plants in the low-price lines, which are not so strongly tied to the fashion centers. . . .

"For an understanding of New York's dominant position within this industry it is necessary to study in a little more detail the structure of New York's garment manufacturing. . . .

"The New York clothing plants are highly concentrated in a small area of Manhattan. . . . Here is found a geographic concentration greater than in any other manufacturing center. About three-fourths of the 369,000 New York garment employees work in an area about 200 acres in size. But, unlike the case in most other manufacturing industries, the geographic concentration is brought about by a clustering of thousands of small plants. The problems arising from rapid changes of style are more easily mastered by small units than by the huge firm with its top-heavy, bureaucratic organization. The individual producer is highly specialized, not only to a particular type of garment but often also to a specific price class within this type, and therefore he is dependent upon other producers and auxiliary services, which are available close at hand in the New York clothing district. The concentration of thousands of plants in a small area allows every manufacturer to be in touch with and get 'ideas' from the others. For buyers coming from all over the country it is convenient to have . . . most of the show rooms located in a few blocks."

Alexandersson adds this note that sheds light on the historical factors that shaped the present distribution: "During the nineteenth century large quantities of fine clothing were imported from Europe. Merchants from all parts of the United States went to the landing port, New York, which became established as the leading wholesale center. This historic development goes far to explain why New York . . . became the American apparel center."

See Gunnar Alexandersson, *The Industrial Structure of American Cities* (Lincoln: University of Nebraska Press, 1956), pp. 70-71.

[20]The development of air freight has also played a role.

wages associated with the anthracite cities of Scranton and Wilkes-Barre. Pennsylvania accounted for almost half of the net upward shift in men's and boys' suits and coats and almost a third of the upward shift in women's and misses' outerwear—items for which access to the styling center is more important. In contrast, it did not share in the upward shift in men's and boys' furnishings or children's clothes.

The upward shift in New England is not large, but the fact that it is taking place at a time when these states are losing heavily in the textiles industry is interesting. Although the wage differential is favorable to the Southeast, New England has a labor surplus created by the migration of the textiles industry; it also has the advantage of proximity to the major style center. What are high wages for textiles are still feasible wages for apparel industries that gain from being close to the fashion market. Here, as in Pennsylvania, it is men's suits and coats and women's and misses' outerwear that account for much of the shift—especially in Rhode Island and Massachusetts. Upper New England is more like the Southeast. Here the wage differential is greater, the distance from the fashion market is greater, and there tends to be specialization in men's and boys' furnishings and children's clothing.

The net upward shift in Minnesota reflects a rise in employment in children's clothing and men's and boys' furnishings. A factor in this upward shift is the "surplus" female labor in the iron-ore mining districts.

The shifts in Texas and California represent in part a limited shift in the fashion market itself, arising out of the distance of these markets from New York City. But probably more important is the fact that climate and habits of living make different requirements upon fashion in these areas. In any case, Los Angeles and Dallas have been emerging as fashion centers. The same is true to a lesser degree of Miami, Florida. Casual fashions and sports clothes are a specialty. Los Angeles, in particular, has gained because of the influence of the motion picture industry.

Next to Pennsylvania, California and Texas show the largest upward shifts in women's and misses' outerwear. Texas also shows strong upward shifts in men's and boys' furnishings and children's clothing, indicating that it shares these trends, and presumably some of the labor cost advantage, with the Southeast.

In general, then, the apparel industry is one that has a somewhat mixed orientation—to fashion markets (essentially wholesale and intermediate rather than terminal) on the one hand and to relatively low-cost labor on the other. The balance between these two factors seems to be changing markedly and bringing about important shifts out of which a far-reaching reorganization of this industry may be emerging.

Lumber and Lumber Products

The net shift in lumber and lumber products employment between 1939 and 1954 is shown for each state in Figure 78. Although this sector employs only 4.5% of the manufacturing labor force, it exerts a relatively important influence upon the observed changes in total employment. It is particularly important in explaining the 1-digit proportionality effect, for its rates of growth is considerably below the national average for all industry sectors (Table 147). The states that specialize in this activity are located in the Southeast, upper New England, and the Far West, Southwest, and Mountain regions. All of these states except California and Arizona show a downward proportionality shift in total manufacturing employment between 1939 and 1954. And in all but nine of the thirty-five states that had downward total shifts over these years, specialization in this industry contributed to the decline.

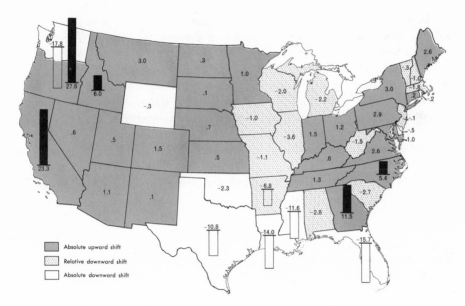

Figure 78. Net Shift in Lumber and Products Employment, 1939-54.
   State figures represent % of total net shift. Total net shift as % of incremental change: 66.4. Total net shift as % of 1939 lumber and products employment: 15.0. Source: Appendix Table K.

The contribution of the lumber products sector to the 1-digit differential shift is also important. Over half of the net upward shift between 1939 and 1954 was in California and Oregon and roughly one-fourth in the Southeast. The downward shifts were concentrated in the Gulf states and the Great Lakes states. The shifts in this industry were sufficiently important in ten states to account for over 10% of the total differential shifts in these states;[21] and in the Pacific Northwest and four of the Gulf states, they explain a large part of the total. Differential changes in relative regional access to basic inputs seem to be the most important explanatory factor.

[21]Arizona, Arkansas, Florida, Idaho, Louisiana, Minnesota, Montana, Nevada, Oregon, and Washington.

Actually, except for wood containers, 50% or more of the output of this sector goes to construction and final demand. This strong transaction tie with terminal markets exerts only slight influence upon location, however, because the principal non-labor input comes from logging, and the processing of forest products is characterized by considerable weight loss. It follows that the industry is closely associated in space with the supply of standing timber. The relative unimportance of the market as a locational determinant is seen in the fact that the coefficient of association with population (.576) is lower for this industry than for any other manufacturing activity (see Table 150).

It should also follow, therefore, that the principal shifts in this industry would be associated with regional changes in access to standing timber. A comparison of the net shifts in lumber products employment (Figure 78) with the shifts in logging employment (Figure 68) reveals a general consistency. The upward shifts in lumber products in the West and Southeast are associated with upward shifts in logging employment; and the strong net downward shifts in lumber products employment in Florida and Washington are associated with strong downward shifts in logging employment in these states. There are, however, important differences in detail that require some explanation.

(1) Oregon, California, and the Mountain states display a much greater upward shift in lumber products employment than in logging employment. The reasons for this would seem to be as follows: (a) The species type and virgin character of many of their tracts lend themselves more to specialization in lumber products than in pulp; and (b) two-thirds of the employment in the "lumber and lumber products" group is in basic lumber products, such as sawmill products. The western states specialize in these basic lumber products. Their employment in this category is almost twice as large a share of the national total as is their share of logging employment.

(2) While the Southeast accounts for 85% of the upward shift in logging employment, it accounts for only 24% of the upward shift in lumber products. A reverse explanation applies here. The Southeast specializes in pulp logs and much of the upward shift in logging has been in this area. In fact this specialization has become so strong that, in spite of the great increase in logging employment, most of the Gulf states have had absolute downward shifts in lumber and lumber products employment.

(3) The states in the Manufacturing Belt show a 9% upward shift despite net downward shifts for all except Pennsylvania and Ohio. Three comments are in order here. (a) These net downward shifts have been relative and, hence, are consistent with absolute increments in output that could support expanding lumber products employment. (b) Such a phenomenon might reflect a move to bring lumber products employment into a better relationship with logging capacity. (Both of these points apply to some of the Mountain states as well.) (c) More than anything else, this probably indicates that the market does exert some influence on a portion of this industry. This is especially true for the fabricated wood products sector (SIC 349). The major sources of inputs for this sector are saw and planing mills, while two-thirds of the output goes to terminal markets highly associated with population. Since a substantial portion

of the weight-loss has already been realized in the previous stage and the fabricating often adds bulk, there would be grounds to suppose that market attraction might exert greater influence here. The same is true for wood containers, except that over half of the market here is in other manufacturing sectors. This generalization is given some confirmation by the fact that the Manufacturing Belt states contain about 10% of the total logging employment but less than 8% of the employment in basic sawmill products. At the same time they claim about 30% of the total employment in millworks and wood containers and about 40% of the total employment for miscellaneous fabricated wood products.

Furniture and Fixtures

The furniture and fixtures sector accounts for only a little over 2% of total manufacturing employment; and, while it is a slow-growth sector, its rate of growth does not depart much from the national average. Hence, it does not contribute significantly to the 1-digit proportionality effect. Its influence upon the differential effect has also been limited. There is no state in which as much as 10% of the total differential shift in manufacturing employment is attributable to changes in the furniture industry.

The shifts for this industry between 1939 and 1954 are shown in Figure 79. Almost half of the net upward shift occurred in the Southeast and 70% of the net downward shift in the Great Lakes states. We might offer a few words of explanation for these shifts.

The production of furniture adds considerable bulk to a relatively cheap product. Only the quality grades can carry the costs of long-distance transport. At the same time the industry is not one that enjoys significant scale economies, and moderate-sized plants can realize competitive efficiency. In combination, these factors create an industry that is primarily oriented to markets. As a symptom of this, it has a higher rank correlation with population (.924) than any other manufacturing industry except printing and publishing (see Table 150).

This fact of market orientation is, nevertheless, consistent with some concentration and specialization of activity.[22] The Great Lakes states and the Southeast (especially the states nearer the prime markets) show the major concentrations. Texas and California show a trace.

The net upward shifts of the industry in California and Texas seem clearly to

[22]The concentrations that exist can be attributed to these factors: (1) While the industry is primarily oriented to markets, access to important inputs does exert an influence. (2) Something of the style center influence at work in the apparel industry is at work here. Chicago-Grand Rapids, New York, and, more recently, High Point (North Carolina) and Los Angeles are important furniture centers where a large number of producers establish common markets and displays. Fashion centers exert a certain agglomerating influence—especially upon the production of quality goods. (3) A segment of the industry is engaged in producing office and professional furniture. Since it concentrates more on metals, both input sources and markets tend to be concentrated in the Manufacturing Belt region.

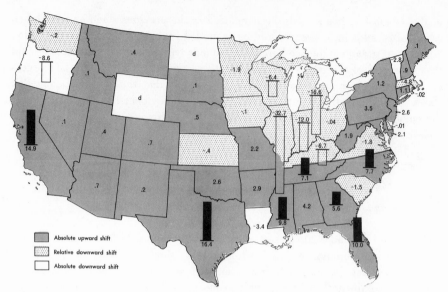

Figure 79. Net Shift in Furniture and Fixtures Employment, 1939-54.

State figures represent % of total net shift. Total net shift as % of incremental change: 26.3. Total net shift as % of 1939 furniture and fixtures employment: 13.5. (d = not available because of disclosure problem.) Source: Appendix Table K.

be a response of an essentially market-oriented industry to a pronounced regional shift in markets.[23] The significant expansion in the Southeast, however, comes in the face of an apparent relative decline in the regional market. Further, the relative decline in the Great Lakes region runs counter to a relative increase in the regional market. However, these developments are not really inconsistent with the basic market orientation of the industry.

Basically, the adjustment taking place has resulted from the fact that the Great Lakes region was "overdeveloped" relative to its total access to inputs and markets and the Southeast has been "underdeveloped" relative to its total access.[24] The two regions have roughly equal access to regional supplies of furniture-grade lumbers and to final markets. In spite of this, the Great Lakes

[23]In California, the development of Los Angeles as a fashion center has been a factor in aiding this growth. Alexandersson has suggested: "The style-forming influence of the movie industry must be great. It can hardly be a mere coincidence that Los Angeles during the last few decades has become an important furniture center, an apparel center and a style center for modern American architecture (California bungalows, 'ranch' houses)." *Op. cit.*, p. 17.

[24]The Great Lakes states (and their best-known furniture city—Grand Rapids) represent the region of origin in the United States for the production of furniture using factory methods. During the last century this area was a leading lumbering area and the furniture industry was an outgrowth of lumbering. At the outset it concentrated on factory-produced cheap furniture (referred to by the trade as "borax"). As factory organization for furniture production became more widely established, the region moved gradually into furniture styling and quality production in order to retain its position in the face of competitive pro-

states, largely for historical reasons, developed a disproportionately larger share of the total output. In 1910 they employed 47% of the total labor force in contrast to the Southeast's 10%.

It is only natural, then, that subsequent shift patterns should bring production in both regions more nearly into balance with their relative access characteristics. This adjustment was undoubtedly accelerated by the fact that a wage differential that favored the Southeast existed between these regions. By 1954 the share of the Great Lakes states in the output had fallen and the Southeast's share had risen to the point where each region had about 30% of the total.

The expansion in the Middle Atlantic states could be partly associated with the expanding regional market along the Middle Atlantic seaboard. It is more probably associated, however, with an expanding total market for a segment of the industry that is by nature more concentrated, and centered in the Manufacturing Belt. First, upholstered furniture makes proportionally much less use of lumber and much more use of textile products. This weakens the pull of resource inputs. It requires more styling and skilled fabric workers. This favors agglomeration near styling centers. It tends more towards a quality product without the same mass market as the standard wood furniture items. In short, a larger portion of the total output can be supplied from production facilities that are regionally concentrated. These factors have made New York City the largest producer of upholstered furniture in the country. The Middle Atlantic region seems to have gained most from an expansion in the total demand for this product.

Second, the Middle Atlantic region has come to specialize in office and professional furniture. Here metal is a more important input than lumber, and intermediate markets are just as important as terminal markets. This branch of the industry also lends itself to greater standardization and economies of scale. The number of firms required to satisfy the market is not large. The result is considerable concentration of production in the Manufacturing Belt region. These states make all but 10% of the office furniture and all but 15% of the public and professional furniture produced in the United States.

Paper and Allied Products

Paper and allied products employment, like furniture employment, does not make an important contribution to the 1-digit proportionality effect upon total manufacturing employment. This is a rapid-growth sector, but its rate of growth is only slightly above average.

Its influence on the 1-digit differential effect in total manufacturing employ-

---

ducers oriented more to markets. The chief regional competition for the Great Lakes states came from the Southeast. Even before the turn of the century, the Southeast was producing wood furniture aimed at the local market. With decades of experience, it has evolved an industry that has some of the largest and most advanced plants in the country. It has moved into quality furniture and has become an important style center with permanent exhibitions at High Point, North Carolina.

ment, however, has been greater than that of the furniture sector. In four states (and the District of Columbia) it generated more than 10% of the total differential shift between 1939 and 1954, and in nine other states it accounted for between 5% and 10% of the total.[25]

Figure 80 shows the shifts in paper and allied products employment during this period. The net downward shift was concentrated in the Northeast. The major upward shifts were in the Southeast and in California and Texas. The downward shifts in New York, Massachusetts, and the upper New England states and the upward shifts in the Southern states and Minnesota were an important part of the total differential shift in manufacturing employment in these states.

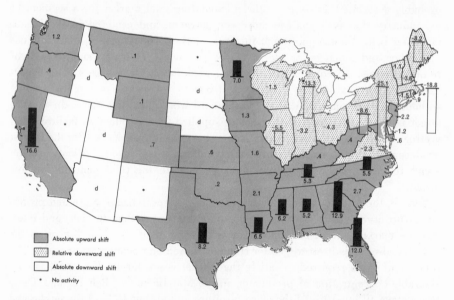

Figure 80. Net Shift in Paper and Allied Products Employment, 1939-54.

State figures represent % of total net shift. Total net shift as % of incremental change: 28.6. Total net shift as % of 1939 paper and allied products employment: 17.5. (d = not available because of disclosure problem.) Source: Appendix Table K.

Except in upper New England, the 2-digit proportionality effect tends to run counter to the over-all shifts observed here. The rapid-growth segments of the industry are paper coating and glazing, paper bags, and miscellaneous paper products. The manufacture of these products is concentrated principally in the Manufacturing Belt states. In contrast, the slow-growth segments—pulp, paper, and paperboard—are concentrated more heavily in the Southeast. It follows that

[25]Alabama (5.0), Delaware (9.0), Florida (12.5), Georgia (7.3), Louisiana (7.4), Maine (20.4), Massachusetts (6.5), Minnesota (13.3), Mississippi (8.7), New Hampshire (12.9), New York (8.1), Tennessee (6.1), and Vermont (8.3).

the shifts shown in Figure 80 would have been even more pronounced were it not for the 2-digit proportionality effect.

The contrasting orientation tendencies of these two major segments of the industry are important in explaining the differential shifts. The pulp and paper segments are oriented to resource inputs—an orientation remarkably similar to that for basic lumber products.[26] The segments that produce converted paper products tend more to market-orientation.

Two-thirds of the total employment is concentrated in the Northeastern states. This stems in part from the fact that the production of converted paper products is concentrated in this area with its favorable access to national markets. But it stems also in part from the fact that a disproportionate share of production capacity is still located here, where the industry originated.[27]

In recent years, however, two developments have combined to effect a drastic change in the location picture of the pulp and paper industry: (1) A growing economy has converted paper into a growth industry. Employment increased by two-thirds between 1939 and 1954. This allowed for significant additions to capacity, and these additions could seek a more rational economic location. (2) A practical method for making pulp from the resinous Southern pine was perfected in the 1930's. Thus the Southeast's access to resource inputs was

---

[26]It takes roughly two tons of wood to make a ton of sulphite and sulphate pulp. While 90% of the output of pulp mills goes to paper, this does not represent a significant contrasting pull. Rather, there is considerable production cost advantage to be gained through vertical integration of paper and pulp mill. Paper production, therefore, tends to take on this same resource-oriented character.

[27]Before the invention of the process for producing paper from wood pulp, the industry was essentially market-oriented. The chief raw materials were straw, rags, and waste paper, all of which were readily available in urban districts, and economies of scale did not require large producers. The advent of pulp changed all of that. Sizable investment in plant and machinery was necessary, and these plants needed to be placed with reference to supplies of pulp species adequate to cover the long period over which large fixed investments would be amortized.

Despite the drastic change in the logical orientation of the industry occasioned by the new process, the industry's investors and managers continued to show a strong preference for locations near the traditional sites of paper production. This was true in New England and the Middle Atlantic states—particularly New York and Massachusetts. As a consequence the new plants were not established near supplies of pulpwood that were adequate to cover the reasonable life of production facilities. Competition with lumber for the remaining stands and the rapid decline in the available stands in the East considerably aggravated the consequence of these poor location decisions. Apparently the same phenomenon took place later in Michigan and Wisconsin. Construction of new pulp and paper capacity continued there for a decade after wood supplies began to grow scarce.

This seemingly displaced production capacity persisted for a number of reasons: (1) Fixed costs are a high proportion of total costs and capacity is long-lived. When faced with competition from mills better situated, the mills reorganized to scale down fixed costs. The losses were real; but as long as variable costs were covered, the mills continued to operate. (2) Since paper-making machinery can be adapted to different grades of paper, the mills in the most competitive position have moved progressively into the production of higher grades. (3) These mills could import foreign pulp without an impossible cost disadvantage.

For an account of these developments, documented in considerable detail, see Helen Hunter, "Innovation, Competition, and Locational Change in the Pulp and Paper Industry, 1880-1950," *Land Economics*, Nov. 1955, pp. 314-27.

immeasurably increased through technology at a time when total demand was expanding and significant elements of existing capacity were obsolete. The result is the shift picture presented in Figure 80.[28]

Printing and Publishing

This sector of manufacturing activity has had very little influence on the total changes observed. It is one of the smallest of the manufacturing sectors and, although it is a slow-growth industry, its rate of growth is so close to the national average that its contribution to the total 1-digit proportionality effect has been negligible. Nor has it contributed significantly to the 1-digit differential effect. There is no state in which employment shifts in this industry have accounted for as much as 10% of the total differential effect.

Furthermore, the shifts that have occurred can be very simply explained. The industry distributes 75% of its output to final markets. This leads to a strong market association, as reflected in the fact that the printing and publishing industry has the highest coefficient of association with population of any manufacturing industry (Table 150). The shifts observed, therefore, must be largely a response to regional changes in market access. They reveal a general southwestward movement that correlates highly with the major shifts in population.[29]

---

[28]Of the converted paper products, paper coating and glazing (SIC 264) and miscellaneous paper products (SIC 269) are most heavily oriented to intermediate markets.

Converted paper products industries generally add bulk and value to processed inputs for which significant weight loss has been achieved in earlier stages. This, plus the market service aspect, tends to make these sectors strongly market-oriented. They are concentrated in the Manufacturing Belt states and these are the only paper products sectors that displayed any upward shifts in this region.

Paper bags and envelopes (SIC 265-266) are oriented more to terminal markets. The shifts in these sectors are roughly consistent with shifts in population and, hence, out of the Manufacturing Belt area.

Paperboard containers and boxes (SIC 267) are oriented to intermediate markets but more to a wide variety of general manufacturing than paper coating, etc. The shifts in this sector have been roughly consistent with the shifts in manufacturing production. The major shifts are into the Southeast and Southwest. The Southeast's upward shift in box-making seems a little out of proportion with its gains in manufacturing but the discrepancy can be explained by the fact that (1) the type of paper produced in that region is especially suitable for this purpose, and (2) the furniture industry has shifted almost entirely from wood crating to cardboard.

[29]Discrepancies in this picture can be detected when the 3-digit breakdowns are examined. For example, the Southeast claimed 25% of the upward shift in newspaper employment in the face of relative and absolute declines in population. This region alone in the United States has had a deficiency of news outlets. With increasing income, education, and urbanization this deficit is being made up.

Again, publishing and job-printing is essentially a market-service oriented big city operation. Some types of book printing, however, are becoming increasingly labor oriented, leading to shifts into the Southeast and northern Plains states.

Chemicals and Allied Products

Although the chemical products sector accounts for only 4% of manufacturing employment, it has generated important proportionality and differential effects on the total. Its employment shifts among the states between 1939 and 1954 equaled 25% of its 1939 employment.

The rate of employment growth in this sector over these years has been significantly above the national average (82% as compared with 58%). This characteristic helps to explain the upward proportionality shifts in total manufacturing employment shown by the western states of the Manufacturing Belt (see Figure 73). In the remaining areas where the manufacture of chemical products is important—the Southwest, the Plains states, and upper Southeast, Florida, and Washington—the tendency to an upward proportionality shift established by the chemical industries has not been sufficient to offset the opposite tendency set in motion by the food, textiles, apparel, lumber and products, and leather industries. It might help to explain, however, why these states tend to have had more moderate downward proportionality shifts than other states without such a specialization, particularly in the Southeast.

Chemical products also contributed significantly to the 1-digit differential effect in total manufacturing employment. The end results of both effects are shown in Figure 81. In general, Texas and Louisiana have made the greatest

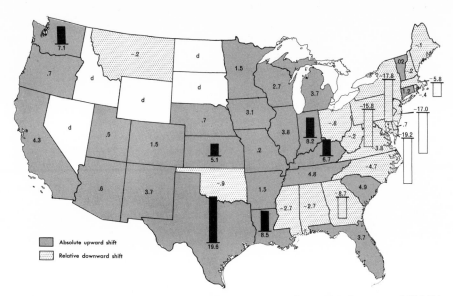

Figure 81. Net Shift in Chemicals and Allied Products Employment, 1939-54. State figures represent % of total net shift. Total net shift as % of incremental change: 30.1. Total net shift as % of 1939 chemicals and allied products employment: 24.6. (d = not available because of disclosure problem.) Source: Appendix Table K.

gains, followed by the western states of the Manufacturing Belt, the Far West, Kansas, and four scattered Southeastern states. The upward shift supports the total upward trend in manufacturing employment in the Southwest, most of the Plains region, and the upper Southeast (compare with Figure 74) and runs counter to the total downward shift in the western end of the Manufacturing Belt. The net downward shifts spread, with minor exceptions, all the way down the Atlantic coast from Maine through the Deep South, with almost three-fourths of the total concentrated in the Middle Atlantic states. It supports the total downward trend in New England and the eastern end of the Manufacturing Belt, but runs counter to it in the Deep South.

These shifts explain an important part of the total shift in specific states. They account for more than 9% of the total differential manufacturing shift in ten states,[30] and for over 5% of the total in eleven others.[31]

The 2-digit proportionality effect offsets to some degree the differential effect. Drugs and medicines and industrial organic and inorganic chemicals have been the rapid-growth sectors. The relative concentration of the rapid-growth and the slow-growth sectors tends to generate an upward proportionality shift along the Atlantic seaboard and a downward proportionality shift through the entire Southeast. In a few cases the upward porportionality shift reinforces the differential effect; this is true for Michigan, Indiana, Kentucky, Tennessee, Louisiana, and Washington. In general, however, the shifts shown in Figure 81 would be more marked were it not for the 2-digit proportionality effect.

The industry is in a state of rapid change.[32] Between 1939 and 1954, employment in industrial inorganic materials and drugs and medicines increased by almost 150%, and employment in industrial organic chemicals more than doubled. The rate of technological change has been staggering; DuPont reports that over half of its output represents products that were either unknown or in their commercial infancy in the 1930's.

The task of analyzing these employment changes is further complicated by the fact that the chemical products sector of manufacturing is a catch-all for a wide variety of industries. There are, for example, over 2,500 chemical products based upon petroleum and natural gas chemicals alone. Indeed, there is wide disagreement about a proper definition for chemical industries.[33]

These complicating factors, together with the fact that there is little published material that deals adequately with the problems of location for the chemical industries, make it impossible to do more here than point out some of the elements at work within specific segments of this heterogeneous set of activities.

[30]Indiana, Iowa, Kentucky, Louisiana, Maryland, New Jersey, Colorado, New Mexico, Texas and Washington.

[31]Arizona, Delaware, Florida, Georgia, Kansas, Mississippi, New York, Pennsylvania, South Carolina, Tennessee and Virginia.

[32]For an excellent analysis of the development of the chemical industry, based on its structure, see Harold J. Barnett and Frederick T. Moore, "Long-Range Growth of Chemical Industries," *Chemical and Engineering News*, Volume 36 (April 7, 1958), pp. 78-84, 142.

[33]See Alderfer and Michl, *Economics of American Industry* (New York: McGraw-Hill, 1950), p. 245.

INDUSTRIAL INORGANIC CHEMICALS

In this sector, Texas and Louisiana have displayed the greatest upward shifts. Florida, Maryland, and West Virginia also show some strength. The downward shifts are concentrated in the Manufacturing Belt.

The industries in this group produce a wide variety of inorganic acids and salts, the most important of which are chlorine and caustic soda, sulphuric acid, and alumina. The production of sulphuric acid is a strongly market-oriented process.[34] All of the markets for the product are intermediate markets, however. The fertilizer industry takes more than a third of the output, and petroleum and petrochemicals from 10% to 15%. The balance is widely distributed among a variety of chemical and mechanical process industries. Sulphuric acid, as could be expected, has figured importantly in the expansion in Texas and Louisiana. These states have excellent access to petroleum-refining and fertilizer markets, as well as to the largest sulphur deposits in the United States.

The pattern for the production of chlorine and caustic soda in remarkably similar. The production of these chemicals tends to be market-oriented.[35] Petroleum-refining is an important user of heavy alkalies and some petrochemicals are important users of chlorine (such as the production of ethylene glycol from ethane by the chlorohydrin process). There are expanding markets in the Southwest in close juxtaposition to some of the nation's largest salt deposits.

Alumina production has also contributed to the shift of inorganic chemicals into this region. A major concentration of alumina production is located along the Gulf coast—particularly at sites with ready access to the Mississippi and its network of inland waterways. The production of alumina is a process where bauxite is reduced to aluminum-hydroxide preparatory to electrolytic refining. There is a large weight loss (two tons of bauxite yield one ton of alumina). The process is, therefore, heavily oriented to resource materials. In 1947, 72% of the U. S. bauxite supply was imported—primarily from Dutch Guiana. The Gulf ports were the nearest transshipment points. The production of alumina takes place here rather than at the mines primarily because of an import duty of $5.00 a ton on alumina (as compared to $.50 a ton on bauxite).[36] The expanding total market for aluminum has resulted in an expansion of alumina capacity in this area.

INDUSTRIAL ORGANIC CHEMICALS

The Great Lakes and Plains states, Texas and Louisiana, and the Far West showed upward shifts in industrial organic chemicals; the New England and

[34]The manufacture of sulphuric acid is a weight-adding process. It is made with a combination of crude sulphur and water, which is a ubiquitous material. The acid equivalent in crude sulphur has only about ⅓ the weight of an equivalent amount of sulphuric acid. In addition, the freight rate on crude sulphur is much cheaper.

[35]The electrolysis of salt solution produces both. There is no weight loss but higher transport costs prevail on the finished product than on salt.

[36]See John V. Krutilla, "Locational Factors Influencing Recent Aluminum Expansion," *Southern Economic Journal*, Vol. 21 (January 1955), pp. 275-6.

Middle Atlantic states accounted for virtually all of the net downward shifts. The shifts that are characteristic of plastic intermediates, shown in Table 154, are remarkably similar to those described for all organic chemicals. It is also true that this sector of organic chemicals has been the most dynamic one over our period. This suggests that the shifts in organic chemicals can be explained in large part by explaining the shifts in plastic materials.

There are some sixteen intermediate chemicals based upon petroleum and natural gas alone that are used in the production of plastic materials. Isard and Schooler have examined the production orientation of these (and other) chemical intermediates.[37] Their findings can be briefly summarized as follows: For all markets in the Southeast and West (other than the Pacific Coast states) production is resource-oriented and would tend to be centered in the major supply areas in the Southwest—particularly Texas and Louisiana. For all markets along the Eastern seaboard there is a strong tendency to resource-orientation, although a few of the chemical intermediates continue to show a tendency to market-

Table 154. Percentage net shift in employment in plastic materials and plastic products, by region, 1947-1954

Region	Plastic materials		Plastic products	
	Absolute upward shifts %	Relative downward shifts %	Absolute upward shifts %	Relative downward shifts %
New England		73		25
Middle Atlantic		27		75
Great Lakes and Plains	25		61	
Southeast	44		31	
Far West	31		6	

SOURCE: *Census of Manufactures 1947*, Volume II, Table 2, pp. 394 and 818; *Census of Manufactures 1954*, Vol. II, Table 2, pp. 28b-9 & 39d-7.

orientation in this area. Production to serve markets in the Great Lakes and Plains states shows a decidedly mixed tendency. About two-fifths of the processes seem to be resource-oriented and about two-fifths market-oriented. Another 20% of the processes do not show any clear-cut cost advantage at either place. Production to serve markets in the Pacific states is oriented to the market as the low-cost production site.[38]

[37]Walter Isard and Eugene W. Schooler, *Location Factors in the Petrochemical Industry with Special Reference to Future Expansion in the Arkansas-White-Red River Basins* (Area Development Division, Office of Technical Services, Business and Defense Services, U. S. Department of Commerce, 1955); also Eugene W. Schooler, *Regional Advantage in the Production of Chemicals from Petroleum and Natural Gas*, unpublished doctoral dissertation, Harvard University.

[38]See Schooler dissertation, *op. cit.*, pp. 416-419.

With these generalizations in mind, let us examine the regional changes in input-output access. As suggested by Table 154, New England and the Middle Atlantic states have been losing their earlier advantage in access to the intermediate markets. For plastic materials (according to Schooler), the latest technology tends to make it more economical to produce chemical intermediates close to their oil and natural gas sources. Declining access to both total markets and resource inputs in an area that dominated the early production of plastic materials has led to a net downward shift.

The Great Lakes and Plains states made a striking gain in access to markets for plastic materials.[39] But production of plastic materials in these states has not increased correspondingly. For some chemical intermediates there is a tendency to market orientation, but for a number of others the petroleum-producing areas are most economic for serving this market.

The Southeast has made a more striking gain in the production of plastic materials than would seem to be accounted for by the gain in markets. The explanation may be that newer technology has given this region access to important markets for plastics products in other regions. The Pacific area shows an important gain because it has access to an expanding regional market and has its own oil and natural gas sources.

These chemical intermediates that form plastic materials are a good example of mixed location orientation. In some cases the same process can be oriented both to intermediate markets and to resource inputs, depending upon which of several regional markets it is serving.

Two other organic chemicals should be touched upon here. The production of synthetic fibers as such has not contributed to the major shifts into the Plains states and the Southwest. This production is basically labor-oriented.[40] Since its major markets are in the textile industry concentrated in the Southeast, where there is also an abundance of cheap labor, 85% of the synthetic fiber production is in this region. Production changes between 1939 and 1954 have only served to strengthen this pattern and do not seem important in explaining major interregional shifts in organic chemicals.

On the other hand, the Texas and Louisiana Gulf area has gained a part of its strength from the production of the chemical intermediates that form the synthetic fibers. The Isard-Schooler study reveals that these processes would be strongly resource-oriented for serving the Southeastern market.

Synthetic rubber is another petrochemical that has made a significant contribution to the expansion in organic chemicals in the Southwest. The Isard-Schooler study reveals that this process is firmly oriented to resource inputs except for a few of the chemical intermediates that might serve the "Eastern Interior" markets. Since the preponderant tendency is to resource orientation, the Eastern Interior has been losing employment in the rubber industry; the South-

---

[39] We know of no study of the orientation of the production of plastic products, but *a priori* logic tells us that greater bulk and value of products should lead to a degree of market orientation. The shifts pictured in Table 154 seem to support this motion.

[40] See Joseph Airov, "Location Factors in Synthetic Fiber Production," *Papers and Proceedings of the Regional Science Association*, Vol. 2 (1956), pp. 291-303.

east and West have claimed all of the recent expansion in the industry and now account for 87% of the total employment. (Texas alone accounts for a third.)

OTHER CHEMICAL INDUSTRIES

The remaining chemical industries can be referred to only briefly.

In drugs and medicines, 90% of the employment is in the Manufacturing Belt. Agglomeration economies appear to be important for this industry. Product research is essential to its existence. It collects inputs from a wide variety of sources—often other drug and medicine firms. The scale of production for many lines is large relative to the size of the total market. All of these factors encourage a certain amount of concentration in reasonably close contact with the drug and medicine community. The shift in drugs and medicines has, therefore, been limited principally to a shift toward the western end of the Manufacturing Belt— particularly Indiana. Since almost two-thirds of the total output goes to terminal markets, the shift in the national market is pulling this industry westward although it stays firmly entrenched in the Manufacturing Belt. Of the states west of the Mississippi River, California alone shows an absolute upward shift.[41]

Soap and related products and paint and allied products show roughly similar shift patterns for approximately the same reasons. Both groups tend towards market orientation. This does not mean, however, that production of these products is widely scattered. Indeed, two-thirds to three-fourths of the total employment in these groups is in the Manufacturing Belt states. There are two reasons for this. (1) Intermediate (as well as final) markets are important for these industries (especially paint products) and these intermediate markets are concentrated. (2) The scale of output relative to total demand precludes widespread distribution.

Nevertheless, changes in market access seem to be most important in explaining the shifts that take place. The output of both groups is produced, without weight loss, from basic chemical inputs that can be assembled in bulk. The products do not gain weight but do gain volume and value in processing. Perhaps more important, particularly for paints, good access to markets allows quick service without requiring large and complex inventories.

The greatest expansion in production between 1939 and 1954 was in Kansas, Missouri, and Iowa. These states had increasing access not only to westward shifting terminal markets, but also to westward shifting intermediate markets in the Manufacturing Belt. At the same time, their location at the heart of the source region for vegetable and animal oils gave them access to the major raw materials used in the production of both paint and soap. Other states that showed upward shifts during these years were Texas, California, North Carolina, Georgia, and Florida. The expansion in Texas and California seems to have been a response to terminal and industrial markets, while the gains in North Carolina and Georgia demonstrate more of a response to intermediate markets,

---

[41]New York and Connecticut showed significant relative gains but these were not sufficient to offset the major decline of this area in chemical products as a whole. See Appendix Table S.

especially furniture and automobile assembly. Florida's growth seems largely
due to the expansion of terminal markets in the construction industry and to the
fact that a good deal of research in paints is conducted there. In the Manufacturing Belt, Pennsylvania was the only state that showed significant relative gains
in the production of these products.

The shifts in fertilizer employment have been striking. In the Southeast, with
the exception of Florida, there were large relative and absolute declines. The
major gains have been in the Corn Belt states and in Arkansas, Louisiana,
Oklahoma and Texas.

These shifts are chiefly explained in terms of changes in market access, for
fertilizer production is strongly market-oriented.[42] The downward shifts in the
Southeast are closely tied to the changes in agricultural practices—that is, the
movement out of row-cropping to cover-cropping and livestock production in
this region. These uses of the soil make much lighter demands for fertilizer than
cotton.

The expansion of fertilizer production in the Great Lakes and Plains states is
tied directly to the corn-soy complex in these states. Here agriculture is dominated by row-cropping, which has steadily reduced the fertility quotient of the
soil.[43] At the same time, research has shown more extensive fertilization to be
profitable.

All of the Southwest has expanded fertilizer production largely because of
the big upward shifts here in the production of field crops, especially cotton.

Florida presents an interesting contrast. While the fertilizer industry is dominated by ordinary superphosphates, there is a growing usage of double superphosphates. Since this material concentrates more usable plant nutrient in a
pound, production tends to be resource-oriented.[44] Florida produces most of the
nation's phosphate; so it has had an expansion of production oriented to this
resource.

The processing of vegetable and animal oils is strongly oriented to resource
inputs. Not only is there substantial weight-loss in the process, but the cake and
other by-products can be profitably returned to agriculture. The process is at the
same time oriented to resource inputs and resource markets.

The shift pattern for this industry has been characterized by substantial absolute downward shifts for the Southeast as a whole. The Great Lakes and Plains
states and California and Arizona have displayed absolute upward shifts.

Changes in access to resource inputs seem to have been the basic cause of
these shifts. The Southeast's heavy loss is attributable to the decline in the pro-

[42]To produce one ton of ordinary superphosphate containing 16% P205 requires about a
half ton of rock one-eighth ton of sulphur (to produce ½ ton 70% sulphuric acid).
Since (a) the total weight of both is less than the weight of the final product and (b) the
transportation rate on each of the two raw materials is less than on the fertilizer, production
locations close to market are desirable. See Sam H. Schurr and Jacob Marschak, *Economic
Aspects of Atomic Power* (Princeton: Cowles Commission and Princeton University Press,
1950), p. 126.

[43]Haystead and Fite, *The Agricultural Regions of the United States* (Norman: University
of Oklahoma Press, 1955), p. 158.

[44]Schurr and Marschak, *op. cit.*, p. 126.

duction of oil crops. The westward shift in cotton culture, together with the shift from row-cropping to cover-cropping, has reduced the Southeast's production of cotton seed. Although the production of soybeans was originally begun in the Southeast, it has found its home in the Corn Belt. The expansion in the Great Lakes and Plains states is tied closely to the soybean, which is virtually a creation of our modern period. The California-Arizona expansion is probably tied to the westward shift of cotton.

SUMMARY

We can now make some generalizations about the shifts shown in Figure 81 for the chemical industries as a whole. The pronounced gains in Texas and the rest of the Southwest, it can be seen, received strong stimulus from both inorganic chemicals and organic chemicals. In the case of organic chemicals, the petrochemicals dominate; the access of this region to some of the world's finest petroleum deposits has certainly been instrumental in this regard. In the case of inorganic acids and salts, access to sulphur and salt has been important, but so also has access to important intermediate markets in the petrochemical industries. In addition, the region (mostly Texas) made gains in the production of fertilizer and of the more market-oriented soaps and paints.

In the Great Lakes states, there was some gain in organic chemicals—primarily plastics—in response to a marked increase in market access, combined with the fact that some chemical intermediates can be profitably produced near production markets. There was also some gain in drugs and medicines. But the greatest gains have been in the production of fertilizer and of vegetable and animal oils.

The West Coast's expansion received some stimulus from organic chemicals and vegetable and animal oils. Its major gains, however, have come from those chemical products attracted to expanding markets—drugs, soaps, and paints.

The East lost out in practically every segment except for scattered upward shifts in drugs and medicines, paints, soaps, and miscellaneous chemicals. The Deep South lost out because of heavy downward shifts in fertilizers and in vegetable and animal oils that offset modest upward shifts in other chemicals oriented to its resources and markets.

Petroleum and Coal Products

This is another sector of manufacturing activity that contributes little to an explanation of the total shift in manufacturing employment. Its growth experience has been sufficiently close to the national average that it cannot exert a significant 1-digit proportionality effect. The differential effect is likewise not very important. Louisiana is the only state in which more than 10% of the total manufacturing shift was attributable to changes in this sector during the 1939-54 period. There is no other state that we can reliably report with more than a 5% boost from this source.

The shift pattern for this sector is primarily a shift out of the Northeast into the Southwest, with the Middle Atlantic states showing the biggest relative losses and Texas and Louisiana dominating the gains.

The explanation lies principally in the performance of petroleum refining. This industry accounts for 70% of the total employment in the petroleum and coal products sector and it is besides the dynamic segment of this sector. In a detailed study of locational factors in oil-refining in the United States, John Robert Lindsay has shown that oil refiners serving the East Coast complex around New York and Philadelphia achieve their greatest economies at the resource site.[45] This characteristic of refining technology, together with the relative decline of the market in the East, is sufficient to explain the relative declines in refining activity in this area. It is also sufficient to explain why the Gulf Coast area of Texas and Louisiana should account for 75% of the total net upward shift. This area has relatively good access (given the nature of the products) to most of the nation's market—the Northeast, the Southeast, and the Southwest.

In contrast, Lindsay points out that refineries serving the Great Lakes region find a market location most advantageous. For consuming areas west of the Mississippi, the market pull is even more pronounced. This seems sufficient to explain the relative gains in the Great Lakes states and the mid-Mountain states. The westward shift of population is increasing their market access. At the same time the mid-Mountain area has significantly increased its access to resource inputs (see Figure 54 and accompanying discussion).

California has both significant markets and access to oil, upon which its refining activity is based. The relative decline there in petroleum-refining in the face of an expanding market is probably due to the fact that exploration and discovery have not expanded well capacity in this area as rapidly as in others. The relative decline in Kansas and Oklahoma is attributable to the same factor plus the fact that, lacking Gulf outlets, their market access is inferior to that of Texas and Louisiana.

[45]John Robert Lindsay, *The Location of Oil Refining in the United States* (unpublished doctoral dissertation, Harvard University, 1955). See also "Regional Advantage in Oil Refining," *Papers and Proceedings of the Regional Science Association*, Vol. 2 (1956), p. 304-17.

25 / Regional influence of manufacturing activity:

(3) THE MAJOR COMPONENTS;

SERVICE ACTIVITIES

The Rubber Industry

The rubber industry can be given only passing attention in our analysis of the shifts that have taken place in total manufacturing activity. It is one of the smallest sectors. Its rate of growth does not depart from the national average sufficiently to exert any influence upon the 1-digit proportionality effect; and its contribution to the 1-digit differential effect has not exceeded 5% of the total in any of the states except Iowa and Alabama.

Over all, the configuration presented by the shifts in rubber manufacture are consistent with the differential shifts in total manufacturing. The shifts are, generally, out of the Manufacturing Belt into the Southeast, Far West, and upper New England states.[1]

In its evolution from a craft industry, the rubber industry came to be highly concentrated in Ohio—particularly Akron. The importance of access to a relatively large skilled labor force and other external economies encouraged agglomeration. As the industry has matured and mechanization has reduced the significance of labor skills, distribution economies seem to have become more important and a noticeable decentralization of the industry is now under way.

A little more than a third of rubber employment is in tires and tubes. New plants have been established in Iowa, Kansas, Colorado, Oklahoma, Texas, California, Tennessee, Alabama, and Mississippi. Even Pennsylvania and Massachusetts in the Manufacturing Belt show some gains. Two factors are in effect here: (1) The growing importance of market access. Because of market rivalry there is a service advantage in being closer to markets, and there are usually

---

[1]See Appendix Table K. The major loss is in Ohio, the traditional center of the rubber industry. The greatest gains appear to be in the Southeast, in Ohio's neighboring states (Indiana and Pennsylvania), and in Iowa and California.

transport savings on the final product because the production process adds considerable value and bulk. (2) The fact that there have been important inter-regional shifts in the market stemming from (a) the westward shift in population and (b) a marked regional decentralization in automobile assembly.[2] We might add that the presence of the textile, carbon black, and synthetic rubber industries in the Southeast and Southwest meant that changing market advantage could be exploited without incurring significant penalty in the assembly of inputs. Further, natural rubber, which is imported, can be delivered at many points at approximately the same cost.

Miscellaneous fabricated rubber products account for about half of rubber products employment. This segment has displayed a similar shift to the South and West. The principal difference, when contrasted with the production of tires and tubes, is that the downward shift took place mostly in the Middle Atlantic states and southern New England. This is the area that specialized early in miscellaneous rubber manufacturing and still claimed half of the total employment in 1954.[3]

Leather and Leather Products

Interregional changes in leather products employment are a fairly large part of the shifts observed in total manufacturing employment over the 1939-54 period. Leather is one of the most important of the slow-growth industries and, since there is considerable regional specialization, the industry has contributed significantly to the 1-digit proportionality shifts shown in Figure 74. Like textiles, it was an important factor in the downward proportionality shift in total manufacturing employment in New England; in some of these states, specialization in leather products is from five to ten times greater than the national average. In Missouri, Arkansas, and Tennessee also it is a factor in the total downward proportionality shifts.

The leather industry's contribution to the 1-digit differential effect is also important. Shifts in leather products employment accounted for 5% or more of the total differential shift in manufacturing employment for seven states (10% or more in five cases).[4]

[2]The shifts that have taken place in the automobile industry are discussed later in this chapter, pp. 854-55.

[3]We do not have any accurate information concerning the change factors affecting this polyglot set of production processes. The fact that there has been a substantial shift to the West and Southwest suggests that changing market access may be importantly at work. The fact that there are shifts into the Southeast and upper New England suggests that interregional labor cost differentials might exercise a force. The fact that there are a whole range of new synthetic rubber materials available that have encouraged new products and new specialties (especially those related to mining and airplane manufacture) might create a role for a 3-digit proportionality effect. We are in no position, however, to make a systematic statement concerning this sector of the economy.

[4]Arkansas, Colorado, Delaware, Maine, Missouri, New Hampshire, and Tennessee. See Table 151.

Figure 82 shows the shifts in leather products employment between 1939 and 1954. Like the shifts in total manufacturing employment over these years, they are primarily out of the Manufacturing Belt into the Southeast and West. The Middle Atlantic states, however, form an important exception; certain of these states show significant upward shifts.

The upward shifts in the Middle Atlantic states are in part based on a 2-digit proportionality effect. These states have the highest concentration of production in luggage, handbags, and small leather goods, which are the rapid-growth sectors of the leather industry. For the most part, however, the shifts are based upon genuine differential shifts.

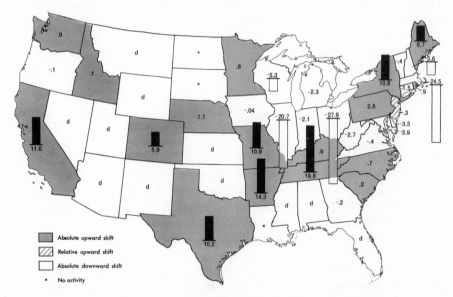

Figure 82. Net Shift in Leather and Leather Products Employment, 1939-54.

State figures represent % of total net shift. Total net shift as % of incremental change: 402.4. Total net shift as % of 1939 leather and leather products employment: 7.4. (d = not available because of disclosure problem.) Source: Appendix Table K.

There are really *two* basic shifts, with contrary results in some instances, reflected in Figure 82. At the risk of some oversimplification, the shift out of the Great Lakes states and into the Middle Atlantic states might be said to represent an eastward shift in leather-tanning and production of footwear cut-stock; and the shift out of New England and into states such as Missouri, Arkansas, Texas and California represents a westward shift of the shoe industry.

As there is substantial weight-loss in the processing of hides, the tanning industry is oriented to the sources of leather inputs. This form of orientation has not always been prevalent. In earlier days the weight of the bark used in tanning was five times the weight of the product and two and a half times the weight of the hide. Production was carried on close to the forests in the East. The development of concentrated and inorganic tanning which diminished the importance of transporting bark, plus the development of large scale meat-packing in the Midwest, caused a widespread migration to the Great Lakes states. Only the light leathers based upon imported hides retained much activity on the Eastern Seaboard.[5]

In our current period the trend is reversing itself, and there is a shift back to the Eastern Seaboard. As before, the reason is a change in the access to materials. The demand for leather has come to exceed the supplies that develop as a by-product of meat-packing. As a consequence, a larger share of the leather output is based upon imported hides; hence the decline in the Great Lakes states and the expansion in the Middle Atlantic states.[6]

The eastern shift in leather tanning has been matched by a shift in leather cut-stock operations.[7] Production of cut-stock tends to be located near the leather source because of the weight losses involved.

Contrasted with these eastern shifts involving leather are the western shifts in the shoe industry. Nearly 70% of the downward shift (absolute) in this industry occurred in New England and the Middle Atlantic states, and the other 30% in the Great Lakes states. Missouri, Tennessee, and Arkansas accounted for about half of the upward shift, and Pennsylvania, Texas, and California for most of the remainder.

The shoe industry developed early in New England. It was essentially handicraft and heavily agglomerated and specialized because of the requirements of skilled labor. New England continued to be the nation's shoeshop long after population trends had carried the markets westward. The segregation of tasks and the invention of shoe machinery significantly reduced the strongest binding force in the agglomerative complex—skilled labor. Further, the leasing policy on shoe machinery wiped out interregional differences in capital costs. These changes exposed the industry to the influence of the location determinants that have been controlling in the present period. Owing to the higher cost of transporting the finished product, the industry became more oriented to terminal markets. And, owing to the importance of labor and a reduction in labor skill requirements, it also tended to be attracted to areas with relatively low labor costs. The shifts that have taken place in the industry and its present distribution represent a compromise between these two forces.

Under the stimulus of the newer pulls, a part of the industry had shifted from New England to the Middle Atlantic states and then to the Great Lakes states—particularly Cincinnati, Detroit, Chicago, and Milwaukee. In our current period, these forces have continued. The importance of the market is certainly reflected in the expansion in California and Texas. The shoemaking complex based on

[5] Edgar M. Hoover, Jr., *Location Theory and the Shoe and Leather Industries* (Cambridge: Harvard University Press, 1937), pp. 137-55.

[6] New England shared in this gain, but it was more than offset by the decline in the shoe industry.

[7] Unassembled soles, heels, uppers, etc.

St. Louis has reaped the major gains associated with a shifting market because it was in an excellent position to realize the best compromise of forces. (1) It is nearer to expanding markets than any other major shoe-producing area. (2) In the nearby states—Kentucky, Tennessee, and Arkansas—it has ready access to relatively cheap labor. (3) Although agglomeration economies are less important than in the earlier period, they are still active. St. Louis has been able to bring to full realization a specialization of function by relegating standard work and cut-stock to nearby states and retaining for itself general assembly and warehousing functions, as well as some production of style goods that require greater labor skill.[8]

The downward shifts in employment in the shoe industry that characterize New England, the Middle Atlantic states, and the Great Lakes states reflect (1) a less favorable position relative to shifting markets and (2) a relative labor-cost disadvantage.

Pennsylvania and Connecticut are interesting exceptions in the East. They seem to reflect market access with a reverse twist. The growing importance of style goods in shoes is reemphasizing the importance of access to markets through style centers. Pennsylvania and Connecticut are favorably situated with reference to the New York style center. In addition, Pennsylvania can claim some labor-cost advantage in the depressed anthracite regions.

Stone, Clay, and Glass Products

The stone, clay, and glass products industry is not a large sector of manufacturing and its growth rate has been sufficiently close to the national average that the 1-digit proportionality effect is not worth considering in our context. Its contribution to the differential shift in total manufacturing employment, however, has been of more consequence. Changes in this industry accounted for more than 25% of the total differential shift in manufacturing employment in West Virginia and for a significant part of the total in Florida, Nevada, Ohio, and Pennsylvania.

The shifts are roughly consistent with the total differential shifts in manufacturing employment. The eastern end of the Manufacturing Belt accounted for 85% of the downward shift. The principal upward shifts were in California, Texas, Florida, and Kansas.

The basic explanation for these shifts lies in changing markets and changing technology that places greater emphasis on market access. The importance of market access is indicated by the very high correlation with population for this industry (Table 150).

The cement industry is a good example. The product has low value per unit

[8]The reference to the St. Louis area here is very broad. Shoe manufacture itself has moved out of the St. Louis metropolitan area in order to take advantage of the cheaper labor in the surrounding states; only a few thousand persons are today producing shoes in the St. Louis metropolitan area. However, the shoe industry does employ many thousands of persons in this area in headquarters operations, particularly warehousing and general assembly and "paper-work" operations, as well as the manufacture of some shoe accessories.

of weight, and transportation costs on the final product amount to almost 20% of the non-labor costs for the industry. This fact, together with the fact that the inputs employed are found in every region, allows production to be market-oriented. Production takes place today in 38 states.

Clay products present a similar picture. The glass industry produces a fragile product that is expensive to prepare for shipping and takes a higher transport rate than glass sand.

The importance of the market helps to explain why the westward shift is so much in evidence here. However, the shift in final markets does not serve to explain the upward shift in stone, clay, and glass employment in parts of the Southeast, in Illinois and Michigan, and in parts of New England. Nor do the downward shifts in the eastern end of the Manufacturing Belt seem proportional to relative declines in market access that are realistic for this area.

The explanation of these discrepancies lies in the fact that the orientation for several important sectors of the industry has been in process of change during our period. The Middle Altantic states, together with West Virginia and Ohio, constitute the original center of the glass industry. These areas had good deposits of glass sand and ample fuel. Natural gas is the logical fuel for the glass industry because of the tremendous advantage of temperature control in glass-making. As new fuel sources became available in the Southwest, some shifts were made to natural gas sites. This type of shift is in evidence during a part of the current period. With the advent of pipelines, however, the natural fuel has been made economically available at the principal intermediate markets in the Manufacturing Belt. This has been mostly responsible for the expansion recorded by Michigan and Illinois. (These changes also help explain the concentration of downward shifts in the eastern end of the Manufacturing Belt.)

Likewise the cement industry has not always been so widespread. In 1900, 70% of the output came from the Lehigh Valley in Pennsylvania, which had especially good access to excellent limestone deposits and cheap coal. Technological changes that permitted economical use of fuels other than coal and of lower-grade raw materials have destroyed this input advantage and allowed the market forces greater play. A major part of the shift into the Southeast stems primarily from the fact that the Southeast was a deficit supply area, rather than from a relative increase in market access. Under the impact of changing technology, an important shift into this region has taken place.[9]

Metal and Metal Products Industries

The location of the metal products industries may be influenced to some degree both by access to resources and by access to final markets, but it is probably not dominated by either. A glance at Table 150 reveals that these industries occupy a middle range in the array recording the degree of association with population.

[9]The South and New England have also enjoyed some upward shifts because these areas are important in the production of cut stone. In this segment the raw materials are not regionally ubiquitous and, therefore, exert more influence upon location.

No other group of industries is so characteristically intermediate or so closely tied together through intra-industry relationships on both the input and output side of the market. With one small exception, a third or more *of the inputs as well as the outputs* of every 2-digit metal and metal products industry comes from or goes to other industries in the metal products group.

These are the industries that have built up the highest concentrations in the Manufacturing Belt. They find their best location orientation within an agglomerated complex of activities (a) because of the important intra-industry ties, (b) because of the important *external* economies that attend clustering and specialization in an urban metropolitan complex, and (c) because these are often industries for which *internal* scale economies are important, and which are oriented more to national markets than to regional markets.

It must follow that the changes taking place in the metal and metal products industries will be explained partly by changes taking place in each region's access to resources and final markets. Most important, however, will be changes that alter each region's access to essential agglomeration advantages.[10]

PRIMARY METALS

The industries in this group make an important contribution to an understanding of the shifts in total manufacturing employment. They comprise one of the largest 2-digit manufacturing sectors (about 8% of the total) and exhibit significant differential and proportionality effects.

They are slow-growth industries (Table 147). The downward proportionality shifts in total employment shown by Alabama and some of the Mountain states, areas of specialization in primary metals, are consistent with this fact. In the Manufacturing Belt states that specialize in primary metals (and possibly in Arizona), this tendency was more than offset by specialization in other rapid-growth sectors; but the upward proportionality shift shown by these states (Figure 74) would unquestionably have been greater were it not for the downward influence exerted by the primary metals industries. However, as usual, it is the differential effect that is most striking.

Figure 83 shows the major employment shifts in these industries between 1939 and 1954. The eastern end of the Manufacturing Belt lost heavily in relative terms. New Jersey, Pennsylvania, West Virginia, and Ohio account for nearly 80% of the net downward shift. Six states experienced significant upward shifts: New York, Michigan, Wisconsin, Texas, California, and Washington. In fifteen states, the differential shifts in the metal products industries were a significant part of the total differential shift.[11]

[10]Unfortunately any adequate discussion of the important changes in agglomeration characteristics is out of the question, because of the lack of existing knowledge on this point. We can, therefore, provide little more than a rather superficial treatment of what is probably the big sector of the economy.

[11]Arizona (15%), Arkansas (7%), Colorado (5%), Connecticut (7%), Iowa (13%), Kentucky (7%), Louisiana (7%), New Jersey (6%), Oregon (6%), Pennsylvania (25%), Texas (11%), Utah (30%), Washington (17%), West Virginia (20%), and Wisconsin (9%). See Table 151.

Needless to say, the changes in access that have stimulated these shifts are a composite of those bringing about changes in the individual metals industries that comprise this sector. It is to these we now turn.

Blast Furnaces and Steel Mills: The most important of the primary metal industries by every measure is the iron and steel industry. Blast furnaces and steel mills account for fully half of the employment in primary metals; and if iron and steel foundries are included fully 75% of the employment in primary metals is covered.

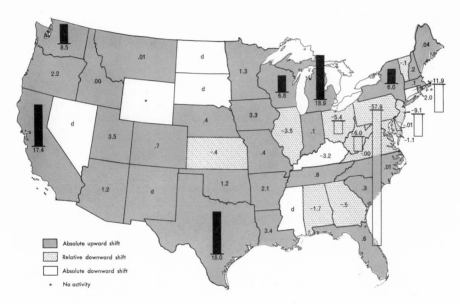

Figure 83. Net Shift in Primary Metal Industries Employment, 1939-54. State figures represent % of total net shift. Total net shift as % of incremental change: 31.4. Total net shift as % of 1939 primary metals industries employment: 12.4. (d = not available because of disclosure problem.) Source: Appendix Table K.

At this level there is both a 2-digit proportionality and differential effect in operation. Of the primary metal industries, blast furnaces and steel mills constitute the only slow-growth sector (but, because of the size of the sub-group, primary metals as a whole appear as a slow-growth category). The heavy specialization in blast furnaces and steel mills in Pennsylvania, Ohio, and West Virginia means that the heavy downward shifts in these states are in part a result of this proportionality effect.

Table 155, based on steel "districts," shows that the Pittsburgh-Youngstown area experienced the greatest relative decline in steel-making capacity over the period 1930-54. In contrast the Eastern, Southern, and Western areas and the

Table 155. Distribution by district of steel-making capacity in the United States, 1930–1954

(per cent of total)

	1930	1940	1946	1950	1954
Eastern	16.1	19.8	19.5	20.0	20.8
Pittsburgh-Youngstown	46.4	42.2	39.7	39.4	35.7
Cleveland-Detroit	7.3	9.7	8.3	9.4	10.3
Chicago	24.6	21.8	22.5	20.9	22.0
Southern	3.0	3.8	4.7	4.6	5.6
Western	2.6	2.7	5.3	5.7	5.6
TOTAL	100.0	100.0	100.0	100.0	100.0

SOURCE: Paul G. Craig, "Location Factors in the Development of Steel Centers," *Papers and Proceedings of the Regional Science Association,* Volume 3 (1957), p. 261.

For historical data on capacity and a map showing the geographic boundaries of the districts (which are the bases for the steel industry reports on capacity and production), see American Iron and Steel Institute, *Steel Facts,* No. 124, February 1954, p. 2.

Cleveland-Detroit area made gains. The Chicago area was roughly static.

The changes in access that have brought about these shifts in the iron and steel industry have been well documented.[12] They are compounded of three important elements: (1) changes in technology that modified the transport orientation of the industry, (2) shifts in raw materials access, and (3) shifts in market access.

In the early phase of iron and steel development in the United States, the general rule of thumb concerning location orientation was "iron moves to coal." In 1810, it took five tons of coal and two tons of ore to produce a ton of steel. In this early phase the steel industry became centered in the Pittsburgh-Youngstown area on top of the nation's richest deposit of good-grade coking coal. Although technological change has been rapidly reducing the dominance of coal in the iron and steel complex, the influence of this early phase is still felt. In 1938, Pennsylvania, West Virginia, and Ohio produced 56.5% of the industry output but consumed only 30.5% of the industry output.[13]

Successive technological changes have reduced the coal content of a ton of finished steel to significantly less than two tons. Add to this the fact that trans-

[12]The reader interested in examining this literature would do well to start with Richard Hartshorne, "Location Factors in the Iron and Steel Industry," *Economic Geography,* Vol. 4 (July 1928), pp. 241-52; Walter Isard, "Some Locational Factors in the Iron and Steel Industry Since the Early Nineteenth Century," *Journal of Political Economy,* Vol. 56 (June 1948), pp. 203-17; Allan Rodgers, "Industrial Inertia—A Major Factor in the Location of the Steel Industry in the United States," *Geographical Review,* Vol. 42 (January 1952), pp. 56-68; Paul Craig, "Location Factors in the Development of Steel Centers," *Papers and Proceedings of the Regional Science Association,* Volume 3 (1957), pp. 249-65.

[13]Craig, *op, cit.,* p. 255.

port rates on finished steel are higher than on the raw material inputs[14] and the fact that scrap—which is most accessible at the markets—can be used to reduce the ore content, and it is plain to see that the market has assumed the major role in the location matrix.

In response to this basic change, steel capacity commenced to move to the deficit supply areas. Early in the century basic capacity began to expand out from the Pittsburgh area to Chicago, Cleveland, Buffalo, and Sparrows Point (Baltimore). More recently has come the development of Detroit; of San Bernardino, Provo, and Pueblo in the West; and of the Texas mills. The construction of the world's most modern integrated steel mill on the tidewater at Morrisville, Pennsylvania, has taken place too recently to be reflected adequately in the period we examine.

In addition to a movement to even out the regional distribution of markets and capacity, these shifts have led in some degree to shifts in the markets themselves. The steel industry is closely associated with manufacturing as an intermediate market (it distributes outputs to 132 of the 197 industries listed in the 1947 input-output table). Figure 72 suggests the extent to which the shifts of the steel industry in the western end of the Manufacturing Belt, as well as in the Southwest and Far West, could have gained strength from the shifts of markets into these areas. Paradoxically even the East Coast expansion has gained to some degree because of the westward shift. The East Coast is often in the best position to serve the deficit supply areas in the South and West by water transport.

The movement to the East Coast has also been aided by a basic change in the availability of iron ore. Venezuela and Labrador ores have become available at tidewater sites at relatively favorable cost.

One point needs to be emphasized. Although significant changes have taken place in the location of the iron and steel industry, the major changes have taken place *within* the Manufacturing Belt. There are several important reasons why this is so. (1) While the present-day steel industry is predominantly market-oriented, it must still expend enormous effort in assembling its raw materials. Interregional differences in the cost of assembling these inputs are substantial, and the fact remains that sites within the Manufacturing Belt still have more favorable access, on the average, to raw material inputs. (2) As the industry's pattern of orientation has changed, there has been a shift to markets stimulated by (a) the existence of regional imbalances between production and consumption and (b) shifts over time and space in the distribution of the steel market. Well over four-fifths of the steel market, however, is contained within the Manufacturing Belt. Only about 10% of the steel output goes to sectors that could be classed as terminal markets. Around 80% goes into the metal products industries, which are highly concentrated in the Manufacturing Belt. (3) Though expanding, the markets in the South and West have not yet reached the size

---

[14]Rodgers has pointed out that, by 1939, the weighted transportation costs for finished steel were 53.2% of the total transport costs for the industry, thereby exceeding the combined transportation costs on the inputs. *Op. cit.*, Table 2, p. 58.

where they will support significant additions of fully integrated capacity.[15]

Primary Aluminum: The refining and milling of non-ferrous metal products account for about one-fourth of the total employment in primary metals. Of these metals, aluminum is by far the most important and accounts for roughly half.[16] Although aluminum refining and milling are both included under primary metals, they are not highly integrated as in the steel industry and their location characteristics are quite different.

The disclosure rules of the census do not allow us to present anything like a shift picture for either segment of the industry. Table 156, however, gives the location of all of the electrolytic reduction plants and the dates that they were established. With it we can identify four major shifts in the industry, three of which took place within the limits of our current period. The industry started in New York and then expanded into the Tennessee Valley. During World War II some expansions took place in the Tennessee Valley but the major change was a shift to the Pacific Northwest. In the postwar period, Texas, Louisiana, and Arkansas gained a share of the industry. Three plants in the Ohio Valley have been announced so recently that they are not at this writing in operation.

Basically the production of pig aluminum is input-oriented, and it is to changes in access to basic inputs that we must look in order to explain these shifts. Superficially one would expect the industry to be transport-oriented, with alumina sources dominating the location pattern. Transportation costs on each ton of alumina amount to about $52,[17] and it takes two tons of alumina to make a ton of pig aluminum. The cost savings of a favorable raw material location, however, are far offset by the cost savings in access to cheap power. Each ton of aluminum requires 18,000 kilowatt hours of electricity. A difference of one mill in the rate will change the cost of electricity by $18.00 per ton—approximately 5% of its price.

It follows, therefore, that the shifts in the industry were a response to changes in access to the most economical sources of power. For a long period cheap water power claimed all additions to capacity—first at Niagara, then the Tennessee Valley and the Pacific Northwest. As the water resources in each case came to be fully utilized, the industry turned to the next. More recently with the best water power sites appropriated, the industry has turned to cheap natural gas and lignite in the Southwest. The Pacific Northwest still has the largest reservoir of

---

[15]The over-all shift picture for iron and steel foundry products and the logic of that shift are not basically too different from that discussed above for blast furnaces and steel mills. There are differences in the detail of the shifts and the detail of the distribution between states because the major markets for foundry products are different from those for mill products. An analysis of this detail, however, is beyond the scope of our present effort.

[16]That part of the aluminum industry that is engaged in converting bauxite into alumina is not considered here. It is classed as a chemical industry and was discussed briefly on page 435 *supra.* The reader who wants to take a closer look at the location characteristics of the aluminum industry is advised to consult John V. Krutilla, *The Structure of Costs and Regional Advantage in Primary Aluminum Production* (unpublished doctoral dissertation, Harvard University) ; also "Locational Factors Influencing Recent Aluminum Expansion," *Southern Economic Journal,* Vol. 21 (January 1955), pp. 275-76.

[17]As of 1954.

Table 156. Aluminum plants of the United States, June 1956

Present owner	Location	Energy source	Date started
1 Alcoa	Massena, New York	Water	1903
2 Alcoa	Alcoa, Tennessee	Water	1914
3 Alcoa	Badin, North Carolina	Water	1916
4 Alcoa	Vancouver, Washington	Water	1940
5 Reynolds	Longview, Washington	Water	1941
6 Reynolds	Listerhill, Alabama	Water	1941
7 Reynolds	Troutdale, Oregon	Water	1942
8 Reynolds	Jones Mill, Arkansas	Gas	1942
9 Kaiser	Spokane, Washington	Water	1942
10 Kaiser	Tacoma, Washington	Water	1942
11 Alcoa	Point Comfort, Texas	Gas	1950
12 Kaiser	Chalmette, Louisiana	Gas	1951
13 Alcoa	Wenatchee, Washington	Water	1952
14 Alcoa	Rockdale, Texas	Lignite	1952
15 Reynolds	Corpus Christi, Texas	Gas	1952
16 Reynolds	Arkadelphia, Arkansas	Gas	1954
17 Anaconda	Columbia Falls, Montana	Water	1955
18 Kaiser	Ravenswood, W. Virginia	Coal	In construction 1956
19 Olin Mathieson	Clarington, Ohio	Coal	In construction 1956
20 Alcoa	Evansville, Indiana	Coal	In construction 1956

SOURCE: *Business Week,* June 16, 1956, p. 88.

underdeveloped water power, but Department of Interior policy provides that all but 70,000 KWH be made available to utilities. Further expansion in the Southwest is unlikely because of rising natural gas prices and the relative exhaustibility of this resource. It is not surprising, then, that the most recent expansions have been announced for the heart of the Ohio Valley. Alumina can be barged in on inland waterways. It is in the heart of the aluminum market and modern steam plants utilizing coal are almost as efficient as any of the alternative power sources.

In contrast to aluminum refining, aluminum rolling and drawing is essentially market-oriented. The freight rate on pig aluminum is only half the rate on sheet aluminum. Since the major portion of metal fabricating takes place in the Manufacturing Belt, the major additions to mill capacity have been in this area.

Other Non-Ferrous Metals: The other non-ferrous metals—primarily copper, zinc, and lead—are mined predominantly in the Mountain states (over 95% of the copper). These states seem to have gained somewhat in production at the expense of Michigan, Illinois, and the tri-state area (Missouri, Oklahoma, and Arkansas). Since the mill-processing that concentrates, smelts, roasts, and converts the ore is located close to the mines (because of significant weight losses) major additions for these metals have come in the expanding mining areas—particularly Arizona.

Summary: Referring briefly once again to Figure 83, we can state these general conclusions. The expansion in the eastern and western ends of the Manufacturing Belt is primarily in iron and steel, with some assistance from non-ferrous rolling and drawing. The expansion in the Pacific Northwest is almost exclusively in aluminum. California's expansion is primarily in iron and steel. In the Mountain states that show upward shifts, the rise is attributable to iron and steel and copper primarily. The Southwest expansion is tied to iron and steel and aluminum reduction. The scattered states in the Southeast and New England that show slight gains owe these gains to an assortment of minor metals that have developed importance during and since the war.

METAL PRODUCTS INDUSTRIES

In this section we have lumped several 2-digit categories together for discussion—specifically fabricated metal products, machinery (except electrical), electrical machinery, and transportation equipment.[18] Separately, these industries constitute some of the largest and most dynamic sectors of the U. S. manufacturing economy. Combined, their significance for understanding regional economic growth in unrivaled. They account for one-third of all manufacturing employment. No sectors surpass them in the importance of their interregional shifts. The inter-state shifts in these industries between 1939 and 1954 amounted to almost 30% of their total combined 1939 employment; in transportation equipment, the shift equaled 71% of the total 1939 employment in that sector.

Their proportionality effect has been most important. Every one of these 2-digit components is among the most rapidly growing elements of manufacturing employment (Table 147). Except for New Jersey, Connecticut, and California, the states that are specialists in these rapid-growth sectors are all concentrated in the western end of the Manufacturing Belt. It is interesting to note, therefore, that over 80% of the net upward *proportionality* shift in total manufacturing employment is also concentrated here (see Figure 73). However, differential shifts across state lines have been even more important, particularly with the decentralization of production in some of these categories, as in the case of transportation equipment. As a result, even the western end of the Manufacturing Belt has lost relative standing. Basically the shift is out of the Manufacturing Belt states and into the Southeast and West, with California exhibiting the major gains and Michigan the major (relative) losses. New York state forms an exception to the general relative decline in the Manufacturing Belt.

---

[18]Our reasons for doing so are as follows: First, there is a kind of homogeneity in these activities that few other 2-digit groups share to the same degree. This has made it possible to construct a shift pattern for the whole group that is to a considerable extent representative of each. Second, as has already been suggested, there has been very little specialized study of the space properties of these industries and we know only general things about them. Last, these industries are too big and too important to be adequately covered in this limited study.

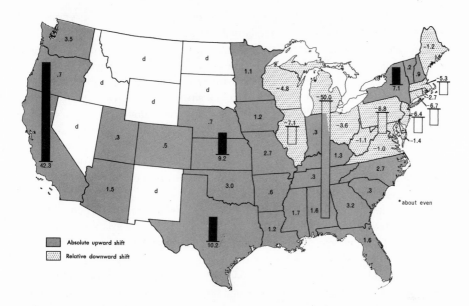

Figure 84. Net Shift in Metal Products Industries Employment, 1939-54.

State figures represent % of tôtal net shift. Total net shift as % of incremental change: 21.2. Total net shift as % of 1939 metal products industries employment: 27.0. Metal products include: fabricated metal products, machinery (except electrical), electrical machinery, and transportation equipment. (d = not available because of disclosure problem.) Source: Appendix Table K.

Indiana also displays a relative gain, but its magnitude is significant only in contrast with the surrounding states.[19] The general configuration of this shift corresponds very closely to the total differential shift in manufacturing employment shown in Figure 73. This is certainly an outstanding element in explaining the total shift picture.

That this is so is supported by additional evidence. There were only eight states in which the total differential behavior was not affected to a significant extent by at least one of these 2-digit metal products sectors.[20] None of these received more than 5% of their total differential shift from these sectors. More important, there were only seventeen states in which these sectors accounted for

[19]This pattern is strikingly similar for each of the component 2-digit groups. The reader can check this by examining the data presented in Appendix Table K. There are, of course, some differences in detail. Component shifts that contrast in direction, however, are limited to the Manufacturing Belt states. Michigan, for example, displays significant gains in fabricated metal products and machinery only to have these more than offset by relative losses in transportation equipment. These internal shifts within the manufacturing belt were not sufficient to counteract the general downward shift for the region as a whole.

[20]Idaho, Montana, Nevada, North Dakota, South Carolina, South Dakota, Vermont and Wyoming. See Table 151.

less than 20% of the total differential behavior. In six states, 60% or more of the total differential behavior is explained by these sectors.[21]

What are the major orientation factors at work here that could contribute to an understanding of the changes in access leading to these extensive shifts?

First of all, regional changes in access to primary metal inputs are not apt to be very important over-all in explaining the shifts in the metal products industries. Although this conclusion runs counter to a common concept, there is evidence to support it. Iron and steel products and all forms of metal rolling and drawing, we have seen, tend to be market-oriented under modern technology. This is the major part of all primary metals activity, and one may tentatively conclude that shifts in primary metals employment are more apt to follow shifts in metal products industries than vice versa.

This is particularly true if these industries are not strongly bound to the inputs that the primary metals industries provide. That they are not is suggested by at least two students of the metal products industries. In investigating this field, both Robert Kuenne and John Waters start with the hypothesis that metal-fabricating industries have tended to locate in areas where large amounts of steel capacity are located.[22] Both conclude that ties to primary metal capacity are not major location factors. Kuenne says, "The twelve regions in the United States which possess more than 1,000,000 tons of steel capacity account for about 90% of the total capacity in the 69 areas. Yet, within these major steel areas, only about 40% of the production employment in fabricating industries is located." He computes the rank correlation between employment in the metal-fabricating industries and population to be .90. Metal-fabricating employment correlated with basic steel capacity yields a coefficient of only .33.[23] Kuenne, therefore, tends to assign an important role to the market in determining the location of metal-fabricating industries. Waters concludes, "In general primary steel producer-consumer industry relationships are unsatisfactory as explanations for the locations of the steel-using industries in Peninsular Ontario. . . . Agglomerating factors might account better for the distribution of these industries. . . ." [24]

We do not mean to rule out altogether a role for changing access to primary metal inputs. The expansion in steel capacity in the Far West and Southwest has probably established a permissive factor which may have allowed cumulative second- or third-round expansions in some fabricating activities that might otherwise have been unfeasible in those areas. What we suggest is that other factors have been more important over-all.

The fact that Kuenne emphasizes markets and Waters emphasizes agglomera-

[21]Connecticut, Kansas, Michigan, California, Ohio, and Oklahoma. See Table 151.

[22]Robert E. Kuenne, *The Use of Input-Output Techniques for the Estimation of Employment in the Delaware Valley*, (unpublished doctoral dissertation, Harvard University). John W. Waters, *The Locational Significance of Primary Steel Producer-Consumer Industry Relationship in Peninsular Ontario* (doctoral dissertation, State University of Iowa, on microfilm).

[23]Kuenne, *op. cit.*, pp. 13-25.

[24]Waters, *op. cit.*, p. 266. Unfortunately Waters does not succeed in giving any dimension to the agglomeration factors.

tion economies as the important elements need not be inconsistent. At the beginning of this section we pointed out that, to a considerable degree, these industries sell to essentially agglomerated markets. This suggests that the shifts in the metal products industries are partly a result of shifts in the markets they serve and partly a result of regional changes in the agglomeration economies that they find so significant. Since there are around thirty 3-digit components that should be considered in this shift, we shall discuss here only a few key industries under three headings.

Agglomeration Not a Necessary Characteristic: Although agglomeration appears to be the major characteristic of the industry groups that we examine here, there are a least five of the 3-digit groups that do not show any strong tendency for this form of orientation. Combined, these account for between 15% and 20% of the total employment in the metal-fabricating groups. All of them are oriented either to final markets or to intermediate markets or inputs that are not tied in with the agglomerations of the Manufacturing Belt.

We might identify these sectors briefly and see how they differ from the industries more characteristic of the metal products group. The production of tin cans (SIC 341) is a strongly market-oriented process. The industry produces a low-value product that acquires great bulk in processing. As a consequence, it is located near major food-processing plants—often to the extent of being connected by a common conveyor. The shift pattern for this industry shows that the groups which have made the major gains (California, Florida and some of the Plains states) have made the greatest gains in the production of food products subject to canning.

The production of mining machinery also seems to be market-oriented—and, again, to an essentially resource market. For example, Texas produces almost half of the oil-mining machinery, with California and Oklahoma being the runners-up. The Southwest (particularly Louisiana and Oklahoma) shows the principal upward shifts here. This industry produces a highly specialized product and, consequently, sells important services as well as machinery. This makes close communication with the market important.

Two sectors appear to be oriented more to final markets (or to intermediate markets closely associated with final markets). The structural metal products industry is an example (SIC 344). Only slightly more than half of this industry group's production is in the Manufacturing Belt. Agglomeration economies seem less important in part because most of its inputs come from primary and secondary metal groups, rather than being distributed widely among the metal fabricators. The shift pattern for this industry is predominately into the Southeast and West, following the more general shifts in construction employment and its association with shifting final and intermediate markets. Another case where the market influence seems strong is in the ships and boats industry (SIC 373). This industry has displayed marked downward shifts from the Middle Atlantic region into the Great Lakes states, the Gulf states, and the Pacific Coast states. This is largely due to an unprecedented boom in the construction of small pleasure craft.

The aircraft industry has been the most dynamic sector in the metal products group. Its growth rate was over 1000% for the period 1939-54. The engine and propeller segments of the industry require considerable skilled labor and seem to enjoy significant agglomeration economies; their production is concentrated in the Manufacturing Belt and has tended to stay there. On the other hand, the production of airframes and finished aircraft has done considerable shifting and has displayed rather remarkable mobility. As early as 1940 one-half of the industry's capacity was in locations other than its original location.[25] Inputs are widespread in source, high in value, and easily shipped. The market is primarily military and highly centralized; and can be served in a matter of hours, regardless of location. The industry started in the East with New York City as a center. It moved to the West Coast—partly in response to actually and potentially available labor supplies, partly because of a climate better for testing planes and for outside work (as well as permitting less expensive buildings), and partly because surplus government buildings were available. In our current period the evidence indicates that the industry is shifting eastward again with Texas, Oklahoma, Kansas, Georgia, and Alabama all showing important expansions. Labor and climate continue to appear as significant factors, but the industry appears to come close to the footloose category. Few industries can match the number of instances in which plant, equipment, and personnel were moved from one region to another.

Currently, also, there are additional factors to be considered. Depending on how the aircraft industry is defined—i.e., to include or exclude missiles—the industry can either be said to be changing in character or to be declining. The bulk of the industry is assigned to defense production, where the ratio of missiles to aircraft is rapidly changing. Missile systems have the following major components: (1) airplanes; (2) guidance and control systems; (3) propulsion units; (4) nose-cones with warheads; (5) ground guidance and launching systems. Usually the airplane manufacturer assembles the missile and acts as prime contractor. Like airplane plants, many missile assembly plants are in California. Here, the advantage of a climate favoring testing is replaced by the advantage of proximity to test firing ranges, i.e., large uninhabited areas. Propulsion units, because of noise and explosion hazards, as well as the warheads, are manufactured outside population centers. Since so much of the missile takes the form of electronic equipment, which requires skills for its research and development activities as well as its production, the electronics phase tends to be close to populated areas. On this basis, it can be assumed that the major industry in Los Angeles in a few years will most likely be the electronics industry rather than the aircraft industry.

It is also worth noting that the civilian aircraft industry is shifting from propeller-driven to jet planes. For example, Douglas Aircraft will produce no more DC-6s. Because of the noise factor and the danger that is associated with test flights, the testing of jets will have to be done more and more outside populated areas. This is likely to be an increasingly important factor in location decisions.

[25] W. G. Cunningham, *The Aircraft Industry: a Study in Industrial Location* (Los Angeles: L. L. Morrison, 1951), p. 191.

It is plain to see that these five sectors, all of which find little significance in agglomeration economies, have concentrated their growth in areas outside the Manufacturing Belt and go far to account for the shifts revealed by Figure 84.

Agglomeration Economies Important but Changing in Significance: Significant shifts out of the Manufacturing Belt have been displayed by a number of industries in the metal products groups for which agglomeration economies appear to be quite important. From this it seems either (1) that other regions are gaining relative access to significant agglomeration economies, or (2) that the agglomeration economies for these industries are becoming less important. Actually there are good reasons to believe that both of these developments are taking place.

One reason why metal-fabricating industries have tended to locate in the Manufacturing Belt is that they usually require large-scale operations for economical production. This means that regional markets are often not large enough to support certain types of production and the major portion of that production becomes concentrated in the region with the largest regional market and the best over-all access to the national market—i.e., the Manufacturing Belt.

Another reason is that these industries often find it more economical to be close to a variety of intermediate suppliers and markets, thereby reducing the effort and expense of communication and taking advantage of certain specialized products and services they would otherwise have to provide for themselves.

However, as the total economy is growing and as other regions, like the Far West, make striking differential gains and become more diversified, these forms of production may be finding that some regional markets are passing a threshold where they become a feasible locus for economical production.

At the same time, there may be some trends under way that have made the Manufacturing Belt less attractive as an agglomeration center. Agglomeration usually creates some diseconomies as well as economies—particularly in areas where the tendency is well established. There is evidence, for example, that rising labor costs in the Manufacturing Belt may be offsetting some of the other advantages that the region has to offer. This may run counter to the common belief that regional differences in wages are disappearing. This belief is probably founded on the fact that the percentage rate of increase in some areas, such as the Southeast, has been greater than for the nation as a whole. However, this is consistent with the fact that the *absolute* differential between Manufacturing Belt wages and external wages may be widening, or at least remains significant.

Other factors may work in the same direction. Technological developments in standardized assembly, automatic machinery, data processing, and management techniques often make it possible to carry on at least parts of an industry's function outside an area with primary agglomeration economies. This has also been a period of rising transportation costs. It is characteristic of such cost increases that they usually penalize the distribution of finished products more severely than the assembly of inputs.

All of these influences have a greater opportunity to become manifest in a period of rapid growth such as has characterized our period. It is much easier to make rational adjustments in incremental capacity than in existing capacity.

A number of industries in the metal products group display behavior suggesting that some combination of the factors just discussed is in operation. Perhaps the key exhibit is the automobile industry. This is a highly concentrated industry with almost three-quarters of its employment in three states—Michigan Ohio, and Indiana. Michigan alone accounts for over half of the total. Few other industries have made so much of external agglomeration economies. The region centered on Detroit has been developed into a vast complex of suppliers and service functions for the gigantic auto industry. This complex has proved to be vulnerable, however. Michigan has incurred large relative losses in this industry. (Over 80% of the net downward shift. In the post-war period the losses have been absolute.) To some extent the shift out of Michigan represents nothing more than a readjustment within the agglomeration complex. The principal gainer was Ohio. Indiana and Illinois also showed relative upward shifts. But this shift was far more fundamental. Savings to be realized in transport and assembly costs are pulling automobile assembly towards expanding markets. Some 60% of the net upward shift appears to be outside the Detroit – Great Lakes complex. Such states as California, Kansas, Texas, and Massachusetts have made important gains. During the past fifty years automobile assembly meant Michigan. Today that state produces only one-third of the new automobiles.

Other industries appear to share in this trend toward decentralization. The agricultural machinery and tractor industry (SIC 352) has displayed a decided shift of production out of Illinois and Wisconsin to areas closer to regional markets. This is largely because a movement is under way to establish branch assembly plants to save on heavy freight costs from the Midwest. Service and household machinery (SIC 359) and communication equipment (SIC 366) also show similar influences.

For proper perspective, however, it is important to take note of two things. (1) The operating core of these industries remains in the Manufacturing Belt. For example, while Michigan produces only one-third of the automobiles, it still claims half of the industry's total employment. The financial heart, the engineering brains, and the management force for this industry are still there. The major shifts involve branch assembly plants—that part of the industry's operation that benefits least from agglomeration economies. (2) The major expansion outside the Manufacturing Belt has been concentrated in California, Texas, Kansas, and Georgia. These states all have prominent nodal characteristics as central points of large multi-state market areas. Perhaps, even in decentralization, agglomeration economies have been instrumental in shaping the location pattern.

Agglomeration Economies Remain Dominant: There remain, of course, some industries for which the Manufacturing Belt retains all of its traditional importance. Such industries as engines and turbines (SIC 351), insulated cable and wire (SIC 363), engine electrical equipment (SIC 364), and railroad equipment, all concentrate close to 100% of their employment in the Manufacturing Belt. Virtually all of the shifts that have taken place in these industries have taken place within that area. Indeed, in the case of railroad equipment, the Manufacturing Belt has strengthened its hold; faced with the completion of dieseli-zation and serious competition from other transport media, most of the other producing areas have experienced absolute declines in employment.

Most of the industries in the metal products groups fall somewhere between those that exhibit an extreme dependence upon the agglomerations of the Manu-facturing Belt and those, like the automobile industry, that display marked decentralization. All of these have contributed a bit here and a bit there to the shifts out of the Manufacturing Belt we have observed. Often these shifts are more limited in scope. *In the aggregate,* however, they are creating a shift out of the Manufacturing Belt that is significant and undeniable. In 1939, the four 2-digit metal products sectors concentrated 87% of their total employment in the Manufacturing Belt; in 1954, only 76%.

These changes could, if continued, bring about important changes in the location structure of American manufacturing, particularly since these industries have so many important input-output ties with other segments of manufacturing activity. This gives rise to considerable speculation. What causes these shifts? We have suggested that regional changes in relative access to certain agglomera-tion economies and internal scale economies might be fundamental. But are they? If they are, how can we come to grips with their true nature in specific industries? Will the direction of these changes persist? Is this a cumulative process that will draw a larger and larger share of metal products industries out of the Manufacturing Belt? Or will it taper off as regional agglomerations reach their optimum relative expansion based upon largely regional markets? Might it even reverse if coal becomes relatively more important in the power complex?

These are all questions that deserve careful and detailed attention in future research in the field of regional analysis.

A great deal more detail concerning the structure and shifts in these metal products industries is available in the Appendix Tables. The reader may wish to carry some aspect of this analysis to greater length with the assistance of these data.

Instruments and Miscellaneous Manufacturing

These two sectors (SIC 38 and 39) tell an important part of the story of inter-regional shifts in total manufacturing employment. They are both important rapid-growth industries and contribute a great deal to the upward proportion-ality shift in total manufacturing employment displayed by the Manufacturing Belt states. Each of them displayed a differential shift between 1939 and 1954 that amounted to more than one-third of its total 1939 employment. Instru-ments and related products explains more than 10% of the differential shift for only one state (Nebraska). However, there are five more states in which between 5% and 10% of the total differential shift was contributed by this sector.[26] Miscellaneous manufacturing is even more important. In Nebraska and Minne-

[26]Arkansas (estimated), Connecticut, Massachusetts, Minnesota, New York, and Wisconsin.

sota, it accounted for more than 20% of the differential shift in total manufacturing employment. In fourteen additional states it was more than 5% (in six of these, more than 10%).[27]

Two generalizations can be made about these shift patterns.[28] (1) Between 70% and 85% of the total activity in these sectors still takes place in the Manufacturing Belt, and an important part of the shift is within the Manufacturing Belt itself. In general, the principal net downward shifts have been in Illinois, lower New England, and the Middle Atlantic states. With the exception of Illinois, the states in the western end of the Manufacturing Belt have shown upward shifts. This is particularly pronounced in the case of instruments; more than half of the total upward shift has been retained within the Manufacturing Belt. (2) A significant part of the downward shift in instruments, and most of it in miscellaneous manufacturing, has been into states outside the Manufacturing Belt. Iowa, Missouri, and Nebraska show important gains, as do California and Texas.

We cannot hope to analyze the forces back of these differential shifts. Miscellaneous manufacturing is a catch-all group that ranges all the way from musical instruments and toys to morticians' supplies. Only the broadest kind of generalization can be offered on such a heterogeneous classification. The movement to the western end of the Manufacturing Belt and into the Southeast and West suggests considerable influence of the expanding market access of these regions. On the other hand, the concentration of these shifts in the western end of the Manufacturing Belt and in a few states outside suggests an important role for internal scale economies and some agglomeration economies.

A Review of Regional Shifts in Manufacturing

We have examined so many facets of change in manufacturing activity that some review of the ground covered seems called for.

Manufacturing is one of the largest and most dynamic sectors of total employment. In explaining shifts in total employment its role is especially important because it is the basic link between the resource sectors and consuming sectors of the economy. Because internal and external economies of scale are often important, a significant segment of manufacturing activity is characterized by a large *intra*-industry absorption of inputs and outputs and a locational orientation towards "intermediate" inputs and outputs.

In some segments of manufacturing activity, access to resource inputs and to final markets is also important. Taken as a whole, however, the major characteristic of the manufacturing industries is a kind of pull between access to final markets and access to intermediate markets and important agglomeration economies. Over the period under review, the interregional shift in final markets

[27]California (8), Colorado (9 est.), Connecticut (7), Delaware (16), Illinois (15), Kentucky (5), Massachusetts (9.5), Missouri (15), New Hampshire (7), New Jersey (10), New Mexico (over 5), Rhode Island (15), Tennessee (9), Vermont (9), West Virginia (5). See Table 151.

[28]See Appendix Table K.

has had a *secondary* influence upon the location of intermediate markets that has, in general, reduced the relative access to markets for manufactured products in the Manufacturing Belt—particularly in the eastern end of the Belt. There is evidence to suggest that regions outside the Manufacturing Belt are also augmenting their locational advantages with regard to agglomeration economies.

Changes in transportation costs played a role during this period. The relative decline in the cost of short overland hauls and of small lots, compared to long hauls and large lots, has been a favorable factor for the Southeast and the West. The lower wages in the Southeast could also become a significant factor when joined with the growth of regional markets.

The total effect has been to produce a general shift out of the Manufacturing Belt in to the Southeast and the West. While this shift is marked, it is less marked than it would be if the states in the Manufacturing Belt had not had net upward proportionality shifts in manufacturing employment at the 1-digit level. These states tend to specialize in the most rapidly growing manufacturing sectors. As a matter of fact, this proportionality effect is sufficiently important to generate a total upward shift in manufacturing employment in the western end of the Manufacturing Belt in the face of net differential downward shifts (see Figures 72-73-74).

Among the 1-digit employment groups, manufacturing as a whole is a rapid-growth sector. Thus, it explains in large part why the proportionality upward shifts in total employment are concentrated in the Manufacturing Belt (see Figure 47.) These total proportionality shifts are, in turn, important in explaining the upward shifts in total employment at the extreme eastern and western ends of the Manufacturing Belt.

The detail that supports these generalizations is the subject matter of the chapters preceding.

Trade, Service, and Government Activities

Thus far we have given attention to only three of the major sectors of employment (that is to three of the ten 1-digit Census sectors). We forego a detailed treatment of the remaining sectors for two reasons: first, because our central concern is with natural resource activities and the sectors which are most related to these; second, because there is little of the supplementary detail available for analysis that we have for the other sectors.[29]

In order to present a brief statement about the shifts in the "service" sectors of economic activity between 1939 and 1954, we have combined them into a

---

[29]Researchers have, on the whole, failed to recognize the importance of this area of research. Even Stigler's pioneering study restricts its view of the service industries to the national aggregates. Stigler acknowledges that he has only scratched the surface at the national level. Even less has been attempted in the way of an understanding of the functional and regional components of the service industries. See George Stigler, *Trends in Employment in the Service Industries*, National Bureau of Economic Research, 1956 (Princeton: Princeton University Press, 1956).

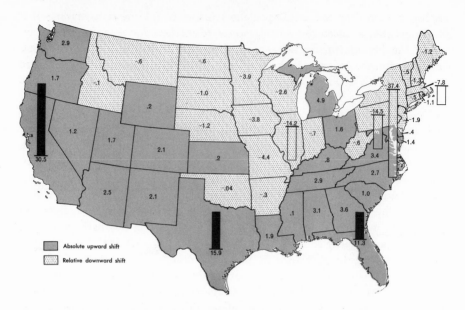

Figure 85. Net Shift in Trade, Service, and Government Activities
Employment, 1939-54.

State figures represent % of total net shift. Total net shift as % of
incremental change: 15.7. Total net shift as % of 1939 trade, service, and
government activities employment: 8.7. Source: Appendix
Tables F-1 and F-2.

composite shift picture shown in Figure 85.[30] Their configuration corresponds
closely with that presented by the shifts in total employment and population (see
Figure 45). Every one of the major growth regions shares in the upward shift
in trade and service activity—the Pacific Coast, the Southwest, Florida, the
western end of the Manufacturing Belt, and some of the Middle Atlantic seaboard states. The areas displaying downward shifts in total employment also

---

[30]This composite shift includes wholesale and retail trade, transportation and public
utilities, finance and real estate, miscellaneous services and government.

We do not include construction in this composite picture for several reasons. (1) Construction is basically a processing industry. The only reason this activity is not included in
manufacturing is its uniqueness in producing an immobile product that is highly market-
oriented. (2) Construction is essentially a "multiplier" industry. It may generate upward
shifts in a region that are a multiple of other initiating shifts that give rise to increases in
private and public overhead. For this reason the shifts are more erratic and particularly
subject to the influence of the cycle. Since our terminal year (1954) was characterized by a
slight recession, the shifts in construction employment are particularly erratic—although they
present a picture that is roughly consistent with the total shifts in population and
employment.

The 1-digit shifts and related data are presented in greater detail for construction and the
service sectors in Appendix Table H.

display downward shifts in trade and service employment with the exception of the Southeastern states.[31]

These shifts in trade-service-government activities have been a very important part of the total shift in employment; about half of all employment is in these sectors. There is good reason to believe, however, that they do not provide a major part of the explanation for total growth behavior. On the whole, these activities are so strongly oriented to final markets that their response to change is essentially a passive one rather than an initiating one. In short, these sectors on the whole[32] appear to follow and reinforce the changes initiated by the other sectors.

There are several bits of evidence that give support to this view. (1) Table 144 reveals that 83% of all inputs in these sectors come from final demand or from intra-industry sources.[33] Some 88% of all outputs go to final demand or intra-industry markets. The ties with final markets are so close that these activities must be intimately associated with changes in the regional distribution of final demand and respond directly to them. (2) These activities have a very close spatial association with population, as shown in Table 136. Even more impressive is the fact that the dispersion of the states about a coefficient of one (signifying a spatial distribution identical with population) was never more than 50% and only occasionally more than 15% for these service sectors. In contrast, the dispersion ran as high as 100% for manufacturing, 300% for agriculture and 700% for mining. (3) The fact that the shifts in service employment revealed by Figure 85 correspond so closely with the shifts in final demand is evidence consistent with the view that these sectors are market-oriented and adaptive.[34]

[31]This discrepancy appears to rest upon several factors. (1) "Nodal" functions such as wholesale trade and finance and insurance appear to be undergoing some decentralization with the major nodes in the Northeast and North Central states displaying relative losses. The Southeast has gained from this trend. (2) The Southeast is going through its phase of urbanization later than much of the rest of the nation. This has required a more rapid expansion of social overhead activities in the transportation, public utilities and government sectors. (3) Although the Southeast has been experiencing downward shifts in population and total employment, it has made gains in per capita income. This, coupled with the fact that most of the service sectors allocated a smaller share of their employment to the Southeast than was consistent with the Southeast's share of total population, made the Southeast an attractive area for relative expansion of these activities. (4) Our period embraces a period of war and war preparedness. The Southeast has received a generous share of the Federal employment associated with military activities.

[32]There are important exceptions, as in the case of service activities related to recreation, but we cannot undertake to treat these activities within the confines of our study.

[33]It should be noted, however, that the high percentage of "household" inputs in the case of trade is partly a direct result of the manner in which trade was defined for the 1947 input-output table—as consisting of a gross margin, so that its inputs necessarily are essentially "households."

[34]We do not feel completely comfortable with this rationalization. The evidence that we have used to support these comforting generalizations is built upon levels of aggregation that are most general. The mass of activity represented by the service industries is so large it suppresses a great deal of detail that may prove to be very important to an understanding of the location of economic activity and the growth of regions. For example, some segments

We conclude that the differential shifts in service activities will tell an important part of the story as we proceed to analyze specific regions, but that the changes in access that have brought them about are rather simply identified with relative regional changes in final demand. While not completely satisfied with such a condensed and simplified treatment, we feel that this procedure will not introduce gross error in our tentative generalizations. The reader is also reminded that these service sectors are all rapid-growth industries and contribute a tendency toward upward shift for those states that specialize in them. The nodal states and the most sparsely settled states are the ones that tend to specialize in service activities for exactly opposite reasons—the nodal states because they are service centers for a region, the sparsely settled states because so-called minimum services cannot be provided on a scale that will allow optimum efficient utilization. The Pacific Coast states, the Mountain states, Texas, Florida, and the nodal states associated with New York City, Boston, Baltimore-Washington, and Chicago are the areas that can be said to specialize in service activities.

may not be oriented to final demand. This is certainly true to some degree of transportation and business services. These may play an important role in determining where and when external agglomeration economies can serve to generate and/or sustain regional growth. Or again, some service functions may exhibit significant economies of scale that require specific levels of final demand to justify their regional existence. Once some developmental stimulus has carried a region's final demand to the point where it will justify certain specialized services, access to these services may become very important to further growth. Still further, these service functions contain transportation services as an important component. The distribution of these services between regions is inextricably bound up with each region's access to inputs and markets. We should be bending every effort to a study of the changes in transport and the way these changes have been modifying regional access characteristics. Certainly this is an area of research that is begging for more careful attention.

26 / The resulting regional patterns of growth

Early in our discussion of regional economic growth we suggested that an understanding of this process called for a knowledge both of the kind of stimuli that initiate and maintain development and of the nature of the region that receives such stimuli. We suggested, further, that an understanding of a region's economic behavior requires a knowledge of its access to important inputs and markets. There were two necessary consequences of this conceptual focus: (1) Each region must be viewed with a considerable degree of functional disaggregation. The concept of "access" becomes an operational research concept only when we are talking about specific economic activities in a regional context. Various stimuli operate primarily upon the input-output relationships for specific functions, and their influence must be analyzed at the activity level in order to arrive at a real understanding of regional economic behavior. (2) Each economic activity must be examined for the nation and all of its regional components. There is no absolute scale for measuring a region's "access" characteristics or its exhibited development. These attributes take on meaning only as the performance of one region is compared with that of other regions and of the nation as a whole.

The materials that we have presented here have been determined by this conceptual focus. We have examined numerous resources, processing, and marketing activities on an "across the board" basis for the United States and its regional components. In each case we have attempted to come to some understanding of the access characteristics that have led to the observed regional structure and to the changes in economic activity that were found to have occurred during the period under review. We have been at pains to make clear that this effort was primarily exploratory and did not constitute an adequate exploitation of the research design.

Only in brief summaries for specific activities have we turned our attention to the analysis of specific regions. Our design would be incomplete, therefore, if we did not return to the regional focus once more. We can now talk about the characteristics of specific regions with the insight gained from an analysis of specific activities. For some of the more important regions of relative growth and decline, we shall now bring together the vertical shift dimensions that

Table 157. State total, differential, and proportionality net shifts in employment and the industry components of the differential shifts, 1939–1954

State	Total employment shift	Total differential shift (ABS & %*)	Total proportionality shift (ABS & %*)	Agriculture	Mining	Construction	Manufacturing	Trans. and pub. utilities	Wholesale trade	Retail trade	Finance, ins. & real estate	Service & miscellaneous	Government
New England													
Maine	−34,687	−40,091	+5,404	13,321	−88	−616	−33,006	−2,989	70	−4,406	−417	−3,404	−8,556
		−88.1	+11.9	+19.9	−.1	−.9	−49.4	−4.5	+.1	−6.6	−.6	−5.1	−12.8
New Hampshire	−36,155	−55,248	+19,093	−8,797	−22	−5,352	−24,588	−1,646	973	−2,599	588	−4,463	−14,342
		−74.3	+25.7	−6.5		−9.2	−42.1	−2.8	+1.7	−4.5	+1.0	−7.6	−24.6
Vermont	−24,371	−18,778	−5,593	−1,420	−253	−3,672	−5,766	−1,588	−470	−3,042	306	−1,783	−1,090
		−77.1	−22.9	−7.3	−1.3	−18.9	−29.7	−8.2	−2.4	−15.7	+1.6	−9.2	−5.6
Massachusetts	−119,129	−368,577	+249,448	−16,338	−325	−6,009	−220,229	−16,745	−8,251	−46,794	−1,394	−7,224	−45,288
		−59.6	+40.4	−4.4	−.1	−1.6	−59.8	−4.5	−2.2	−12.7	−.4	−2.0	−12.3
Rhode Island	−50,832	−101,772	+50,940	−1,430	−73	−3,202	−79,962	−1,224	296	−8,657	879	−3,642	−4,757
		−66.6	+33.4	−1.4	−.1	−3.1	−76.8	−1.2	+.3	−8.3	+.8	−3.5	−4.5
Connecticut	+85,728	−70,713	+106,441	−8,238	68	−7,420	−45,928	−965	5,930	−357	1,723	−4,575	−10,951
		−39.9	+60.1	−9.6	+.1	−8.6	−53.3	−1.1	+6.9	−.4	+2.0	−5.3	−12.7
Middle Atlantic													
New York	−79,626	−777,501	+697,875	−20,294	1,407	−92,646	−80,440	−107,768	−94,253	−113,294	−160,255	−52,380	−57,578
		−52.6	+47.4	−2.6	+.2	−11.9	−10.3	−13.8	−12.1	−14.5	−20.5	−6.7	−7.4
New Jersey	+123,322	−100,699	+224,021	8,930	464	346	−85,263	−5,246	19,783	−6,679	−13,511	−6,128	−13,345
		−31.0	+69.0	+5.6	+.8	+.4	−.7	−3.3	+12.4	−4.2	−8.5	−3.8	−8.4
Pennsylvania	−276,399	−545,910	+269,511	4,734	−86,653	−3,742	−240,017	−29,609	3,797	−64,242	−4,483	−22,999	−102,696
		−66.9	+33.1	+5.6	−15.4	−.7	−42.6	−5.3	+.7	−11.4	.8	−4.1	−18.2
Delaware	+14,919	+5,943	+8,976	967	−7	−1,759	−94	1,506	2,263	2,497	433	581	−444
		+39.8	+60.2	+.8		−16.7	−.9	+14.3	+21.4	+23.7	+4.1	+5.5	−4.2
Maryland and D. C.	+105,893	−49,567	+155,460	−4,780	−1,582	−30,770	−20,255	−7,120	−4,810	1,197	4,349	−8,852	23,056
		−24.2	+75.8	−4.5	−1.5	−28.8	−19.0	−6.7	−4.5	+1.1	+4.1	−8.3	+21.6
Great Lakes													
Ohio	+304,790	+128,436	+176,354	−7,645	−5,897	39,364	71,812	2,812	12,284	298	5,047	19,944	−9,583
		+41.2	+57.9	−4.4	−3.4	+22.5	+41.1	+1.6	+7.0	+.2	+2.9	+11.4	−5.5
Indiana	+68,052	+35,339	+27,713	19,726	−2,775	−1,529	27,900	−2,039	6,580	4,142	2,457	−14,903	−4,220
		+56.0	+44.0	+22.9	−3.2	−1.8	+32.3	−2.4	+7.6	+4.8	+2.8	−17.3	−4.9
Illinois	+498	−249,193	+249,691	5,934	−11,699	23,226	−54,784	−17,055	−15,499	−58,935	−45,615	−46,594	−28,172
		−50.0	+50.0	+1.9	−3.8	+7.6	−17.9	−5.5	−5.0	−19.2	−14.8	−15.2	−9.0
Michigan	+227,725	+98,019	+129,706	4,132	2,352	18,388	−3,320	22,421	14,010	14,801	7,274	20,232	−2,271
		+43.0	+57.0	+3.8	+2.2	+16.8	−3.0	+20.5	+12.8	+13.6	+6.7	+18.5	−2.1
Wisconsin	−52,577	−14,966	−37,611	21,112	1,801	−5,028	11,020	629	3,931	−1,508	2,118	−4,100	−44,941
		−28.5	−71.5	+21.9	+1.9	−5.2	+11.5	+.7	+4.1	−1.6	+2.2	−4.3	−46.7

1-Digit components of total differential shift in employment

Southeast

State	(1)	(2)	(3)	(4)	(5)	(6)	(7)	(8)	(9)	(10)	(11)	(12)	(13)
Virginia	−13,591	+36,141 / +42.1	−49,732 / −57.9	−1,712 / −1.8	−2,631 / −2.7	−6,229 / −6.4	−6,311 / −6.5	−1,424 / −1.5	−11,919 / −12.3	26,374 / +27.3	12,781 / +18.2	2,126 / +2.2	25,086 / +26.0
West Virginia	−159,903	−88,733 / −55.5	−71,170 / −44.5	−25,852 / −26.7	−23,600 / −24.4	−6,889 / −7.1	−24,480 / −25.3	−385 / −.4	−1,129 / −1.2	−3,364 / −3.5	944 / +1.0	3,053 / +3.1	−7,031 / −7.3
North Carolina	−103,806	+41,250 / +22.1	−145,056 / −77.9	60,358 / +30.1	1,739 / +.9	−7,450 / −3.7	−52,889 / −26.3	−19,494 / −9.7	15,254 / +7.6	18,475 / +9.2	6,847 / +3.4	5,415 / +2.7	12,945 / +6.4
South Carolina	−211,282	−78,006 / −86.9	−133,276 / −77.9	−94,316 / −70.1	125 / +.1	6,382 / +6.3	−4,672 / −26.3	391 / +.3	4,190 / +8.1	3,922 / +9.2	7,522 / +5.6	−7,251 / −5.4	5,701 / +4.2
Georgia	−273,931	−115,711 / −42.2	−158,220 / −57.8	−171,044 / −64.3	772 / +.3	−12,471 / −4.7	10,760 / +4.0	4,710 / +1.8	14,285 / +5.4	8,232 / +2.9	9,561 / +3.6	−7,252 / −2.7	26,736 / +10.1
Florida	+250,586	+230,706 / +92.1	+19,880 / +7.9	6,130 / +2.6	3,620 / +1.6	24,450 / +10.6	17,691 / +7.7	7,955 / +3.4	5,237 / +2.3	55,349 / +24.0	20,487 / +8.9	45,579 / +19.7	44,258 / +19.2
Kentucky	−118,309	+23,258 / +14.1	−141,567 / −85.9	3,535 / +4.8	−10,737 / −14.5	−3,655 / −4.9	21,515 / +29.1	−2,273 / −3.1	2,164 / +2.9	6,700 / +9.1	3,232 / +4.4	11,434 / +15.5	−8,657 / −11.7
Tennessee	+14,034	+129,041 / +52.9	−115,007 / −47.1	60,108 / +45.3	−1,887 / −1.4	15,231 / +11.5	11,592 / +8.7	3,250 / +2.4	9,050 / +6.8	8,284 / +6.2	9,373 / +7.1	1,665 / −1.3	12,375 / +9.3
Alabama	−239,053	−62,175 / −26.0	−176,878 / −74.0	−94,401 / −56.8	−10,501 / −6.3	−8,319 / −5.0	3,802 / +2.3	−1,034 / −.6	6,807 / +4.1	11,994 / +7.2	7,708 / +4.6	968 / +.6	20,851 / +12.5
Mississippi	−299,100	−36,903 / −12.3	−262,197 / −87.7	−30,259 / −36.2	3,822 / +4.6	−14,782 / −17.7	5,658 / +6.8	−1,073 / −1.3	3,632 / +4.3	3,790 / +4.5	4,743 / +5.7	1,656 / +2.0	−14,090 / −16.9
Arkansas	−211,474	−13,987 / −6.6	−197,487 / −93.4	−13,541 / −25.3	−194 / −.4	−5,495 / −10.2	10,337 / +19.3	−2,445 / −4.6	1,476 / +2.7	1,466 / +2.7	2,946 / +5.5	3,570 / +6.7	−12,107 / −22.6

Plains

State	(1)	(2)	(3)	(4)	(5)	(6)	(7)	(8)	(9)	(10)	(11)	(12)	(13)
Minnesota	−80,226	−1,054 / −1.3	−79,172 / −98.7	24,500 / +17.3	8,862 / +6.3	−5,314 / −3.8	33,770 / +23.9	2,886 / +2.0	−4,490 / −3.2	−15,467 / −10.9	96 / −.1	−4,509 / −3.2	−41,388 / −29.3
Iowa	−117,559	−18,593 / −15.8	−98,966 / −84.2	41,395 / +29.6	−3,064 / −2.2	−14,977 / −10.7	17,000 / +12.1	−6,151 / −4.4	−1,607 / −1.1	−17,696 / −12.6	2,308 / +1.7	−10,808 / −7.7	−24,993 / −17.9
Missouri	−97,364	−53,463 / −54.9	−43,901 / −45.1	6,399 / +6.4	−2,278 / −2.3	4,614 / −4.6	6,160 / +6.2	5,844 / +5.9	−14,475 / −14.5	−14,875 / −15.0	−2,267 / −2.3	−13,514 / −13.6	−29,071 / −29.2
North Dakota	−71,289	−2,393 / −3.4	−68,896 / −96.6	3,351 / +12.6	898 / +3.4	4,299 / +16.1	−1,098 / −4.1	799 / +3.0	−1,330 / −5.0	1,445 / +5.0	1,340 / +5.0	−3,847 / −14.4	−8,250 / −30.9
South Dakota	−39,548	+4,520 / +9.3	−44,068 / −90.7	21,900 / +49.1	204 / +.5	842 / +1.9	−629 / −1.4	−1,475 / −3.3	342 / +5.4	88 / +.2	1,175 / +2.6	−1,409 / −3.2	−16,518 / −37.0
Nebraska	−30,847	+21,314 / +29.0	−52,161 / −71.0	26,591 / +35.9	1,048 / +1.4	−3	13,344 / +18.0	2,642 / +3.6	−1,465 / −2.0	−2,835 / −3.8	4,053 / +5.5	−4,502 / −6.1	−17,559 / −23.7
Kansas	+28,708	+92,087 / +59.2	−63,329 / −40.8	17,648 / +14.3	5,433 / +4.4	10,854 / +8.8	55,064 / +44.8	7,640 / +6.2	382 / +.3	6,279 / +5.1	2,977 / +2.4	1,270 / +1.0	−15,510 / −12.6

Table 157—continued

State	Total employment shift	Total differential shift (ABS & %*)	Total proportionality shift (ABS & %*)	1-Digit components of total differential shift in employment									
				Agriculture	Mining	Construction	Manufacturing	Trans. and pub. utilities	Wholesale trade	Retail trade	Finance, ins. & real estate	Service & miscellaneous	Government
Southwest													
Louisiana	−36,947	+63,854	−100,801	−967	25,085	8,695	1,860	11,606	1,513	8,998	7,611	1,059	−1,556
		+38.8	−61.2	−1.4	+36.3	+12.6	+2.7	+16.8	+2.2	+13.1	+11.1	+1.5	−2.3
Oklahoma	−79,746	−19,168	−98,914	−5,435	7,819	2,554	17,396	5,919	1,492	−5,612	3,546	−15,316	6,805
		+16.2	−83.8	−7.6	+10.9	+8.6	+24.2	+8.2	+2.1	−7.8	−4.9	−21.3	+9.5
Texas	+112,286	+408,869	−296,583	−64,896	80,347	−6,911	142,854	35,060	24,166	54,224	33,328	83,436	77,261
		+58.0	−42.0	−11.7	+14.5	−1.3	+25.9	+6.3	+4.4	+9.8	+6.0	+6.1	+14.0
New Mexico	+36,201	+59,403	−23,202	8,403	6,168	4,377	8,225	4,606	3,686	9,236	4,092	−25	10,635
		+71.9	−28.1	+14.1	+10.4	+7.4	+13.8	+7.8	+6.2	+15.5	+6.9		+17.9
Arizona	+68,058	+81,238	−13,180	17,912	3,547	8,185	12,596	4,008	6,124	13,284	4,962	1,512	9,158
		+86.0	−14.0	+22.0	+4.4	+10.0	+15.5	+4.9	+7.5	+16.4	+6.1	+1.9	+11.3
Mountain													
Montana	−45,079	−17,927	−27,152	−4,539	29	−2,023	−1,376	−989	977	−2,015	1,895	2,240	−12,126
		−39.8	−60.2	−16.1	+.1	−7.2	−4.9	−3.5	+3.5	−7.1	+6.7	+7.9	−43.0
Idaho	−8,246	+20,045	−28,291	17,868	218	549	2,736	2,050	564	−945	1,972	429	−5,896
		+41.5	−58.5	+54.6	+.7	+1.7	+8.3	+6.3	+1.7	−2.9	+6.0	+1.3	−16.5
Wyoming	−4,986	+3,892	−8,878	60	3,288	−2,215	−1,338	−714	640	1,106	1,013	3,358	−1,306
		+30.5	−69.5	+.4	+21.9	−14.7	−8.9	−4.7	+4.3	+7.4	+6.7	+22.3	−8.7
Colorado	+89,695	+51,779	−12,084	12,312	−250	−3,311	9,877	3,619	2,679	3,709	3,264	6,949	12,931
		+81.1	−18.9	+20.9	−.4	−5.6	+16.8	+6.1	+4.6	+6.3	+5.5	+11.8	+22.0
Utah	+43,631	+48,968	−5,337	13,821	2,993	1,856	3,533	−157	976	2,705	3,077	2,514	17,650
		+90.2	−9.8	+28.0	+6.1	+3.8	+7.2	−.3	+2.0	+5.5	+6.2	+5.1	+35.8
Far West													
Washington	+68,812	+60,810	+8,002	−2,068	−872	666	17,382	−11,062	2,289	4,695	5,198	15,376	29,206
		+88.4	+11.6	−2.3	−1.0	+.7	+19.6	−12.5	+2.6	+5.3	+5.9	+17.3	+32.9
Oregon	+48,839	+58,317	−9,478	12,095	23	5,105	13,633	1,609	3,517	5,308	4,627	10,215	2,185
		+86.0	−14.0	+20.7		+8.8	+23.4	+2.8	+6.0	+9.1	+7.9	+17.5	+3.7
California	1,303,805	+1,133,188	+170,617	139,333	3,163	77,708	435,374	74,799	12,267	91,303	28,860	45,615	224,766
		+86.9	+13.1	+12.3	+.3	+6.9	+88.4	+6.6	+1.1	+8.1	+2.5	+4.0	+19.8
Nevada	+25,478	+26,290	−812	270	147	4,149	3,507	1,170	841	3,473	1,279	9,283	2,171
		+97.0	−3.0	+1.0	+.6	+15.8	+13.3	+4.5	+3.2	+13.2	+4.9	+35.3	+8.2

*%'s are based upon sum without regard to sign in order to avoid the extreme distortions of the algebraic sum. First line for each state is absolute shift, second line is % shift.
SOURCE: Appendix Table H.

describe how these regions share in the shift behavior of a specific activity and the horizontal shift dimensions that describe the way in which different activities have contributed to the total shift behavior of these regions. The horizontal shifts have been shown in the maps throughout the text and in the Appendix tables. The vertical shifts for the 1-digit components of total employment are presented in Table 157. With these tools we should be able to arrive at a better understanding of the differences we have observed in the total growth performance of various regions.

California

The Far West shows the most spectacular growth of all the rapid-growth regions over the 1939-1954 period, and California is the prime mover in this development. In absolute terms, California's population increased by close to 6,000,000 during these years, an increase almost three times greater than that of any other state. In relative terms, California claims almost half of the nation's total net upward shift in population between 1939 and 1954—a relative gain nearly four times as great as that of its nearest competitor (Florida).

The growth in employment was equally spectacular. Indeed, the economic opportunity offered by expanding employment and relatively high per capita incomes was largely responsible for the population growth—and the population growth, in turn, generated new employment opportunities. To some degree, however, population seems to have served here as an independent stimulus to growth. (1) California's share of the nation's population has increased more rapidly than its share of the employment at a time when the employment-population ratio was already relatively low. This suggests that the amenities of coast and climate have been a direct stimulus to population growth—for example, by attracting retired persons *with income*—and, hence, to regional development.[1] (2) The rate of urbanization has been one of the highest in the nation. These internal population migrations are important growth generators. They require significant investments in social overhead and generate new service and production processes that expand employment opportunities.

We are now in a position to look beneath these aggregates and examine the influence of more detailed sectors. Some 13% of California's upward shift in employment is a result of the total proportionality effect. Thus, a part of its phenomenal growth has been achieved by specialization in the rapid-growth sectors of the economy. Although agriculture and mining—the slow-growth sectors—are very important in this state and contribute significantly to its performance, the proportion of employment in these sectors is less than the average for the nation as a whole.[2]

[1] The situation in California contrasts with that in the Southeast, where a high population-employment ratio signifies a stretching of limited family income in the support of many children and other persons without income.

[2] California also fails to show manufacturing specialization although it comes closer than any other state west of the Mississippi. Thus the service, trade, and government sectors carry most of the burden of supplying the upward proportionality shift.

Differential shifts in the ten 1-digit components of total employment, however, comprise 87% of the employment shift. Table 158 shows California's share of the national shift in each of these major components and also the share of each component in California's total shift. Two facts stand out here: (1) Every 1-digit component makes a contribution to the upward shift in employment in California; and (2) California's shifts comprise a major portion of the total national shift in almost every employment component. Only mining and wholesale trade fall below 10% of the national total.

Within the state, manufacturing contributed 38% of the total differential upward shift; this is twice as large a gain as that of any of the other 1-digit components. Both the proportionality effect and the differential effect contributed to the upward shift in manufacturing. California was one of only four states in which this occurred. As a matter of fact, California and Arizona are the only states outside the Manufacturing Belt that specialize in the rapid-growth sectors of manufacturing activity.

Table 158. Employment shifts in California, by industry, 1939–1954

1-digit industry	California's share of the total national shift for each component	Each component sector's share of the total differential shift in California
Agriculture	24.32%	12.30%
Mining	1.92	.30
Manufacturing	44.14	38.40
Construction	29.68	6.90
Transp. and pub. util.	33.52	6.60
Wholesale trade	6.85	1.10
Retail trade	24.46	8.10
Finance, ins. and real est.	12.66	2.50
Service and misc.	18.28	4.00
Government	39.87	19.80
		100.00%

SOURCE: Appendix Table H and Table 157.

California accounted for 44% of the net differential 1-digit shift in manufacturing for the nation as a whole—a share that is almost three times greater than that of any other state. Table 159 shows the types of manufacturing that contributed most to this result. Some 80% of the state's upward shift in manufacturing employment was in primary metals, metal products, and miscellaneous manufacturing. In none of these sectors was the upward shift less than 17% of the national upward shift, and fabricated metal products, transportation equipment, and miscellaneous manufacturing accounted for more than one-third of the national upward shift for these sectors. This suggests that California has passed the threshold for minimum internal and external scale economies that are so important for these activities. It has become the only major diversified center for metal and metal products industries outside the Manufacturing Belt.

It is worth noting, however, that 42% of California's differential upward shift is supplied by one manufacturing sector—transportation equipment. Expansion of the airplane industry on the West Coast is the dominant element in this development, but the decentralization of automobile assembly is also a part of it. The fact that one industry sector dominates the shift to this extent may raise some questions concerning the stability of this relative growth performance over time.

Other manufacturing sectors have also played a role in the total upward differential shift. As a matter of fact, every sector except tobacco manufacturing shows relative gains. The large upward shifts in publishing and printing and in stone, clay, and glass products, like the lesser gains in apparel, leather, and furniture products, are in industries that are principally oriented to the final market. The significant upward shifts in lumber and pulp and paper products reflect the great relative increase in California's access to logging production.[3]

In general, food products, textiles, chemical and petroleum products, and rubber manufacturing have not contributed much to the upward shifts observed for the state.

Second only to manufacturing employment, government employment contributed 20% of the total differential shift displayed by California. The state's share of the total national shift was 40%—three times that of the nearest competing state. Two things appear to be especially important in explaining this development. (1) State and local government employment is a kind of internal social overhead activity. When a state is growing as rapidly as California, these social overhead services must not only expand, but must also often expand at an accelerated rate. (2) This was a period of hot and cold war and California occupies a strategic position with reference to national security interests. Expanding federal employment, both military and civilian, has been an important part of this picture.

Next in importance is agriculture with 12% of the total differential shift for the state. California shows 24% of the total national shift in agricultural employment between 1939 and 1954 and 36% of the upward shift in the value of agricultural products sold. This amounted to 22% of the upward shift in field crops, 12% in fruits and nuts, 57% in vegetables, 25% in dairy products, 15% in poultry products, and 12% in meat animal products. To a considerable degree this impressive showing in agriculture was generated by the greatly enlarged access to markets in the Far West. However, in field crops (primarily cotton), vegetables, fruits and nuts, and horticultural

[3] Because some of these segments are small in the national picture and because the total differential shift in California is quite large, these sectors can claim a large portion of the total national shift for its activity without contributing more than a small portion to the total differential upward shift displayed by the state as a whole.

Table 159. Manufacturing employment shifts in California, by manufacturing industry group, 1939-1954

S.I.C. code & title	California's share of the total national shift for each component	Each component sector's share of the total differential manufacturing shift in California
20 Food	2.16%	.50%
21 Tobacco	—	—
22 Textiles	.33	.20
23 Apparel	13.00	5.40
24 Lumber and prod.	23.34	4.60
25 Furniture	14.86	1.20
26 Pulp and paper	16.61	2.40
27 Printing and publ.	22.74	1.90
28 Chemicals	4.30	.90
29 Petrol. and coal prod.	1.01	—
30 Rubber	d	d
31 Leather	11.62	.90
32 Stone, clay and glass	31.47	3.20
33 Primary metal	17.38	4.50
34 Fab. metals	35.45	7.00
35 Machinery	22.95	7.40
36 Electrical mach.	31.77	8.20
37 Transportation equip.	34.56	41.60
38 Instruments	19.55	2.00
39 Miscellaneous	34.36	7.60
		100.00%

Source: Appendix Table K and Table 151.

specialties, California has gained in production on a scale that cannot be explained solely on the basis of population within the region. The state is highly successful in gaining access to national markets for these selected agricultural commodities, primarily because of its superior agricultural inputs. The fact that it has succeeded in supplying so large a part of its expanding requirements for agricultural products at home and has even succeeded in developing significant export specialties attests to a quality of access to agricultural resources that has been a significant element in its growth.

These three components of employment—manufacturing, government, and agriculture—together account for 70% of the total differential shift displayed by the state. The remaining 30% is dominated by trade and service activities that are more inclined to be responsive to regional changes in final demand and have less significance in our context here.

The phenomenal growth shown by California seems to have resulted from a combination of favorable circumstances. In the broadest terms, the picture is as follows: California has immediate access to significant home markets.

It has excellent access to regional markets because of its strategic nodal position; Los Angeles is the point of highest market potential and minimum transport costs in serving the Pacific Coast and Mountain states. For selected products it also has favorable access to national markets. It has excellent access at home to an amazingly wide variety of basic resource inputs and competitive access to regional and national sources for many others. More than any other state outside the Manufacturing Belt, it has access to a wide range of intermediate inputs and markets.

At the beginning of the period under review, there appears to have been a significant gap between California's potential for growth and the stage of development achieved at that time. Consequently, its access to inputs and markets improved continuously between 1939 and 1954. Its dominant access advantages to local and regional markets is a product of the remoteness of the Far West from the major producing areas of the nation. When the economic cost for many commodities of serving the West Coast from the major manufacturing area is taken into account, it is probable that California has not needed such large-sized markets in order to bring into play the operation of internal and external scale economies. In short, the market threshold where new functions requiring scale economies become feasible has probably been lower in California than in the East. The fact that the metal products industries, for which agglomeration economies are so important, dominate the employment gains in California gives support to this view. So also does the fact that California is the only state outside the Manufacturing Belt that has developed a truly diversified set of these agglomeration activities.

As a result of such factors, California has been growing somewhat like a nation; and in its growth performance it has had a particular advantage over (a) those regions that have not yet reached the threshold where regional markets will allow a multiplication of new functions, and (b) those regions that are more mature and whose facilities and economic function are already highly developed.

Florida

There are certain obvious similarities between Florida and California. Both exhibit considerable growth; both offer the amenities of coast and climate; and both have access to a specialized form of agricultural resource that makes them competitors in the national market for fruits and vegetables. But the differences between the two states are greater than the similarities.

Florida is not, like California, the nodal center of a large regional market. The market center for the Southeast is Atlanta.[4] Florida is especially disadvantaged in this regard because it is a peninsula and can find adjacent markets only in one quadrant of a radius based upon Florida. Its most favor-

[4]See Chauncy D. Harris, "The Market as a Factor in the Localization of Industry in the United States," *Annals of the Association of American Geographers*, Vol. 44 (December 1954), p. 332.

able market access is in the local market. And while the local market has been growing, it is less than a third the size of California's. For specialized products and services, of course, Florida can claim favorable access to national and regional markets, but the general picture remains. Further, Florida has little of the diversity of economic function that provides for California access to a wealth of intermediate markets and supply sources. California is in the first quartile of a crude index of diversity; Florida is at the bottom of the third quartile.

Florida is also in a relatively poor position over-all in its access to a vast majority of resource inputs.

Another point of difference needs mention. The outstanding institutions of higher learning on the West Coast seem likely to be one reason why important modern industries requiring highly skilled labor are attracted to California but not to Florida. The persons who guided the development of education in California evidently did not have their counterpart in Florida.

In spite of these general indicators, Florida shows a 12% net upward shift in population for the 1939-54 period—second only to that of California. The major factor in this growth is clearly the in-migration of families seeking the amenities of climate and coast. As a result, Florida's share of the national population is increasing much more rapidly than its share of the national employment; only three states have as low an employment-population ratio as Florida. Not surprisingly, the major increments in employment have been supplied by construction and the trades and services (Table 157). Indeed, in 1950, two-thirds of Florida's employment was in tertiary activities—a higher proportion than that of any other state in the nation.[5]

Table 157 shows that the three basic producing sectors—agriculture, mining, and manufacturing—account for only 12% of Florida's total differential upward shift. Even here, however, the lines of sequence seem to run from population and expanding local markets. Among the most important contributors to growth in manufacturing are apparel (largely market response, though possibly labor costs played a part; beach wear is significant), furniture, and printing and publishing (both market-oriented industries), stone, clay, and glass (mostly tied to expansion in construction), fabricated metal products (dominated by structural metal products supplying construction), and transportation equipment (dominated by pleasure craft oriented to market). Further, an important part of the state's mining activity was in non-metallic minerals tied to expanding construction activity, and an important part of its agriculture— particularly the dairy products sector—expanded in response to the expanding local markets.

In a few instances access to resources and markets independent of this dominant population movement has given rise to activities that have contributed to the development of the state. The most important of these activities are phosphates and associated fertilizers, pulp and paper, fruits and vegetables

[5] Since these sectors are rapid-growth sectors, Florida claims 8% of its upward shift in total employment as a result of the proportionality effect. It is one of only three states outside the Manufacturing Belt to receive such a stimulus.

and associated food products industries, and synthetic fibers used as intermediate inputs by the Gulf states oil and Southeastern textiles industries.

Even allowing for exceptions such as these, the contrast is very great—Florida's growth led and stimulated by population migration based largely upon amenities, California's growth aided by this factor but built upon favorable access to important markets and input sources and showing a range of diversity unmatched outside the Manufacturing Belt. The two states are widely different types of regions and therefore in a position to receive and respond to widely different types of stimuli.

Texas

Texas is a third state with a significant growth performance (see Table 160). It accounted for 6.5% of the net upward shift in population during 1939-1954 and also experienced better than average gains both absolutely and relatively in total income and per capita income. The pattern of its access and growth,

Table 160. Employment shifts in Texas, by industry, 1939-1954

1-digit industry	Texas' share of the total national shift for each component	Each component sector's share of the total differential shift in Texas
Agriculture	−11.33%	11.70
Mining	48.58	14.50
Manufacturing	14.48	25.90
Construction	−2.64	1.30
Transportation & public utilities	15.71	6.30
Wholesale trade	13.49	4.40
Retail trade	14.52	9.80
Finance, insurance & real estate	14.62	6.00
Service & miscellaneous	13.40	6.10
Government	13.70	14.00
		100.00%

SOURCE: Appendix Table H and Table 157.

however, offers further contrast to the two cases already examined.

Its access to national markets does not differ significantly in the aggregate from that of either Florida or California. It does have good access to regional markets,[6] but its nodal position is probably inferior to California's and its regional markets are probably smaller. The increase in its share of the nation's population is slightly greater than its increase in the share of employment. It may appear, therefore, to share with California and Florida some stimulus from

[6]Chauncy Harris, *op. cit.,* p. 332.

population migration independent of economic opportunity. We feel, however, that this evidence is misleading. Texas exhibited the same agricultural readjustment as the Southeast and recorded a very large absolute decline in agricultural employment; this downward shift amounted to 12% of its total differential shift. Thus, the marginal amount by which the increase in population share exceeds the increase in employment share is probably more a product of the necessity for an internal readjustment of the labor force than a product of the independent influence of amenities in the sense that they operate in Florida and California.

As a matter of fact, Texas overcame two factors to record a spectacular growth performance. (1) The downward shift in agricultural employment in the state has been so marked that it was an important counter to the growth trend. Without this, Texas might have displayed as much as 20% more growth in population and employment.[7] (2) In contrast to Florida and California, Texas specialized in slow-growth sectors of employment. As a result, it had to overcome a proportionality downward shift in employment that was equal to 42% of its total gross employment shift.

It follows that Texas must have had exceptionally great upward differential shifts in employment for some sectors. Since we conclude that no sizeable independent shifts of population (and, therefore, final markets) have taken place, some basic production activities must have generated this growth behavior.

The principal stimulus to growth in this state has been the amazing increase in its access to basic mineral inputs. Texas accounts for almost half of the net upward shift in mining employment in the United States. This has come about because of its specialization in the rapid-growth sector of mining activity—i.e., crude petroleum and natural gas. It has also had the benefit of a large 1-digit differential effect. Texas produces half of the nation's petroleum and a substantial portion of its sulphur and salt. It claims half of the net upward shift in crude petroleum and natural gas. In recording this performance, mining employment made one of the largest contributions (14.5%) to the total differential shift displayed by the state.

But even these data do not adequately reflect the contribution that mining activities have made to the growth of the state. These shifts are based upon employment data, and oil and sulphur mining are capital-intensive and labor-extensive relative to output. The impact of this expanding resource base needs to be evaluated, therefore, in terms of the supplementary activities it has generated.

The largest direct contribution to the total gross differential shift displayed by Texas has been manufacturing employment, with 26% of the total. This amounts to 14.5% of the total manufacturing shift of the nation. However, this does not vitiate mining's claim to primary importance. A large part of the manufacturing activity is directly related to the increase in access to basic mineral inputs.

---

[7] It should be noted in this connection, however, that the movement out of agriculture signified a more productive utilization of human resources and, with this, a relative per worker gain in output and income.

Some indication of this is given by an examination of the manufacturing activity. Texas claims one-fifth of the nation's upward shift in chemicals and allied products (10% of its own total differential manufacturing shift). This is dominated by petrochemicals and their derivatives and by inorganic chemicals based upon the area's sulphur and salt. Some 27% of the nation's petroleum refining is conducted in Texas, which showed one-fourth of the nation's total upward shift in petroleum refining over the 1939-54 period. There is substantial production of paving and roofing materials based upon petroleum products. Some of the region's expansion of rubber products production may be associated with petrochemical-based synthetic rubber. The expansions in the glass industry would probably not have taken place without access to cheap natural gas. Texas accounts for 18% of the nation's upward shift in primary metals (11% of its own differential manufacturing shift). Primary aluminum reduction has been an important part of this gain, attracted to the area by cheap power based upon lignite and natural gas. Basic steel capacity—which, we have seen, is market-oriented within the limits imposed by economies of scale—has been attracted to the area primarily because of the large market for petroleum and chemical piping and the demands for metal for other petroleum equipment. Much of the expansion in the production of machinery is tied to mining machinery and industrial machinery related to the petroleum and chemical complex. Even an important part of the expanding service employment consists of specialized mining and business services.

All of this activity has carried with it expanding markets and, hence, expanding trade, service, and utility employment.

There have been other elements, to be sure. Government employment has expanded, partly in response to the area's growth but also partly in relation to military activities. Transportation equipment accounts for 26% of the state's total employment increment, and this sector is made up of three types of production—decentralized automobile assembly, private aircraft construction, and pleasure boat construction—none of which is closely related to the expansion of the mineral resource base. Such industries as food products, furniture, and apparel have shown a strong response to expanding markets. The fact remains, however, that the growth of Texas is largely a story of oil and its geological associates—sulphur and salt, and the cumulative sequences of development they have inspired. And this growth has been accomplished in the face of a strong downward proportionality effect.

Western End of the Manufacturing Belt

Michigan, Indiana, and Ohio in the western end of the Manufacturing Belt also displayed significant growth between 1939 and 1954. Both in absolute and in relative terms, they all displayed above average gains in population, total income, and per capita income over these years—the only states in the Manufacturing Belt to do so. While these states exhibit individual differences, their general behavior is sufficiently similar to justify discussing them together.

The pattern of development is not like any of the patterns observed in the regions previously discussed. One difference is that the share of total national employment increased faster here than the share of total population. This, combined with the fact that the area is a high income area and that its employment-population ratio is higher than that of the nation as a whole, suggests that there is little of the amenity-seeking factor in the population movement here. The growth of population in these states seems largely a direct response to economic opportunity.

In examining the data to see why economic opportunity and development have been expanding in this area, we observe first that about half of the upward shift in employment is generated here by the total proportionality effect. These states tend to specialize rather heavily in the manufacturing, trade, and service sectors that are the rapid-growth sectors of the economy—with particular emphasis upon manufacturing specialization (in contrast to the proportionality effect in Florida and California).

While this has been an important element in the expansion in these three Great Lake states, they shared the proportionality effect with the entire Manufacturing Belt. However, they are the *only* major Manufacturing Belt states that add to this proportionality effect net upward differential shifts in employment.

The major differential gains in employment in this area have been in manufacturing.[8] Interestingly enough, at this 1-digit level the upward shift in manufacturing employment is, in turn, primarily dependent upon the proportionality effect. As we have seen, the rapid-growth sectors of manufacturing are primarily the metal hard goods, rubber, chemicals, and paper sectors. The slow-growth sectors are the soft goods and primary resource-processing sectors. These three states specialize in the rapid-growth sectors—so much so that they claim two-thirds of the total upward proportionality shift in manufacturing employment for the nation. This specialization, with its resultant proportionality effect, is largely responsible for the strong showing in manufacturing (and, hence, total employment) that these states have displayed.

They have also displayed net upward differential shifts in metal products industries and chemicals, but the latter have only been successful in dampening the downward differential shift and allowing the proportionality effect to exert greater influence.[9]

---

[8] Michigan was an exception to this, but for the sole reason that the decentralization of automobile assembly offset rather important gains in the other metal and metal products sectors. Some 78% of the total differential effect upon manufacturing employment in Michigan was provided by the transportation equipment industry. While the growth of manufacturing employment in Michigan was just about on a par with the national average, Illinois displayed a marked downward shift. Practically every manufacturing segment in this state displayed net downward shifts. These differential downward shifts overshadowed a favorable proportionality effect. The relative losses in food, apparel, machinery and miscellaneous manufacturing were particularly serious.

[9] Although the differential upward shifts in metal products and chemicals in this area was strong it could not forestall a moderate downward differential shift primarily because of four factors. (1) The decentralization of automobile assembly created a decline of generous proportions in Michigan and Indiana. (2) The striking gains in metal products were offset to some degree by absolute declines in the soft goods—tobacco, textiles, apparel, and

Except for manufacturing, the principal upward differential shifts in the 1-digit sectors have been in the service, trade, and construction sectors of the economy.[10] Apparently the relative gains that this area has derived from manufacturing in the current period and in previous periods have stimulated gains in these tertiary sectors that have, in turn, made important contributions to the differential gains.

The performance of these states appears to be tied to the fact that their total access to inputs and markets is probably unexcelled. They are located in the part of the country that has the most favorable access to national markets; Fort Wayne, Indiana, represents the point of minimum transport costs in serving a national market.[11] This part of the country is also one of the most concentrated regional and local markets in the United States. Furthermore, the Westward drift of the population has increased the access of these states to the national market relative to that of states in the eastern end of the Manufacturing Belt. Add to this the fact that one of the largest concentrations of intermediate markets and input sources in the world is located here.

The access of this region to important basic resources is also very favorable. While these states themselves produce only about 6% of the coal output, they are ringed by the five largest coal-producing states. Through pipelines, they have favorable access to natural gas. All have low-cost access to Mesabi ores and, together, they still account for around 6% of the employment in petroleum extraction, although the fields are old and well past peak production. A list of lesser metallic and non-metallic minerals available in these states would be extensive.

The extent to which metal products industries have been dominant in the performance of this region, therefore, is not surprising. These are the industries for which internal scale economies so often require locations with good access to the national market and for which external scale economies so often place a premium on being in an agglomeration of producers with good access to many intermediate markets and supply sources. This region fulfills these requirements better than most and its favorable access characteristics have been augmented by virtue of its western orientation.

Middle Atlantic Seaboard States (from Connecticut to Maryland)

This is the last of the major states or groups of states that displayed upward shifts in population during the 1939-54 period. The same states displayed upward

leather. These industries favor a low wage structure and have been bid out of competitive advantage by the relatively high-wage and skilled metal products industries. (3) Some industries that were once strong in this area like furniture and paper production are losing out to more favorable resource and market access in the Southeast. (4) These states represent relatively older industrial areas with a large manufacturing base. It takes a much larger absolute gain in these areas to maintain their share of the employment.

[10] Indiana also displayed a strong relative gain in agriculture employment.

[11] Chauncy Harris, *op. cit.*, p. 328.

shifts of employment. A unique characteristic of these states is that they experienced upward employment shifts over-all *in spite of* significant total differential downward shifts in employment. In short, their growth in employment and population was due almost exclusively to the fact that they were specialists in the rapid-growth sectors of total employment.

Although the total differential shift is downward, these shifts have made an *indirect* contribution to the upward shift in total employment. All of the rest of the Manufacturing Belt states (i.e., Illinois, Massachusetts, Rhode Island, New York, Pennsylvania, and also West Virginia) experienced downward differential shifts in virtually every 1-digit employment sector. In these few Atlantic Seaboard states there were enough 1-digit sectors that displayed upward differential shifts to keep the downward *total* differential shift small enough to allow the proportionality effect to dominate. For example, Connecticut and New Jersey benefited from the decentralization of wholesale trade and finance; New Jersey and Delaware from an expansion in agriculture based upon market-oriented vegetables, horticultural specialties, and poultry; Maryland and the District of Columbia from expanding government employment.

The most striking feature of the employment shifts during the 1939-1954 period is that these states experienced over-all relative growth *in spite of*, not because of, the contribution of manufacturing employment. It is true that these states do display an upward proportionality manufacturing shift because of their specialization in rapid-growth sectors of manufacturing activity. The differential downward shift is so dominant, however, that the total manufacturing employment in these areas displays significant downward shifts. As a matter of fact, more than half of the differential effect embodied in the differential shifts in total employment in Connecticut and New Jersey were provided by the downward shifts in manufacturing employment. To the extent that these states did display upward shifts in any of the more detailed manufacturing sectors, they were restricted pretty much to two types—(1) industries such as transportation equipment and rubber that were undergoing a decentralization phase; (2) industries such as furniture, printing, converted paper products, chemicals, and miscellaneous foods that gained from an expanding market in the area.

Delaware is the sole exception to this general pattern. Here, there was an upward differential shift as well as an upward proportionality shift. These differential gains were partly in agriculture, as mentioned, but were concentrated primarily in the transportation, public utility, retail trade, and service sectors of employment. Delaware showed this exceptional behavior partly because it is a small state, closely linked with the Philadelphia-Baltimore urban complex.

These employment data also explain why Virginia shared in the population gains of this section of the country but did not share in the relative employment gains. Virginia, like Delaware, experienced upward total differential shifts, and largely for the same reasons. It has become linked increasingly with Washington, D. C. But, alone among the Middle Atlantic Seaboard states, it shared the Southeast's specialization in the slow-growth employment sectors.

Its resultant downward total proportionality shift overbalanced its differential shift.

Regions That Experienced Relative Decline

The regions that experienced relative economic decline during the period 1939-54 show at least four broad patterns of behavior.

(1) THE DECLINING MANUFACTURING BELT STATES

A group of Manufacturing Belt states display a remarkably similar pattern. Massachusetts, Rhode Island (as well as Maine and New Hampshire of the New England states), New York, Pennsylvania, and Illinois all experienced the net upward total proportionality shifts that are characteristic of the states in the Manufacturing Belt because of their specialization in the rapid-growth employment sectors. In these states, however, downward differential shifts overbalanced the upward proportionality shifts and created a downward shift in total employment. Most of the employment sectors contributed to this downward total differential shift, but manufacturing was chiefly at fault. In most of these states manufacturing accounted for between 40 and 77% of the total differential shift displayed.

The depressing influence of the manufacturing shift has been due not only to differential losses in this area's share of manufacturing activity, but also to the fact that these states tended, on the whole, to specialize in slow-growth sectors of manufacturing such as textiles, apparel, leather, tobacco, and primary metals. The upshot of this situation is that downward shifts in total manufacturing employment accounted for a large portion of the total differential effect in these states—two-thirds or more in the case of Massachusetts and Rhode Island. To the extent that the states in this area enjoyed any differential upward shifts in segments of manufacturing activity, they were restricted largely to three types of situations: (1) industries seeking to utilize the surplus labor created by the migrating textile industry (apparel and electronics), (2) industries that are in a decentralizing phase (rubber and transportation equipment), and (3) industries adjusting to a regional surplus supply situation (primary metals).

In Pennsylvania, relative declines in mining also made a big contribution. In general terms, the explanation is fairly simple. These states are the early core states of the Manufacturing Belt. As the national economy has grown and shifted westward, their *relative* access to national markets and to important basic and intermediate inputs has declined.

New York and Illinois offer an interesting variation on the pattern. Their downward shift in manufacturing was much more modest. The main sources of the downward differential shifts in these states were the functions that have become concentrated in these two great centers. Wholesale trade, finance and insurance, transportation and public utilities all display a strong tendency to regional decentralization and dominate the downward differential shifts in these states.

(2) THE LOWER (OR DEEP) SOUTH

South Carolina, Georgia, Alabama, Mississippi, and Arkansas in the Deep South (plus West Virginia) all display a similar pattern—downward shifts generated by both the differential and proportionality effects. They all specialize in the slow-growth sectors of employment that generate downward proportionality shifts. In addition they all generate substantial downward differential shifts. Most of this has been due to developments in agriculture. In these states, where agriculture is undergoing a substantial transition from labor-intensive to labor-extensive systems of land culture, the downward shifts in agricultural employment run between 40% and 70% of the total differential shift.[12] In West Virginia, mining and manufacturing also helped generate the downward shift. The rest of the states, however, display slight gains in most manufacturing, trade, and service sectors—too slight, however, to offset the downward agricultural shift.[13]

(3) THE UPPER SOUTH

North Carolina, Tennessee, and Kentucky all share the Deep South's downward proportionality shifts. They also tend to share its downward shift in total employment. However, these states all experienced net upward total differential shifts. Indeed, were it not for the dominance of the proportionality effect, their performance would show up quite differently. Several elements account for the difference. (1) These states do not share the Deep South's large relative declines in agricultural employment. (2) Kentucky and Tennessee made gains in manufacturing.[14]

In general these states perform somewhat better than the Deep South because of better access to national markets and to basic mineral resources plus the fact that agriculture has not exerted so depressing an influence.[15]

Throughout the whole Southeast, whatever gain there was in manufacturing employment was due to differential shifts. The proportionality net shifts in manufacturing employment have been downward because of specialization in the slow-growth sectors. The net differential shifts, however, have all been upward and have been strong enough to generate upward shifts in total manu-

---

[12] These shifts, however, signify an improved use of human resources and a gain in per worker output and income.

[13] The general pattern for Vermont looks something like these Deep South states except the differential shifts take on more of the pattern of the Manufacturing Belt states with manufacturing being the principal source of decline.

[14] North Carolina displayed a minus for manufacturing because of its specialization in the slow-growth textile industry, but it showed up with plusses in every other sector.

[15] A somewhat similar pattern, with minor variations, is displayed by some of the Southwest states (Oklahoma and Louisiana), the northern Mountain states of Idaho and Wyoming, and the Plains states—South Dakota and Nebraska.

facturing employment over the area. The principal exceptions are Virginia, North Carolina, and South Carolina. The Carolinas have specialized so heavily in textiles, one of the major slow-growth sectors, that the proportionality effect has created net downward shifts in manufacturing employment in these states. The differential upward shifts in the Southeastern states have been dominated by food products, textiles, and apparel. Tobacco products and furniture in the Upper South and pulp and paper in the Lower South are important. The decentralization of automobile assembly and rubber products has contributed to the strength of the nodal states. Metal products industries are important in Alabama, Kentucky, Tennessee, and the states adjacent to the western end of the Manufacturing Belt.

The net effect of the manufacturing shifts in the states characterized by relative decline was not great. In general the states in the Southeast did not receive more than 6% or 7% of their total differential effect from manufacturing. An upward shift of this dimension was easily offset by declines in other sectors of the economy.

(4) IOWA, WISCONSIN, AND MINNESOTA

These states offer an interesting contrast to the Deep South states. They are like the latter in that both the differential and proportionality effects have contributed to the relative decline in employment. The differential effect in their case, however, is much smaller and is generated by a quite different set of sectors. The Deep South sustained a double-barreled effect on its agricultural employment. Rapidly advancing farm technology has forced large declines in labor requirements for almost every farming system. Added to this, the Southeast was shifting to less intensive farming systems. These north central states, however, experienced only the effect of the technological decline in labor requirements. As a consequence agriculture did not contribute directly to the differential downward shift but did contribute indirectly. These states experienced upward shifts in agricultural employment but these shifts were relative—which means that they were consistent with absolute declines in agricultural employment. Therefore, the same level of agricultural production in these states required a smaller share of total employment and population. This had two effects. (1) Since they were accessible to the western end of the Manufacturing Belt, some of this displaced farm labor was absorbed by expansions in manufacturing employment (and mining in Minnesota). (2) For the most part, however, this change in the requirements agriculture makes upon employment and population has resulted in a relative decline in the trade, service, and government sectors sufficient to generate net downward total differential shifts.[16]

This concludes our effort to summarize the regional shifts in employment and to show how the developments within the various major industries have influenced economic growth or decline within various states and regions of the

[16] Montana and North Dakota share this pattern to some extent, but without the gains in manufacturing. Montana also displayed a modest downward shift in agricultural employment.

country. We have attempted little more than to outline the major features for the areas which have experienced the most significant economic changes during the period on which we have focused our attention. An examination of this sort, in spite of its obvious limitations, does serve to highlight the extent to which growth patterns among regions can be expected to differ in response to nation-wide industrial changes. We have seen that each industry has its own requirements in terms of inputs and markets, that these change over time—and often at a rapid rate—so that the relative advantages and disadvantages of the various parts of the country for any given industry are subject to continuing revaluation. Also, we have seen that there is a regional version of "one man's meat." Because of the great differences among regions—in human and material resources, position with regard to centers of population, and previous development—regions can be expected to experience quite different results from a given nation-wide change, such as a decline in agricultural employment or an increase in demand for petroleum. Finally, we have touched upon the fact that as the various industries within a given region expand or decline or change in nature, the consequence for the region is not merely the sum total of these individual industry changes. What evolves is a total pattern of economic development which is itself a significant force in future changes. This influence extends in many directions, but particularly in determining the size and character of the regional markets for the products and services of industry which is evolving. To understand the process, then, one has to go from the individual industry to the total regional economy and again back to the individual industry so that the concrete elements at work take on substance and form.

Part

V / *Variations in levels and rates of*

growth of per capita income

27 / Inter-state differences in per capita income and in rates of growth in per capita income

So far in this study of regional economic growth in the United States, we have focused our attention mainly on the *volume* of economic activities in the various parts of the country and on the forces behind the varying rates of growth. We have touched only in passing upon the *welfare* aspect of growth as represented by changes in family incomes. But, as the income level that a given region or state achieves can be said to be a rather significant part of its "pay-off" on the workings of the economic system, differences in income levels as between one part of the country and another have particular relevance to our subject. In this final section of our study, therefore, we shall examine in some detail the income levels and rates of growth in per capita income in the various regions and states and try to explain why they differ from place to place.

Determinants of Per Capita Income

In our society, personal income is derived primarily from the sale of productive services.[1] It depends, then, both upon one's ownership of factors of production and upon the prices per unit one receives for the services of these factors of production. The prices per unit which persons receive for their production services are determined through a series of interrelated factor markets: markets for the services of different kinds of labor and of capital in different areas of the country. Factor prices affect not only the current incomes of persons; they also induce changes over time in the quantity and location of those factors which are reproducible, and hence they affect future as well as current incomes.

The study of factor markets is part of the special province of economics. Indeed, it is principally in the generalizations as to the nature and operation of

---

[1] A second, and much less important, source is the collection of money receipts called "transfer payments," that is, payments such as pension and relief which are not related to current productive activities.

these markets that economic analysis contributes to the understanding of areal differences in per capita income. Taking certain data as given,[2] economic analysis shows how the prices of final products and of production factors in different places, as well as the quantities of final products produced and of production factors employed in the various places, are arrived at through a process of mutual determination. This process of mutual determination is often referred to as the general equilibrium system. Its workings determine both factor prices and the rate at which factor services are utilized in market activities in different places and the composition of output in these places; in other words, what is often called the industrial structure.

It is not our purpose to attempt a detailed analysis of the workings of this general equilibrium system as it affects areal differentiation of economic activity. Rather, we shall attempt to discover those specific variables within its operation which influence levels of per capita income in different places and to assess the importance of these variables. But in so doing, it is helpful to remember how they fit into the workings of the economic system.

State Per Capita Income Estimates

The distinction between *ownership of* and *rate of return to* different factors of production is partially reflected in the types of income which, taken together, comprise the Department of Commerce estimates of per capita personal income levels in the various states. These are: wages and salaries, other labor income, proprietors' income, property income, and transfer payments.

In our analysis, we treat the first three of these types of income—wages and salaries, other labor income, and proprietors' income—as a distinct category. We refer to this category, using Simon Kuznets' term, as "participation income."[3]

Participation income consists largely of income from labor services. (However, proprietors' income includes income received from the sale of the services of non-human capital owned by unincorporated enterprises as well; this cannot be readily separated out.) It is the most important income category, amounting to about five-sixths of the national personal income in recent years. Because of its quantitative importance, most of our attention will be directed to it.

Property incomes consist of dividends, interest, and rent payments. These depend primarily upon the pattern of ownership of capital, which at any given moment is historically determined. The property income category is small relative to participation income; however, it is a significant source of income differences among states.[4]

---

[2] Data on tastes and location of consumers; quantity, quality, and location of all factors of production; technological factors; institutional factors; distance from markets, etc.

[3] Simon Kuznets, "Industrial Distribution of Income and Labor Force by States, United States, 1919-21 to 1955," Part III of "Quantitative Aspects of the Economic Growth of Nations," *Economic Development and Cultural Change*, Vol. 6 (July 1958), p. 3.

[4] The owner of labor services must sell them in person; thus, most persons live in the state in which they contribute labor services to production. Except in a few instances,

Interstate and interregional differentials in participation income per capita[5] arise in part from differences in the proportion of the total population that is in the labor force of the various states and regions. They also arise in part from differences in the skills of the various populations. But, in addition, there are genuine differentials in the wages of workers of identical skill in different parts of the country.

We shall begin the presentation of our material with a description of income and its components in the different states in 1950. This will be followed by data on income by place of residence and color for the regions and states and then by data on incomes in standard metropolitan areas by size of area.

The sources used here are the state personal income estimates of the Department of Commerce[6] and the tabulations of family and individual income contained in the 1950 census reports.[7]

---

participation income *received* corresponds closely to participation income *produced* within a state. In the case of property income, however, there is no presumption that the recipient lives in the state where the factor services he sells are used in production. Indeed, it is principally in the property income category that income received in a particular state differs from income produced in that state.

[5] About three-quarters of the interstate variation in per capita personal income (that the data reveal) can be attributed to variations of the regional means around the national average. But the variations of the state data around their regional means is too large to be ignored. For this reason, our tables will show data for selected individual states in each of the eight regions to give some idea of the intra-regional variation in each. So far as possible, the individual states shown are chosen to indicate the extremes of variation within each region. But, of course, where a single table contains data on several income variables, or data for several years, the two states shown will not always indicate the regional extremes for every column of the table.

In our analysis of the data we have considered agricultural and non-agricultural income separately. This seemed advisable for two reasons: First, because of the greater importance of the unincorporated enterprise in the agricultural sector, income from capital is probably a greater fraction of agricultural than of nonagricultural income. Second, since the prices of consumer goods, particularly food, appear to be lower for farm families than for non-farm families, equivalent *real* wages per worker in agricultural and nonagricultural employment would mean lower *money* wages in agriculture. The money incomes of the two groups, therefore, are not strictly comparable. However, the real wage as well as the money wage of labor in agriculture appears to be below that in nonagricultural employment, especially in the Southeast. This fact further suggests the advisability of studying the two groups separately.

[6] U.S. Department of Commerce, Office of Business Economics, *Personal Income by States since 1929* (Washington: U.S. Government Printing Office, 1956).

The Commerce data include the current income received by the residents of a state from all sources, before the deduction of personal income taxes and other direct taxes, but after the deduction of personal contributions to social insurance programs. In addition to money income receipts, which account for about 95% of personal income for the nation, estimates of income in kind are included as well.

[7] U.S. Department of Commerce, Bureau of the Census, *1950 Census of Population*, Vol. II (Washington: U.S. Government Printing Office, 1952), Part I, p. 63.

These data were obtained from a 20-percent sample of persons fourteen years of age and over who were enumerated in the 1950 census. The census data include money income received in 1949 from wages and salaries, net income from other sources such as rents, royalties, dividends and interest, before deduction for personal taxes, social security pay-

Per Capita Personal Income and Its Components, 1950

The Department of Commerce estimates of personal income per capita and its components in 1950 are shown for the eight regions and selected states in Table 161.[8] (See also Figure 86.) Per capita personal income in the various

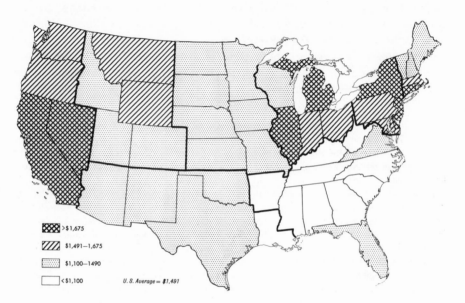

Figure 86. Per Capita Personal Income, 1950.

states in this year ranged from $2,153 in Delaware to $729 in Mississippi. In the Middle Atlantic, Great Lakes, and Far West states, it was 10-20% above the national average; in the Southeast, 34% below the national average. All states in the Southeast, Southwest, and Plains regions were below the average for the

ments, etc. Income in kind is not covered in these data; while income in kind is only about 5% of personal income for the whole nation, it may be a much more important source of income for persons in some areas, particularly rural areas in the South.

[8] While data for 1949 would be more comparable as to time with the census data presented in later tables, the data for 1950 are probably subject to less variation about secular trend lines because of short-term fluctuations than the data for 1949. Entries shown for the eight regions are simple averages for the states making up the respective regions. The U. S. average value shown is the weighted average for the forty-eight states and the District of Columbia, which is not included in any of the regional averages. Two measures calculated from the observations for the forty-eight states are included also. The relative variation —the standard deviation of the state values divided by the mean of the state values— describes the variability of the observations for the several states about the mean of these values. The statistic H—the Kruskal-Wallis statistic—is used to test the significance of the differences of the mean values for the various regions. For a description of this statistic, see the note at the end of this chapter.

nation as a whole. So also were the upper New England states—Maine, New Hampshire, and Vermont—and three of the Mountain states, Colorado, Idaho, and Utah.[9]

The pattern of distribution for income received from current production—that is, participation plus property income—closely paralleled that for personal income per capita. This is explained by the fact that net transfer payments were an insignificant part of personal income received by residents of the United States; they averaged $80 per capita or about 5% of total personal income in 1950 and varied from $127 per capita in Washington to $55 in Virginia. Furthermore, there was no significant tendency for net transfer payments per capita to be either positively or negatively associated with participation plus property income per capita.[10] Thus, the inter-state distribution of participation plus property income is substantially the same as the distribution of personal income.[11]

The most variable of all income components is property income per capita. Its relative variation was 45.1% in 1950 or about twice that of participation income and personal income per capita. The per capita level was highest in Delaware ($519) and lowest in Mississippi ($58). Property income was concentrated primarily in the northeastern part of the country—the New England, Middle Atlantic, and Great Lakes states. In the Middle Atlantic states it was about one-sixth of personal income, as compared with about one-eighth for the nation as a whole and about one-tenth in the Southeast.

Participation and property income per capita were highly correlated positively.[12] While the relative variation for participation income per capita was about the same as for personal income per capita, the (absolute) regional differentials were somewhat smaller for the former.

An important part of the variation in participation income per capita arises from variations in the proportion of the population employed in different areas. The relative variation of participation income *per person employed*[13] was only about two-thirds as great as the relative variation of participation income per capita and personal income per capita. In the Middle Atlantic, Great Lakes, and Far West regions in 1950, where personal income per capita was about 18% above the national average, participation income per person employed was only

[9] Actually, Montana and Wyoming had unusually high per capita incomes in 1950 because of the unusually high returns to agriculture. Generally, these states—as is true of all the other Mountain states—fall below the national average in per capita income.

[10] Spearman's rank correlation coefficient rho is equal to $+0.11$. For a description of this statistic and its distribution on the null hypothesis that the two series being compared are independent, see M. G. Kendall, *The Advanced Theory of Statistics*, Vol. I, 5th ed. (New York; Hafner Publishing Co., 1952), pp. 388-403.

[11] For more information on the distribution of transfer payments see Howard G. Schaller, "Veterans' Transfer Payments and State Per Capita Incomes, 1929, 1939, and 1949." *Review of Economics and Statistics*, Vol. 35 (Nov. 1953), pp. 325-32 and "Social Security Transfer Payments and Differences in State Per Capita Incomes, 1929, 1939, and 1949," *Review of Economics and Statistics*, Vol. 37 (Feb. 1955), pp. 83-89.

[12] Spearman's rho for the two series is $+0.84$.

[13] Computed by multiplying participation income per capita by the ratio of employment to population as reported in the 1950 census.

Table 161. Per capita personal income and its components, by region, selected states, 1950

Region and state[a]	Personal income per capita	Participation plus property income per capita	Property income per capita	Participation income per capita	Participation income per person employed
New England	$1,484	$1,398	$226	$1,172	$3,029
Vermont	1,185	1,114	177	937	2,572
Connecticut	1,908	1,835	312	1,523	3,664
Middle Atlantic	1,796	1,717	289	1,428	3,588
Pennsylvania	1,566	1,453	199	1,253	3,332
Delaware	2,153	2,091	519	1,572	3,934
Great Lakes	1,623	1,559	190	1,369	3,500
Wisconsin	1,467	1,411	179	1,232	3,117
Illinois	1,827	1,756	233	1,523	3,705
Southeast	988	920	99	821	2,335
Mississippi	729	659	58	601	1,792
Florida	1,288	1,200	195	1,006	2,653
Plains	1,372	1,302	150	1,151	3,032
South Dakota	1,213	1,144	109	1,035	2,755
Nebraska	1,468	1,407	165	1,242	3,196
Southwest	1,204	1,122	134	988	2,918
Louisiana	1,089	989	117	872	2,640
Texas	1,340	1,267	159	1,109	2,990
Mountain	1,449	1,372	157	1,215	3,324
Idaho	1,279	1,211	122	1,090	3,108
Wyoming	1,629	1,567	182	1,385	3,508
Far West	1,765	1,669	220	1,449	3,717
Oregon	1,602	1,520	174	1,346	3,534
Nevada	1,938	1,870	278	1,593	3,841
U.S.[b]	$1,491	$1,411	$187	$1,224	$3,224
Relative variation[c]	23.2%	24.4%	45.1%	22.4%	17.6%
H[d]	34.5***	34.7***	33.9***	35.3***	35.5***

    [a] Regional averages are simple averages of the data for states in the region.

    [b] The per capita values for the nation are those obtained by dividing total income for the nation by population (or employed labor force); thus, they are also averages of the state values weighted by population (or employed labor force).

    [c] Standard deviation divided by the mean of the state observations.

    [d] The Kruskal-Wallis statistic for judging the significance of regional variation. (See note on the H statistic at the end of this chapter.) Asterisks in this and later tables indicate significance level as follows:

       * Significant at the 0.05 level, but not the 1 per cent level

     ** Significant at the 0.01 level, but not the 0.1 per cent level

   *** Significant at the 0.001 level

Unless indicated otherwise, we shall use these designations of significance level for H throughout Tables 161-166.

12% above average. In the Southeast, similarly, while personal income per capita in 1950 was about 34% below the national average, participation income per person employed was only 28% below. However, the rank order of the states was almost identical for participation income per person employed and personal income per capita.[14] Employment per capita depends upon the proportion of the population of working age and the proportion of these who are employed. Both tended to be significantly associated positively with participation income per person employed in 1950.[15]

In summary, states with relatively high per capita personal incomes have relatively high property incomes per capita and relatively high labor force participation ratios. Differences in participation income per person employed reflect differences in ownership of productive services, differences in the skills of the labor force, and differences in the price per unit received for identical labor services in different areas.

Median Family Income, 1949

The 1950 census data on median incomes of families, shown in Table 162, permit a more detailed examination of the state income differentials. The totals in this table tell almost the same story as the per capita personal income estimates of the Department of Commerce. The relative variation for the median family income series is only slightly less than for the per capita personal income series—21.7% as compared with 23.2%.[16] The median incomes averaged about 14% above the national level for the Middle Atlantic, Great Lakes, and Far West regions and about 34% below the national level for the Southeast.

However, the pattern of income differentials between regions changes substantially when the families are classified by place of residence and color.[17] The

[14]As judged by a rho of +0.95.

[15]The rank correlation coefficient rho for participation income per person employed and proportion of the population 14 years old and over was +0.65; for participation income per person employed and labor force per population 14 years old and over was +0.52. (For forty-eight observations, the two-tail five per cent point for rho is +0.29). For a detailed analysis of labor force participation, see Clarence D. Long, *The Labor Force Under Changing Income and Employment*. National Bureau of Economic Research, No. 65 (Princeton: Princeton University Press, 1958).

[16]Spearman's rank correlation coefficient for the two series is +0.90.

[17]Actually, the 1950 Census tabulations do not show incomes for white and non-white families separately, except for the census South. Therefore, the data in the last two columns of Table 162 are based upon the reported figures for white families in the census South and for white *and* non-white families outside the census South. To the extent that incomes of white families exceed those of non-whites outside the census South, the data in Table 162 underestimate the incomes of white families, except for the South, and underestimate the regional differences in incomes.

SOURCE: Computed from data in *Personal Income by States since 1929;* participation income per person employed was computed by multiplying participation income per capita by the ratio of employment to population as computed from data in *1950 Census of Population*, Vol. II.

Table 162. Median income of families and unrelated individuals, by region, selected states, 1949

Region and state[a]	Total	Urban "white"[e]	Rural-farm "white"[e]
New England	$2,572	$2,727	$2,003
Vermont	2,101	2,427	1,579
Connecticut	3,155	3,187	2,593
Middle Atlantic	2,935	3,227	2,016
Pennsylvania	2,834	2,968	2,140
New Jersey	3,285	3,372	2,203
Great Lakes	3,014	3,234	2,213
Indiana	2,827	3,062	2,327
Michigan	3,195	3,380	2,125
Southeast	1,733	2,762	1,266
Mississippi	1,028	2,472	1,035
Virginia	2,172	3,154	1,483
Plains	2,435	2,802	2,103
Missouri	2,200	2,667	1,350
Minnesota	2,683	3,066	2,105
Southwest	2,162	2,759	1,590
Louisiana	1,810	2,969	1,424
Texas	2,273	2,867	1,718
Mountain	2,776	3,037	2,290
Colorado	2,514	2,704	2,182
Utah	3,001	3,136	2,473
Far West	2,973	3,156	2,243
Oregon	2,933	3,076	2,338
Washington	2,955	3,182	2,380
U. S. average [b]	$2,619	—	—
Relative variation[c]	21.7%	9.3%	23.7%
H[d]	36.6***	25.6***	30.9***

[a] Regional averages are simple averages of the data for states in the region.
[b] Tabulated value for the United States.
[c] Standard deviation divided by the mean of the state observations.
[d] See note d, Table 161.
[e] The data are for white families and unrelated individuals in the census South (our Southeast plus Delaware, Maryland, Louisiana, Oklahoma, and Texas) and for white and non-white for the remaining states. The data thus underestimate the incomes of white families outside the census South.

SOURCE: *1950 Census of Population*, Vol. II, Pt. 1, T. 175 and Pts. 2-8 and 10-50, T. 32.

incomes of "white" urban families show much less regional variation than the incomes of all families—the relative variation of the former is only 9.3% as against 21.7% for the latter. The incomes of "white" urban families in the Southeast are only 15% below those of "white" urban families in the Great Lakes states. But, while the regional differentials in income are much smaller for "white" urban families than for all families, they are statistically significant.

The relative variation for the incomes of "white" rural-farm families is slightly greater than the relative variation for the incomes of all families. But, while state variations are substantial, there is little over-all *regional* variation in "white" rural-farm family incomes outside the South. The incomes of these families are only about 3% higher in the Mountain region than in the Great Lakes region, and only about 9% lower in New England than in the Great Lakes region. In the Southeast, however, they are about 43% below those in the Great Lakes region. The comparison of incomes of "white" urban and "white" rural-farm families in the same region is also interesting. The incomes of "white" urban families were about one-third greater than those of "white" rural-farm families in the New England, Plains, and Mountain states, about 40% greater in the Great Lakes states, but *over twice as* great in the Southeast.[18]

Median Incomes of Individuals

In addition to the data on family incomes presented above, the 1950 census contains tabulations of the incomes of individuals classified by place of residence and by color. These are summarized for the regions and selected states in Table 163. The data here on incomes for all individual and for white rural-farm individuals show about the same relative variation as the data for all families and white rural-farm families in the corresponding columns in Table 162. The relative variation shown in column two, Table 163, is about half again as great as that in the corresponding column of Table 162, but the former includes the incomes of rural non-farm as well as urban individuals.

The income differentials between the Southeast and the Great Lakes states for white individuals are likewise similar to those for white families—24% for urban and rural non-farm individuals and 43% for rural-farm individuals. The income levels of the lowest income states in the non-South are about the same as those of the highest income states in the Southeast for rural-farm individuals. Again one notices that the principal variation in white rural-farm incomes is that between the Southeast and the rest of the nation. Particularly striking is the fact that the average incomes of white rural-farm individuals in the Great

---

[18]Cf. D. Gale Johnson, "Functioning of the Labor Market," *Journal of Farm Economics*, Vol. 33 (Feb. 1951), pp. 75-87 and "Some Effects of Region, Community Size, Color, and Occupation on Family and Individual Income," in *Studies in Income and Wealth*, Vol. 15 (New York: National Bureau of Economic Research, 1952), pp. 51-66. Because the money value of income in kind is not included in the census income data, however, these data may overestimate somewhat the differentials in income between the South and the rest of the nation for white rural families and between white urban and rural-farm families within the South.

Table 163. Median income, persons with income, 14 years old and over, by region, selected states, 1949

Region and state[a]	Total	White		Non-white	
		Urban & rural non-farm	Rural-farm	Urban & rural non-farm	Rural-farm
New England	$1,828	$1,872	$1,464	$1,240	$ 772
Vermont	1,485	1,581	1,156	933	625
Connecticut	2,255	2,289	1,839	1,595	1,464
Middle Atlantic	2,192	2,356	1,552	1,344	918
Maryland	2,044	2,325	1,385	1,229	734
New Jersey	2,389	2,476	1,798	1,034	881
Great Lakes	2,214	2,330	1,625	1,753	810
Wisconsin	1,995	2,150	1,388	1,572	629
Michigan	2,419	2,554	1,532	2,189	898
Southeast	1,255	1,766	933	855	486
Mississippi	759	1,576	798	591	370
West Virginia	1,840	2,045	1,079	1,562	689
Plains	1,788	1,881	1,596	1,104	759
Missouri	1,682	1,970	1,019	1,227	419
Iowa	1,916	1,914	1,941	1,315	1,325
Southwest	1,524	1,857	1,230	878	499
Oklahoma	1,416	1,670	1,119	854	519
Arizona	1,716	1,912	1,572	889	478
Mountain	1,918	2,017	1,616	1,127	878
Colorado	1,748	1,802	1,500	1,384	1,383
Wyoming	2,037	2,205	1,632	869	634
Far West	2,128	2,226	1,611	1,463	1,004
Oregon	1,967	2,064	1,461	1,347	909
Nevada	2,294	2,434	1,694	1,394	1,075
U.S. average[b]	$1,917	$2,157	$1,273	$1,121	$ 443
Relative variation[c]	22.5%	13.5%	23.8%	32.3%	39.4%
H[d]	36.9***	29.8***	28.0***	25.8***	24.1***

[a-d] See corresponding footnotes, Table 162

SOURCE: *1950 Census of Population*, Vol. II, Pt. 1, Table 175.

Lakes, Middle Atlantic, Plains, Mountain, and Far Western states differ by very little.

As the last two columns of Table 163 show, the inter-state variation is considerably greater in the incomes of non-white individuals than of white—32.3% as against 13.5% for urban and rural non-farm individuals and 39.4% as against 23.8% for rural-farm individuals. For non-whites, the income differentials between the Southeast and the Great Lakes states were 52% for urban and rural non-farm persons and 40% for rural-farm. The differentials in the

Table 164. Median income, white males with income, 14 years old and over, standard metropolitan areas, by size, 1949

	Population		
Regional average[a]	500 thous. & over	250 thous. to 500 thous.	100 thous. to 250 thous.
New England	$2,610	$2,806	$2,557
Middle Atlantic	3,033	2,628	2,628
Great Lakes	3,149	3,125	2,959
Southeast	2,825	2,627	2,466
Plains	3,030	2,715	2,794
Southwest	2,733	2,702	2,745
Mountain & Far West	2,965	2,730	2,799
Relative variation[b]	9.0%	10.4%	13.4%
H[c]	7.1	12.3*	21.1**

[a] Regional averages are simple averages of the data for SMA's in the states of the region.
[b] Standard deviation divided by the mean of the observations.
[c] See note d, Table 161. For purposes of these tests the regions were combined as follows:
SMA's 500 thous. or more: New England with Middle Atlantic, Southeast with Southwest, Lakes with Plains; thus, H is distributed approximately as Chi-square with three degrees of freedom.
SMA's 250 thous. to 500 thous.: Lakes with Plains; thus, H is distributed approximately as Chi-square with five degrees of freedom.
SOURCE: *1950 Census of Population*, Vol. II, Pt. 1, Tables 28 and 185.

incomes of white and non-white individuals in the same region also vary from region to region. Incomes of non-white urban and rural non-farm individuals were 52% below those of white individuals in the Southeast, as compared with 25% in the Great Lakes region. For all four cells of the two-way classification of individuals, significant regional variation in individual income existed in 1949.

Median Incomes of Males, by Community Size and Color: It has long been known that incomes vary with the size of the community in which they are earned. In fact, some studies have suggested that there is little or no regional variation in incomes of white families or individuals in communities of the same size.[19] In this section we shall examine some data on the earnings of white and Negro males in 1949 in standard metropolitan areas of three size groups. These

[19]See, in particular, Herbert E. Klarman, "A Statistical Study of Income Differences among Communities," in *Studies in Income and Wealth*, Vol. VI (New York: National Bureau of Economic Research, 1943), pp. 206-226 and the two articles by D. Gale Johnson cited earlier in this chapter. For a list of important studies of the relation of income and community size see Edwin Mansfield, "City Size and Income, 1949"; in *Regional Income (Studies in Income and Wealth, Vol. 21, op. cit.)*, p. 271. Mansfield's study is unique in that he examines the dispersion of income of communities of comparable size as well as their mean values.

data, presented in Table 164 for whites and in Table 165 for Negroes, show some tendency for the incomes of males in all regions to be higher the larger the community, although there are several exceptions to this tendency; and, as would be expected from the data for states, the incomes of Negro males tend to be below those of white males for all three community size groups in all regions. But the white-Negro differential varies from region to region and is greatest in the Southeast, where it was from 42% to 47% in 1949 for the three size groups.

Table 165. Median income, Negro males with income, 14 years old and over, standard metropolitan areas, by size, 1949

| | Population | | |
| | 500 thous. | 250 thous. to | 100 thous. to |
Regional average[a]	& over	500 thous.	250 thous.
New England	$1,777	$2,050	$1,845
Middle Atlantic	2,111	1,955	1,800
Great Lakes	2,270	2,323	2,295
Southeast	1,619	1,619	1,314
Plains	2,002	2,035	2,039
Southwest	1,572	1,548	1,436
Mountain & Far West	2,109	1,667	1,932
Relative variation[b]	15.0%	19.8%	29.4%
H[c]	16.2**	20.7**	39.9***

[a-c] See corresponding footnotes, Table 164.

SOURCE: 1950 Census of Population, Vol. II, see Table 164.

For both whites and Negroes, the income differentials between communities in the same size class tend to increase as community size decreases. But for all community size classes the variation in income is greater for Negro males than for white males.

While there is less regional variation in the incomes of males in the same community size class than for all urban and rural non-farm individuals, some regional variation remains, even for white males. For standard metropolitan areas with a population of 500,000 or more, the incomes of white males were about 6% lower in the Southeast than in the Great Lakes states. For cities with populations of 250,000 to 500,000 the differential between these two regions was about 16%, and for cities of 100,000 to 250,000, about 18%. The comparable differentials for Negro males were 29%, 30%, and 43%, respectively.[20] This suggests that *significant differentials in individual income among the various*

[20]While H is not quite significant at the 5% level for white males in the 500,000 and over class, it is significant at this level for both other community size classifications and for all three size classes for Negro males.

states remain even when the effect of sex, color, and community size are re-moved.[21]

Note on the H statistic: The H statistic[22] is used throughout this study as a means of testing the significance of the differences of mean values of a variable between regions. This statistic is analogous to the F ratio used in the more familiar parametric analysis of variance. But unlike the latter, it requires no assumption of normality for its validity. Rather it assumes that all observations are independent, that all observations in a single sample come from a single population, and that the several populations are of approximately the same form. The null hypothesis it tests is that the several samples come from identical populations.

Where:

C = the number of samples,
n_i = the number of observations in the i-th sample,
N = the number of observations in all samples combined,
R_i = the sum of the ranks in the i-th sample, where all observations are ranked together from 1 to N,

H is defined as follows:

$$(1) \quad H = \frac{12}{N(N+1)} \times \sum_{i=1}^{c} \frac{R_i^2}{n_i} - 3(N+1)$$

If there are tied observations this is modified slightly. On the null hypothesis that the C samples come from identical populations, H is asymptotically (in large samples) distributed as Chi-square with C-1 degrees of freedom. (Tables are available for small samples.)

Thus, if we were to assign the integers one through forty-eight at random and compute H for each possible assignment, the resulting values of H would follow the distribution of Chi-square with C-1 degrees of freedom, approximately. A value of H which is significant at the five per cent level might be interpreted as follows: the probability is not more than one in twenty that a value of H as large as the one observed or larger could arise from randomly assigning the integers one through forty-eight to the several states.

It should be emphasized that we shall use H only as a means for testing the significance of the difference between a set of regional means. Its value as a descriptive statistic is limited by the fact that the original values of the observations, upon which a meaningful description of the proportion of inter-state variance explained by the variance of regional means must depend, are transformed into ranks. In doing so, much of the information upon which a descriptive statistic ought to depend is "lost."

[21]Cf. Herman P. Miller, *Income of the American People*, Census Monograph Series (New York: John Wiley & Sons, 1955), pp. 43-46. Miller presents some data derived from the 1950 census which show that the incomes of white urban males 25 to 44 years old in the South are below those of the North Central and West for all city size groups. He also suggests that these differences cannot be explained by differences in occupational structure. On p. 46 Miller also shows that the incomes of white males 35 to 44 years old, when classified by educational attainment, are lower in the South than in the North and West for all groups except for those completing four years or more of college.

[22]W. H. Kruskal and W. A. Wallis, "Use of Ranks in One-Criterion Variance Analysis," *Journal of the American Statistical Association*, Vol. 47 (Dec. 1952), pp. 583-621.

28 / *Rates of income change, 1920-1955*

We shall now examine differentials in rates of income change among the various states for the period 1920-1955. In examining these differentials over time we are handicapped by the fact that income data are much less plentiful for this period than for the year 1950 alone. In particular, there are no data on income in sub-state areas comparable to those that the 1950 census provides. The data presented in this chapter, therefore, will relate exclusively to states. They are based on the Commerce estimates for the years 1929 to 1955 and on the Easterlin estimates for 1920.

The analysis of income changes over this 35-year period also poses difficult problems. Perhaps the most striking observation to emerge from an examination of these changes is the persistence of income differentials among states. There has been remarkably little change in income differences among states over these years. While it is true that some states have had more rapid increases in per capita income than others and there has been some tendency toward equalization of differentials in relative terms, the narrowing of the differentials appears to be related primarily to short-run fluctuations and year-to-year random movements. For example, the movement of income in the Plains states relative to the national average was as great from 1950 to 1955, owing principally to the fall in demand for farm products, as it was from 1929 to 1955. Thus it is difficult both to discern the direction of changes in per capita income in the various states and to analyze these differential changes. Furthermore, the time period we are considering has been characterized by two great economic upheavals, the depression of the 1930's and the inflation associated with World War II. As we shall show, whatever tendencies are observable toward the equalization of per capita personal income among states occurred primarily during these periods. This makes it still more difficult to determine secular trends in the movement of relative real incomes by states.

In presenting our material in this chapter, we shall first describe the changes that occurred in per capita personal income between 1929 and 1955 and show how the rates of change varied within these years. We shall then show changes in the principal components of personal income—participation income and property income—between 1920 and 1950. Finally, we shall discuss changes in participation income per worker over the period as a whole and attempt to discover why the rates of change have differed in different states.

Changes in Per Capita Personal Income, 1929-1955

Per capita personal incomes for the years 1929 and 1955 are summarized in Table 166. Here, as before, we have presented simple averages for the eight regions of the nation as well as data for selected states, in this case the states with lowest and highest per capita personal income in each region in 1929.[1]

The most striking observation emerging from the data shown (and from similar data for *all* the states not shown separately here) is the remarkable stability in the rank order of states with respect to per capita real income over this period. The rank correlation coefficient rho between per capita real income in 1929 and in 1955 is +0.96, which indicates that the two rankings are almost identical. There were a few shifts in position. Vermont fell in rank by 11.5 places over the period (it was tied with Virginia in 1955), New Hampshire fell seven places and West Virginia six. On the other hand, Montana rose in rank by eight places and Florida, Texas, and Indiana by seven. However, these shifts were almost insignificant as compared with the over-all pattern of stability in the rank order of per capita income in 1955 as compared with 1929.

Almost as striking is the lack of any apparent relation between level of income in 1929 and the absolute increase in per capita personal income from 1929 to 1955. (The latter is also shown in Figure 87.) Over this period, per capita personal income increased by $559 (1950 dollars) for the nation as a whole. The increase for the various states (in constant dollars) tended strongly to cluster about the national average. All but twelve states had increases of from $450 to $650 (1950 dollars); all but five, increases of from $400 to $700. The states at the extremes of the distribution were Nevada, with an increase of $813, and New York with an increase of $228. If we compare the absolute increase in real per capita personal income with the level of income in 1929 for the forty-eight states, we find no apparent relation between the two variables. The coefficient of rank correlation rho is —0.04. Likewise, in all of the eight regions, at least one state had an absolute increase in real per capita income which was below the national average and at least one had an above-average absolute increase. If we take the simple averages of the absolute increases in real per capita income for each of the eight regions, we find that increases were below

[1] These income data are current dollar per capita personal income estimates of the Department of Commerce deflated by the implicit G.N.P. deflator to remove the effects of changes in the general price level for the nation as a whole. No attempt has been made to allow for the possibility of differential changes in the general level of prices in different parts of the country. However, a recent study by Hurwitz and Stallings ("International Differentials in Per Capita Real Income Change," in *Regional Income, Studies in Income and Wealth*, Vol. 21, pp. 195-265) suggests that differential price trends among the various states from 1929 to 1953 were too small to affect trends in the relative real incomes of these states. The data in Table 166, therefore, are indicative of trends in real per capita personal income in the various states.

See U. S. Department of Commerce, Office of Business Economics, *National Income, 1954 Edition* (Washington: U. S. Government Printing Office, 1954), Part IV, pp. 153-58, for a discussion of the implicit G.N.P. deflator, and Table 41, pp. 216-17, for the data.

Table 166. Per capita personal income, by region, selected states, 1950 dollars,[a] 1929-1955

Region and state[b]	1929	1955	1955 — 1929	1955/1929
New England	$1,213	$1,690	$477	1.404
Maine	925	1,415	490	1.530
Connecticut	1,584	2,220	636	1.402
Middle Atlantic	1,434	1,951	517	1.377
Pennsylvania	1,192	1,690	498	1.418
New York	1,783	2,011	228	1.128
Great Lakes	1,177	1,799	622	1.546
Indiana	941	1,683	742	1.789
Illinois	1,473	2,005	532	1.361
Southeast	567	1,118	552	1.998
South Carolina	416	985	569	2.368
Florida	802	1,470	668	1.833
Plains	818	1,380	563	1.713
North Dakota	577	1,219	642	2.113
Missouri	966	1,599	633	1.655
Southwest	722	1,326	604	1.858
New Mexico	626	1,271	645	2.030
Arizona	909	1,401	492	1.541
Mountain	914	1,489	575	1.634
Idaho	774	1,300	526	1.680
Wyoming	1,042	1,558	516	1.495
Far West	1,271	1,894	623	1.500
Oregon	1,051	1,630	579	1.551
California	1,530	2,018	488	1.319
U. S.[c]	$1,082	$1,641	$559	1.517
Relative variation	35.8%	22.9%	—	—
H[d]	—	—	9.4	34.8***

[a] The current dollar data were deflated by the implicit G.N.P. deflator for the U. S. from *National Income, 1954 Edition, op. cit.*, Table 41, pp. 216-17; thus, adjustment is made only for the national change in the price level.

[b] Regional averages are simple averages of the data for states in the region.

[c] Values for the U. S. are total personal income for the nation divided by population, hence the weighted (by population) average of per capita personal income for the several states.

[d] See note d, Table 161.

SOURCE: Computed from current dollar data in *Personal Income by States Since 1929*, pp. 146-203.

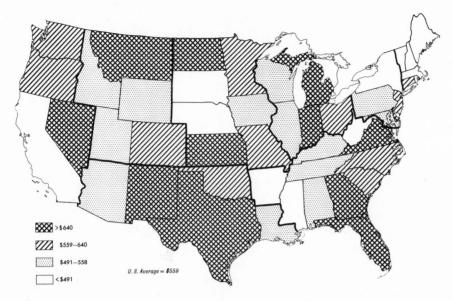

>$640
$559—640
$491—558
<$491

U. S. Average = $559

Figure 87. Absolute Increases in Real Per Capita Personal Income, 1929-55.

average in the east—the New England, Middle Atlantic, and Southeastern states —and above average elsewhere. However, as judged by the Kruskal-Wallis statistic H, there was no significant regional concentration of absolute increases in real per capita personal income.

In view of the fact that the rank order of the states remained roughly unchanged, and in the absence of any relation between income level in 1929 and the *absolute* increase from 1929 to 1955, it is not surprising to find that the greatest *relative* increases in real per capita income occurred in the states that had the lowest per capita income in 1929.[2] These were primarily the Southeastern and Southwestern states. Over the period 1929 to 1955, the standard deviation of per capita personal income in 1950 dollars remained roughly unchanged; owing to the sameness of absolute increases in real income throughout the country, the relative variation in per capita real income fell from about 35.8% to 22.9%.

Changes in Income From Current Production 1920-1955—By Time Interval

We shall now consider changes in per capita income in somewhat greater detail by examining these changes over several shorter time intervals in the period since 1920. This more detailed examination will enable us to locate the

[2]Comparing the relative increase in real per capita income with real per capita income in 1929 is virtually the same thing as comparing per capita personal income in 1929 with its reciprocal, rho is equal to −0.90.

principal sources of the differences among states in the rate of change.

Table 167 presents data on per capita income from current production for the eight regions and two states in each region for selected years during the 1920-1955 period.[3] Income from current production is the sum of participation income and property income and differs from personal income only in that net transfer payments are included in the latter. As net transfer payments are small,[4] for all practical purposes the two income concepts are identical. In Table 167, and in the remaining tables in this chapter, per capita income magnitudes are presented as ratios to the national average. This form of presentation was selected because it enables the reader to evaluate differences in income levels at a given point in time as well as differences in rates of change over time. Obviously, if per capita income in a particular state increases (decreases) relative to the national average over a given time period, it has grown at a more rapid (slower) rate than average for the nation. The U. S. average (in 1950 dollars) is given in each table also so that the reader may easily approximate the constant dollar value for any region or state shown in the table.

The data presented in Table 167 show the same tendency toward elimination of relative differentials in per capita income as the data presented in the previous section. From 1929 to 1955, per capita incomes on the average tended to move toward the national average in seven of the eight regions (in all but the Great Lakes region, where there appears to have been no strong tendency either to increase or decrease relative to the national average). An even stronger tendency toward the elimination of relative differentials is seen in the data for all forty-eight states. Form 1929 to 1955, thirty-nine states moved toward the national average in relative terms and one remained unchanged. And a comparison of the years 1920 and 1947, two years of unusually high demand for farm products, gives similar results.

However, this movement toward equality of real per capita income proceeded at different rates within the different intervals in the period 1920 to

---

[3]Examination of annual data for the period since 1929 suggests that essentially the same story can be told by presenting data for certain selected years, as we have done, as by presenting annual time series either in graphic or tabular form. However, in interpreting the data presented here, it should be kept in mind that the years 1920 and 1947 (or 1950) were years of unusually high demand for farm products, resulting from the two World Wars. Hence a comparison of, say, 1920 with 1929 or of 1947 with 1955 may give a misleading impression as to the direction of the secular trend in income in states such as the Plains states, where income from farming is an unusually high proportion of total income. For such states, a comparison of 1920 with 1947 or 1950, or of 1929 with 1955, would be a better indicator of the secular trend in per capita income relative to the national average.

Graphic presentations of the annual time series can be found in *Personal Income by States since 1929* (*op. cit.*, p. 27) for eight regions (slightly different from ours), or in Frank Hanna's *State Income Differentials, 1919-1954* (Durham, N. C.: Duke University Press, 1959) for the various states.

[4]For the nation they averaged $17 and $67 (1950 dollars) in 1929 and 1955 respectively—and are uncorrelated with income from current production, at least in 1950. They were probably smaller still in 1920, although no estimates of this class of money income receipts are available for this date.

Table 167. Per capita income from current production, participation plus property income, by region, selected states, selected years, 1920-1955

Region and state[a]	Ratio to national average				
	1920	1929	1941	1947	1955
New England	1.114	1.120	1.146	1.008	1.020
Vermont	0.886	0.885	0.872	0.833	0.816
Connecticut	1.200	1.469	1.609	1.295	1.366
Middle Atlantic	1.230	1.328	1.327	1.171	1.190
New York	1.586	1.651	1.381	1.312	1.230
Delaware	1.101	1.451	1.606	1.266	1.384
Great Lakes	1.038	1.087	1.102	1.087	1.104
Illinois	1.235	1.363	1.246	1.251	1.233
Indiana	0.886	0.863	1.012	1.004	1.034
Southeast	0.567	0.523	0.604	0.655	0.675
West Virginia	0.781	0.655	0.692	0.780	0.683
Florida	0.673	0.741	0.826	0.859	0.884
Plains	0.844	0.752	0.782	0.967	0.839
Nebraska	0.852	0.836	0.755	0.950	0.836
Missouri	0.893	0.889	0.897	0.917	0.970
Southwest	0.802	0.666	0.691	0.771	0.802
Arizona	1.061	0.839	0.861	0.867	0.854
Louisiana	0.647	0.591	0.621	0.659	0.706
Mountain	1.041	0.844	0.920	1.019	0.907
Wyoming	1.360	0.965	1.087	1.148	0.959
Utah	0.844	0.793	0.823	0.885	0.845
Far West	1.302	1.175	1.280	1.228	1.159
Oregon	1.134	0.967	1.166	1.159	0.990
California	1.472	1.416	1.396	1.281	1.233
U. S. dollar average [b]					
1950 dollars	$ 889	$1,065	$1,190	$1,345	$1,574

[a] Regional averages are simple averages of the data for states in the region.
[b] Excludes District of Columbia for 1920.

SOURCE: For 1920, computed from data supplied by Richard Easterlin; for other years the data were computed from data in *Personal Income by States since 1929*, pp. 146-203.

1955. From 1920 to 1929, relative differentials tended to widen; six of the eight regional averages and the averages of thirty-five states tended to move away from the national average. This tendency can be attributed in part to the fall in the demand for farm products that occurred in the 1920's, since decreases in per capita income relative to the national average occurred principally in the Southeast, the Southwest, the Plains, and the Mountain regions— those regions with the largest percentage of the labor force employed in agriculture in that decade. But changes in the demand for farm products are not the whole of the explanation. Data from the manufacturing censuses indicate that wages in manufacturing increased less rapidly than the national average in the Southeast, Southwest, and Mountain regions for the ten-year period 1919-1929 and more rapidly than average in the New England, Middle Atlantic, and Great Lakes regions.

The trend towards elimination of relative differentials in per capita income appears to have been strongest for the intervals 1929-1941 and 1941-1947. During the earlier of these two intervals, changes in per capita income were most noticeable in the Southeast; between 1929 and 1941 the regional average rose 8 percentage points and the averages of ten of the eleven Southeastern states increased relative to the national average. During the 1941-47 interval, the average for the Southeast rose another 5 percentage points and the average for the Southwest rose by 9 percentage points relative to the national average. While this relative increase in the Southeast and Southwest between 1941 and 1947 may have been partly due to increased demand for farm products, manufacturing wages increased more rapidly than for the nation as a whole both in both regions during these years. It would also appear that the relative decline in per capita incomes in New England and the Middle Atlantic states was confined primarily to the years during and immediately following World War II. Since 1947, the relative increase in per capita income in the Southeast and Southwest has proceeded more slowly than during the two previous intervals. However, per capita levels have continued to rise relative to the national average in every state in these two regions except West Virginia, North Carolina, and Arizona.

Changes in the Components of Per Capita Personal Income

Table 168 presents data on differential changes in the components of per capita personal income—participation income and property income—between 1920 and 1950 for the eight regions and selected states in each region.[5]

There were wide differences among states in property income per capita in 1950. Property income, however, is a relatively small part of personal income, and the national average, in 1950 dollars, shown in Table 168, indicates that it has become a smaller part of total personal income over time. From 1920 to 1950, property income per capita increased only 10% (in 1950 dollars);

---

[5] We have concentrated upon the changes that occurred between 1920 and 1950 for two reasons. First, when ratios to the national averages for per capita participation income and per capita property income were examined, it appeared that the time pattern of change for both of these components of personal income has been very similar to the time pattern of changes in personal income itself. Second, and perhaps more important, to estimate participation income per worker by states, we need estimates of the labor force by states. Such estimates are most readily available for census years, which do not coincide with the selected turning point years we have used for our analysis of income from current production. The years 1920 and 1950 are probably as satisfactory as any pair of years for making comparisons. In particular, both were years of unusually high demands for farm products, so that comparisons for these years are not likely to be biased by differences in the contribution of agriculture to personal income.

Table 168. Per capita participation and property income, by region, selected states, 1920 and 1950

| | Ratio to national average | | | |
| Region and state[a] | Property income | | Participation income | |
	1920	1950	1920	1950
New England	1.230	1.207	1.087	0.958
Vermont	0.740	0.947	0.921	0.766
Connecticut	1.550	1.668	1.118	1.244
Middle Atlantic	1.488	1.544	1.170	1.167
New York	2.041	1.567	1.479	1.228
Delaware	1.586	2.775	0.987	1.284
Great Lakes	0.927	1.017	1.065	1.119
Illinois	1.349	1.246	1.208	1.244
Indiana	0.669	0.818	0.937	1.071
Southeast	0.400	0.529	0.606	0.671
West Virginia	0.651	0.561	0.811	0.759
Florida	0.669	1.043	0.674	0.822
Plains	0.722	0.804	0.872	0.941
Nebraska	0.852	0.882	0.851	1.015
Missouri	0.787	0.941	0.918	0.968
Southwest	0.641	0.719	0.839	0.807
Arizona	0.746	0.738	1.133	0.883
Louisiana	0.574	0.626	0.664	0.712
Mountain	0.753	0.841	1.109	0.993
Wyoming	0.929	0.973	1.461	1.132
Utah	0.615	0.701	0.897	0.883
Far West	1.206	1.176	1.324	1.184
Oregon	1.006	0.930	1.162	1.100
California	1.769	1.332	1.403	1.218
U. S. Dollar average[b]	$169	$187	$720	$1,224

[a] Regional averages are simple averages of the data for states in the region.
[b] Excludes District of Columbia for 1920.

SOURCE: Same as Table 167.

on the other hand, participation income per capita increased by about 71%. Further examination reveals that property income per capita increased from $169 to $236 (1950 dollars) between 1920 and 1929 and then fell to $159 in 1947; since 1947 it has tended to increase, reaching $202 in 1955. Between 1920 and 1950, the standard deviation of property income per capita by states increased only slightly, and the relative variation fell from 50.8% to 45.1%. However, between 1920 and 1929, the standard deviation—a measure of the absolute differential—increased from about $73 to $124, and the relative variation rose from 50.8% to 67.1%. Thus, since 1929, inter-state differences in per capita property income have made a smaller contribution to differentials in per capita personal income, both because property income has become a smaller fraction of personal income and because inter-state differentials in property income per capita have declined, both in relative and in absolute terms.

In seven out of the eight regions, the averages of property income per capita have moved toward the national average. In the eighth, the Middle Atlantic region, the average rose a little less than 6 percentage points. However, in this region, it rose from 49% to 82% above the national average between 1920 and 1941 and fell to a little under 38% above the national average by 1955. The rise between 1929 and 1941 here was due solely to Delaware; every other state in this region rose relative to the national average from 1920 to 1929, but fell from 1929 to 1941.

On a state basis the movement toward the national average in property income per capita was even more striking. From 1920 to 1950, averages moved toward the national average in forty-two states. A part of this trend toward equalization might be attributed to the fact that the states have tended to become more alike in the proportion of the labor force employed in agriculture. Since a large part of the income from capital employed in agriculture accrues to recipients in the form of participation income, some of the equalization of property income per capita may be due to the fact that, in states where the movement out of agriculture has been quantitatively most important, a greater fraction of the income from capital was received as property income in 1950 as compared with 1920.

The tendency towards reduction of relative differentials in income is also apparent in the regional averages of participation income per capita. During the period 1920 to 1950, six of the eight regional averages moved toward the national average, the exceptions being the Southwest and Great Lakes regions. Although the average for the Middle Atlantic region was virtually the same in 1950 as in 1920, it increased from 1920 to 1941 and fell relative to the national average after 1941. The average for the Great Lakes region increased from 1920 to 1929 and remained virtually unchanged from 1929 to 1955. The average for the Southwest fell from 84% of the national average in 1920 to 72% in 1929, remained at about this level in 1939, and rose again to 82% of the national average in 1955.

Like personal income per capita, participation income per capita tended to become more unequal by states between 1920 and 1929, during which time the Southeast, Southwest, Plains and Mountain states tended to move away from the national average. After 1929 the most notable relative changes in income were in New England, the Southeast, and the Southwest. Between 1929 and 1955, New England fell from 110% to 99% of the national average, while the Southeast rose from 57% to 69% and the Southwest from 72% to 82% of the national average. During this same interval, income in the Middle Atlantic and Far Western regions fell about 5 percentage points, while incomes in the Great Lakes and Mountain regions remained about the same in relation to the national average. The tendency toward relative equalization of per capita participation income was also apparent on a state basis, but less so than for property income. From 1920 to 1950, thirty-two states moved toward the national average. The tendency was particularly strong in the Southeast, where eight out of eleven states moved toward the national average and in the Far West, where all four states declined relative to the national average. The relative variation of participation income per capita fell from 27.7% in 1920 to 22.4% in 1950.

But, while relative differentials in participation income per capita have tended to decline over the past thirty-five years, these tendencies should not be over-emphasized. For four of the eight regions, the changes were either away from the national average or were quite small relative to the difference between the regional average and the national average. Except for the Far West, the regions with the highest per capita participation incomes showed no tendency to fall relative to the national average over this same period. And during this time, while the relative variation of participation income per capita fell, the standard deviation—a measure of absolute differentials—rose about 35%, from $189.5 to $256.2 (1950 dollars). The equalization of participation income in *relative* terms has been due largely to the increase of incomes everywhere, since *absolute* differentials have actually widened.

Participation Income Per Worker and Its Components

The data on changes in participation income *per worker* relative to the national average, shown in Table 169, tell roughly the same story as the data on participation income per capita. The two are not identical because of differences in labor force per capita in different states at the same time and because of differential changes in labor force per capita over time. However, the pattern of changes in participation income per worker between 1920 and 1950 was very similar to that in participation income per capita; in each of the eight regions the averages for both moved in the same direction relative to the national average. Thirty-six states moved toward the national average, and the relative variation in participation income per worker fell from 22.4% to 17.5% over these years.

These data suggest two conclusions. First, that differential changes in labor force have not contributed very importantly to the observed pattern of differential change in participation income per capita by states. Secondly, that the equalization effect during this period has not been very great. This is true, interestingly enough, not only over all, but when agriculture and non-agricultural industries are considered separately. Over all, while relative differentials declined between 1920 and 1950, the absolute differentials in constant dollars actually widened. In 1920 the standard deviation of participation income per worker was $393.4 (1950 dollars) and in 1950 it was $506.2, or almost 29% greater.

When agriculture and non-agriculture are considered separately, although there are some significant differences in the patterns of change, the total impact is not too unlike.

Table 169. Participation income per worker, all industry, agricultural and non-agricultural, by region, selected states, 1920 and 1950

| Region and state[a] | All industry | | Ratio to national average | | | |
| | | | Agricultural | | Non-agricultural | |
	1920	1950	1920	1950	1920	1950
New England	0.995	0.920	1.390	0.946	0.892	0.907
Vermont	0.913	0.811	1.409	0.686	0.818	0.843
Connecticut	1.029	1.096	1.606	1.318	0.917	1.065
Middle Atlantic	1.103	1.109	1.302	1.096	1.015	1.084
New York	1.319	1.195	1.685	0.855	1.191	1.172
Delaware	0.927	1.265	0.988	1.477	0.884	1.227
Great Lakes	1.071	1.099	1.247	1.091	1.007	1.094
Illinois	1.196	1.151	1.247	1.412	1.124	1.121
Indiana	0.966	1.074	0.959	1.294	0.969	1.052
Southeast	0.644	0.717	0.662	0.664	0.760	0.756
West Virginia	0.946	0.916	0.905	0.632	0.946	0.932
Florida	0.656	0.807	0.717	1.162	0.651	0.773
Plains	0.959	0.971	1.182	1.261	0.956	0.941
Nebraska	0.945	1.006	1.087	1.461	0.984	0.937
Missouri	0.926	0.979	0.839	1.019	0.970	0.990
Southwest	0.912	0.908	1.021	1.252	0.969	0.878
Arizona	1.146	1.004	1.383	2.042	0.808	0.841
Louisiana	0.689	0.819	0.575	0.751	1.104	0.889
Mountain	1.139	1.042	1.652	1.506	1.042	0.980
Wyoming	1.371	1.090	2.296	1.774	1.170	0.989
Utah	1.064	1.056	1.390	1.232	1.006	1.042
Far West	1.177	1.126	1.966	1.636	1.033	1.08ᶜ
Oregon	1.108	1.056	1.831	1.188	0.960	1.040
California	1.286	1.161	2.110	1.754	1.132	1.113
U. S. Dollar average	$1,846	$3,055	$1,202	$2,302	$2,069	$3,154

[a] Regional averages are simple averages of the data for states in the region.

Source: Computed from unpublished data supplied by Richard Easterlin.

The regional averages and data for all the states show that there has been some narrowing of differentials in agricultural participation income per worker. Five of the eight regional averages moved toward the national average from 1920 to 1950. But the average for the Southeast remained virtually unchanged. On a state basis, thirty-four states moved toward the national average, but there was a tendency for regional clustering of the exceptions to this tendency. Six of the eleven Southeastern states fell relative to the national average, and four of the seven Plains states rose relative to the national average.

When the change in relative variation of agricultural participation income per worker is examined by states, it would appear that even the relative differentials failed to decline from 1920 to 1950. In fact, there was a slight increase, from 36.7% in 1920 to 37.3% in 1950. The standard deviation, which measures absolute differentials, increased almost proportionally with the average for the forty-eight states, from $531.7 to $949.2 (1950 dollars). These statistics suggest that on the whole the pattern of differentials in agricultural participation income per worker remained roughly unchanged form 1920 to 1950.[6]

The failure of participation income per worker to become more equal in different states over time is even more apparent when we look at the data for non-agricultural workers. Three of the eight regional averages were virtually unchanged, those for the New England, Southeast, and Plains regions. In the Middle Atlantic, Great Lakes, and Far Western regions, where non-agricultural participation income per worker was relatively highest in both 1920 and 1950, it tended to increase relative to the national average. The data for the forty-eight states show that in only twenty-eight states has participation income of non-agricultural workers tended to move toward the national average. In six of the eleven Southeastern states, where even for non-agricultural workers participation income is farthest below average, participation income per worker fell relative to the national average. From 1920 to 1950, the relative variation of non-agricultural participation income per worker increased very slightly, from 14.0% to 14.6%; during the same time the standard deviation of non-agricultural participation income per worker increased from $269.4 to $431.5 (1950 dollars). Thus, for both agricultural and non-agricultural workers, inter-state differentials in participation income remained unchanged in relative terms and actually widened markedly in absolute terms between 1920 and 1950.

While the relative variation of participation income per worker fell from 1920 to 1950, the relative variation of both agricultural and non-agricultural

[6]In an article by Robert J. Wolfson, "An Econometric Investigation of Regional Differentials in American Agricultural Wages," *Econometrica*, Vol. 26 (April, 1958), pp. 225-57, indices of annual average monthly farm wage rates for census divisions, 1910-42, are presented. His data reveal little or no tendency for farm wage rates to converge toward the national average for the period examined. Only for the West North Central (Plains) and Mountain regions does it appear that farm wage rates have tended toward the national average; as between 1910 and 1940 farm wage rates remained roughly the same relative to the national average in the East North Central (Lakes) and South Atlantic regions and have tended away from the national average in the other five regions. Wolfson comments that "There is a stable and persistent pattern of significantly large differentials in money wages paid to hired agricultural labor in the United States." *Ibid.*, p. 228.

participation income per worker remained unchanged over this period. In the Southeast, participation income per worker increased relative to the national average from 1920 to 1950 in ten out of eleven states, but both agricultural and non-agricultural participation income per worker increased relative to the national average in only five of these states. This seeming contradiction is resolved when it is noticed that from 1920 to 1950 the proportion of the labor force employed in agriculture declined, particularly in the Southeast and Southwest. Table 170 shows the per cent distribution of the labor force in agriculture in 1920 and 1950, together with the decline in this percentage over this period. For the nation as a whole the proportion of the labor force employed in agriculture fell from 25.6% to 11.6%. The fall was least marked in the New

Table 170. Per cent of labor force employed in agriculture, by region, selected states, 1920 and 1950

Region and state[a]	1920	1950	1950−1920
New England	12.5	6.1	− 6.4
Vermont	30.2	17.2	−13.0
Connecticut	6.2	2.5	− 3.7
Middle Atlantic	10.7	4.5	− 6.2
New York	6.8	2.6	− 4.2
Delaware	19.1	8.2	−10.9
Great Lakes	20.8	9.7	−11.1
Illinois	14.4	6.6	− 7.8
Indiana	26.2	11.1	−15.1
Southeast	48.7	22.5	−26.2
West Virginia	24.2	9.3	−14.9
Florida	27.9	11.0	−16.9
Plains	41.4	28.4	−13.0
Nebraska	40.9	28.6	−12.3
Missouri	29.8	16.9	−12.9
Southwest	40.8	16.5	−24.3
Arizona	27.1	14.2	−12.9
Louisiana	41.0	16.5	−24.5
Mountain	33.9	18.8	−15.1
Wyoming	31.4	18.6	−12.8
Utah	28.9	11.8	−17.1
Far West	20.4	8.9	−11.5
Oregon	24.5	11.4	−13.1
California	17.2	6.7	−10.5
United States[b]	25.6	11.6	−14.0

[a] Regional averages are simple averages of the data for states in the region.
[b] Average for the nation as a whole, or the weighted average of state data.

SOURCE: Lee, Miller, Brainerd, and Easterlin, *Population Redistribution and Economic Growth, United States, 1870–1950* (Philadelphia: American Philosophical Society, 1957), Table L-4, pp. 609-21, Cols. 6 and 9.

England and Middle Atlantic regions, the regions with the smallest proportion of the labor force in agriculture. It was most marked in the Southeast and Southwest, the regions with the greatest percentage of employment in agriculture. The relative decline in employment in agriculture was much less in the other regions where agriculture is relatively important, the Plains and Mountain regions. The relative shift out of agriculture was particularly striking in South Carolina, where the proportion of the labor force employed in agriculture fell from 62.1% in 1920 to 25.6% in 1950; similar changes occurred in Georgia, Alabama, and Texas.

Some notion of the quantitative importance of the shift out of agriculture in the South during the three decades from 1920 to 1950 can be gained from the data in Table 171. For the nation as a whole, participation income per worker in real terms increased by almost two-thirds over these years. Of the total increase of 65.5%, 15.2% was due to the increase in participation income per worker in agriculture, 43.8% to the increase in non-agricultural income, and 6.6% to the movement of the labor force out of agriculture.[7] However, there was considerable regional variation in the relative importance of these various components of change. The contribution of the increase in agricultural income was greatest, as would be expected, in the Southeast, the Southwest, the Plains, and the Mountain regions, where employment in agriculture is relatively most important. (See Figure 88.) In five of the seven Plains states and in all states but Oklahoma in the Southwest, increases in agricultural participation income per worker were above the national average. But only five states in the Southeast and only Montana in the Mountain region had above-average increases.

The non-agricultural component of change was relatively greatest in the New England, Middle Atlantic, and Great Lakes states and in the Far West (Figure 89).

[7] The percentage of change in participation income per worker attributable to change in agricultural participation income per worker for any state is the percentage of change in agricultural income per worker weighted or multiplied by the fraction of the labor force in agriculture and the ratio of agricultural to all industry participation income per worker (and similarly for non-agricultural participation income per worker). The percentage of change in participation income per worker due to the decline in the percentage of the labor force in agriculture is the latter multiplied by the ratio of the difference between non-agricultural and agricultural participation income per worker to participation income per worker for all industry. The formula may be expressed as follows:

Letting y stand for participation income per worker, p for per cent of labor force, and the subscripts 1 and 2 for agriculture and non-agriculture respectively, we have:

$$y = p_1 y_1 + p_2 y_2$$

Hence:

$$\frac{dy}{y} = p_1 \frac{(y_1)}{y} \frac{(dy_1)}{y_1} + p_2 \frac{(y_2)}{y} \frac{(dy_2)}{y_2} - \frac{(y_2 - y_1)}{y} dp_1$$

The first term represents the contribution of change in agricultural participation income per worker, the second non-agricultural, and third the contribution of the movement of the labor force out of agriculture.

For the computations shown in Table 171, we used 1920 data to weight the percentage change from 1920 to 1950. Since the formula is only approximate, the components of change do not equal the actual change exactly.

Table 171. Per cent change in participation income per worker, by components of change,[a] by region, selected states, 1920-1950

Region and state[b]	Percentage increase in participation income per worker	Due to increase in participation income per worker		Due to decrease in % labor force in agriculture
		in agric.	in non-agric.	
New England	52.9	2.2	48.4	0.2
Vermont	47.0	2.0	40.1	0.1
Connecticut	76.3	3.6	72.2	—
Middle Atlantic	69.1	7.4	58.9	2.1
New York	49.9	0.2	47.3	0.8
Delaware	125.9	24.7	96.6	4.1
Great Lakes	70.2	10.2	54.8	3.3
Illinois	59.2	11.4	46.9	2.9
Indiana	84.0	26.8	54.5	7.2
Southeast	86.3	29.9	35.7	18.4
West Virginia	60.2	5.1	42.7	7.4
Florida	103.6	41.8	65.0	6.8
Plains	67.9	34.3	33.1	4.0
Nebraska	76.3	48.2	31.2	5.1
Missouri	74.9	23.3	45.9	7.5
Southwest	67.4	37.2	27.9	12.3
Arizona	45.0	38.9	18.0	3.8
Louisiana	96.8	33.5	45.6	18.9
Mountain	52.9	25.1	30.0	1.5
Wyoming	31.6	16.4	19.0	−1.7
Utah	64.2	17.2	43.7	3.6
Far West	58.6	13.1	47.2	−1.1
Oregon	57.7	6.4	47.8	−1.4
California	49.4	10.9	40.8	−0.9
United States[c]	65.5	15.2	43.8	6.6

[a] Using 1920 weights. For a more complete discussion of the components of change in participation income per worker, see the description in the text.

[b] Regional averages are simple averages of the data for states in the region.

[c] Obtained by applying the same method to national data as was applied to the state data for state figures.

SOURCE: Computed from unpublished data supplied by Richard Easterlin.

The only regions in which the movement of the labor force out of agriculture made a significant contribution to the increase in participation income per worker were the Southeast and the Southwest (Figure 90). Indeed, had it not been for the movement out of agriculture in the Southeast, other things being equal, these states would have had only average percentage increases in par-

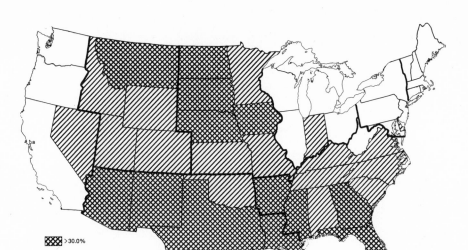

Figure 88. Increase in Participation Income per Worker Due to Increase in Agricultural Participation Income per Worker, 1920-50.

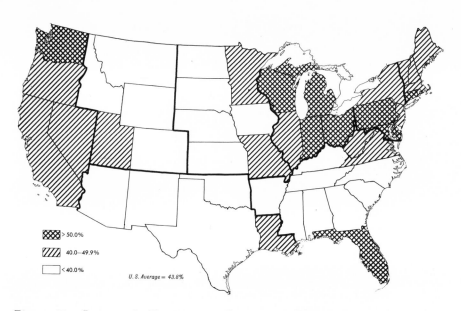

Figure 89. Increase in Participation Income per Worker Due to Increase in Non-Agricultural Participation Income per Worker, 1920-50.

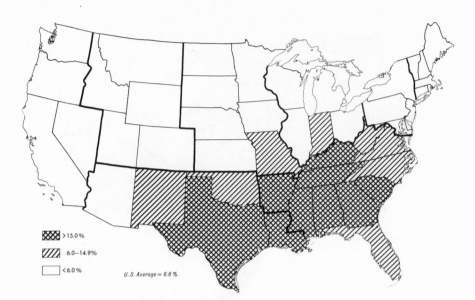

Figure 90. Increase in Participation Income per Worker Due to Fall in % Labor Force Employed in Agriculture, 1920-50.

ticipation income per worker. The contributions due to this factor were particularly striking in the Deep South—South Carolina, Georgia, Alabama, Mississippi, and Arkansas. In these five states the movement of labor out of agriculture resulted in increases of from 24% to 28% in participation income per worker. In the Southwest it meant increases of from 10% to 19% except for Arizona, where it made a below-average contribution. The shift out of agriculture had as important an effect upon incomes as it did in the South both because of the relatively large fall in the proportion of the labor force in agriculture and because of the great differentials in income between agricultural and non-agricultural pursuits in these regions.[8]

In summary, then, it would appear that the strongest force for reduction in

[8]It should be noted here that the increase in participation income per worker due to the movement of the labor force out of agriculture is partly overstated in real terms because of the difference in the prices of consumer goods on the farm and in the city. The basket of goods consumed by farm families costs from twenty-five to thirty per cent less on the farm than in cities. Because of this, an increase in money income due to movement from the farm to city does not carry with it a corresponding increase in command over consumer goods. But in 1920, participation income per worker in the Southeastern states averaged about one-half that per worker in non-agricultural pursuits. Hence, though the data in Table 171 probably over-state the increase in well-being in the Southeast due to the movement off the farm, the increase in "real" income due to the movement off the farm cannot be attributed wholly to differences in prices of consumer goods between the agricultural and non-agricultural sectors of the economy.

inter-state income differentials as between 1920 and 1950 was differential change among the states in the proportion of the labor force employed in agriculture. Over this period, the relative decline in agricultural employment was greatest in the Southeast and Southwest, where the incomes of farm persons are farthest below those of others. The narrowing of the differentials among states in participation income per worker seems to be mainly explained by this factor. The decline in the relative variation of property income made a small contribution to the decline in per capita income differentials over this same period also. Finally, while there has been a clear tendency toward the elimination of inter-state income differentials over the period since World War I, such reduction as has occurred has been small relative to the income differentials that existed among the states at the start of the period under consideration.

29 / *Income and industrial structure*

The association between income and industrial structure as among nations has long been subject to economic investigation, and more recently some attention has also been directed to this association at the sub-national level. In this connection the thoroughgoing study by Simon Kuznets of the industrial distribution of income and workers in the United States is particularly valuable.[1] He shows the nature of this relationship at four points in time—1920, 1930, 1940, and 1950—for six groups of eight states each, arrayed each year in descending order of personal income per capita. Thus, for example, his group "VI" consists of the eight states with the lowest per capita income in the nation in each of the four years under review (with only one exception for one year, these being states in the Southeast). The industrial structure is taken to be characterized by the distribution of employment among three sectors, which Kuznets designates as the A, M, and S sectors. The A sector covers agriculture and the related industries, fishing and forestry.[2] The M sector is a combination of mining, manufacturing, and construction. The S sector is the total of all "service" activities, including transportation and public· utilities, trade, finance, government, and personal, professional, domestic, and business services. His results, with regard to the distribution of the labor force, are reproduced in Table 172.

The association between the relative level of per capita income and the proportion of the labor force in the A sector is clearly negative. Its association with the share of the M sector is positive, although the trough is reached, at least in two of the four years, in group IV or V rather than in group VI. The association with the S sector is also positive, though weaker than with A or M, and it is less close in 1950 than in the earlier years. In general, Kuznets points out, these associations are not very different in character from those found through international comparisons (although the range of differences in the shares of the S sector is narrower in the interstate than in the international comparisons).

A more detailed analysis of the association between income and industrial

[1] Simon Kuznets, "Industrial Distribution of Income and Labor Force by States, United States, 1919-21 to 1955," Part III of "Quantitative Aspects of the Economic Growth of Nations," *Economic Development and Cultural Change,* Vol. 6 (July 1958), pp. 1-128.
[2] Except in 1920—actually the average for 1919-21—when it covers only agriculture.

Table 172. Arithmetic means of percentage share of three major sectors in labor force, groups of states by total income per capita, selected years, 1920 to 1950

	Groups of states by total income per capita						Arith. mean I–VI (unweighted)	Ratio of I+II to V+VI
	I	II	III	IV	V	VI		
	(1)	(2)	(3)	(4)	(5)	(6)	(7)	(8)
Share of A Sector								
1 1920	12.6	17.4	28.35	33.0	37.7	48.6	29.6	0.35
2 1930	10.6	13.9	27.3	34.0	38.85	51.8	29.4	0.27
3 1940	7.8	12.7	21.25	26.95	34.1	40.05	23.8	0.28
4 1950	5.7	10.2	18.3	19.2	18.4	27.0	16.5	0.35
Share of M Sector								
5 1920	39.8	40.3	32.7	24.15	22.2	19.2	29.7	1.93
6 1930	39.0	41.4	29.05	21.4	22.6	17.8	28.5	1.99
7 1940	37.45	37.25	30.6	22.2	20.0	23.6	28.5	1.71
8 1950	37.95	34.0	29.7	24.0	29.1	28.3	30.5	1.25
Share of S Sector								
9 1920	47.5	42.3	38.9	42.9	40.05	32.2	40.6	1.24
10 1930	50.4	44.7	43.65	44.6	38.6	30.4	42.1	1.38
11 1940	54.75	50.05	48.1	50.85	45.9	36.35	47.7	1.27
12 1950	56.35	55.8	52.0	56.8	52.5	44.7	53.0	1.15

SOURCE: Simon Kuznets, "Industrial Distribution of Income and Labor Force by States, United States, 1919.21 to 1955," Part III of "Quantitative Aspects of the Economic Growth of Nations," *Economic Development and Cultural Change*, Vol. 6 (July 1958), p. 58. For details on classification and measurement problems involved, see *ibid.*, pp. 2-10, 55-56.

structure is provided by Kuznets in terms of the industrial distribution of participation income. A similar pattern of association is shown to exist, although the positive association between the level of per capita income and the S sector's share of participation income is less clear cut than is its share in the labor force, and also the range of the shares of the M and S sectors is narrower for participation income than it is for labor force.

With the greater detail provided for participation income by industrial origin (as characterizing the industrial structure of the various states) it can be seen that, of the categories that comprise Kuznets' M sector—mining, manufacturing, and construction—only the latter two are positively associated with per capita income levels; the association in the case of mining is negative (as it is for agriculture). Kuznets "breaks out" another set of significant subcategories in his M sector; material-oriented branches of manufacturing and fabricating branches. Here, taking percentage distribution of manufacturing wages and salaries (rather than participation income) for two years, 1939 and 1955, he shows that only in the case of *fabricating* industries—such as machinery and equipment of various types, printing, and miscellaneous manufactures—do the shares in total manufacturing wages and salaries tend to increase as we move from low to high income states. Thus, for example, in 1955, the sixteen states with the lowest per capita income derived some 5.9% of their total manufacturing wages and salaries from "machinery (including electrical)"; the sixteen states with middle level income, 16.3%; the sixteen states with the highest per capita incomes, 20.1%. Kuznets suggests that, on the other hand, the shares of the raw-material-oriented industries in general tend to be *negatively* associated with per capita income; thus the shares of such industries as food and tobacco, textiles, lumber, chemicals, petroleum, and stone, clay, and glass tend to be lower in the high-income states as compared with low-income states.[3] Kuznets makes this observation:

> "The reasons for this finding can only be conjectured. . . . It may be suggested that the material-oriented industries tend to be located close to the supply of raw materials, many of which are products of agriculture and some of which are products of mining. Since there is negative association between the shares of agriculture and mining and total output (inferrable from their shares in participation income), the low income states in which the shares of agriculture and mining are large would also tend to have, within whatever manufacturing industries they possess, a preponderance of the material-oriented branches. On the other hand, the fabricating branches, with a presumably higher ratio of value added to cost of materials and a greater orientation to consumer markets would be relatively more important within total manufacturing in those states in which per capita income is high and the density and potential of the domestic market great."

Our inquiry into the association between per capita income and industrial structure focuses attention directly on the specific states and regions. The general picture which emerges is, of course, similar to the one shown by the Kuz-

[3]*Ibid.*, pp. 20-25.

nets data (which treat only classified groups of states), but this particular focus permits us to tie the income problem more specifically to the materials discussed in Parts III and IV of our study. It also opens up some significant questions concerning the major forces determining differentials in income levels and rates of growth: To what extent is the level of per capita income in a given area, as compared to other areas within the nation, associated with the relative proportions of its labor force in the various employment sectors at a given point in time? And to what extent is the rate of increase in per capita income related to changes in the industrial distribution of the labor force within the area over a given period of time?

Industrial Distribution of Employment, 1950

A partial breakdown of the labor force by industry of employment, based on data in the 1950 census, is presented in Table 173.[4] The first column of this table tells a familiar story: agricultural employment is relatively most important in the Southeast, Plains, Southwest, and Mountain states, and relatively least important in the New England, Middle Atlantic, Great Lakes, and Far West states. In all but one of the former group of states, West Virginia, the percentage of the labor force employed in agriculture in 1950 exceeded the national average; in the latter group, it was greater than the national average in only five states. Similarly, employment in manufacturing is relatively most important in the New England, Middle Atlantic, and Great Lakes states; of these states, only Vermont and Maryland fall below the national average in the proportion of their total employment that was in manufacturing in 1950. Outside these states, the national average was exceeded only in the Carolinas. It is also interesting to note that in the states where manufacturing as a whole is relatively most important, employment in the resource-processing industries (shown in Figure 91) is relatively least important. In the New England, Middle Atlantic,

[4]The first three columns of this table, headed agriculture, mining, and manufacturing, need no comment. The next two columns present a breakdown of tertiary employment based upon the principal user of the industry's output. The various tertiary employment categories were first broken down into those selling primarily to consumers, those selling primarily to other than consumers, and a mixed group. (For this purpose, "primarily" means two-thirds or more of gross output, as determined from the 1947 Input-Output table.) The latter two groups, here labelled "business," were combined since they tended to vary similarly between states. Those tertiary industries selling primarily to consumers, the consumer category in Table 173, include the following: local and highway passenger transportation, air transportation, retail trade, auto services, personal services, entertainment, medical services, and educational services, both public and private.

Because of our special interest in natural resources, another column was included in Table 173, the percent of manufacturing in the "processing" industries. The processing industries are the (essentially two-digit) manufacturing industries which include those firms for which the output of agricultural and mining industries is a significant input ("significant" meaning 10 per cent or more of all inputs in value terms as determined from the 1947 Input-Output table). They are: food, tobacco, textiles, lumber and furniture, petroleum and coal products, and metals. It should be noted that not all the *sub-industry categories* in each of these industries are significant resource users in the sense of the above.

Table 173. Industrial distribution of employment, by region, selected states, 1950

Region and state[a]	Percent of labor force employed in					Per cent mfg. employment in processing[d]
	Agriculture[c]	Mining	Manufacturing	Business services[d]	Consumer services[d]	
New England	7.2	0.31	37.0	14.3	30.0	47.0
Vermont	18.6	1.35	24.5	13.9	31.1	53.1
Connecticut	3.0	0.06	42.2	15.2	28.5	50.7
Middle Atlantic	5.1	1.13	31.8	17.8	30.4	41.9
New York	2.9	0.16	29.5	22.3	33.3	36.5
Pennsylvania	4.2	4.89	35.2	16.3	28.6	52.7
Great Lakes	10.2	0.82	34.7	15.6	28.6	38.4
Michigan	6.8	0.64	40.6	13.7	28.7	24.3
Wisconsin	18.7	0.22	30.3	13.8	27.4	41.7
Southeast	23.8	3.46	19.4	12.3	29.6	66.4
Mississippi	42.5	0.50	12.5	8.7	26.6	64.9
Florida	13.3	0.53	10.7	17.7	42.1	63.1
Plains	29.5	0.87	11.6	16.6	29.7	54.4
Missouri	17.6	0.62	21.5	18.2	30.2	38.1
South Dakota	40.5	1.12	4.8	12.9	28.6	70.6
Southwest	17.7	4.16	10.5	16.7	35.2	62.9
Oklahoma	20.6	5.30	9.8	15.3	34.0	61.4
Arizona	14.9	4.40	8.7	18.3	38.1	71.2
Mountain	20.2	4.48	9.5	18.3	32.5	72.8
Colorado	15.2	2.16	12.0	19.4	35.9	56.3
Idaho	27.2	2.61	9.1	16.9	31.2	82.0
Far West	10.2	1.69	17.1	19.2	36.3	52.3
Nevada	10.6	5.22	5.1	18.4	42.5	51.7
California	7.6	0.78	19.5	20.6	36.3	45.4
United States[b]	12.4	1.65	25.9	16.1	31.8	47.2

[a] Regional averages are simple averages of data for states in the region.

[b] Weighted average of the state data.

[c] Includes forestry and fisheries.

[d] For description, see footnote, p. 523.

SOURCE: Computed from data in the 1950 Census of Population.

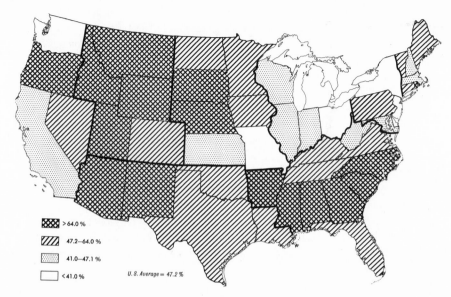

Figure 91. % Manufacturing Labor Force Employed in Processing
Industries, 1950.

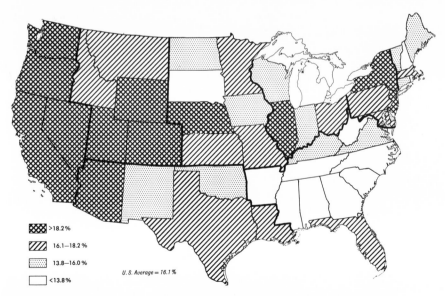

Figure 92. % Labor Force Employed in Business Service
Industries, 1950.

and Great Lakes regions, the percentage of manufacturing employment in the resource-processing industries in 1950 tended to be below the national average in all but four states (Maine, Vermont, Connecticut, and Pennsylvania). Outside these regions it was below average only in West Virginia, Missouri, Kansas, Washington, and California.

Employment in the business service industries is relatively most important in the Far West and the Mountain states, relatively least important in the Southeastern states. (See Figure 92.) In the Southeast, Florida was the only state in which employment in these industries exceeded the national average in 1950. Less than 10% of total employment was in these categories in the Carolinas and Mississippi, and only around 12% in Alabama, Arkansas, and Georgia. The data suggest that, except in the Great Lakes states, employment in the business services tends to vary—admittedly in a very rough way—with the level of per capita income in the various states. Not so with employment in the consumer service industries. The relative importance of this employment category was greatest in the Far West and Southwest and least in the Plains and Lakes states in 1950. It was almost as great in the Southeast as in the New England and Middle Atlantic states.

Relation of Income and the Industrial Structure, 1950

In our analysis of the association between income level and the industrial structure, we have made separate comparisons for rural-farm persons and other persons. Our reason for following this procedure is that the money incomes of the two groups are not strictly comparable because of differences in the level of prices of consumer goods for farm and city people. (This is discussed more fully in the following chapter.) There is considerable evidence that the prices of consumer goods are lower for farm families than for city families. Equal real incomes for the two groups, then, would mean lower money incomes for farm persons than for non-farm persons. Hence, even if real incomes were the same for farm and non-farm persons in all states, money income would be lower in those states where the proportion of the labor force employed in agriculture is greater.

In making our comparisons, therefore, we have compared the median income of persons with income, urban and rural non-farm on the one hand and rural-farm on the other, as reported in the 1950 census, with the relative importance of the different employment categories. For each of these income measures, the relationship with the various categories of employment is summarized by the rank correlation coefficient rho. These correlations are given in Table 174.

Table 174 indicates that the incomes of both rural-farm persons and urban and rural non-farm persons tend to vary inversely with the percentage of the labor force employed in agriculture. For the rural farm group, however, rho is small (−0.30), although significant at the 5% level. The figures shown in this table are for the nation as a whole, and in this instance they hide some significant regional differences—particularly the different situation of the "South" and the "non-South."

Table 174. Rank correlations of income and the relative importance of various employment categories, by state, 1950

| Median income, persons with income | Agri- culture | Percent of labor force employed in | | | | Percent mfg. employ- ment in processing |
		Mining	Manu- facturing	Business services	Consumer services	
Urban and rural non-farm	−0.65***	−0.10	+0.33*	+0.57***	+0.09	−0.60***
Rural farm	−0.30*	−0.18	+0.08	+0.48***	+0.02	−0.35*

Note: Asterisks denote significance level as follows:
  * Significantly different from zero at the 0.05 level
  ** Significantly different from zero at the 0.01 level
  *** Significantly different from zero at the 0.001 level

If we look at the rural-farm group of the Southeast and Southwest on the one hand and the other thirty-two states on the other, the results are quite different. For the sixteen Southern (i.e., Southeastern and Southwestern) states, considered separately, rho equals -0.70^{**}, while for the other thirty-two states rho equals $+0.04$. In the North and West, farmers in the agricultural states do not seem to be worse off than farmers in the non-agricultural states. But this is not the case in the South. Here the poorer farmers tend to be found in the states which rely most heavily on agriculture.

The correlation between the percentage of the labor force employed in agriculture and the median income of urban and rural non-farm persons is much higher than for rural-farm persons (-0.65 as compared to -0.30), both for the sixteen Southern states and for the thirty-two Northern and Western states.[5] This would seem to suggest that the higher urban incomes, on the whole, are to be found in the states where farming is less important and that this is true both North and South.

For 1950, there appears to be a small but significant correlation between the percentage of the labor force employed in manufacturing and the median income of urban and rural non-farm persons ($+0.33$) but none for rural-farm persons ($+0.08$). Of the twelve states that ranked highest in percentage of employment in manufacturing in 1950, eight also ranked among the top twelve in income of urban and rural non-farm persons; of the twelve that ranked lowest in the relative importance of manufacturing employment, two were in the top twelve and two in the bottom twelve states ranked by income.

The income of urban and rural non-farm persons and the income of rural-farm persons are both significantly associated with the percentage of employment in the business service industries ($+0.57$ and $+0.48$). Of the twelve states that ranked highest in the relative importance of employment in the business services in 1950, six were also in the top twelve in income of urban and rural non-farm persons and four in the top twelve in income of rural-farm persons. There is no apparent association, however, between income and the relative importance of employment in the consumer service industries. This is possibly due to the fact that where incomes are relatively high, wages are also, so these services are relatively more costly in such states. Finally, as in the Kuznets data, an inverse association is observed between income and the percentage of manufacturing employment in the processing industries, both for urban and rural non-farm persons and for rural-farm persons.

In comparing income with industrial structure, we might rank states by income level and compare the top twelve states in the relative importance of different kinds of employment. When such a comparison is made for the twelve states that ranked highest in rural-farm income in 1950, the following facts emerge: In the relative importance of agricultural employment, five of these states were also among the nation's top twelve and six were in the bottom twelve; in manufacturing employment, six ranked among the top twelve and four among the bottom twelve; in business services, three were among the top twelve and two among the bottom twelve. Hence, while there is a tendency for

[5]Rho equals -0.72^{**} for the former and -0.56^{**} for the latter.

income levels to vary from state to state with the broad classes of employment characteristic of the various states, one finds relatively high income associated with many different kinds of specialization in employment.

Additional Information Through Disaggregation

The association between per capita income and industrial structure becomes more meaningful as we get away from the broadest categories of employment. This was demonstrated when mining was separated out, when manufacturing was subdivided into processing and fabricating industries, and when services were broken down into business and consumer services.

A recent study has shown that a fairly limited amount of disaggregation of employment classes—essentially down to the 2-digit Census classes, and consisting of 58 groups of industries—reveals the expected close association between per capita income within a state and its industrial structure.[6] This is shown by a standardization procedure; the data are reproduced in Table 175, comparing income per capita expected within a state on the basis of its industrial structure and the actual per capita income in 1950.[7]

The correlation coefficient between observed per capita income (income-payments basis) and expected per capita income is .861.[8]

Two features of the relationship between income and industrial structure are highlighted by this type of comparison. One is that, as we move away from the very aggregate employment categories (as agriculture, manufacturing, and services), the large differences among the industries falling within such broad classes with reference to association with state income levels becomes apparent. Thus the study referred to above presents data—reproduced in Table 176— showing income per worker for industries at both ends of the income spectrum for various non-agricultural 1-digit Census classes. Clearly, *within* all the broad categories there are very large differences in per worker income. These data suggest why states with similar proportions of their labor force in the broad

[6]Harvey S. Perloff, "Interrelations of State Income and Industrial Structure," *Review of Economics and Statistics*, Vol. 39 (May 1957), pp. 162-71.

[7]The "expected" total state income is arrived at by taking the figures for income produced per employed person in each industry in 1950 (i.e., the national averages) and multiplying them by the number of workers within each industry in the given state. This is placed on a per capita basis by dividing total expected income of each state by its population as reported in the U. S. Department of Commerce, Bureau of the Census, *Census of Population: 1950*, Vol. I, pp. 1-8. Observed per capita income are those reported by the Department of Commerce *(Survey of Current Business, August 1953)*, and therefore are based on the earlier income-payments basis of income estimation by the Office of Business Economics of the Department of Commerce. See Perloff, *loc. cit.*, pp. 167-68.

[8]Since this is the correlation of an observed and a standardized variable, the correlation reflects not only the independent influence of the standardized variable but also the correlation of the standardized variable with the difference between the observed and the standardized variable. A measure of the independent effect of the standardization is obtained by comparing the standard deviation of the standardized variable with the standard deviation of the observed variable.

Table 175. Observed and "expected" income per capita (income–payments basis), 1950, on basis of industrial structure*

State	Expected income per capita	Observed income per capita
New England		
Connecticut	$1,747	$1,789
Maine	1,281	1,157
Massachusetts	1,595	1,602
New Hampshire	1,413	1,310
Rhode Island	1,564	1,542
Vermont	1,337	1,162
Middle Atlantic		
Delaware	1,741	1,956
Maryland	1,564	1,557
New Jersey	1,793	1,708
New York	1,745	1,872
Pennsylvania	1,581	1,537
Great Lakes		
Ohio	1,676	1,584
Indiana	1,652	1,459
Illinois	1,760	1,757
Michigan	1,859	1,596
Wisconsin	1,572	1,442
Southeast		
Alabama	1,219	847
Arkansas	1,059	821
Florida	1,405	1,201
Georgia	1,296	967
Kentucky	1,200	913
Mississippi	1,072	703
North Carolina	1,243	949
South Carolina	1,210	844
Tennessee	1,280	967
Virginia	1,311	1,147
West Virginia	1,273	1,050
Plains		
Minnesota	1,472	1,343
Iowa	1,412	1,413
Missouri	1,526	1,396
North Dakota	1,198	1,273
South Dakota	1,253	1,275
Nebraska	1,403	1,474
Kansas	1,445	1,349

State	Expected income per capita	Observed income per capita
Southwest		
Oklahoma	1,341	1,077
Texas	1,443	1,273
Louisiana	1,279	1,049
New Mexico	1,146	1,133
Arizona	1,165	1,233
Mountain		
Montana	1,405	1,568
Idaho	1,282	1,260
Wyoming	1,488	1,514
Colorado	1,421	1,384
Utah	1,332	1,270
Far West		
Washington	1,423	1,627
Oregon	1,464	1,517
California	1,550	1,750
Nevada	1,530	1,882

*The regional groupings have been rearranged to conform with those employed throughout Parts IV and V of this study.

employment categories might have widely different per capita incomes, and why a focus on any given level of disaggregation of industry is appropriate only to the extent that it is revealing of significantly different "income-generating powers" of different groupings of industry (essentially, of significant differences in productivity per worker). That is why, for example, the breaking out of the fabricating industry grouping and the business service grouping turned out to be so suggestive for the examination of the income-industrial structure association.

The second feature is related to the fact that the major divergence between the calculated and observed per capita incomes among the states (as shown in Table 175) occur in the lower-income states of the Southeast. The implications with regard to the tendency for wages to be below the national average for given industries within certain parts of the country are discussed at a later point.

Industrial Structure and Increases in Income

The question arises as to whether the type of association between per capita income and industrial structure revealed by cross-section analysis persists when

Table 176. Average income per full-time employed person in selected industries, 1949–51

Secondary industries	
Mining	$ 5,211
Anthracite mining	3,537
Crude petroleum & natural gas	6,821
Construction	3,476
Manufacturing	4,882
Apparel & other finished fabricated products	2,893
Products of petroleum & coal	12,423
Tertiary industries	
Trade	3,837
Retail trade & auto services	3,437
Wholesale trade	5,115
Transportation	4,641
Local & highway passenger transp.	3,504
Pipeline transportation	8,815
Communications & public utilities	5,641
Local utilities & public service, n.e.c.	3,957
Electric & gas utilities	7,377
Services	2,943
Misc. repair services & hand trades	2,078
Legal services	5,858
Government & government enterprises	3,170
State & local—general government	2,938
Federal government enterprises	3,682

SOURCE: Income originating in each industry is from Table 13 of *National Income: A Supplement to the Survey of Current Business,* 1954 ed., prepared by the Office of Business Economics of the U.S. Dept. of Commerce. The number of persons employed in each industry includes "active proprietors of unincorporated enterprises devoting the major proportion of their time to the business," given in Table 28 of the above publication, *ibid.,* p. 166.

changes over time are examined. That is, is there an association between the percentage change in per capita income in a given state over a given period of time and the industrial structure of the state at the initial point in time (or percentage change in the structure over the period)? Once again, the Kuznets data provide a useful summary of the relationships (Table 177).

Since the rate of growth in per capita income between 1920 and 1950 was above average for the states with initially low incomes and below average for those with initially high incomes, the Southeastern states fall into the I+II grouping in Table 177. It can be seen that there is a positive association between the percentage growth in income per capita and the changes in the shares of the A and M sectors. In the states with the highest rise in per capita income, the decline in the share of the A sector in the labor force and the rise in the share

Table 177. Changes in percentage shares of three major sectors in labor force, 1920 to 1950, groups of states by rise in total income per capita over the period

	Groups of states by rise in total income per capita		
	I + II	III + IV	V + VI
% change in per capita income, 1920–1950	194%	152%	115%
Change in share of A Sector, 1920–1950 (arith. mean)	−17.3	−11.85	−10.3
Change in share of M Sector, 1920–1950 (arith. mean)	+ 4.3	+ 0.75	− 2.75
Change in share of S Sector, 1920–1950 (arith. mean)	+13.0	+11.1	+13.0

SOURCE: Same as source for Table 172, pp. 66-67.

Table 178. Rank correlation coefficients of changes in per capita income and in industrial structure of the states, 1920–1950

Agriculture	−0.45**
Mining	+0.22
Manufacturing	+0.57***
Rest (services, etc.)	+0.07

**Significant at the 0.01 level.
***Significant at the 0.001 level.

of the M sector are both greater than the average for all states; and conversely for the states with the smallest rises in per capita income. No definite association can be observed for changes in the share of the S sector in the labor force.

A similar picture emerges if the basic income and employment data are examined in terms of rank correlation coefficients, as we have done in Table 178.[9] This table highlights the significant and rather large correlation between the differential change in per capita income among the states and the changes in the relative importance of agricultural and manufacturing activities within each. Where the percentage of the labor force employed in agriculture tends to decline most and the percentage in manufacturing tends to increase most, per capita income increases relatively most (or the relationship can be described the other way around, to suggest that certain changes in industrial structure are

[9] The coefficients refer to the comparison of the relative change in per capita income with the relative change in the proportion of the state's employment in the several employment categories.

observed to accompany changes in per capita income). In the case of mining, where a negative association appeared in the cross-section analysis, it is interesting to note that a small positive (but not quite significant) association appears in the time series analysis; also, in the case of services, where a generally positive association was evident in the cross-section data, no association at all appears in the time series. Kuznets sums up this set of relationships as follows:[10]

". . . When an increase in per capita income over time is accompanied by the changes in the shares that are indicated by cross-section correlation, the association between the rate of growth of income per capita and the change in the share of a sector is also clearly positive. For example, the downward trend in the shares of the A sector in income and the labor force is consilient with the negative association in cross-section analysis between its shares and per capita income; and the states in which per capita income grew at the highest rates are those in which the share of the A sector declined most. If, however, the trend over time runs counter to the association suggested by cross-section analysis, the correlation of the rate growth of per capita income with the changes in the shares tends to be irregular. . . .

"In other words, the faster the rate of growth of per capita income, the faster the change in industrial structure—provided that the change is in the direction suggested by cross-section analysis. A similar finding but of much narrower scope (referring to the share of the A sector alone) was observed in the international comparison; and if the data for nations were as plentiful as those for states, we might well find the same widespread association there."

The association of income levels (and changes) with the importance of a given sector in the industrial structure of a state arises from the fact that the sector is characterized—on the average—by a given level of "income-producing power" as compared to the other sectors. It reflects, then, the given level of socio-technical development on the part of each employment sector. Thus, for example, one would *not* expect the same association between income and, say, agriculture in the case of the subnational units in a country like Australia or New Zealand, where the relative income per worker in the agricultural sector is above the average for all industries. Even within the United States itself, when we get away from the national averages, we note very great differences in association between income and agriculture for the Northern and Western states as compared to the Southern states.

Over time, the income-structure association, it is clear, is greatly affected by (1) how large the income differentials are—on the average—as between employment sectors at the start and the end of the period, (2) how large the sectoral changes have been, i.e., the shift in employment between sectors, and (3) how large the changes in per capita income have been nationally and regionally. Thus, the size of the income gain actually recorded for a given state as accompanying a given structural change within the state reflects specific conditions and not any generalized pattern of change. A per capita income gain accompanying a very substantial shift in employment from certain manufacturing

[10]Kuznets, *loc. cit.*, p. 93.

categories to certain service categories within a Western state might be no larger than that accompaning a relatively small shift out of low-productivity agricultural industries to high-productivity agricultural industries within a Southern state.

While it is important to appreciate the general relationships between different sectors of the economy and income, it is even more important to appreciate the characteristics which make a given sector more or less productive with regard to the relative level of output per worker.

30 / Factors related to money income differentials

In our examination earlier of money incomes in the various states, we found significant differentials in the money returns to labor in different places. These differentials do not in themselves, however, necessarily imply a corresponding difference in welfare in the various states. They might be accompanied by differences in the level of prices of consumer goods; and to the extent that consumer prices vary from place to place, the money expenditure needed to achieve a given level of consumption likewise varies. Thus different levels of money income might be equivalent with similar levels of consumer welfare.

Nor do they in themselves necessarily imply differentials among the various states in the real returns to labor of equivalent skill. They might reflect differences in the industrial or occupational composition of the labor force or differences in skill of workers in the same industry in different places. To the extent that low labor incomes per worker are associated with a concentration of an area's employment in the lower paying occupations or industries, and to the extent that differentials in the labor incomes of workers in identical industries in different places are due to differences in skill, interstate differentials in labor income might be consistent with equality in the real returns to labor of the same skill in different states. Of course, in each of these two circumstances, differentials in labor income might result in differences in the level of consumer welfare in one state as compared with another.

In order to appraise the relevance of these factors to money income differentials, we shall inquire further into their meaning in this chapter. But first we shall touch upon the meaning of the effects of color on money income received.

The Effects of Color

We have already seen that in virtually every state and place of residence the incomes of non-white persons are substantially lower than those of white persons. Several reasons suggest themselves for this. First, although there are no data on property incomes by color, it seems quite likely that non-whites own less capital and so receive smaller incomes from property. Second, it would seem that they have less capital invested in themselves. In almost every state the median years of school completed is lower for non-whites than for whites. This is particularly true in the South.[1] Because they are generally less well educated, and also because they are more concentrated in the younger age groups, non-whites are presumably less skilled and earn smaller labor incomes.

However, neither of these factors can account completely for the color-income differential. Data given both by Miller[2] and by Becker[3] indicate that, for a given class of men of comparable age and education, the average income of non-whites is less than that of whites. In almost all cases the differential is greater in the South, and it increases with educational attainment. Data on the distribution of white and non-white males of a given age in the South show a higher relative concentration of non-whites in the lower paying occupations for any given degree of educational attainment.[4]

The implications of these data are that, in explaining the white-Negro income differential, the factor of racial discrimination must be taken into account.[5] Because of racial discrimination, education appears to be more costly for non-whites than for whites, especially in the South, and the marginal monetary returns to education are lower.

Further evidence on the white-Negro differential is provided in a recent study by Robert Weintraub.[6] This study is based on a sample of men employed as production and maintenance workers between September 1947 and March 1953 in an International Harvester plant in Memphis, Tennessee; the company policy is one of non-discrimination in employment. In this plant, Negro workers earned about 9% less than white workers of the group studied; and if workers (all white) in managerial positions are excluded, and account is taken of previous experience and the level of vocational training of the workers, the earnings of Negroes averaged only 3% less than those of whites. In contrast, in 1949 the median income of Negroes in metropolitan Memphis was only 50% that of whites. Weintraub's study strongly suggests that there are no inherent differences

[1]Cf. Gary S. Becker, *The Economics of Discrimination* (Chicago: University of Chicago Press, 1957), p. 107. Becker found that relative education of non-whites is negatively related to their relative numbers in the South, if relative incomes are held constant.

[2]H. F. Miller, *Income of the American People*, Census Monograph Series, (New York: John Wiley and Sons, 1955), Table 20, p. 46. These data are on the median incomes in 1949 of men 35 to 44 years old, for the South and for the North and West, by years of school completed.

[3]Becker, *op. cit.*, Table 10, p. 92. These data are on wage and salary incomes for urban males in 1939, by age, and are from M. Zeman, "A Quantitative Analysis of White-Non-White Income Differentials in the United States in 1939" (Unpublished Ph. D. dissertation, Department of Economics, University of Chicago, 1955). They cover more age groups than Miller's data, and refer only to urban males.

[4]Miller, *op. cit.*, Table 21, p. 47.

[5]Becker, *op. cit.* pp. 91-107, examines and rejects some alternative explanations, including the one that differences in quality of education account for this differential. He concludes also that "tastes" for discrimination are almost twice as strong in the South as elsewhere.

[6]"Negro-White Earnings in a Southern Industrial Plant," (abstract), *Econometrica*, Vol. 25 (April, 1957), pp. 368-69.

in the productivity of white and Negro workers and that, for those workers studied, differences in training and experience had little effect upon the earnings of whites and Negroes, as compared with the relative incomes for all whites and Negroes in Memphis. This study also suggests that the white-Negro differential might be largely explained by racial discrimination.

Differences in Consumer Prices

Economists have long recognized that differences in money incomes may be compensated for by many factors, and that one such factor is a difference in the level of consumer prices in one area as compared to another. It is conceivable that money prices of consumer goods and money incomes might differ from area to area in the same fashion. If this were the case, differentials in money incomes might not mean differences in the real incomes of consumers or in the real labor returns to workers in different areas.

We shall now examine some of the available data on price differences in various areas to see whether they are associated with the money income differences observed as between these areas. We shall present two kinds of comparisons: a comparison of the money prices paid by farm families and by urban families and a comparison of the money prices paid by urban families in different regions of the country. In making such comparisons, one is faced with two difficult problems—first, the limited availability and reliability of data on price differences and, second, the problem of what prices to compare. Consumers in different areas may consume different bundles of commodities because of conditions unrelated to relative prices (e.g., fewer overcoats in warmer climates). And, if relative prices differ in different areas, consumers tend to consume more of the commodities that are less expensive; these may be different commodities in different areas.

The only published study we have come across which compares the prices of consumer goods for farm and urban residents is that of Nathan Koffsky.[7] Using data for 1941, Koffsky compared two budgets, farm and urban, both evaluated in terms of prices paid on the farm and prices paid in urban communities. The comparison was made only for the nation as a whole; no regional comparisons were made.[8] He found that the farm budget would cost 30% more in terms of

[7]"Farm and Urban Purchasing Power," *Studies in Income and Wealth*, Vol. XI (New York: National Bureau of Economic Research, 1949), pp. 153-78. See also the comment by Margaret G. Reid, *ibid.*, pp. 179-206.

[8]In a more recent study by Robert J. Wolfson, "An Econometric Investigation of Regional Differentials in American Agricultural Wages," *Econometrica*, Vol. 26 (April 1958), pp. 231-33, crude price indices for farm areas of five census regions were constructed. These are simple averages of prices of thirty-six basic food and clothing items reported for 1952 by the U.S. Department of Agriculture. (No data are available to determine relative weights for these various prices.) The interregional variation in prices found was quite small relative to the difference between farm and urban price levels found by Koffsky. The maximum difference Wolfson found was between the West North Central and West South Central regions, prices in the latter averaging about 6 per cent below those in the former. In the South Atlantic and East South Central regions, prices averaged about 2 and 4 per cent, respectively, below those in the West North Central region.

urban prices and that the city budget cost 14% more in terms of urban prices than in terms of farm prices.[9]

Koffsky's finding on the difference between the cost of a farm budget in farm prices and in urban prices in 1941 is unquestionably too high to be used as a measure of present-day differences between farm and urban prices.[10] But it does reveal a tendency, or relationship, that must be taken into account in comparing farm and urban incomes.

Keeping in mind the fact that there is an apparent urban-farm price differential, how do urban and farm incomes within the same region compare? In Table 179 we make such a comparison for each of the eight regions, first of the incomes of urban and rural "white" persons and then of the incomes of white and non-white persons, urban and rural non-farm *vs.* rural-farm.[11] For three regions—the New England, Plains, and Mountain regions—the money income differentials for whites as between farm and non-farm areas are only slightly greater than the differentials in money prices of consumer goods. But even

Table 179. Median family and individual incomes, non-farm vs. farm, by region, 1949

Region	Families and unrelated individuals, urban/rural-farm "white"	Individuals with income, urban & rural non-farm/rural-farm	
		White	Non-white
New England	1.36	1.28	1.61
Middle Atlantic	1.60	1.52	1.46
Great Lakes	1.46	1.43	2.16
Southeast	2.18	1.89	1.76
Plains	1.33	1.18	1.45
Southwest	1.74	1.51	1.76
Mountain	1.33	1.25	1.28
Far West	1.41	1.38	1.46

SOURCE: Computed from the regional averages shown in Tables 162 and 163.

[9]The greatest source of difference was in food; food tends to cost less on the farm because much of it is produced on the farm, and farm families tend to consume more food than urban families.

D. Gale Johnson suggests a figure similar to Koffsky's—25 per cent—as an estimate of the difference between the cost of a farm budget in farm prices and in urban prices. See "Functioning of the Labor Market," *Journal of Farm Economics,* Vol. 33 (February 1951), p. 76.

[10]And the differences can be expected to diminish further as agriculture becomes more and more oriented to large-scale commercial farming.

[11]The fact should be kept in mind here that, in the comparisons of the incomes of white and non-white persons, rural non-farm incomes as well as urban incomes are included in the numerator and that price differentials are possibly smaller between rural non-farm and rural-farm areas than between urban and rural-farm areas.

Table 180. B.L.S. city worker's budget, four regions, October 1949

Region[a]	25 Cities over 500 thousand	33 Cities over 100 thousand
Northeast	$3,578	$3,533
South	3,491	3,503
North Central	3,510	3,510
West	3,569	3,569
All cities	3,538	3,523
Relative variation	3.0%	3.3%
H[b]	1.6	0.9

[a] For this comparison the eight regions were combined as follows:
    Northeast—New England and Middle Atlantic
    South—Southeast and Southwest
    North Central—Great Lakes and Plains
    West—Mountain and Far West
Data presented in this table are simple averages of all cities in the region for which data are available.

[b] Since we have four classes, H is distributed approximately as Chi-square with three degrees of freedom. The five per cent point for Chi-square with three degrees of freedom is about 7.8.

SOURCE: Computed from data given in U. S. Department of Labor, Bureau of Labor Statistics, "Family Budget of City Worker, October 1950," *Monthly Labor Review,* Vol. 72 (February 1951), pp. 152-55.

allowing for the urban-rural price differential, real incomes in the Southeast, Middle Atlantic, and Southwest regions are substantially lower for farm than for non-farm persons. In evaluating this comparison it should be noted that the data refer to 1949, a year in which farm incomes were influenced by the unusually high post-war demand for farm products. If a similar comparison were made for, say, 1955 the data might show *greater* differentials between farm and non-farm money incomes. On the other hand, the census income data do not include the money value of income in kind. Hence, the comparisons here may overstate the difference in consumption levels as between rural-farm and other persons; this overstatement is likely to be relatively greatest in the Southeast, where income in kind is relatively more important than in other agricultural regions.

Such evidence as is available suggests that the prices of consumer goods in cities do not differ appreciably among regions. Table 180 shows the average cost of the city worker's budget in 1949 for cities of two size groups (over 500,000 and over 100,000) in the Northeast, the South, the North Central, and the Western regions of the country as computed from Bureau of Labor Statistics data.[12] The averages show surprisingly little variation among the four

[12]The BLS city worker's budget is the total cost of a given collection of goods and services in different cities. The cost of this budget in 1949 varied from $3,773 in Washington, D. C., to $3,295 in New Orleans—a difference of about 14 per cent.

regions in the cost of this budget; the Southern cities averaged only about 1% below all cities, and the Western cities only about 1% above all cities. The regional differences were not significant for the cities within either of the two size groups.[13] Furthermore, there seems to be no significant difference between cities of the two size groups;[14] the average for the eight cities of between 100,000 and 500,000 was $3,477 as compared with $3,538 for the twenty-five cities of 500,000 or more. If the money incomes of white males in the twenty-five cities of over 500,000 are compared with the city worker's budget for these same cities, the rank correlation coefficient, rho, between the two series is +0.32, which is not statistically significant at the 5% level.

Thus differences in the city worker's budget among regions are insignificant and the city worker's budget is not significantly related to money incomes in the different cities. While a more detailed study for a larger number of cities, particularly smaller cities, might show significant regional and city-size differences in the prices of consumer goods, the data examined above show no such difference.[15]

Differences in Occupational and Industrial Structure

Differences in earnings among workers in a given area depend in part upon differences in skills as reflected in the occupational or industrial classifications of these workers.[16] Hence, considerable variation in the money returns to workers in different occupations within the same labor market could be consistent with equilibrium, defined as a position in which there is no incentive

[13]As judged by the statistic H, equally great or greater differences among cities in the four regions could arise in seven out of ten samples for the twenty-five cities in the first size group (over 500,000) and in eight out of ten samples for the thirty-three cities in the second size group, even if no true regional differences existed.

[14]Again using H as a criterion, as great a difference as was observed, or greater, could occur in about three samples out of ten if no true difference existed between cities in these two groups.

[15]We should point out in passing that differences in the level of consumer prices are only one of many possible factors compensating for differences in money income. Many persons might achieve a given level of satisfaction with a lower money income in Florida, with its climatic and recreational advantages, than in states which lack these advantages. Likewise, in a very large city as compared with a small city, many persons might achieve a given level of satisfaction only with a larger money income because of the time spent in transportation, the "crowding," and the unpleasant atmospheric conditions, such as "smog," in the large city. But, so far as we know, no systematic data have been collected for evaluating such advantages and disadvantages in monetary terms.

[16]There is some evidence that industrial and occupational wage differences are relatively stable over time and between different places and reflect lasting differences. Stanley Lebergott, in comparing wage differentials in similar industries in the United States, Canada, the United Kingdom, Switzerland, Sweden, and the U.S.S.R., found that the pattern among industries was very similar in all these countries, except possibly the U.S.S.R. He found also a close similarity between wage differentials by industries in four regions of the United States and between selected occupations in the United States over the period 1900 to 1940. See "Wage Structures," *Review of Economic Statistics*, Vol. 29 (November 1947), pp. 274-85.

for any worker to change employment. And even if workers in all occupations were of equal skill, money wage differentials between occupations might be compatible with equilibrium in the sense in which we have defined this term. Such differentials would reflect a variety of factors other than current money income that influence the choice of employment; for example, the relative cost of training for the different occupations, the time pattern of expected earnings, the variability of earnings within a single year or over a lifetime, and various nonpecuniary considerations—the pleasantness of a particular occupation, the social prestige connected with it, and so on.

In this section we shall seek to determine the extent to which differences in the labor income of persons in the various states are associated with differences in the industrial and/or occupational distribution of the labor force in these various states. We shall also seek to determine whether there are any systematic tendencies for workers in all industries and/or occupations in a given area to receive above or below average earnings. If labor income differences are associated solely with the industrial and/or occupational composition of the labor force in different areas, they would be consistent with an optimal allocation of labor area-wise, even though they could contribute to differentials in consumer welfare in these different areas. If workers in the same industry and/or occupation earn the same money wages everywhere, occupational rather than geographic factors would account for the labor income differentials among states.

The most comprehensive set of data relating labor income differences to differences in occupational and/or industrial structure are the "rate-constant" occupational and industrial earnings computed by Hanna.[17] Table 181 presents regional averages and data for selected states based on Hanna's data. The "rate-constant" earnings for each state were obtained here by multiplying the national average earnings of wage and salary workers in a given occupation (industry) by the proportion of the labor force in the state employed in that occupation (industry) and summing over-all occupations (industries).[18] If inter-state differences in labor incomes are due solely to differences in structure, and workers in a given occupation receive the same wage in every state, rate-constant earnings would duplicate exactly the inter-state distribution of actual or reported earnings, apart from certain technical problems of calculating rate-constant earnings.[19]

---

[17] Frank Hanna, *State Income Differentials, 1919-1954* (Durham, N. C.: Duke University Press, 1959), chapters 5 and 6.

[18] Both the average earnings of wage and salary workers for the nation and the occupational and industrial distributions of the labor force in the various states were obtained from special tabulations of 1950 census data. For the occupational distribution, over 400 classes for both males and females-were used, while the industrial distribution was made up of about 140 classes.

[19] These calculations refer only to earnings of wage and salary workers but might include income other than wage and salary income. Self-employed workers were omitted in the calculations of earnings, and their earnings consist in part of labor income. The omission is particularly important in the case of agriculture, in which most labor income accrues to self-employed farmers rather than to recipients of wages and salaries. To the extent that

The data reveal a strong tendency for states with above-average reported earnings to have above-average rate-constant earnings as well. In all but seven states, both reported and rate-constant earnings deviate from their national averages in the same direction.[20] But there is also at least as strong a tendency for states with above (below) average rate-constant earnings, or a "favorable" ("unfavorable") industrial structure, to have reported earnings which exceed (fall below) rate-constant earnings. This tendency holds in all but two states for occupational rate-constant earnings and in all but three states for industrial rate-constant earnings. The difference between reported and rate-constant earnings, when adjusted for the difference in the national averages of these two series, is the sum of wage differentials by industry (occupation), as between the state and the national average, weighted by the proportion of workers employed in the corresponding industry (occupation).[21] Thus, in the Far West, earnings per worker averaged $267 above the national average wage in comparable occupations; in the Southeast, $437 below. Dividing by state rate-constant occupational earnings, earnings averaged about 11% above the national average in the Far West and about 19% below it in the Southeast. (See Figure 93).

Hanna's data suggest that reported earnings and rate-constant occupational and industrial earnings tend to be above average in the Middle Atlantic, Great Lakes, and Far Western states (except as noted earlier) and below average in the Southeast, Southwest, and the Plains states. Likewise, in the Middle Atlantic, Great Lakes, and particularly the Far Western states, reported earnings exceed rate-constant earnings; this means that, on the average, earnings exceed the national average in each occupation and/or industry in these states. Reported earnings are less than rate-constant earnings principally in the Southeast, but also in the Southwest and Plains states. In these states, therefore, earnings on the average tend to be below the national average in all occupations and/or industries. Examination of the state data reveals that in eight of the eleven Southeast states (all except Virginia, West Virginia, and Florida), earnings in

---

the money prices of consumer goods are lower on the farm, the money incomes of wage and salary recipients are not really comparable in terms of real income. But the computation of rate-constant earnings accounts for this difference, at least in part.

[20]The principal exception to this tendency is found in the Far West. All four of the states in this region have above average reported earnings, but two have below average rate-constant occupational earnings and all four have below average rate-constant industrial earnings.

[21]In symbols, let:

P_{ij} equal proportion of labor force in the i-th industry in the j-th state,

w_{ij} equal average earnings of workers in the i-th industry and the j-th state,

w_i equal average earnings of workers in the i-th industry in the nation.

Then:

reported earnings in the j-th state equal $\Sigma_i \ p_{ij} w_{ij}$, rate-constant industry earnings in the j-th state equal $\Sigma_i \ p_{ij} w_i$, and reported minus rate constant earnings in the j-th state equal $\Sigma_i \ p_{ij} \ (w_{ij} - w_i)$.

Thus, reported minus rate constant earnings for a particular state is the average of $(w_{ij} - w_i)$, the difference between earnings in the i-th industry for the state and for the nation, weighted by the proportions of the labor force in the various industries in that state.

Table 181. Reported earnings and Hanna's "rate-constant"[a] occupational and industrial earnings, all wage and salary workers, by region, selected states, 1949

Region and state[b]	Reported earnings	Rate-constant occupational earnings	Difference[c]	Rate-constant industrial earnings	Difference[d]
New England	$2,337	$2,469	−171	$2,450	−165
Vermont	1,997	2,363	−405	2,353	−408
Connecticut	2,795	2,636	120	2,608	135
Middle Atlantic	2,783	2,576	167	2,556	175
Pennsylvania	2,630	2,542	49	2,569	9
New Jersey	2,959	2,646	274	2,603	304
Great Lakes	2,789	2,616	134	2,617	120
Wisconsin	2,586	2,562	275	2,529	226
Michigan	2,974	2,660	−437	2,696	−464
Southeast	1,904	2,302	15	2,316	5
Mississippi	1,408	2,180	−811	2,183	−827
West Virginia	2,412	2,490	−117	2,508	−148
Plains	2,268	2,484	−255	2,454	−239
North Dakota	2,007	2,400	−432	2,355	−400
Minnesota	2,472	2,546	−113	2,502	−82
Southwest	2,278	2,432	−193	2,443	−217
Louisiana	2,114	2,383	−308	2,411	−349
Arizona	2,397	2,382	−24	2,363	−18
Mountain	2,468	2,492	63	2,470	−54
Idaho	2,300	2,397	−136	2,364	−116
Utah	2,610	2,594	−23	2,579	−21
Far West	2,788	2,482	267	2,430	306
Oregon	2,668	2,430	199	2,354	262
California	2,870	2,551	280	2,497	321
United States average[e]	$2,556	$2,517	—	$2,504	—
Relative variation	16.0%	5.1%	—	4.8%	—
H[t]	—	—	35.8***	—	36.3***

A computation of what average state earnings would have been had the earnings per worker in each state been equal to the average in each occupation or industry; this gives a money value of the occupational or industrial earnings less the U. S. average.

b Data for regions are simple averages of the data for the states in the region.

c State reported earnings less U. S. average minus state rate-constant occupational earnings less the U. S. average; note that the U. S. average figures differ for the two.

d State reported earnings less U. S. average minus state rate-constant industrial earnings less the U. S. average; again note that the U. S. average figures differ.

e The national figure or weighted state average.

f For purposes of this test the eight regional grouping was used.

***Significantly different from zero at the 0.001 level.

SOURCE: Computed from data in Hanna, *State Income Differentials, 1919-1954*, cited above, chapters 5 and 6. The reader is referred to this work for the details of the computations.

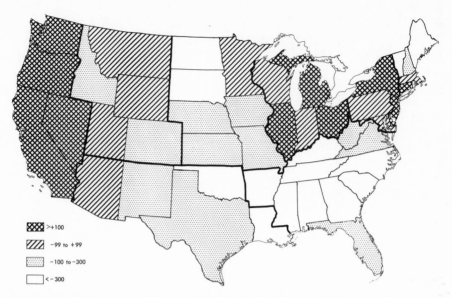

Figure 93. Reported Earnings Minus Industry Rate-Constant Earnings, 1949.

all occupations averaged at least $400 below the national average. In Mississippi they averaged $811, or 37% below. In New York, New Jersey, Michigan, Illinois, and the Far West states they were $200 or more above the national average in all occupations ($380 above in Nevada). As Table 181 indicates, the relative variation of rate-constant earnings is only about one-third of the relative variation of reported earnings.

Thus, part of the variation in the earnings of wage and salary workers is due to variations in the occupational and industrial structure; states with greater than average reported earnings tend to have employment concentrated in the higher paying occupations and industries. But this is only a part of the explanation of differentials, for in states with greater than average reported earnings, reported earnings exceed rate-constant earnings—that is, earnings tend to be greater than average in all occupations or industries.[22] To the extent that differences in labor skills and other factors influencing the equilibrium money earnings of workers are associated with differences in the occupational and/or industrial structure, these factors account for only a part of the differ-

[22]Because of the correlation of high-paying occupational/industrial structure and higher wages in all occupations, it is impossible to assign a fraction of the variation in earnings to either factor alone. The magnitude of the variance in earnings explained by the independent effects of structure alone can be judged by the square of the ratio of relative variation of rate-constant to reported earnings. Both for occupation and industry this is about ten per cent. See Frank A. Hanna, "Analysis of Interstate Income Differentials: Theory and Practice," *Regional Income, (Studies in Income and Wealth,* Vol. 21, *op. cit.),* pp. 150-51, the comment by George H. Borts, pp. 186-89, and Hanna's reply, pp. 191-93.

ences in money labor income between states. It should also be noted that, to the extent that employment in any occupation or industry tends to be regionally concentrated, and to the extent that there is a regional effect on the level of wages in all occupations or industries, the computed rate-constant earnings tend to reflect regional wage differences in part and to overestimate the effect due to occupation or industry. Wages in the cotton-textile industry are below the national average partly because the majority of textile workers are employed in the Southeast, where wages in all occupations tend to be below the national average. And, because the data in Table 181 refer to wage and salary workers only, and thus exclude a large proportion of agricultural workers, the comparison of rate-constant earnings with reported earnings probably tends to understate inter-state differentials in labor income (since inter-state differentials in income are greater for agricultural than for non-agricultural workers).

Thus, it seems clear that inter-state differences in labor incomes cannot be explained solely by the hypothesis that all workers in a given occupation or industry earn the same wage everywhere but that the distribution of employment differs among states. However, it might be argued that differences in the industrial structure as among states cause wage differences in the sense that the presence of "high-wage" industries in a given state forces wages up in all industries. Alternatively, an industry might be a "high-wage" industry nationally at least partly because employment in the industry is concentrated in areas where wages in all industries are above the national average. This could result either from coincidence or from the operation of other forces that also produce relatively high wages in these areas. In such a case, the "favorable" industrial structure would be a symptom rather than a cause of the above-average wages. The really relevant question, however, is why the demand for labor of all kinds is higher relative to its supply in certain areas than in others. We shall postpone consideration of this question until later.

Studies other than Hanna's suggest that there are wage differentials between workers in the same industry or occupation in different states. One of the best of these is the Bureau of Labor Statistics study of regional wage differentials in various industries in 1945 and 1946.[23] This study, which paid particular attention to industries which are important in the South, showed that substantial wage differentials in the same industry existed. Wages were highest in the Pacific region (our Far West) in twenty-six out of twenty-nine industries for which data were available for this region; in only one of these twenty-nine industries were wages here below the national average. Wages were lowest in the Southeast (our Southeast without West Virginia and Arkansas) in twenty-three out of thirty-six industries which were compared for this region; wages here were above the national average in only one of these industries. The magni-

[23]Bureau of Labor Statistics, U.S. Department of Labor, "Regional Wage Differentials," *Monthly Labor Review*, Vol. 63 (October 1946), pp. 511-25. The data presented are straight-time average hourly earnings, the closest available measure of wages.

The industries included in the study were primarily manufacturing industries, although data for three kinds of retail stores, electric light and power companies, power laundries, and telephone companies were included as well. Data were presented only for eight regions, which do not coincide exactly with the regional grouping of states we have employed.

tude of the wage differentials varied from industry to industry. But wages in the Southeast tended to be from 10% to 30% below the national average in the majority of industries, while in the Pacific region they tended to be clustered between 20% and 30% above the national average. These results are consistent with the inferences drawn from Hanna's data on reported and rate-constant earnings in 1949.

Further evidence on the relation of income to region, city size, occupation, as well as age and color can be derived from data Miller presents on the median incomes in 1949 of white urban men 25 to 44 years old, by size of place and region, and data for seven major non-farm occupational groups classified in the same way. Miller suggests that income differences by size of place can be largely attributed to occupation, although occupation apparently does not account for regional differences in income.[24] However, if the occupational distributions he gives are weighted by the data on median earnings in 1951 of employed men by occupation and age,[25] the occupational differentials of white urban men 25 to 44 do not explain either the city size differential or the regional differentials observed in the income data he presents. In the South, the median incomes of this group of males averaged about 18% greater in urbanized areas of one-quarter million to one million population than in urban places (not in urbanized areas) of less than ten thousand population; in the Northeast, the differential in incomes was about 6% between these two size places; in the North Central region, about 12%; and in the West, 3%. Allowing for differences in occupational structure only, these income differentials would have been only about 2% in the South, 1% in the Northeast, 1% in the North Central states, and about 2% in the West.[26]

Likewise, allowing for differences in occupational structure only, incomes of this group in the South would have been a little more than 2% above those in the Northeast in urbanized areas of one-quarter million or more, and 1% and 2% above in the North Central states and in the West, respectively. But observed incomes for this group were 4% above those of the Northeast in the South, 11% above in the North Central states, and 12% above in the West.

This comparison suggests that not only are incomes in the same occupation greater than average in states with above average incomes, but that incomes in the same occupation tend to be greater in larger than in smaller cities.

In summary, the data Hanna presents suggest that in states where labor income per worker is above the national average, workers tend to be concentrated in those occupations and industries in which earnings per worker for the

[24]Miller, *op. cit.*, pp. 44-45. The regions he uses are the four census regions: Northeast, North Central, South, and West.

[25]*Ibid.*, p. 54. For this purpose we used the average of the median earnings by occupation for men in the 25 to 34 and the 35 to 44 age groups.

[26]Both Otis Dudley Duncan and Albert J. Reiss, Jr., *Social Characteristics of Urban and Rural Communities, 1950,* A Volume in the Census Monograph Series (New York: John Wiley & Sons, Inc., 1956) p. 103-6, and Johnson in his comment on Mansfield's study, *op. cit.,* pp. 310-11, examine data for the whole nation and conclude that the income differential by size of place can be explained only in part by differences in occupational structure.

nation as a whole are above average. But this concentration of employment in high-paying occupations and industries accounts only in part for above-average earnings, since in states where earnings per worker are above the national average, they tend to be higher than the national average in *all* occupations and industries. This latter tendency is verified by the data contained in the B.L.S. study of wages in 1945 and 1946. This study showed that if the effect of industry is held constant, wages average 10% to 30% below the national average in the Southeast and 20% to 30% above the national average in the Far West. Miller's data suggest that, when occupation, age, and color are held constant, incomes of workers tend to be greater in the North Central and Western regions than in the South in cities of comparable size and that in all regions they tend to be higher in larger cities.

These observed income differentials might be explained by one or both of two factors—differences in skill of workers in a given occupation or industry in different areas or differences in productivity of workers of identical skill. We shall now examine the first of these two possibilities.

Differences in Skill

Differences in the occupational and/or industrial composition of the labor force in the various states, we have seen, cannot account completely for the labor income differentials that exist among these various states. Is there a possibility, then, that differences in the degrees of skill possessed by comparable types of workers (e.g., unskilled, semi-skilled, etc.) in the *same* occupation or industry in different states are a contributing factor? The fact that wages in the same occupation or industry are lower in one state as compared with another might imply such differences in skill or they might, instead, imply differences in the productivity of workers of identical skill due to differences in factor proportions. Few studies are available that help to determine which implication is correct, and market data alone are of little use in this regard.

A study by D. Gale Johnson, however, touching upon this question, suggests that there are no essential differences in skill as between farm and non-farm populations and none as between the farm populations in different areas.[27] There is also a study by Robert J. Wolfson that seeks to determine the extent to which interregional differences in agricultural wage rates can be explained by "equalizing differences."[28] Wolfson computed averages of regional wage rate indices for the period 1910-42 for five census regions and adjusted these for differences in prices, race, sex, age, and education. Three of these factors—sex, age, and

[27]"Comparability of Labor Capacities of Farm and Nonfarm Labor," *American Economic Review*, Vol. 43 (June 1953), pp. 296-313. Johnson found the earnings of recent migrants from farm areas to be about 90% as great at the median earnings of non-farm workers. The differences might be attributable to short-run differences in adjustment and to differences in education. He found also that, if only whites were included, there were no important differences in earnings to be attributed to the region of origin or the occupational experience of migrants.

[28] *Op. cit.* pp. 232-33.

education—represent differences in skills of the agricultural labor force; the first—prices—represents differences in money wages due to differences in consumer prices. In view of our previous comments on color as a factor influencing income received, it is not clear what interpretation should be placed on his correction for racial composition of the farm labor force. To the extent that income differentials between white and non-white workers are the result of racial discrimination, differences in average wage rate arising from differences in race would be equalizing. Therefore, in Table 182 we present Wolfson's wage indices both uncorrected and corrected for race. Other data Wolfson

Table 182. Regional farm wage rate indices, average, 1910-1942, and corrections for equalizing differences[a]

		Corrected	
Region[b]	Uncorrected	Excluding race	Including race
East North Central	0.837	0.854	0.854
West North Central	1.000	1.000	1.000
South Altantic	0.544	0.630	0.730
East South Central	0.505	0.572	0.625
West South Central	0.612	0.692	0.740

[a] Interregional differences in price, age composition, sex composition, educational attainment, and race composition of farm labor force.

[b] As defined by the census.

SOURCE: Robert J. Wolfson, *op. cit.* The correction factors are based in part on Zeman's unpublished work, *op. cit.*

provides, which are not presented here, indicate that the corrections for price differences and sex are small. The effect of standardizing for these two factors plus age and education raises wages from 54% to 63% of the West North Central regional average in the South Atlantic region, from about 50% to 57% in the East South Central region, and from about 61% to 69% in the West South Central region. This suggests that age, sex composition, and educational attainment account for a relatively small part of the differences in real farm wages among regions. Even if race is considered as an equalizing difference, substantial interregional variation in agricultural wages remains.

The productivity of labor in three occupations in selected Northern and Southern plants of two corporations in the cotton textile industry has been compared in a study by Jesse W. Markham.[29] For both companies, the plants in the North and the South were roughly the same as to product, machinery, supervisory practices, and labor-recruiting policies. The study showed no essential difference in the productivity of labor as between plants in the two areas. This

[29]"Regional Labor Productivity in the Textile Industry," *American Economic Review*, Vol. 33 (March 1943), pp. 110-15.

result is consistent with the hypothesis that labor in the same industry in different areas is of equivalent skill.[30]

To the extent that differences in skill are reflected in educational attainment, Miller's data also throw some light on the nature of skill differences.[31] His study of median incomes in 1949 of men in the 35 to 44 year age group by year of school completed indicates that, for both whites and non-whites, incomes are lower in the South than in the North and West for all levels of educational attainment, except for whites who have completed four or more years of college.

Thus, although the data on skill differences between workers in the same occupation or industry in different areas are very scanty, such data as exist seem to contradict the hypothesis that these differences in skill contribute significantly to the observed income differentials. While such factors as sex, age, and educational attainment may explain part of the interregional differences of incomes of workers in a given industry, it would appear that genuine differentials in real incomes of workers of equal skill exist among regions.

[30]However, Markham notes that the same wages were paid to workers in the two areas. The study thus admits of an alternative interpretation—that labor in the Southern plants surveyed was of greater than average skill for the South. But if workers of equivalent skill in the cotton textile industry received the same wages in the South as in the North, there would seem to be no explanation for the movement of the industry to the South beginning around 1920.

[31]*Op. cit.*, p. 46.

31 / Differences in labor incomes in the same industry:

(1) AGRICULTURE

The extent to which the various factors that we have so far considered "explain" the observed differentials in labor income may be summed up as follows: (1) While there is evidence of a difference in the level of consumer prices between the farm and the city, there is no evidence of significant price differentials among cities in different regions that would account for the interregional differentials in labor income. (2) Although states where the earnings of workers exceed the national average tend to have employment concentrated in the higher-paying occupations and industries, this factor does not completely account for the observed differentials in earnings. (3) As there is a significant interstate variation in earnings of workers even within the same industry, the labor income differentials observed cannot be attributed to differences in the skills of the labor forces in the various states.

In this and the following chapter we shall examine differentials among states in the labor incomes of workers in the same industry. Our purpose here is to determine whether these differentials are related to differences in the marginal productivity of labor arising from differences in the proportions with which labor is combined with capital in production. We shall begin with the differences observed among states in the labor returns to agriculture.

Differentials in Agriculture: Cross-Sectional

In our analysis of median incomes earlier in this study, we found the incomes of white rural-farm persons to vary substantially more from state to state than those of white urban and rural non-farm persons. The principal variation, however, was between the South and the rest of the nation. The averages for white rural-farm persons in the New England, Middle Atlantic, Great Lakes, Mountain, and Far Western states differed by only a few dollars. But the average for the Southeast was 42% below that of the non-South, and the average of the Southwest 23% below. We also found the real incomes of white rural-farm persons in the Southeast to be only about 60% as great as those of white urban and rural non-farm persons in this region. These data refer to the total money income received, including non-labor income and labor income from occupations other than farming as well as agricultural labor income. But they suggest that differentials in the earnings of workers in agriculture are a significant source of interstate variations in per capita income and that the states with the lowest labor return to agriculture are to be found primarily in the Southeast.

We shall advance the hypothesis that differences among states in the returns to labor in agriculture are due to differences in the marginal productivity of labor which reflect differences in the amount of capital per worker used in production. So long as agricultural labor markets are competitive, the return to labor is equal to the money value of the marginal product of labor in production. The marginal product of labor depends, in turn, upon the relative scarcity of labor as a factor in production. By capital, we mean all non-human agents of production, including land as well as reproducible non-human capital.

In testing this hypothesis, we have adopted the value of output per worker employed in agriculture as a measure of the labor income of workers in different states.[1] If the production function which governs production possibilities in agriculture is linear in the logarithms of the various inputs and outputs,[2] the output per unit of labor would be proportional to the marginal product of labor, or the logarithm of output per worker would equal the logarithm of the marginal product of labor except for an additive constant.[3]

[1]Several problems arise in attempting to measure labor income and capital in agriculture. The income of persons classified as rural-farm by the census includes not only their agricultural labor income, but their non-agricultural earnings and non-labor income as well. Hence, for states where off-farm employment and ownership of property are a significant source of income to rural-farm persons, the census income data might be poor measures of agricultural labor income. One alternative would be to use some series on agricultural wage rates as a measure of labor income in agriculture. The basic difficulty with this approach is that most agricultural labor is performed by self-employed farm operators and unpaid family workers, and no market measures of the labor return to this class of workers is available. Most of the published agricultural wage data are not comparable from state to state because part of the payment to hired labor consists of perquisites, which need not be comparable between states. A comparison of agricultural wage statistics might also be misleading if the duration of employment is not specified. The marginal product per week of a worker employed for one or two weeks at harvest time might differ from the marginal product per week of a worker employed on a yearly basis. It is because of such considerations that we have adopted the alternative measure of labor income described here.

[2]The comparison of output per worker and value of land and buildings per worker described below suggests that the relation between these two variables is roughly linear in the logarithms of these two variables. If this relation were exactly linear in the logarithms, the production function for agriculture would be linear in output and the various inputs if the logarithms of these variables are used.

[3]It is possible that production functions for different types of agriculture might differ and that for some purposes this difference should be taken into account. For our purpose, if production functions for agriculture differed among regions because of differences in the major types of farming, we would expect to find differences among regions in the relation of output per worker to value of land and buildings per worker. (See the Appendix to the

To measure output per worker in agriculture, measures of farm output and agricultural employment by states are needed. The 1950 agricultural census contains data on the total value of farm products sold by states. However, for 1949, these data represented the total sales of the farm, regardless of who shared in the receipts, and included the value of government payments for specific crops.[4] As the value of consumption on the farm is a significant part of total agricultural output, particularly for the Southeastern states, we have estimated the total value of agricultural output for 1949 by multiplying the reported value of farm products sold by the following ratio: value of farm products sold plus value of consumption on the farm *to* value of farm products sold, both for 1944, as reported in the 1945 agricultural census.[5]

Two published sources of data by which to measure employment in agriculture by states are available for 1950—the 1950 population and agricultural censuses. According to the population census, agricultural employment in 1950 was about six and three tenths million, while the agricultural census gives a figure of about eight and one-half million. The discrepancy between the two totals is partly due to differences in methods of enumeration and partly to differences in the definition of employment. In the population census only persons fourteen years old and over were counted, and workers were classified by industry according to the job in which the greatest number of hours were worked in the week preceding the enumeration. In the agricultural census, no age limit was specified, and workers were counted as agricultural workers if they worked a specified minimum number of hours on the farm, regardless of time worked in other pursuits.[6] Thus, it seems likely that the population census data underestimate agricultural employment at the time of the enumeration by excluding children under fourteen and some part-time agricultural workers. On the other hand, the agricultural census data might overestimate agricultural employment by including workers who worked the greater part of their time in non-agricul-

following chapter.) But, as we show below, such differences as exist can be attributed to sampling variation.

[4] For further discussion of these data, see U. S. Department of Commerce, Bureau of the Census, *1950 Census of Agriculture*, Vol. II (Washington: U. S. Government Printing Office, 1952), Chapter IX, pp. 745-46.

[5] Before turning to the discussion of the measure of employment used, one particular shortcoming of output per worker as a measure of the return to labor should be noted. Since there is reason to believe that the forces leading to differentials in agricultural labor income among states have persisted for several decades at least, we would like our measure of labor income to reflect secular differences in labor incomes among states. However, the value of output of agriculture in any state, or for the whole nation, in any particular year reflects variability due to forces operating over relatively short periods of time. Because output per worker probably fluctuates more from year to year than does the value of land and buildings, which we use as a measure of capital inputs, we shall estimate the relation of output per worker to value of land and buildings per worker from the regression with output per worker as the "dependent" variable—dependent in the statistical sense of dependence upon random fluctuations. Economic analysis would specify simply that, apart from short-run fluctuations, output per worker and value of land and buildings per worker would be related.

[6] For a more complete discussion of the two sources of agricultural employment data, see *ibid.*, Chap. IV, pp. 237-40.

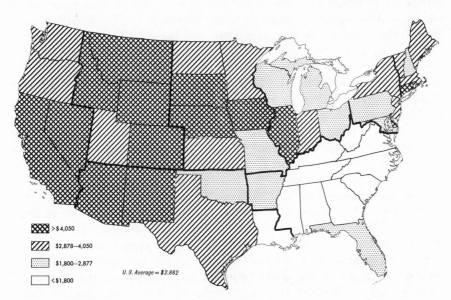

>$4,050

$2,878—4,050

$1,800—2,877

<$1,800

U. S. Average = $2,882

Figure 94. Output per Worker in Agriculture, 1950.
Source: Appendix Table N.

tural pursuits. Since agricultural employment varies from month to month, either set of data might differ from the yearly average. For our purposes, these shortcomings are not important, however, unless they have a systematic effect on the data for groups of states. We have chosen the data from the agricultural census to estimate agricultural employment.[7]

Table 183 shows the average value of output per worker for the eight regions and selected states, using the data described in the above paragraphs. (Also see Figure 94). The table contains a few suspicious-looking entries: Delaware, for example, with an output per worker of over $6,000, ranked second among the forty-eight states; and even more doubtful is the average for the Southwest.[8] Otherwise, the estimates here show much the same pattern of inter-state variation as do the census data on the median incomes of persons with income (including both whites and non-whites) for rural-farm persons. The rank

[7] The second of the comparisons described below suggests that roughly the same results would be obtained here by using either of the two measures of employment.

[8] The estimate of output per worker averaged for the Southwestern states is only slightly below the average for the Plains states, while the median income of white rural farm persons with income in the Southwest (Table 162) was about twenty-three per cent below that in the Plains states. Easterlin's estimates of participation income per worker in agriculture for 1950 (see Table 183 below) indicate, however, that this income measure was almost the same in these two regions. Similar estimates of output per worker for 1940 and 1954 indicate that output per worker was thirty-nine per cent below that in the Plains states in the Southwest in 1940, and twenty-nine per cent below in 1954. Therefore, the average of the estimates of the Southwestern states for 1950 may overestimate the secular level of the return to labor in agriculture in these states, relative to other states.

correlation coefficient rho between the two series is +0.72, with deviations in relative ranking occurring primarily in the Southwest (in Texas, Arizona, and New Mexico), and also in Delaware, Ohio, and Indiana. The relative variation of output per worker was over 40% for 1950, and the principal source of variation was between the Southeast and other parts of the country. In only one of the states in the Southeast, Florida, did output per worker in 1950 exceed $2,000 per year, while at the same time it exceeded this figure in every state outside the South.

To compare output per worker with capital per worker, it is necessary to have estimates of the value of agricultural capital as well, and so far as we know there are no published estimates of the total value of agricultural capital by states for the period around 1950. However, the agricultural census contains data on the value of land and buildings by states for 1950.[9] Tostlebe's estimates for the whole nation put the value of land and buildings at about three-quarters of the total value of physical capital, which also includes machinery and crop and livestock inventories.[10] As a check, we plotted output per worker against the value of land and buildings per worker and against the value of physical assets per worker, using Tostlebe's data for 1950 for the ten types of farming regions for which he presents estimates of the last. The two scatter diagrams were virtually identical. Likewise, using data for these same ten regions, we prepared separate scatter diagrams for comparing output per worker with the value of land and buildings per worker, using in turn the population and agricultural census tabulations of agricultural workers as the deflator. These two scatter diagrams were also practically identical. Therefore, we shall use the value of land and buildings divided by the agricultural census employment data to measure the value of capital per worker in agriculture.

We now turn to the comparison of output per worker with value of land and buildings per worker by states. In making this comparison, we wish to arrive at answers to two questions. First, is output per worker significantly related to the value of land and buildings per worker in different states? And, second, when the variation in the value of land and buildings per worker has been taken into account, does any variation remain in the value of output per worker among regions? The first of these questions can be answered by taking the regression of the value of output per worker in agriculture on the value of land and buildings per worker. But such a procedure is of no help in itself in answering the second question. In fact, if there were no relation between these two variables within regions, but the average values of the two varied together among regions, we might find a significant relation between them. Thus, as a check, we shall use the analysis of covariance. We shall assume that the true values of the residual variance and the slope of the relation between output per worker and land and buildings per worker are the same in all regions.[11] We then ask

[9] *Ibid.*, Chap. I, Table 10, pp. 30-31.

[10] Alvin S. Tostlebe, *The Growth of Physical Capital in Agriculture, 1870-1950* (New York: National Bureau of Economic Research, 1954).

[11] Inspection of the scatter diagram on which output per worker and value of land and buildings per worker were plotted reveals no apparent difference in slope or variation about the regression line as among regions.

Table 183. Output per worker in agriculture, by region, selected states, 1950

Region and state[a]	Output per worker
New England	$3,652
New Hampshire	2,778
Connecticut	4,604
Middle Atlantic	3,832
Pennsylvania	2,530
Delaware	6,462
Great Lakes	3,222
Ohio	2,700
Illinois	4,830
Southeast	1,568
South Carolina	1,089
Florida	2,750
Plains	3,935
Missouri	2,443
Iowa	5,198
Southwest	3,851
Louisiana	1,583
Arizona	7,417
Mountain	4,658
Utah	3,443
Colorado	5,320
Far West	4,412
Oregon	3,471
California	5,573
United States	2,878
Relative variation[b]	42.9%
H[c]	25.6***

[a] Regional averages are simple averages of the data for states in the region.

[b] Standard deviation of the observations for the various states divided by their mean value.

[c] For this test the New England and Middle Atlantic states were combined into the Northeast, the Lakes and Plains into the North Central, and the Mountains and Far West into the West. This was done for comparability with the covariance analysis discussed below.

***Significantly different from zero at the 0.001 level.

whether the regional means of output per worker differ significantly when adjusted for the effect of differences in the value of land and buildings per worker (as estimated from the covariation within regions of output per worker and value of land and buildings per worker). For this purpose we have combined the eight regions into five as follows: the New England and Middle Atlantic states; the Great Lakes and Plains states; the Mountain and Far West states; the Southeast; and the Southwest. This was done because it was felt that these five regions provided sufficient "control" and that the use of more regional means for control would have severely limited the within-region variation of value of land and buildings per worker, upon which the quality of the estimate of the regression depends in part. In fact, over two-thirds of the inter-state variation in the value of land and buildings per worker is associated with variations in the means of this variable between these five regions.[12]

The analysis of covariance is summarized in the measures presented in Table

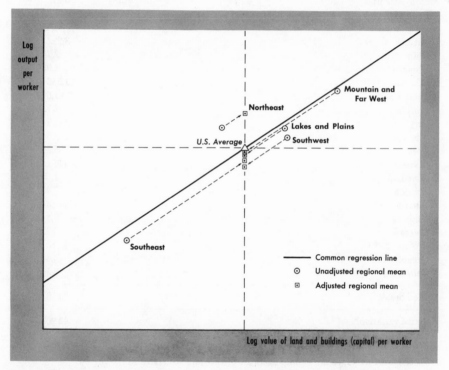

Figure 95. Illustration of Covariance Analysis: Output per Worker Adjusted for Capital per Worker.
Source: Appendix Table N.

184 and illustrated graphically in Figure 95. In this analysis we compared the logarithms of output per worker with the logarithms of value of land and buildings per worker. The regression of the former on the latter was estimated from the covariation of output per worker and value of land and buildings per worker within the five regions. (The common regression line is the solid line in Figure

[12]We note that, to the extent that there are differences in skills of the farm labor force in different places which might account for a part of the differences in agricultural labor income among regions, these differences are reflected in the analysis described here. That is, differences in skills might be one factor leading to differences both in output per worker and value of land and buildings per worker.

95.) The regression of output per worker on value of land and buildings per worker is significantly greater than zero at the 0.05 level. Before the adjustment for differences in the value of land and buildings per worker, output per worker in agriculture varied significantly among regions, as Table 183 and the circled crosses in Figure 95 indicate. But, once the regional means of output per worker are so adjusted,[13] the remaining variation as between the five regions is not sta-

Table 184. Summary of the relation of output per worker and the value of land and buildings per worker, by states, 1950

Residual degrees of freedom	Regional effect[a] F	Regression[b] t
42	1.90	10.2

[a] With 4 degrees of freedom in the numerator; not significant at the 0.05 level of significance.
[b] Significantly greater than zero at the 0.05 level of significance.

tistically significant at the 0.05 level. In fact, an equally great or greater difference would occur in about one out of every six samples if there were no true difference.[14]

Furthermore, it would seem that relatively less capital per worker is used in all types of farming in states where output per worker is relatively low. In Table 185, output per worker (for all agriculture) is compared with the value of land and buildings per worker for eight types of farming on which the 1950 agricultural census presents data.[15] For all of these types of farms, value of land and buildings per worker was significantly correlated with agricultural output per worker.

The results of our analysis imply that interstate variations in the labor incomes of agricultural workers are significantly associated with variations in marginal labor productivity reflecting variations in capital per worker used in agricultural production. They also imply that regional variations in output per

[13]By moving the regional averages parallel to the common regression line to the national average capital per worker, as shown by the squared crosses in Figure 95.

[14]After this analysis was performed, a report on a much more detailed and sophisticated analysis by Robert J. Wolfson, "An Econometric Investigation of Regional Differentials in American Agricultural Wages," *Econometrica*, Vol. 26 (April 1958), appeared. Wolfson related agricultural wage rates to marginal labor productivity and concluded that "It seems quite clear that for the year 1939 there was a strong interregional relationship between agricultural wage rates and the marginal value productivity of labor," which was related to differences with which labor is combined with other factors of production. *Op. cit.*, p. 255.

[15]Value of land and buildings per worker was computed from data in the *1950 Census of Agriculture, op. cit.*, Vol. I, *Counties and State Economic Areas*, Economic Area Table 7. For a given type of farming only those states for which one thousand or more workers were reported were included in the comparisons.

Table 185. Comparison of value of land and buildings per worker, by type of farm, with agricultural output per worker, by states, 1950

Type of farm	Number of states included	Rank correlation coefficient, rho[a]
All	48	+0.88
Cash grain	37	+0.77
Cotton	15	+0.74
Other field crops	34	+0.80
Vegetables	23	+0.71
Fruit & nut	20	+0.57
Dairy	47	+0.75
Poultry	40	+0.76
Livestock	40	+0.87

[a] All significantly greater than zero at the 0.01 level.

worker are due to variations in capital per worker. Not all the variation in output per worker in 1950 can be explained by variation in the value of land and buildings per worker—the correlation between the two variables is not perfect. But such variation as remains once the value of land and buildings per worker is taken into account could quite conceivably be due to chance (short-term as opposed to secular) variation.

Urbanization and Agricultural Incomes

We have shown that agricultural labor income as measured by output per worker is significantly associated with the value of land and buildings per worker, a measure of capital per worker, and that this latter variable largely "explains" the regional variation in output per worker. In this section we shall seek to determine whether state data reveal any influence of urbanization upon agricultural incomes and through what channels such an influence operates.

Urbanization could affect agriculture in many ways. In our inquiry here we shall be concerned only with its influence upon the working of factor markets. One aspect of the working of factor markets—value of capital per worker in agriculture—has already been related to agricultural labor incomes. If capital per worker is greater near urban centers, we would find a positive association between urbanization and agricultural labor incomes. Agricultural labor incomes might also be affected by other variables associated with urbanization. We shall examine three such variables related to the operation of factor markets— manufacturing earnings, off-farm employment, and the change over time in agricultural employment—and seek to determine whether these variables are associated with urbanization. Finally, we shall ask whether these variables exert any influence upon the median incomes of rural-farm persons, which include property income and non-agricultural labor income as well as agricultural labor income, apart from the influence upon agricultural labor income.[16]

In our comparisons we shall confine our attention to the rank correlation coefficient rho. These correlation coefficients have been computed for the nation as a whole and separately for the sixteen states in the Southeast and Southwest and the thirty-two other states, to determine whether the relation between these variables differed regionally. In particular, the influence of urbanization might be expected to be different in the South, where the differences between the real income of rural-farm persons and other persons are substantially greater than in other parts of the country.

In Table 186 output per worker in agriculture, which measures agricultural labor income, is compared with several variables related to the operation of factor markets. It is seen to be significantly associated with the value of land and buildings per worker, both for the nation as a whole and for the South and the North and West separately. Output per worker tends to vary significantly with urbanization in the sixteen Southern states, but not in the thirty-two Northern and Western states. The relation between ouput per worker and urbanization in the case of the South would appear to be due to the fact that value of land and buildings per worker varies significantly with urbanization. There is a positive relationship between output per worker in agriculture and manufacturing earnings for all forty-eight states which appears to be due to the direct association between value of land and buildings per worker and average hourly earnings in manufacturing. Manufacturing earnings and off-farm employment are positively associated, though not significantly so, with output per worker in the South. It would appear that these associations can be explained statistically by the intercorrelation of these variables with the value of land and buildings per worker. Off-farm employment, however, is significantly associated with urbanization and manufacturing earnings. Finally, for the whole nation and for the South, agricultural employment tended to decrease least over the period 1939–1954 in the states where output per worker in agriculture was highest in 1950, but the change in agricultural employment was not significantly associated with urbanization.

[16]In making our comparisons we shall use the same measures of output per worker and value of land and buildings per worker used in the previous section of this chapter. The only aspect of urbanization considered here is the percentage of the population of a state classified as urban (new definition) as computed from data in the 1950 population census. Manufacturing earnings, a measure of labor income in other than agricultural employments, have been computed from average hourly earnings data for 1950 in U.S. Department of Labor, Bureau of Labor Statistics, *Employment and Earnings*, Vol. II (June 1956), Table SC-2, pp. 122-32. Data for four states were not available for 1950. These were estimated by interpolating their trend relative to the national average for the period 1947-55.

Off-farm employment has been measured by data from the 1950 agricultural census on the percentage of farm operators working 100 or more days off the farm. To measure change in farm employment, the ratio of family and hired workers 1954 to 1939 was computed from the 1954 agricultural census. Income was measured by the 1950 population census data on the median income of rural-farm persons. And, finally, as a measure of ownership of capital, we have used the percentage of farm operators who are owners, as computed from the 1950 agricultural census.

Table 186. Agricultural labor incomes

Variables analyzed:
X_1 = Output per worker, agriculture, 1949
X_2 = Value of land and buildings per worker, 1950
X_3 = Per cent of population, urban, 1950 (new definition)
X_4 = Average hourly earnings, manufacturing, 1950
X_5 = Per cent of farm operators working 100 or more days off the farm, 1949
X_6 = Ratio agricultural workers, 1954/1939

Rank Correlation Coefficients

48 States

	X_2	X_3	X_4	X_5	X_6
X_1	+0.88***	+0.32*	+0.53***	−0.08	+0.45**
X_2		+0.32*	+0.66***		
X_3					−0.02

16 Southern states

	X_2	X_3	X_4	X_5	X_6
X_1	+0.92***	+0.69**	+0.43	+0.41	+0.56*
X_2		+0.79***	+0.54*	+0.48	
X_3			+0.45	+0.64**	+0.31
X_4				+0.66**	

32 Northern and Western states

	X_2	X_3	X_4	X_5	X_6
X_1	+0.71***	−0.13	+0.11	−0.34	+0.32
X_2		−0.17			

Note: Asterisks indicate significance as follows:
*Significantly different from zero at the 0.05 level
**Significantly different from zero at the 0.01 level
***Significantly different from zero at the 0.001 level

Thus it would appear from this examination of state data that the impact of urbanization on agriculture is most noticeable in the South, the area of the nation where incomes are lowest and where rural-farm incomes are farthest below the national average. Capital per worker, as measured by the value of land and buildings per worker, tends to vary directly with urbanization as well as with manufacturing earnings in the South. For the thirty-two Northern and Western states, there is no apparent relationship of output per worker in agriculture with urbanization by state. However, if data for sub-state areas were to be used, one might find these variables related for the states outside the South as well.

In Table 187, the median incomes of rural-farm persons are compared with urbanization and other variables reflecting the influence of different sources of income. For the nation as a whole, as well as for the South and the North and West considered separately, the incomes of rural-farm persons are significantly associated with output per worker in agriculture, which measures labor income from agriculture.[17] Incomes of rural-farm persons are significantly associated with urbanization in the South but not in the North and West. For the South, this association would appear to be due primarily to the correlation between output per worker and urbanization and between urbanization and off-farm employment (see Table 186). Also for the South, both manufacturing earnings and off-farm employment are significantly associated with the incomes of rural-

Table 187. Median income, rural farm persons

Variables Analyzed:
X_1 = Output per worker, agriculture, 1949
X_3 = Per cent of population urban, 1950 (new definition)
X_4 = Average hourly earnings, manufacturing, 1950
X_5 = Per cent of farm operators working 100 or more days off the farm, 1949
X_7 = Median income, persons with income, rural farm, 1949
X_8 = Per cent of farm operators owners, 1950

Rank Correlation Coefficients

48 States	X_1	X_3	X_4	X_5	X_8
X_7	+0.72***	+0.42**	+0.63***	−0.02	+0.35*
16 Southern states					
X_7	+0.70**	+0.51*	+0.84***	+0.72**	+0.81***
X_3	+0.69**		+0.45	+0.64**	+0.42
32 Northern and western states					
X_7	+0.49**	+0.11	+0.18	−0.24	−0.28

Note: Asterisks indicate significance as follows:
   *Significantly different from zero at the 0.05 level
   **Significantly different from zero at the 0.01 level
   ***Significantly different from zero at the 0.001 level

farm persons, and these associations appear to be too strong to be explained by the intercorrelations of manufacturing earnings and off-farm employment with output per worker. The percentage of owners, which is included in an attempt to measure income from sources other than labor, is significantly associated with median income of rural-farm persons for the South. The lack of correlation between these variables in the North and West may be due to the fact that part owners as well as full owners are included in the percentage of owners variable.

Apart from its influence upon agricultural labor income through its influence upon value of capital per worker, urbanization would seem to influence the income of rural-farm persons in the South in additional ways. It is positively

[17]The fact that rho is much smaller for the Northern and Western states than for the Southern or for all states may be due to the fact that secular differences among them are much smaller than for the other two groups.

associated with off-farm employment, which in turn is significantly associated with the income of rural-farm persons. It is also associated positively, though not quite significantly, with manufacturing earnings in the Southern states, and manufacturing earnings significantly influence farm incomes in the South. Both of these latter two associations indicate that labor income from non-farm employment tends to vary significantly with urbanization. Finally, for the South, there is a positive though not quite significant association of the owner-ship variable with urbanization, and there is a high positive correlation of the ownership variable with the median incomes of rural-farm persons. The latter association reflects the effect of property incomes on the incomes received by rural-farm persons.[18]

Differential Changes in Agriculture, 1930-1954

We have used output per worker as a measure in analyzing the differences in labor income among the various states at a given point in time. In this section we shall use a similar measure in order to analyze differentials in the rate of change in labor income from agriculture. Changes in output per worker over the years are shown for the eight regions and selected states in Table 188 in the form of ratios of the years 1940 to 1930 and 1954 to 1940.[19] For the nation

[18]Before leaving this section it seems appropriate to compare our results with those of Vernon W. Ruttan, "The Impact of Urban-Industrial Development on Agriculture in the Tennessee Valley and the Southeast," *Journal of Farm Economics*, Vol. 37 (Feb., 1955), pp. 38-56, also reproduced in *Papers and Proceedings of the Regional Science Association*, Vol. I (processed), pp. R1-R14. Ruttan studied the impact of urbanization on the incomes of rural-farm persons in counties of the Tennessee Valley area and arrived at conclusions somewhat at variance with ours, which relate to variations among sixteen Southern states. In the counties Ruttan studied, the impact of urbanization on agricultural labor productivity was much less pronounced than its impact on the incomes of rural-farm persons through greater off-farm employment. The results summarized in our Table 186 suggest that the impact of urbanization on rural-farm persons' incomes through its effect on farm labor productivity was about as important as its effect through off-farm employment in the sixteen Southern states. No significant influence of value of land and buildings per worker on agricultural labor productivity was found by Ruttan, although he found that the level of other capital inputs did significantly influence agricultural labor productivity. The differ-ence between our results and his might be due to one or both of two factors. First, it seems likely that there is much less secular, as opposed to short-term or random, variation among the counties he studied as compared with the sixteen states studied here. And, second, while he recognizes that the appropriate relation between labor productivity and the various capital inputs is some curvilinear one, Ruttan fitted only linear relations. Since we have used rank correlations in the analysis above, our results are independent of the specific mathematical form of the true relation up to a monotonic (order-preserving) transforma-tion. The latter property of non-parametric methods is one of their principal strengths in an analysis such as this.

[19]The output data for the earlier two years were obtained from U. S. Department of Commerce, Bureau of the Census, *16th Census of the United States: 1940, Agriculture*, Vol. III (Washington: U. S. Government Printing Office, 1942), Tables 8, pp. 905-11. The data are for the years 1929 and 1939 and include the value of farm products sold, traded, or used by farm households.

For 1954, estimates of output were obtained by adding A.M.S. estimates of the value of

as a whole, output per worker in agriculture remained virtually unchanged between 1930 and 1940 but almost doubled between 1940 and 1954. However, in each of these periods, there was great diversity among the various states in the rate of change.

Over the period 1930 to 1940, the increases in agricultural output per worker were greatest in the states along the Atlantic seaboard and in the Great Lakes states. They were smallest in the Plains states. During this decade output per worker increased 25% or more in New Hampshire, Massachusetts, Rhode Island, Connecticut, North Carolina, and Florida and decreased 25% or more in North Dakota, South Dakota, Nebraska, and Kansas. However, the regional concentration of rates of growth was not significant at the 0.05 level, as judged by the statistic H, although it exceeded the 10% point.[20]

Over the period 1940 to 1954, the greatest increases tended to be in the lower Southeast and the Southwest. The smallest increases were in New England, the Middle Atlantic states, and the Upper South—Virginia, West Virginia, Kentucky, Tennessee, and North Carolina. Output per worker more than doubled in Delaware, Texas, Arizona, Nebraska, Montana, and Washington, and in the states of the lower South—South Carolina, Georgia, Alabama, Mississippi, Arkansas, and Florida. It increased by less than one-half in the upper New England states—Maine, New Hampshire, and Vermont—and in Tennessee, Oklahoma, Wyoming, and Utah.

There was no tendency for the states with high rates of growth in the 1930-40 period to have high rates in the 1940-54 period, and no significant tendency for the states with high rates of growth to be regionally concentrated in either period.

Earlier we found that agricultural output per worker in the various states was significantly related to the value of land and buildings per worker in 1950 and that no significant regional effect exists once account is taken of differ-

home consumption to the 1954 agricultural census data on the value of farm products sold or traded. These data are from U. S. Department of Agriculture, Agricultural Marketing Service, *Farm Income Situation*, FIS-160, Table 4, pp. 15-25, and U. S. Department of Commerce, Bureau of the Census, *1954 Census of Agriculture*, Vol. II (Washington: U. S. Government Printing Office, 1956), Table 3, p. 915, respectively.

For the comparison between 1940 and 1930, the output data were deflated by the number of agricultural workers as estimated by Carol Brainerd from population census data (Lee, Miller, Brainerd, and Easterlin, *Population Redistribution and Economic Growth, United States, 1870-1950* (Philadelphia: American Philosophical Society, 1957), Table L-4. For the comparison of 1954 with 1940, the output data were deflated by agricultural census data on the number of family and hired workers. (From *1954 Census of Agriculture*, Vol. II, Table 21, p. 298. The counts of the number of workers were taken in the last week of September 1939 and a specified week in September or October 1954.) Adjustment was made for the change in the national price level by deflating the output data by the implicit G.N.P. deflator, 1949 = 100. (From U. S. Department of Commerce, Office of Business Economics, *National Income, 1954 Edition* (Washington: Government Printing Office, 1954), Table 41, p. 216, for 1929; from (U. S. Department of Commerce, Office of Business Economics, *Survey of Current Business*, July 1956, Table 41, pp. 24-25, for 1954.)

[20] For purposes of this test and the similar test for the period 1940-1954 the five regions used earlier for analysis were employed so that this test might be comparable with the covariance analysis to be discussed below.

Table 188. Changes in agricultural output per worker, by region, selected states, 1949 U. S. dollars, 1930-1954

Region and state[a]	Ratio	
	1940/1930	1954/1940
New England	1.383	1.557
Maine	0.868	1.407
Connecticut	1.540	1.960
Middle Atlantic	1.179	1.844
New York	1.064	1.616
Delaware	1.245	2.482
Great Lakes	1.113	1.778
Wisconsin	0.871	1.621
Illinois	1.311	1.899
Southeast	1.086	2.070
Tennessee	0.982	1.367
Florida	1.300	2.905
Plains	0.850	1.833
Kansas	0.731	1.893
Iowa	1.036	1.735
Southwest	1.029	2.025
Oklahoma	0.914	1.452
Arizona	1.107	3.136
Mountain	1.008	1.677
Utah	1.111	1.216
Montana	1.018	2.331
Far West	1.016	1.872
Nevada	1.018	1.575
Washington	0.960	2.316
United States[b]	1.032	1.920
H[c]	9.0	6.2

[a] Regional averages are simple averages of the data for states in the region.
[b] Change for the nation as a whole.
[c] For these tests the data were combined into the five regions used for the analysis in earlier sections.

ences in the value of land and buildings per worker. We now ask: Are changes in output per worker over time significantly related to changes in the value of land and buildings per worker? Once the effect of changes in the value of land and buildings per worker is removed, is there any significant regional effect? Measures of the value of land and buildings from the agricultural census were deflated by the same employment data as were used to deflate output figures. In addition, the value of land and buildings was adjusted for changes in the national level of prices.[21] We shall compare the logarithm of change in output

[21]Since changes in the national price level enter only as a constant term in the logarithmic regression of change in output per worker on change in value of land and buildings per worker, the choice of deflator makes no difference for this purpose. Actually, for this

per worker with the logarithm of change in value of land and buildings per worker. We first estimate the regression of the former on the latter from the covariation of the two variables within regions, using the same five regions as were used in the cross-section comparison discussed earlier. We then test whether, after the regional means of changes in output per worker are adjusted for differences in changes in the value of land and buildings per worker, any significant regional effect in the change in value of output per worker exists. The results of these comparisons are shown in Table 189, for the 1930-1940 and the 1940-1954 periods. For both periods, the regression of change in output per worker on change in value of land and buildings per worker was significantly

Table 189. Covariance analysis of changes in agricultural output per worker

Period	Residual degrees of freedom	Regional effect F^a	Regression t
1930–1940	42	2.26	+6.27*
1940–1954	42	2.81*	+5.60*

^{a} With four degrees of freedom in the numerator.
* Significantly different from zero at the 0.05 level.

greater than zero at the 0.05 level. For the earlier period there was no significant regional effect, but for the period 1940-1954 the regional effect differed significantly from zero at the 0.05 level. However, further investigation revealed that for the later period, of the five regions, only for the West (Mountain and Far West) did the regional mean differ significantly from zero.

In general, the evidence suggests that differences in the rate of growth of output per worker in agriculture are significantly related to differential change in value of land and buildings per worker, an indication of the capital/labor ratio. Yet this relationship does not come out as strongly when it is examined over time as when it is examined at one point in time. Also, a statistically significant regional effect was found for changes in output per worker for the period from 1940 to 1954, suggesting that variables other than value of land and buildings per worker are responsible for regional differences in the changes over time of output per worker. As shown in the note attached to the next chapter, regional differences in farm price changes or in the rate adoption of new production techniques could account for the latter finding.

purpose we used the deflator implicit in Tostlebe's estimates of current and constant dollar value of land and buildings for 1930 and 1940, from Table 6, p. 35, and Table 8, p. 43, and an index of average value per acre from U. S. Department of Agriculture, Agricultural Research Service, *Current Developments in the Farm Real Estate Market*, ARS 43-25 (CD-42), November 1955, Table 3, p. 8, for 1954. The latter is also available for earlier years and is virtually identical with the deflator implicit in Tostlebe's estimates for 1930 and 1940. The base for both indexes is 1950 = 100.

32 / Differences in labor incomes in the same industry:

(2) MANUFACTURING

We shall now examine differences among states in labor income from manufacturing to determine whether they are associated, like those in agriculture, with differences in the marginal productivity of labor reflecting differences in the proportion of labor and capital employed in production.

The earnings of manufacturing workers in a given state depend partly on the structure of manufacturing in this state, just as the wage and salary earnings of all workers in a given state depend partly on the industrial composition of these workers. It is not surprising, then, that a comparison of reported and rate-constant earnings of manufacturing production workers by states is much the same as the comparison for all wage and salary workers. Such a comparison is made in Table 190 for the eight regions and selected states. The rate-constant earnings shown in this table were computed in the same manner as Hanna's occupational and industrial rate-constant earnings.[1] For each state, the proportion of manufacturing production workers in a particular industry was weighted by the national average hourly earnings in that particular industry and summed over all industries. For this computation, 430 different industrial categories were used.

The data here show that, where reported earnings of manufacturing production workers exceed (fall below) the national average, there is a strong tendency for rate-constant earnings to exceed (fall below) the national average as well. In fact, in all but eight of the forty-four states in which both reported earnings and rate-constant earnings deviate from the national average, both deviate in the same direction. The rank order of the states in the two series is also very similar—the rank correlation coefficient rho is +0.73. And, in states where the reported hourly earnings of manufacturing workers exceed (fall below) the national average, the wages of these workers in all industries tend strongly to exceed (fall below) the national average for their particular indus-

[1] Frank Hanna, *State Income Differentials, 1919-1954* (Durham, N. C.: Duke University Press, 1959), Chapter 6.

Table 190. Reported and Hanna's "rate-constant" manufacturing production worker hourly earnings, by region, selected states, 1947

Region and state[a]	Reported earnings	Rate-constant earnings	Difference
New England	$1.12	$1.18	—$0.06
Vermont	$1.02	$1.15	—$0.13
Connecticut	1.27	1.29	— 0.02
Middle Atlantic	1.25	1.25	0.00
Delaware	1.17	1.20	— 0.03
New Jersey	1.33	1.26	+ 0.07
Great Lakes	1.35	1.32	+ 0.03
Wisconsin	1.25	1.28	— 0.03
Michigan	1.48	1.39	+ 0.09
Southeast	0.95	1.09	— 0.14
Mississippi	0.78	1.03	— 0.25
West Virginia	1.24	1.26	— 0.02
Plains	1.11	1.21	— 0.10
North Dakota	1.00	1.15	— 0.15
Minnesota	1.17	1.23	— 0.06
Southwest	1.10	1.20	— 0.10
Louisiana	0.99	1.16	— 0.17
Arizona	1.22	1.17	+ 0.05
Mountain	1.24	1.21	+ 0.05
Utah	1.17	1.24	— 0.07
Wyoming	1.38	1.33	+ 0.05
Far West	1.43	1.19	+ 0.24
Nevada	1.38	1.23	+ 0.15
Washington	1.46	1.18	+ 0.28
U. S.	$1.24	$1.24	—
Relative variation	14.9%	7.6%	—
H	—	—	31.0***

[a] Regional averages are simple averages of the data for states in the region.
*** Significantly different from zero at the 0.001 level.

Source: Hanna, *State Income Differentials, 1919-1954,* cited above, Chapter 6.

try. In forty-two states in which reported earnings deviate both from national average reported earnings and from the state's rate-constant earnings, the deviations take the same direction; that is, if reported earnings exceed (fall below) the national average, they also exceed (fall below) rate-constant earnings. When the forty-eight states are ranked by reported earnings and by reported earnings minus rate-constant earnings, the two rankings are almost identical—Spearman's rho is equal to +0.91. (These same tendencies were also observed in the comparison made earlier of the reported and rate-constant earnings of all wage and salary workers by states.)

Part of the variation in the earnings of manufacturing production workers, as reflected in rate-constant earnings, might be attributable to differences in the skills required in the different occupations and industries and to factors other than current money income, such as stability of earnings and non-pecuniary advantages, that influence the choice between occupations. However, Hanna's data suggest that there are significant state and regional variations in manufacturing earnings in all industries. In the Southeast, for example, manufacturing earnings in 1947 averaged 14% below the level for the nation as a whole (in Mississippi, 29% below). They also tended to be below the national average in the New England, Southwest, and Plains states. On the other hand, in the Far West, wages were 20% above the national average in all industries (35% above in Oregon), and they tended to be above the national average in all industries in the Great Lakes and Mountain states as well.

The structure of manufacturing industry, therefore, accounts for only a part of the interstate variation in earnings.[2] To some extent the comparison of Hanna's rate-constant and reported earnings overestimates the effect of structure on manufacturing earnings. As Hanna points out, in 108 of the 430 industries 50% or more of the production worker man-hours for the nation were expended in a single region.[3] The data in Table 190 strongly suggest that location has a significant effect upon earnings; the national average earnings in at least one-fourth of the industries used in Hanna's standardization are greatly influenced by locational effects upon wages.

Thus, to explain the differentials among states in the earnings of manufacturing production workers, it is necessary to explain the differentials in earnings of workers in the same industry in different states. But the relation observed above of "favorable" industrial composition—or an above-average proportion of workers in the higher paying industries when weighted by national average industry earnings—and above-average earnings in all industries also presents a challenge to explanation.

While we might expect earnings to vary from industry to industry because of differences in skills and conditions other than current money income that affect the relative attractiveness of different industrial employments, there is no *a priori* reason to expect that, for these reasons, above-average earnings would be associated with "favorable" industrial structure. In the remainder of this chapter we shall present evidence bearing on the hypothesis that interstate differences in labor income in manufacturing are reflective, in part, of variations in the proportions with which labor is combined with other factors, particularly capital, in production. If differences in factor proportions significantly affect labor productivity as between states, we would expect to observe two closely related phenomena: in states in which the average wage in manufacturing is below (above) the national average, we would expect to find—everything else being equal—first, a concentration of employment in the labor (capital) intensive manufacturing industries and, second, a greater (smaller) proportion of labor used relative to other production factors and hence lower (higher) labor

---

[2]The independent effects of structure account for only about one-fourth of the inter-state variation in manufacturing earnings as indicated by the square of the ratio of the relative variations of rate-constant to reported earnings.

[3]*Ibid.*, p. 156.

productivity in each industry. In other words, our hypothesis has two implications: (1) that interstate variations in manufacturing wages are related to the relative factor endowments of the various states; and (2) that in states with below (above) average earnings in manufacturing, more (less) labor will be used relative to other factors of production and hence the marginal productivity of labor will be lower (higher).[4]

As the theory of interregional and international trade suggests,[5] the pattern of specialization is determined, in part, by the relative endowments of the different factors of production. To illustrate, we shall take the case of two areas, each producing two commodities with two factors of production, labor and capital. We shall assume that, for each of these two commodities, the production possibilities are the same in both areas, as are the production factors employed in the production of each commodity. Let the ratio of labor to capital, however, differ between the two areas. Then, provided that the production function for the two commodities differs sufficiently and conditions of demand are not too different as between the two areas, the area in which labor is the relatively more plentiful factor will tend to specialize in the production of the labor-intensive commodity; in this area, more labor will be used relative to capital in each of the two "industries," and the ratio of labor to capital return will be lower. If transport costs are at zero and if certain other conditions exist, including the lack of complete specialization, trade between the two areas will equalize the ratio of factor prices between them.[6] But even if transport costs are not zero, trade between the two areas will serve as a partial substitute for the movement of factors of production in equalizing factor returns, and relative wages will be higher in the labor-plentiful area than if no trade were to take place.[7] Suppose, that transport costs are not zero in the instance that we are considering, so that relative factor prices are not equal in the two areas. If we were to compute the average wage in each of the two industries, or in the production of each of the two commodities, for the two areas, we would find that the average wage was lower in the labor-intensive commodity industry and that the area which specialized in the production of this commodity would have lower relative wages in the production of both of the two commodities. Hence, we would observe the coincidence of greater than average wages in both industries and a "favorable"

[4] An exception to the second of these implications would be the case of fixed proportions. If production possibilities require that labor and capital be combined in fixed proportions in a given industry, there would of course be no such relation between factor proportions and the average manufacturing wage in that industry.

[5] See, in particular, Bertil Ohlin, *Interregional and International Trade* (Cambridge: Harvard University Press, 1952).

[6] See Paul A. Samuelson, "International Trade and the Equalization of Factor Prices," *Economic Journal*, Vol. 68 (June 1948), pp. 163-84.

[7] In the above discussion, no attempt has been made to state these results with rigor, nor has an attempt been made to discuss the complications to this simple model. For either, the reader is referred to one of the standard texts on the theory of international trade. Nor is it claimed that this relatively simple model is a "realistic" description of the American economy. The effect of factor endowments on specialization, trade, and factor prices is a logical possibility. It is the task of empirical investigation to discover whether any such tendencies prevail in the American economy.

industrial composition in the area in which labor is relatively scarce, and vice versa for the area in which labor is relatively plentiful.

In presenting this rather simple example, we do not mean to imply that relative factor endowments are the only determinants of the structure of manufacturing or that they are the only conditions that could lead to the observed coincidence between a "favorable" industrial structure and greater than average earnings in all industries. Obviously, the geographic distribution of natural resources can be expected to influence the pattern of regional specialization and trade. And we have already mentioned several other factors that might affect differentials in manufacturing earnings in different industries in our economy. But the coincidence of above-average reported earnings in manufacturing and above-average earnings in all industries is consistent with these propositions derived from the theory of interregional trade. We now ask, is there any other evidence of an association between interstate specialization and manufacturing earnings?

Before an answer to any such question can be attempted, measures of these variables are needed. To measure earnings of labor in manufacturing, we used Bureau of Labor Statistics data on average hourly earnings in 1950.[8] To measure the percentage of each state's manufacturing workers employed in capital-intensive industries, we had to have some criterion for choosing these industries. Actually, we used two different measures of capital per worker in different manufacturing industries: first, total capital in various kinds of manufacturing in the United States for the year 1948 [9] and, second, national income by industrial origin less compensation of employees in 1948.[10]

To obtain two estimates of capital per worker in the different manufacturing industries, both these measures of capital were divided by the number of full-time equivalent employees in these same manufacturing industries.[11] Eight industries were found to be below the average for all manufacturing on both measures. These were: electrical machinery, machinery except electrical, printing, textiles, lumber and furniture, transportation equipment except motor vehicles, leather, and apparel. For our purposes here, these eight were identified as labor-intensive industries. Nine industries were identified as capital-intensive or high-capital/labor-ratio industries. Five of these nine—petroleum products and coal, chemicals, motor vehicles, tobacco, and paper—were above

[8]See U. S. Department of Labor, Bureau of Labor Statistics, *Employment and Earnings*, Vol. II (June 1956), Table SC-2, pp. 122-32. Data on average hourly earnings in manufacturing were not available for four states for 1950. Thus, we estimated them by interpolating the ratio of the trend to the national average for the period 1947-1955.

[9]Unpublished estimates made available to us by Daniel Creamer. See also his *Capital and Output Trends in Manufacturing Industries, 1880-1948*, Occasional Paper No. 41 (New York: National Bureau of Economic Research, 1954).

[10]Computed from Department of Commerce, Office of Business Economics estimates in *National Income, 1954 Edition* (Washington: Government Printing Office, 1954). Tables 13 and 14, pp. 176-79. This figure is a measure of the total returns to capital engaged in the different manufacturing industries. Assuming that the rate of return to capital is the same for all manufacturing in the nation as a whole, this figure is proportional to total capital employed in the various manufacturing industries.

[11]Also as estimated by the Department of Commerce (*Ibid.*, Table 25, pp. 196-97.)

the average on both measures. In 1950, average wage and salary earnings were about $3,100 nationally in the industries classified here as labor-intensive and about $3,500 in those classified as capital-intensive.[12]

Using data from the 1950 census, we computed the percentage of manufacturing employment in the high-capital/labor-ratio industries for each of the forty-eight states. Regional averages of these data, together with data for selected states, are shown in Table 191 and Figure 96. The concentration of employment in high-capital/labor-ratio industries varied widely among states; it was highest

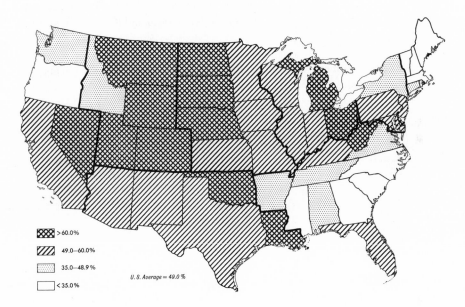

> 60.0%

49.0—60.0%

35.0—48.9 %

< 35.0%

U. S. Average = 49.0 %

Figure 96. % Manufacturing Employment in High Capital-Labor-Ratio Industries, 1950.

in Michigan (77%) and lowest in South Carolina (a little under 13%). In Oregon and Washington it was also much below average.[13] The lowest regional concentrations were in New England—particularly in Maine, New Hampshire, and Vermont—and in the Southeast, especially in the Carolinas, Georgia, and Mississippi. States which ranked highest in percentage of employment in the

[12] It should be noted here that the manufacturing employment data were disaggregated only to what is essentially the 2-digit level. Further disaggregation might well result in reclassification of many of the 3-digit industries in the 2-digit groups. For example, the food industries are among our nine industries classified as capital-intensive; but a further breakdown might result in many of the 3-digit food industries being reclassified as labor intensive.

[13] It is interesting to note that these two states are the principal exception to the generalization derived from Table 190, that states with above average reported earnings of manufacturing production workers tend to have above average rate-constant earnings also.

high-capital/labor-ratio industries were located primarily in the Great Lakes, Southwest, Plains, and Mountain regions.

When the percentage of manufacturing employment in high-capital/labor-ratio industries is compared with the average hourly earnings in manufacturing by states for 1950, there is a rank correlation coefficient rho of +0.38 for the nation as a whole. While this value is fairly small, it is too large to be attributed to chance variation. The association between these two variables is examined further in Table 192. The mean ranks of the two variables are shown here for three broad regions, each consisting of sixteen states, as well as the rank correlation between the two variables within each of these three regions. Both the percentage of manufacturing in high-capital/labor-ratio industries (C) and the

Table 191. Employment in high-capital per labor ratio[a] manufacturing, by region, selected states, 1950

Region and state	Per cent
New England	33.9
New Hampshire	20.2
Connecticut	48.6
Middle Atlantic	54.8
New York	41.1
Delaware	72.1
Great Lakes	60.0
Wisconsin	50.1
Michigan	77.0
Southeast	38.6
South Carolina	12.7
West Virginia	71.2
Plains	59.6
Missouri	49.7
Nebraska	70.0
Southwest	58.1
Arizona	53.7
Oklahoma	64.7
Mountain	62.7
Idaho	41.9
Utah	72.7
Far West	43.2
Oregon	24.7
Nevada	60.0
United States	49.0
H	23.3**

[a] Employment in those industries in which the ratio of capital to labor (see text for further description) is above the average for all manufacturing as a percentage of total employment in manufacturing.

**Significantly different from zero at the 0.01 level.

SOURCE: Computed from data in 1950 Census of Population.

manufacturing wage rate (W) averaged highest in rank in the West and lowest in the South. Within both the North and the South, the correlation is positive and significantly so, but a negative correlation is observed for the West. The mean ranks of W and C in the three regions and the correlation within the North and the South are consistent with the first implication of our hypothesis—that interstate differentials in manufacturing wages are associated with the relative factor endowments of the various states. But the correlation for the West is not.

Table 192. Relation of the manufacturing wage rate (W) to the per cent of manufacturing employment in high capital per labor ratio industries (C) by and within regions, 1950

Region[a]	Mean rank, 1950[b]		Within region rank correlation coefficient rho[c]
	(W)	(C)	
North	20.9	26.6	+0.72
South	36.1	28.5	+0.79
West	16.5	18.4	−0.43

[a] The three broad regions are defined as follows:
   North: New England, Middle Atlantic, and Lakes.
   South: Southeast and Southwest.
   West: Plains, Mountain, and Far West.
[b] When all states are ranked from one to forty-eight.
[c] For the North and South, the correlation is significantly greater than zero at the 0.01 level.

In interpreting these results, it must be remembered that the level of wage rates is only one of many factors affecting the location of manufacturing industry. Considerations of markets and material inputs are much more significant in the location of many industries than are differential wage rates (even though the cost of labor is rarely ruled out of consideration entirely). The correlation within the states of the West suggests that these other factors tend to predominate here.[14] However, the comparisons shown in Table 192 lend some support to our hypothesis.

The second implication of our hypothesis is that, in states with below-average

[14] In Oregon and Washington—the most striking exceptions to the general tendency for the two variables, W and C, to be positively associated—employment in the labor-intensive manufacturing industries might be attributed in part to a comparative advantage in lumber product manufacturing based on favorable location relative to natural resources. (In these two states, employment in the lumber products industries accounted for 61 and 35 per cent, respectively, of all manufacturing employment.) Likewise, in the Dakotas and Nebraska, the relatively large employment in capital-intensive industry results largely from the concentration of employment in the food-processing industries. These facts suggest that, for at least certain of the Western states, natural resources might be the principal determinant of manufacturing activity located there.

earnings in manufacturing, more labor will be used relative to other factors in production and, hence, the marginal productivity of labor will be lower.[15]

The 1947 Census of Manufactures provides data on the earnings of production workers by industry and state. Average hourly earnings in 1947, by industry, computed from these data are shown in Table 193 for each of the eight regions. These averages follow a familiar pattern and need only passing comment. In nine out of the seventeen industries analyzed, wages were lowest in the Southeast; in fourteen, they were highest in the Far West. The statistic H, computed separately for each of the seventeen industries, was significant at the 0.05 level in thirteen of them (in eight of these, at the 0.001 level); and in three of the four "non-significant" cases, it was significant at about the 0.1 level. Since the test ignores differences between the New England and Middle Atlantic states, the Plains and Great Lakes states, and the Mountain and Far West states —differences which are readily apparent from the regional averages in Table 193—these data strongly confirm the existence of interstate differentials in 2-digit manufacturing industries.

But while the average hourly earnings of manufacturing workers can be readily obtained from the manufacturing census data, there are no comparable estimates available of capital employed in manufacturing in the various states in 1947. The latest census to contain such data was the 1919 census. However, value-added minus production worker wages can be computed from the 1947 census data. This quantity consist of capital returns plus the returns to certain other factors such as earnings of non-production workers, payments for business services, and some taxes; it excludes payments for material and power inputs. It is easy to show that average hourly earnings and value-added minus wages per production worker man-hour in a given industry both vary directly with the price per unit of output f.o.b. factory, capital per man-hour, other factors (whose returns are included in value-added) per man-hour, and materials and power inputs per man-hour, as well as external economies, provided that the production function for the industry is the same everywhere and linear in the logarithms of output and the various inputs, and that product and factor markets are competitive.[16]

Thus, we would expect to find that wages per man-hour and value-added minus wages per man-hour vary together by states for the same industry. Further-

[15]After the following pages were written, we discovered a report of a similar study by Jerome Stein, "The Predictive Accuracy of the Marginal Productivity Theory of Wages," *Review of Economic Studies*, Vol. 25 (June 1958), pp. 182-89. Stein found, as we do, a significant association between average wage and value added per employee in several manufacturing industries within the United States.

[16]Evidence for linearity in the logarithms of production functions is provided by the observation that the scatter of wages per man-hour (or worker) and value-added minus wages per man-hour (or worker) appeared to be approximately linear in the logarithms for all the industries for which this relation is examined in Table 195. The assumption that product and factor markets are competitive seems the most natural one to make for a study such as ours, even though the model should be judged only by its consistency with observable magnitudes and not by the so-called "realism" of its assumptions. These conditions are sufficient to obtain the stated result, though they need not be necessary. The appendix to this chapter contains the proof of these statements.

Table 193. Average hourly earnings of manufacturing production workers, by industry, by region, 1947

Industry	Region[a]								H[b]
	New England	Middle Atlantic	Great Lakes	Southeast	Plains	Southwest	Mountain	Far West	
Food	$1.00	$1.07	$1.14	$0.80	$1.08	$0.89	$1.05	$1.22	29.0***
Textiles	1.14	1.14	1.09	0.92	0.96	0.85	0.82	1.20	17.1***
Apparel	0.92	1.05	0.99	0.75	0.85	0.73	0.80	1.11	19.1***
Lumber	0.96	0.98	1.03	0.69	0.95	0.94	1.20	1.55	28.7***
Furniture	1.00	1.16	1.18	0.83	1.08	0.88	1.07	1.35	25.9***
Paper	1.15	1.17	1.22	1.11	1.09	1.11	—	1.44	8.8
Printing	1.24	1.49	1.47	1.21	1.21	1.32	1.30	1.71	10.1*
Chemicals	1.08	1.29	1.30	1.04	1.22	1.22	1.24	1.41	11.4*
Petroleum & coal	1.41	1.60	1.51	1.30	1.29	1.57	1.65	1.55	13.9**
Leather	0.97	1.11	1.06	0.88	0.92	0.82	0.94	1.20	10.8*
Stone, clay & glass	1.18	1.14	1.23	0.94	1.05	1.02	1.13	1.32	18.9***
Primary metals	1.23	1.44	1.50	1.14	1.31	1.20	1.40	1.48	15.6**
Fabricated metals	1.14	1.26	1.33	1.05	1.15	1.22	1.27	1.49	18.7***
Machinery, except elec.	1.29	1.37	1.43	1.06	1.17	1.14	1.23	1.54	18.6***
Electrical machinery	1.14	1.33	1.30	1.08	1.09	1.07	0.85	1.34	6.8
Transportation equipment	1.28	1.45	1.51	1.20	1.26	1.31	1.18	1.58	7.3
Instruments	1.14	1.33	1.23	1.15	1.12	1.08	1.05	—	2.2

[a] Regional averages are simple averages of the data for the states in the region for which data are available.

[b] For this purpose the regions were regrouped into five: Northeast (New England and Middle Atlantic); North Central (Lakes and Plains); West (Mountain and Far West); Southeast; and Southwest, primarily for comparability with the covariance analysis. For the same reason, the Southeast and Southwest were combined for textiles and electrical machinery, and the West was combined with the North Central for instruments. These latter combinations were also made to avoid too few observations for a single region in order that the distribution of H might be better approximated by that of Chi-square.

Note: Asterisks denote significance level as follows:

* Significantly different from zero at the 0.05 level

** Significantly different from zero at the 0.01 level

*** Significantly different from zero at the 0.001 level

Source: Computed from data in U. S. Department of Commerce, Bureau of the Census, *1947 Census of Manufactures*, Vol. III (Washington: U. S. Government Printing Office, 1950).

more, if the inter-state variation of wages of the workers in the same industry is explained by variation in factor proportions, we would expect to find no significant regional effect in the relation of wages per man-hour and value-added minus wages per man-hour.

Several problems arise in interpreting the relation of production worker wages per man-hour and value-added minus wages per man-hour. First, there is the question of which of the industries for which census data are available should be used in making the comparisons. The comparison would show a significant regional effect if the production functions of the industry differed among regions. This difference would result either if the production functions of all industries aggregated into a particular classification differed regionally or if the classification contained several industries with identical production functions everywhere, the relative importance of which differed from region to region. If the latter situation obtained, then by disaggregating—that is, by going from, say, 2-digit to 3-digit industries—the regional effect would disappear. But if the regional effect persisted, one might presume that production functions are not the same for the same industry in all regions. Thus, we shall begin with all manufacturing treated as a single industry and proceed to examine the 2-digit and 3-digit industries.

A second problem is that the data on wages and value-added refer to a single year. Income data suggest that, as in agriculture, the forces operating to produce inter-state variation in labor income in non-agricultural industries have persisted for at least several decades. What we want is a measure which reflects secular differences, but the annual data reflect short-run as well as secular differences. However, it would seem likely that value-added minus production worker wages for a single year would be more subject to errors as a measure of secular values than production worker wages. Hence, in comparing wages with value-added minus wages, we shall choose value-added minus wages as the dependent variable in the regression analysis. As in output per worker in agriculture, value-added minus wages is dependent in the statistical sense of dependence on random fluctuations only; our model implies simply that wages and value-added minus wages are co-related. To the extent that wages are measured with some error from their secular values, the relation between wages and value-added minus wages will be biased. However, our model implies that the slope of the regression should be equal to unity (see the appendix at the end of the chapter). For the twenty-one comparisons made in Table 195, the estimated slope differed significantly from unity in only one case. This consideration suggests that we introduce no obvious bias into the relation of wages and value-added minus wages by neglecting the possibility of errors in the former. But in all these comparisons, if wages per worker is taken as the dependent variable, the estimated slope is substantially less than one.

Finally, we noted above that wages per man-hour will vary not only with capital per man-hour, but with other factors whose returns are included in value added per man-hour and material and power inputs per man-hour, as well as with price, f.o.b. factory, and external economies. While the relation of production worker wages to value-added minus wages may reflect differences in marginal labor productivity due to differences in factor proportions, it does not necessarily imply that these differences are due to differences in capital per worker. But we can go to the 1919 manufacturing census for data enabling us to compute capital per worker as well as wages per worker and value-added minus wages per worker. The data on capital contained in this census are probably none too good; at best, they represent accounting book values rather than a measure of physical capital. However, they do provide some guide for interpretation. Wages per worker, or average annual earnings of production workers (X_1), capital per worker (X_2), and value-added minus production worker wages per worker (X_3) were all computed for all manufacturing, by states, for 1919. Simple and partial correlation coefficients of the logarithms of these three variables were then computed. These are presented in Table 194. The three simple correlation coefficients are all significant at the 0.05 level; those for wages per worker and capital per worker and for capital per worker and value-added minus wages per worker at the 0.001 level. The partial correlation of wages per worker and capital per worker, with value-added minus wages per worker held constant, is also significant at the 0.001 level; but the partial correlation of wages per worker and value-added minus wages per

Table 194.   Comparison of wages per worker, capital per worker, and value added minus wages per worker, all manufacturing, by states, 1919

---

a. *Simple correlation coefficients*

$$r_{12} = +0.63$$
$$r_{13} = +0.37$$
$$r_{23} = +0.62$$

b. *Partial correlation coefficients*

$$r_{12.3}{}^x = +0.55$$
$$r_{13.2}{}^x = -0.04$$

---

worker with capital per worker held constant, does not differ significantly from zero. This result suggests that the relation of wages per worker to value-added minus wages per worker depends only upon the relation of wages per worker and capital per worker, and not upon any relation of other variables which might affect labor productivity. These other variables, however, might be inter-correlated with capital per worker. The comparison also suggests that value-added minus wages measures total capital with a relatively large error. The latter consideration also suggests that value-added minus wages is the appropriate dependent variable for regression analysis.

Using covariance analysis, we shall compare the logarithms of production worker wages per man-hour with the logarithms of value-added minus production worker wages per man-hour.[17] It is assumed that the true value of the slope of this relation and the residual variance are the same for all regions; we estimate the regression of value-added minus wages on wages from the within-region covariation of these variables. The regional mean values of value-added minus wages per man-hour are then adjusted for regional differences in wages per man-hour, and the significance of the differences between the adjusted mean values of value-added minus wages is tested. The latter is equivalent to testing whether wages per worker in different industries differ significantly between regions when differences in value-added minus wages per worker are eliminated. Thus, we can determine not only whether wages per worker and capital per worker are related, but also whether this relation explains the observed regional differences in wages per worker in the same industry.[18]

The analysis of covariance for several manufacturing industries is presented in Table 195. All manufacturing, treated as a single industry, was first examined. For all manufacturing the regional effect is significantly different from zero at the 0.001 level and the regression slope is not significantly greater than zero. However, when we disaggregate by examining data for 2-digit industries, the results are quite different.[19] One of these industries—petroleum and coal products—revealed no association between wages per man-hour and value-added minus wages per man-hour when the scatter diagrams were examined. Of the remaining sixteen 2-digit industries, a significant regional effect was found for only five. However, for thirteen of these sixteen, the regression slope was significantly greater than zero at the 0.05 significance level.

To determine whether the regional effect in these 2-digit industries was due to aggregation into a category of industries whose production functions are the same in every state but which differ among themselves, data were examined for 3-digit industries in the food, lumber, chemicals, and fabricated metals categories.[20] In none of these was a significant regional effect found, but for all four the regression slope was significantly greater than zero at the 0.05

[17] As in the case of agricultural differentials, differences in skills of workers in different states are reflected here, since such differences would lead to differences both in wages per worker and value added minus wages per worker, even if no differentials existed in terms of workers of identical skill.

[18] As in the analysis of regional differences in output per worker in agriculture, the eight regions are combined for this analysis into five. This combination was made in order that there remain some within-region variation in wages per worker, on which the regression estimate partly depends. In three cases examined in Table 195, two regions were further combined since only two observations were available for a region in these cases. For textiles and electrical machinery the Southeast and Southwest were combined, and for instruments the West and North were combined.

[19] The comparisons were not made for the miscellaneous industries, for obvious reasons, nor for the tobacco and rubber industries, since for each of the latter two industries too few observations were available to permit analysis.

[20] For the 3-digit industries, no man-hour data were published by states. Hence, production worker wages and value-added minus production worker wages were both deflated by the average number of production workers for the year. None of the 3-digit industries in the petroleum and coal or the paper categories were analyzed, since data were not available for enough states to allow for about 20 degrees of freedom in the estimate of the residual variance.

Table 195. Summary of the relation between wages per production worker man-hour and value added less wages per production worker man-hour, manufacturing industries, by states, 1947

Industry	Residual degrees of freedom	Regional effect, $F^{a,b}$	Regression t^b
All manufacturing	42	10.65*	2.02*
Food	42	2.71*	4.10*
Textiles	30	1.49	5.14*
Apparel	36	2.13	3.42*
Lumber	39	2.83*	8.43*
Furniture	36	0.50	2.27*
Paper	31	3.35*	1.84*
Printing	42	2.56	3.28*
Chemicals	41	4.19*	2.52*
Petroleum & coal[c]	—	—	—
Leather	32	0.39	1.58
Stone, clay & glass	41	1.61	2.36*
Primary metals	34	1.90	2.36*
Fabricated metals	40	3.29*	0.92
Machinery, except electrical	39	0.65	2.32*
Electrical machinery	21	0.94	3.79*
Transportation equipment	26	1.51	0.57
Instruments	19	0.16	2.96*
Bakery products[d]	31	0.35	2.47*
Lumber & timber, basic products[d]	28	0.76	5.55*
Vegetable & animal oils[d]	25	1.11	3.74*
Structural metal products[d]	31	1.35	2.50*

[a] For all but three of the two-digit industries, the numerator of the F ratio has four degrees of freedom. For textiles and electrical machinery the Southeast and Southwest were combined, and for instruments the West and North Central were combined; hence, for these latter three, the numerator of the F ratio has three degrees of freedom.

[b] A single asterisk means significantly different from zero for F, significantly greater than zero for t, at the 0.05 level.

[c] Scatter diagram showed no relation between wages and value added minus wages man-hour.

[d] For the three-digit industries no man-hour data were available by states; hence production worker wages and value added minus production worker wages were both deflated by the average number of production workers for the year.

level. This result suggests that the regional effect observed in the 2-digit and all manufacturing categories is due to the aggregation of industries whose production functions differ in these categories. Taken as a whole, our results suggest that the inter-state variation in wages per production worker man-hour can be explained to a significant extent by differences in the marginal productivity of labor resulting from differences in the proportions with which labor is combined with other factors of production. The evidence clearly suggests that differences in the marginal productivity of labor as among industries, at one point in time, are at least partly the result of differences in the relative amounts of capital and labor used in production. Once this variable is held constant, there is no evidence of any regional variation in production worker wages for most industries. This is not to minimize in any way the important role of certain qualitative aspects, such as those related to the quality of management; rather, it serves to pinpoint what would seem to be a really critical element characterizing the relative "income-producing power" of industries in the various parts of the country.

Differential Change in Manufacturing, 1919-1954

Table 196 shows changes in manufacturing wages over the 1919-1954 period in the form of ratios for the years 1929 to 1919, 1939 to 1929, 1947 to 1939, and 1954 to 1947. [21] Except for the depression decade, real wages of production workers in manufacturing increased by about 25% for the nation as a whole during each of these four time periods. But, as with agriculture, there were wide differences in the changes for the various states.

In the 1919-1929 period, the increases were most rapid in the Northeast, where real wages rose at least 20% in every state except Maine, Delaware, and Maryland. They were least rapid during this decade in the Southern and Mountain states; in all of these states except West Virginia, Kentucky, Oklahoma, and Montana, the increases were less than 20%. During the 1930's, when little change occurred nationally, there was no marked regional concentration of rates of growth in manufacturing wages, although all states in the Far West had greater than average increases.

From 1939 to 1947—the war period—the rates of increases were greatest in New England and the South. The growth in the Southeast was particularly striking; in the Carolinas, Georgia, Alabama, Mississippi, Arkansas, and Florida, real wages in manufacturing were 40% greater in 1947 than in 1939. In the Southwest, Oklahoma was the only state that fell below the national average in its rate of growth during these years. Outside these three regions, however, only New Jersey, Delaware, Idaho, Utah, and Oregon exceeded the national average. The lowest rates of growth were in the Great Lakes states.

[21] In each case total wages of production workers by states were obtained from the census of manufactures; for the comparisons in the first three columns of Table 196, total production worker wages were deflated by the average number of production workers for the year; in the fourth column, by total production worker man-hours. All the wage data were converted to constant dollars by deflating by the implicit G.N.P. deflator, 1947 = 100. For 1929 and later years the deflator was obtained from *National Income*, 1954 edition; for 1919, from Raymond W. Goldsmith, *A Study of Saving in the United States*, Vol. I (Princeton: Princeton University Press, 1955), Table T-16, p. 377. The wage and production worker data used were taken from the *1947 Census of Manufactures*, Vol. III, and earlier years. For 1954 the preliminary state reports of the 1954 census were used.

Table 196. Changes in wages of manufacturing production workers, by region, selected states, 1947 U. S. dollars, 1919-1954

Region and State [a]	1929/1919	1939/1929	1947/1939	1954/1947
New England	1.253	1.042	1.334	1.186
Rhode Island	1.279	1.048	1.356	1.110
Connecticut	1.295	1.095	1.302	1.238
Middle Atlantic	1.224	1.060	1.283	1.212
New York	1.383	0.983	1.278	1.153
Maryland	1.185	1.178	1.271	1.232
Great Lakes	1.299	1.111	1.210	1.252
Illinois	1.328	1.025	1.269	1.232
Indiana	1.282	1.131	1.257	1.257
Southeast	1.068	1.073	1.441	1.247
W. Virginia	1.212	1.055	1.209	1.280
S. Carolina	0.940	1.227	1.595	1.153
Plains	1.224	1.050	1.236	1.300
N. Dakota	1.287	0.899	1.224	1.253
Kansas	1.228	1.055	1.265	1.406
Southwest	1.152	0.985	1.377	1.326
Oklahoma	1.323	1.006	1.269	1.299
Louisiana	1.099	0.973	1.542	1.360
Mountain	1.148	1.013	1.235	1.269
Montana	1.242	0.987	1.132	1.273
Utah	1.046	0.991	1.346	1.306
Far West	1.169	1.117	1.271	1.210
Nevada	1.295	1.128	1.184	1.234
Oregon	1.053	1.103	1.380	1.192
United States [b]	1.235	1.071	1.275	1.232
H [c]	16.85**	6.42	23.45***	18.85***

[a] Regional averages are simple averages for the states in the region.

[b] Change for the nation as a whole.

[c] For these tests the data were combined into the five regions used for analysis in this chapter.

** Significantly different from zero at the 0.01 level.

*** Significantly different from zero at the 0.001 level.

During the postwar period, 1947-1954, wages grew more rapidly than average again in six of the Southeastern states, but only two of these states ranked among the twelve with the highest rates of increase in the nation as a whole. The average for the region only slightly exceeded the national average. Increases during this period tended to be most rapid in the Southwest and in the Plains and Mountain states and least rapid in New England, the Middle Atlantic states, and the Far West.

For each of these time periods except 1929-1939, there was a significant regional concentration of states in the rate of growth of real wages in manufacturing. But there was no strong tendency for above-average rates of growth to persist from period to period in any group of states.

We shall now ask whether there is any association between the changes in wages observed over these four time periods and the changes in value-added minus wages. Table 197 summarizes the results of a comparison of these two variables, both deflated by the average number of production workers or production worker man-hours.[22] The data for 1929-1939, when plotted, indicated that there was no relation between changes in wages and changes in value-added

Table 197. Covariance analysis of changes in manufacturing production worker wages

Period	Residual degrees of freedom	Regional effect F^a	Regression t^b
1919-1929	42	1.94	+2.72*
1929-1939[c]	—	—	—
1939-1947	42	0.09	+3.86*
1947-1954	42	2.57	+2.79*

[a] With four degrees of freedom in the numerator.
[b] Asterisk indicates significantly greater than zero at the 0.05 level.
[c] Scatter diagram indicated no relationship between changes in wages and changes in value added minus wages.

minus wages, hence the covariance was not computed. For the other time periods, the regression of wages on value-added minus wages was significantly greater than zero at the 0.05 level. The regional effect (F) was not significant in any of the three periods, although for 1947-1954 it was almost significant at the 0.05 level. These results indicate that, to the extent that value-added minus

[22]Value-added was obtained from the same source as total production worker wages, and was adjusted for changes in the national price level by using the same deflator.

Our procedure here is much the same as the one we employed in the cross-sectional comparisons. We estimate the regression of value-added minus wages on wages, both per worker or per man-hour, from the within-regional covariation of these variables, adjust the regional means of value-added minus wages for regional differences in the means of wages using this relationship, and ask whether the differences in the adjusted regional means are too great to be attributed to random variation. For this purpose, we again divide the states into five regions. However, comparison was not made of the logs of value-added minus wages and wages, but of their untransformed values. We have done this because it can be shown that, if our hypothesis is correct, wages will be proportional to value-added minus wages; hence the relative change in wages would equal change in value-added minus wages. (See the Technical Appendix to this chapter.) Also, we made the comparison for all manufacturing only; it can be shown that the constant of proportionality depends upon the kind of manufacturing located in the state, but this constant drops out when we take the ratios of wages and value-added minus wages, both per worker or per man-hour, in two different years.

wages varies with capital per worker, changes in manufacturing wages by states are significantly associated with changes in capital per worker. They provide no specific evidence that any regional effect remains once account is taken of changes in marginal labor productivity. However, regional differences in price changes of manufactured products or technological change would not show up in these comparisons as regional effects since either would affect wages and value-added minus wages proportionally (see the appendix to this chapter).

Thus, both in agriculture and in manufacturing, we find that differences in labor income at a given point in time are significantly associated with differences in the marginal productivity of labor, and that differences in rates of change of labor income are significantly associated with differences in rates of change in marginal labor productivity. For agriculture, differences in productivity can be related directly to differences in capital per worker, measured by the value of land and buildings per worker. For manufacturing, we have no direct measures of capital per worker for the years since 1919, but examination of data for 1919 suggests that value-added minus wages per worker varies directly with capital per worker. Value-added minus wages per worker and its change over time were found to be significantly associated with differences in wages and differences in the rates of change in wages, respectively. Once differences in the marginal productivity of labor are taken into account, our results reveal no evidence of systematic regional variation in labor income at a given point of time or in changes in labor income over time, as would be expected if other variables were important in accounting for regional differences. Other such variables, however, may be related to the variations in labor income *within* regions, and there is good reason to believe that such is the case.

TECHNICAL APPENDIX

In this short appendix we shall demonstrate some of the assertions made in this and the preceding chapter. First, consider the case of agriculture. Let Y be the total agricultural output for the state, L be the number of workers employed, K be the amount of capital used in production, and O be the amount of all other factors affecting output (we could consider them separately with no essential change in the argument). If the production function for agriculture is linear in the logarithms of output and the various inputs, and exhibits constant returns to scale, we have:

(1) $Y = a_0 L^{a_1} K^{a_2} O^{a_3}$, where $a_1 + a_2 + a_3 = 1$.

The wage per worker, w, is equal to the marginal product of labor in value terms assuming competitive conditions in the product and factor markets; so where p is the price per unit of output received in the state:

(2) $\dfrac{\partial Y}{\partial L} = a_1 a_0 L^{a_1-1} K^{a_2} O^{a_3} = a_1 \dfrac{Y}{L}$ and

$w = p \dfrac{\partial Y}{\partial L} = a_1 p \dfrac{Y}{L}$, that is, under the conditions assumed here, the wage per worker is proportional to the average product per worker in value terms. The latter depends upon the price received for farm products in the state and upon the proportions with which labor is combined with capital and other factors, if any, in production. From (1) it follows that:

(3) $p \dfrac{Y}{L} = p \, a_0 \, (K/L)^{a2} \, (O/L)^{a3}$ or

(4) $\log p \dfrac{Y}{L} = \log p + \log a_0 + a_2 \log (K/L) + a_3 \log (O/L)$.

Equation (4) states that the logarithm of output per worker, which is equal to the logarithm of the wage per worker except for an additive constant, is a linear function of the logarithms of prices, capital per worker, and other factors per worker. (Since we use the value of land and buildings as a measure of capital inputs, the other factors variable might be interpreted as including other capital inputs.) We also see that if the production function differed systematically among regions, both the intercept and the slope of the relation between output per worker and value of land and buildings per worker would be different for different regions. Likewise, if other factors influenced labor productivity and these factors took different mean values in different regions, the intercept of the relation between output per worker and value of land and buildings per worker would differ among regions.

In considering changes in output per worker over time, suppose that the production function (1) is unchanged over time except that the constant a_0 may increase because of changes in technology. Then in the initial and final years of the period being considered, call these i and f, respectively, an equation such as (4) would determine output per worker. Subtracting and rearranging:

(5) $\log \left(\dfrac{p \, Y/L}{p \, Y/L} \right)^{f}_{i}$

$= \log \dfrac{p_f}{p_i} + \log \dfrac{a_{0f}}{a_{0i}} + a_2 \log \left(\dfrac{K/L}{K/L} \right)^{f}_{i} + a_3 \log \left(\dfrac{O/L}{O/L} \right)^{f}_{i}$.

Thus, from (5) we would expect that differential change among states in output per worker would be related to differential change in capital per worker. Other factors that might influence changes in output per worker are changes in prices received for farm products in different states—the "terms of trade"—and differential change in technology and in other factors of production.

Now consider manufacturing. Because we have no estimates of capital in manufacturing by state for recent years we must adopt a different approach than for agriculture. Again let the symbol Y equal manufacturing output and the symbol L equal labor input in production worker man-hours or in workers per year. Let K stand for capital input and O for all other factors of production whose returns are included in value added by manufacture. Let M be the quantity of material and power inputs, the returns to which are excluded from value added, and X stand for all factors external to the firm which affect the firm's output and are responsible for any external economies. Let the production function for manufacturing be linear in the logarithms of output and the several inputs:

$$(6) \quad Y = a_0 \, L^{a_1} \, K^{a_2} \, O^{a_3} \, M^{a_4} \, X^{a_5}, \text{ where } \sum_{1}^{5} a_i = 1 \, .$$

Since we have included all the possible factors that might affect the output of the firm, (6) is homogeneous of degree one and can be rewritten:

$$(7) \quad (Y/L) = a_0 \, (K/L)^{a_2} \, (O/L)^{a_3} \, (M/L)^{a_4} \, (X/L)^{a_5} \, .$$

Now let the symbol V stand for value added and V′ for value added minus wages. If all factors, except external factors, receive their marginal product we have:

$$(8) \quad w = p \, \frac{\partial Y}{\partial L} = a_1 \, p \, \frac{Y}{L} \text{ and } m = p \, \frac{\partial Y}{\partial M} = a_4 \, p \, \frac{Y}{M} \, ,$$

where w stands for wages per man-hour or per worker, depending upon how L is defined, m is the price per unit of material and power inputs, and p is the price received per unit of output. Then we have:

$$(9) \quad V = pY - mM = (1 - a_4) \, pY \text{ and } V' = V - wL = (1 - a_1 - a_4) \, pY \, .$$

Thus, value-added minus wages per man-hour or per worker is:

$$(10) \quad (V'/L) = (1 - a_1 - a_4) \, (pY/L) \, .$$

Equation (10) states that value-added minus wages per worker varies proportionally with the value of output per worker, as does the wage per worker. Value of output per worker as seen by multiplying both members of (7) by p, depends upon the price received per unit of output and upon the quantities of capital, other factors, materials and power, and external factors relative to the amount of labor employed.

From (8) and (10),

$$(11) \quad (V'/L) = \frac{(1 - a_1 - a_4)}{a_1} \, w, \text{ or}$$

$$(12) \quad \log (V'/L = \log \frac{(1 - a_1 - a_4)}{a_1} + \log w \, .$$

Equation (12) states that the logarithms of value-added minus wages per worker and wages per worker differ only by an additive constant, which depends upon the parameters of the production function, and that the slope of the relation between the two should be equal to unity. Also, if the parameters of the production function (7) differ as among regions, we would expect that the intercept of (12) would differ as among regions.

Finally, consider changes in manufacturing over time. Again let the symbols i and f as subscripts stand for the initial and final periods being compared. If the a's in the production function remain unchanged over time, except for a_0 if a time factor representing technological change is included, we have:

$$(13) \quad w_f/w_i = \left(\frac{V'}{L}\right) f \Big/ \left(\frac{V'}{L}\right) i \, .$$

Equation (13) states that, under these conditions, the ratio of wages in the final to the initial period is equal to the ratio of value-added minus wages in the final to the initial period. Thus, we need not take logarithms of these rates of change. Again we would expect the slope of the relation to be unity. Provided the a's remain unchanged, the constant term cancels out; the a's might change, however, for an aggregate of industries such as all manufacturing if the composition of industries changed, even if for each separate industry the a's remained unchanged. Both members of (13) vary with the ratio of output per worker in the final to the initial period; an additional factor now affecting output per worker is the time factor T representing technological change. Since the latter operates so as to affect both members of (13) equally, a differential impact of technological change between regions would not be revealed by the comparison of changes in wages with change in value-added minus wages. Likewise, if the price received for manufacturing products, p, were to increase more rapidly in some states than in others, both members of equation (13) would be affected in the same proportion.

33 / Migration and income

We have made a number of references to the ways in which per capita income is related to population numbers, characteristics, and movements. Thus, we have noted the influence on per capita income of the ratio of productive workers to total population within a given region, the influence of the population structure particularly with regard to racial composition and residence, and the influence of labor supply and price (by way of the capital-labor ratio and labor productivity).

What becomes evident from a review of population-income relationships in the various regions of the country is that large numbers and high rates of population growth have quite different effects under different economic circumstances. Where job opportunities are expanding rapidly, population growth can itself be a force for growth in per capita income; but where job opportunities are not expanding at all or expanding only slowly, it may well have an opposite effect.

Here we are dealing with factors and interrelationships of seemingly endless complexity, and while some parts of the picture can be brought into focus rather sharply, the larger picture introduces so many unresolved questions that we can deal with it in only a generalized and speculative manner. It seems evident, however, that the rapidity with which new and better-paying job opportunities are introduced within an area sets the range within which population growth can be absorbed at the same time that per capita income levels are increased.

Conceivably, low wage levels and large numbers of unemployed or under-employed workers in a given area (say, a Southeastern state) might attract industry and capital investment in sufficient volume to bring the per capita income level up to the national average. However, industrial location has a logic of its own; for many industries, closeness to national or major regional markets or to input sources may carry more weight than lower wage levels in the final locational decisions. It is not a foregone conclusion, therefore, that the inflow of capital and the creation of job opportunities will be fully adequate to absorb the natural increase in labor force and effect any significant improvement in living levels.

A sizeable number of industries might well be attracted to the area over a certain period of time. Yet the demand for labor which is generated might still not be enough to absorb the labor force at wage rates comparable to the national average for the categories of labor involved. Then not only would the "surplus" of labor persist, but the tendency for per capita income to be relatively low in this area would be reinforced by the fact that the industries coming in would have an incentive to use more labor and less capital than in higher-wage areas of the country.

Under such circumstance, migration out of the area might serve to raise average wages and per capita income. One can conjecture that the amount of out-migration required to bring wages and income within a given area close to national averages would depend on many factors, and that important among them would be:

1) the rate of natural increase in population, and of in-migration if any;

2) the ratio of labor force to population and the number of new entrants into the labor force;

3) the existing amount of unemployment and underemployment;

4) the extent of the decline in the demand for labor as a result of mechanization and related technological and organizational changes;

5) the rate at which new job opportunities are being created (including opportunities for the earning of supplemental income, as in the case of off-farm work and work for more than one member of the family).[1]

Aside from population numbers, of course, there are significant qualitative considerations to be taken into account. The over-all effect of migration upon per capital income levels can be expected to vary with the characteristics of those who leave the area and of those who remain behind—whether they are in the labor force or not and whether they are older or younger persons, skilled or unskilled, white or non-white, and so on. The numbers-quality aspects are inter-related in a highly complicated fashion. One suspects that there are always both gains and losses income-wise and that the net result evolves in a highly dynamic fashion. Thus, for example, the characteristics of the out-migrants will influence the over-all productivity level of the community, the nature of the local market (e.g., the demand for new homes and other new-family-oriented purchases), the costs of public services—such as education—and the ability of the community to finance them. What happens to the spirit of a community or region under the impact of out-migration is also no small matter. The qualitative aspects are extremely elusive and hard to evaluate, but some useful things can be said about numbers.

One feature of the movement of persons within the continental United States that seems to play a major role in the population-income relationship has to do with certain basic differences between in-migration and out-migration situations. When a region offers unusually attractive job (and living) opportunities, and when it can absorb new labor force from outside its borders at relatively high wages, it can and does draw persons from many parts of the nation. Even if only small numbers should come from each of the various outside states,

---

[1] Cf. Vernon W. Ruttan, "The Impact of Urban-Industrial Development on Agriculture in the Tennessee Valley and the Southeast," *Papers and Proceedings of the Regional Science Association*, Vol. 1 (1955), pp. R1-R14. Our own data indicate that off-farm employment plays a larger role in the Southeast than in any other part of the country.

Table 198. Regional real income per capita, 1880–1950, weighted average of state incomes per capita, 1929 dollars

(Percentage of national average in parentheses)

	1880			1900			1920			1930			1940			1950	
		$	%		$	%		$	%		$	%		$	%		$	%
F.W.		638.2	(211.3)	F.W.	674.6	(162.9)	M.A.	780.6	(135.1)	M.A.	912.9	(142.6)	M.A.	965.8	(132.8)	F.W.	1279.4	(120.4)
MT.		501.5	(166.0)	MT.	601.0	(145.2)	F.W.	772.5	(133.7)	F.W.	837.0	(130.8)	F.W.	959.7	(131.9)	M.A.	1255.2	(118.1)
N.E.		425.0	(140.7)	M.A.	570.2	(137.7)	N.E.	719.3	(124.4)	N.E.	826.7	(129.2)	N.E.	925.4	(127.2)	G.L.	1183.9	(111.4)
M.A.		422.8	(140.0)	N.E.	551.7	(133.3)	G.L.	623.5	(107.9)	G.L.	701.6	(109.6)	G.L.	815.4	(112.1)	N.E.	1160.4	(109.2)
G.L.		307.4	(101.8)	G.L.	439.6	(106.2)	MT.	590.7	(102.2)									
U.S.		302.1		U.S.	414.0		U.S.	578.0		U.S.	640.0		U.S.	727.4		U.S.	1062.7	
PL.		271.2	(89.8)	PL.	401.5	(97.0)	PL.	501.0	(86.7)	MT.	551.8	(86.2)	MT.	649.2	(89.2)	MT.	1017.8	(95.8)
S.W.ᵃ		182.7	(60.5)	S.W.	283.2	(68.4)	S.W.	466.2	(80.7)	PL.	523.1	(81.7)	PL.	590.5	(81.2)	PL.	1003.6	(94.4)
S.E.ᵃ		150.6	(49.9)	S.E.	197.7	(47.8)	S.E.	326.2	(56.4)	S.W.	411.3	(64.3)	S.W.	511.0	(70.2)	S.W.	916.6	(86.3)
										S.E.	321.0	(50.2)	S.E.	419.3	(57.6)	S.E.	719.2	(67.7)

[a]Louisiana in the Southeast region throughout.

Deflators: 1929 = 100

1880—57.3	1920—121.2	1940— 81.8
1900—48.9	1930— 97.5	1950—140.3

1880–1920 are GNP deflators used by Easterlin.
1930–1950 are based on BLS Consumers Price Index, Stat. Abstract 1958, Table 419.

SOURCE: Same as for Table 9.

the cumulative in-migration can be large. Quite a different situation obtains in a region which, in terms of relative job and income opportunities, is "over-populated." All the personal migration decisions must be made within the one area. Thus, the proportion of persons who are willing to leave the area to improve their economic situation becomes a critical factor. For the region that can absorb in-migrants, the characteristics of the resident population are not significant; it can draw migration-prone persons from anywhere and every-where (including other high-income areas). This suggests that migrants are likely to keep arriving into a region offering unusually attractive wages until the interregional wage differential is dampened, but that out-migration from any given area will not always be at the volume and rate called for by the objective situation (i.e., the wage and income differentials). In other words, under the the conditions existing in the continental United States, no one region can long be far ahead of all the others in its wage and income levels, but any one region *can* continue to be at per capita income levels well below the national average.

The Historical Record

The historical data suggest population-income adjustments within and among the various regions that cover a range from quite sensitive adjust-ments to fairly inadequate adjustments, following the pattern suggested above. Table 198 shows regional real income per capita over the period 1880 to 1950 as a percentage of the national average. The data here highlight the rapid convergence downward of the high income regions over this period, and especially between 1880 and 1920. The Far West's per capita income dropped from 211% of the national average in 1880 to only 135% in 1920; since 1920 it has come even closer to the national average (120% in 1950 and 118.7% in 1957). The downward convergence in the Mountain region was even sharper —from 166% of the national average in 1880 to 102% in 1920; since 1920, per capita income in this region has been below the national average.

On the other side, the upward convergence of per capita income in the South-east between 1880 and 1940 was quite unimpressive—from 50% of the national average to 58%—and even today the average is still well below the national average (32% below in 1950 and 30% below in 1957).

Viewed in relation to the data in Table 198, the data in Table 199 are instruc-tive with regard to the broad migration patterns. Thus, for example, net in-migration continued into the Mountain region until about 1920, when per capita income in the region had converged to the national average. By contrast, the movement into the Plains—where per capita income was already below the national average by 1880—was much more limited during the latter part of the 19th century, and by the last decade of the century gave way to a net outward movement. The continuous growth of income-earning opportunities in the Far West has attracted migrants in every decade of the period covered; and although the inflow of persons has served to dampen the wage levels, unlike the other regions of the West, the Far West continues to attract investment in sufficient volume to maintain an above-average wage level. The Northeast (the New England, Middle Atlantic, and Great Lakes regions), with per capita incomes which over-all are more or less representative of the national average for the industrial sections of the country, continues to attract migrants—mainly from the South—but in relatively small numbers.[2]

Table 199. Net regional migration per 1000 average population, 1870-1950

	1870-80	1880-90	1890-00	1900-10	1910-20	1920-30	1930-40	1940-50
N.E.	42	102	107	91	48	4	− 6	− 1
M.A.	14	75	82	113	47	54	12	5
G.L.	3	37	46	33	72	55	− 4	13
S.E.	− 18	− 26	− 39	− 33	− 47	− 64	− 23	− 58
Pl.	210	170	− 10	− 9	− 26	− 56	− 46	− 73
S.W.	311	98	249	176	41	27	− 39	− 10
Mt.	695	548	196	289	96	− 74	− 11	− 13
F.W.	282	396	160	481	220	307	145	284

SOURCE: Lee, Miller, Brainerd, and Easterlin, *Population Redistribution and Economic Growth, United States, 1870–1950* (Philadelphia: American Philosophical Society, 1957), Table P–1, pp. 107-231. (See pp. 54-55 on "Negroes.")

The complexities of the population-income relationship are too great, and the data too gross, for the historical materials to do more than suggest in a general way, first, that the movements have on the whole been into the areas with expanding income-earning opportunities and out of the areas with relatively limited opportunities and, second, that the forces working for convergence of regional per capita incomes *downward* toward the national average seem to work more powerfully and consistently than those working for movement *upward* toward the national average.[3]

[2]A more detailed description of the population-income relationship is presented in Chapter 17 of Part III, with a focus on the regional *shares of population and income* (i.e., percentages of national totals at various census years). These data serve to throw light on the changing levels of living in the various (multi-state) regions of the country during the period of rapid national growth after 1870.

[3]There is a simple but important point to which we want to bring attention in passing. One must always be aware of the fact that there is a significant difference between focusing attention on income in a given area (either at one point in time or over a period of time) and focusing attention on income over a period of time of families *originally* coming from a given area. The families living in a given area at one period may all leave for other parts of the country and thereby improve their income status, while their places are taken by families from neighboring areas who were worse off at the starting point. Thus, all the families involved may improve their income situation and yet, if the "filtering up" was diffused, only the poorest of the *areas* involved need necessarily show any net average income improvement. Although we do not have adequate data about the "filtering up" process, hypothesizing its existence is the only way by which certain regional income phenomena can be explained.

Migration From Farm Areas [4]

Our earlier discussion has highlighted the fact that in the United States today low per capita income is associated essentially with farming, particularly with farming in the South, and that this situation is largely a matter of under-employment or low over-all productivity of labor. The areas with the lowest per capita income are precisely the areas (1) where the rates of natural increase are highest, (2) where the products produced are products that tend to have a low income elasticity of demand, and (3) where increases in productivity are associated with a sharp reduction in the labor required for a given value of product. All these circumstances add up to what may justifiably be called areas of "surplus" labor, where outward migration becomes necessary if per capita income levels are to be improved or even maintained. To what extent have persons living in such areas responded to this situation? Data available for recent decades throw some light on this matter.

First, migration from farm areas has been subject to major cyclical variations. In the prosperous decade 1940-50, it was two and one-half times as great as in the preceding decade, when job opportunities in the nonfarm sectors were scarce as a result of the depression. During the 1930-40 decade, net migration was not sufficient to balance the high natural increases of the rural-farm population, which grew in numbers from 30,158,000 to 30,216,000 over the decade. But the high net migration of the 1940's reduced the rural-farm population to 23,077,000 (based on the old urban definition) by 1950.

Otis Dudley Duncan and his associates have examined the relationship of migration to levels of living in farm areas during these two decades by way of a sample of State Economic Areas. They found no evidence that increases in the Farm-Operator Family Level of Living (FOLL) were greater for areas with substantial out-migration over-all than for the average SEA during the 1930-1940 decade (if anything, the reverse appears to have been the case). Thus, migration did not help to equalize levels of living in the manner expected. Even for 1940-50, there was only a small association between the relative amount of out-migration and increases in the Farm-Operator Family Level of Living.

Duncan explains the findings as follows: The correlation between deviations from the inter-annual regression of 1950 on 1940 FOLL index and the 1940-50 net migration rate was —.19, not quite significant at the 0.05 level of probability, but in conformity with the assumption that areas experiencing rapid out-migration improved their levels of living more rapidly than the national average. The small magnitude of the correlation suggests—if accepted at face value—that the effect of migration in equalizing levels of living among agricultural areas was slight. It is perfectly possible, therefore, for migration to flow disproportionately from areas of low levels of living without reducing appreciably the relative disadvantage of such areas. In part, this

[4]Most of the factors considered in this section on farm areas hold equally well for other types of areas which are subject to secular unemployment and underemployment (relatively low productivity of labor)—such as mining and some textile areas, so that it seems appropriate to concentrate on the major areas in this category—the agricultural areas.

is explained by the fact that areas with low levels of living generally have higher rates of natural increase than those with higher levels of living and must, therefore, have higher out-migration rates to get equal relief from population pressure.

Data for the 1940-50 decade demonstrate the independent effect of natural increase as a source of population pressure. On the basis of the age distribution of the 1940 rural-farm male population, it is possible to calculate the expected number of males of working age in 1950, assuming an applicable set of mortality rates, no migration, and an allowance for older males reaching retirement age. The "replacement ratio" is defined as the ratio of the expected number of entrants into selected working ages (in this case, 25-69) during a decade per 100 expected departures from these ages during the same decade through death or attaining retirement age. The ratio is an index of the potential replacement if no net migration occurs into or out of an area. In theory, the higher the replacement ratio, the greater the impetus to migration, assuming that economic opportunities for the surplus over exact replacement must be found outside the area.

The correlation between the 1940-50 net migration rate and the 1940-50 replacement ratio [5] was —.57, approximately the same absolute magnitude as the correlation between FOLL and net migration for this decade.

When combined, the level of living of a given area (the FOLL index) and the replacement ratio explain 42% of the variance in net migration rates ($r = .65$). Within the combination both FOLL and the replacement ratio make separate significant contributions.[6] The following illustrative data compare net migration rates expected on the basis of FOLL and replacement ratios with the rates that were actually observed. It is evident from this analysis that population pressure, as a determinant of migration, has two aspects: the relative disadvantage of an area in terms of its level of living, and its potential population growth from natural increase. Inasmuch as high natural increase typically occurs in association with low levels of living, the two factors reinforce one another in impelling migration—or, if migration is blocked off, in generating unrelieved population pressure.

Not much is added to the explanation of the net migration of the rural-farm population by taking into account indexes of population distribution in space. Net migration rates correlated significantly with two nodal factors—closeness to the major centers of population (the population potential) and closeness to a metropolis. However, when the effects of the replacement ratio and FOLL index were taken into account, the relationship of these two nodal factors became insignificant. Population potential was significantly associated with rural-farm

[5]Data taken from Gladys K. Bowles and Conrad Taeuber, "Rural-Farm Males Entering and Leaving Working Ages, 1940-50 and 1950-60," *Farm Population*, Series Census-AMS (P-27), No. 22 (August 1956).

[6]If the FOLL index (X_1) and the replacement ratio (X_2) are combined in a multiple regression to estimate the 1940-50 net migration rate (Y), the resulting equation is $_cY = - 19 + .100 X_1 - .103 X_2$. That each independent variable contributes separately to the explanation of the dependent variable is indicated by the partial correlations. The correlation between Y and X_1 holding constant X_2 is .37. The correlation between Y and X_2 holding constant X_1 is — .38.

Table 200. Illustrative migration rates, expected and observed

SEA		FOLL 1940	Replacement ratio 1940-50	Rural farm net migration rate 1940-50	
				Expected	Observed
Illinois	1	142	150	−20.2	−20.5
Georgia	3	36	193	−35.3	−31.3
Montana	2a	84	136	−24.6	−27.4
Wisconsin	5	90	146	−25.0	−26.3

net migration rates, $r=.21$. There is a slight but significant tendency for areas with low population potential to have comparatively greater out-migrations for the 1940-50 decade. Such areas, however, are also typified by higher replacement ratios and lower levels of living. Net migration rates also correlated significantly with distance to metropolitan center, $r=.29$. When population potential and closeness to a metropolitan center were combined with FOLL and the replacement ratio, the result was little better than that obtained by using FOLL and the replacement ratio in combination. Together, these two variables explained 42% of the variance in net migration rates. When the nodal indexes were added, it was possible to explain 45% of the variance in migration. Analysis of the effect of each variable within the combination revealed that only FOLL and the replacement ratio were having a significant effect; the contribution of the nodal indexes was not significant.

This analysis suggests, at least for the 1940-50 decade, that the migration of the rural-farm population was affected more by "push" factors in the form of low levels of living and relatively high population pressures than by the "pull" factors of accessibility to centers of population, assuming that the nodal variables provide an adequate index of accessibility for this purpose.

Both the movement out of farming and the movement out of farm areas were very high, on the whole, during the period 1940-50 (and have also been since that date), the rates in the movement out of farming running as high as 90% in some of the Southeastern states. This suggests that it is not *lack* of movement out of agriculture and agricultural areas that is the basic difficulty, but rather that the magnitude of out-migration—even though very great—is not sufficient to obtain equality of income for farm people under the existing circumstances, particularly given the very high replacement rates in the poorer agricultural areas.

Charles H. Berry highlights this in a recent study.[7] Between 1940 and 1950, he shows, some 465,000 persons left agriculture in Alabama and some 453,000 persons in Mississippi. This amounted to a rate of movement out of farming of 93.4% in Alabama and 84% in Mississippi during this decade. However, the rural-farm replacement rate during this same decade was 203% in Alabama

[7]Charles H. Berry, *Occupational Migration from Agriculture* (unpublished Ph.D. dissertation, University of Chicago, no date available on microfilm).

and 181% in Mississippi. (By comparison, New York State has a replacement rate of 115%, Ohio of 138%, and California of 122%.) Altogether, then, farm employment in Alabama declined by only some 127,000 persons—a decrease of 25%; in Mississippi, the total reduction in employment was 142,000 persons— an over-all reduction rate of 26%.[8]

In some instances, the rural-farm replacement rates were even higher than in Alabama and Mississippi, thus offsetting to an even greater degree very high rates of movement out of agriculture. The replacement rate in North Carolina was 217% and in South Carolina, 215%. That is, the number of young persons entering the agricultural labor force was more than double the number required to replace retiring farm workers and maintain the farm labor force at existing levels. In North Carolina, where over a half million persons left farming, the actual net reduction—because of replacement—was only 65,000 persons, a rate of decrease of only 11%.

Clearly, then, the number of persons who leave agriculture is not by itself the determining factor; the replacement rate must be taken into consideration.[9] Translated into geographic terms, a predominantly agricultural region may continue to be subject to underemployment and limited improvements in income levels, despite substantial out-migration, as long as birth rates continue relatively high and there is a "filtering up" process (with the same size farms merely changing hands).

Berry has tested a number of variables that have been advanced to explain the varied rates of "occupational migration" from agriculture for employment elsewhere, including the level of labor income in agriculture, the change in farm income (from 1940 to 1950), the age structure of the population, the ratio of farm employment to total employment in the area considered, the schooling of adults, the ratio of non-white to total farm employment, and the proportion of hired farm workers.

His findings indicate that, for the 1940-50 decade, the most important variable in the analysis of mobility was *age*; that is, the greater the proportion of young farm workers (aged 15-24) in the farm population in 1940, the greater the rate of farm labor exodus from agriculture during the ensuing ten years. There are well-known reasons why younger persons tend to out-migrate more readily than older persons. One is the lower earnings of the younger persons. Another is the deeper roots that the older persons have in the area. And a third is the greater ability of the younger persons to obtain jobs in new occupations. In fact, the difficulty of an older farmer to get a nonfarm job—except in periods of extreme labor shortage—may be one of the main reasons for the inadequate migration from the poor farm areas.[10]

[8]The rate base is the mean number of persons who would have been employed in agriculture during the 1940-50 decade had there been no occupational migration to or from agriculture during the decade. *Ibid.* Table 2, pp. 18-20.

[9]The relationship between poverty and relatively high fertility rates is too well known to require comment here.

[10]Berry makes this useful observation, in the face of his findings regarding the clear relationship between age and the rate of mobility from agricultural employment, suggesting that the bulk of the farm migrants are young. "These younger migrants could have been

Berry found income level to be a significant factor in influencing migration from farming, but not quantitatively as important as age. However, *changing* levels of income during the ten-year period were largely ignored in the migration decision of farm workers (or the changes were insufficiently varied regionally to be quantitatively important in the analysis). No relationship was observed between migration and the industrial character of the area as reflected in the ratio of farm to nonfarm employment. This again suggests the possible importance of the "push" factor as against the "pull." (Although, as Berry points out, the finding may be largely a reflection of the inadequacy of the variable used to describe the extent of outside opportunity.) Education, race, and farm ownership do not appear to compete strongly with age and farm income level in determining occupational migration from agriculture, when the whole nation is considered. The race factor, however, would seem to be significant in the Southeastern states taken by themselves.[11]

Migration, Plus . . .

Out-migration from farm areas, even if involving reductions in total numbers, cannot be expected by itself necessarily to increase levels of living within such areas. The out-migration would normally have to be accompanied by a number of changes—such as the creation of larger farms, a higher ratio of capital inputs, or a more efficient use of labor—which add up to a higher productivity per farm worker.[12] This is highlighted by the Duncan data for State Economic Areas examining the relationship between differential change in Farm-Operator Family Level-of-Living Indexes for the 25-year interval between 1930 and 1954 and differential change in a number of selected explanatory factors (such as size of farm, % of farmland in cropland, % tenants, value of farm, etc.). It was

influenced by factors such as distance to nonfarm jobs, education, race, and the nature of their farm employment opportunities, yet, when all migrants are considered as a whole, these relationships might not be evident if older migrants reacted differently or to different incentives. A check against this possibility could be made, and in view of the importance of the age factor should be made, by computing migration rates separately for two or more age classes and then repeating the analysis of this dissertation separately for each age class. The hypothesis that different age groups of the farm population react differently to the incentives responsible for occupational migration from agriculture would then be tested. The impact of income would be more completely determined, the significance of the other variables of the analysis could be more carefully investigated, and the impact of age would also be more clearly shown." *Ibid.*, p. 65.

[11] Eleanor H. Bernert, *County Variation in Net Migration from the Rural Farm Population, 1930-1940* (Washington, D. C.: United States Government Printing Office, 1944) and *Volume and Composition of Net Migration from the Rural Farm Population, 1930-1940* (Washington, D. C.: United States Government Printing Office, 1944); Gladys K. Bowles, *Migration Patterns of the Rural Farm Population, Thirteen Economic Regions of the United States, 1940-1950* (Washington, D. C.: United States Government Printing Office, 1955).

[12] In poor farm areas, there may be serious hurdles to the accomplishment of such changes, e.g., existing land tenure institutions, inadequacy of farm credit for certain purposes, limited knowledge concerning advanced methods of farming, and even lack of strong motivation for economic accomplishment.

found, not unexpectedly, that two factors—differential change in average size of farm and change in value of land and buildings per farm—were capable of explaining a sizeable share of the variation in differential change in FOLL indexes. In other words, the areas in which farmers enlarged their farms and in other ways invested capital were the areas that on the whole enjoyed the greatest increases in levels of living.

A very high replacement rate within a farm area and/or an inability on the part of farmers to raise productivity substantially (for whatever reasons) can be expected to result in painfully slow increases in family levels of living. It is significant in this respect that, as a matter of fact, Farm-Operator Family Level-of-Living Indexes have been highly stable in their distribution or areal pattern. That is, an area which is relatively low in level of living in one year is very likely to be relatively low several years later. The correlation between the 1930 FOLL index and the 1954 FOLL index for the 346 non-metropolitan State Economic Areas was .92. There would seem to have been few changes in the relative standing of SEA's with respect to level of living of the agricultural population—notwithstanding the heavy out-migration from the poorer agricultural areas. Between 1930 and 1954 there *was* a tendency for the poorer areas to experience somewhat greater absolute changes in level of living. However, the difference in absolute change in level of living between "poor" as opposed to "wealthy" areas was quite slight. Thus, if the 1930-54 differences in change in FOLL were to hold in the future, it would take an area with a FOLL index of 50 in 1930 (the national average being 100) more than 350 years to catch up to one with an index of 150.[13]

---

[13]This figure is used only to illustrate the modest nature of the difference in relative change in level of living over the actual period studied and, of course, is not a forecast.

34 / Regions and income:

A SUMMARY

Our inquiry into interstate differentials in per capita personal income has provided some answers to two key questions: (1) what are the determinants of income differentials, and (2) have these differentials declined or increased over time, and why? The attempt to get at the problem of wide income differences—given the highly complex, inter-related, and fluid nature of our economy—has involved us in a long and fairly technical search.

Regional Income Determinants

Differences in each of the major types of income contribute to the per capita income differentials among the states. The most variable of all income components is property income per capita. In 1950 (the census year on which we focused attention), it ranged from $519 (in Delaware) to $58 (in Mississippi); its relative variation among the states[1] was twice that of total income per capita. High levels of property income are concentrated in the northeastern part of the country—the New England, Middle Atlantic, and Great Lakes states. However, property income contributes on the average only one-eighth of total personal income, so that actually its contribution to income differentials is modest. Transfer payments (pensions, social security payments, and the like) are an even smaller part of total income and therefore have little influence over-all on average levels of living. Of the major income components, it is "participation income"—wages and salaries and other labor income, plus income of unincorporated enterprises—that is the main contributor to state per capita income differentials.

The analysis of interstate differences in per capita participation income points to two key determinants: per cent of population employed and average earnings of employed persons. In states of high participation income, a relatively large proportion of the population is found to be 14 years or older and a high proportion of this group is in the labor force. The fact that

[1] The standard deviation divided by the mean of the state data.

the populations of the poorer states include a larger percentage of children is no small matter income-wise. When participation income is expressed in terms of persons *employed* rather than in terms of population, the relative variation of per capita income among the states (the standard deviation divided by the mean of the state data) drops from 22.4% to 17.6%.

Place of residence and color greatly influence income levels. This is shown by the 1949 Census income data (the only such data available). Average incomes varied less by state for urban and rural nonfarm persons than for rural farm persons and less for white than for nonwhite persons. For example, the median income of all persons in the Southeast averaged about 43% below those of persons in the Lakes states, but for white urban and rural nonfarm persons it averaged only about 24% less. An especially interesting finding is that, except for the Southeast, there was relatively little regional variation in the incomes received by white farm persons.

Color thus emerges as an extremely important factor in income levels and in interstate income differentials. Its role is especially striking in the Southeast farm sector. In 1949 the median income of rural farm nonwhites in the Southeast was only $485 compared with $933 for rural farm whites. Great, if less striking, differences appear in the nonfarm sectors and in other regions. For example, in the case of urban and rural nonfarm persons in the Middle Atlantic region, the median income of nonwhites was $1,344 compared with $2,330 for whites, or 42% less. When account is taken of differences in education, occupation, etc., among the races, it strongly appears that the white-Negro income differentials can only be explained by racial discrimination.

The census data also indicate that incomes received vary directly with the size of place in which the recipient lives, with higher income levels generally found in the larger cities. In addition, income differentials were found to be larger among small cities than among bigger ones. For example, for white males residing in cities over 500,000 population, incomes in the Southeastern states averaged only about 10% below those in the Lakes states. For cities of 100,000 to 250,000 population, however, this differential was almost 17%. This finding raises some interesting questions: Do our large cities offer more equal opportunities in general than do the smaller ones? Over time, will incomes tend to become more equal for residents of large cities than for those of smaller ones? We will have some additional insights on these questions when the 1960 Census data are available, and comparisons over time can be made.

The relationship between the relative importance of various kinds of economic activities within a state and its relative level of per capita income is also worth noting. For the nation as a whole, the states with the largest proportion of persons working in farming generally have lower average per capita incomes than the states in which manufacturing and service activities predominate. However, farm persons are influenced by the proportion of workers in agriculture within a state in a different way than are urban and rural nonfarm persons. For the latter group, higher incomes are found where farming is less important, and this holds both North and South. For the farmers, however, the situation seems to be different, with substantial differences between the North and South. For the sixteen Southern (i.e., Southeastern and Southwestern) states taken as a separate unit, average income of farmers was found to be highly correlated with the relative importance of farming within the state. For the other thirty-two states, however, no such correlation appeared. In the North and West, the farmers in the states in which farmers make up a large proportion of the total labor force were no worse off—taken as a whole—than their counterparts in the states where farming was less important and other activities more important. As a matter of fact, in some of the Northern and Western regions—when account is taken of the differences in the cost of living on and off the farm—the income of farmers is comparable to those of the nonfarm families. Thus, if price adjustments are made for commodities consumed by farm families, the 1949 *real* income of farm and nonfarm persons in New England, the Plains, and the Mountain region were roughly comparable. In the Southeast, by contrast, the median income of white urban and rural nonfarm persons was about one and a half times as great as that of white rural farm persons.

There is a positive association between income levels and the relative importance of manufacturing employment within a state. This arises from the fact that the incomes of urban and rural nonfarm persons in states where a relatively high proportion of the labor force is in manufacturing tend to be higher than their counterparts in states with less manufacturing employment. However, the incomes of rural farm persons do not seem to be affected (or least did not in 1949) by the relative importance of manufacturing in the state.

Within manufacturing as an employment category, there is an important difference between "fabricating" and "processing" industries as far as effect on income levels is concerned. The 1949 data show a strong association between *fabricating* industries and relatively high per capita income levels. Persons living in areas with a large percentage of manufacturing employment in *processing* industries (those for which the products of agriculture and mining are important inputs) were found to have relatively low incomes. The fabricating industries are of course important in the Manufacturing Belt states and in the Far West, and these are the very areas with the highest incomes. Another noteworthy finding was that the level of state per capita income tends to be associated positively with the relative importance of employment in the business services (industries at least one-third of whose output is purchased by other than final consumers), but there was no significant association between income and employment in consumer services. These findings should be particularly interesting to those who have been assuming that a shift of employment to *any* type of manufacturing and *any* type of services within a state is a sure path to high income levels.

It is clear from the data that the average money wage in a state depends, in broadest terms, on the industrial and occupational composition of its labor force—that is, whether the major industries in the state provide low-paying or high-paying jobs. But wage levels, in turn, have an influence on the occupational and industrial structure of a state, so that these reinforce each other. Thus, the data indicate that in states where the average wage and salary earnings of workers are above the national average, workers tend to be concentrated in the higher paying occupations and industries. Moreover, in states in which average earnings are above the national average, the average earnings in *all* occupations and industries tend to be above the national average for that occupation or industry. In other words, workers in relatively high-wage industries, like chemicals, as well as workers in low-wage industries, like apparel or personal services, will usually get a lower wage for the same work in poor sections of the country as compared with the higher income states. Thus, it would seem that income effects are self-reinforcing in several ways: in terms of the types of industries attracted to a given state, the degree to which industries tend to be labor-intensive or capital-intensive, and the general wage levels set by local labor supply and demand conditions within a given labor market.

Among the many interrelated factors that determine differentials in wage levels and therefore in income generally, the two that stand out are (1) the marginal productivity of labor (or the relative value of the product that a worker will turn out on the average within a given period), and (2) the relationship between labor supply and the job opportunities available within given areas. The latter is highly influenced on the supply side by birth rates and migration; on the job-opportunity side, by the relative input-output access advantages for industry (as discussed in Parts II and IV of this book).

The marginal productivity of labor has a distinct bearing on interstate differentials in wage levels of workers in the same industry. In turn, marginal productivity differences appear to be related to differences in the proportion with which labor is combined with other factors, especially capital. This is true for both agriculture and manufacturing.

Output per worker in agriculture, which varies greatly in the different states, was found to be significantly associated with capital per worker (as measured by the value of land and buildings). Once variations in capital per worker are taken into account, no significant regional variation in output per worker can be detected. This helps to pinpoint an important aspect of the low-income problem. From this finding it can be inferred that, while at present the output per worker in agriculture is, for example, very low in the Southeast, the introduction of more capital into its agriculture (assuming of course that it is sensibly applied) is likely greatly to improve output and income per worker in that region.

Interstate differentials in labor income from manufacturing were also found to be highly associated with differentials in the marginal productivity of labor and this in turn, as in agriculture, to be associated with the amount of capital that labor had to work with. Once the differences in the relative amounts of capital and labor used in production were held constant as among regions, our results suggest that for most industries there is no evidence of any significant regional variation in production worker wages. This is not to minimize in any way the important role of certain qualitative aspects, such as the caliber of management, but rather serves to pinpoint what would seem to be a really critical element characterizing the relative "income-producing power" of industries in the various parts of the country. Also worth noting is the fact that the data reveal a significant tendency—with important exceptions in the West where natural resource orientation plays an especially important part in industrial composition—for the relative importance of employment in capital-intensive industries to vary directly with average hourly earning in manufacturing. Thus, differences in the factor endowments in the various states appear to influence labor incomes in manufacturing in two ways, through the location of the various types of manufacturing and through the marginal productivity of labor in each given type of industry.

Declining Regional Income Differences

Per capita income differentials among the states have declined since the end of World War I, but the force of income convergence has not been constant. From 1920 to 1929 relative differentials among the states in per capita income actually widened. From 1929 on, the forces of equalization have had the upper hand, particularly during the depression of the 1930's and World War II. Since 1947 income levels have continued to become more alike, but at a slower rate than during the preceding eighteen years. From 1929 to 1955 the relative interstate variation in per capita income fell from 36% to 23%.

Both property and participation income contributed to the decline in income differentials. Between 1920 and 1950, for example, property income increased only about 10% in real terms nationally, as compared with an increase of about 70% in participation income (mostly salaries and wages), and its relative variation among states fell slightly. More importantly, however, the relative variation of participation income per capita fell from 28% in 1920 to 22% in 1950. But over this same period, *absolute* differentials in participation income per capita (as measured by its standard deviation among states) increased by about 35%, from $190 to $256 (1950 dollars). This is a significant phenomenon.

Although per capita personal incomes among the different states have converged more closely toward the national average during 1929-55, (the period especially examined), *absolute* increases in real income were about the same everywhere. They were unrelated to the level of state per capita income in 1929 and did not differ significantly among regions. Furthermore, the rank order of the forty-eight states in per capita personal income was virtually unchanged from 1929 to 1955. Thus, despite the tendency toward equality of per capita incomes, in the Southeast—where per capita incomes are lowest —the increase relative to the national average since 1920 has been small compared with the income differential in either 1929 or 1955.

What contributed to the decline in income differentials? Perhaps the most important single factor pulling the per capita income of the Southeast and Southwest closer to the national average was the decline in agricultural employment in these regions. Thus it was found that in states where the proportion of the labor force employed in farming fell most from 1920 to 1950, per capita income increased the most. There was an even stronger tendency for per capita incomes to increase in states where the proportion of the labor force employed in manufacturing increased very rapidly.

During this period changes in labor incomes in both agriculture and manufacturing went hand in hand with changes in the marginal productivity of labor and in the relative use of capital. Thus, changes in agricultural output per worker were significantly related to changes in the value of land and buildings per worker. Except for the depression years, changes in manufacturing wages during 1919-55 were also significantly associated with changes in capital used. When capital was held constant, no significantly regional effects were found.

The historical record covering the years 1870 to 1950 suggests that people have tended to move away from low-income regions and toward higher-income areas. However, it would appear that migration has been more important in bringing about a downward convergence of per capita income in above-average-income regions than the reverse. Immigration into the Far West, for instance, appears to have kept per capita income from increasing faster than it otherwise would have done. About the same picture emerged in the Mountain region prior to 1920. By contrast, in the Southeast, out-migration, while taking place, was not rapid enough to bring about an upward convergence of incomes comparable in extent to the Far West's downward convergence. Farm areas with below-average incomes tended to have above-average out-migration from 1940 to 1950. However, a high population replacement rate or a high proportion of the labor force in the younger age groups was at least as important a factor leading to above-average out-migration from farm areas. It is not the lack of shift out of agriculture—which ran as high as 90% of the farm labor force in some states in 1940-50 (that is, the number of migrants out of the state during the decade was equal to 90% of the number of farmers shown by the 1940 Census)—but the magnitude of out-migration required to achieve income equality, coupled with high rates of population replacement in certain areas, that is the basic difficulty facing farm people.

In conclusion, interstate differentials in personal income have been declining ever since the end of World War I; absolute increases in real income were, however, about the same everywhere. Among the important determinants of per capita personal income in a region, the following stood out—per cent of population employed, average earnings of employed persons, place of residence, type of industrial employment, marginal labor productivity and capital per worker.

Some Policy Questions

The broad picture that emerges would seem to have the following features:

Structural changes in our highly dynamic national economy (associated with changes in taste, income elasticity of demand, labor productivity, and similar elements) set up the forces within which individual regions and local areas become more or less attractive for the investment of capital and the creation of new job opportunities and within which existing labor force can be supported at wage levels rising at rates comparable to the national average. While relative wage levels among different areas of the country are always a consideration in locational decisions made by the various industries, factors such as markets and material inputs are also very important in determining the location of new investment. Thus, the fact that wages within given regions have lagged behind those in other regions of the country, partly as a result of the structural changes under way, is not enough by itself to attract a large inflow of capital. Flows of capital, therefore, by themselves need not bring about an equilibrium in which wages for similar levels of skill are more or less comparable throughout the nation, even under circumstances where goods are freely traded among regions. Increments to the labor force within a given region, and even members of the existing labor force, will, therefore, not necessarily be fully employed and wage levels will be depressed. Under such circumstances, it is only through out-migration that upward pressures on wage levels can be exerted and per capita income raised.

Historically, the American people have shown a high degree of mobility, both occupationally and geographically. Wherever wages and salaries rose to unusually high levels, for whatever reasons, in-migrants could be expected to stream in until the wage levels settled at points not much above those characterizing other sections of the country with similar industrial structures. However, where significant secular changes in the industrial structure took place—and particularly where the number of agricultural workers that could be employed at high productivity levels declined—out-migration and related adjustments needed to raise productivity levels often have not occurred in sufficient volume to bring per capita income in such areas up to national averages. The adjustments have been made at a painfully slow rate; as a result, levels of living in agricultural areas in various parts of the country, but especially in the Southeast, continue to be substantially below the national average in spite of very heavy migration from farming and from farm areas.

The different reaction of farm persons during the prosperity years since 1940 as compared with the depression years of the 1930's suggests that, with a continuation of national prosperity, the magnitude of the low-income problem will *continue* to be reduced, if slowly. It is equally clear that if national or state policy were to aim seriously at a more rapid rate of improvement in the income levels of the poorer areas, rather substantial programs serving to influence migration and/or replacement rates, as well as programs to increase employment opportunities where economic and feasible, would be called for.

In recent years, and particularly since the end of World War II, localities, states, and regions have come increasingly to realize that there are useful measures that can be taken to attract industries and capital. This could be done in large part by building on the special natural and locational advantages of the area or by overcoming existing deficiencies. Thus, there have been efforts to improve the social overhead facilities and services—such as the provision of transport facilities and the establishment of industrial estates—thereby enhancing the play of external economies for different industries. There have been efforts to develop local material input sources through research and development activities, including experiments with new uses of local resources. There have been efforts centered on improving the skills of local labor as an attraction for industry. Some communities have improved their recreation facilities greatly, with the aim of becoming important recreation centers. The list is very long. Much of the effort is still in the pure publicity stage and, in general, a great deal remains to be learned about sensible and effective ways of enhancing the growth potentialities of a given area.

The population side of the equation has received very little if any attention in cases where industrial growth opportunities are obviously limited. Economic decline in an area is an extremely difficult thing to face, particularly in our growth-minded culture, and yet the relative decline of certain areas in the *volume* of economic activities is an inevitable feature of a rapidly changing economy. It seems important that we learn to face up to problems involved in declines in volume if we are to achieve the important objective of rapid increases in *family* levels of living, particularly for those currently in the lower income groups.

Statistical appendix

Source notes and tables:

historical data 1870-1950

Six principal series are used in the historical section of this study (Part III):

1) United States Population, 1870-1950, by States
2) Urban Population in the United States, 1870-1950, by States
3) Value-added by Manufacture, 1870-1950, by States
4) Personal Income, 1880-1950, by States
5) Labor Force, 10 years old and over, 1870-1950, by States
6) Gross Value of Extracted Resources, 1870-1950, by States

The first four of these six series are readily available in published form as follows:

1) 17th U. S. Census of Population, 1950, Vol. II, Part 1, Table 6; Lee, Miller, Brainerd, and Easterlin, *Population Redistribution and Economic Growth, United States, 1870-1950* (Philadelphia: American Philosophical Society, 1957), Table P-4A.
2) 17th U. S. Census of Population, 1950, Vol. II, Part 1, Table 15; Lee, Miller, Brainerd, and Easterlin, *op. cit.*, Tables P-4B and P-4C.
3) Lee, Miller, Brainerd, and Easterlin, *op. cit.*, Table M-8.
4) *Ibid.*, Table Y-1; C. F. Schwartz and R. E. Graham, Jr., *Personal Income by States since 1929*, Office of Business Economics, U. S. Department of Commerce (Washington: Government Printing Office, 1956), Table 1.

The other two, Labor Force, 10 years old and over, 1870-1950, by States, and Gross Value of Extracted Resources, 1870-1950, by States, are reproduced in Appendix Tables A1–A7 and B1–B5, respectively. The notes and sources for these tables are given below, prior to the tables.

Historical analysis of census data is complicated by frequent changes in census categories, definitions, and coverage. The occupational categories and definitions used in the enumeration of manufacturing workers, for example, were radically changed in 1899 to exclude the "hand trade industries"; an even greater difficulty is posed by the conceptual change from "gainful worker" to "labor force" after 1930. Complexity is further compounded by the fact of census miscounts, for example, the undercount of population in 13 Southern states in 1870 (mostly rural Negroes) and the unusually inclusive count of agricultural workers in 1910. Another census shortcoming, from the standpoint of historical study, is the fact that decennial counts do not permit of annual series which are necessary for the determination of points of inflection in cyclical and secular trends. Thus most of the series listed above are for intercensal intervals approximating decades but which in fact range from 9¾ to 10¼ years. Adjustments made as a consequence of these and many other census deficiencies are explained in the notes to Appendix Tables given below.[1]

There are certain compensatory features of the present study, nevertheless, which reduce the effects of distortion arising from the use of census materials. In the first place, it is an exploratory study concerned only with very broad relationships between industrial structures and economic growth; it focuses on four major categories of resource activities: agriculture, mineral extraction, forestry and logging, and fisheries. Manufactures and service activities are, for the most part, treated as gross categories of non-resource activities. Hence the many involved questions concerning definitions and coverage of particular manufactures and services do not arise. Secondly, although our spatial units (the states) are not homogeneous in shape or area, they are, for all practical purposes, unvarying throughout the period covered in this study. Historical and geographical facts represented by state boundaries, moreover, are part of the essential data of economic history however much they may vex the theoretician. Thirdly, because our concern is with the changing industrial structures of multi-state groups (regions) over long periods, the economic growth of intercensal years is subsumed in a series of "focal" years which extend over sufficiently long intervals, 1870-1910 and 1910-1950, to register leading secular movements and minimize the influence of short-run fluctuations. One further point warrants special mention: the choice of a particular source among a number of alternatives is governed by one over-riding criterion, namely, the extent to which it provides the most comprehensive breakdown by states of a given national total. There are a number of items for which revised and improved *national* totals exist; because of our concern with *state* and *regional* shares of the national total, however, we have been unable to use such improved figures except where their state components could be readily identified or inferred. More often we have had to be content with an unrevised total or have simply distributed the revised one according to the weight of state components indicated in the original census report. The whole operation of preparing consistent and comparable series for

---

[1]For a full explanation of these and other problems connected with the development of consistent and comparable historical series from census data, see, 16th U. S. Census, 1940, *Population*, "Comparative Occupation Statistics for the United States, 1870 to 1940," by A. M. Edwards (Washington: Government Printing Office, 1943). Also the invaluable commentary and results of E. S. Lee, A. R. Miller, C. P. Brainerd, and R. A. Easterlin, *op. cit.*, and the eight dittographed studies listed on page 1 of that volume. D. Carson, "Changes in the Industrial Composition of Manpower since the Civil War," *Studies in Income and Wealth*, Vol. XI, Pt. 1 (New York: National Bureau of Economic Research, 1949), pp. 46-134, for further commentary on the problems of developing historical series for the nation as a whole.

the period 1870-1950 has been greatly facilitated by the comprehensive and careful analyses made of census materials by the University of Pennsylvania group, E. S. Lee, A. R. Miller, C. P. Brainerd, and R. A. Easterlin, under the direction of Simon Kuznets and Dorothy S. Thomas, referred to above.

Appendix Tables A1–A7 Notes

LABOR FORCE, 10 YEARS OLD AND OVER, 1870-1950, BY STATES

Labor force estimates used in this study cover the following sectors: Total Labor Force, Agriculture, Mining, Forestry and Logging, Fishing, Manufactures, and Services (rest). Development of labor force estimates covering eight or more decades from census reports is complicated by frequent changes in concepts, categories, and coverage, errors of enumeration, and, most recently, by a sharpening of the time reference for which the report is made. The most reliable returns on the working population appear to be those of 1880, 1900, and 1930; all others are subject to more or less serious reservation, particularly those which deal with agricultural labor where part-time, seasonal, and family workers may comprise a sizeable fraction of the total. For the most recent and comprehensive analysis of historical labor force estimates since 1870, see the dittographed volumes by C. P. Brainerd, *Agricultural and Non-Agricultural Workers by States, 1870-1950* (1954) and A. R. Miller, *Statistics on the Labor Force by Sex and Age, 1870-1950* (1954) ; some of this commentary is included in Lee, Miller, Brainerd, and Easterlin, *op. cit.*, pages 363-631.

The primary source of labor force estimates used in this study is the adjusted census series of Brainerd and Miller. Since those authors provide a full explanation of their series in the volumes referred to, no further account of their figures need be given here. From their tables we have acquired the following components of the present series: total labor force, 10 years old and over, and their allocation between the agricultural and non-agricultural sectors. The remaining components—mining, forestry and logging, fishing, manufactures, and services (rest)—have been developed independently from the original census reports and the adjusted comparative occupation statistics of A. M. Edwards referred to above. Edwards' adjustments cover the years 1870-1930 and 1930-1940; the 17th U. S. Census, 1950, presents certain retabulated occupational data in terms of 1940 classifications. Adjustments since 1930 present data in terms of the labor force, 14 years old and over, and we have not attempted to readjust these in terms of the labor force, 10 years old and over, except for those components taken from Brainerd: total labor force, agriculture, and the residual category of services. This is not a major defect, however, since the numbers of children under 14 employed in manufactures, mining, fishing, forestry and logging since 1930 are very small. Unfortunately, the adjustments by Edwards, Carson, and other authorities are for national totals and only on rare occasions do they provide hints on the appropriate breakdown of their revised totals by states. The commentaries by Brainerd and Miller on the shortcomings of the several censuses, however, provide many clues which help toward the distribution of national totals among the states and we are further indebted to their work in making distributions for mining, forestry and logging, fisheries, and manufactures, although their studies only treat such matters in detail for the years 1880, 1900, 1940, and 1950; see Lee, Miller, Brainerd and Easterlin, *op. cit.*, Table L-5. Where such leads are not available we have distributed the revised national totals according to the weights indicated by the original census returns. The residual sector "Services" is simply the total labor force less all four resource sectors and manufactures.

The labor force estimates used in the present study are derived as follows:

A-1) *Total labor force, 10 years old and over, 1870–1950, by states*

SOURCE: C. P. Brainerd, *op. cit.*, Table I, "Growth of the American Labor Force by states, 1870–1950."

A-2) *Agricultural labor force, 10 years old and over, 1870–1950, by states*

SOURCE: C. P. Brainerd, *op. cit.*, Table I, "Growth of the American Labor Force by states, 1870–1950."

A-3) *Mining labor force, 10 years old and over, 1870–1950, by states*

SOURCE:
1870: 9th U. S. Census, Vol. III, Table 12, adjusted to Edwards, Table 8; includes oil borers, peatcutters, quarrymen, and additions in Edwards, Table 8, Note 15.
1880: 10th U. S. Census, *Statistics of the Population of the U. S.* Tables 33, 34, adj. to Edwards, Table 8; includes quarrymen and additions in Edwards, Table 8, Note 14.
1890: 11th U. S. Census, *Report on the Population of the U. S.*, Pt. II, Table 79, adj. to Edwards, Table 8; includes quarrymen and additions in Edwards, Table 8, Note 14.
1900: 12th U. S. Census, Special Reports, *Occupations*, Tables 1, 41 no adjustments required.
1910: 13th U. S. Census, Vol. IV, "Occupation Statistics," Table I, II, adj. to Edwards, Table 8, includes quarrymen, oil, gas, and salt well operatives.
1920: 14th U. S. Census, Vol. IV, "Occupations," Tables 4, 23, no adjustments necessary.
1930: 15th U. S. Census, Vol. IV, "Occupations by States," Table 3 and States' Tables 4, no adjustments necessary. (For 1930 comparable with 1940, see Edwards, Table 7.)
1940: 16th U. S. Census, Vol. III, States' Tables 17, and Edwards, Table 7.
1950: 17th U. S. Census, Vol. II, States' Tables 80, (comparable with 1940).

A-4) *Forest labor force, 10 years old and over, 1870–1950, by states*

SOURCE:
1870: 9th U. S. Census, Vol. I, Tables 29, 30, adjusted to Edwards, Table 8, including additions in Edwards, Table 8, Note 12.
1880: as for Mining, adjusted to Edwards Table 8, includes lumbermen, raftsmen, woodchoppers, and additions in Edwards, Table 8, Note 11.

1890: as for Mining, adj. to Edwards, Table 8, includes lumbermen, raftsmen, woodchoppers, and additions in Edwards, Table 8, Note 11.

1900: as for Mining, adj. to Edwards, Table 8, includes lumbermen, raftsmen, woodchoppers, and additions in Edwards, Table 8, Note 11. Edwards total of 140,599 may be a misprint, since following his sources and adjustments we obtain a total of 140,959.

1910: as for Mining, adj. to Edwards, Table 8, includes lumbermen, raftsmen, woodchoppers, owners and managers of log and timber camps, foresters, forest rangers, and timber cruisers.

1920: as for Mining, adj. to Edwards, Table 8, includes same categories as 1910.

1930: as for Mining. No adjustments necessary. (Comparability with 1940 not available.)

1940: as for Mining. Includes loggers transferred from Manufacturing.

1950: as for Mining. (Comparable with 1940.)

A-5) *Fishing labor force, 10 years old and over, 1870–1950, by states*

SOURCE:
1870: as for Mining, adjusted to Edwards, Table 8, includes oystermen and additions in Edwards, Table 8, Note 13, but excludes whale fishery.

1880: as for Mining, adj. to Edwards, Table 8, includes oystermen.

1890: as for Mining, no adjustment required, includes oystermen but excludes shore workers who are counted in manufactures.

1900: as for Mining, adj. to Edwards, Table 8, includes same categories as 1890.

1910: as for Mining, no adjustment required, includes same categories as 1900.

1920: as for Mining, no adjustment required, categories as for 1910.

1930: as for Mining, no adjustment required, categories as for 1920. (For 1930 comparable with 1940, see Edwards, Table 7.)

1940: as for Mining.

1950: as for Mining. (Comparable with 1940.)

A-6) *Manufacturing labor force, 10 years old and over, 1870–1950, by states*

SOURCE:
1870: as for Forest, adjusted to Edwards, Table 8, less lumbermen, raftsmen, woodchoppers, fishermen, oystermen, and certain mining operatives transferred to resource sectors, but including additions in Edwards, Table 8, Note 20.

1880: as for Mining, adj. to Edwards, Table 8, less categories transferred to resource sectors, but including additions in Edwards, Table 8, Note 19.

1890: as for Mining, adj. to Edwards, Table 8, including additions to Note 19.

1900: as for Mining, adj. to Edwards, Table 8, including additions in Note 19.

1910: as for Mining, adj. to Edwards, Table 8, including additions in Note 18.

1920: as for Mining, adj. to Edwards, Table 8, including additions in Note 17.

1930: as for Mining, no adjustments required. (For 1930 comparable with 1940, see Edwards, Table 7, less loggers transferred to forest sector.)

1940: as for Mining, less loggers transferred to forest sector.

1950: as for Mining. (Comparable with 1940.)

A-7) *Services labor force (rest), 10 years old and over, 1870–1950, by states*

For each year the residual of Total Labor Force less the four resource activities and manufactures.

Appendix Tables B1–B5 Notes

GROSS VALUE OF EXTRACTED RESOURCES, 1870-1950, BY STATES

"Gross Value of Extracted Resources" is an attempt to establish the current values of natural resources actually produced in the various states and regions. While the figures provide some indication of the growth of resource output over two decade intervals, they are intended to show rather the changing local contributions to the growing national aggregate. They are not, of course, a net figure such as "value-added by manufacture," but they do show the relative importance of leading resource activities in different parts of the country; to this extent they supplement labor force data. Perhaps the most serious weakness of the "gross value" concept, over and beyond the problems of enumeration, occurs in relation to agriculture where, for example, considerable duplication of values is entailed. The gross value of agricultural products includes the value of crops fed to livestock and also the value of livestock sold to farmers. Thus the duplication of values is greater where crops are raised and fed on farms than in areas where cash crops like wheat and cotton are raised. These conceptual problems, however, pale in significance when compared with the fundamental problem of sources. Four major resource sectors are covered in the present series: agriculture, minerals, fisheries, and forest products. The sources for the first three sectors are tolerable, however inadequate they may be for any refined analysis; a reliable or comprehensive source for forest products is non-existent. We have been content to compile merely approximate average annual values for hard and soft wood lumber and approximate average annual values for domestic pulpwood. Any close examination of the standard series of lumber prices, however, reveals the extreme artificiality of this method. As far as the sources permit, the values represented are the values to primary producers and an effort has been made to exclude any element of value-added by processing, e.g., the value of fish to fishermen rather than the value at the cannery or market. Needless to add that in many cases this represents an ideal and that the sources do not always allow for such refinement.

The gross value series, unlike the labor force series, does not originate in a single source, the U. S. Census. Much of the material is from the census, but especially in the period since 1910, more definite figures have been obtained from Bureau of Mines' publications, reports of the Fish and Wildlife Service, the annual *Statistical Abstract*, etc. For this reason values do not always apply to the calendar years in question such as 1870 or 1910 but to a period *circa* 1870 or 1910; more especially, 1869-70 or 1909-10, etc. Where revised figures have been issued subsequent to the original enumeration, the revised figure has been adopted where it has been provided or can be estimated on a state basis. The main items included in the four resource sectors are as follows:

B-2) *Agriculture:* includes all major field, orchard, and garden crops, and livestock categories; also the value of forest products produced on farms. It excludes certain poultry values (turkeys, geese, and ducks), apiary, nursery, and green-house products.

B-3) *Mining:* includes value of recovered ores, quarry products, and oil-well output.

B-4) *Forest:* includes lumber products used in mills, more especially values of hard and soft wood lumber; also the value of domestic pulpwood. Excludes lumber used for fuels, cross-ties, and mining. Lumber produced on farms is included in agriculture.

B-5) *Fishing:* includes value of catch to fishermen in coastal regions and inland waters. Excludes the whale fishery.

B-1) Total of B-2, B-3, B-4, B-5.

Particular inclusions and exclusions are noted in the original sources cited below.

1869–70:

Agricultural, 9th U. S. Census, 1870, Vol. III, Table 3, includes betterments, improvements and additions to stock.

Mining, 9th U. S. Census, 1870, Vol. III, Table 12.

Forest, 9th U. S. Census, 1870, Vol. III, Table 8c, value of lumber materials used at mills, and in tar and turpentine production.

Fishing, 9th U. S. Census, 1870, Vol. III, Table 16, excludes whale fishery.

1889–90:

Agricultural, 11th U. S. Census, 1890, *Statistics of Agriculture,* Table 1.

Mining, 11th U. S. Census, 1890, *Compendium,* Pt. II, p. 467, less imported ores and natural gas used at wells.

Forest, 11th U. S. Census, 1890, *Manufacturing Industries,* Pt. III, pp. 593-645, does not include 94,640,000 cubic feet used for woodpulp not available on state basis.

Fishing, *Statistical Abstract of the United States, 1931,* Table 728, based on U. S. Department of the Interior, Fish and Wildlife Service, *Fishery Statistics of the U. S.* The Census *Statistics of Fisheries* for 1890 gives a considerably higher total.

1909–10:

Agricultural, 14th U. S. Census, 1920, Vol. V, p. 18.

Mining, 13th U. S. Census, 1910, Vol. XI, Table 3.

Forest, U. S. Department of Agriculture, *Misc. Pub. No. 669* (1948), and 13th U. S. Census, 1910, Vol. X, Tables 16, 17, less values of pulpwood imports.

Fishing, U. S. Census, *Special Reports,* "Fisheries of the United States, 1908." Tables 2-5, provides the most extensive breakdown by states.

1929–30:

Agricultural, *U. S. Census of Agriculture, 1940,* Vol. III, Tables 4, 6, 7.

Mining, U. S. Bureau of Mines, *Minerals Yearbook, 1932–33,* "Value of mineral products of the U. S., by States," p. A6 (1929 figures).

Forest, U. S. Department of Agriculture, *Misc. Pub. No. 669* (1948), hard and soft wood million feet board measure at average annual price and same for cords pulpwood (census).

Fishing, *Statistical Abstract of the United States, 1931,* Table 728, based on data from U. S. Bureau of Fisheries.

1949–50:

Agricultural, *U. S. Census of Agriculture,* 1950, Vol. II, *General Report,* Table 1, p. 752.

Mining, U. S. Bureau of Mines, *Minerals Yearbook, 1952,* Vol. II, Table 3 (1949 figures).

Forest, *Statistical Abstract of the United States, 1954,* Table 860, total allocated according to 1947 weights of state production; 1949 or 1950 state figures n.a. U. S. Forest Service, *Timber Resources Review,* Ch. IX (1955, prelim.)

Fishing, *Statistical Abstract of the United States, 1953,* Table 837, based on data from U. S. Fish and Wild Life Service.

Appendix Table C

SOURCE: Appendix Tables A1-A7.

Appendix Table D

SOURCE: Appendix Tables A1-A7.

Appendix Table E

SOURCE:

Lee, Miller, Brainerd and Easterlin, *op. cit.,* Tables Y-1, Y-2 and Y-5; *Personal Income by States Since 1929,* p. 142 and pp. 146-203; *Survey of Current Business,* August 1958, Table 2, p. 13 and pp. 14-20.

Appendix Table F-1

SOURCE:

1. Agricultural employment: *U. S. Census of Agriculture, 1940,* Vol. III, Table 13, p. 464.
2. Mining employment: *Census of Mineral Industries, 1939,* Vol. II, State Tables 2.
3. Construction employment (contract): U. S. Department of Labor, Bureau of Labor Statistics, *State Employment 1939-56* (1957), State tables.
4. Manufacturing employment: *Census of Manufactures, 1939,* Vol. II, Part 1, General Summary, Table 6, p. 44.
5. Transportation and public utilities employment: Same as Construction.
6. Wholesale trade employment: *1948 Census of Business,* Vol. IV, Table 1 D, p. 1.09.
7. Retail trade employment: *1948 Census of Business,* Vol. I, Table 1 D, p. 1.06.
8. Finance, insurance and real estate employment: Same as Construction.
9. Service and miscellaneous employment: Same as Construction.
10. Government employment: Same as Construction.
11. Total employment: A simple summation of the employment components identified in sources 1-10.

NOTE: These data, derived from the above sources, indicate the nature and degree of employment specialization in each state and are particularly helpful in analyzing the proportionality effect.

Appendix Table F-2

SOURCE:

1. Agricultural employment: *U. S. Census of Agriculture, 1954,* Vol. II, Table 21, p. 298.
2. Mining employment: *Census of Mineral Industries, 1954,* Vol. I, pp. C-8—C-9.
3. Construction employment: U. S. Department of Labor, Bureau of Labor Statistics, *Employment and Earnings,* Annual Supplement Issue, (Vol. 2, June 1956), Table SA-9, p. 66.
4. Manufacturing employment: *1954 Census of Manufactures,* Vol. I, Table 4A, pp. 34-39.
5. Transportation and public utilities employment: *Employment and Earnings,* Table SA-11, p. 68.
6. Wholesale trade employment: *1954 Census of Business,* Vol. III, Table 2F.
7. Retail trade employment: *1954 Census of Business,* Table 1H, pp. 1-39.
8. Finance, insurance and real estate employment: *Employment and Earnings,* Table SA-13, p. 70.
9. Service and miscellaneous employment: *Employment and Earnings,* Table SA-14, p. 71.
10. Government employment: *Employment and Earnings,* Table SA-15, p. 72.
11. Total employment: A simple summation of the employment components identified in sources 1–10 above.

NOTE: These data, derived from the above sources, indicate the nature and degree of employment specialization in each state and are particularly helpful in analyzing the proportionality effect.

Appendix Table G

SOURCE:
One-digit employment: Same as source for Appendix Tables F-1 and F-2.
Two-digit value of agricultural products sold: Same as source for Appendix Table J.
Two-digit mining employment: Same as source for Appendix Tables F-1 and F-2.
Two- and three-digit manufacturing production workers: Same as source for Appendix Table K.

Appendix Table H

SOURCE:
1. Population:
   1939—U. S. Bureau of the Census, *Current Population Reports—Population Estimates,* Series P-25, No. 139.

1954—U. S. Bureau of the Census, *Current Population Reports—Population Estimates*, Series P-25, No. 145.
2. Personal Income: *Personal Income by States Since 1929*, Table 1, pp. 140-1. The remainder—same as source for Appendix Tables F-1 and F-2.

Appendix Table I

SOURCE: Same as Mining employment in Appendix Tables F-1 and F-2.

Appendix Table J

SOURCE: Value of agricultural products sold: *U. S. Census of Agriculture, 1940*, Vol. III, Table 8, p. 905-11 and *U. S. Census of Agriculture, 1954*, Vol. II, Chap. IX.

Appendix Table K

SOURCE: Manufacturing production workers: *U. S. Census of Manufactures, 1947*, Vol. III, state tables No. 3, and *U. S. Census of Manufactures, 1954*, Vol. III, Table 4A, pp. 34-39.
NOTE: The calculations on shifts in manufacturing production workers were made on the basis of the Census of Manufactures preliminary data for 1954. Some revisions were made by the Census in the final published figures for production workers. This amounted to an increase of 282 to a total of 12,373,030. The components for Tobacco and Lumber Products omit "Tobacco stemming and redrying" and "Logging camps and contractors" respectively, because equivalent data are not given for 1939. Some state figures are approximated because of disclosure problems.

Appendix Table L

SOURCE: U. S. Department of Labor, Bureau of Labor Statistics, *BLS Report No. 3*, "General Explanations of the 200 Sector Tables: The 1947 Interindustry Relations Study."

Appendix Table M

SOURCE: Unpublished data furnished by Richard Easterlin.

Appendix Table N

SOURCE:
1950 Census of Agriculture, Vol. II, Chapter I, Table 10.
Alvin S. Tostlebe, *The Growth of Physical Capital in Agriculture, 1870–1950* (New York: National Bureau of Economic Research, 1954), Table 6, p. 36.

APPENDIX TABLES

Appendix Table A-1

LABOR FORCE, 1870 - 1950: TOTAL

	1870	1880	1890	1900	1910	1920
U. S.	12,505,923	17,392,099	22,735,661	29,073,233	38,167,336	41,614,248
Alabama	365,258	492,790	541,602	763,188	997,524	908,216
Arizona	6,030	22,271	26,416	53,370	87,825	130,579
Arkansas	135,949	260,692	347,208	485,795	672,403	634,564
California	238,648	376,505	544,165	644,267	1,107,668	1,512,760
Colorado	17,583	101,251	191,943	218,263	338,724	366,457
Connecticut	193,421	241,333	317,014	385,610	490,462	589,905
Delaware	40,313	54,580	64,286	72,996	85,863	91,224
D. C.	49,041	66,624	101,119	126,941	157,965	236,027
Florida	60,703	91,536	136,827	201,570	322,087	385,312
Georgia	444,678	597,862	668,713	864,471	1,160,126	1,129,157
Idaho	10,879	15,578	35,172	62,683	131,088	153,459
Illinois	742,015	999,780	1,353,559	1,804,04c	2,296,778	2,627,738
Indiana	459,369	635,080	724,058	898,953	1,036,710	1,117,032
Iowa	344,276	528,302	631,835	789,404	826,313	858,698
Kansas	123,852	322,285	452,346	507,740	621,333	624,391
Kentucky	414,593	519,854	590,324	752,531	866,980	851,122
Louisiana	256,452	363,228	423,074	536,093	679,183	681,233
Maine	208,225	231,993	257,096	276,777	305,457	309,858
Maryland	258,543	324,432	393,267	458,738	541,164	603,478
Mass.	579,844	720,774	982,444	1,208,407	1,531,068	1,728,318
Michigan	404,164	569,204	759,575	905,990	1,112,998	1,474,014
Minnesota	132,657	255,125	469,086	645,874	835,452	907,013
Mississippi	318,850	415,506	462,739	645,123	879,645	721,410
Missouri	505,556	692,959	884,379	1,121,392	1,288,336	1,317,160
Montana	14,048	22,255	72,223	114,799	178,747	214,183
Nebraska	43,837	152,614	368,060	373,970	441,114	457,081
Nevada	26,911	32,233	23,415	19,809	44,910	37,548
N. H.	120,168	142,468	164,703	178,719	191,703	192,827
N. J.	296,036	396,879	570,738	757,759	1,074,360	1,310,653
N. M.	29,361	40,822	54,151	66,020	121,497	122,031
N. Y.	1,491,018	1,884,645	2,435,725	2,996,474	4,003,844	4,503,204
N. C.	351,299	480,187	537,363	716,742	947,839	895,852
N. D.	5,887	57,844	67,771	117,640	217,418	207,082
Ohio	840,889	994,475	1,272,786	1,545,952	1,919,055	2,301,516
Oklahoma				20,906	266,405	598,629	681,428
Oregon	30,651	67,343	126,781	169,637	305,164	322,283
Penn.	1,020,544	1,456,067	1,959,091	2,448,589	3,130,681	3,426,359
R. I.	88,574	116,979	155,878	191,923	251,901	275,000
S. C.	263,301	392,102	440,854	570,995	728,627	674,257
S. D.	Included in North Dakota		114,093	137,156	219,077	216,571
Tennessee	367,987	447,970	553,753	727,587	855,546	830,096
Texas	237,126	522,133	696,208	1,033,033	1,556,866	1,719,023
Utah	21,517	40,055	66,901	84,604	131,540	149,201
Vermont	108,763	118,584	128,771	134,933	144,089	138,484
Virginia	412,665	494,240	551,839	662,415	795,568	833,576
Washington	9,760	30,122	164,696	225,387	521,501	578,667
W. Va.	115,229	176,199	223,788	325,663	448,490	491,116
Wisconsin	292,808	417,455	576,290	732,538	892,412	995,549
Wyoming	6,645	8,884	30,630	44,268	73,606	81,536

Appendix Table A-1 (continued)

	$\dfrac{1930*}{1920}$	$\dfrac{1930*}{1940}$	$\dfrac{1940*}{1930}$	$\dfrac{1940*}{1950}$	1950
U. S.	48,829,920	47,404,000	53,299,000	49,625,354	60,200,847
Alabama	1,026,295	996,325	1,037,315	965,818	1,099,233
Arizona	165,296	160,469	181,303	168,807	266,535
Arkansas	667,845	648,343	681,281	634,324	655,326
California	2,500,644	2,427,621	3,023,656	2,815,250	4,417,471
Colorado	402,867	391,102	415,141	386,527	514,708
Connecticut	677,208	657,432	791,287	736,747	880,624
Delaware	98,104	95,239	118,416	110,254	131,158
D. C.	243,853	236,732	354,414	329,986	403,952
Florida	598,939	581,449	796,825	741,904	1,102,887
Georgia	1,162,158	1,128,221	1,263,855	1,176,744	1,350,079
Idaho	162,232	157,494	190,326	177,208	219,148
Illinois	3,184,684	3,091,686	3,363,852	3,131,998	3,729,628
Indiana	1,251,065	1,214,532	1,334,866	1,242,860	1,572,960
Iowa	912,835	886,179	987,674	919,598	1,024,843
Kansas	694,272	673,998	673,223	626,821	740,833
Kentucky	907,095	880,606	1,002,429	933,336	1,018,864
Louisiana	815,616	791,798	901,829	839,670	934,336
Maine	308,603	299,591	338,021	314,723	345,075
Maryland	672,879	653,230	793,298	738,620	972,027
Mass.	1,814,315	1,761,334	1,829,175	1,703,099	1,959,898
Michigan	1,927,347	1,871,065	2,137,125	1,989,823	2,542,590
Minnesota	992,798	963,807	1,104,396	1,028,275	1,190,950
Mississippi	844,905	820,232	837,805	780,059	775,181
Missouri	1,457,968	1,415,393	1,514,345	1,409,968	1,579,608
Montana	216,479	210,157	222,577	207,236	232,856
Nebraska	507,008	492,202	497,741	463,434	528,206
Nevada	42,884	41,632	48,994	45,617	71,109
N. H.	192,666	187,040	209,793	195,333	217,330
N. J.	1,712,106	1,662,109	1,874,411	1,745,217	2,100,149
N. M.	142,607	138,443	172,007	160,151	230,990
N. Y.	5,523,337	5,362,046	6,097,088	5,676,844	6,347,269
N. C.	1,140,971	1,107,653	1,374,129	1,279,417	1,564,871
N. D.	240,303	233,286	232,509	216,483	233,728
Ohio	2,615,764	2,539,379	2,750,146	2,560,592	3,216,184
Oklahoma	828,004	803,825	789,008	734,625	800,459
Oregon	409,645	397,683	462,883	430,979	621,286
Penn.	3,722,103	3,613,411	3,948,233	3,676,099	4,168,339
R. I.	297,172	288,494	318,741	296,772	343,939
S. C.	687,737	667,654	745,142	693,783	808,707
S. D.	247,653	240,421	234,977	218,781	252,970
Tennessee	958,386	930,399	1,090,927	1,015,735	1,206,704
Texas	2,206,767	2,142,325	2,499,568	2,327,285	2,991,011
Utah	170,000	165,036	177,265	165,047	243,917
Vermont	141,203	137,080	144,417	134,463	145,636
Virginia	880,211	854,507	1,063,090	989,816	1,307,623
Washington	664,730	645,319	722,137	672,364	959,675
W. Va.	570,452	553,794	616,900	574,380	659,501
Wisconsin	1,129,461	1,096,479	1,232,485	1,147,536	1,400,084
Wyoming	92,448	89,748	101,975	94,946	120,390

*The data are for the upper year, expressed in terms of Census occupational
classifications for the lower year.

Appendix Table A-2

LABOR FORCE, 1870 - 1950: AGRICULTURE

	1870	1880	1890	1900	1910	1920
U. S.	6,437,372	8,590,280	9,235,290	11,288,027	12,389,840	10,665,812
Alabama	299,500	410,991	391,629	543,543	662,251	497,791
Arizona	1,823	4,387	7,710	17,635	21,735	35,426
Arkansas	111,812	223,243	266,229	362,554	466,193	402,207
California	57,371	94,871	147,009	161,544	211,898	260,612
Colorado	7,282	15,611	41,732	48,664	84,763	99,158
Connecticut	47,468	48,853	49,878	49,118	46,015	36,553
Delaware	18,502	22,256	21,277	21,857	22,742	17,382
D. C.	1,750	1,821	2,015	1,718	1,217	913
Florida	45,616	64,796	71,678	91,303	117,753	107,468
Georgia	348,101	468,037	433,203	557,339	720,439	601,875
Idaho	1,513	4,485	14,851	29,785	55,457	67,297
Illinois	414,862	493,102	478,513	517,055	447,513	378,128
Indiana	290,399	375,568	357,329	385,008	342,971	292,507
Iowa	227,844	333,671	345,775	403,230	353,724	326,230
Kansas	78,454	222,681	265,811	291,319	274,075	232,790
Kentucky	279,863	350,618	342,826	442,464	452,396	391,715
Louisiana	157,734	244,401	266,407	329,458	335,350	279,003
Maine	88,816	92,394	86,843	85,114	73,331	61,267
Maryland	92,593	105,650	102,669	108,683	108,734	90,691
Mass.	81,896	72,935	75,664	71,471	67,472	51,436
Michigan	208,861	283,499	311,194	345,346	321,877	272,443
Minnesota	84,080	149,296	208,853	280,677	278,695	292,492
Mississippi	272,861	357,260	373,626	516,358	671,955	498,498
Missouri	293,327	396,188	419,383	501,712	453,213	392,559
Montana	2,212	5,213	16,014	31,055	53,411	81,798
Nebraska	26,187	98,573	183,971	201,353	202,491	186,976
Nevada	2,430	5,021	5,686	6,639	8,575	8,450
N. H.	48,958	49,111	44,967	41,690	34,555	25,451
N. J.	74,809	70,312	77,138	77,034	76,068	58,418
N. M.	21,340	22,982	29,941	34,940	66,119	54,070
N. Y.	421,520	433,365	438,207	413,636	372,885	306,069
N. C.	281,305	378,891	385,073	493,638	602,337	468,821
N. D.	2,621	32,261	45,339	76,486	130,822	119,822
Ohio	436,391	458,911	450,949	466,539	417,461	358,606
Oklahoma			14,393	197,916	348,216	313,268
Oregon	14,699	31,851	50,755	64,199	79,382	79,015
Penn.	308,804	371,474	374,888	389,587	352,593	276,732
R. I.	13,406	12,235	12,796	11,764	11,276	7,674
S. C.	215,267	318,753	339,625	419,276	510,853	418,578
S. D.	Included in N. D.		71,682	87,256	124,687	116,954
Tennessee	280,284	328,775	349,825	449,519	464,410	395,483
Texas	177,599	395,937	458,030	695,993	927,768	787,946
Utah	12,545	17,818	23,216	33,017	37,241	43,102
Vermont	62,164	61,870	58,242	54,136	48,701	41,780
Virginia	264,200	301,469	283,112	335,941	348,926	291,895
Washington	4,215	14,112	44,405	60,456	97,998	101,128
W. Va.	78,187	118,733	127,935	168,910	160,075	119,057
Wisconsin	175,712	223,992	257,516	298,595	296,545	292,700
Wyoming	189	2,007	9,481	15,497	24,676	25,578

Appendix Table A-2 (continued)

	$\dfrac{1930*}{1920}$	$\dfrac{1930*}{1940}$	$\dfrac{1940*}{1930}$	$\dfrac{1940*}{1950}$	1950
U. S.	10,471,998	10,175,570	9,003,702	8,700,396	6,962,779
Alabama	492,761	478,813	385,149	372,175	263,582
Arizona	38,423	37,335	37,363	36,104	37,823
Arkansas	384,381	373,500	325,850	314,873	222,672
California	332,024	322,625	299,130	289,053	295,539
Colorado	106,068	103,065	81,527	78,781	73,573
Connecticut	36,500	35,467	26,753	25,852	21,897
Delaware	17,316	16,826	14,734	14,238	10,793
D. C.	1,081	1,050	372	359	470
Florida	133,530	129,750	124,211	120,027	121,305
Georgia	497,941	483,846	402,623	389,060	275,107
Idaho	65,528	63,673	63,045	60,921	55,998
Illinois	351,977	342,014	299,472	289,384	247,648
Indiana	249,884	242,811	216,892	209,586	174,256
Iowa	330,881	321,515	325,251	314,294	282,778
Kansas	229,390	222,897	194,349	187,802	162,140
Kentucky	358,506	348,358	338,601	327,195	251,163
Louisiana	296,801	288,400	266,961	257,968	154,461
Maine	51,462	50,005	40,559	39,193	29,379
Maryland	84,082	81,702	72,349	69,912	53,423
Mass.	55,643	54,068	36,693	35,457	29,523
Michigan	247,652	240,642	228,194	220,507	158,863
Minnesota	303,589	294,995	301,527	291,370	260,477
Mississippi	557,067	541,298	453,809	438,521	316,704
Missouri	370,878	360,380	326,008	315,026	267,391
Montana	79,518	77,267	64,543	62,369	55,103
Nebraska	197,199	191,617	171,700	165,916	150,828
Nevada	8,903	8,651	6,678	6,453	6,449
N. H.	22,067	21,442	16,561	16,003	12,751
N. J.	64,061	62,248	48,822	47,177	45,381
N. M.	58,900	57,233	52,027	50,274	39,319
N. Y.	267,373	259,805	223,464	215,936	167,102
N. C.	499,957	485,805	434,009	419,388	370,468
N. D.	134,393	130,589	115,823	111,921	100,983
Ohio	311,646	302,824	270,748	261,627	209,077
Oklahoma	306,091	297,427	241,171	233,047	156,996
Oregon	81,879	79,561	76,691	74,108	70,539
Penn.	250,925	243,822	205,050	198,143	159,300
R. I.	8,833	8,583	5,051	4,881	3,905
S. C.	344,629	334,874	280,399	270,953	206,858
S. D.	130,742	127,041	104,784	101,254	98,687
Tennessee	376,852	366,185	337,713	326,337	252,920
Texas	841,547	817,726	692,545	669,214	452,427
Utah	41,247	40,079	31,350	30,294	28,688
Vermont	38,114	37,035	32,510	31,415	25,094
Virginia	270,696	262,033	236,855	228,876	168,237
Washington	104,077	101,131	89,734	86,711	79,277
W. Va.	118,200	114,854	87,163	84,227	61,639
Wisconsin	289,989	281,780	289,300	279,554	251,359
Wyoming	30,795	29,923	27,589	26,660	22,427

*The data are for the upper year, expressed in terms of Census occupational classifications for the lower year.

Appendix Table A-3

LABOR FORCE, 1870 - 1950: MINING

	1870	1880	1890	1900	1910	1920
U. S.	186,616	297,784	447,001	694,352	965,169	1,090,223
Alabama	236	1,325	9,707	22,098	28,916	35,639
Arizona	252	5,586	4,138	9,193	15,574	15,437
Arkansas	17	78	953	3,183	4,894	5,556
California	41,078	44,462	26,064	31,605	31,309	24,698
Colorado	2,478	34,675	24,195	34,936	28,386	23,382
Connecticut	2,138	1,798	2,035	1,091	1,314	442
Delaware	21	146	122	311	327	70
D. C.	13	26	42	44	77	79
Florida		35	394	1,472	3,518	2,999
Georgia	274	619	1,692	2,164	3,493	2,466
Idaho	7,410	5,621	6,008	8,581	6,727	5,132
Illinois	8,740	16,695	27,932	47,076	67,797	90,644
Indiana	1,544	4,917	9,264	15,510	24,309	33,322
Iowa	1,692	4,510	9,368	13,659	15,734	14,196
Kansas	530	4,111	6,700	11,772	14,003	20,312
Kentucky	2,073	3,235	6,511	11,468	21,108	51,471
Louisiana	30	14	87	55	1,320	7,669
Maine	381	1,383	1,554	1,195	1,557	748
Maryland	3,360	4,601	5,655	6,439	7,371	6,637
Mass.	883	1,526	2,450	2,295	2,682	1,198
Michigan	3,908	8,446	22,227	28,623	36,515	28,798
Minnesota	78	142	3,182	8,030	19,175	14,994
Mississippi		3	8	21	84	259
Missouri	3,389	5,968	16,295	25,421	26,798	21,516
Montana	7,568	5,748	12,308	20,687	19,409	16,718
Nebraska	54	175	373	261	664	388
Nevada	9,425	7,937	5,595	3,254	9,838	6,178
N. H.	266	327	613	672	574	406
N. J.	3,640	4,940	3,106	3,319	6,190	3,935
N. M.	566	1,799	3,458	4,963	6,131	7,310
N. Y.	5,019	5,294	9,137	6,402	12,269	7,549
N. C.	619	1,035	1,110	1,480	2,103	1,990
N. D.	1	4,265	57	140	506	1,298
Ohio	15,393	7,180	32,144	41,019	54,618	59,573
Oklahoma			18	5,278	11,779	38,349
Oregon	4,467	4,423	2,739	6,352	3,672	2,203
Penn.	50,207	88,066	142,426	222,977	327,787	332,432
R. I.	186	261	224	201	439	160
S. C.	29	168	1,134	1,953	686	624
S. D.	Included in N. D.		2,662	2,981	4,252	1,437
Tennessee	1,233	1,664	6,598	13,473	17,586	17,630
Texas	30	140	1,467	3,979	8,279	31,495
Utah	648	3,145	4,342	8,187	10,023	10,117
Vermont	1,471	1,978	2,541	2,685	2,515	1,899
Virginia	1,301	1,730	5,447	9,117	13,223	16,205
Washington	203	1,176	3,748	14,610	11,407	8,821
W. Va.	1,839	4,511	11,385	25,687	64,519	103,151
Wisconsin	1,272	1,508	4,209	3,593	5,996	3,901
Wyoming	654	392	3,577	4,840	7,716	8,790

Appendix Table A-3 (continued)

	1930* / 1920	1930* / 1940	1940* / 1930	1940* / 1950	1950
U. S.	984,323	1,165,203	1,109,860	913,000	929,421
Alabama	31,415	37,188	36,678	30,172	27,440
Arizona	13,982	16,551	15,567	12,806	10,494
Arkansas	7,392	8,750	7,175	5,902	6,773
California	39,743	47,046	55,593	45,732	30,335
Colorado	17,488	20,702	19,325	15,897	10,275
Connecticut	626	741	722	594	537
Delaware	61	72	130	107	84
D. C.	84	99	152	125	121
Florida	2,253	2,667	3,175	2,612	5,299
Georgia	3,429	4,059	4,957	4,078	5,052
Idaho	5,577	6,602	8,187	6,735	5,374
Illinois	60,536	71,660	59,818	49,208	43,626
Indiana	21,103	24,981	16,374	13,470	15,278
Iowa	8,664	10,256	7,711	6,343	3,308
Kansas	14,286	16,911	18,491	15,211	14,846
Kentucky	61,767	73,117	73,608	60,552	69,715
Louisiana	7,135	8,446	18,014	14,819	24,201
Maine	1,434	1,698	683	562	616
Maryland	5,023	5,946	4,892	4,024	2,781
Mass.	1,435	1,699	1,842	1,515	1,446
Michigan	20,510	24,279	19,263	15,846	15,409
Minnesota	10,736	12,709	9,646	7,935	15,797
Mississippi	511	605	2,330	1,917	3,616
Missouri	16,330	19,331	15,144	12,458	9,486
Montana	14,952	17,700	16,442	13,526	9,301
Nebraska	570	675	737	606	1,062
Nevada	5,000	5,919	7,612	6,262	3,321
N. H.	519	614	386	318	188
N. J.	3,638	4,307	4,328	3,560	4,049
N. M.	7,008	8,296	10,735	8,831	10,526
N. Y.	9,229	10,925	10,818	8,899	9,458
N. C.	2,740	3,244	3,541	2,914	3,076
N. D.	1,088	1,288	1,200	987	755
Ohio	39,418	46,661	39,423	32,430	30,606
Oklahoma	41,286	48,873	42,558	35,009	39,969
Oregon	2,167	2,565	3,590	2,953	1,649
Penn.	299,151	354,123	273,444	224,942	192,230
R. I.	237	281	230	189	175
S. C.	927	1,097	1,618	1,331	1,135
S. D.	1,498	1,773	3,485	2,867	2,736
Tennessee	14,598	17,281	17,501	14,397	14,451
Texas	34,716	41,095	74,216	61,052	89,951
Utah	10,514	12,446	12,280	10,102	12,081
Vermont	2,350	2,782	1,769	1,455	1,852
Virginia	16,006	18,947	29,377	24,166	28,985
Washington	5,720	6,771	6,599	5,429	3,886
W. Va.	109,923	130,123	137,813	113,369	134,329
Wisconsin	3,235	3,829	3,044	2,504	3,031
Wyoming	6,313	7,473	7,637	6,282	8,710

*The data are for the upper year, expressed in terms of Census occupational classifications for the lower year.

Appendix Table A-4

LABOR FORCE, 1870 - 1950: FOREST

	1870	1880	1890	1900	1910	1920
U. S.	32,360	55,931	122,143	140,599	173,531	217,378
Alabama	972	1,344	2,820	3,831	4,370	4,401
Arizona	5	130	455	562	700	768
Arkansas	151	451	1,844	5,833	5,771	6,018
California	3,122	5,716	8,491	8,548	9,661	8,775
Colorado	70	720	1,807	783	875	965
Connecticut	140	320	601	731	590	696
Delaware	13	40	100	105	74	59
D. C.	1	20	34	11	24	23
Florida	502	844	1,921	4,073	5,375	5,628
Georgia	717	1,392	3,021	5,040	4,282	5,727
Idaho	55	288	466	912	2,634	5,551
Illinois	563	988	1,432	1,821	887	1,671
Indiana	805	700	2,029	1,436	1,007	1,329
Iowa	354	470	613	841	309	579
Kansas	223	142	231	291	85	287
Kentucky	298	307	1,814	2,971	2,291	1,876
Louisiana	790	913	3,170	5,532	9,342	8,244
Maine	2,204	1,686	3,466	2,795	4,230	12,542
Maryland	112	273	715	749	915	709
Mass.	310	312	763	1,117	1,248	1,552
Michigan	2,904	11,485	16,959	12,337	11,839	16,517
Minnesota	1,809	2,778	5,061	6,885	7,908	14,726
Mississippi	426	462	1,356	3,077	5,556	5,698
Missouri	498	1,441	3,087	3,928	4,082	4,094
Montana	174	503	1,759	1,511	1,590	3,202
Nebraska	40	133	228	247	53	113
Nevada	763	537	646	191	171	136
N. H.	491	815	1,210	1,508	1,931	4,904
N. J.	151	224	547	509	499	687
N. M.	1	238	459	426	773	962
N. Y.	2,130	2,215	3,541	3,043	3,186	6,807
N. C.	347	660	3,510	4,603	6,686	6,444
N. D.	134	186	51	38	51	59
Ohio	730	893	1,762	1,693	942	1,311
Oklahoma			16	759	1,925	1,348
Oregon	288	828	3,189	3,487	7,058	11,091
Penn.	4,261	5,266	15,837	13,035	8,777	7,281
R. I.	28	53	89	210	239	206
S. C.	125	542	1,308	1,639	1,344	1,739
S. D.	Included in N. D.		456	186	208	295
Tennessee	490	405	1,363	4,403	4,876	4,421
Texas	419	1,217	1,467	3,697	5,156	4,816
Utah	80	226	415	218	135	129
Vermont	366	508	740	626	837	2,458
Virginia	516	711	2,285	2,245	2,909	3,933
Washington	796	1,287	7,424	10,785	23,562	25,439
W. Va.	116	273	1,614	3,200	8,164	6,521
Wisconsin	2,656	4,912	9,749	7,744	7,887	14,177
Wyoming	214	77	222	387	517	464

	1930*	1940**/1930	1940**/1950	1950
U. S.	177,189	250,352	186,688	215,432
Alabama	4,583	8,314	6,200	7,577
Arizona	799	1,147	855	799
Arkansas	5,911	8,967	6,687	8,454
California	7,796	9,490	7,077	12,203
Colorado	1,166	1,266	944	1,007
Connecticut	385	1,090	813	353
Delaware	94	113	84	124
D. C.	46	33	25	61
Florida	6,763	18,078	13,481	8,862
Georgia	4,287	23,458	17,493	17,595
Idaho	5,447	3,708	2,765	2,983
Illinois	1,152	1,336	996	1,517
Indiana	973	1,171	873	1,061
Iowa	340	424	316	408
Kansas	140	397	296	243
Kentucky	1,781	2,885	2,151	3,259
Louisiana	7,669	8,979	6,696	7,095
Maine	5,619	8,410	6,271	7,790
Maryland	759	1,025	764	1,052
Mass.	1,759	2,477	1,847	930
Michigan	10,295	7,760	5,787	5,235
Minnesota	5,146	4,443	3,313	3,880
Mississippi	6,049	8,325	6,208	9,164
Missouri	3,368	3,378	2,519	2,710
Montana	2,586	2,360	1,760	1,931
Nebraska	78	261	195	143
Nevada	110	106	79	92
N. H.	2,111	4,483	3,343	2,054
N. J.	421	629	469	500
N. M.	1,141	841	627	614
N. Y.	3,004	3,940	2,938	3,252
N. C.	5,373	8,957	6,679	11,085
N. D.	30	121	90	60
Ohio	1,301	1,407	1,049	1,489
Oklahoma	2,113	2,590	1,931	1,332
Oregon	16,565	22,871	17,055	28,126
Penn.	5,173	5,359	3,996	5,124
R. I.	173	244	182	119
S. C.	2,809	5,576	4,158	6,852
S. D.	191	555	414	338
Tennessee	3,780	4,873	3,634	4,601
Texas	4,964	8,007	5,971	6,693
Utah	206	591	441	431
Vermont	731	2,155	1,607	2,053
Virginia	3,790	6,060	4,519	5,546
Washington	26,352	30,155	22,487	19,370
W. Va.	5,203	5,462	4,073	5,029
Wisconsin	5,850	5,544	4,134	3,889
Wyoming	807	531	396	347

*1930 is the same in relation to 1940 as in relation to 1920.
**The data are for the upper year, expressed in terms of Census occupational classifications for the lower year.

Appendix Table A-5

LABOR FORCE, 1870 - 1950: FISH

	1870	1880	1890	1900	1910	1920
U. S.	27,871	41,352	60,162	68,940	68,275	52,836
Alabama	179	296	397	612	589	462
Arizona			1		1	5
Arkansas	20	104	184	404	1,295	426
California	978	3,010	1,946	1,969	3,802	3,560
Colorado	1	5	13	10	63	30
Connecticut	946	1,260	1,317	1,041	792	432
Delaware	87	180	409	444	463	253
D. C.	61	80	98	35	21	11
Florida	166	309	991	1,814	3,011	4,318
Georgia	162	170	394	675	648	473
Idaho		6	13	11	15	12
Illinois	314	428	759	1,658	2,888	906
Indiana	108	162	314	326	481	170
Iowa	98	108	217	615	439	315
Kansas	16	65	119	125	75	35
Kentucky	98	175	253	503	384	158
Louisiana	697	726	1,564	2,632	3,418	2,344
Maine	4,006	4,244	3,666	4,166	4,524	3,495
Maryland	1,613	3,560	9,196	9,524	7,450	4,481
Mass.	5,461	6,103	9,254	6,389	5,961	4,567
Michigan	1,105	1,398	1,621	1,731	1,876	1,414
Minnesota	59	74	374	538	552	658
Mississippi	56	190	384	700	710	981
Missouri	144	187	348	617	438	210
Montana	1	5	11	11	20	20
Nebraska	2	41	81	109	53	26
Nevada	8	12	26	50	24	3
N. H.	80	226	172	113	97	71
N. J.	1,159	2,529	3,595	4,769	3,589	2,048
N. M.		3	11		11	1
N. Y.	2,629	3,788	4,674	3,537	2,459	1,898
N. C.	1,244	1,382	2,586	3,080	3,065	2,399
N. D.	1	4	19	8	3	5
Ohio	308	357	944	993	992	738
Oklahoma			1	47	123	41
Oregon	93	3,192	1,478	2,756	1,744	1,894
Penn.	450	598	827	559	496	300
R. I.	717	879	782	725	1,052	474
S. C.	348	479	507	571	458	245
S. D.	Included in N.D.		28	23	11	28
Tennessee	138	199	335	519	458	228
Texas	59	140	431	712	1,032	623
Utah	9	14	23	22	40	28
Vermont	28	16	43	21	21	22
Virginia	3,681	3,625	7,699	9,275	7,570	5,879
Washington	184	613	1,202	3,225	3,711	4,959
W. Va.	7	8	51	27	45	14
Wisconsin	350	402	794	1,247	1,296	1,173
Wyoming			10	2	9	3

Appendix Table A-5 (continued)

	$\frac{1930*}{1920}$	$\frac{1930*}{1940}$	$\frac{1940*}{1930}$	$\frac{1940*}{1950}$	1950
U. S.	73,280	71,568	68,633	60,027	76,877
Alabama	893	872	749	655	1,261
Arizona	10	10	23	20	37
Arkansas	1,088	1,063	1,182	1,034	1,302
California	5,148	5,028	6,155	5,383	8,093
Colorado	84	82	122	107	197
Connecticut	845	825	615	538	606
Delaware	260	254	178	156	217
D. C.	10	10	22	19	12
Florida	6,084	5,942	5,944	5,199	6,885
Georgia	885	864	664	581	975
Idaho	26	25	86	75	136
Illinois	1,237	1,208	874	764	863
Indiana	320	313	184	161	256
Iowa	432	422	270	236	286
Kansas	34	33	48	42	45
Kentucky	391	382	325	284	239
Louisiana	5,719	5,585	6,923	6,055	7,754
Maine	3,494	3,412	3,485	3,048	4,989
Maryland	5,300	5,176	4,673	4,087	4,030
Mass.	5,932	5,793	5,310	4,644	5,655
Michigan	2,246	2,194	1,771	1,549	1,475
Minnesota	909	888	437	382	612
Mississippi	1,596	1,559	1,062	929	1,650
Missouri	388	379	276	241	364
Montana	32	31	64	56	65
Nebraska	77	75	82	72	130
Nevada	10	10	9	8	31
N. H.	65	63	165	144	138
N. J.	2,426	2,369	1,818	1,590	2,342
N. M.	5	5	19	17	51
N. Y.	2,198	2,147	2,258	1,975	2,460
N. C.	3,658	3,573	3,036	2,655	3,100
N. D.	5	5	7	6	17
Ohio	912	891	806	705	808
Oklahoma	98	96	93	81	202
Oregon	2,067	2,019	1,122	981	1,373
Penn.	264	258	361	316	439
R. I.	895	874	591	517	730
S. C.	543	530	370	324	561
S. D.	26	25	18	16	32
Tennessee	642	627	821	718	739
Texas	1,438	1,404	2,186	1,912	3,067
Utah	29	28	49	43	100
Vermont	18	18	43	38	30
Virginia	7,568	7,391	7,404	6,475	6,046
Washington	5,569	5,439	4,475	3,914	5,147
W. Va.	5	5	37	32	43
Wisconsin	1,392	1,359	1,396	1,221	1,259
Wyoming	7	7	25	22	28

*The data are for the upper year, expressed in terms of
Census occupational classifications for the lower year.

Appendix Table A-6

LABOR FORCE, 1870 - 1950: MANUFACTURING

	1870	1880	1890	1900	1910	1920
U. S.	2,643,417	3,841,487	5,525,692	7,199,208	10,656,545	12,860,914
Alabama	16,892	22,534	42,347	67,020	107,830	151,209
Arizona	861	2,617	2,966	9,541	18,290	24,134
Arkansas	6,495	11,865	23,790	36,312	66,846	76,586
California	44,154	80,719	125,311	151,170	293,512	432,055
Colorado	2,575	19,526	42,740	47,318	75,562	74,168
Connecticut	88,605	124,011	158,887	195,113	259,028	319,258
Delaware	9,984	15,151	19,648	24,555	29,901	34,764
D. C.	12,357	16,691	25,300	29,601	38,795	44,652
Florida	3,957	8,163	19,701	32,618	73,683	101,060
Georgia	27,683	37,725	64,026	92,547	142,263	182,234
Idaho	689	1,748	4,327	7,444	23,182	24,646
Illinois	132,464	208,804	346,368	492,774	754,265	878,897
Indiana	78,534	115,487	151,410	216,100	310,335	378,694
Iowa	48,265	72,043	97,303	126,185	158,072	177,106
Kansas	18,546	35,863	59,339	69,412	114,928	121,946
Kentucky	44,636	64,002	89,729	108,190	147,929	147,521
Louisiana	25,988	32,062	45,219	57,722	117,304	139,604
Maine	59,481	72,331	86,883	92,371	115,769	120,646
Maryland	62,335	85,227	110,718	131,788	172,117	208,101
Mass.	304,141	397,709	516,228	623,115	774,229	890,834
Michigan	80,466	124,513	175,928	225,722	362,335	620,470
Minnesota	18,062	41,062	90,893	124,771	190,885	204,677
Mississippi	10,179	13,812	21,312	33,511	65,750	75,207
Missouri	81,048	113,477	165,952	219,905	303,803	331,977
Montana	1,242	3,085	12,768	21,533	33,589	32,737
Nebraska	6,035	19,701	60,552	54,426	75,059	84,178
Nevada	5,097	6,751	3,321	2,579	7,620	7,206
N. H.	48,696	62,408	77,500	83,993	94,742	99,651
N. J.	104,993	168,586	242,994	333,521	492,008	630,654
N. M.	1,902	2,941	4,338	6,666	15,680	16,171
N. Y.	497,176	679,876	898,880	1,144,455	1,591,180	1,762,919
N. C.	19,707	34,219	54,995	96,674	158,377	211,720
N. D.	368	5,901	5,206	10,707	21,334	19,250
Ohio	193,810	257,978	359,226	479,201	702,728	962,555
Oklahoma			2,353	17,176	74,201	105,132
Oregon	4,680	10,879	24,919	30,931	82,080	88,717
Penn.	326,944	493,337	682,543	894,037	1,251,300	1,431,423
R. I.	48,994	71,308	88,505	111,870	141,889	162,455
S. C.	14,159	20,462	33,794	63,118	93,657	109,906
S. D.			11,394	13,259	25,244	26,369
Tennessee	29,145	37,480	63,134	77,681	123,727	151,201
Texas	16,419	31,963	63,018	85,041	184,355	269,007
Utah	3,674	8,103	14,491	15,337	31,136	33,705
Vermont	22,294	26,482	32,236	37,910	44,084	44,820
Virginia	47,017	62,987	84,235	104,366	161,849	196,791
Washington	1,755	5,154	40,137	48,950	150,142	180,133
W. Va.	16,932	24,445	33,473	52,347	93,165	117,418
Wisconsin	53,013	88,871	140,326	192,283	279,459	340,935
Wyoming	968	1,428	5,029	6,342	11,327	15,415

	1930*/1920	1930*/1940	1940*/1930	1940*/1950	1950
U. S.	14,110,652	10,481,019	11,574,807	10,425,807	14,398,854
Alabama	185,681	137,919	167,236	159,635	219,057
Arizona	34,704	25,777	13,386	12,057	20,535
Arkansas	81,960	60,878	57,030	51,369	77,699
California	636,564	472,823	456,160	410,878	754,614
Colorado	76,734	56,996	38,925	35,061	57,735
Connecticut	309,465	229,862	327,880	295,332	352,302
Delaware	33,604	24,960	32,823	29,565	40,972
D. C.	46,658	34,656	30,875	27,810	27,356
Florida	141,951	105,437	81,902	73,772	103,388
Georgia	233,060	173,111	221,803	199,785	280,918
Idaho	26,652	19,796	11,592	10,441	16,735
Illinois	1,035,696	769,287	910,864	820,445	1,134,927
Indiana	433,095	321,692	382,614	344,633	526,876
Iowa	173,149	128,610	109,147	98,312	151,618
Kansas	131,715	97,834	58,591	52,775	88,694
Kentucky	162,873	120,978	109,627	98,745	147,776
Louisiana	154,889	115,047	103,878	93,566	126,625
Maine	113,985	84,665	94,987	85,558	99,790
Maryland	223,412	165,945	199,589	179,776	222,159
Mass.	773,293	574,382	624,939	562,903	682,166
Michigan	786,031	583,843	771,157	694,606	973,580
Minnesota	206,139	153,115	125,306	112,867	183,657
Mississippi	82,464	61,252	68,844	62,010	82,491
Missouri	361,227	268,310	269,249	242,521	329,726
Montana	33,618	24,971	14,095	12,696	17,378
Nebraska	80,989	60,156	32,854	29,593	46,775
Nevada	7,991	5,936	2,051	1,847	3,234
N. H.	89,303	66,332	74,002	66,656	80,067
N. J.	689,715	512,302	634,328	571,360	738,964
N. M.	23,322	17,323	9,552	8,604	11,905
N. Y.	1,866,374	1,386,294	1,503,574	1,354,318	1,770,420
N. C.	290,719	215,938	354,353	319,177	398,618
N. D.	21,995	16,337	5,510	4,963	6,488
Ohio	991,242	736,269	868,413	782,208	1,119,336
Oklahoma	139,923	103,931	54,190	48,811	72,964
Oregon	107,166	79,600	72,816	65,588	104,359
Penn.	1,416,590	1,052,206	1,186,996	1,069,166	1,391,521
R. I.	151,462	112,502	134,448	121,102	133,910
S. C.	147,590	109,626	162,652	147,407	204,543
S. D.	27,682	20,561	9,956	8,968	11,614
Tennessee	201,614	149,754	187,263	168,674	235,539
Texas	385,307	286,196	228,143	205,496	366,735
Utah	36,969	27,460	17,993	16,207	27,846
Vermont	41,450	30,788	28,970	26,094	32,122
Virginia	212,855	158,103	203,455	183,259	230,604
Washington	188,411	139,947	121,421	109,368	160,757
W. Va.	133,698	99,307	97,433	87,761	113,786
Wisconsin	364,511	270,749	296,112	266,718	411,723
Wyoming	15,155	11,256	4,823	4,344	6,250

*The data are for the upper year, expressed in terms of Census occupational classifications for the lower year.

Appendix Table A-7

LABOR FORCE, 1870 - 1950: REST (SERVICES, ETC.)

	1870	1880	1890	1900	1910	1920
U. S.	3,178,287	4,565,265	7,345,373	9,682,107	13,913,976	16,727,085
Alabama	47,479	56,300	94,702	126,084	193,568	218,714
Arizona	3,089	9,551	11,146	16,439	31,525	54,809
Arkansas	17,454	24,951	54,208	77,509	127,404	143,771
California	91,945	147,727	235,344	289,431	557,486	783,060
Colorado	5,177	30,714	81,456	86,552	149,075	168,754
Connecticut	54,124	65,091	104,296	138,516	182,723	232,524
Delaware	11,706	16,807	22,730	25,724	32,356	38,696
D. C.	34,859	47,986	73,630	95,532	117,831	190,349
Florida	10,462	17,389	42,142	70,290	118,747	163,839
Georgia	67,741	89,919	166,377	206,706	289,001	336,382
Idaho	1,212	3,430	9,507	15,950	43,073	50,821
Illinois	185,072	279,763	498,555	743,656	1,023,428	1,277,492
Indiana	87,979	138,246	203,712	280,573	357,607	411,010
Iowa	66,023	117,500	178,559	244,874	298,035	340,272
Kansas	26,083	59,423	120,146	134,821	218,167	249,021
Kentucky	87,625	101,517	149,191	186,935	242,872	258,381
Louisiana	71,213	85,112	106,627	140,694	212,449	244,369
Maine	53,337	59,955	74,684	91,136	106,046	111,160
Maryland	98,530	125,121	164,314	201,555	244,577	292,859
Mass.	187,153	242,189	378,085	504,020	679,476	778,731
Michigan	106,920	139,863	231,646	292,231	378,556	534,372
Minnesota	28,569	61,773	160,723	224,973	338,237	379,466
Mississippi	35,328	43,779	66,053	91,456	135,590	140,767
Missouri	127,150	175,698	279,314	369,809	500,002	566,804
Montana	2,851	7,701	29,363	40,002	70,728	79,708
Nebraska	11,519	33,991	122,855	117,574	162,794	185,400
Nevada	9,188	11,975	8,141	7,096	18,682	15,575
N. H.	21,677	29,581	40,241	50,743	59,804	62,344
N. J.	111,284	150,288	243,358	338,607	496,006	614,911
N. M.	5,552	12,859	15,944	19,025	32,783	43,517
N. Y.	562,544	760,107	1,081,286	1,425,401	2,021,865	2,417,962
N. C.	48,077	64,000	90,089	117,267	175,271	204,478
N. D.	2,762	15,227	17,099	30,261	64,702	66,648
Ohio	194,257	269,156	427,761	556,507	742,314	918,733
Oklahoma			4,125	45,229	162,385	223,290
Oregon	6,424	16,170	43,701	61,912	131,228	139,363
Penn.	329,878	497,326	742,570	928,394	1,189,728	1,378,191
R. I.	25,243	32,243	53,482	67,153	97,006	104,031
S. C.	33,373	51,698	64,486	84,438	121,629	143,165
S. D.			27,871	33,451	64,675	71,488
Tennessee	56,697	79,447	132,498	181,992	244,489	261,133
Texas	42,600	92,736	171,795	243,611	430,276	625,136
Utah	4,561	10,749	24,414	27,823	52,965	62,120
Vermont	22,440	27,730	34,969	39,555	47,931	47,505
Virginia	95,950	123,718	169,061	201,471	261,091	318,873
Washington	2,607	7,780	67,780	87,361	234,681	258,187
W. Va.	18,148	28,229	49,330	75,492	122,522	144,955
Wisconsin	59,805	97,770	163,696	229,076	301,229	342,663
Wyoming	4,620	4,980	12,311	17,200	29,361	31,286

Appendix Table A-7 (continued)

	$\frac{1930*}{1920}$	$\frac{1930*}{1940}$	$\frac{1940*}{1930}$	$\frac{1940*}{1950}$	1950
U. S.	23,012,448	25,333,451	31,291,646	29,339,436	37,617,484
Alabama	310,962	336,950	439,189	405,981	580,316
Arizona	77,378	79,997	113,817	106,965	196,847
Arkansas	187,113	198,241	281,077	254,459	338,426
California	1,479,369	1,572,303	2,197,128	2,057,127	3,316,687
Colorado	201,327	209,091	273,976	255,737	371,921
Connecticut	329,387	390,152	434,227	413,618	504,929
Delaware	46,769	53,033	70,438	66,104	78,968
D. C.	195,974	200,871	322,960	301,648	375,932
Florida	308,358	330,890	563,515	526,813	857,148
Georgia	422,556	462,054	610,350	565,747	770,432
Idaho	59,002	61,951	103,708	96,271	137,922
Illinois	1,734,086	1,906,365	2,091,488	1,971,201	2,301,047
Indiana	545,690	623,762	717,631	674,137	855,233
Iowa	399,369	425,036	544,871	500,097	586,445
Kansas	318,707	336,183	401,347	370,695	474,865
Kentucky	321,777	335,990	477,383	444,409	546,712
Louisiana	343,403	366,651	497,074	460,566	614,200
Maine	132,609	154,192	189,897	180,091	202,511
Maryland	354,303	393,702	510,770	480,057	688,582
Mass.	976,253	1,123,633	1,157,914	1,096,733	1,240,178
Michigan	860,613	1,009,812	1,108,980	1,051,528	1,388,028
Minnesota	466,249	496,954	663,037	612,408	726,527
Mississippi	197,218	209,469	303,435	270,474	361,556
Missouri	705,777	763,625	900,290	837,203	969,931
Montana	85,773	87,602	125,073	116,829	149,078
Nebraska	228,095	239,601	292,107	267,052	329,268
Nevada	20,870	21,006	32,538	30,968	57,982
N. H.	78,601	96,478	114,196	108,869	122,132
N. J.	951,845	1,080,462	1,184,486	1,121,061	1,308,913
N. M.	52,231	54,445	98,833	91,798	168,575
N. Y.	3,375,159	3,699,871	4,353,034	4,092,778	4,394,577
N. C.	338,524	393,720	570,233	528,604	778,524
N. D.	82,792	85,037	109,848	98,516	125,425
Ohio	1,271,245	1,451,433	1,569,349	1,482,573	1,854,868
Oklahoma	338,493	351,385	448,406	415,746	528,996
Oregon	199,801	217,373	285,793	270,294	415,240
Penn.	1,750,000	1,957,829	2,277,023	2,179,536	2,419,725
R. I.	135,572	166,081	178,177	169,901	205,100
S. C.	191,239	218,718	293,527	269,610	388,758
S. D.	87,514	90,830	116,179	105,262	139,563
Tennessee	360,900	392,772	542,756	501,975	698,454
Texas	938,795	990,940	1,494,471	1,383,640	2,072,138
Utah	81,035	84,817	115,002	107,960	174,771
Vermont	58,540	65,726	78,970	73,854	84,485
Virginia	369,296	403,243	579,939	542,521	868,205
Washington	334,601	365,679	469,753	444,455	691,238
W. Va.	203,423	204,302	288,992	284,918	344,675
Wisconsin	464,484	532,912	637,089	593,405	728,823
Wyoming	39,371	40,282	61,370	57,242	82,628

*The data are for the upper year, expressed in terms of Census occupational classifications for the lower year.

Appendix Table B-1

VALUE OF EXTRACTIVE RESOURCES, 1870 - 1950: TOTAL

	1870	1890	1910	1930	1950
U. S.	$ 2,745,463	$ 3,280,974	$10,512,395	$17,426,866	$35,030,981
Alabama	68,261	79,366	220,486	335,309	528,193
Arizona	305	8,356	48,214	211,089	397,164
Arkansas	41,298	57,193	192,410	310,803	559,017
California	60,718	110,113	311,093	1,241,522	3,105,693
Colorado	3,368	54,673	132,696	244,373	572,453
Connecticut	29,901	23,183	44,861	65,038	129,287
Delaware	8,462	7,419	15,610	23,279	80,732
D. C.	445	439	862	1,527	633
Florida	10,185	15,615	72,918	145,960	444,389
Georgia	82,438	89,389	280,541	301,787	505,654
Idaho	2,647	12,518	72,734	192,956	394,190
Illinois	225,423	204,825	667,947	697,388	1,815,020
Indiana	130,412	114,233	374,352	411,381	874,512
Iowa	119,460	177,664	615,032	730,129	1,673,808
Kansas	28,629	101,070	408,270	583,022	1,102,029
Kentucky	90,110	74,659	247,038	377,224	806,431
Louisiana	52,815	58,183	149,701	297,162	959,824
Maine	42,183	37,448	91,020	131,389	198,925
Maryland	39,974	38,264	78,301	117,402	208,511
Mass.	45,750	39,881	76,301	113,952	192,428
Michigan	104,366	196,050	355,230	445,761	734,164
Minnesota	35,857	96,297	360,700	567,020	1,249,169
Mississippi	74,017	75,553	211,747	353,769	548,142
Missouri	110,572	129,432	473,708	478,449	844,288
Montana	5,880	40,399	123,406	241,806	401,110
Nebraska	8,754	67,172	327,470	442,114	789,658
Nevada	12,968	12,872	35,956	56,651	71,707
N. H.	25,318	16,732	41,870	44,276	66,831
N. J.	47,681	41,375	75,540	171,390	266,230
N. M.	2,288	6,509	31,785	101,898	359,971
N. Y.	273,890	197,800	389,777	516,533	813,768
N. C.	61,349	55,556	212,270	331,325	660,422
N. D.	534	21,363	205,479	220,151	410,204
Ohio	213,030	167,531	463,363	597,205	959,644
Oklahoma		1,807	244,143	829,154	959,603
Oregon	7,976	23,380	110,581	265,492	797,126
Penn.	279,214	283,069	657,602	1,232,523	1,615,407
R. I.	5,138	6,230	11,159	13,509	20,015
S. C.	42,952	55,693	170,922	174,608	265,653
S. D.	Incl. in N.D.	25,854	184,391	243,880	458,125
Tennessee	89,042	66,350	228,494	291,590	463,178
Texas	49,839	118,593	471,320	1,286,833	4,202,136
Utah	2,257	16,674	53,065	179,840	309,605
Vermont	38,842	29,089	69,029	75,890	117,024
Virginia	53,145	54,100	198,328	280,600	492,216
Washington	3,475	24,708	173,438	414,116	679,186
W. Va.	26,702	29,900	173,234	453,443	825,276
Wisconsin	86,601	112,292	312,545	469,195	826,898
Wyoming	992	4,103	45,456	115,153	275,332

Appendix Table B-2

VALUE OF EXTRACTIVE RESOURCES, 1870 - 1950: AGRICULTURAL

	1870	1890	1910	1930	1950
U. S.	$ 2,447,541	$ 2,460,003	$ 8,494,231	$11,011,329	$22,052,255
Alabama	67,522	66,240	170,939	212,280	274,037
Arizona	278	1,046	13,113	48,885	203,937
Arkansas	40,702	53,128	153,835	225,279	392,851
California	49,856	87,033	224,982	623,103	1,741,961
Colorado	2,335	13,137	84,871	187,299	426,448
Connecticut	26,482	17,924	37,457	53,009	121,269
Delaware	8,172	6,482	13,356	21,202	76,228
D. C.	320	373	713	462	570
Florida	8,910	12,086	43,689	92,009	338,645
Georgia	80,390	83,371	257,351	241,187	375,152
Idaho	638	3,849	54,963	135,802	281,025
Illinois	210,861	184,759	586,484	509,866	1,361,578
Indiana	122,914	94,759	341,313	306,671	731,894
Iowa	114,386	159,348	598,799	690,302	1,635,350
Kansas	27,631	95,070	389,413	458,531	764,728
Kentucky	87,477	65,948	218,456	228,699	417,061
Louisiana	52,007	54,344	90,402	161,079	245,730
Maine	33,470	22,049	61,318	92,373	125,515
Maryland	34,344	26,443	64,171	89,828	172,157
Mass.	32,192	28,073	59,875	75,199	135,350
Michigan	81,509	83,651	253,749	266,155	473,612
Minnesota	33,446	71,238	279,063	418,801	960,553
Mississippi	73,138	73,343	172,703	274,214	339,661
Missouri	103,036	109,751	429,670	388,921	719,878
Montana	1,677	6,273	64,066	138,514	279,059
Nebraska	8,605	66,838	327,145	437,250	779,521
Nevada	1,660	2,706	12,684	19,875	34,007
N. H.	22,474	13,761	28,884	28,584	46,500
N. J.	42,725	28,997	62,895	90,018	214,319
N. M.	1,905	1,785	24,902	61,165	154,740
N. Y.	253,526	161,593	352,396	384,192	630,401
N. C.	57,846	50,071	176,262	278,488	556,628
N. D.	496	21,265	204,914	216,685	400,822
Ohio	198,257	133,232	388,191	367,810	711,681
Oklahoma		440	214,868	307,061	471,002
Oregon	7,123	19,026	80,842	137,009	298,079
Penn.	183,946	121,328	281,649	323,552	545,927
R. I.	4,761	4,218	8,086	9,911	16,084
S. C.	41,909	51,238	156,350	140,605	213,562
S. D.	Incl. in N.D.	22,047	177,513	233,480	430,399
Tennessee	86,473	55,194	192,932	219,256	340,542
Texas	49,185	111,699	430,006	749,324	1,753,052
Utah	1,973	4,891	30,802	64,577	130,288
Vermont	34,647	20,365	49,706	55,873	86,988
Virginia	51,775	42,244	150,872	204,653	309,644
Washington	2,112	13,675	104,689	197,745	365,209
W. Va.	23,380	20,439	70,770	81,149	82,146
Wisconsin	78,027	70,991	267,641	400,104	764,629
Wyoming	43	2,242	34,481	63,293	121,836

Appendix Table B-3

VALUE OF EXTRACTIVE RESOURCES, 1870 - 1950: MINERAL

	1870	1890	1910	1930	1950
U. S. $	152,596	$ 582,133	$ 1,238,415	$ 5,164,968	$10,579,973
Alabama	52	9,828	24,351	65,402	143,905
Arizona	25	7,249	34,218	157,960	181,094
Arkansas		568	4,604	41,325	109,523
California	8,282	19,699	63,382	555,001	1,075,612
Colorado	859	41,127	45,680	55,332	139,858
Connecticut	1,227	3,090	1,376	7,053	4,887
Delaware	11	507	516	467	335
D. C.		40		1,065	63
Florida		139	8,847	14,804	55,018
Georgia	49	2,989	2,875	15,294	35,508
Idaho	1,989	8,385	8,649	32,143	64,292
Illinois	6,968	17,110	76,659	182,791	449,894
Indiana	1,137	9,705	21,934	96,962	141,025
Iowa	1,063	10,267	13,878	35,955	37,458
Kansas	174	5,936	18,723	124,472	337,162
Kentucky	509	4,712	12,100	132,650	372,229
Louisiana	1	480	6,547	62,726	631,813
Maine	622	8,126	2,056	6,749	6,742
Maryland	3,444	5,089	5,782	18,470	20,461
Mass.	1,494	3,701	3,468	16,031	12,449
Michigan	7,199	70,881	67,714	151,976	201,260
Minnesota	35	11,542	58,665	136,350	257,540
Mississippi		41		2,573	103,711
Missouri	3,473	15,932	31,668	78,948	111,293
Montana	4,030	33,738	54,992	93,842	98,070
Nebraska	30	257	323	4,845	10,102
Nevada	11,166	10,144	23,272	36,776	37,372
N. H.	324	920	1,309	3,726	1,384
N. J.	2,554	8,276	8,348	71,892	38,584
N. M.	343	4,612	5,588	37,128	198,825
N. Y.	4,325	24,165	13,335	109,361	138,493
N. C.	638	1,238	1,359	10,964	19,755
N. D.		61	565	3,466	8,818
Ohio	7,752	26,653	63,767	220,061	242,080
Oklahoma		1,334**	25,638	516,685	484,264
Oregon	418	1,238	1,192	6,877	21,845
Penn.	76,208	150,877	349,060	892,914	1,035,970
R. I.	59	987	898	940	929
S. C.	20	3,022	1,253	3,592	9,026
S. D.		3,685	6,432	8,914	26,723
Tennessee	776	6,456	12,693	40,720	77,333
Texas	1	1,986	10,742	495,820	2,379,793
Utah	15	11,681	22,083	115,131	177,825
Vermont	905	5,674	8,221	14,603	17,384
Virginia	410	6,023	8,796	39,753	116,408
Washington	109	2,998	10,538	22,435	40,863
W. Va.	2,539	6,970	76,288	346,565	718,119
Wisconsin	511	10,184	7,459	24,222	35,878
Wyoming	850	1,811	10,572	51,237	150,998

** Includes Indian Territory.

Appendix Table B-4

VALUE OF EXTRACTIVE RESOURCES, 1870 - 1950: FOREST

	1870	1890	1910	1930	1950
U. S.	$ 134,229	$ 199,937	$ 725,737	$1,137,180	$2,086,249
Alabama	686	3,143	24,809	57,627	108,129
Arizona	2	61	883	4,244	12,133
Arkansas	594	3,422	33,764	42,922	55,836
California	2,430	2,290	20,759	50,548	206,515
Colorado	174	404	2,145	1,742	6,147
Connecticut	1,422	611	3,046	1,341	1,017
Delaware	272	163	1,197	1,274	1,028
D. C.	125		149		
Florida	1,173	2,106	16,993	33,027	35,022
Georgia	1,998	2,905	19,614	44,429	91,410
Idaho	20	225	9,122	25,011	48,873
Illinois	7,577	2,679	3,368	2,269	1,392
Indiana	6,359	9,709	10,882	7,608	1,496
Iowa	4,010	7,894	2,140	2,777	440
Kansas	822	36	106	Incl. in Iowa	139
Kentucky	2,120	3,913	16,372	14,769	16,580
Louisiana	798	2,699	51,183	68,853	56,476
Maine	7,111	5,162	24,389	27,370	51,979
Maryland	995	713	5,042	4,809	7,005
Mass.	5,849	2,249	5,863	4,670	3,861
Michigan	15,090	40,696	32,294	25,062	56,207
Minnesota	2,376	13,443	22,780	10,514	29,683
Mississippi	879	1,923	38,488	74,843	100,840
Missouri	4,062	3,621	12,099	9,305	12,522
Montana	173	380	4,348	9,450	23,981
Nebraska	119	57	Incl. in Kan.	Incl. in Ia.	35
Nevada	142		Included in Calif.		328
N. H.	2,520	1,962	11,624	11,914	18,728
N. J.	2,027	655	1,228	749	3,126
N. M.	40	109	1,295	3,605	6,406
N. Y.	15,803	7,315	19,452	17,706	28,578
N. C.	2,599	3,219	32,873	39,329	77,239
N. D.	38	36			564
Ohio	6,638	7,146	10,565	8,668	3,280
Oklahoma		31	3,636	5,329	3,962
Oregon	380	2,105	27,191	119,001	470,051
Penn.	19,022	10,411	26,380	15,836	32,716
R. I.	193	90	423	223	214
S. C.	1,023	1,230	13,031	30,136	40,255
S. D.	Incl. in N.D.	111	442	1,486	1,003
Tennessee	1,790	4,642	22,757	30,479	43,367
Texas	653	4,594	30,126	40,712	58,026
Utah	267	97	180	132	1,492
Vermont	3,290	3,037	11,102	5,414	12,652
Virginia	873	2,197	33,944	28,908	50,045
Washington	964	7,144	54,698	184,373	254,043
W. Va.	783	2,486	26,174	25,729	25,011
Wisconsin	7,849	30,766	36,378	42,364	23,919
Wyoming	99	50	403	623	2,498

Appendix Table B-5

VALUE OF EXTRACTIVE RESOURCES, 1870 - 1950: FISH

	1870	1890	1910	1930	1950
U. S.	$ 11,097	$ 38,901	$ 54,012	$113,389	$312,504
Alabama	1	155	387		2,122
Arizona					
Arkansas	2	75	207	1,277	807
California	150	1,091	1,970	12,870	81,605
Colorado		5			
Connecticut	770	1,558	2,982	3,635	2,114
Delaware	7	267	541	336	3,141
D. C.		26			
Florida	102	1,284	3,389	6,120	15,704
Georgia	1	124	701	877	3,584
Idaho		59			
Illinois	17	277	1,436	2,462	2,156
Indiana	2	60	223	140	97
Iowa	1	155	215	1,095	560
Kansas	2	28	28	19	
Kentucky	4	86	110	1,106	561
Louisiana	9	660	1,569	4,504	25,805
Maine	980	2,111	3,257	4,897	14,689
Maryland	191	6,019	3,306	4,295	8,888
Mass.	6,215	5,858	7,095	18,052	40,768
Michigan	568	822	1,473	2,568	3,085
Minnesota		74	192	1,355	1,393
Mississippi		246	556	2,139	3,930
Missouri	1	128	271	1,275	595
Montana		8			
Nebraska		20	2	19	
Nevada		22			
N. H.		89	53	52	219
N. J.	375	3,447	3,069	8,731	10,201
N. M.		3			
N. Y.	236	4,727	4,594	5,274	16,296
N. C.	266	1,028	1,776	2,544	6,800
N. D.		1			
Ohio	383	500	840	666	2,603
Oklahoma		2	1	79	375
Oregon	55	1,011	1,356	2,605	7,151
Penn.	38	453	513	221	794
R. I.	125	935	1,752	2,435	2,788
S. C.		203	288	275	2,810
S. D.		11	4		
Tennessee	3	58	112	1,135	1,936
Texas		314	446	977	11,265
Utah	2	5			
Vermont		13			
Virginia	87	3,636	4,716	7,286	16,119
Washington	290	891	3,513	9,563	19,071
W. Va.		5	2		
Wisconsin	214	351	1,067	2,505	2,472
Wyoming					

Appendix Table C

NET SHIFT BY STATES IN SELECTED LABOR FORCE COMPONENTS, 1870 - 1910

	TOTAL LABOR FORCE			AGRICULTURE		
	Actual Change	Downward Shift	Upward Shift	Actual Change	Downward Shift	Upward Shift
U. S.	25,661,413	-5,372,116	5,372,125	5,952,468	-2,838,949	2,838,952
Alabama	632,266	-117,222		362,751		85,811
Arizona	81,795		69,422	19,912		18,226
Arkansas	536,454		257,495	354,381		250,991
California	869,020		379,329	154,527		101,478
Colorado	321,141		285,062	77,481		70,748
Connecticut	297,041	-99,847		-1,453	-45,345	
Delaware	45,550	-37,170		4,240	-12,868	
D. C.	108,924		8,295	-533	-2,151	
Florida	261,384		136,825	72,137		29,957
Georgia	715,448	-197,005		372,338		50,458
Idaho	120,209		97,886	53,944		52,545
Illinois	1,554,763		32,193	32,651	-350,961	
Indiana	577,341	-365,257		52,572	-215,952	
Iowa	482,037	-224,397		125,880	-84,801	
Kansas	497,481		243,344	195,621		123,077
Kentucky	452,387	-398,333		172,533	-86,249	
Louisiana	422,731	-103,493		177,616		31,764
Maine	97,232	-330,033		-15,485	-97,611	
Maryland	282,621	-247,894		16,141	-69,477	
Mass.	951,224	-238,581		-14,424	-90,151	
Michigan	708,834	-120,486		113,016	-80,112	
Minnesota	702,795		430,591	194,615		116,868
Mississippi	560,795	-93,466		399,094		146,787
Missouri	782,780	-254,591		159,886	-111,346	
Montana	164,699		135,873	51,199		49,154
Nebraska	397,277		307,326	176,304		152,090
Nevada	17,999	-37,221		6,145		3,898
N. H.	71,535	-175,043		-14,403	-59,673	
N. J.	778,324		170,876	1,259	-67,915	
N. M.	92,136		31,889	44,779		25,046
N. Y.	2,512,826	-546,653		-48,635	-438,403	
N. C.	596,540	-124,304		321,032		60,917
N. D.	430,608		418,528	252,888		250,464
Ohio	1,078,166	-647,288		-18,930	-422,449	
Oklahoma	598,629		598,629	348,216		348,216
Oregon	274,513		211,619	64,683		51,091
Penn.	2,110,137		16,042	43,789	-241,754	
R. I.	163,327	-18,422		-2,130	-14,526	
S. C.	465,326	-74,952		295,586		96,534
S. D.	Included in North Dakota					
Tennessee	487,559	-267,528		184,126	-75,045	
Texas	1,319,740		833,172	750,169		585,948
Utah	110,023		65,871	24,696		13,096
Vermont	35,326	-187,849		-13,463	-70,944	
Virginia	382,903	-463,861		84,726	-159,573	
Washington	511,741		491,714	93,783		89,885
W. Va.	333,261		96,818	81,888		9,591
Wisconsin	599,604	-1,220		120,833	-41,643	
Wyoming	66,961		53,326	24,487		24,312
Total Net Shift as % of 1870 Labor Force		43.0			44.1	

	MINING			FOREST		
	Actual Change	Downward Shift	Upward Shift	Actual Change	Downward Shift	Upward Shift
U. S.	778,553	-372,280	372,281	141,171	-69,001	68,998
Alabama	28,680		27,695	3,398	-842	
Arizona	15,322		14,271	695		673
Arkansas	4,877		4,806	5,620		4,961
California	-9,769	-181,144		6,539	-7,081	
Colorado	25,908		15,570	805		500
Connecticut	-824	-9,744		450	-161	
Delaware	306		218	61		4
D. C.	64		10	23		19
Florida	3,518		3,518	4,873		2,683
Georgia	3,219		2,076	3,565		437
Idaho	-683	-31,597		2,579		2,339
Illinois	59,057		22,594	324	-2,132	
Indiana	22,765		16,324	202	-3,310	
Iowa	14,042		6,983	-45	-1,589	
Kansas	13,473		11,262	-138	-1,111	
Kentucky	19,035		10,387	1,993		693
Louisiana	1,290		1,165	8,552		5,106
Maine	1,176	-414		2,026	-7,589	
Maryland	4,011	-10,007		803		314
Mass.	1,799	-1,885		938	-414	
Michigan	32,607		16,303	8,935	-3,734	
Minnesota	19,097		18,772	6,099	-1,793	
Mississippi	84		84	5,130		3,272
Missouri	23,409		9,270	3,584		1,411
Montana	11,841	-19,732		1,416		657
Nebraska	610		385	13	-162	
Nevada	413	-38,908		-592	-3,921	
N. H.	308	-802		1,440	-702	
N. J.	2,550	-12,636		348	-311	
N. M.	5,565		3,204	772		768
N. Y.	7,250	-13,689		1,056	-8,236	
N. C.	1,484	-1,098		6,339		4,825
N. D.	4,757		4,753	125	-460	
Ohio	39,225	-24,994		212	-2,973	
Oklahoma	11,779		11,779	1,925		1,925
Oregon	-795	-19,431		6,770		5,514
Penn.	277,580		68,118	4,516	-14,073	
R. I.	253	-523		211		89
S. C.	657		536	1,219		674
S. D.				Incl. in N.D.		
Tennessee	16,353		11,209	4,386		2,248
Texas	8,249		8,124	4,737		2,909
Utah	9,375		6,672	55	-294	
Vermont	1,044	-5,093		471	-1,126	
Virginia	11,922		6,494	2,393		142
Washington	11,204		10,357	22,766		19,293
W. Va.	62,680		55,008	8,048		7,542
Wisconsin	4,724	-583		5,231	-6,356	
Wyoming	7,062		4,334	303	-631	
Total Net Shift as % of 1870 Labor Force		199.5			213.2	

	FISHING			MANUFACTURING		
	Actual Change	Downward Shift	Upward Shift	Actual Change	Downward Shift	Upward Shift
U. S.	40,404	-22,469	22,473	8,013,128	-1,674,341	1,674,346
Alabama	410		151	90,938		39,733
Arizona	1		1	17,429		14,819
Arkansas	1,275		1,246	60,351		40,662
California	2,824		1,406	249,358		115,512
Colorado	62		61	72,987		65,181
Connecticut	-154	-1,525		170,423	-98,170	
Delaware	376		250	19,917	-10,348	
D. C.	-40	-128		26,438	-11,020	
Florida	2,845		2,604	69,726		57,731
Georgia	486		251	114,580		30,663
Idaho	15		15	22,493		20,404
Illinois	2,574		2,119	621,801		220,256
Indiana	373		216	231,801	-6,263	
Iowa	341		199	109,807	-36,501	
Kansas	59		36	96,382		40,163
Kentucky	286		144	103,293	-32,014	
Louisiana	2,721		1,711	91,316		12,537
Maine	518	-5,289		56,288	-124,020	
Maryland	5,837		3,499	109,782	-79,177	
Mass.	500	-7,417		470,088	-451,870	
Michigan	771	-831		281,869		37,948
Minnesota	493		407	172,823		118,071
Mississippi	654		573	55,571		24,715
Missouri	294		85	222,755	-22,930	
Montana	19		18	32,347		28,582
Nebraska	51		48	69,024		50,730
Nevada	16		4	2,523	-12,928	
N. H.	17	-99		46,046	-101,569	
N. J.	2,430		750	387,015		68,744
N. M.	11		11	13,778		8,012
N. Y.	-170	-3,981		1,094,004	-413,110	
N. C.	1,821		18	138,670		78,931
N. D.	13		12	46,210		45,094
Ohio	684		238	508,918	-78,588	
Oklahoma	123		123	74,201		74,201
Oregon	1,651		1,516	77,400		63,213
Penn.	46	-606		924,356	-66,726	
R. I.	335	-704		92,895	-55,623	
S. C.	110	-394		79,498		36,577
S. D.	Included in North Dakota					
Tennessee	320		120	94,582		6,233
Texas	973		887	167,936		118,164
Utah	31		18	27,462		16,325
Vermont	-7	-48		21,790	-45,791	
Virginia	3,889	-1,447		114,832	-27,693	
Washington	3,527		3,260	148,387		143,069
W. Va.	38		28	76,233		24,906
Wisconsin	946		439	226,446		65,745
Wyoming	9		2	10,359		7,425
Total Net Shift as % of 1870 Labor Force		80.6			63.3	

Appendix Table C (continued)

	Actual Change	Downward Shift	Upward Shift
		REST (Services, etc.)	
U. S.	10,735,689	-2,162,800	2,162,807
Alabama	146,089	-14,287	
Arizona	28,436		18,002
Arkansas	109,950		50,994
California	465,541		154,967
Colorado	143,898		126,411
Connecticut	128,599	-54,222	
Delaware	20,650	-18,891	
D. C.	82,972	-34,775	
Florida	108,285		72,946
Georgia	221,260	-7,557	
Idaho	41,861		37,767
Illinois	838,356		213,216
Indiana	269,628	-27,549	
Iowa	232,012		8,998
Kansas	192,084		103,980
Kentucky	155,247	-140,734	
Louisiana	141,236	-99,309	
Maine	52,709	-127,454	
Maryland	146,047	-186,770	
Mass.	492,323	-139,846	
Michigan	271,636	-89,521	
Minnesota	309,668		213,167
Mississippi	100,262	-19,070	
Missouri	372,852	-56,638	
Montana	67,877		58,247
Nebraska	151,275		112,366
Nevada	9,494	-21,541	
N. H.	38,127	-35,094	
N. J.	384,722		8,825
N. M.	27,231		8,477
N. Y.	1,459,321	-440,851	
N. C.	127,194	-35,201	
N. D.	126,615		117,285
Ohio	548,057	-108,108	
Oklahoma	162,385		162,385
Oregon	124,804		103,105
Penn.	859,850	-254,419	
R. I.	71,763	-13,503	
S. C.	88,256	-24,472	
S. D.	Included in North Dakota		
Tennessee	187,792	-3,720	
Texas	387,676		243,781
Utah	48,404		32,998
Vermont	25,491	-50,307	
Virginia	165,141	-158,961	
Washington	232,074		223,268
W. Va.	104,374		43,073
Wisconsin	241,424		39,414
Wyoming	24,741		9,135
Total Net Shift as % of 1870 Labor Force		68.0	

Note: Underscored data indicate Absolute Upward or
Downward Shift. Other shift data are Relative
Upward or Downward Shift.

Appendix Table D

NET SHIFT BY STATES IN SELECTED LABOR FORCE COMPONENTS, 1910 - 1950

	TOTAL LABOR FORCE			AGRICULTURE		
	Actual Change	Downward Shift	Upward Shift	Actual Change	Downward Shift	Upward Shift
U. S.	22,033,512	-6,322,295	6,322,294	-5,427,061	-824,389	824,388
Alabama	101,709	-474,149		-398,669	-108,586	
Arizona	178,710		128,010	16,088		25,608
Arkansas	-17,077	-405,247		-243,521	-39,317	
California	3,309,803		2,670,361	83,641		176,458
Colorado	175,984	-19,557		-11,190		25,938
Connecticut	390,162		107,025	-24,118	-3,962	
Delaware	45,295	-4,273		-11,949	-1,987	
D. C.	245,987		154,796	-747	-214	
Florida	780,800		594,863	3,552		55,131
Georgia	189,953	-479,773		-445,332	-129,762	
Idaho	88,060		12,385	541		24,833
Illinois	1,432,850		106,950	-199,865	-3,843	
Indiana	536,250	-62,229		-168,715	-18,485	
Iowa	198,530	-278,490		-70,946		83,994
Kansas	119,500	-239,188		-111,935		8,117
Kentucky	151,884	-348,612		-201,233	-3,072	
Louisiana	255,153	-136,931		-180,889	-33,997	
Maine	39,618	-136,718		-43,952	-11,831	
Maryland	430,863		118,456	-55,311	-7,683	
Mass.	428,830	-455,036		-37,949	-8,395	
Michigan	1,429,592		787,073	-163,014	-22,024	
Minnesota	355,498	-126,798		-18,218		103,857
Mississippi	-104,464	-612,272		-355,251	-60,918	
Missouri	291,272	-452,468		-185,822		12,697
Montana	54,109	-49,079		1,692		25,087
Nebraska	87,092	-167,557		-51,663		37,033
Nevada	26,199		273	-2,126		1,630
N. H.	25,627	-85,041		-21,804	-6,668	
N. J.	1,025,789		405,575	-30,687		2,633
N. M.	109,493		39,354	-26,800		2,162
N. Y.	2,343,425		32,057	-205,783	-42,450	
N. C.	617,032		69,857	-231,869		31,970
N. D.	16,310	-109,203		-29,839		27,464
Ohio	1,297,129		189,283	-208,384	-25,526	
Oklahoma	201,830	-143,751		-191,220	-38,693	
Oregon	316,122		139,955	-8,843		25,928
Penn.	1,037,658	-769,644		-193,293	-38,848	
R. I.	92,038	-53,381		-7,371	-2,432	
S. C.	80,080	-340,547		-303,995	-80,229	
S. D.	33,893	-92,577		-26,000		28,616
Tennessee	351,158	-142,738		-211,490	-8,067	
Texas	1,434,145		535,386	-475,341	-68,955	
Utah	112,377		36,441	-8,553		7,759
Vermont	1,547	-81,634		-23,607	-2,275	
Virginia	512,055		52,784	-180,689	-27,851	
Washington	438,174		137,118	-18,721		24,205
W. Va.	211,011	-47,896		-98,436	-28,319	
Wisconsin	507,672	-7,506		-45,186		84,708
Wyoming	46,784		4,292	-2,249		8,560
Total Net Shift as % of 1910 Labor Force	16.6			6.7		

Appendix Table D (continued)

	MINING			FOREST		
	Actual Change	Downward Shift	Upward Shift	Actual Change	Downward Shift	Upward Shift
U. S.	-35,748	-292,712	292,712	41,901	-55,289	55,291
Alabama	-1,476	-405		3,207		2,152
Arizona	-5,080	-4,503		99	-70	
Arkansas	1,879		2,060	2,683		1,290
California	-974		186	2,542		209
Colorado	-18,111	-17,060		132	-79	
Connecticut	-777	-728		-237	-379	
Delaware	-243	-231		50		32
D. C.	44		47	37		31
Florida	1,781		1,911	3,487		2,188
Georgia	1,559		1,688	13,313		12,279
Idaho	-1,353	-1,104		349	-287	
Illinois	-24,171	-21,660		630		416
Indiana	-9,031	-8,131		54	-189	
Iowa	-12,426	-11,843		99		24
Kansas	843		1,362	158		137
Kentucky	48,607		49,389	968		415
Louisiana	22,881		22,930	-2,247	-4,503	
Maine	-941	-883		3,560		2,539
Maryland	-4,590	-4,317		137	-84	
Mass.	-1,236	-1,137		-318	-619	
Michigan	-21,106	-19,753		-6,604	-9,463	
Minnesota	-3,378	-2,668		-4,028	-5,937	
Mississippi	3,532		3,535	3,608		2,266
Missouri	-17,312	-16,319		-1,372	-2,358	
Montana	-10,108	-9,389		341	-43	
Nebraska	398		423	90		77
Nevada	-6,517	-6,153		-79	-120	
N. H.	-386	-365		123	-343	
N. J.	-2,141	-1,912		1	-119	
N. M.	4,395		4,622	-159	-346	
N. Y.	-2,811	-2,357		66	-703	
N. C.	973		1,051	4,399		2,785
N. D.	249		268	9	-3	
Ohio	-24,012	-21,989		547		320
Oklahoma	28,190		28,626	-593	-1,058	
Oregon	-2,023	-1,887		21,068		19,364
Penn.	-135,557	-123,416		-3,653	-5,772	
R. I.	-264	-248		-120	-178	
S. C.	449		474	5,508		5,183
S. D.	-1,516	-1,359		130		80
Tennessee	-3,135	-2,484		-275	-1,452	
Texas	81,672		81,979	1,537		292
Utah	2,058		2,429	296		263
Vermont	-663	-570		1,216		1,014
Virginia	15,762		16,252	2,637		1,935
Washington	-7,521	-7,098		-4,192	-9,881	
W. Va.	69,810		72,200	-3,135	-5,106	
Wisconsin	-2,965	-2,743		-3,998	-5,902	
Wyoming	994		1,280	-170	-295	
Total Net Shift as % of 1910 Labor Force		30.3			31.9	

Appendix Table D (continued)

	FISHING			MANUFACTURING		
	Actual Change	Downward Shift	Upward Shift	Actual Change	Downward Shift	Upward Shift
U. S.	8,602	-16,689	16,689	3,742,309	-1,972,805	1,972,804
Alabama	672		598	111,227		73,360
Arizona	36		36	2,245	-4,178	
Arkansas	7	-156		10,853	-12,622	
California	4,291		3,812	461,102		358,028
Colorado	134		126	-17,827	-44,362	
Connecticut	-186	-286		93,274		2,310
Delaware	-246	-304		11,071		571
D. C.	-9	-12		-11,439	-25,063	
Florida	3,874		3,495	29,705		3,829
Georgia	327		245	138,655		88,696
Idaho	121		119	-6,447	-14,588	
Illinois	-2,025	-2,389		380,662		115,783
Indiana	-225	-286		216,541		107,559
Iowa	-153	-208		-6,454	-61,965	
Kansas	-30	-39		-26,234	-66,594	
Kentucky	-145	-193		-153	-52,102	
Louisiana	4,336		3,905	9,321	-31,873	
Maine	465	-105		-15,979	-56,634	
Maryland	-3,420	-4,359		50,042	-10,401	
Mass.	-306	-1,057		-92,063	-363,953	
Michigan	-401	-637		611,245		484,002
Minnesota	60	-10		-7,228	-74,262	
Mississippi	940		851	16,741	-6,349	
Missouri	-74	-129		25,923	-80,765	
Montana	45		42	-16,211	-28,007	
Nebraska	77		70	-28,284	-54,643	
Nevada	7		4	-4,386	-7,062	
N. H.	41		29	-14,675	-47,946	
N. J.	-1,247	-1,699		246,956		74,175
N. M.	40		39	-3,775	-9,281	
N. Y.	1	-309		179,240	-379,542	
N. C.	35	-351		240,241		184,623
N. D.	14		14	-14,846	-22,338	
Ohio	-184	-309		416,608		169,828
Oklahoma	79		64	-1,237	-27,295	
Oregon	-371	-591		22,279	-6,545	
Penn.	-57	-119		140,221	-299,204	
R. I.	-322	-455		-7,979	-57,807	
S. C.	103		45	110,886		77,996
S. D.	21		20	-13,630	-22,495	
Tennessee	281		223	111,812		68,362
Texas	2,035		1,905	182,380		117,639
Utah	60		55	-3,290	-14,224	
Vermont	9		6	-11,962	-27,443	
Virginia	-1,524	-2,478		68,755		11,918
Washington	1,436		968	10,615	-42,111	
W. Va.	-2	-8		20,621	-12,096	
Wisconsin	-37	-200		132,264		34,125
Wyoming	19		18	-5,077	-9,055	
Total Net Shift as % of 1910 Labor Force	24.4			18.5		

Appendix Table D (continued)

	REST (Services, etc.)		
	Actual Change	Downward Shift	Upward Shift
U. S.	23,703,508	-4,851,842	4,851,781
Alabama	386,748		56,989
Arizona	165,322		111,617
Arkansas	211,022	-6,021	
California	2,759,201		1,809,479
Colorado	222,846	-31,115	
Connecticut	322,206		10,923
Delaware	46,612	-8,509	
D. C.	258,101		57,366
Florida	738,401		536,106
Georgia	481,431	-10,905	
Idaho	94,849		21,471
Illinois	1,277,619	-465,873	
Indiana	497,626	-111,586	
Iowa	288,410	-219,316	
Kansas	256,698	-114,967	
Kentucky	303,840	-109,5_2	
Louisiana	401,751		39,827
Maine	96,465	-84,193	
Maryland	444,005		27,349
Mass.	560,702	-596,840	
Michigan	1,009,472		364,572
Minnesota	388,290	-187,924	
Mississippi	225,9(	-5,022	
Missouri	469,929	-381,864	
Montana	78,350	-42,141	
Nebraska	166,474	-110,859	
Nevada	39,300		7,474
N. H.	62,328	-39,553	
N. J.	812,907	-32,079	
N. M.	135,792		79,944
N. Y.	2,372,712	-1,071,696	
N. C.	603,253		304,665
N. D.	60,723	-49,502	
Ohio	1,112,554	-152,037	
Oklahoma	366,611		89,975
Oregon	284,012		60,455
Penn.	1,229,997	-796,800	
R. I.	108,094	-57,163	
S. C.	267,129		59,924
S. D.	74,888	-35,291	
Tennessee	453,965		37,458
Texas	1,641,862		908,852
Utah	121,806		31,576
Vermont	36,554	-45,100	
Virginia	607,114		162,325
Washington	456,557		56,759
W. Va.	222,153		13,427
Wisconsin	427,594	-85,574	
Wyoming	53,267		3,248
Total Net Shift as % of 1910 Labor Force		34.9	

Note: Underscored data indicate Absolute Upward or
Downward Shift. Other shift data are Relative
Upward or Downward Shift.

Appendix Table E

PER CAPITA PERSONAL INCOME AND ITS COMPONENTS, 1880, 1900, 1920*, 1940, 1950, AND 1957**

	1880			1900			1920*		
	Total Personal Income	Property Income	Partici- pation Income	Total Personal Income	Property Income	Partici- pation Income	Total Personal Income	Property Income	Partici- pation Income
	Per Capita in Dollars			Per Capita in Dollars			Per Capita in Dollars		
U. S.	175	27	148	203	33	170	658	125	533
Alabama	82	8	74	88	9	78	313	34	279
Arizona	399	18	381	321	34	287	701	94	608
Arkansas	79	7	72	89	9	80	329	40	290
California	392	54	338	365	76	289	998	228	770
Colorado	371	23	348	318	37	282	728	124	603
Connecticut	268	46	222	278	47	231	789	194	596
Delaware	199	34	165	220	45	175	708	194	514
Florida	79	10	69	112	16	96	437	83	354
Georgia	86	11	75	86	10	75	348	46	302
Idaho	281	4	277	221	15	205	597	65	529
Illinois	208	32	176	260	45	215	829	172	657
Indiana	150	20	130	182	21	161	582	83	499
Iowa	168	23	145	202	27	175	564	104	460
Kansas	120	13	107	187	23	164	588	97	491
Kentucky	107	14	93	120	16	104	400	53	348
Louisiana	138	14	124	128	17	111	426	72	354
Maine	149	23	127	187	27	161	611	104	506
Maryland	171	33	138	204	40	163	726	165	563
Mass.	292	58	234	304	59	246	907	203	704
Michigan	175	23	152	185	27	158	719	124	596
Minnesota	175	22	153	207	29	178	574	107	466
Mississippi	82	7	75	84	7	77	281	30	251
Missouri	157	21	136	188	26	162	584	98	486
Montana	456	16	440	415	38	377	627	85	543
Nebraska	156	14	142	212	27	185	557	106	451
Nevada	606	36	570	395	54	340	939	125	797
N. H.	198	28	171	214	28	186	657	120	537
N. J.	253	46	207	277	49	228	812	169	644
N. M.	105	4	101	148	17	131	477	51	426
N. Y.	280	53	227	323	73	250	1,026	251	775
N. C.	64	8	56	72	8	64	354	40	315
N. D.	186	12	174	209	14	195	458	45	413
Ohio	177	30	147	222	34	188	707	122	585
Oklahoma				114	17	97	504	89	416
Oregon	234	13	221	248	29	219	744	126	617
Penn.	222	44	178	250	48	202	744	144	601
R. I.	279	57	222	293	64	228	849	210	640
S. C.	72	9	64	74	8	66	336	40	296
S. D.				183	15	168	539	71	466
Tennessee	81	12	70	101	10	91	361	45	316
Texas	98	12	86	138	20	118	539	97	442
Utah	134	13	122	183	22	161	556	77	480
Vermont	168	23	144	190	24	169	580	92	487
Virginia	85	13	72	110	14	97	420	59	361
Washington	234	15	219	296	32	264	770	130	640
W. Va.	89	11	77	117	12	105	513	81	430
Wisconsin	156	19	137	179	25	154	608	83	524
Wyoming	321	18	303	311	31	280	902	117	779

* 1919-21 average

Appendix Table E (continued)

	1940				1950				1957			
	Total Personal Income	Property Income	Participation Income	Net Transfer Payments	Total Personal Income	Property Income	Participation Income	Net Transfer Payments	Total Personal Income	Property Income	Participation Income	Net Transfer Payments
	Per Capita in Dollars				Per Capita in Dollars				Per Capita in Dollars			
U. S.	595	96	475	24	1,491	187	1,224	80	2,027	252	1,649	126
Alabama	282	28	244	10	867	78	721	68	1,324	111	1,110	102
Arizona	497	62	405	28	1,297	138	1,081	78	1,750	179	1,466	106
Arkansas	256	23	222	11	805	71	655	79	1,151	117	924	110
California	840	146	650	44	1,848	249	1,491	108	2,523	335	2,034	154
Colorado	546	85	424	37	1,446	192	1,146	108	1,996	269	1,593	134
Connecticut	917	199	695	23	1,908	312	1,523	73	2,821	421	2,261	139
Delaware	1,004	353	632	19	2,153	519	1,572	62	2,740	637	1,998	103
Florida	513	111	381	20	1,288	195	1,006	88	1,836	274	1,422	140
Georgia	340	38	291	11	1,016	102	848	66	1,431	135	1,200	96
Idaho	464	38	406	21	1,279	122	1,090	68	1,630	161	1,359	111
Illinois	754	117	609	28	1,827	233	1,523	71	2,447	282	2,041	124
Indiana	553	65	466	22	1,521	153	1,311	57	2,010	198	1,700	111
Iowa	501	58	424	20	1,447	168	1,216	64	1,806	228	1,469	110
Kansas	426	56	351	20	1,374	158	1,151	65	1,787	249	1,424	114
Kentucky	320	40	268	12	958	92	798	67	1,372	139	1,123	110
Louisiana	363	49	300	14	1,089	117	872	100	1,566	159	1,291	115
Maine	523	102	395	24	1,188	168	944	75	1,663	215	1,313	136
Maryland	712	139	550	22	1,588	210	1,313	65	2,156	255	1,784	117
Mass.	784	171	578	35	1,662	254	1,305	103	2,335	366	1,786	182
Michigan	679	84	573	22	1,684	185	1,436	63	2,141	227	1,797	118
Minnesota	526	71	427	28	1,397	164	1,149	83	1,850	229	1,500	121
Mississippi	218	19	191	9	729	58	601	70	958	88	784	85
Missouri	524	80	424	20	1,443	176	1,185	82	1,940	239	1,570	131
Montana	570	57	487	27	1,606	159	1,374	72	1,896	207	1,564	126
Nebraska	439	55	364	19	1,468	165	1,242	61	1,818	246	1,468	104
Nevada	876	150	690	35	1,938	278	1,593	68	2,423	273	2,045	109
N. H.	579	112	441	24	1,314	212	1,017	85	1,862	271	1,449	143
N. J.	822	147	653	23	1,792	223	1,501	68	2,504	292	2,070	141
N. M.	375	43	318	15	1,163	121	971	71	1,686	161	1,431	92
N. Y.	870	187	647	36	1,883	293	1,503	87	2,578	393	2,033	151
N. C.	328	33	286	9	1,009	87	864	58	1,317	129	1,108	80
N. D.	350	31	303	17	1,260	113	1,081	66	1,435	152	1,183	99
Ohio	665	94	545	25	1,614	201	1,344	70	2,255	264	1,868	123
Oklahoma	373	49	305	18	1,133	137	905	92	1,619	189	1,295	135
Oregon	623	74	523	27	1,602	174	1,346	82	1,914	232	1,543	139
Penn.	648	110	511	28	1,566	199	1,253	113	2,112	268	1,703	141
R. I.	743	163	548	32	1,644	231	1,307	106	1,990	313	1,505	172
S. C.	307	27	270	9	881	78	741	62	1,180	111	992	76
S. D.	359	33	306	19	1,213	109	1,035	69	1,531	174	1,262	95
Tennessee	339	36	288	14	995	105	816	74	1,383	134	1,151	99
Texas	432	64	355	13	1,340	159	1,109	73	1,791	218	1,477	95
Utah	487	54	409	25	1,283	131	1,081	71	1,694	172	1,420	103
Vermont	507	88	399	19	1,185	177	937	71	1,665	234	1,295	133
Virginia	466	58	395	13	1,222	118	1,049	55	1,660	174	1,398	87
Washington	662	83	549	30	1,671	179	1,365	127	2,128	246	1,726	155
W. Va.	407	42	352	13	1,095	105	929	61	1,554	143	1,297	114
Wisconsin	554	78	454	22	1,467	179	1,232	56	1,920	237	1,570	114
Wyoming	608	72	512	24	1,629	182	1,385	62	2,038	263	1,668	108

**Detail will not necessarily add to totals due to rounding.

651

Appendix Table F-1

TOTAL EMPLOYMENT AND ITS ONE-DIGIT COMPONENTS, 1939

	Total	Agri-culture	Mining	Construc-tion	Manufac-turing	Transp't Pub. Util.
U. S.	40,908,238	11,250,252	827,410	1,177,000	9,622,923	2,912,000
Alabama	852,549	465,111	27,078	17,800	130,492	36,500
Arizona	140,440	48,905	10,432	4,500	8,255	11,600
Arkansas	630,568	441,750	6,456	9,300	41,857	23,100
California	2,106,122	345,430	37,805	76,400	362,609	183,100
Colorado	326,752	98,151	14,884	13,100	32,690	28,100
Connecticut	604,938	45,575	725	22,000	282,099	30,900
Delaware	84,819	14,944	86	5,400	24,028	6,700
D. C.	Included in Maryland					
Florida	503,100	120,571	3,480	26,800	64,554	49,700
Georgia	1,015,012	511,246	3,910	26,900	179,161	46,200
Idaho	164,624	80,781	4,989	3,500	12,936	9,700
Illinois	2,518,204	333,649	44,724	62,800	759,710	227,400
Indiana	1,068,169	263,300	12,588	26,700	340,563	73,700
Iowa	769,712	350,645	6,260	21,800	88,789	46,100
Kansas	500,880	214,250	13,327	11,400	43,498	40,700
Kentucky	720,645	351,419	54,001	18,900	76,887	42,800
Louisiana	717,341	333,430	11,782	19,600	88,723	50,600
Maine	269,828	73,264	439	6,600	83,978	16,500
Maryland	887,163	82,932	3,876	42,400	181,684	78,300
Mass.	1,380,159	70,581	1,617	35,000	552,310	96,700
Michigan	1,634,953	302,983	16,144	44,800	621,173	86,200
Minnesota	897,538	359,019	8,027	25,700	104,445	61,500
Mississippi	787,145	585,200	644	13,900	52,593	19,300
Missouri	1,184,681	387,042	11,066	27,900	233,467	86,400
Montana	188,838	80,094	11,738	5,700	12,440	16,500
Nebraska	400,145	184,312	557	9,800	26,739	28,300
Nevada	41,746	7,980	5,714	2,100	1,558	5,500
N. H.	161,042	25,251	316	6,300	61,607	8,900
N. J.	1,250,876	70,925	4,010	43,600	533,475	109,100
N. M.	143,848	66,200	8,266	4,300	4,147	9,800
N. Y.	4,355,449	310,701	8,887	146,100	1,221,843	426,800
N. C.	1,164,638	545,645	1,997	25,400	294,314	32,400
N. D.	230,527	157,364	1,078	2,800	4,125	9,300
Ohio	2,106,679	354,423	28,028	56,100	735,277	154,400
Oklahoma	583,556	272,895	30,949	12,800	38,227	31,200
Oregon	365,178	114,792	1,485	7,900	74,396	32,000
Penn.	2,958,315	311,924	207,494	79,900	1,021,636	245,100
R. I.	238,595	6,352	259	8,400	122,886	12,200
S. C.	679,221	382,237	1,400	13,600	136,713	18,100
S. D.	200,879	115,815	2,924	4,000	7,485	8,200
Tennessee	845,078	390,494	12,578	17,100	153,166	39,900
Texas	1,971,998	924,223	52,149	69,500	166,438	136,200
Utah	149,176	39,141	10,789	4,400	15,656	15,900
Vermont	112,743	39,604	1,735	3,600	25,566	7,200
Virginia	815,553	292,621	20,122	28,100	152,255	59,200
Washington	565,090	152,088	4,317	21,600	108,834	53,100
W. Va.	514,851	144,768	107,488	11,600	88,423	35,600
Wisconsin	1,016,809	350,667	2,396	25,300	254,625	53,900
Wyoming	82,066	29,558	6,394	3,800	4,591	11,400

	Wholesale Trade	Retail Trade	Finance, Ins., & Rl. Est.	Services & Misc.	Govern-ment
U. S.	1,605,347	4,821,806	1,364,700	3,339,700	3,987,100
Alabama	14,494	54,774	9,400	36,000	60,900
Arizona	3,824	17,524	1,700	15,000	18,700
Arkansas	8,045	35,560	3,900	19,700	40,900
California	136,083	341,295	96,400	276,700	250,300
Colorado	14,211	46,616	9,300	29,000	40,700
Connecticut	16,095	73,044	27,300	55,400	51,800
Delaware	2,962	11,499	3,200	7,700	8,300
D. C.	Included in Maryland				
Florida	37,083	77,312	14,600	51,000	58,000
Georgia	24,849	83,346	15,100	57,600	66,700
Idaho	5,819	17,499	1,500	9,700	18,200
Illinois	124,835	353,486	138,000	258,500	215,100
Indiana	28,761	129,757	27,600	72,700	92,500
Iowa	24,281	92,137	16,100	50,500	73,100
Kansas	15,149	58,256	10,000	33,600	60,700
Kentucky	17,302	57,636	9,900	31,900	59,900
Louisiana	24,013	66,893	10,300	45,600	66,400
Maine	7,454	28,093	5,100	18,700	29,700
Maryland	35,265	126,306	35,400	100,100	200,900
Mass.	59,235	210,116	56,300	138,400	159,900
Michigan	53,308	208,645	39,700	117,700	144,300
Minnesota	38,308	109,539	25,900	66,000	99,100
Mississippi	7,224	34,884	3,000	21,000	49,400
Missouri	64,055	139,851	40,500	99,400	105,000
Montana	4,252	20,714	2,000	10,800	24,600
Nebraska	15,419	45,818	9,500	30,200	49,500
Nevada	767	6,027	400	5,300	6,400
N. H.	2,570	18,198	3,100	14,800	20,000
N. J.	36,089	158,377	57,600	115,400	122,300
N. M.	2,522	13,813	1,100	14,100	19,600
N. Y.	297,738	587,180	376,900	522,900	456,400
N. C.	43,635	85,147	14,400	52,700	69,000
N. D.	6,335	16,025	2,100	11,100	20,300
Ohio	76,788	282,963	58,400	160,500	199,800
Oklahoma	16,011	62,774	10,600	45,400	62,700
Oregon	15,696	43,909	8,100	25,700	41,200
Penn.	100,232	368,329	86,700	250,200	286,800
R. I.	7,624	31,174	7,100	19,400	23,200
S. C.	8,874	43,997	3,400	29,000	41,900
S. D.	4,957	17,798	2,400	10,400	26,900
Tennessee	23,343	76,897	12,000	53,100	66,500
Texas	69,068	222,120	42,500	141,500	148,300
Utah	6,693	20,397	3,300	12,600	20,300
Vermont	2,364	12,174	1,800	8,600	10,100
Virginia	33,008	79,147	14,700	54,600	81,800
Washington	28,780	69,771	16,300	41,100	69,200
W. Va.	11,830	44,942	6,800	24,200	39,200
Wisconsin	26,893	111,028	22,600	69,500	99,900
Wyoming	1,204	9,019	700	4,700	10,700

Appendix Table F-2

TOTAL EMPLOYMENT AND ITS ONE-DIGIT COMPONENTS, 1954

	Total	Agri-culture	Mining	Construc-tion	Manufac-turing	Transp't Pub. Util.
U. S.	56,689,380	9,597,343	754,238	2,617,600	15,683,317	4,039,600
Alabama	942,383	302,375	14,182	31,100	216,476	49,600
Arizona	262,675	59,632	13,056	18,100	26,050	20,100
Arkansas	662,348	363,307	5,691	15,100	78,555	29,600
California	4,222,404	434,012	37,625	246,900	1,026,350	328,800
Colorado	492,498	96,043	13,318	25,700	63,154	42,600
Connecticut	874,033	30,642	729	41,300	413,833	41,900
Delaware	132,459	13,716	71	10,200	39,067	10,800
D. C.	Included in Maryland					
Florida	947,767	108,987	6,792	83,800	122,900	76,900
Georgia	1,132,641	265,089	4,336	47,100	302,754	68,800
Idaho	219,885	86,781	4,766	8,300	23,819	15,500
Illinois	3,490,148	290,563	29,070	162,300	1,183,381	298,400
Indiana	1,543,288	244,342	8,700	57,600	582,945	100,200
Iowa	949,084	340,523	2,642	33,300	161,707	57,800
Kansas	722,812	200,420	17,581	36,100	125,956	64,100
Kentucky	880,339	303,323	38,488	38,200	146,824	57,100
Louisiana	957,122	283,475	35,775	52,100	146,460	81,800
Maine	339,232	75,821	312	14,000	103,860	19,900
Maryland	1,335,296	65,968	1,951	74,200	275,851	101,500
Mass.	1,793,453	43,874	1,149	71,500	679,919	117,400
Michigan	2,493,393	262,601	17,068	117,600	1,009,059	142,000
Minnesota	1,163,555	330,772	16,179	51,600	203,993	88,200
Mississippi	791,701	468,963	4,409	16,000	91,373	25,700
Missouri	1,544,331	336,577	7,809	66,400	370,364	125,700
Montana	216,607	63,788	10,729	10,600	18,899	21,900
Nebraska	523,662	183,824	1,556	21,700	56,923	41,900
Nevada	83,328	7,078	5,356	8,800	6,046	8,800
N. H.	187,012	17,745	266	8,600	75,818	10,700
N. J.	1,856,748	69,458	4,119	96,900	787,593	146,100
N. M.	235,541	64,877	13,703	13,900	14,984	18,200
N. Y.	5,956,021	244,759	9,508	230,900	1,910,904	484,300
N. C.	1,510,114	525,836	3,559	48,800	426,830	60,200
N. D.	248,168	137,595	1,881	10,500	5,625	13,700
Ohio	3,224,161	294,706	19,652	163,600	1,270,157	217,000
Oklahoma	728,928	227,366	36,031	30,900	79,698	49,200
Oregon	554,891	110,022	1,377	22,600	134,883	46,000
Penn.	3,823,143	270,830	102,491	173,200	1,425,032	310,400
R. I.	279,806	3,989	163	15,400	120,316	15,700
S. C.	729,962	231,762	1,401	36,500	218,141	25,500
S. D.	238,824	120,699	2,869	9,700	11,570	9,900
Tennessee	1,185,117	393,285	9,579	53,100	261,220	58,600
Texas	2,845,020	723,539	127,884	147,000	414,113	224,000
Utah	250,355	47,212	12,828	11,600	29,049	21,900
Vermont	131,865	32,366	1,329	4,300	35,901	8,400
Virginia	1,116,577	247,917	15,712	56,000	241,832	80,700
Washington	851,896	127,675	3,063	48,500	194,758	62,600
W. Va.	553,562	97,674	74,382	18,800	119,631	49,000
Wisconsin	1,356,486	320,259	3,985	51,400	426,005	75,400
Wyoming	108,739	25,276	9,117	6,200	6,144	15,100

	Wholesale Trade	Retail Trade	Finance, Ins., & Rl. Est.	Services & Misc.	Govern-ment
U. S.	2,581,007	7,121,351	2,118,400	5,430,000	6,746,600
Alabama	30,110	92,840	22,300	59,500	9,000
Arizona	12,272	39,165	7,600	25,900	35,600
Arkansas	14,410	53,985	9,000	40,800	57,100
California	231,055	595,362	178,500	495,500	648,300
Colorado	25,527	72,556	17,700	54,100	81,800
Connecticut	31,807	107,522	44,100	85,500	76,700
Delaware	7,025	19,480	5,400	13,100	13,600
D. C.	Included in Maryland				
Florida	64,857	169,531	43,100	128,500	142,400
Georgia	54,236	131,326	33,000	86,400	139,600
Idaho	9,920	24,899	4,300	16,200	25,400
Illinois	185,205	463,129	168,600	373,700	335,800
Indiana	52,821	195,780	45,300	103,300	152,300
Iowa	37,431	118,381	27,300	71,300	98,700
Kansas	24,738	92,317	18,500	55,900	87,200
Kentucky	29,981	91,823	18,600	63,300	92,700
Louisiana	40,120	107,792	23,600	75,200	110,800
Maine	12,054	37,105	7,500	27,000	41,700
Maryland	51,888	187,738	59,300	153,900	363,000
Mass.	86,984	263,527	86,000	217,800	225,300
Michigan	99,716	322,949	68,900	211,600	241,900
Minnesota	57,100	146,311	40,300	102,800	126,300
Mississippi	15,246	55,310	9,400	35,800	69,500
Missouri	88,540	191,671	60,600	148,100	148,600
Montana	7,813	28,578	5,000	19,800	29,500
Nebraska	23,325	64,834	18,800	44,600	66,200
Nevada	2,074	12,374	1,900	17,900	13,000
N. H.	5,105	24,278	5,400	19,600	19,500
N. J.	77,755	227,228	75,900	181,500	193,600
N. M.	7,741	29,636	5,800	22,900	43,800
N. Y.	384,437	753,913	424,800	797,800	714,700
N. C.	50,660	144,229	29,200	91,100	129,700
N. D.	8,855	25,112	4,600	14,200	26,100
Ohio	135,740	418,206	95,700	280,900	328,500
Oklahoma	27,234	87,099	20,000	58,500	112,900
Oregon	28,752	70,157	17,200	52,000	71,900
Penn.	164,946	497,744	130,100	383,800	382,600
R. I.	12,554	37,384	11,900	27,900	34,500
S. C.	18,457	68,901	12,800	39,900	76,600
S. D.	8,312	26,374	4,900	15,500	29,000
Tennessee	46,580	121,853	28,000	88,000	124,900
Texas	135,211	382,273	99,300	263,500	328,200
Utah	11,737	32,829	8,200	23,000	52,000
Vermont	3,331	14,938	3,100	12,200	16,000
Virginia	41,150	143,266	35,600	90,900	163,500
Washington	48,560	107,740	30,500	82,200	146,300
W. Va.	17,891	63,011	11,500	42,400	59,300
Wisconsin	47,168	162,469	37,200	108,900	124,100
Wyoming	2,576	14,426	2,100	11,000	16,800

Appendix Table G

PERCENTAGE INCREASES IN EMPLOYMENT IN THE UNITED STATES in 1-,2-, and 3-DIGIT GROUPS, 1939 - 1954

SIC Code	Industry Title	Per Cent Change	SIC Code	Industry Title	Per Cent Change
372	Aircraft & Parts	1101.8	346	Metal Stamping & Coating	91.0
274	Misc. Publishing	1005.0	357	Off. & Store Machines	89.9
397	Plastics Prod., nec	401.5	384	Med. Instr. & Supplies	85.4
381	Scientific Instr.	371.7	34	Fabric. Metal Prod.	82.0
366	Communication Equip.	344.5	28	Chem. & Allied Prod.	81.8
383	Optical Instr. & Lenses	327.7	323	Prod. of Purchased Glass	81.8
351	Engines & Turbines	221.9	253	Public & Prof. Furniture	81.2
382	Mech. Measuring Instr.	219.9	209	Misc. Food Prep.	80.9
202	Dairy Products	203.4	289	Misc. Chem. Prod	79.4
36	Elec. Machinery	191.4	243	Millwork & Rel. Prod.	79.0
362	Elec. Appliances	184.9	254	Partitions & Fixtures	78.3
399	Misc. Manufactures	179.5	347	Lighting Fixtures	77.6
236	Children's Outerwear	177.1	352	Tractors & Farm Mchy.	75.4
264	Paper Coating & Glazing	168.7	208	Beverages	75.2
359	Misc. Mach. Parts	166.5	234	Undergarments, Wom. & Children	71.6
336	Non-Ferrous Foundries	163.6	329	Misc. Non-Met. Min. Prod.	71.2
361	Elec. Indus. Apparatus	162.7	267	Paperboard Cont. & Boxes	70.9
299	Misc. Petrol. & Coal Prod.	161.3		GOVERNMENT	69.2
344	Struct. Metal Prod.	160.0	239	Misc. Fabric. Textiles	69.1
354	Metalworking Mach.	154.9	324	Cement. Hydraulic	68.1
266	Paper Bags	150.6	316	Luggage	67.7
386	Photographic Equip.	149.9	201	Meat Products	65.8
283	Drugs & Medicines	147.5	395	Office Supplies	64.1
37	Transp. Equipment	143.7	341	Tin Cans & Other Tinware	64.0
327	Concrete & Plaster Prod.	143.0		MANUFACTURES	63.0
269	Pulp Gds. & Misc. Paper	131.9	252	Office Furniture	62.7
281	Indus. Inorganic Chem.	130.8		SERVICE & MISC.	62.6
38	Instr. & Rel. Prod.	130.5	30	Rubber Prod.	62.5
39	Misc. Manufactures	129.9	333	Prim. Non-Ferrous Metals	62.4
303	Reclaimed Rubber	129.5	26	Pulp, Paper & Prod.	61.2
276	Lithographing	123.3	374	Railroad Equip.	61.1
349	Misc. Fabr. Metal Prod.	122.0		WHOLESALE TRADE	60.8
	CONSTRUCTION	121.5	373	Ships & Boats	60.2
339	Misc. Prim. Metal Indus.	119.9	348	Fabricated Wire Prod.	59.2
358	Svce. & Hsehld. Machines	119.4	355	Spec.-Indus. Mchy., nec	58.7
35	Mach., (except electrical)	118.5	285	Paints & Allied Prod.	57.9
364	Engine Elec. Equip.	118.4	342	Cutlery, Hand Tools, & Hdwre.	56.7
353	Const. & Mining Mach.	116.9	204	Grain-Mill Prod.	56.6
356	Gen. Indus. Machinery	115.5	233	Women's & Misses Outerwear	56.6
394	Toys & Sporting Gds.	107.8	291	Petroleum Refining	56.0
309	Rubber Indus., nec	105.2	328	Cut-Stone & Stone Prod.	55.5
277	Greeting Cards	103.4		FIN., INS. & RL. EST.	55.2
282	Indus. Organic Chem.	102.8	335	Non-Ferr. Met. Rllngt. Drwing.	54.5
273	Books	102.3	32	Stone, Clay & Glass	54.3
365	Electric Lamps	99.2	27	Printing & Publ.	54.0
	Crude Petrol. & Nat. Gas	92.4			

656

Appendix Table G (continued)

SIC Code	Industry Title	Per Cent Change	SIC Code	Industry Title	Per Cent Change
271	Newspapers	54.0	375	Motorcycles & Bicycles	14.3
29	Petrol. & Coal Prod.	52.1	226	Finishing Tex., wool, etc.	13.7
25	Furn. & Fixtures	51.4	229	Misc. Textile Goods	12.9
317	Handbags & Sm. Lea. Gds.	51.1	227	Carpets & Rugs	12.5
334	Sec. Non-Ferrous Metals	50.5	207	Confectionery & Prod.	12.0
238	Misc. Apparel & Acces.	50.2	325	Structural Clay Prod.	12.0
385	Ophthalmic Gds.	50.0	379	Transp. Equip., nec	8.5
265	Envelopes	49.8	272	Periodicals	6.1
322	Pressed & Blown Glassware	49.0	302	Rubber Footwear	6.1
332	Iron & Steel Foundries	48.7	343	Heating & Plumbing Equip.	5.7
295	Paving & Roofing Mat.	48.4		Livestock & Prod.	(2.4)
369	Misc. Elec. Prod.	48.3		Metal Mining	2.2
371	Motor Veh. & Equip.	48.1	211	Cigarettes	1.0
	RETAIL TRADE	47.7	222	Yarn & Thread Mills, Wool exc.	-1.4
251	Hsehold. Furniture	45.5	31	Leathers & Leather Gds.	-1.8
279	Printing Trds. Serv. Ind.	44.8	319	Misc. Leather Goods	-2.1
312	Indus. Leather Belting	43.0	314	Footwear (exc. Rubber)	-3.9
23	Apparel & Rel. Prod.	42.1	286	Gum & Wood Chem.	-5.0
20	Food & Kindred Prod.	41.9	313	Footwear Cut Stock	-6.4
284	Soap & Rel. Prod.	41.3	224	Narrow Fabric Mills	-7.0
391	Jewelry & Silverware	41.1	223	Cotton & Rayon Broad-Woven	-8.7
275	Comm. Printing	40.2	231	Men's & Boys' Suits & Coats	-8.7
396	Costume Jewelry & Notions	39.8		MINING	-8.8
33	Primary Metal Ind.	39.6		Vegetables	(-11.8)
	TRANSPORTATION	38.7	22	Textile Mill Prod.	-12.4
	TOTAL EMPLOYMENT	38.5	206	Sugar	-12.8
301	Tires & Inner Tubes	36.7	225	Knitting Mills	-14.6
326	Pottery & Rel. Prod.	35.2		AGRICULTURE	-14.7
232	Men's & Boys' Furnishings	34.0	244	Wooden Containers	-17.2
	Poultry & Prod.	(33.0)	311	Leather Tanning & Finsh'g.	-18.2
287	Fertilizers	30.8		Fruits & Nuts	(-18.9)
203	Canning, Pres. & Freezing	29.8	21	Tobacco Mfg.	-19.8
293	Coke & By-Products	28.9		Field Crops	(-19.8)
261	Pulp, Paper & Paper board	28.8		Horticultural Spec.	(-20.6)
321	Flat Glass	27.8	235	Millinery	-24.1
249	Misc. Wood Prod.	26.9		Dairy Products	(-25.3)
256	Screens, Shds., & Blinds	24.7	363	Insulated Wire & Cable	-26.2
393	Mus. Instr. & Parts	22.4	212	Cigars	-29.1
278	Bookbinding & Indus. Rel.	22.2	213	Chewing & Smoking Tob.	-30.0
24	Lumber & Prod., Furn. exc.	21.5	315	Leather Gloves & Mittens	-35.2
387	Watches & Clocks	19.5	237	Fur Goods	-39.4
	Non-Met. Minerals (Fuels exc.)	18.3	221	Woolen & Worsted Mfg.	-45.3
242	Lumber & Timber Prod.	16.9		Bit. Coal & Lignite	-45.4
331	Blast Furn. & Steel Mills	15.0		Anthracite Coal	-48.0
288	Veg. & Animal Oils	14.6	228	Hats (exc. Cloth & Millinery)	-52.5

Note: Total - All Employment is written with all capitals and underlined; 1-Digit Industries are all
capitals only; 2-Digit Industries are initial capitals and underlined; 3-Digit Industries are
initial capitals only. Numbers in parentheses are estimates.
3-Digit Industries 214 - Tobacco Stemming & Redrying and 259 - Misc. Furniture & Fixtures not
shown above - no information for 1939.
nec - not elsewhere classified.

Appendix Table H

NET SHIFT BY STATES IN POPULATION, TOTAL PERSONAL INCOME, TOTAL EMPLOYMENT

AND ONE-DIGIT EMPLOYMENT CATEGORIES, 1939 - 1954

	POPULATION			TOTAL PERSONAL INCOME		
	Actual Change	Downward Net Shift	Upward Net Shift	Actual Change	Downward Net Shift	Upward Net Shift
	000 omitted			000,000 omitted		
U. S.	30,311	-9,460	9,453	71,784.6	11,348.3	11,348.3
Alabama	259	-393		940.1		245.5
Arizona	446		334	523.3		295.4
Arkansas	-141	-592		433.0	-31.7	
California	5,723		4,152	8,523.3		3,336.3
Colorado	372		113	700.7		130.4
Connecticut	481		88	1,202.2	-194.0	
Delaware	106		45	211.3	-26.5	
D. C.	Included in Maryland					
Florida	1,553		1,128	1,819.6		939.5
Georgia	510	-213		1,275.6		321.5
Idaho	77	-44		211.1	-11.9	
Illinois	1,261	-566		4,477.4	-1,014.5	
Indiana	838		50	2,100.4		356.9
Iowa	146	-438		1,075.3	-92.0	
Kansas	199	-223		1,036.9		352.1
Kentucky	169	-485		969.3		125.7
Louisiana	554		13	1,065.4		242.5
Maine	55	-141		244.9	-166.5	
Maryland	1,004		436	1,606.8	-288.6	
Mass.	481	-526		1,633.8	-1,486.1	
Michigan	1,920		726	3,978.7		806.5
Minnesota	360	-282		1,191.8	-221.1	
Mississippi	-37	-539		475.3		37.2
Missouri	341	-535		1,672.7	-215.8	
Montana	64	-65		251.2	-38.9	
Nebraska	41	-264		614.0		99.9
Nevada	105		80	166.9		78.1
N. H.	62	-51		179.8	-90.6	
N. J.	1,089		133	2,797.8	-260.9	
N. M.	246		125	362.7		181.1
N. Y.	2,305	-827		6,195.2	-4,808.4	
N. C.	712	-102		1,406.2		310.0
N. D.	-8	-157		183.8	-15.5	
Ohio	1,958		363	4,476.4		268.2
Oklahoma	-147	-687		798.5		4.2
Oregon	567		317	844.6		224.0
Penn.	955	-1,338		4,039.3	-1,815.3	
R. I.	106	-57		272.6	-220.7	
S. C.	394	-40		702.7		198.5
S. D.	28	-121		238.4		22.3
Tennessee	490	-176		1,163.7		289.5
Texas	2,102		629	4,151.1		1,585.7
Utah	219		93	330.7		83.0
Vermont	16	-67		100.1	-69.6	
Virginia	831		213	1,509.0		397.0
Washington	812		415	1,461.2		417.3
W. Va.	123	-310		505.0	-208.4	
Wisconsin	509	-214		1,538.2	-55.3	
Wyoming	50	-7		127.1	-16.0	
Total Net Shift as % of 1939 Total	7.23			15.60		

	TOTAL EMPLOYMENT			AGRICULTURAL EMPLOYMENT		
	Actual Change	Downward Net Shift	Upward Net Shift	Actual Change	Downward Net Shift	Upward Net Shift
U. S.	15,781,142	-2,916,062	2,916,060	-1,652,909	-572,934	572,934
Alabama	89,834	-239,053		-162,736	-94,401	
Arizona	122,235		68,058	10,727		17,912
Arkansas	31,780	-211,474		-78,443	-13,540	
California	2,116,282		1,303,805	88,582		139,333
Colorado	165,746		39,695	-2,108		12,313
Connecticut	269,095		35,728	-14,933	-8,237	
Delaware	47,640		14,919	-1,228		968
D. C.	Included in Maryland					
Florida	444,667		250,586	-11,584		6,131
Georgia	117,629	-273,931		-246,157	-171,044	
Idaho	55,261	-8,246		6,000		17,869
Illinois	971,944		498	-43,086		5,934
Indiana	475,119		63,052	-18,958		19,727
Iowa	179,372	-117,559		-10,122		41,395
Kansas	221,932		28,708	-13,830		17,648
Kentucky	159,694	-118,309		-48,096		3,535
Louisiana	239,781	-36,947		-49,955	-967	
Maine	69,404	-34,687		2,557		13,321
Maryland	448,133		105,893	-16,964	-4,779	
Mass.	413,294	-119,129		-26,707	-16,337	
Michigan	858,440		227,725	-40,382		4,133
Minnesota	266,017	-80,226		-28,247		24,501
Mississippi	4,556	-299,100		-116,237	-30,258	
Missouri	359,650	-97,364		-50,465		6,400
Montana	27,769	-45,079		-16,306	-4,538	
Nebraska	123,517	-30,847		-488		26,591
Nevada	41,582	25,478		-902		270
N. H.	25,970	-36,155		-7,506	-3,796	
N. J.	605,872		123,322	-1,467		8,953
N. M.	91,693		36,201	-1,323		8,403
N. Y.	1,600,572	-79,626		-65,942	-20,293	
N. C.	345,476	-103,806		-19,809		60,358
N. D.	17,641	-71,289		-19,769		3,351
Ohio	1,117,482		304,790	-59,717	-7,644	
Oklahoma	145,372	-79,746		-45,529	-5,435	
Oregon	189,713		48,839	-4,770		12,095
Penn.	864,828	-276,399		-41,094		4,734
R. I.	41,211	-50,832		-2,363	-1,430	
S. C.	50,741	-211,282		-150,475	-94,316	
S. D.	37,945	-39,548		4,884		21,900
Tennessee	340,039		14,034	2,791		60,163
Texas	873,022		112,286	-200,684	-64,896	
Utah	101,179		43,631	8,071		13,822
Vermont	19,122	-24,371		-7,238	-1,419	
Virginia	301,024	-13,591		-44,704	-1,712	
Washington	286,806		68,812	-24,413	-2,068	
W. Va.	38,711	-159,903		-47,094	-25,824	
Wisconsin	339,677	-52,577		-30,408		21,113
Wyoming	26,673	-4,986		-4,282		61
Total Net Shift as % of 1939 Total		7.13				

Appendix Table H (continued)

	MINING EMPLOYMENT			CONSTRUCTION EMPLOYMENT		
	Actual Change	Downward Net Shift	Upward Net Shift	Actual Change	Downward Net Shift	Upward Net Shift
U. S.	-73,172	-165,388	165,392	1,435,600	-261,789	261,790
Alabama	-12,896	-10,501		13,300	-8,319	
Arizona	2,624		3,547	13,600		8,135
Arkansas	-765	-194		5,800	-5,495	
California	-180		3,163	170,500		77,708
Colorado	-1,566	-250		12,600	-3,311	
Connecticut	4		68	19,300	-7,420	
Delaware	-15	-7		4,800	-1,759	
D. C.						
Florida	3,312		3,620	57,000		24,450
Georgia	426		772	20,200	-12,471	
Idaho	-223		218	4,800		549
Illinois	-15,654	-11,699		99,500		23,226
Indiana	-3,888	-2,775		30,900	-1,529	
Iowa	-3,618	-3,064		11,500	-14,977	
Kansas	4,254		5,433	24,700		10,854
Kentucky	-15,513	-10,737		19,300	-3,655	
Louisiana	23,993		25,035	32,500		8,695
Maine	-127	-88		7,400	-616	
Maryland	-1,925	-1,582		26,800	-30,770	
Mass.	-468	-325		36,500	-6,009	
Michigan	924		2,352	72,800		18,388
Minnesota	8,152		8,862	25,900	-5,314	
Mississippi	3,765		3,822	2,100	-14,782	
Missouri	-3,257	-2,278		38,500		4,614
Montana	-1,009		29	4,900	-2,023	
Nebraska	999		1,048	11,900	-3	
Nevada	-358		147	6,700		4,149
N. H.	-50	-22		2,300	-5,352	
N. J.	109		464	53,300		346
N. M.	5,437		6,168	9,600		4,377
N. Y.	621		1,407	84,800	-92,646	
N. C.	1,562		1,739	23,400	-7,450	
N. D.	803		898	7,700		4,299
Ohio	-8,376	-5,897		107,500		39,364
Oklahoma	5,082		7,819	18,100		2,554
Oregon	-108		23	14,700		5,105
Penn.	-105,003	-86,653		93,300	-3,742	
R. I.	-96	-73		7,000	-3,202	
S. C.	1		125	22,900		6,382
S. D.	-55		204	5,700		842
Tennessee	-2,999	-1,887		36,000		15,231
Texas	75,735		80,347	77,500	-6,911	
Utah	2,039		2,993	7,200		1,856
Vermont	-406	-253		700	-3,672	
Virginia	-4,410	-2,631		27,900	-6,229	
Washington	-1,254	-872		26,900		666
W. Va.	-33,106	-23,600		7,200	-6,889	
Wisconsin	1,589		1,801	25,700	-5,028	
Wyoming	2,723		3,288	2,400	-2,215	
Total Net Shift as % of 1939 Total		19.99			22.15	

	GOVERNMENT EMPLOYMENT		
	Actual Change	Downward Net Shift	Upward Net Shift
U. S.	2,759,500	-563,772	563,776
Alabama	63,000		20,851
Arizona	22,100		9,158
Arkansas	16,200	-12,107	
California	398,000		224,766
Colorado	41,100		12,931
Connecticut	24,900	-10,951	
Delaware	5,300	-444	
D. C.			
Florida	84,400		44,258
Georgia	72,900		26,736
Idaho	7,200	-5,396	
Illinois	120,700	-28,172	
Indiana	59,800	-4,220	
Iowa	25,600	-24,993	
Kansas	26,500	-15,510	
Kentucky	32,800	-8,657	
Louisiana	44,400	-1,556	
Maine	12,000	-8,556	
Maryland	162,100		23,056
Mass.	65,400	-45,268	
Michigan	97,600	-2,271	
Minnesota	27,200	-41,388	
Mississippi	20,100	-14,090	
Missouri	43,600	-29,071	
Montana	4,900	-12,126	
Nebraska	16,700	-17,559	
Nevada	6,600		2,171
N. H.	-500	-14,342	
N. J.	71,300	-13,345	
N. M.	24,200		10,635
N. Y.	258,300	-57,578	
N. C.	60,700	12,945	
N. D.	5,800	-8,250	
Ohio	128,700	-9,583	
Oklahoma	50,200	6,805	
Oregon	30,700	2,185	
Penn.	95,800	-102,696	
R. I.	11,300	-4,757	
S. C.	34,700		5,701
S. D.	2,100	-16,518	
Tennessee	58,400		12,375
Texas	179,900		77,261
Utah	31,700		17,650
Vermont	5,900	-1,090	
Virginia	81,700		25,086
Washington	77,100		29,206
W. Va.	20,100	-7,031	
Wisconsin	24,200	-44,941	
Wyoming	6,100	-1,306	
Total Net Shift as % of 1939 Total		14.14	

	WHOLESALE TRADE			RETAIL TRADE		
	Actual Change	Downward Net Shift	Upward Net Shift	Actual Change	Downward Net Shift	Upward Net Shift
U. S.	975,660	-179,192	179,163	2,299,525	-373,322	373,324
Alabama	15,616		6,807	38,066		11,944
Arizona	8,448		6,124	21,641		13,284
Arkansas	6,365		1,476	18,425		1,466
California	94,972		12,267	254,067		91,303
Colorado	11,316		2,679	25,940		3,709
Connecticut	15,712		5,930	34,478	-357	
Delaware	4,063		2,263	7,981		2,497
D. C.						
Florida	27,774		5,237	92,219		55,349
Georgia	29,387		14,285	47,980		8,232
Idaho	4,101		564	7,400	-945	
Illinois	60,370	-15,499		109,643	-58,935	
Indiana	24,060		6,580	66,023		4,142
Iowa	13,150	-1,607		26,244	-17,696	
Kansas	9,589		382	34,061		6,279
Kentucky	12,679		2,164	34,187		6,700
Louisiana	16,107		1,513	40,899		8,998
Maine	4,600		70	8,992	-4,406	
Maryland	16,623	-4,810		61,432		1,197
Mass.	27,749	-8,251		53,411	-46,794	
Michigan	46,408		14,010	114,304		14,801
Minnesota	18,792	-4,490		36,772	-15,467	
Mississippi	8,022		3,632	20,426		3,790
Missouri	24,455	-14,475		51,820	-14,875	
Montana	3,561		977	7,864	-2,015	
Nebraska	7,906	-1,465		19,016	-2,835	
Nevada	1,307		841	6,347		3,473
N. H.	2,535		973	6,080	-2,599	
N. J.	41,666		19,733	68,851	-6,679	
N. M.	5,219		3,686	15,823		9,236
N. Y.	86,699	-94,253		166,733	-113,294	
N. C.	7,025	-19,494		59,082		18,475
N. D.	2,520	-1,330		9,087		1,445
Ohio	58,952		12,284	135,243		298
Oklahoma	11,223		1,492	24,325	-5,612	
Oregon	13,056		3,517	26,248		5,308
Penn.	64,714		3,797	111,415	-64,242	
R. I.	4,930		296	6,210	-8,657	
S. C.	9,583		4,190	24,904		3,922
S. D.	3,355		342	8,576		88
Tennessee	23,237		9,050	44,956		8,284
Texas	66,143		24,166	160,153		54,224
Utah	5,044		976	12,432		2,705
Vermont	967	-470		2,764	-3,042	
Virginia	8,142	-11,919		64,119		26,374
Washington	19,780		2,289	37,969		4,695
W. Va.	6,061	-1,129		18,069	-3,364	
Wisconsin	20,275		3,931	51,441	-1,508	
Wyoming	1,372		640	5,407		1,106
Total Net Shift as % of 1939 Total		11.16			7.74	

Appendix Table H (continued)

	FIN., INS. & REAL ESTATE			SERVICE & MISCELLANEOUS		
	Actual Change	Downward Net Shift	Upward Net Shift	Actual Change	Downward Net Shift	Upward Net Shift
U. S.	753,700	-227,942	227,941	2,090,300	-249,480	249,479
Alabama	12,900		7,708	23,500		968
Arizona	5,900		4,962	10,900		1,512
Arkansas	5,100		2,946	15,900		3,570
California	82,100		28,860	218,800		45,615
Colorado	8,400		3,264	25,100		6,949
Connecticut	16,800		1,723	30,100	-4,575	
Delaware	2,200		433	5,400		581
D. C.						
Florida	28,500		20,437	77,500		45,579
Georgia	17,900		9,561	28,800	-7,252	
Idaho	2,800		1,972	6,500		429
Illinois	30,600	-45,615		115,200	-46,594	
Indiana	17,700		2,457	30,600	-14,903	
Iowa	11,200		2,308	20,800	-10,808	
Kansas	8,500		2,977	22,300		1,270
Kentucky	8,700		3,232	31,400		11,434
Louisiana	13,300		7,611	29,600		1,059
Maine	2,400	-417		8,300	-3,404	
Maryland	23,900		4,349	53,800	-8,852	
Mass.	29,700	-1,394		79,400	-7,224	
Michigan	29,200		7,274	93,900		20,232
Minnesota	14,400		96	36,800	-4,509	
Mississippi	6,400		4,743	14,800		1,656
Missouri	20,100	-2,267		48,700	-13,514	
Montana	3,000		1,895	9,000		2,240
Nebraska	9,300		4,053	14,400	-4,502	
Nevada	1,500		1,279	12,600		9,283
N. H.	2,300		588	4,800	-4,463	
N. J.	18,300	-13,511		66,100	-6,128	
N. M.	4,700		4,092	8,800	-25	
N. Y.	47,900	-160,255		274,900	-52,380	
N. C.	14,800		6,847	38,400		5,415
N. D.	2,500		1,340	3,100	-3,847	
Ohio	37,300		5,047	120,400		19,944
Oklahoma	9,400		3,546	13,100	-15,316	
Oregon	9,100		4,627	26,300		10,215
Penn.	43,400	-4,483		133,600	-22,999	
R. I.	4,800		879	8,500	-3,642	
S. C.	9,400		7,522	10,900	-7,251	
S. D.	2,500		1,175	5,100	-1,409	
Tennessee	16,000		9,373	34,900		1,665
Texas	56,800		33,328	122,000		33,436
Utah	4,900		3,077	10,400		2,514
Vermont	1,300		306	3,600	-1,783	
Virginia	20,900		12,781	36,300		2,126
Washington	14,200		5,198	41,100		15,376
W. Va.	4,700		944	18,200		3,053
Wisconsin	14,600		2,118	39,400	-4,100	
Wyoming	1,400		1,013	6,300		3,358
Total Net Shift as % of 1939 Total		16.70			7.47	

	MANUFACTURING EMPLOYMENT			TRANSPORTATION & PUBLIC UTILITIES		
	Actual Change	Downward Net Shift	Upward Net Shift	Actual Change	Downward Net Shift	Upward Net Shift
U. S.	6,060,394	-986,395	986,398	1,127,600	-223,176	223,185
Alabama	85,984		3,802	13,100	-1,034	
Arizona	17,795		12,596	8,500		4,008
Arkansas	36,698		10,337	6,500	-2,445	
California	663,741		435,374	145,700		74,799
Colorado	30,464		9,877	14,500		3,619
Connecticut	131,734	-45,928		11,000	-965	
Delaware	15,039	-94		4,100		1,506
D. C.						
Florida	58,346		17,691	27,200		7,955
Georgia	123,593		10,760	22,600		4,710
Idaho	10,883		2,736	5,800		2,050
Illinois	423,671	-54,784		71,000	-17,055	
Indiana	242,382		27,900	26,500	-2,039	
Iowa	72,918		17,000	11,700	-6,151	
Kansas	82,458		55,064	23,400		7,640
Kentucky	69,937		21,515	14,300	-2,273	
Louisiana	57,737		1,860	31,200		11,606
Maine	19,882	-33,006		3,400	-2,989	
Maryland	94,167	-20,255		23,200	-7,120	
Mass.	127,609	-220,229		20,700	-16,745	
Michigan	387,886	-3,320		55,800		22,421
Minnesota	99,548		33,770	26,700		2,886
Mississippi	38,780		5,658	6,400	-1,073	
Missouri	146,897		6,160	39,300		5,844
Montana	6,459	-1,376		5,400	-989	
Nebraska	30,184		13,344	13,600		2,642
Nevada	4,488		3,507	3,300		1,170
N. H.	14,211	-24,588		1,800	-1,646	
N. J.	250,713	-85,263		37,000	-5,246	
N. M.	10,837		8,225	8,400		4,606
N. Y.	689,061	-80,440		57,500	-107,768	
N. C.	132,516	-52,839		27,800		15,254
N. D.	1,500	-1,098		4,400		799
Ohio	534,880		71,812	62,600		2,812
Oklahoma	41,471		17,396	18,000		5,919
Oregon	60,487		13,633	14,000		1,609
Penn.	403,396	-240,017		65,300	-29,609	
R. I.	-2,570	-79,962		3,500	-1,224	
S. C.	81,428	-4,672		7,400		391
S. D.	4,085	-629		1,700	-1,475	
Tennessee	108,054		11,592	18,700		3,250
Texas	247,675		142,854	87,800		35,060
Utah	13,393		3,533	6,000	-157	
Vermont	10,335	-5,766		1,200	-1,588	
Virginia	89,577	-6,311		21,500	-1,424	
Washington	85,924		17,382	9,500	-11,062	
W. Va.	31,208	-24,480		13,400	-385	
Wisconsin	171,380		11,020	21,500		629
Wyoming	1,553	-1,338		3,700	-714	
Total Net Shift as % of 1939 Total		10.25			7.66	

Note: Underscored data indicate Absolute Upward or Downward Shift. Other shift data are Relative Upward or Downward Shift.

Appendix Table I

NET SHIFT BY STATES IN 2-DIGIT MINING EMPLOYMENT, 1939 - 1954

	METAL MINING			COAL MINING		
	Actual Change	Downward Net Shift	Upward Net Shift	Actual Change	Downward Net Shift	Upward Net Shift
U. S.	2,091	-18,043	17,912	-232,146	-28,424	28,537
Alabama	-1,333	-1,445		-11,490	-1,838	
Arizona	2,313		2,090	(-37)	(-16)	
Arkansas	(64)		(43)	(-2,335)	(-990)	
California	(-7,640)	(-7,861)		(4)		(4)
Colorado	(-874)	(-999)		-5,676	(-1,694)	
Connecticut	(2)		(2)			
Delaware						
D. C.						
Florida	(441)		(441)			
Georgia	11		8	(-35)	(-14)	
Idaho	-676	-782		(-21)	(-11)	
Illinois	110		110	-19,657	-3,379	
Indiana				-4,708	-235	
Iowa				-4,387	-1,969	
Kansas	-1,018	-1,049		-2,100	-853	
Kentucky	(-133)	(-136)		-17,600		5,958
Louisiana						
Maine	(2)		(2)			
Maryland				-1,947	-834	
Mass.	(-26)	(-27)				
Michigan	1,624		1,414	-882	-459	
Minnesota	7,467		7,310			
Mississippi						
Missouri	463		395	-2,816	-1,058	
Montana	(-280)	(-442)		-992	-316	
Nebraska						
Nevada	-809	-927				
N. H.	(3)		(3)			
N. J.	(816)		(796)			
N. M.	(490)		(427)	-2,228	-1,082	
N. Y.	(2,216)		(2,189)			
N. C.	(491)		(490)			
N. D.				(-672)	(-165)	
Ohio				-8,212		964
Oklahoma	(-2,170)	(-2,237)		(-283)		(478)
Oregon	(-695)	(-714)		(-21)	(-11)	
Penn.	(997)		(985)	-101,824	-11,632	
R. I.						
S. C.	(32)	(31)				
S. D.	-639	-693		(-22)	(-3)	
Tennessee	-239	-264		-3,412		217
Texas	(-7)	(-18)		-657	-342	
Utah	(-83)	(-250)		468		1,725
Vermont	210		210			
Virginia	234		218	-4,444		3,158
Washington	178	-199		(-1,703)	(-547)	
W. Va.	(27)		(27)	-31,178		16,033
Wisconsin	555		536			
Wyoming	(186)		(185)	(-3,066)	(-976)	
Total Net Shift as % of 1939 Empl.	18.84				5.90	

	CRUDE PETROL. & NATURAL GAS			NON-METALLIC MINERALS		
	Actual Change	Downward Net Shift	Upward Net Shift	Actual Change	Downward Net Shift	Upward Net Shift
U. S.	140,448	-63,983	63,806	17,388	-18,065	18,242
Alabama	266		266	-251	-575	
Arizona				(343)		(309)
Arkansas	482	-1,452		1,024		915
California	4,092	-16,223		3,423		2,458
Colorado	(4,259)		(4,000)	(742)		(636)
Connecticut				(2)	(-130)	
Delaware				-15	-31	
D. C.						
Florida	(285)		(283)	(2,585)		(1,951)
Georgia				(449)	(-232)	
Idaho				(474)		(455)
Illinois	2,886	-3,331		1,063		326
Indiana	786		231	34	-454	
Iowa				774		552
Kansas	7,006	-327		370		115
Kentucky	2,710		1,154	(-490)	(-1,058)	
Louisiana	22,090		12,746	1,903		1,597
Maine				(-129)	(-209)	
Maryland	(60)		(60)	-27	-310	
Mass.				(-442)	(-733)	
Michigan	(-697)	(-3,339)		(877)		(369)
Minnesota				702		552
Mississippi	3,581		3,526	184		77
Missouri	-556	-1,112		-314	-983	
Montana	1,366		499	(-1,104)	(-1,466)	
Nebraska	563		563	436		334
Nevada				(451)		(395)
N. H.				(-53)	(-111)	
N. J.				(-697)	(-1,259)	
N. M.	4,829		3,042	(2,346)		(2,155)
N. Y.	(-725)	(-2,601)		(-236)	(-1,149)	
N. C.				(1,071)		(712)
N. D.	1,247		1,247	(228)		(224)
Ohio	225	-2,261		-303	-1,425	
Oklahoma	7,534	-15,735		13	-189	
Oregon				(616)		(508)
Penn.	-845	-8,824		(-3,286)	(-5,183)	
R. I.				-96	-143	
S. C.				(-33)	(-279)	
S. D.	(23)	(-20)		544		467
Tennessee	-10	-40		685	-12	
Texas	74,430		31,274	1,969		1,183
Utah	(1,272)		(1,239)	(390)		(300)
Vermont				-616	-933	
Virginia	51		51	-222	-868	
Washington	(71)		(54)	(558)		(389)
W. Va.	-1,959	-8,718		(4)	(-333)	
Wisconsin				1,034		754
Wyoming	5,012		3,571	(591)		(511)
Total Net Shift as % of 1939 Empl.		42.11			19.16	

Note: Underscored data indicate Absolute Upward or Downward Shift.
Other shift data are Relative Upward or Downward Shift.
Figures in parentheses are estimates.

Appendix Table J

NET SHIFT BY STATES IN VALUE OF AGRICULTURAL PRODUCTS SOLD, 1940 - 1954

	VALUE OF AGRICULTURAL PRODUCTS SOLD			FIELD CROPS			VEGETABLES		
	Actual Change	Downward Net Shift	Upward Net Shift	Actual Change	Downward Net Shift	Upward Net Shift	Actual Change	Downward Net Shift	Upward Net Shift
	000,000 omitted			000 omitted			000 omitted		
U. S.	$17,960.1	$-1,647.6	$1,650.8	$7,451.5	$-1,204.6	$1,205.2	$445.6	$-122.7	$122.7
Alabama	226.7		22.9	118.3	-39.9		2.4	-.6	
Arizona	288.8		182.8	183.7		136.8	28.0		22.4
Arkansas	373.5		55.5	281.5		19.4	1.2	-1.4	
California	1,809.1		594.5	592.1		269.0	157.3		70.4
Colorado	278.3		5.2	73.3	-26.8		3.3	-4.5	
Connecticut	78.7	-38.7		17.0	-9.8		1.9	-1.1	
Delaware	65.3		21.7	11.7		6.1	4.0		.7
D. C.	Included in Maryland								
Florida	385.7		169.5	49.2		15.0	58.2		13.3
Georgia	326.1	-2.5		133.5	-121.5		5.3	-2.7	
Idaho	248.2		22.7	145.4		25.6	2.3	-.7	
Illinois	1,090.8	-24.2		484.4	-89.3		9.5	-1.3	
Indiana	689.0		105.7	293.8		102.6	4.0	-8.5	
Iowa	1,327.6	-49.9		278.1	-207.5		1.4	-1.4	
Kansas	598.8		51.8	339.5		86.0	.0	-1.4	
Kentucky	296.4	-48.4		185.0	-7.6		.5	-1.2	
Louisiana	219.7	-22.5		159.3	-52.2		1.3	-2.7	
Maine	97.5	-15.7		37.2	-19.8		1.3	-1.2	
Maryland	139.5	-9.9		32.7	-12.0		5.1	-7.8	
Mass.	61.4	-106.8		6.0	-9.4		1.8	-7.0	
Michigan	367.3	-110.5		122.3	-15.9		11.1	-6.3	
Minnesota	683.0	-126.0		228.0	-71.3		7.6		1.2
Mississippi	344.5		34.3	250.9	-32.9		.9	-2.8	
Missouri	519.1	-57.9		192.0	-6.1		-.1	-3.7	
Montana	255.4		29.4	144.1		28.3		-.7	
Nebraska	690.1		173.9	246.0		65.9		-.9	
Nevada	22.5	-7.7		3.1	-1.3		.3		.1
N. H.	25.8	-26.2		.4	-2.9		.3	-.5	
N. J.	168.2	-31.9		14.5	-11.0		22.2	-2.5	
N. M.	112.4	-2.2		63.3		22.1	2.6		.8
N. Y.	426.1	-225.5		45.6	-42.0		18.0	-20.3	
N. C.	533.8	-1.3		412.6	-80.4		5.2	-2.9	
N. D.	274.2		4.3	193.6		9.8		-.2	
Ohio	590.1	-92.4		240.0		43.3	6.6	-9.2	
Oklahoma	263.6	-128.5		137.7	-83.2		.6	-1.5	
Oregon	249.3	-10.2		99.0		17.5	14.6		7.0
Penn.	405.5	-126.8		58.8	-52.5		8.4	-8.0	
R. I.	7.7	-12.8		1.2	-.9		.1	-.6	
S. C.	164.3	-70.5		103.5	-109.6		4.5	-3.0	
S. D.	339.8		81.2	126.8		29.4		-.5	
Tennessee	246.1	-42.4		141.2	-15.6		1.7	-2.5	
Texas	1,203.0		22.8	842.5		262.8	20.0	-4.0	
Utah	86.7	-20.5		17.7	-15.0		1.1	-2.3	
Vermont	53.4	-35.3		.3	-5.0		.1	-.3	
Virginia	255.3	-35.8		91.4	-31.4		5.2	-5.6	
Washington	388.3		72.5	185.6		65.5	11.9		2.8
W. Va.	60.0	-21.7		4.2	-4.8		.1	-1.0	
Wisconsin	553.9	-88.4		48.3	-16.3		13.7		3.7
Wyoming	69.2	-54.3		15.2	-10.7		.4		.2
Total Net Shift as % of 1940 Value		24.71			48.78			61.50	

	FRUITS AND NUTS			HORTICULTURAL SPECIALTIES			DAIRY PRODUCTS		
	Actual Change	Downward Net Shift	Upward Net Shift	Actual Change	Downward Net Shift	Upward Net Shift	Actual Change	Downward Net Shift	Upward Net Shift
	000 omitted			000 omitted			000 omitted		
U. S.	$903.3	$-146.3	$146.3	$324.3	$53.1	$53.1	$2215.9	$-260.7	$260.8
Alabama	1.6	-4.0		4.8		2.6	16.0		3.5
Arizona	5.9		2.9	1.9		1.6	10.1		4.1
Arkansas	1.6	-8.7		1.1		.2	15.1		1.9
California	396.2		17.7	51.3		23.1	197.4		64.4
Colorado	8.0		3.0	4.6	-1.1		16.9	-.2	
Connecticut	3.1	-.7		9.2	-.1		20.0	-11.8	
Delaware	-.1	-3.4		2.2		.8	4.7		.3
D. C.	Included in Maryland								
Florida	163.1		84.5	23.7		13.8	34.7		18.0
Georgia	6.9	-10.6		3.1	-.3		22.8		5.5
Idaho	4.8	-.3		1.1		.2	27.1		6.1
Illinois	2.5	-9.8		15.3	-8.2		72.5	-23.6	
Indiana	2.2	-4.3		10.0	-.3		61.3	-4.0	
Iowa	-.2	-2.5		5.7	-2.9		66.1	-34.1	
Kansas	-.1	-2.9		2.0	-1.2		27.6	-15.2	
Kentucky	1.3	-2.8		1.6	-1.2		32.0		7.7
Louisiana	1.2	-9.1		2.6		1.5	19.2		7.1
Maine	2.8	-.4		.8	-1.4		15.1	-3.1	
Maryland	3.0	-3.1		3.3	-2.5		40.3		9.6
Mass.	5.7	-12.2		8.3	-8.5		14.6	-29.8	
Michigan	35.8		2.1	14.9		2.4	99.7	-2.5	
Minnesota		-2.9		6.8		.1	125.9	-18.5	
Mississippi	1.6	-1.4		.9	-.2		23.4		9.3
Missouri	1.3	-5.5		4.8	-1.3		59.8		11.5
Montana	.6	-.3		.5	-.4		5.8	-5.4	
Nebraska	-.1	-1.3		1.2	-.9		19.9	-11.7	
Nevada		-.1			-.1		1.5	-.9	
N. H.	1.6	-.3		.8	-.5		9.1	-4.8	
N. J.	12.8		.8	15.2	-3.2		29.4	-16.1	
N. M.	3.1		1.5	.4		.2	5.2		.3
N. Y.	41.0		.1	24.4	-8.9		222.7		1.4
N. C.	4.3	-4.3		4.2		1.4	26.4		7.5
N. D.				.3	-.1		14.7	-10.1	
Ohio	7.0	-11.1		25.0	-3.2		97.2	-5.8	
Oklahoma	.1	-4.7		1.5	-1.7		18.0	-16.8	
Oregon	31.0		1.6	7.8		2.6	23.7	-6.8	
Penn.	17.4	-6.9		28.5		.5	148.8		13.6
R. I.	.2	-.4		1.5	-.1		2.4	-5.1	
S. C.	8.2		2.8	1.3		.5	11.5		3.6
S. D.				.6	-.4		10.0	-10.4	
Tennessee	1.9	-4.6		3.0	-.2		36.3		9.7
Texas	-.9	-25.3		9.4		1.2	56.9	-11.3	
Utah	3.3	-.3		.8	-.1		13.7		4.4
Vermont	1.8	-.2		.1	-.6		42.6	-.4	
Virginia	17.8		.2	4.4	-.9		38.5		10.4
Washington	87.9		26.5	6.2	-.5		34.0	-7.7	
W. Va.	9.9		2.7	1.5		.1	10.1	-2.2	
Wisconsin	6.0	-1.8		5.0	-1.9		312.6		60.8
Wyoming		-.1		.3		.2	2.3	-2.4	
Total Net Shift as % of 1940 Value	49.53			41.07			23.32		

	POULTRY AND PRODUCTS			LIVESTOCK AND PRODUCTS			FARM FOREST PRODUCTS		
	Actual Change	Downward Net Shift	Upward Net Shift	Actual Change	Downward Net Shift	Upward Net Shift	Actual Change	Downward Net Shift	Upward Net Shift
	000 omitted			000 omitted			000 omitted		
U. S.	$1361.4	$-325.0	$324.3	$5166.8	$-779.0	$778.0	$91.3	$-33.2	$33.3
Alabama	31.2		20.9	45.3		21.7	7.1		3.8
Arizona	2.2	-.5		56.2		11.9	.8		.6
Arkansas	43.9		28.6	27.4	-6.4		1.6	-1.4	2.3
California	147.3		47.9	264.0		91.4	3.5		2.3
Colorado	5.7	-6.2		166.3		35.6	.2	-.1	
Connecticut	25.4		1.0	2.2	-3.9		-.04	-.7	
Delaware	40.0		19.1	2.4		.6	.2		.03
D. C.	Included in Maryland								
Florida	13.5		3.0	40.2		22.9	3.1		2.2
Georgia	90.1		77.5	52.6		23.9	11.9		5.2
Idaho	2.9	-3.4		63.3	-12.1		1.3		.6
Illinois	29.0	-27.4		477.2		106.5	.4	-.3	
Indiana	50.9		1.1	266.3		24.0	.5	-1.0	
Iowa	62.6	-20.3		913.5		193.1	.2	-.4	
Kansas	8.8	-27.4		221.0		.3	.01	-.3	
Kentucky	6.6	-11.8		68.4	-43.2		1.0	-1.1	
Louisiana	7.8		2.9	27.0		11.1	1.4		.2
Maine	35.4		21.5	1.1	-7.5		2.6	-2.3	
Maryland	33.7		11.5	20.6		4.7	.7	-.1	
Mass.	21.4	-13.2		3.7	-6.5		-.1	-1.9	
Michigan	23.6	-17.5		57.6	-49.5		2.3		.1
Minnesota	75.7		9.3	238.1	-22.0		.9	-1.3	
Mississippi	24.3		16.9	38.1		19.2	4.5		1.5
Missouri	28.9	-25.7		231.7	-30.7		.7	-1.3	
Montana	1.5	-4.1		102.2		1.1	.7		.3
Nebraska	16.2	-14.4		406.9		125.5	-.1	-.4	
Nevada	.1	-1.0		17.4	-4.6		.1		.03
N H.	13.0	-2.5		.7	-4.3		-.1	-3.8	
N. J.	63.2		22.7	10.9	-.5		.1	-.1	
N. M.	1.6	-.6		36.3	-30.1		-.02	-.4	
N. Y.	46.1	-32.8		25.6	-38.3		2.5	-3.2	
N. C.	39.7		20.4	35.6		12.6	5.8		.5
N. D.	3.8	-6.6		61.8		.2	-.1	-.2	
Ohio	40.6	-31.5		173.2	-53.3		.6	-1.6	
Oklahoma	6.1	-16.1		99.5	-16.1		.04	-.5	
Oregon	14.9	-9.3		45.2	-32.7		13.1		11.0
Penn.	78.8	-10.5		63.0	-16.5		1.9	-1.0	
R. I.	2.2	-1.4		.2	-1.0		-.1	-.3	
S. C.	13.3		6.1	18.6		8.8	3.5		1.6
S. D.	12.1	-4.4		190.3		62.9	-.01	-.2	
Tennessee	8.5	-10.0		51.4	-24.7		2.1	-1.3	
Texas	56.3	-2.0		217.7	-238.4		1.1	-1.8	
Utah	13.8		1.5	36.1	-8.5		.1		.1
Vermont	3.9	-1.3		2.4	-8.7		2.2	-3.1	
Virginia	42.2		4.2	50.8	-12.3		5.0	-.6	
Washington	17.7	-12.0		40.4	-6.5		4.6		3.2
W. Va.	19.9		8.2	13.5	-20.5		.9	-.9	
Wisconsin	34.6	-8.4		131.1	-38.0		2.6	-1.6	
Wyoming	.1	-2.5		50.6	-42.3		.2		.1
Total Net Shift as % of 1940 Value	58.52			41.57			84.94		

Note: Underscored data indicate Absolute Upward or Downward Shift. Other shift data are Relative Upward or Downward Shift.

Appendix Table K

NET SHIFT BY STATES IN 2-DIGIT MANUFACTURING PRODUCTION WORKER EMPLOYMENT, 1939 - 1954

	TOTAL MANUFACTURING			20--FOOD & KINDRED PROD.			21--TOBACCO MFG.		
	Actual Change	Downward Net Shift	Upward Net Shift	Actual Change	Downward Net Shift	Upward Net Shift	Actual Change	Downward Net Shift	Upward Net Shift
U. S.	4,564,543	-835,997	836,172	336,106	-75,916	75,901	-17,309	-11,158	11,158
Alabama	72,716		5,081	5,428		3,445	(685)		(685)
Arizona	14,362		10,910	1,285		732			
Arkansas	31,809		10,956	5,584		4,066			
California	500,506		341,915	31,166		1,639	(-562)	(-392)	
Colorado	24,553		10,881	3,761		373	(-150)	(-120)	
Connecticut	98,836	-42,360		1,932	-320		-286	-188	
Delaware	11,163	-426		2,249		1,170	(-95)	(-65)	
D. C.	4,145	-342		683	-475				
Florida	46,189		16,288	11,318		7,253	(-1,466)		(458)
Georgia	104,212		13,093	12,676		7,824	(235)		(324)
Idaho	10,412		4,652	2,591		1,424			
Illinois	312,789	-32,697		20,905	-13,647		-335	-166	
Indiana	182,693		21,774	7,073	-4,301		-463	-202	
Iowa	57,990		20,125	12,038		1,416	-17	-14	
Kansas	67,252		49,168	1,714	-4,561				
Kentucky	56,737		20,212	9,352		5,411	(2,433)		(3,333)
Louisiana	43,925		2,739	2,860	-5,072		(-525)	(-286)	
Maine	17,052	-26,231		3,132		803	(-26)	(-21)	
Maryland	54,986	-27,399		7,134	-1,268		(-21)		(15)
Mass.	78,084	-189,872		3,636	-8,165		16		73
Michigan	289,151	-14,929		10,699	-1,170		-1,331	-961	
Minnesota	73,109		27,498	9,892	-929		(-39)	(-30)	
Mississippi	33,941		7,113	3,082		1,244			
Missouri	109,395		6,518	9,053	-2,385		(-1,124)	(-756)	
Montana	5,875		730	550	-439				
Nebraska	25,015		14,249	9,749		5,177			
Nevada	3,401		2,802	205		68			
N. H.	10,553	-21,853		583		126	(-161)	(-62)	
N. J.	173,537	-78,747		12,281		325	-6,696	-4,670	
N. M.	6,161		4,279	894		594			
N. Y.	520,775	-34,206		21,744	-13,015		(-1,254)	(-771)	
N. C.	110,851	-46,541		8,733		6,109	-1,483		1,839
N. D.	1,308	-215		312	-490				
Ohio	390,762		42,631	10,321	-7,067		(-2,240)	(-1,559)	
Oklahoma	32,930		16,771	1,972	-1,422				
Oregon	56,977		23,371	4,127	-38		(-150)	(-120)	
Penn.	283,870	-214,996		16,059	-9,089		-1,848		1,399
R. I.	-2,289	-64,307		903	-288		(-24)	(-18)	
S. C.	63,711	-10,185		2,043		694	(1,019)		(1,049)
S. D.	2,993	-176		1,817		212			
Tennessee	83,003		6,409	6,880		2,377	(-118)		(108)
Texas	188,823		115,683	18,968		8,431	(42)		(101)
Utah	11,086		4,383	723	-1,299		(-150)	(-120)	
Vermont	9,431	-2,552		843		375			
Virginia	70,565	-6,652		10,503		6,335	-535		1,423
Washington	66,498		18,410	5,673	-101				
W. Va.	22,911	-20,588		1,533		186	176		351
Wisconsin	133,657		17,531	19,400		8,092	(-818)	(-637)	
Wyoming	1,236	-723		33	-375				
Total Net Shift as % of 1939 Total	10.71			9.46			12.75		

Appendix Table K (continued)

	22--TEXTILE MILL PROD.			23--APPAREL & REL. PROD.			24--LUMBER & PROD. (exc. Furn.)		
	Actual Change	Downward Net Shift	Upward Net Shift	Actual Change	Downward Net Shift	Upward Net Shift	Actual Change	Downward Net Shift	Upward Net Shift
U. S.	-134,208	-146,268	145,297	316,904	-133,194	132,959	95,802	-63,617	63,612
Alabama	4,371		9,324	13,706		12,175	2,924	-1,806	
Arizona				708		708	986		677
Arkansas	d			3,455		2,791	251	-4,297	
California	-83		485	26,686		17,296	20,303		14,848
Colorado	(293)		(293)	651		252	1,228		958
Connecticut	-13,521	-8,986		-3,541	-11,784		321		104
Delaware	-138		157	736	-140		-129	-346	
D. C.				84		53	78		66
Florida	134		169	4,527		4,205	-5,968	-10,007	
Georgia	17,320		27,177	16,711		9,402	10,854		7,331
Idaho				d			5,099		3,834
Illinois	-2,974	1,577		-7,299	-28,788		46	-2,267	
Indiana	-6,586	-5,500		-3,562	-10,843		2,449		965
Iowa	-584	-457		575	-613		276	-660	
Kansas	(293)		(293)	1,565		1,314	434		302
Kentucky	-119		316	9,023		6,126	1,662		360
Louisiana	d			1,228	-544		-4,402	-8,917	
Maine	-4,607	-1,846		1,571		1,112	3,217		1,641
Maryland	-2,358	-1,614		-2,496	-12,469		1,296		643
Mass.	-59,610	-44,446		16,818		1,340	13	-1,114	
Michigan	-2,834	-2,115		1,192	-1,994		797	-1,399	
Minnesota	-988	-597		2,946		938	1,499		604
Mississippi	13		621	11,452		8,547	-2,617	-7,356	
Missouri	433		721	4,169	-7,362		449	-723	
Montana				d			2,409		1,911
Nebraska	d			877		692	511		418
Nevada				d			387		363
N. H.	-3,068	-1,140		556		343	322	-640	
N. J.	-16,659	-9,647		6,826	-20,534		786	-37	
N. M.				d			406		67
N. Y.	-19,518	-10,047		81,849	-23,628		4,241		1,930
N. C.	28,684		51,171	13,379		10,648	7,865		3,442
N. D.	d			-3,511	-14,184		(161)		(157)
Ohio	1,113		2,229	1,967		1,865	2,142		741
Oklahoma	d						-859	1,430	
Oregon	369		590	510	-137		24,743		17,580
Penn.	-50,936	-33,417		52,892		13,573	3,686		1,823
R. I.	-27,283	-19,917		1,355		310	-5	-94	
S. C.	27,248		39,004	15,703		14,512	1,214	1,744	
S. D.				(31)		(31)	178		45
Tennessee	-2,647		1,518	11,551		5,582	3,669		855
Texas	927		1,804	15,781		11,499	-2,373	-6,876	
Utah	-203	-151		785		545	340		299
Vermont	-2,512	-1,933		1,465		1,192	570	-193	
Virginia	5,517		8,997	8,618		4,471	4,992		1,643
Washington	78		135	1,168		332	-2,733	-11,296	
W. Va.	-1,296	-887		1,946		1,094	444	-921	
Wisconsin	-3,211	-1,936		1,984	-174		1,657	-1,277	
Wyoming	(293)		(293)	(11)		(11)	-22	-217	
Total Net Shift as % of 1939 Total		13.52			17.69			15.04	

Appendix Table K (continued)

	25--FURNITURE & FIXTURES			26--PAPER & ALLIED PROD.			27--PRINTING & PUBLISHING		
	Actual Change	Downward Net Shift	Upward Net Shift	Actual Change	Downward Net Shift	Upward Net Shift	Actual Change	Downward Net Shift	Upward Net Shift
U. S.	97,267	-25,610	25,605	165,488	-47,256	47,396	175,295	-27,209	27,198
Alabama	1,279		1,062	4,373		2,461	1,743		1,025
Arizona	213		188	d			930		703
Arkansas	1,943		747	1,968		1,000	847		371
California	8,840		3,805	11,171		7,849	14,832		6,186
Colorado	360		181	404		312	1,973		970
Connecticut	912		273	2,180	-706		3,172		128
Delaware	(6)	(-3)		-71	-554		434		238
D. C.	84		35	(-122)	(-409)		2,919		1,231
Florida	2,988		2,553	7,184		5,663	3,033		1,847
Georgia	3,018		1,428	8,060		6,095	2,602		1,156
Idaho	(29)		(25)	d			152	-107	
Illinois	2,054	-8,368		7,719	-2,582		15,642	-9,147	
Indiana	4,293	-3,082		1,923	-1,531		4,064		2
Iowa	640	-18		1,055		613	2,441		231
Kansas	130	-111		738		267	2,727		1,461
Kentucky	283	-1,713		464		191	2,272		764
Louisiana	-177	-877		7,545		3,051	1,142		161
Maine	237		26	3,299	-3,872		182	-371	
Maryland	1,541		529	2,790		626	1,950	-909	
Mass.	2,837	-1,233		5,032	-8,899		5,195	-5,011	
Michigan	3,008	-4,261		5,386	-6,268		5,779	-160	
Minnesota	423	-481		6,144		3,323	4,139		77
Mississippi	2,617		2,515	4,528		2,954	652		320
Missouri	2,322		563	3,856		757	5,498	-47	
Montana	(117)		(109)	(36)		(36)	359		7
Nebraska	376		137	d			1,082		64
Nevada	(22)		(22)				288		230
N. H.	691		217	952	-1,717		984		314
N. J.	2,764		668	8,402		1,019	5,605	-610	
N. M.	68		60				368		205
N. Y.	10,924		315	13,018	-11,865		28,973	-5,933	
N. C.	11,419		1,975	4,621		2,601	2,621		1,392
N. D.	d						351		104
Ohio	5,912	-11		9,655	-2,038		13,162	-482	
Oklahoma	902		671	219		101	1,343		204
Oregon.	-893	-2,190		2,071		197	1,187		250
Penn.	7,286		901	9,224	-4,080		11,752	-3,869	
R. I.	159	-4		294	-440		657	-274	
S. C.	481	-382		2,770		1,280	777		325
S. D.	(23)		(23)	d			378		106
Tennessee	4,168		1,800	4,041		2,516	2,878		778
Texas	5,574		4,203	4,834		3,884	7,397		3,836
Utah	183		89	d			457		76
Vermont	-70	-714		309	-508		337	-9	
Virginia	3,973	-472		2,781	1,086		2,289		798
Washington	859	-49		5,542		564	1,392	-119	
W. Va.	610		477	d			585	-115	
Wisconsin	1,821	-1,641		10,134	-701		5,605		1,638
Wyoming	d			(36)		(36)	81	-46	
Total Net Shift as % of 1939 Total		13.52			17.54			8.39	

	28--CHEMICALS & PROD.			29--PETROL. & COAL PROD.			30--RUBBER PROD.		
	Actual Change	Downward Net Shift	Upward Net Shift	Actual Change	Downward Net Shift	Upward Net Shift	Actual Change	Downward Net Shift	Upward Net Shift
U. S.	225,603	-68,301	67,298	56,116	-11,564	11,384	75,498	-27,822	13,327
Alabama	1,486	-1,831		1,089		188	3,327		2,457
Arizona	663		422	(30)	(30)		(10)		(10)
Arkansas	2,468		1,015	446		91	d		
California	10,949		2,913	5,066		114	d		
Colorado	1,429		1,044	322		91	d		
Connecticut	3,465		806	127	-27		2,430	-2,502	
Delaware	2,199		490	40		8	d		
D. C.	93		32	(15)		(15)	(10)		(10)
Florida	4,664		2,522	d			d		
Georgia	173	-5,886		107	-55		d		
Idaho	d			d			1,273	-948	
Illinois	16,478		2,591	4,396		33	5,244		1,128
Indiana	10,934		5,543	3,037	-1,498		2,588		2,357
Iowa	3,152		2,080	53		49	d		
Kansas	5,129		3,471	252	-1,349		d		
Kentucky	5,386		4,509	237	-231		d		
Louisiana	8,962		5,783	5,818		4,261	(10)		(10)
Maine	163	-64		d			(111)		(62)
Maryland	-3,105	-12,989		1,046		272	3,258		2,126
Mass.	2,375	-3,928		-284	-1,350		5,388	-3,529	
Michigan	13,273		2,532	935	-197		2,142	-2,798	
Minnesota	2,162		1,009	526		195	295		129
Mississippi	1,060	-1,796		190		190	d		
Missouri	5,156		137	1,184		550	-517	-1,240	
Montana	187	-118		(94)	(-135)				
Nebraska	780		464	(130)		(99)	d		
Nevada	d						422		422
N. H.	38	-143		15		(15)	806	-5,604	
N. J.	17,271	-11,499		3,152	-1,466				
N. M.	2,605		2,535	d					
N. Y.	14,230	-12,092		278	-1,938		1,393	-2,586	
N. C.	1,928	-3,177		d			d		
N. D.	d			d			(10)		(10)
Ohio	12,425	-536		3,821		608	17,907	-5,259	
Oklahoma	160	-614		1,789	-464		d		
Oregon	726		485	246		234	d		
Penn.	7,516	-10,705		5,517	-2,522		5,932		3,041
R. I.	244	-272		d			420	-2,011	
S. C.	5,403		3,306	28	-20		d		
S. D.	d			d			(10)		(10)
Tennessee	15,613		3,277	d			2,534		1,218
Texas	18,906		13,303	12,751		2,866	d		
Utah	579		348	1,043		845	(290)		(290)
Vermont	94		16	d			d		
Virginia	10,850	-2,545		(49)	(-82)		351		47
Washington	5,473		4,792	79		40	d		
W. Va.	7,052	-106		940		265	d		
Wisconsin	3,663		1,842	118	-230		703	-1,345	
Wyoming	(33)		(26)	848		325			
Total Net Shift as % of 1939 Total		24.78			10.74			23.04	

	31--LEATHER & PROD.			32--STONE, CLAY & GLASS			33--PRIMARY METAL INDUS.		
	Actual Change	Downward Net Shift	Upward Net Shift	Actual Change	Downward Net Shift	Upward Net Shift	Actual Change	Downward Net Shift	Upward Net Shift
U. S.	-6,028	-24,600	23,914	144,937	-33,001	32,254	266,073	-84,137	83,005
Alabama	d			3,193		1,490	8,184	-1,414	
Arizona	d			554		410	1,779		987
Arkansas	(3,463)		(3,463)	1,263		657	1,899		1,772
California	2,773		2,818	16,270		10,267	19,592		14,523
Colorado	(1,430)		(1,436)	1,091		420	2,397		568
Connecticut	-415	-366		1,252	-153		-679	-9,934	
Delaware	-907	-859		278		188	591	-6	
D. C.				-278	-537				
Florida	d			2,883		2,133	565		510
Georgia	-95	-51		2,818		997	345	-384	
Idaho	(20)		(20)	192		91	(228)		(3)
Illinois	-5,496	-5,026		10,224		798	19,495	-2,911	
Indiana	-557	-509		6,619	-898		20,633		69
Iowa	-19	-9		1,489	-188		3,282		2,752
Kansas	d			2,942		2,173	2	-309	
Kentucky	171		211	1,076	-450		-398	-2,675	
Louisiana				2,399		1,515	2,982		2,872
Maine	1,310		1,619	-32	-400		87		30
Maryland	-1,014	-952		1,494	-912		6,992	-943	
Mass.	-7,152	-5,943		2,831		280	4,483		98
Michigan	-650	-568		5,547		790	30,068		15,774
Minnesota	164		185	843	-963		2,089		1,067
Mississippi	d			1,196		689	d		
Missouri	2,060		2,642	3,894	-436		3,311		289
Montana	d			131	-25		(908)		(10)
Nebraska	(269)		(272)	321	-99		381		325
Nevada	d			622		524	d		
N. H.	-1,755	-1,369		488		41	278		191
N. J.	-119		71	7,838	-1,901		2,889	-7,615	
N. M.	d			141		51	d		
N. Y.	1,633		2,621	9,597	-1,830		21,089		5,032
N. C.	138		157	2,452		731	533		2
N. D.				164		138	d		
Ohio	-7,112	-6,773		14,803	-7,083		38,745	-4,509	
Oklahoma	d			2,765		1,503	1,706		1,017
Oregon	-31	-27		522		233	2,085		1,876
Penn.	116		630	13,002	-10,103		21,581	-43,368	
R. I.	202		210	1,087		781	2,652		1,647
S. C.	(45)		(45)	1,663		651	314		238
S. D.				78	-41		d		
Tennessee	4,712		4,813	2,444	-258		3,262		623
Texas	2,469		2,481	6,395		3,629	16,241		14,999
Utah	d			719		396	3,919		2,912
Vermont	-108	-97		1,334		226	113	-41	
Virginia	-191	-102		2,013		119	789	-3	
Washington	216		220	1,158		333	8,077		7,107
W. Va.	-692	-663		3,254	-6,705		1,354	-5,025	
Wisconsin	-1,591	-1,286		d			9,915		5,705
Wyoming	d			94	-19				
Total Net Shift as % of 1939 Total		7.52			12.35			12.51	

Appendix Table K (continued)

	34--FABRIC METAL PROD.			35--MACHINERY (EXC. ELEC.)			36--ELEC. MACHINERY		
	Actual Change	Downward Net Shift	Upward Net Shift	Actual Change	Downward Net Shift	Upward Net Shift	Actual Change	Downward Net Shift	Upward Net Shift
U. S.	370,085	-65,073	64,005	635,241	-103,087	102,814	474,513	-83,874	80,486
Alabama	3,601		675	3,692		2,411	2,073		1,740
Arizona	d			1,042		982	(193)		(193)
Arkansas	1,312		1,049	355		212	1,468		1,468
California	38,349		22,811	38,560		23,610	33,635		26,213
Colorado	1,246		635	2,311		932	700		629
Connecticut	5,069	-20,297		23,333	-17,938		10,922	-15,260	
Delaware	408	-107		1,257		223	d		
D. C.	(278)		(34)	76		46	208		137
Florida	5,426		5,003	1,693		1,391	713		654
Georgia	2,442		798	3,579		1,094	1,651		1,148
Idaho	281		252	97		18	(46)		(46)
Illinois	41,653	-2,966		71,787	-23,005		66,831	-7,442	
Indiana	15,627		1,809	23,210	-5,116		36,614		1,014
Iowa	1,646	-850		14,246		1,138	6,178		4,515
Kansas	3,104		2,067	5,215		3,819	(727)		(679)
Kentucky	5,738		1,644	8,110		5,315	5,304		1,241
Louisiana	2,327		1,072	1,206		155	d		
Maine	1,135		365	-82	-3,432		d		
Maryland	4,473	-3,326		4,799		790	6,224		2,385
Mass.	9,279	-6,817		23,219	-15,797		37,795		1,473
Michigan	37,020		5,677	85,022		32,621	10,252	-389	
Minnesota	4,058		1,041	10,021		1,197	4,209		2,578
Mississippi	1,495		1,427	1,067		879	d		
Missouri	8,822		171	11,692		4,750	8,631	-6,288	
Montana	85		32	25	-70				
Nebraska	1,106		354	1,819		991	1,834		1,660
Nevada	d			d			(46)		(46)
N. H.	675	-85		2,640	-165		5,175		4,683
N. J	18,887	-134		26,410	-1,566		42,939	-22,413	
N. M.	d			d			(46)		(46)
N. Y.	34,626	-2,482		59,179		3,288	63,024		5,626
N. C.	3,178		2,657	3,667		2,029	7,216		7,120
N. D.	57	-21		d			d		
Ohio	37,801	-11,739		81,409	-19,233		39,376	-17,595	
Oklahoma	3,125		1,980	5,976		3,767	d		
Oregon	2,993		1,885	1,590		233	765		574
Penn.	35,795	-4,379		51,468	-1,822		45,621	-10,454	
R. I.	1,621	-2,273		2,425	-5,807		880	-4,033	
S. C.	(407)		(332)	1,670		948	d		
S. D.	199		125	d			d		
Tennessee	5,213	-1,705		4,642		2,438	3,233		2,923
Texas	10,589		7,157	16,159		6,255	3,180		2,336
Utah	1,191		937	653		405	d		
Vermont	377		106	3,501		100	d		
Virginia	3,269		1,352	1,116		200	d		
Washington	2,253		558	2,276		70	440		136
W. Va.	765	-4,572		1,693		324	2,881		1,811
Wisconsin	9,894	-3,320		30,863	-9,136		19,682		7,412
Wyoming				(198)		(183)	d		
Total Net Shift as % of 1939 Total	14.43			19.23			33.83		

Appendix Table K (continued)

	37--TRANSP. EQUIPT.			38--INSTR. & REL. PROD.			39--MISC. MFG.		
	Actual Change	Downward Net Shift	Upward Net Shift	Actual Change	Downward Net Shift	Upward Net Shift	Actual Change	Downward Net Shift	Upward Net Shift
U. S.	782,525	-389,378	382,019	110,730	-33,591	32,370	314,021	-59,161	70,183
Alabama	7,060		4,183	d			1,598		1,145
Arizona	d			d			271		253
Arkansas	363		287	(1,924)		(1,924)	1,802		1,236
California	171,175		133,287	8,246		6,589	29,779		24,429
Colorado	547		349	421		332	1,786		1,100
Connecticut	40,567		27,885	3,080	-8,748		18,099	-9,097	
Delaware	(1,663)		(544)	d			502	-1,043	
D. C.	(115)		(115)	(97)		(28)	47	-40	
Florida	3,188		752	d			1,166		325
Georgia	15,354		12,793				1,656	-7	
Idaho	d			d			d		
Illinois	24,089		3,565	12,936	-986		13,355	-19,934	
Indiana	40,253	-3,854		1,834		1,236	10,047		2,397
Iowa	3,464		2,804	1,210		918	4,269		329
Kansas	39,914		38,333	d			1,278		900
Kentucky	1,034	-1,260		d			3,328		1,837
Louisiana	7,030		4,920	d			2,036		1,497
Maine	688	-3,041		(265)		(265)	936	-11	
Maryland	16,031	-5,619		796		437	5,660		616
Mass.	7,886	-6,277		4,319	-7,336		13,999	-12,870	
Michigan	62,794	-302,992		6,142		5,163	11,686		2,694
Minnesota	4,106		2,152	(387)	(-1,460)		8,949		6,008
Mississippi	5,511		4,953	(225)		(225)	329		234
Missouri	25,436		13,036	1,281		154	12,501		7,590
Montana	26		26	d			57	-7	
Nebraska	971		948	(2,166)		(2,145)	4,357		3,470
Nevada	d			(214)		(214)	d		
N. H.	(202)		(188)	(500)		(488)	633	-978	
N. J.	15,218	-20,324		12,128		4,798	12,799	-12,711	
N. M.	d			d			547		434
N. Y.	76,133		27,416	27,795	-11,454		70,996	-2,479	
N. C.	839	-118		600		600	880		346
N. D.	d						121		102
Ohio	90,238		41,083	3,674		566	20,883		836
Oklahoma	8,584		8,410	360		342	372		91
Oregon	1,618		987	d			966		345
Penn.	20,910	-23,653		7,684	-4,185		19,242	-4,357	
R. I.	(497)		(129)	573	-882		10,848	-6,957	
S. C.	204	-65		d			1,674		1,428
S. D.	(100)		(100)	d			48		3
Tennessee	3,056		1,521	d			5,413		3,529
Texas	39,139		35,163	1,569		1,397	7,175		5,642
Utah	d			d			238		90
Vermont	d			d			1,482		578
Virginia	6,935	-7,124		d			1,048	-164	
Washington	23,696		16,090	288		235	1,346		55
W. Va.	439	-489		d			44	-1,376	
Wisconsin	7,972	14,562		4,750		4,100	5,812		644
Wyoming	d			(214)		(214)	d		
Total Net Shift as % of 1939 Total	71.50			39.58			29.03		

d = disclosure problem.
Note: Underscored data indicate Absolute Upward or Downward Shift. Other shift data are Relative Upward or Downward Shift. Figures in parentheses are estimates.

IMPORTANT INPUT-OUTPUT RELATIONSHIPS FOR

PRIMARY RESOURCE EXTRACTORS AND 1st and 2nd STAGE RESOURCE USERS, 1947

Sector Number	Industry Title	% Input from 21 Primary Resource Ext.	% Input from 27 First Stage Resource Users	% Input from Households	% Input from Transportation*	Important Foreign Resource Supplements (% Addition to Domestic Supply)	Intra-industry Consumption (% of Total Output Absorbed within Total)	% Output Going to Final Demand**
	I 21 PRIMARY RESOURCE EXTRACTORS (Produced 6.86% of total gross domestic output)							
1	Meat Animals and Products	51.12	3.57	#	3.09	3.30	9.6	10.98
2	Poultry and Eggs	41.16	34.10	#	3.45		8.0	68.45
3	Farm Dairy Products	35.36	12.47	#	3.05		0.0	54.46
4	Food Grains and Feed Crops	11.61	5.64	#	2.15		7.4	.41
5	Cotton	7.75	2.26	#	.69		1.2	.00
6	Tobacco	2.59	5.38	#	.74		0.0	.00
7	Oil Bearing Crops	14.20	3.93	#	.82	10.83	8.8	.30
8	Vegetables and Fruits	6.12	4.80	#	1.88		3.0	68.80
9	All Other Agriculture	6.54	5.07	#	1.09	5.24	3.1	32.80
10	Fisheries, Hunting, and Trapping	.76	9.21	#	3.16	36.39	.7	21.32
11	Iron Ore Mining	1.66	4.60	29.0	.92	11.79	0.0	.00
12	Copper Mining	.89	9.44	25.3	2.84	11.12	0.0	.00
13	Lead and Zinc Mining	.77	10.00	38.2	1.10	18.22	0.0	.00
14	Bauxite Mining	.00	3.52	47.1	1.17	250.58	0.0	.00
15	Misc. Metallic Minerals	.89	10.92	42.4	1.79	252.82	0.0	.00
16	Coal	1.90	3.20	58.3	.31		0.5	2.02
17	Crude Petroleum and Natural Gas	1.18	.90	17.4	.08	3.04	1.1	.80
18	Stone, Sand, Clay, and Abrasives	2.61	4.60	33.1	.96	2.88	2.1	9.69
19	Sulfur	.00	2.93	14.1	.33		0.0	.00
20	Misc. Nonmetallic Minerals	1.97	7.78	26.3	.77	55.94	0.0	.40
36	Logging	.70	5.25	39.1	1.17	5.85	0.0	.12
	II 27 1st STAGE RESOURCE USERS (Produced 9.70% of total gross domestic output)							
21	Meat Packing and Whole Poultry	75.8	2.95	8.3	1.30		1.6	77.27
22	Processed Dairy Products	54.5	15.22	7.6	1.70		9.8	60.34
23	Canning, Preserving and Freezing	32.1	14.75	15.7	1.80		1.6	77.72
24	Grain Mill Products	63.1	12.72	6.1	5.60		6.9	19.41
26	Miscellaneous Food Products	10.3	30.64	12.7	2.55		9.9	62.15
27	Sugar	16.3	59.03	7.9	2.10	64.80	58.0	44.81
28	Alcoholic Beverages	13.2	19.56	15.8	3.00		15.2	44.40
29	Tobacco Manufacture	30.6	34.75	8.5	1.46		34.1	57.90
30	Spinning, Weaving, and Dyeing	24.8	14.57	24.6	1.58		12.2	13.17
37	Sawmills, Planing, & Veneer Mills	15.95	13.18	27.2	4.37		10.6	.85
38	Plywood	17.13	14.52	25.7	6.67		.4	.00
44	Pulp Mills	31.43	6.31	15.1	11.50	25.56	.3	.00
48	Industrial Inorganic Chemicals	10.34	17.32	19.4	5.43		6.6	2.82
57	Gum and Wood Chemicals	36.09	3.30	15.9	4.01		.8	.95
59	Vegetable Oils	42.73	15.87	3.8	1.81	4.09	4.3	1.15
62	Petroleum Products	52.46	10.52	7.8	6.31		9.4	35.24
63	Coke and Products	41.03	6.14	11.0	11.45		2.8	.20
71	Cement	12.05	9.05	25.3	10.22		.1	.02
72	Structural Clay Products	14.28	6.44	43.6	4.94		0.0	.00
77	Other Misc. Nonmetallic Minerals	17.44	5.54	26.5	7.76		1.1	2.27
78	Blast Furnaces	23.70	35.07	7.5	14.53		.6	.00
82	Primary Copper	33.21	46.35	4.1	1.69	8.46	43.9	.11
84	Primary Lead	42.00	30.36	4.5	1.92	1.14	27.8	.02

Sector Number	Industry Title	% Input from 21 Primary Resource Ext.	% Input from 27 First Stage Resource Users	% Input from Households	% Input from Transportation*	Important Foreign Resource Supplements (% Addition to Domestic Supply)	Intra-industry Consumption (% of Total Output Absorbed within Total)	% Output Going to Final Demand**
85	Primary Zinc	34.67	10.23	14.4	4.99		4.1	.03
86	Primary Metals, n.e.c.	55.52	19.06	5.9	.89	109.3	0.0	.00
167	Electric Light and Power	8.66	12.57	18.1	3.40		8.9	6.14
168	Natural, Manufactured & Mixed Gas	11.75	27.43	19.6	1.44		20.0	.33

III 32 2nd STAGE RESOURCE USERS
(Produced 15.33% of total gross
domestic output)

Sector Number	Industry Title	% Input from 21 Primary Resource Ext.	% Input from 27 First Stage Resource Users	% Input from Households	% Input from Transportation*	Important Foreign Resource Supplements (% Addition to Domestic Supply)	Intra-industry Consumption (% of Total Output Absorbed within Total)	% Output Going to Final Demand**
25	Bakery Products	1.8	42.53	26.2	2.80		.3	90.05
31	Special Textile Products	.9	15.36	25.3	1.59		9.4	57.71
32	Jute, Linen, Cordage, and Twine	7.7	11.88	19.6	3.72		3.6	22.24
33	Canvas Products	.1	37.47	25.7	.61		7.5	51.74
34	Apparel	2.3	28.17	26.3	.67		15.6	80.49
35	House Furnishings & Other Nonapparel	.1	51.71	13.9	1.23		3.3	53.61
39	Fabricated Wood Products	1.52	28.60	29.1	7.36		2.4	6.28
40	Wood Containers and Cooperage	2.80	35.35	24.3	7.36		3.4	1.90
41	Wood Furniture	1.10	21.35	30.3	4.19		.8	76.17
42	Metal Furniture	.12	10.53	26.1	1.53		.6	44.33
43	Partitions, Screens, Shades, etc.	.13	14.69	27.6	2.95		.7	14.25
45	Paper and Board Mills	2.25	40.00	16.7	4.06		0.0	.46
49	Industrial Organic Chemicals	3.75	20.98	17.6	3.22		15.8	3.27
50	Plastics Materials	.54	10.73	16.0	3.61		0.0	.32
51	Synthetic Rubber	.07	25.94	9.9	3.04		0.0	.00
52	Synthetic Fiber	1.63	17.26	31.1	2.72		0.0	.39
53	Explosives and Fireworks	.62	14.35	26.4	2.45		.7	10.01
55	Soap and Related Products	.63	14.46	10.3	1.87		2.5	60.78
56	Paint and Allied Products	3.42	21.70	16.1	2.16		10.4	4.33
58	Fertilizers	9.00	22.36	14.3	10.38		11.6	2.00
60	Animal Oils	2.34	46.30	6.6	.94		5.3	.02
61	Miscellaneous Chemical Industries	4.74	13.24	14.9	1.81		2.4	26.99
64	Paving and Roofing Materials	1.13	25.03	18.0	4.66		.3	.04
65	Tires and Inner Tubes	.58	22.35	25.2	1.44		0.0	27.24
74	Concrete and Plaster Products	7.22	16.05	28.9	9.56		.3	3.51
75	Abrasive Products	2.93	12.59	25.9	1.33		11.9	.61
79	Steel Works and Rolling Mills	1.07	27.54	23.5	2.87		21.3	.13
80	Iron Foundries	.86	16.62	39.4	3.13		.1	.16
83	Copper Rolling and Drawing	.16	48.82	14.5	1.87		5.7	.08
87	Nonferrous Metal Rolling, n.e.c.	.09	33.94	13.4	1.44		1.0	.00
88	Primary Aluminum	.63	29.79	9.1	1.72		0.0	.00
90	Secondary Nonferrous Metals	.05	14.70	6.6	3.08		10.7	.04
102	Metal Coating and Engraving	.26	10.30	42.3	.68		2.8	.00
142	Storage Batteries	.09	11.10	17.6	.49		0.0	1.69
155	Medical, Dental Instruments & Supplies	1.24	13.60	29.5	.48		1.7	35.46
180	Eating and Drinking Places	6.82	28.34	22.5	2.59		0.0	98.80
183	Real Estate and Rentals	2.65	10.76	3.6	1.83		.8	70.81
211	New Construction	1.57	10.16		4.78		.0	.00

IV 109 INDUSTRIES FOR WHICH RESOURCES
HAVE THE MOST INDIRECT SIGNIFICANCE
(Produced 28.3% of total gross
domestic output)

A. Manufacturing Industries
(Produced 11.8% of total
gross domestic output)

Sector Number	Industry Title	% Input from 21 Primary Resource Ext.	% Input from 27 First Stage Resource Users	% Input from Households	% Input from Transportation*	Important Foreign Resource Supplements (% Addition to Domestic Supply)	Intra-industry Consumption (% of Total Output Absorbed within Total)	% Output Going to Final Demand**
46	Converted Paper Products	.17	1.87	21.4	3.34		2.8	12.13
47	Printing and Publishing	.02	.51	36.9	1.33		11.9	26.94
54	Drugs and Medicines	1.38	4.00	19.7	1.46		11.7	44.15
66	Miscellaneous Rubber Products	.38	8.62	29.6	1.49		2.6	22.95
67	Leather Tanning and Finishing	.73	4.71	14.4	2.78		3.7	.38
68	Other Leather Products	.03	4.87	28.5	.83		1.8	79.12
69	Footwear (excluding rubber)	.05	2.42	27.8	1.00		11.9	79.57
70	Glass	1.76	9.35	33.4	3.47		6.6	13.02

Sector Number	Industry Title	% Input from 21 Primary Resource Ext.	% Input from 27 First Stage Resource Users	% Input from House-holds	% Input from Transportation*	Important Foreign Resource Supplements (% Addition to Domestic Supply)	Intra-industry Consumption (% of Total Output Absorbed within Total)	% Output Going to Final Demand**
73	Pottery and Related Products	3.52	5.59	47.0	2.92		1.0	33.25
76	Asbestos Products	8.97	8.45	26.9	3.68		2.9	.55
81	Steel Foundries	.81	8.28	39.4	2.08		.7	.04
89	Aluminum Rolling and Drawing	.36	2.86	18.2	.95		8.7	.38
91	Nonferrous Foundries	.26	9.10	33.2	1.42		.2	3.11
92	Iron and Steel Forgings	.46	3.61	27.7	1.79		.4	.16
93	Tin Cans and Other Tin Ware	.04	1.65	20.0	2.93		.8	2.53
94	Cutlery	.06	.79	36.3	.79		1.6	68.46
95	Tools and General Hardware	.16	2.51	34.9	1.45		1.6	12.38
96	Hardware, n.e.c.	.20	1.50	33.9	1.33		1.3	5.64
97	Metal Plumbing & Vitreous Fixtures	.26	5.19	31.3	1.55		1.0	13.81
98	Heating and Equipment	.09	2.17	24.9	1.52		2.9	26.59
99	Structural Metal Products	.06	.90	27.2	1.83		2.7	.59
100	Boiler Shop Products & Pipe Bending	.08	1.33	66.4	1.69		4.2	.60
101	Metal Stampings	.11	1.15	27.9	1.50		.8	14.01
103	Lighting Fixtures	.07	1.06	25.3	1.42		2.2	.00
104	Fabricated Wire Products	.06	.86	19.5	1.02		2.1	2.46
105	Metal Barrels, Drums, etc.	.04	.73	15.3	2.16		1.9	.24
106	Tubes and Foils	.11	1.01	23.6	1.91		10.8	9.00
107	Misc. Fabricated Metal Products	.06	.67	21.7	1.15		.7	6.95
108	Steel Springs	.07	1.56	20.3	1.56		1.4	.00
109	Nuts, Bolts, & Screw Machine Products	.09	1.26	30.9	1.30		.9	2.31
110	Steam Engines and Turbines	.38	1.65	45.7	1.39		1.6	8.00
111	Internal Combustion Engines	.14	1.05	28.2	1.64		4.4	7.35
112	Farm and Industrial Tractors	.11	1.56	24.1	1.86		4.3	2.42
113	Farm Equipment	.17	2.23	28.1	1.98		3.6	8.42
114	Construction & Mining Machinery	.12	1.02	24.7	1.39		2.2	5.91
115	Oil-field Machinery and Tools	.42	2.11	30.0	1.58		.9	.28
116	Machine Tools & Metalworking Machinery	.22	1.65	37.5	.26		3.3	4.03
117	Cutting Tools, Jigs, and Fixtures	.10	1.18	40.9	.18		3.2	.14
118	Special Industrial Machinery	.11	3.02	35.2	.32		2.1	1.09
119	Pumps and Compressors	.12	1.07	26.6	.27		1.2	2.50
120	Elevators and Conveyors	.09	.94	29.5	.21		1.6	.00
121	Blowers and Fans	.11	.93	26.3	.23		3.0	.00
122	Power Transmission Equipment	.11	2.69	35.9	.23		1.2	.95
123	Industrial Machinery, n.e.c.	.16	1.74	29.1	.35		1.3	3.67
124	Commercial Machines, Equipment, n.e.c.	.11	1.08	66.5	.23		3.0	3.84
125	Refrigeration Equipment	.11	1.32	26.3	.44		8.7	34.69
126	Valves and Fittings	.24	2.76	34.9	.28		1.1	.35
127	Ball and Roller Bearings	.15	1.57	41.3	.23		4.3	.00
128	Machine Shops	.06	.80	35.2	.15		.8	.89
129	Wiring Devices & Graphite Products	.24	3.84	25.2	.44		1.6	4.06
130	Electrical Measuring Instruments	.05	.58	32.7	.21		1.2	3.31
131	Motors and Generators	.20	3.14	36.2	.34		1.8	1.96
132	Transformers	.17	1.99	28.4	.40		2.2	2.19
133	Electrical Control Apparatus	.21	1.05	32.2	.28		2.7	2.19
134	Electrical Welding Apparatus	.28	.77	23.9	.28		1.0	2.11
135	Electrical Appliances	.08	1.07	22.9	.34		3.0	60.48
136	Insulated Wire and Cable	.13	4.60	18.2	.55		4.8	6.77
137	Engine Electrical Equipment	.10	2.76	33.1	6.33		2.9	1.03
138	Electrical Lamps	.71	1.43	25.4	.32		10.3	43.08
139	Radio and Related Products	.16	1.30	30.0	.49		14.0	44.78
140	Tubes	.07	1.48	48.2	.40		0.0	4.97
141	Communication Equipment	.14	1.40	39.3	.32		14.1	1.20
143	Primary Batteries	2.89	4.49	29.9	.23		0.0	68.08
144	X-ray Apparatus	.15	1.55	35.7	.46		2.8	.90
145	Motor Vehicles	.12	1.48	17.6	.50		26.3	26.21*
146	Truck Trailers	.06	1.95	21.3	.42		2.3	1.15
147	Automobile Trailers	.07	5.06	19.5	1.01		.5	85.68
148	Aircraft and Parts	.05	1.48	44.2	.26		8.9	59.97
149	Ships and Boats	.08	2.06	50.5	.57		2.1	42.38

Sector Number	Industry Title	% Input from 21 Primary Resource Ext.	% Input from 27 First Stage Resource Users	% Input from Households	% Input from Transportation*	Important Foreign Resource Supplements (% Addition to Domestic Supply)	Intra-industry Consumption (% of Total Output Absorbed within Total)	% Output Going to Final Demand**
150	Locomotives	.14	.82	24.6	.33		5.4	2.39
151	Railroad Equipment	.17	2.96	25.3	.57		11.5	.16
152	Motorcycles and Bicycles	.08	.84	23.4	.32		12.2	47.51
153	Instruments, etc.	.13	1.04	37.8	.19		3.9	11.16
154	Optical, Ophthalmic, Photo Equipment	.14	4.78	39.1	.33		6.7	33.56
156	Watches and Clocks	.30	.45	28.1	.82		28.6	75.21
157	Jewelry and Silverware	5.87	1.96	30.1	.99		6.1	97.30
158	Musical Instruments and Parts	.23	4.94	36.9	1.25		17.3	65.10
159	Toys and Sporting Goods	.18	3.13	31.8	.98		1.3	79.40
160	Office Supplies	.06	2.60	29.4	1.03		1.9	39.32
161	Plastic Products	.18	8.76	30.8	.95		1.4	18.88
162	Cork Products	.25	2.80	17.9	9.43		.8	1.76
163	Motion Picture Production	.00	2.23	63.5	.28		10.2	1.67
164	Misc. Manufactured Products	.82	4.46	21.2	1.51		2.3	22.86
951	Small Arms	.35	1.89		1.20		.9	75.90
961	Small Arms Ammunition	.25	4.64		1.38		0.0	62.70
212	Maintenance Construction	1.49	6.87		3.55		0.0	1.70*
	B. Service Industries (Produced 15.6% of total gross domestic output)							
169	Railroads	4.17	3.88	41.9	5.13		4.1	30.89
170	Trucking	.01	5.40	50.8	1.05		.4	25.54
171	Warehousing and Storage	1.57	5.33	40.7	5.21		.3	40.16
172	Overseas Transportation	.13	5.00	34.7	11.57		10.6	11.61
173	Other Water Transportation	1.81	8.78	33.9	13.63		11.6	20.70
174	Air Transportation	.002	6.67	40.9	2.69		2.3	82.20
175	Pipeline Transportation	1.76	3.68	27.6	.08		0.0	2.51
176	Wholesale Trade	.07	1.56	43.5	.29		.3	38.88
177	Retail Trade	.02	1.99	37.7	1.50		.3	83.83
178	Local & Highway Transportation	.01	5.20	44.1	1.18		.3	91.84
179	Telephone and Telegraph	.08	.72	50.8	2.20		1.6	50.85
181	Banking, Finance, and Insurance	.01	.59	34.2	.22		14.6	55.44
182	Hotels	.17	3.82	27.9	.25		0.0	.00
184	Laundries and Dry Cleaning	.11	6.24	48.9	.64		2.6	73.53
185	Other Personal Services	.06	3.52	31.2	.48		0.0	96.20
186	Advertising, Including Radio	.00	.38	14.1	10.90		1.7	1.64
187	Business Services	.01	.97	39.2	.16		.5	15.37
188	Auto, Repair Services, & Garages	.07	3.45	24.9	.13		1.8	47.41
189	Other Repair Services	.03	2.41	25.9	.86		2.3	49.54
190	Motion Pictures, Other Amusements	.05	2.39	22.9	.29		13.7	81.60
191	Medical, Dental, Other Professional Services	1.52	3.43	13.0	.05		1.1	75.36
192	Nonprofit Institutions	.56	1.61	15.3	.49		0.0	100.00
265	Waste Products, Metal	0.00	0.00					
266	Waste Products, Non-Metal							
267	Stockpile of Byproducts							

Labor input data for agriculture are omitted because they are unsatisfactory and misleading.

* Since the 1947 input-output table is constructed on a "producer's value" basis, these transport costs represent the cost of transporting inputs only. The corresponding transport costs in distributing the product could only be estimated from this table and then only by a complex statistical analysis.

** Final demand consists of households and state and local government. This figure for some industries such as autos and new construction may be misleadingly low, because the output was arbitrarily assigned to "gross private capital formation." The figure is also misleading for coal, as the private consumption was arbitrarily assigned to "real estate and rentals."

ACTUAL AND PER CENT CHANGE, PARTICIPATION (WAGE AND PROPRIETOR'S) INCOME, BY COMPONENTS, 1920 - 1950

	ACTUAL CHANGE, WAGE AND PROPRIETOR'S INCOME	Per Cent Change Due To:		
		AGRI-CULTURE	NON-AGRI-CULTURE	Change in % Labor Force in Agriculture
U. S.	65.5	15.2	43.8	6.6
Alabama	104.4	29.6	37.7	28.2
Arizona	45.0	38.9	18.0	3.8
Arkansas	90.0	58.6	19.2	23.8
California	49.4	10.9	40.8	-0.9
Colorado	42.2	15.2	28.0	1.3
Connecticut	76.3	3.6	72.2	0.1
Delaware	125.9	24.7	96.6	4.1
D. C.				
Florida	103.6	41.8	65.0	6.8
Georgia	100.8	33.1	37.0	25.2
Idaho	47.1	21.4	26.6	-0.9
Illinois	59.2	11.4	46.9	2.9
Indiana	84.0	26.8	54.5	7.2
Iowa	74.1	49.3	29.6	3.7
Kansas	56.2	20.4	33.1	3.3
Kentucky	71.1	23.2	30.3	16.4
Louisiana	96.8	33.5	45.6	18.9
Maine	48.3	3.5	41.3	-
Maryland	63.2	7.6	50.7	4.2
Mass.	45.8	1.1	44.4	0.2
Michigan	73.4	5.7	58.8	3.9
Minnesota	71.0	23.5	43.9	4.4
Mississippi	91.8	40.4	21.5	26.8
Missouri	74.9	23.3	45.9	7.5
Montana	79.2	55.5	32.7	5.1
Nebraska	76.3	48.2	31.2	5.1
Nevada	61.0	29.9	40.7	-
N. H.	50.8	1.6	45.1	0.9
N. J.	51.6	2.9	48.7	0.4
N. M.	69.5	41.8	29.0	10.1
N. Y.	49.9	0.2	47.3	0.8
N. C.	72.8	26.2	31.1	11.2
N. D.	64.5	32.7	28.7	1.5
Ohio	71.1	6.5	58.8	3.4
Oklahoma	48.6	19.3	18.3	13.2
Oregon	57.7	6.4	47.8	-1.4
Penn.	54.7	1.4	51.0	0.9
R. I.	49.3	1.1	47.6	0.5
S. C.	92.5	24.3	28.7	26.4
S. D.	58.5	42.4	19.5	2.2
Tennessee	84.7	22.2	36.7	19.9
Texas	77.3	52.6	28.6	15.3
Utah	64.2	17.2	43.7	3.6
Vermont	47.0	2.0	40.1	-
Virginia	77.3	24.3	43.3	10.3
Washington	66.5	5.2	59.7	-2.2
W. Va.	60.2	5.1	42.7	7.4
Wisconsin	63.3	0.7	55.2	-0.9
Wyoming	31.6	16.4	19.0	-1.7

OUTPUT PER WORKER AND VALUE OF LAND AND BUILDINGS PER WORKER IN AGRICULTURE, 1950

	OUTPUT/WORKER	VALUE LAND AND BUILDINGS/WORKER
U. S.	$2,882	$ 8,815
Alabama	1,228	3,262
Arizona	7,416	21,209
Arkansas	1,831	4,311
California	5,573	17,742
Colorado	5,320	14,402
Connecticut	4,604	10,996
Delaware	6,462	7,904
D. C.		
Florida	2,750	7,162
Georgia	1,452	3,401
Idaho	4,456	13,865
Illinois	4,830	17,984
Indiana	3,370	11,333
Iowa	5,198	16,373
Kansas	3,913	15,348
Kentucky	1,714	5,274
Louisiana	1,583	4,854
Maine	3,624	5,716
Maryland	2,822	7,482
Mass.	3,957	8,416
Michigan	2,487	7,917
Minnesota	3,478	9,022
Mississippi	1,188	3,164
Missouri	2,443	6,585
Montana	5,049	17,158
Nebraska	4,567	14,889
Nevada	5,038	19,083
N. H.	2,778	6,532
N. J.	4,020	9,054
N. M.	4,106	17,379
N. Y.	3,324	7,084
N. C.	1,556	4,395
N. D.	3,857	10,665
Ohio	2,700	9,756
Oklahoma	2,586	8,800
Oregon	3,471	13,161
Penn.	2,530	6,080
R. I.	3,803	9,672
S. C.	1,089	3,372
S. D.	4,089	12,362
Tennessee	1,427	4,575
Texas	3,561	12,235
Utah	3,443	11,641
Vermont	3,142	6,250
Virginia	1,779	5,785
Washington	3,563	13,456
W. Va.	1,235	3,247
Wisconsin	2,720	6,709
Wyoming	5,021	17,781

INDEX

Indexes

PREFATORY NOTE

The index which follows is in two parts, an author index and a general index. The latter, longer and fuller than most, has been constructed on the premise that many users of this volume will desire to obtain information concerning individual regions and states with minimum searching. Therefore the editors have repeated significant listings, principally those referring to key tables, figures and maps, under several headings.

The principal regions indexed are the eight about which many of the tables and analyses in the text are built, as follows: New England, Middle Atlantic, Southeast, Great Lakes, Plains, Southwest, Mountain, and Far West. The three "great regions" are also indexed: Northeast, Southeast, and West. Source material has sometimes required use of various other regional groupings, which are listed under their special designations.

Because the book deals principally with the years 1939 to 1954, the tables usually cover that time period. Where no dates are given in the main index reference to a table, the reader may assume that the matter either covers the 1939-54 period or refers to matters in which year dates are not essential to index references.

In view of the 1954 "cut-off" date, the two newest States are not listed (Alaska and Hawaii). There are few references to the District of Columbia as such; such statistics as appear are usually combined with those of Maryland (where indicated).

Where most aspects of a subject are covered in one group of pages, such as 100-120 or 63-65, the individual aspects (except for a few important ones) are not usually indexed by individual page number within the group. If such aspects of a subject are also mentioned elsewhere in the book, they may sometimes be indexed only for such pages as fall outside the main group.

Within state and regional sections of the index, items in the "employment and labor force" category all appear under that heading, with modifications or sub-headings where needed. In the main body of the index, however, general references appear under the "employment and labor force" heading but specific industry information appears under individual industry names.

The authors of most source books and tables are listed in the author index.

However, the Bureau of the Census, which has been drawn upon as a source hundreds of times, is not listed nor are other government agencies or private companies.

Certain production problems have made it necessary that references to the appendix tables be given by the page number of the *first* page of each multi-page table.

Abbreviations are used in many index entries. Perhaps special note should be made of the abbreviations used with the term "shift", these being: "prop." for proportionality, "diff." for differential, "up" for upward, "down" for downward. Also note that "prod." is used for product or products, "indus." for industry or industries.

INDEX OF AUTHORS

INDEX

Livestock and products (*see also* specific industries, products), 361-63, 412-13; output and land building value, 560(t); sold value shifts, 345(t), 346(t), 362(map)

Location (*see also* under specific industry): factors, 75-86; household decisions re, 296n; industry shifts and income per capita, 99; in low-wage areas, 101, 589; rapid- and slow-growth industries, 305, 306; theory, 75, and sector theory, 59

Logging (*see* Forestry)

Louisiana

agriculture, 557(t), 638(t), 667(t), 681(t)

employment and labor force, 622(t), 652(t), 654(t); agriculture, 143(t), 241(t), 337(t), 514(t), 624(t), 638(t), 642-44(t); construction, 638(t); fisheries, 246(t), 630(t), 642-44(t); forestry, 245(t), 628(t), 642-44(t); industries, rapid- and slow-growth, 304(t); manufacturing, 156(t), ·399-407(t), 632(t), 638(t), 642-44(t), 670(t); mining, 242(t), 312(t), 626(t), 638(t), 642-44(t), 665(t); services and misc., 634(t), 638(t), 642-44(t); shifts, 301(t), 468-70(t), 642-44(t), 658(t)

fisheries, 641(t)

forestry, 640(t)

income, 544(t); median, 496(t); participation, 509(t), 512(t), 516(t), 681(t); per capita and personal, 26n, 37(t), 113, 494(t), 507(t), 530-31(t), 650(t); shifts, 185(t), 658(t)

manufacturing, wages and earnings, 569(t), 583(t)

mining, value, 639(t)

population, 128(t), 230(t), 658(t)

regional classification, 6n, 7

resources, extractive, value, 637(t)

SEA's, income, 41n

Louisville, Ky., 118(t)

Lumber and products: access factors, 425, 426, 429; cost increase, 215n; demand, 373; diff. effect, 425; employment and labor force, 119(t), changes, 391(t), and population correlation, 398(t), share of total, 158(t), shifts, 399(t), 409(t), 424-27, 425(map), 473, 670(t), specialization, 425; institutional factors, 216, 217; labor-intensive character, 572-73; location factors, 218, 426; paper and pulp (*see* Paper and allied prods., Pulp and pulpwood); production, shifting pattern, 215-18; technology, 216-18, 218; value added, 119(t); wages and earnings, 577(t), 581(t)

Machinery: employment, 119(t), 391(t), 398(t), 409(t), 670(t); inputs-outputs, intra-industry absorption, 396(t); production, 479; value added, 119(t), 581(t); wages and earnings, 577(t), 581(t), electrical only, 572-73

Maine

agriculture, 566(t), 638(t), 667(t), 681(t)

economic growth, 39(map), 40

employment and labor force, 622(t), 652(t), 654(t); agriculture, 143(t), 342(t), 624(t), 638(t), 642-44(t); construction, 638(t); fisheries, 630(t), 642-44(t); forestry, 245(t), 628(t), 642-44(t); industries, rapid- and slow-growth, 304(t); manufacturing, 156(t), 388(t), 399-407(t), 632(t), 638(t), 642-44(t), 670(t); mining, 626(t), 638(t), 642-44(t), 665(t); services and misc., 634(t), 638(t), 642-44(t); shifts, 257(t), 301(t), 468-70(t), 483, 642-44(t), 658(t)

fisheries, value, 641(t)

forestry, value, 640(t)

income, 185(t), 275(t), 504(t), 530-31(t), 650(t), 658(t), 681(t)

mining, value, 639(t)

population, 125, 126(t), 128(t), 225(t), 658(t)

resources, extractive, value, 637(t)

Manganese, 331

Manufacturing

access characteristics, 393-98

agglomeration, 395

before 1870, 110, 115, 117-19(t)

capital per worker, 572, 603

demand, 387, 392

economies of scale, 462

employment and labor force: areas of econ. decline, 483-85; before 1870, 117, 119(t), changing structure, 1870-1910, 151-61, 1910-50, 251-55, 1939-54, 303(t); distrib. by components, 408-41, geographic, 120(t), 152(t), 153(t), 183(t), 524(t); and econ. growth, 104; growth rate, 385; in high capital/labor ratio ind., 573-75, 573(map), 574(t); and income, 527(t), 602; population correlation, 315(t), 393, 397, 398(t); in processing industries, 525(map); production workers, 391(t), 656(t), 670(t); prop. effect., 389, 463; resources and resource using groups, 394; rapid-growth industries, 69(map), 70(map); by regions (*see above*, distrib., geographic also see *below*, total and regional); share of total, 1870-1910, 131(t), 1910-50, 234(t), 264(t), 1950, 282(t), 1954, 382, 386(t); shifts, diff., 73(t), 388(t), 389(map), 399-407(t), 468-70(t); interregional, 384; net, 382-87, 384(map); 1870-1910, 155(map), 156(t), 1910-50, 254(map), 1939-54, 658(t); principal state, 255(t), 256(t); production worker, 409(t), 670(t); prop., 390(map), 399-407(t); relative importance, 300(t); by SEA's, 381(map); total and by regions, 1870-1910, 152(t); 1870-1954, 158-59(t); 1910-50, 252(t); total and by states,